id

vo

void

Remarkable
Graphic
Styles

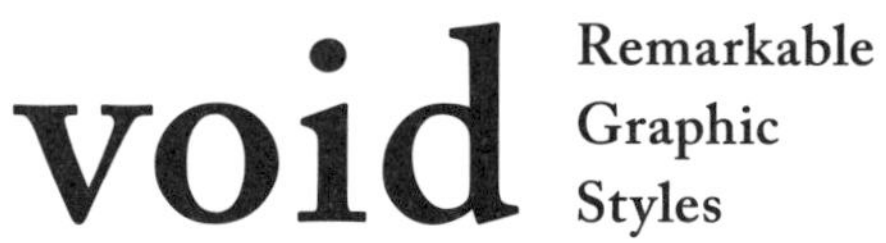

EDITED & PUBLISHED BY SendPoints Publishing Co., Ltd.

PUBLISHER: Lin Gengli

PUBLISHING DIRECTOR: Lin Shijian

ASSISTANT PUBLISHING-DIRECTOR: Chen Ting

CHIEF EDITOR: Lin Shijian

LEAD EDITOR: Li Weiji

EXECUTIVE EDITOR: Peggy Deng

DESIGN DIRECTOR: Lin Shijian

EXECUTIVE ART EDITOR: Kit Leung

PROOFREADING: James N. Powell, Peggy Deng

REGISTERED ADDRESS: Room 15A Block 9 Tsui Chuk Garden, Wong Tai Sin, Kowloon, Hong Kong

TEL: +852-35832323 / **FAX:** +852-35832448

OFFICE ADDRESS: 7F, 9th Anning Street, Jinshazhou, Baiyun District, Guangzhou, China

TEL: +86-20-89095121 / **FAX:** +86-20-89095206

BEIJING OFFICE: Room 107, Floor 1, Xiyingfang Alley, Ande Road, Dongcheng District, Beijing, China

TEL: +86-10-84139071 / **FAX:** +86-10-84139071

SHANGHAI OFFICE: Room 307, Building 1, Hong Qiang Creative, Zhabei District, Shanghai, China

TEL: +86-21-63523469 / **FAX:** +86-21-63523469

SALES MANAGER: Sissi

TEL: +86-20-81007895

EMAIL: sales@sendpoints.cn

WEBSITE: www.sendpoints.cn / www.spbooks.cn

ISBN 978-988-78494-9-0

- CONTENTS -

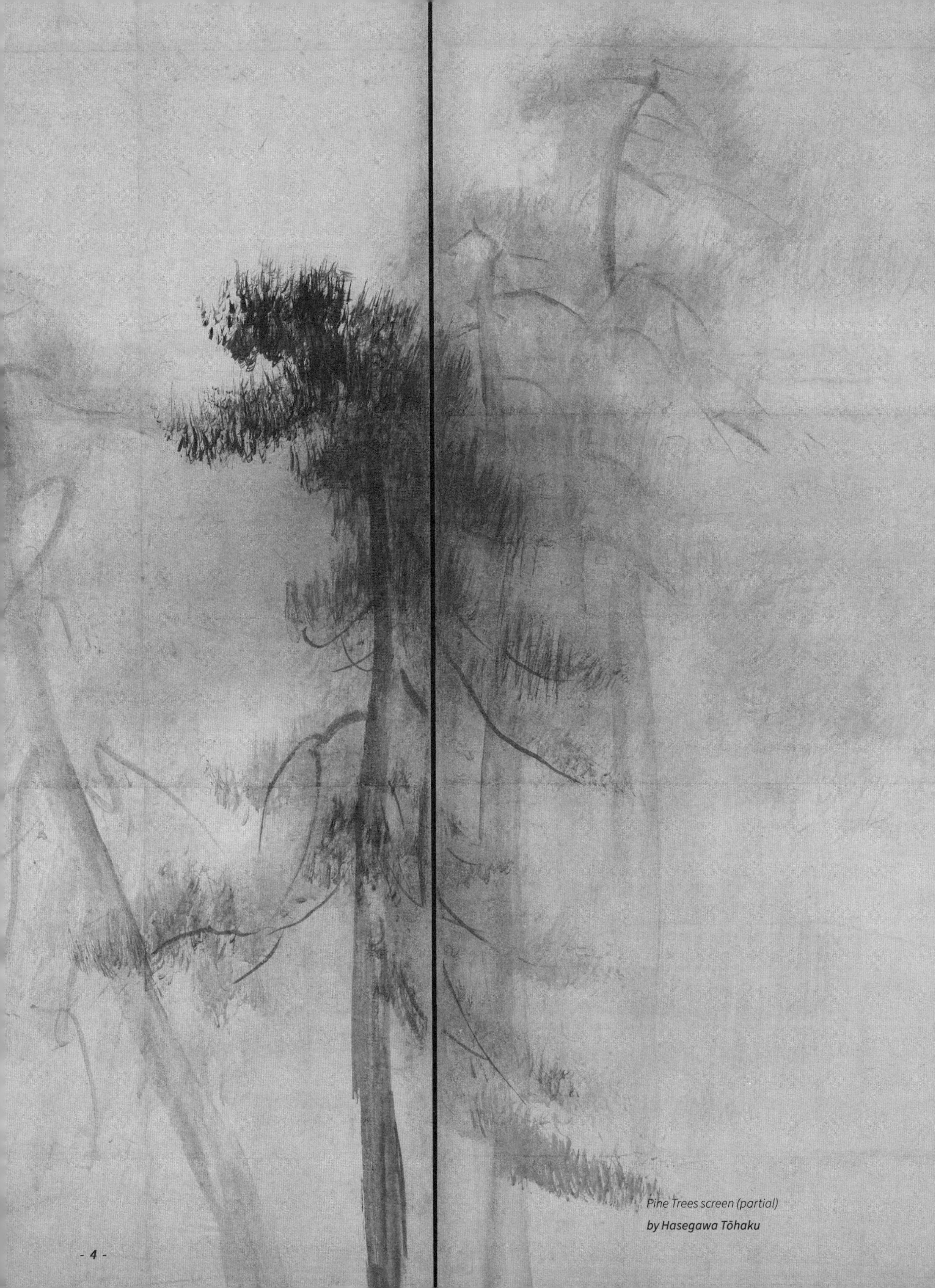

Pine Trees screen (partial)

by Hasegawa Tōhaku

THE VOID HERITAGE

Void in Oriental Art

Centuries before the culmination of reductive art in 1960s America, the concept of minimal art was bred in the Far East. Yet the oriental equivalent of minimalism, or emptiness, is more of a philosophical or emotional statement than mere aesthetics. In Buddhism, emptiness, or Śūnyatā, is considered the essence of all beings because the world is a tentative reality where connections are made and severed constantly. Similarly, Taoism regards void as the source and the end of the universe, calling for one's return to the original mind. Extended with the endorsements by Asian imperial leaders, Taoism and Buddhism played vital roles in shaping Asian cultures, and the concept of emptiness greatly influenced different aspects of life. Therefore, artistic expressions including painting, poetry, and architecture in the Eastern world have always reflected the creators' inner quests for emptiness.

Just as the enjoyment of reciting a poem or appreciating a noh play lies as much or more in the lapse of interval pauses as in the voice, of relishing a painting as much or more in the unpainted as in the filled, and of savoring a story as much or more in the untold as in the depicted, the emptiness, the space, the void within or between is never meaningless. Rather, it is the result of condensation, of extracting the essentials, and of deliberately concealing. This vacuum engages viewers to interact with indefinite potentials. This void could actually be the inclusiveness of everything.

Chinese Ink Wash Painting

Chinese ink wash painters often use the formless to indicate subtle forms, such as cloud, sky, or water, and also abstract ideas such as Zen spirit. The visual absence itself conveys information and gives clarification to the solid space. This lack of an image is interdependent with the space filled, and the two combined bring out rhythm and consonance in an artistic work.

With years of refinement of the nuance in tonality of black, grey, and white and flexibility of brushstrokes that run from thick to thin, square to round, the practitioners of this art mastered their instruments of ink and brush so well as to grasp the essence of a work. A monochrome painting sparsely composed can deliver a full play of vitality.

With less importance attached to anatomical studies or shading techniques, these artists do not aim to replicate the observed effect or concrete natural details. They strip away the unnecessary elements, using a great economy of brushstrokes to distinguish the subject matter. What they are seeking is to capture an emotion or an atmosphere, to explore the understanding of cosmic self-identification, and to depict inner quietude. In this way, their works have been transformed from mere artistic performance into philosophical or emotional declarations that strike their audiences deeply, evoking contemplation and a lingering aftertaste.

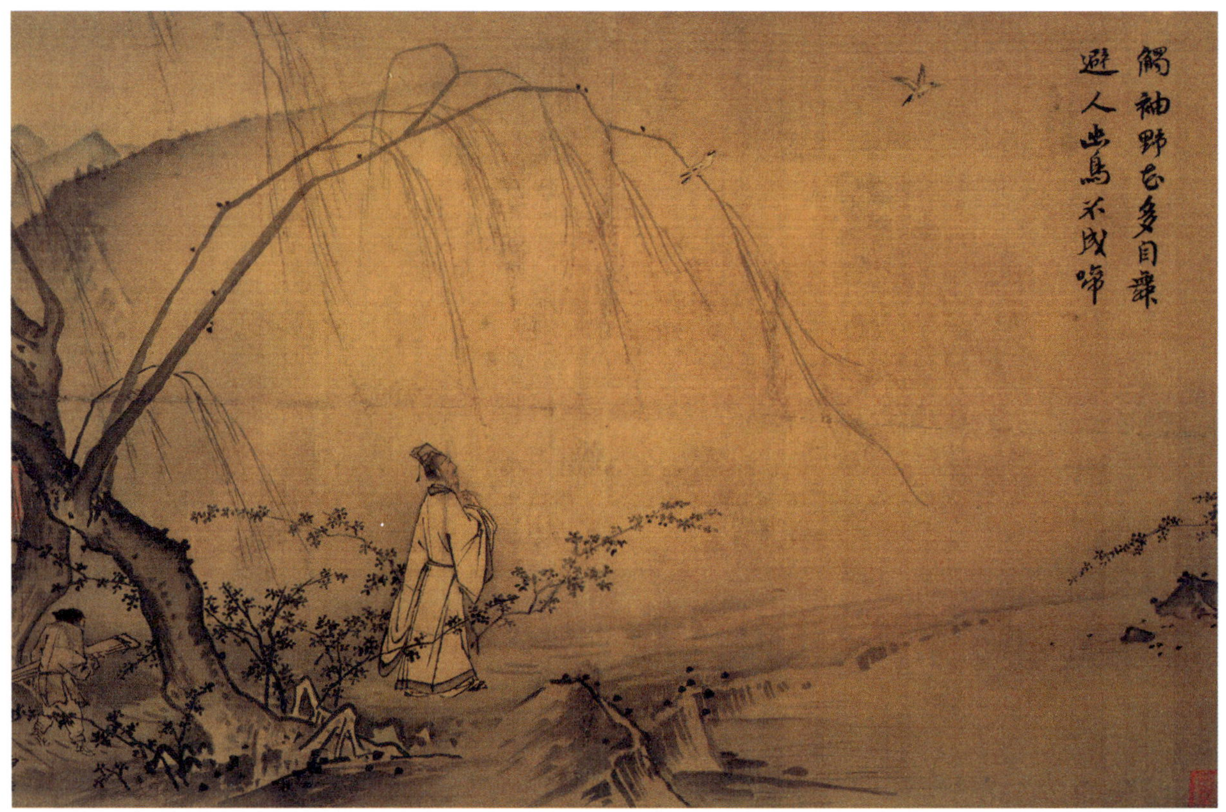

Walking on Path in Spring
by Ma Yuan

Ru Ware

Ceramics produced in the Song dynasty have been ranked by many as the finest in Chinese ceramic history. Among them Ru ware stands out as the best—though fired only for imperial use for a brief period (late 11th – early 12th century). Ru ware distinguishes itself as the paragon of celadon. Nowadays, only less than 70 pieces survive in museums or private collections around the world.

With an ash-gray paste as the base, Ru ware is covered completely by a layer of smooth, transparent, lustrous glaze, forming a special jade-like or vitreous texture. The monochrome stoneware glaze is in a soothing bluish or greenish color and has been eulogized by some as the heavenly blue after rain. When viewed from different angles, a slight tinge of rose-pink luster can be discerned. This celebrated type of ware is mostly undecorated, contrary to the sophistication and splendor favored in the precedent art works of the Tang Dynasty. The form and shape were refined to minimalist to attain simple elegance. Over the surface, only subtle and irregularly veined cracks, naturally formed during the firing process, can be observed. These endow the porcelain with delicate patterns. The austerity, elegance, and balanced tone—hovering somewhere between green and blue—embodies imperial beliefs in Taoist notions of non-action, naturalness, and moderation.

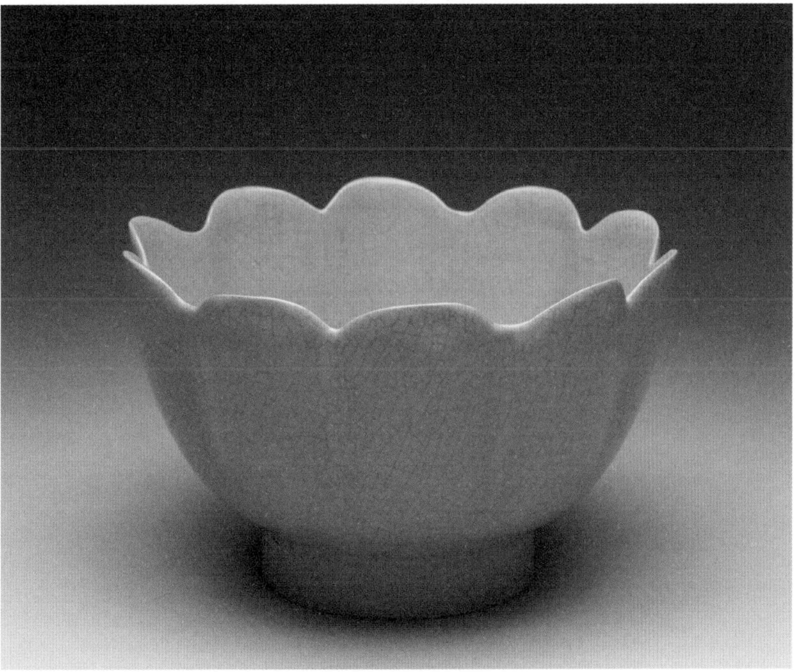

Warming bowl with celadon glaze Ru ware from Northern Song dynasty

Karesansui

Traditional Japanese gardens are renowned for their incorporation of nature, and among them karesansui is especially a unique one. Literally translated as "dry landscape," karesansui refers to waterless gardens that normally employ only a small number of static natural elements such as rocks, sand, gravel, or moss to recreate a natural landscape. Originally a place enveloped in Zen temples for assisting meditation, karesansui features white gravel carefully raked into ripple or wave patterns encircling rocks. Monks daily do the raking, with the rippled sand symbolizing waves or clouds surrounding mountains. The intermediate spaces of the austere composition bring in rhythm and flow of energy. They parallel the immeasurable empty spaces that distinguish transcendental Chinese ink-wash painting. The arrangement of subtle and symbolic elements also tinge the garden with a slight sensation of mysticism and obscurity, adding spiritual depth and profundity. Karesansui, by showing less and eliminating limitations for the viewer's mind, is actually showing more.

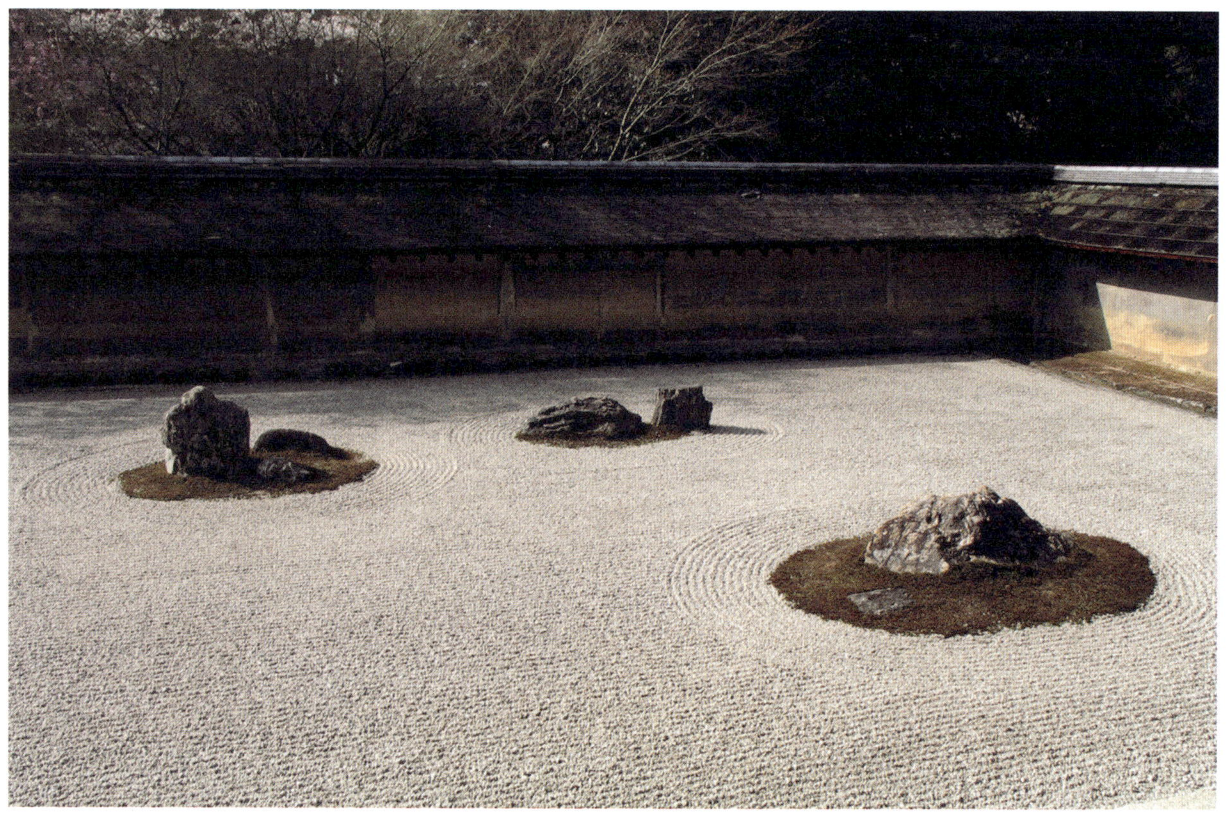

Dry Garden in RyoanJi

Tokonoma

Like karesansui, tokonoma is another embodiment of classical Japanese aesthetics. A tokonoma, an alcove of spiritual importance for traditional Japanese houses, consists mainly of an elevated wooden floor. The floor is often covered with tatami. It also has a corner pillar, normally a tree trunk with natural finish, and a ceiling. This recessed space, with plain wood and plain walls, is in such a simple style that in it only beautiful artistic works such as a calligraphy scroll and flower arrangement—called "ikebana" and "bonsai"—are displayed. These artistic works vary according to seasons and taste, in honor of guests. Tokonoma is cut out of the room in a way that direct light is blocked out. Thus, only dim shadows fill this space of void: imparting a quality of profound stillness. Through containing less, this empty area of measurable size opens up an infinite world of subjective awareness.

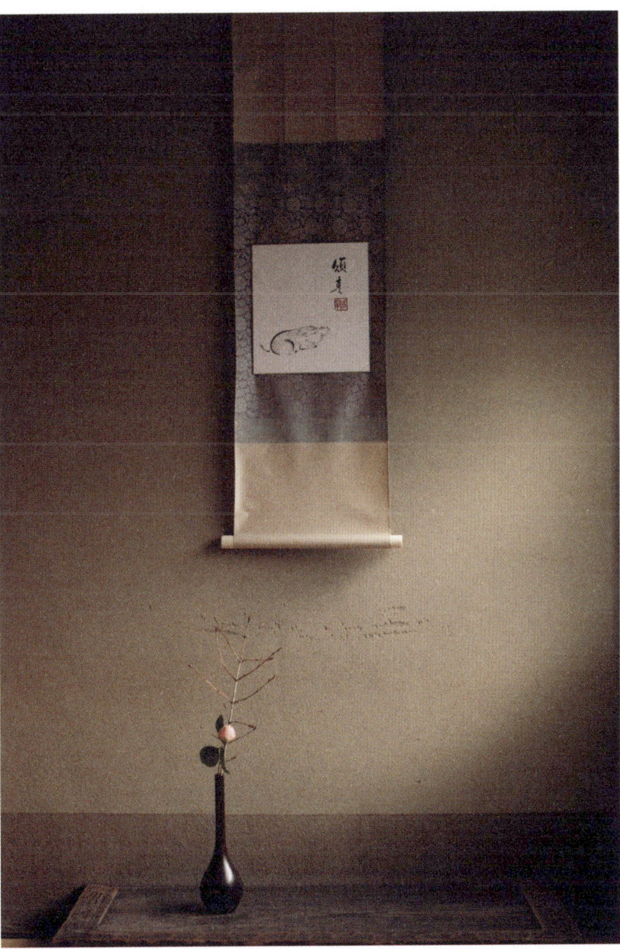

A Tokonoma Display

Contemporary Japanese Architecture

Characterized as being clean-shaped, straightforward, and intimate with nature, contemporary Japanese architecture could well exemplify Japanese values of simplicity, flexibility, and space. Although the buildings are always structurally simple and economical in their use of materials in order to reduce damage brought by earthquakes, they in no way compromise on aesthetics. Rather, many deliver incomparable modernity, marked by geometric succinctness and a soft palette. Unessential decorative elements, such as the sophisticated ornamental touches common in classic European and Chinese constructions, can rarely be found. Many components were devised ingeniously: such as sliding doors and tatami mats to allow flexible configurations of one specific area to attain greater practicality. With inherited respect for and connection to nature, they incorporate the delicacy and vitality of nature into their complexes. This blurs the boundary between man-made and natural and enlarges the perceptive depth and breadth of a space. While retaining a concentration on essentials and cares of human needs, this architecture declutters, stills, and achieves a humane focus that is tender to the touch, easy on the eye, and soothing to the mind.

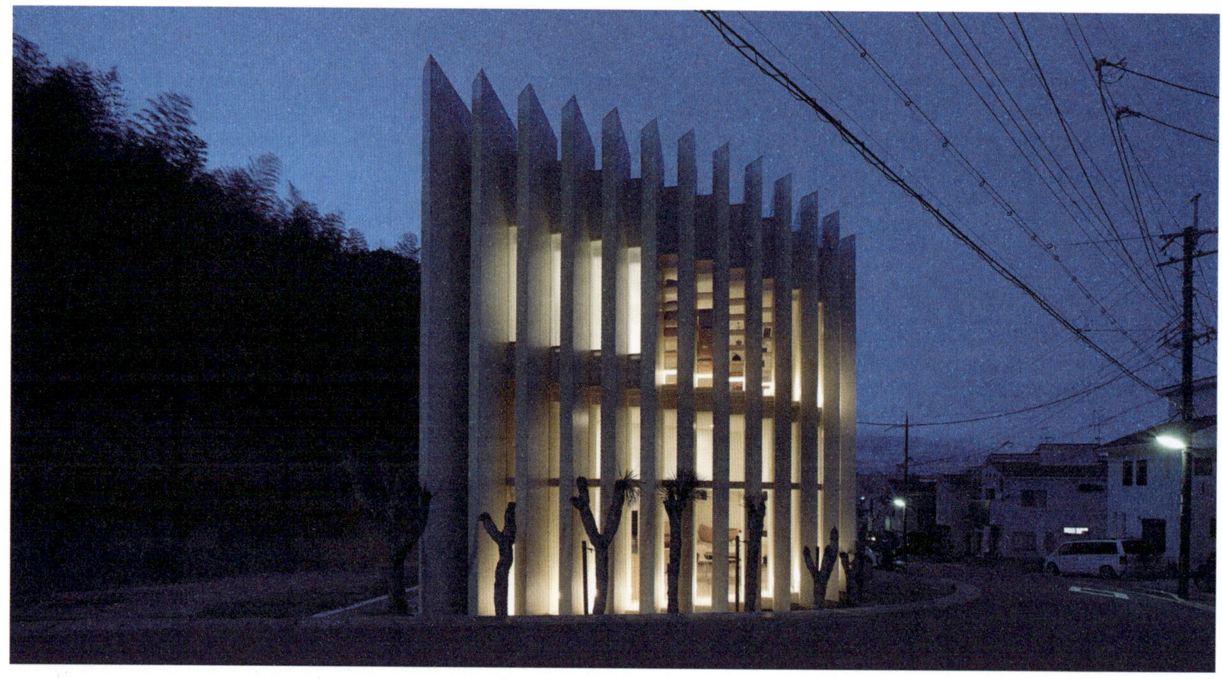

House in Muko

Designed by FujiwaraMuro Architects

Photo by Toshiyuki Yano

Modern Japanese Product

Japanese products have come to the forefront of the international arena for their adeptness at bridging Western concepts with traditional Japanese aesthetics. This involves a predilection for simplicity, empty space, lightness, functionality, superior craftsmanship, mobility, and sustainability. The application of organic elements, materials, and patterns has also been favored in order to highlight a spiritual connection with nature. The designers have adopted a groundbreaking mindset to reconstitute everyday objects and remake them into superb designs, hoping for a "democratization" of goods and beauty. This notion was put forward by the great industrial designer Kenji Ekuan. Designs shall be "without thought," and unnecessary elements shall be pared down to a minimum for products to pass the test of time and the cycles of taste. Products gain both visual appeal and practicality through the physical form of the products themselves, without additional embellishments. By returning to the original objective of a product, maximum usability can be attained. Modern Japanese products also display their creators' zeal for employing technologies to realize their ideal combination of greater functionality and maximum beauty.

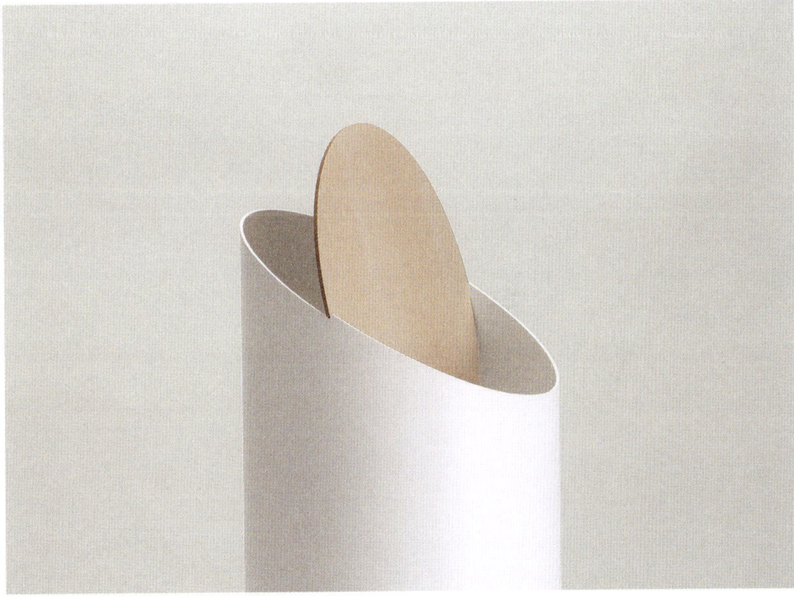

Swing Bin

Product designer: Shigeichiro Takeuchi

© SHIGEICHIRO STUDIO

THE VOID HERITAGE

Void in Western Art

For Westerners, the discovery of the idea of void was long a path less trodden. From as early as the 18th century, however, this changed when concepts and representations of voidness began to emerge. On the canvases of artists, who are often at the cultural forefront, forms melted into abstractions, reflecting a sense of some unfathomable infinity. Canvases became spiritually resonant pronouncements: with Joseph Mallord William Turner's canvases becoming atmospheric interplays of color and light, and Caspar David Friedrich's paintings becoming romanticized and empty landscapes. Alongside a subsequent array of groundbreaking technological innovations and ideological revolutions, the very idea of art was rewritten, unleashing an unbounded potential for modern art.

This probe into void has evolved beyond enigmatic obscurity and into forms oriented toward pictorial reductionism and geometric abstraction. Continuing this reductive philosophy, more recent minimalists have emptied a unique, calming niche for minds crammed with the demands of industrialization and urbanization, offering practical solutions to everyday problems.

Today's graphic design regards "void" as increasingly relevant. Whether it is to simplify form or to leave space for the mind, the aesthetics of "void" will continue to emanate its unique fascination.

Rain, Steam and Speed –
The Great Western Railway
by J. M. W. Turner

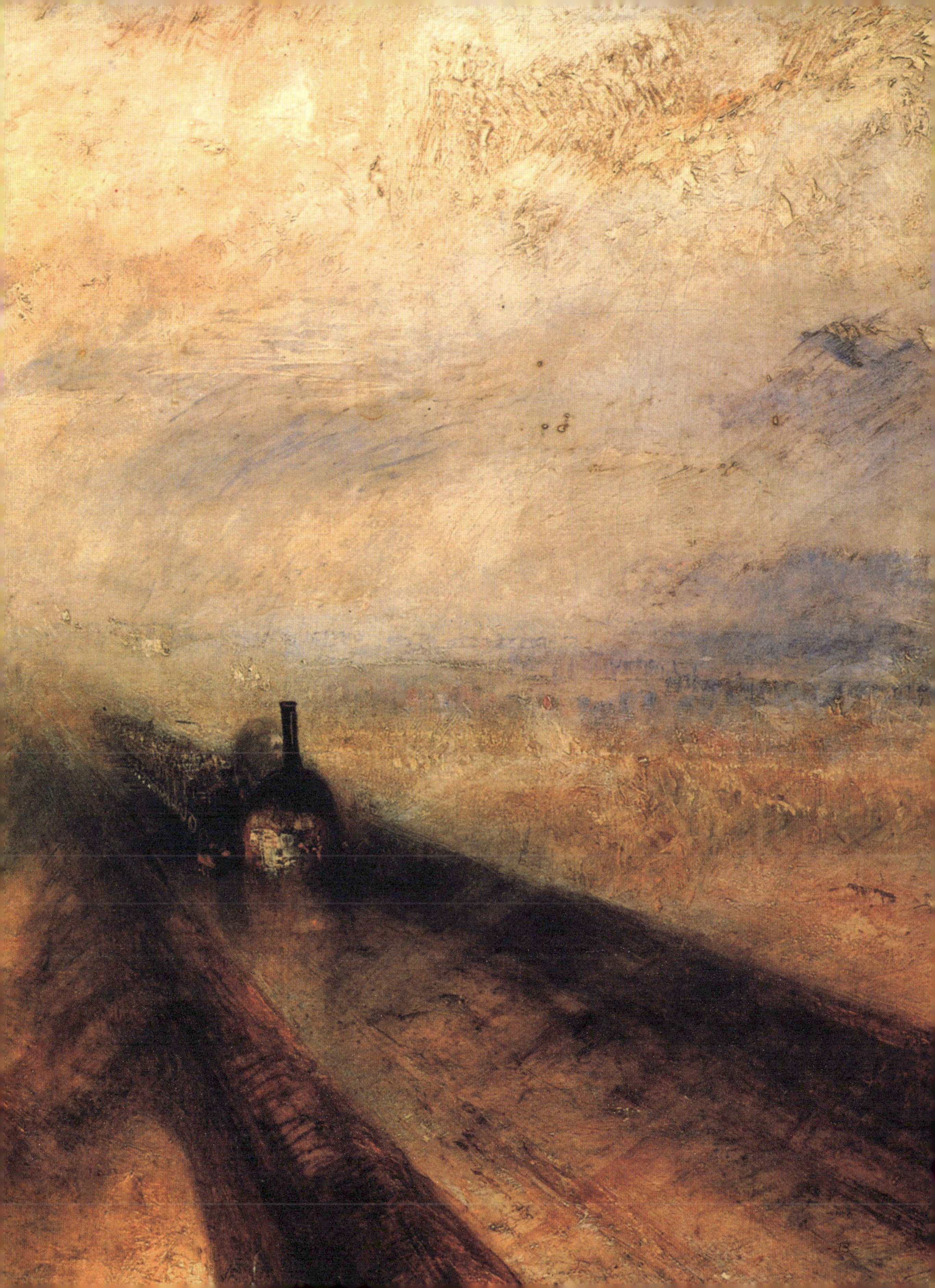

Caspar David Friedrich

"The Vanity of existence is revealed. . . in the infiniteness of time and space contrasted with the finiteness of the individual in both." This lament by German philosopher Arthur Schopenhauer (1788 – 1860) on the emptiness of life resonates with the atmosphere of void exuding from the empty landscapes of one of his contemporaries, Caspar David Friedrich (1774 – 1840), Germany's greatest Romantic painter. His enigmatic landscapes and seascapes have captivated gazes and thoughts throughout the ages.

Before Friedrich, rarely had canvases as empty as his ever been seen in the West. In his paintings, large portions of space are dedicated to empty air. Unnecessary middle-grounds and backgrounds, if there are any, often fall into obscurity. The emptiness of such abstraction was so novel that the painter's visitors often mistook mountain views for seascapes, or complimented pictures that hung upside down on the easel.

"Nothing is incidental in a picture," the painter said. Through a deliberate purification of landscape painting's subject and composition, with details faithful to precise studies of nature, he sought to recreate moodscapes.

Maybe it was the demise of those around him that incited him to relentlessly contemplate the transience of an individual's existence against the almighty and inclusive universe, or, God, and then to portray this sentiment passionately in his canvas. Through the leitmotif in Rückenfigur (figure seen from behind), viewers are constantly invited into the same position, sharing the same view of the barren landscape as the artist. Thus positioned, they face the all-encompassing, sublimity of inscrutable infiniteness, in which they feel individual existence gradually diminish into nothingness.

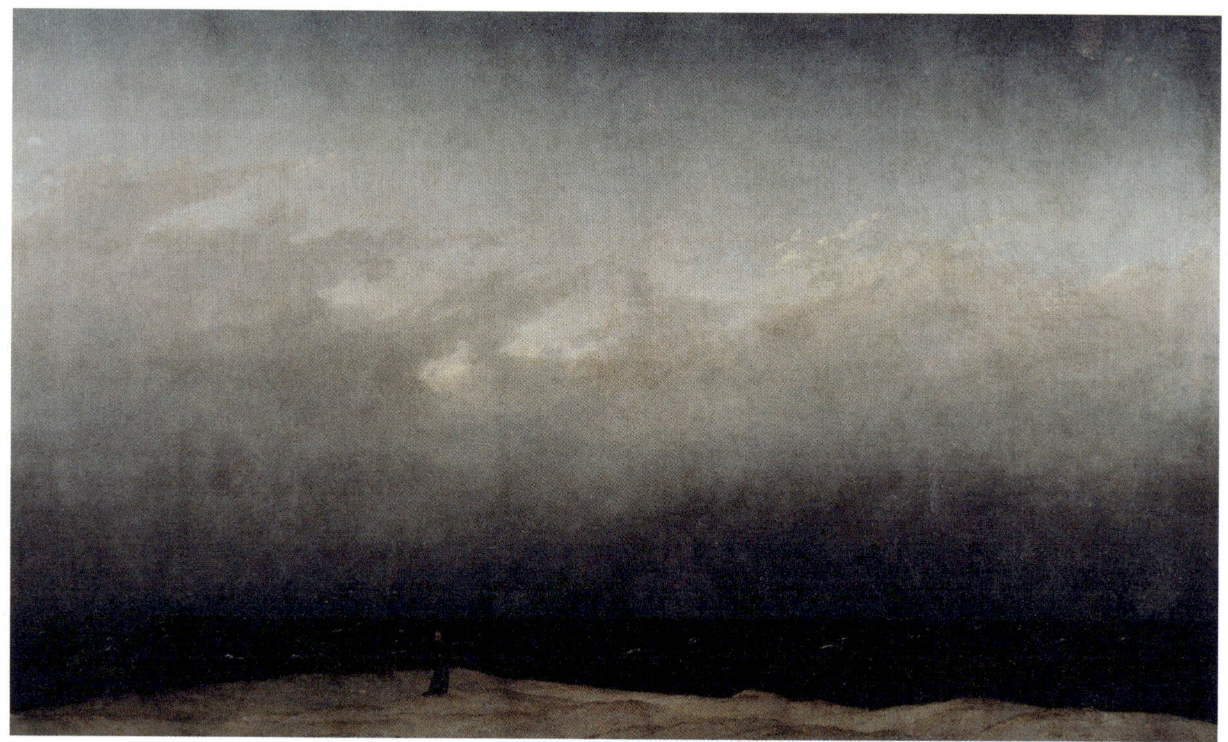

The Monk by the Sea
by Caspar David Friedrich

Geometric Abstractionists

Russian painter Kasimir Malevich's (1878 – 1935) *Black Square*, dubbed the "Suprematist Manifesto," displays a black rectangle against a white background. It is shockingly simple. In defiance of all pictorial conventions, Malevich challenged viewers to seek truth solely in basic forms and limited colors, on a canvas that, radically, no longer functioned as a representation of the experienced world. This elevated colors and forms to supreme dominance. He hoped to engage viewers in a pure experience of enjoying the "non-objective." By the extreme of reducing painting to nothing but shape and color, he opened up a new possibility that cut art off from logic and reason, heralding a new era of modern art of content-free forms.

Echoes of this reductive logic continue to strike notes in the West, as later shown in the colored squares in *Composition with Yellow, Blue and Red*, by Piet Cornelies Mondrian (1872 – 1944), a Dutch pioneer of abstract art and one of the founders of the De Stijl. Intending to disclose a universal order of harmony in pure forms, the painter reduced the elements within his canvas to a grid of vertical and horizontal lines on a white background, with sparsely patched primary colors. Composed with strict adherence to asymmetrical balance, this simplified pictorial vocabulary acquired a ubiquitous appeal that transcended divisions and has been readily married with various artistic media since its emergence.

Black Square
by Kasimir Malevich

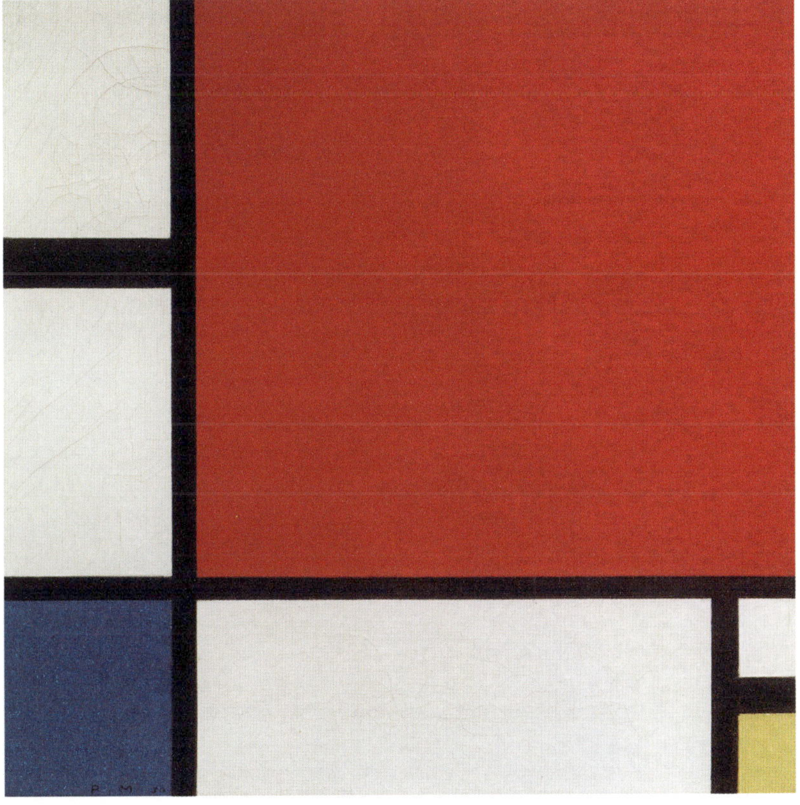

Composition with Yellow, Blue and Red
by Piet Cornelies Mondrian

Less Is More

The famous principle "less is more," advocated by German-born American architect Ludwig Mies van der Rohe (1886 – 1969), means that the proper employment of fewer elements can generate greater impacts. This slogan summarizes the very architectural language of the International style, giving rise to trends of future architects seeking to pare down buildings to their bare essentials.

Influenced by his association with the Deutscher Werkbund (the German Association of Craftsmen), which advocated an innovative link between aesthetics and technology, Mies adopted the most modern materials in search for an architectural Gesamtkultur (a new universal culture in line with the industrialized society of the 20th century). In Mies's design, sophisticated decorations commonly seen in traditional buildings, regarded by the designer mostly as distractions, gave way to functionality and rationality. His most iconic buildings are characterized by an imposing clarity of exposed structural steel sheathed in glass curtain-walls with elegant simplicity. This Miesian principle of "skin-and-bones construction" contributed to steel-and-glass skyscrapers that silhouetted urban skylines all over the world, decisively framing the persuasive tectonic expression of modern architecture.

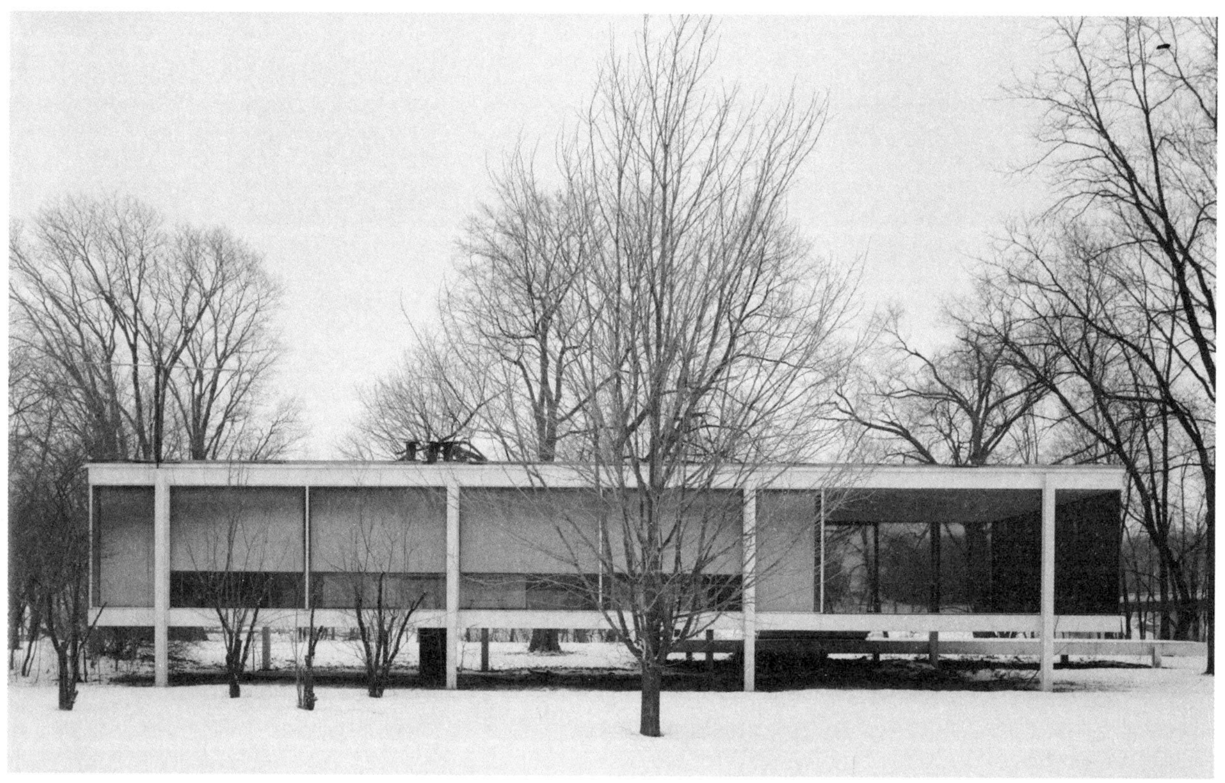

Edith Farnsworth House

Designed by Ludwig Mies van der Rohe

© Library of Congress,

Prints & Photographs Division, ILL,47-PLAN.V,1-9

Less but Better

"Less but better" represents the design philosophy of industrial designer Dieter Rams (1932 –), who had spearheaded a groundbreaking design current in the 20th century, and whose designs have touched the lives of millions of people. Foreseeing the irreversibly diminishing supply of natural resources, including raw materials, energy, food, and land, Rams called for a rationalist and economizing mindset in design to counter the "impenetrable confusion of forms, colors, and noises."

His designs are featured by clean lines, muted color palettes, and restrained subjectivity. By concentrating on less, but essential elements and omitting the superfluous, he responsively contributed to the world with household appliances and interiors distinguished by their comfort, legibility, and timelessness.

According to Rams, a good designer, rather than merely packaging products as the final touch according to his or her aesthetics and preferences as an artist, shall assume the responsibilities of a creative engineer to synthesize the various elements to produce an "ergonomically correct" product. In this sense, at the helm of every design process lies functionality, the understanding of which becomes the touchstone to justify every aesthetic decision.

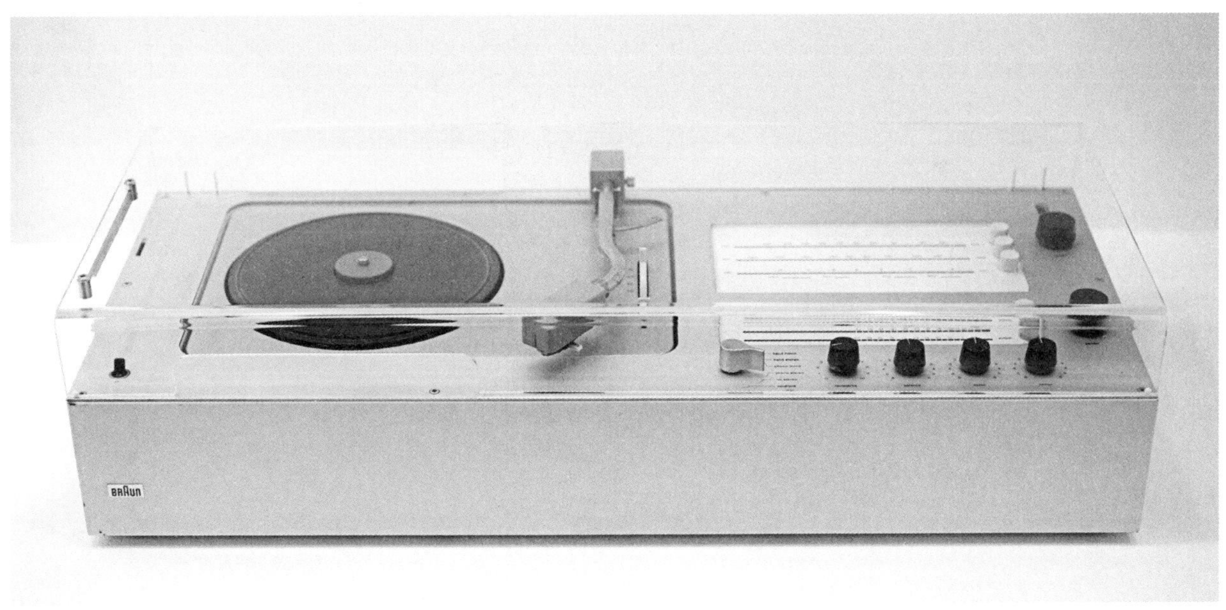

Record player and radio

Designed by Dieter Rams

© René Spitz

Bauhaus

In 1919, to counter the enlarging segregation of art and manufacturing against the backdrop of the growing industrialization, the most influential modernist art institute of the 20th century, Bauhaus, was established by the distinguished architect Walter Gropius (1883-1969), in the hope to achieve a harmonious integration of functionality, simplicity, and aesthetics.

Although the Bauhaus output has shown surprising diversity, the core that binds everything together must not be overlooked. Encompassing the totality of almost all design genres, the Bauhaus artists emphasized the use of simplified geometric forms, the deliberate reduction of ornamentation, the adoption of new production materials and technologies, and a high valuation on the practicality as well as feasibility of satisfying mass demands.

Among the many Bauhaus classics, the Wassily chair (also called the "Club Chair" or "Model B3") is one that perfectly embodies Bauhaus's groundbreaking innovations. This chair represents a revolutionary combination of seamless tubular steel, a new material with great potential for physical tension, endurance, and shaping, with fabric covering. Adopting only essential elements, the chair is lightweight, sleek, and legible. Arriving at an optimal fusion of comfort, elegance, and concerns over manufacturing availabilities, it has proven to be a timeless piece that is still being produced today.

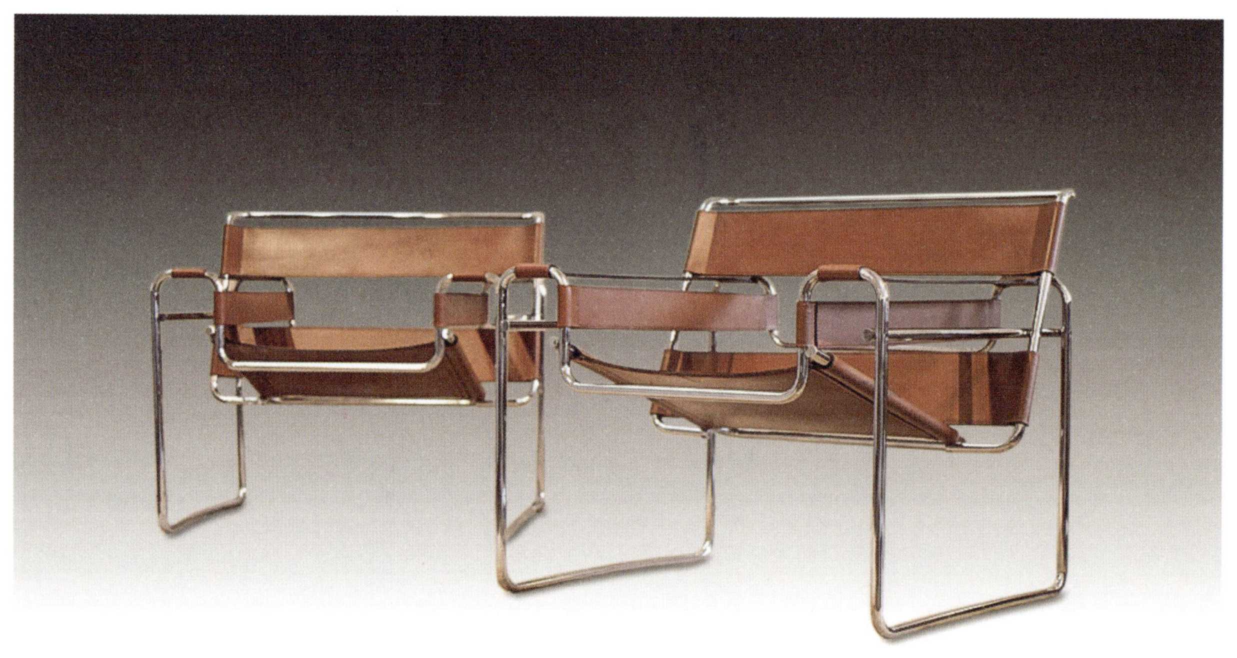

Oxblood Wassily Chairs

© David Costa, Flickr / CC BY 2.0

The Scandinavian Design

Scandinavian design has gained unceasing popularity all around the world since its emergence in the 1950s. The cornerstone behind its success is an ethos of appropriateness, moderation, and balance, or, as Swedish proverb humbly suggests, "Lagom är bäst"— the right amount is the best.

Scandinavian minimalist designs serve functional and aesthetic ends exceptionally well. Excessive adornment or extravagance is not advised because most people prefer a modest and frugal lifestyle. The typical Nordic look is highlighted by simple contours; elegant and succinct geometrical shapes; the dominance of white, grey, and black colors; superb craftsmanship; and sustainable and organic materials. With a democratic mindset for the well-being of the masses, Nordic designers seek to create practical, affordable, and beautiful designs that embody functionality and usability. Caring for people, as shown by the meticulous study on ergonomics by Kaare Klint (1888 – 1954), namely the father of modern Danish furniture design, also embraces minimal expression as a component of spiritual warmth.

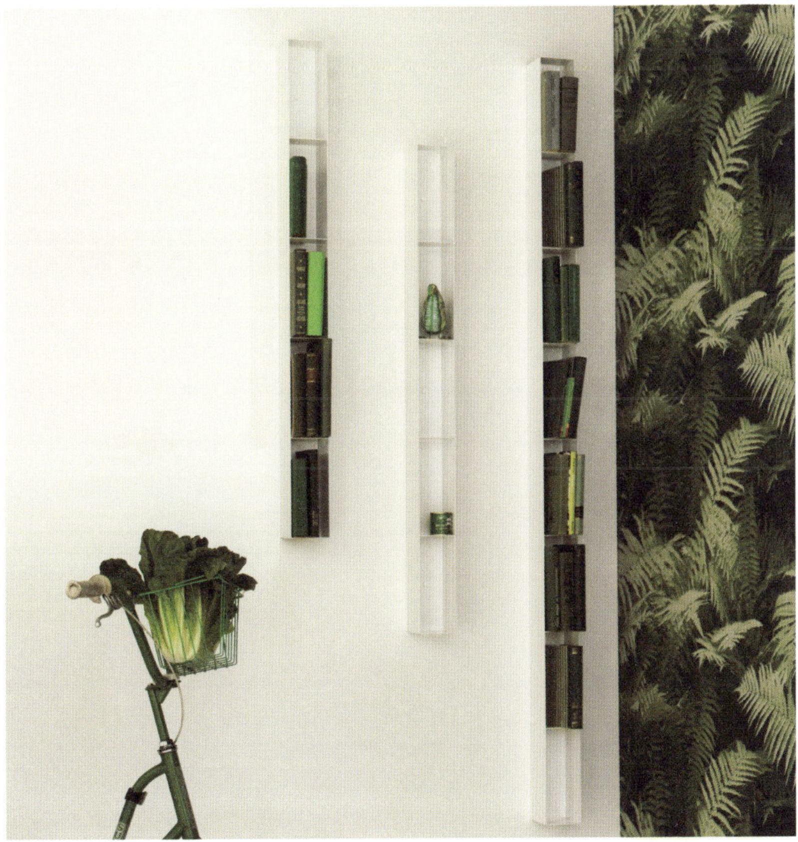

Luft Bookshelf

Designed by MottoWASABI Design Office

EMPTY SPACE

By a conscious control of the primary and secondary relation of design elements and their proportional relationship with the whole picture, a sense of space is produced in terms of visual psychology. In this way, more legible information, clearer hierarchy, and higher mobility are acquired.

image ©Yuta Takahashi

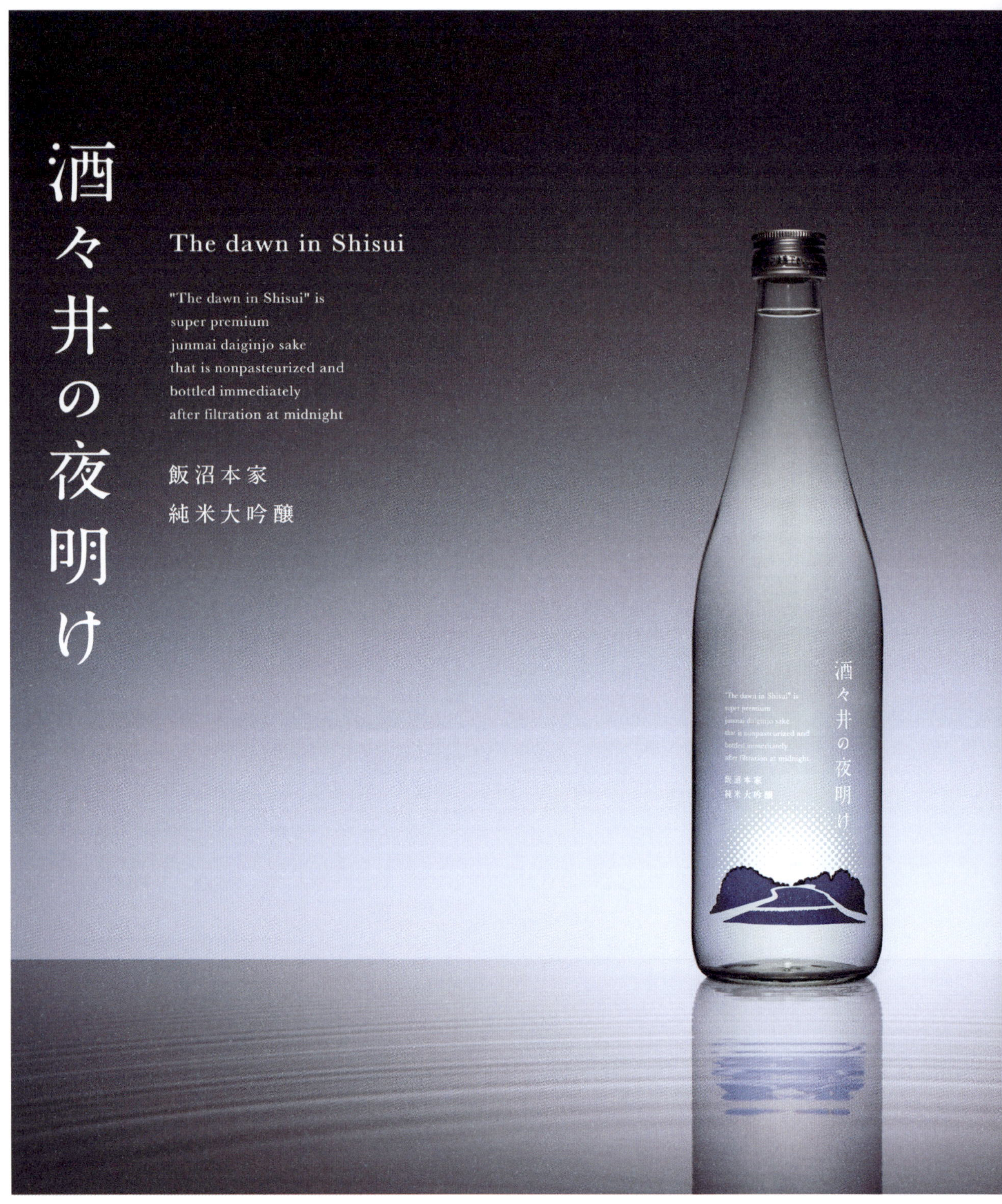

- Studio: **tegusu Inc**
- Designer: **Masaomi Fujita**

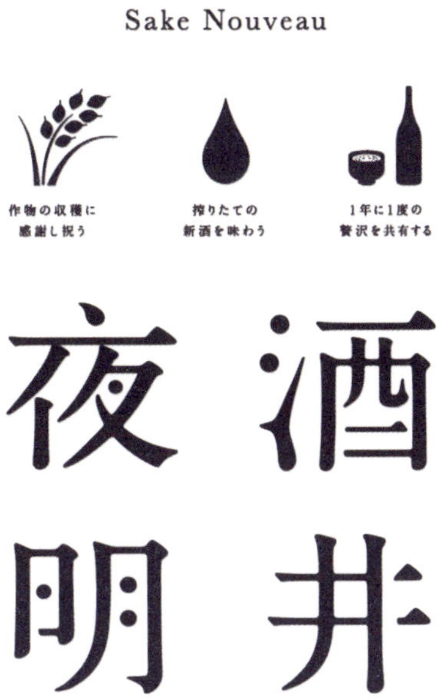

Sake Nouveau

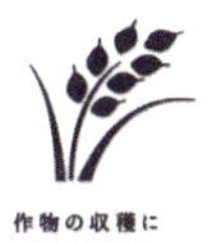

作物の収穫に
感謝し祝う

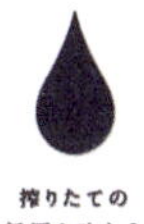

搾りたての
新酒を味わう

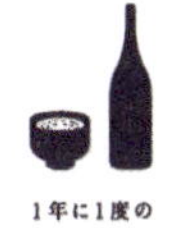

1年に1度の
贅沢を共有する

夜酒
明井

For the advertisement for Sake Nouveau, dark blue, a color of the sky before sunrise, and a combination of rural landscape's silhouette with gradation of dots were employed to capture the crack of dawn when the sake was bottled and delivered after filtration at midnight in Shisui Town, where the established sake brewery makes freshly pressed sake. Printed directly on the bottle, the design accentuates the transparency of the liquid, suggesting the refreshing and clear taste.

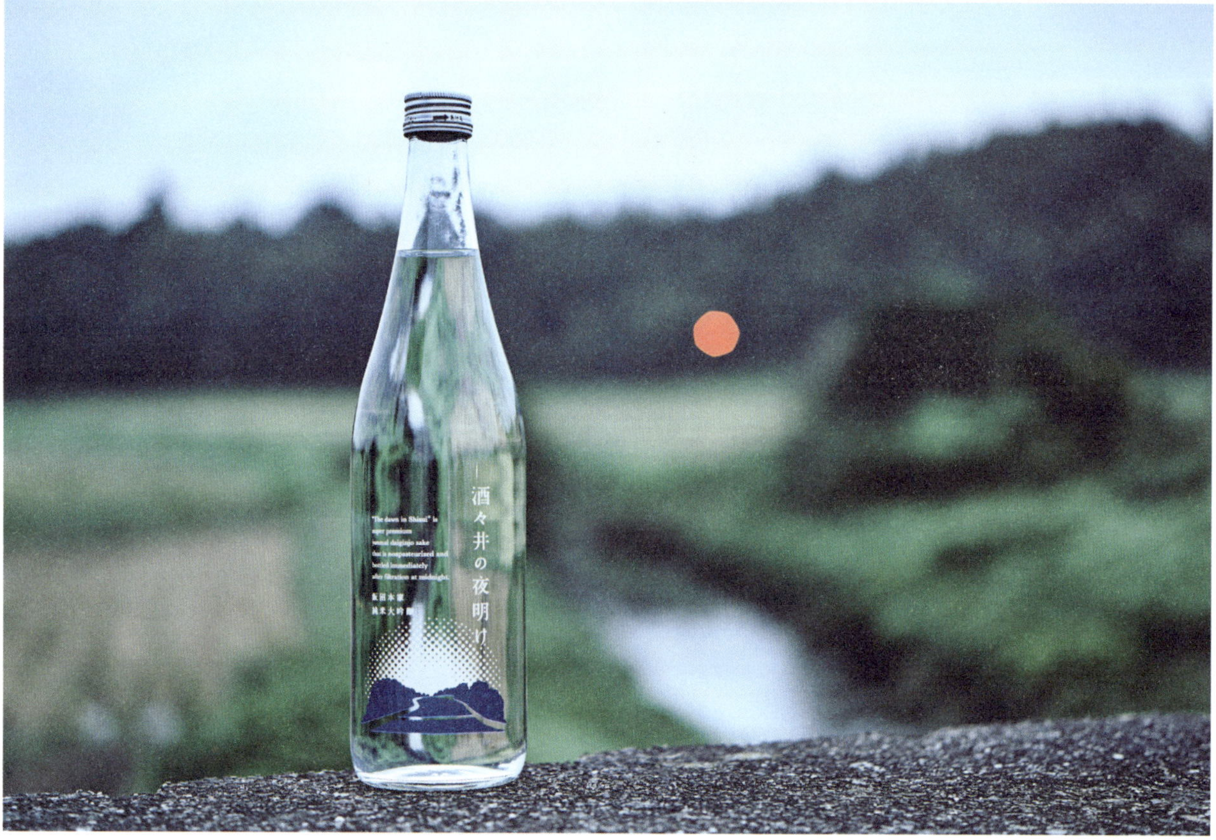

酒々井の夜明け

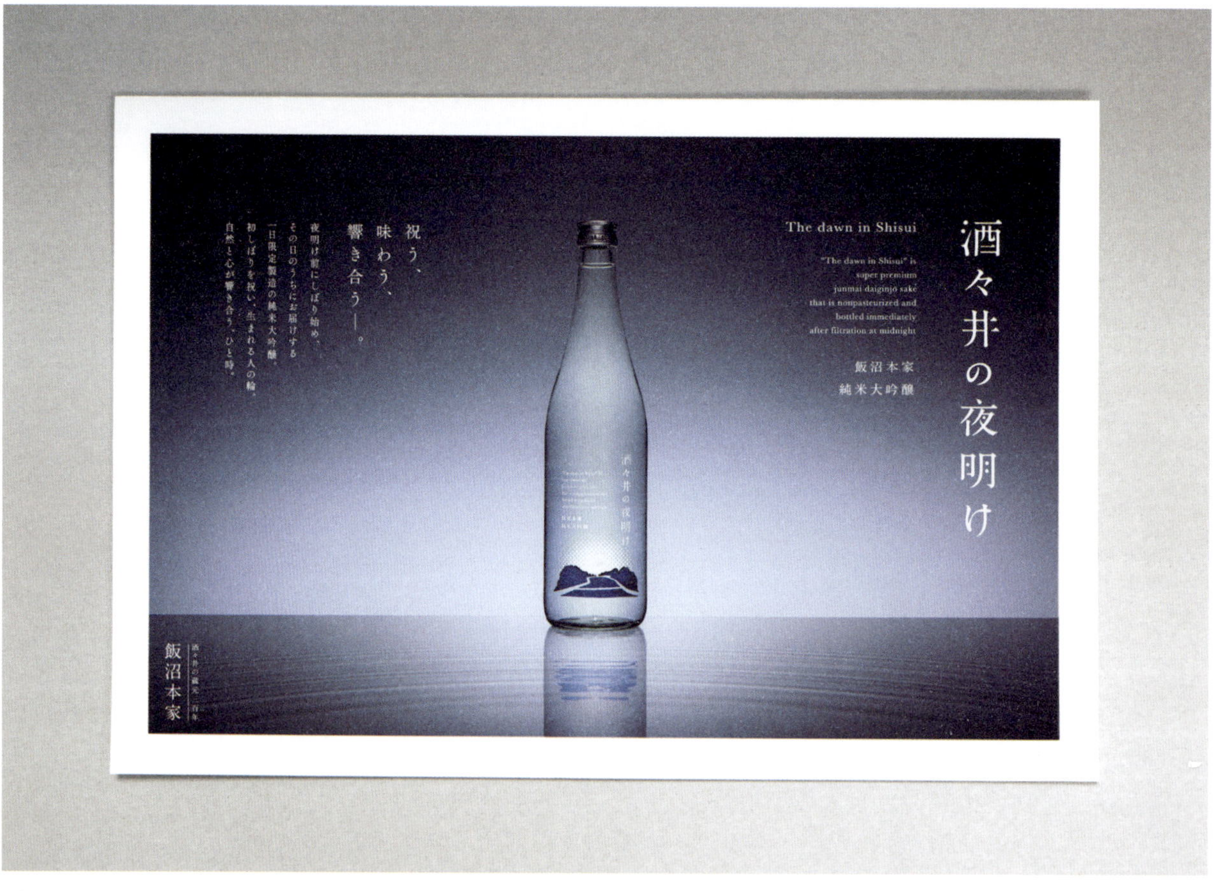

The dawn in Shisui

"The dawn in Shisui" is
super premium
junmai daiginjo sake
that is nonpasteurized and
bottled immediately
after filtration at midnight

飯沼本家
純米大吟醸

祝う、
味わう、
響き合う―。

夜明け前にしぼり始め、
その日のうちにお届けする
一日限定製造の純米大吟醸。
初しぼりを祝い、生まれる人の輪。
自然と心が響き合う、ひと時。

飯沼本家

Interview

- As a kind of visual experience, what do you think about the "voidness" in graphic design?

- I'd suggest that void means to communicate the message through visuals or designs to the recipients. It is to empty a space in design to let viewers feel and think. I think designs that minimalize what to convey often speaks more and arouse more imaginations than designs that are filled with words or visuals.

- What are your common approaches to produce a VOID visual effect?

- I would develop a system to invite perception of the stories concealed behind the objective. For example, Sake Noubeau project pictured ripples stirred up by a drop of water as its main visual to suggest as vividly the beginning of dawn as symbolically the spread of Japanese sake culture. It is this unique approach of void that helps the design achieve a greater result.

ANTHROPOSOPHISCHE GESELLSCHAFT UND FREIE HOCHSCHULE FÜR GEISTESWISSENSCHAFT

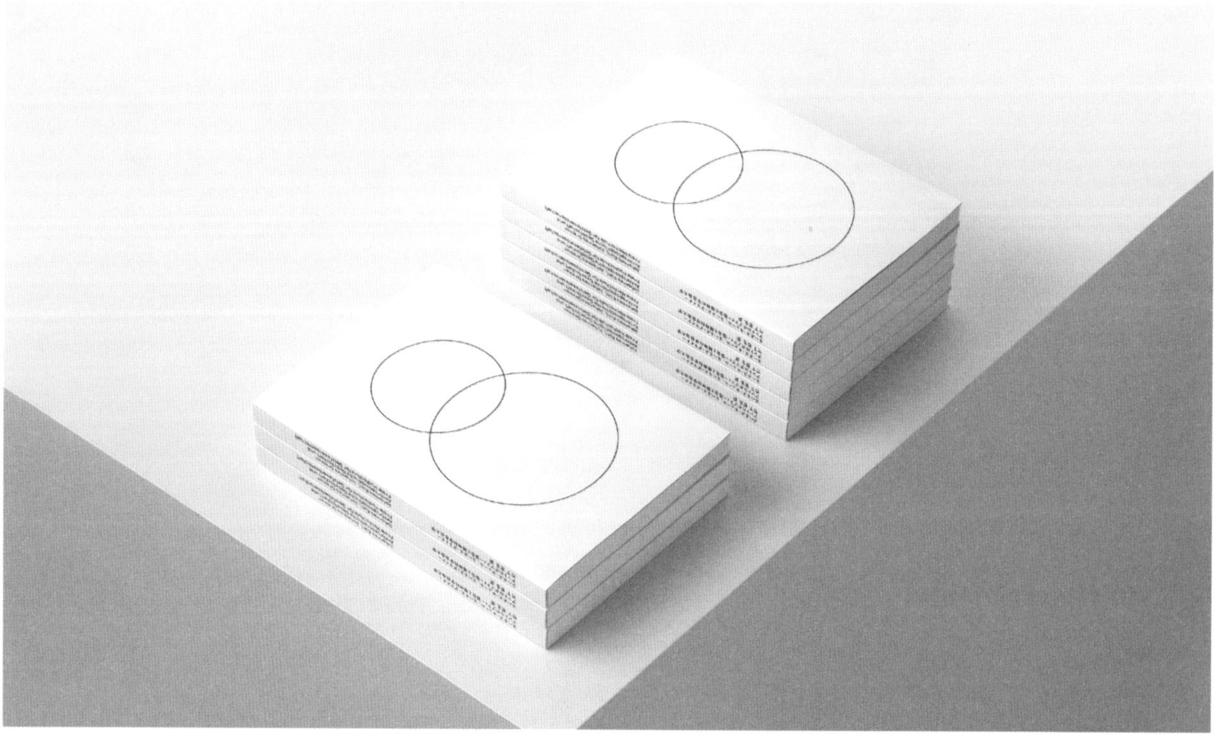

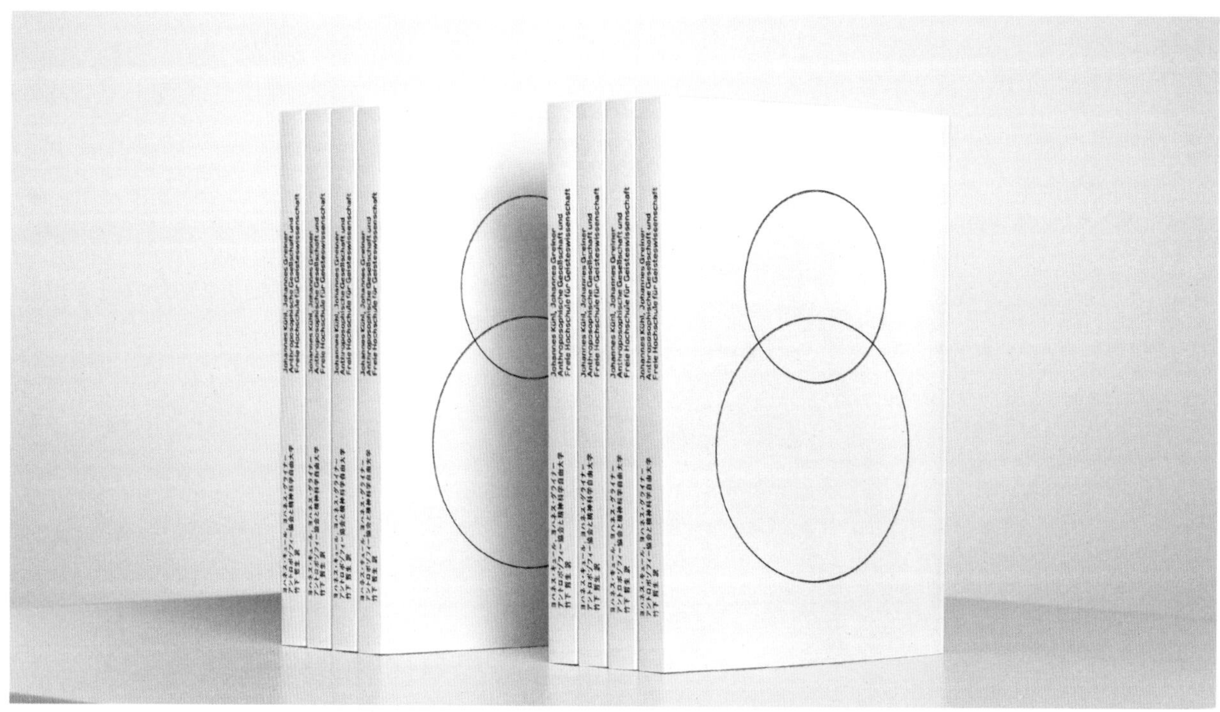

- *Designer:* ***Yuta Takahashi***

This modern book design of minimalist and elegant beauty was constructed with simulation from art, interior design and lifestyle. The key visuals on the cover clearly depict the book's intention to explore the relationship between the society and school. Presenting the content of thought on a white background is uniform throughout this series. The artistic touch of attention to details can be traced from even the minute gimmicks.

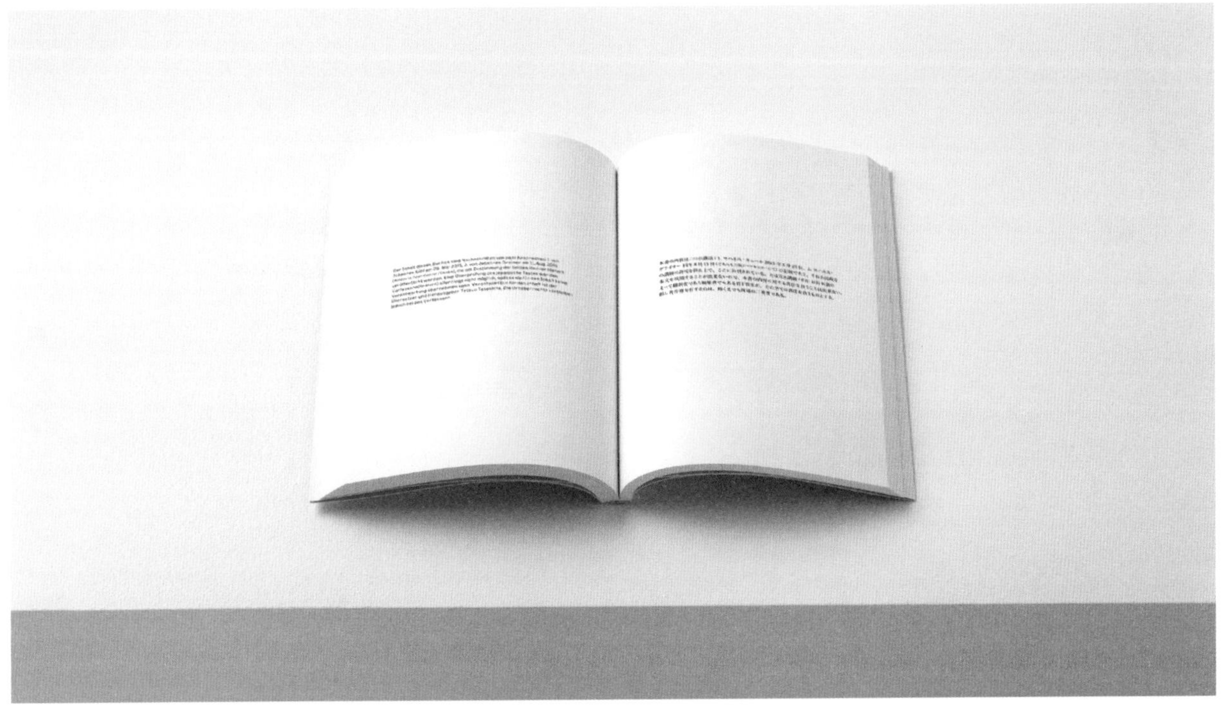

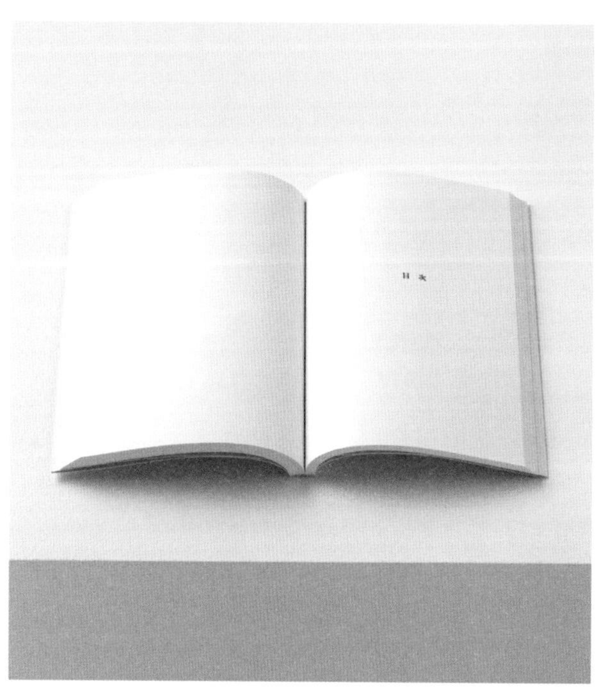

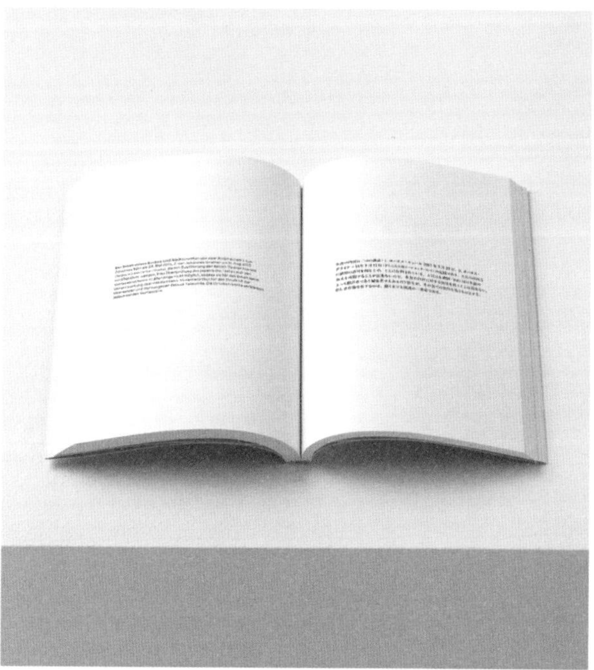

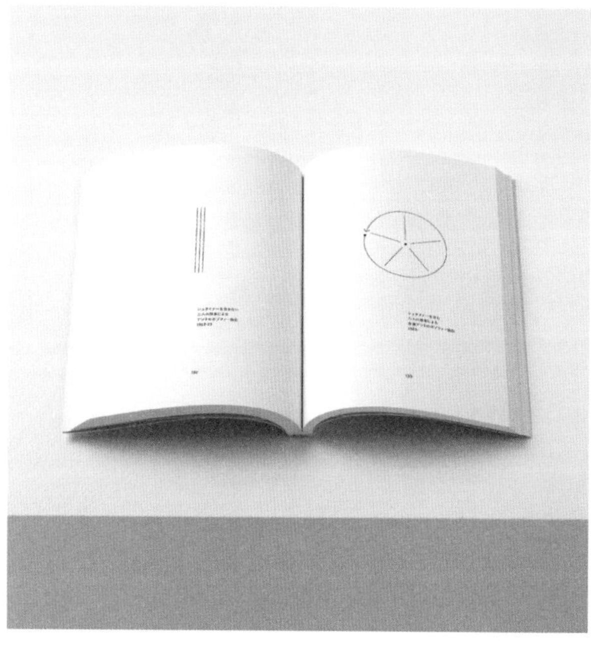

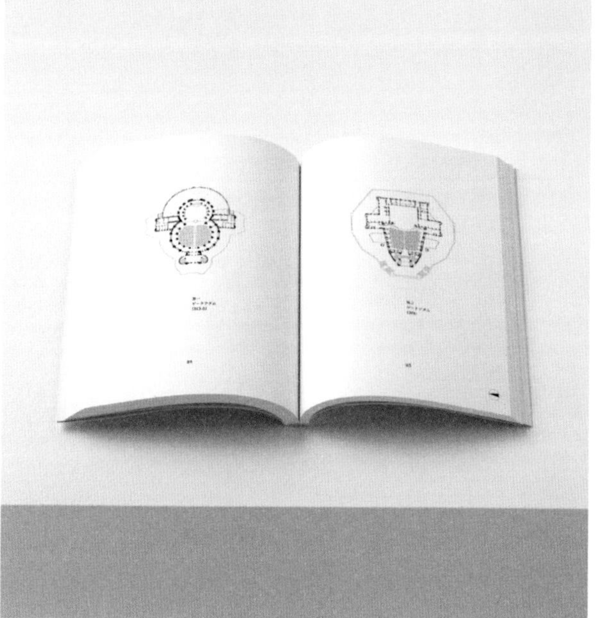

Interview

- As a kind of visual experience, what do you think about the "voidness" in graphic design?

- In Japan we have gardens called dry landscape or zen gardens. It's not that we watch the scenery or nature of each season there; Just that with the static materials there (rocks or gravel), a space with nothing in it comes into being. So what are people gazing at? Their own hearts. To talk with the inner self, you need to keep the things in front of you at a distance for a while.

So, is it possible to do the same thing with graphic design?

And why do we need to do that? We create things and information to improve people's lives, helping them live more actively and independently. However, if things and information stop enriching and instead start to overshadow people's lives, they can't be considered as good. Since the moments we live in are flooded with things and information, "THE VOIDNESS" offers a way to help us present a freer cultural life and contributes to a design that makes people feel more comfortable and relaxing.

- What are your common approaches to produce a VOID visual effect?

- When people look at the things in front of them, how do they perceive? The interesting thing is that people don't just see a thing in front of them as what it is. They are also looking at the philosophy behind it, and seeing through it for what is beyond.

To produce a "VOID" visual effect is not simply learning human patterns of recognition and then setting out to make the first design. More importantly, it is about constructing the underlying philosophy or vision of the subject. Along with this process, the answer will naturally come forth just like water dripping out of a wet towel when it is wrung.

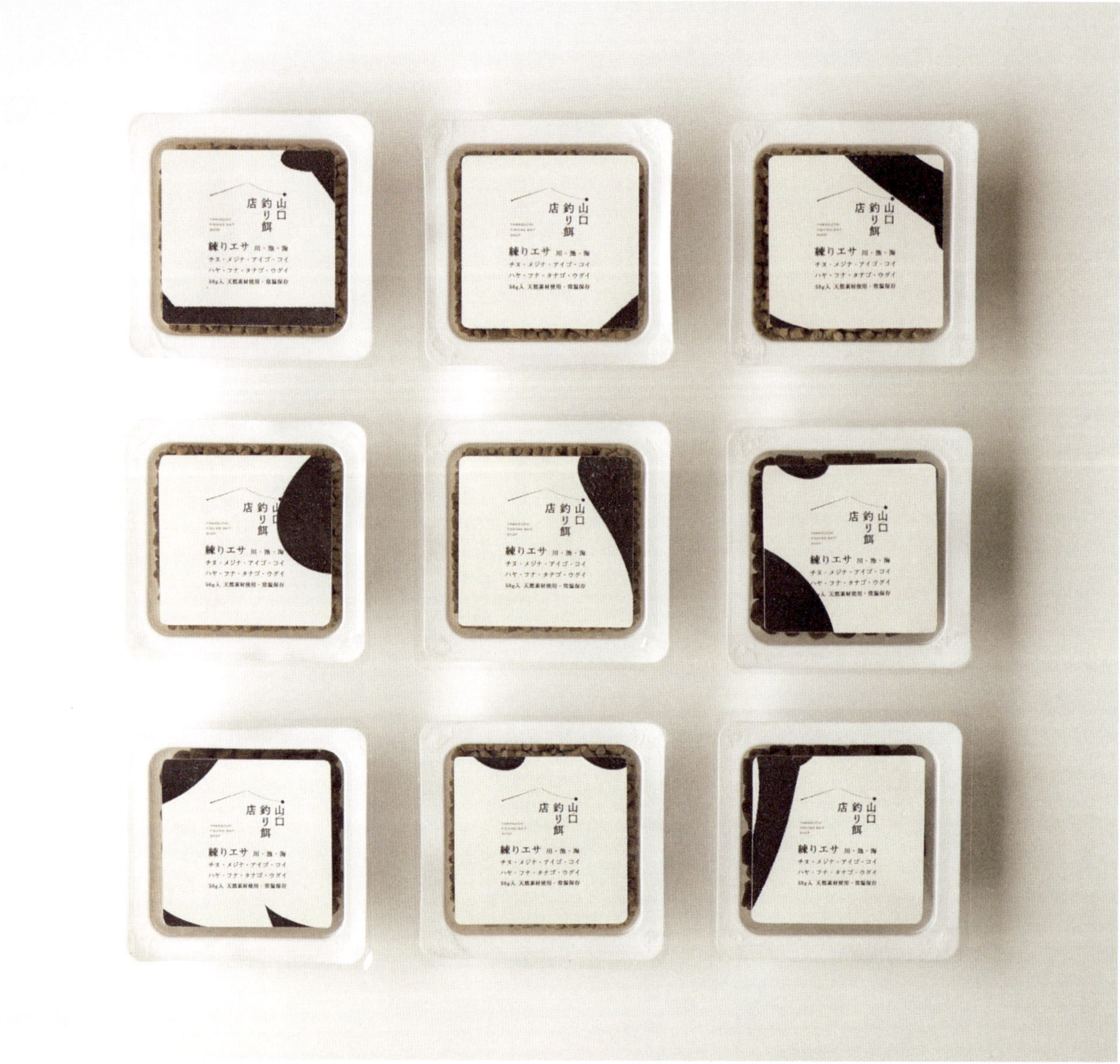

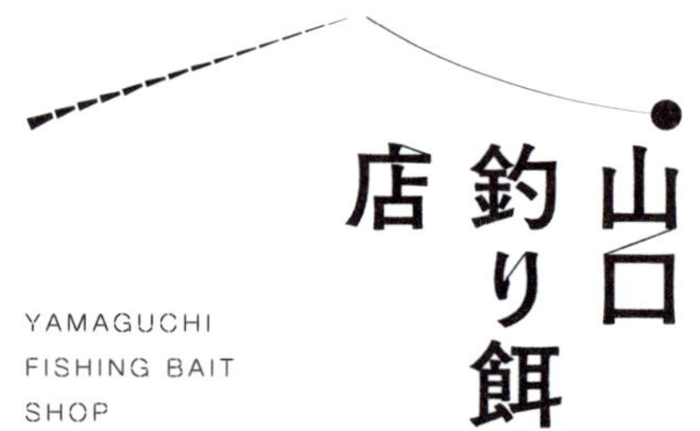

Brand Identity for this fishing baits shop was inspired by the silhouette of the kanji "魚" (pronounced "sakana", meaning "fish" in English). By using only black and white, the designer intended to emphasize the outline of this character. In the poster, the designer also tried to break the original structure of the kanji and make its broken pieces collapse while maintaining its recognizability.

The Yamaguchi Bait Shop

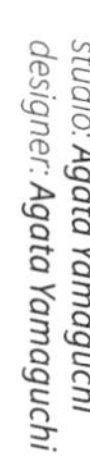

studio: Agata Yamaguchi
designer: Agata Yamaguchi

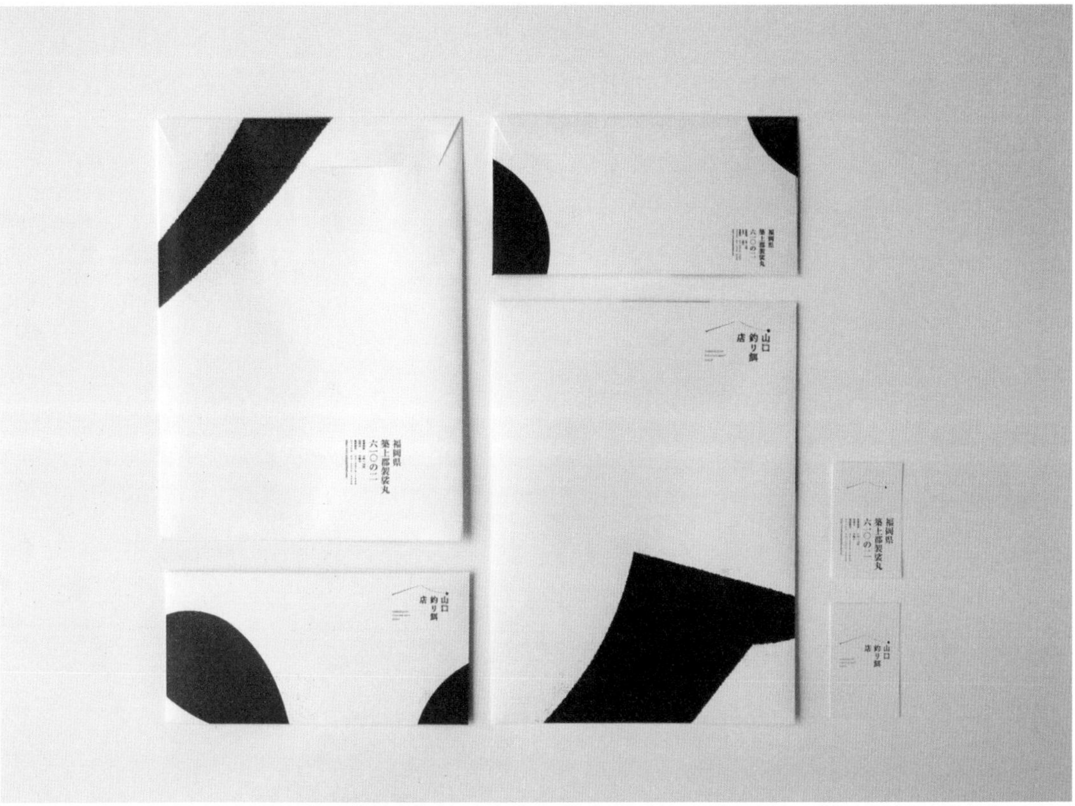

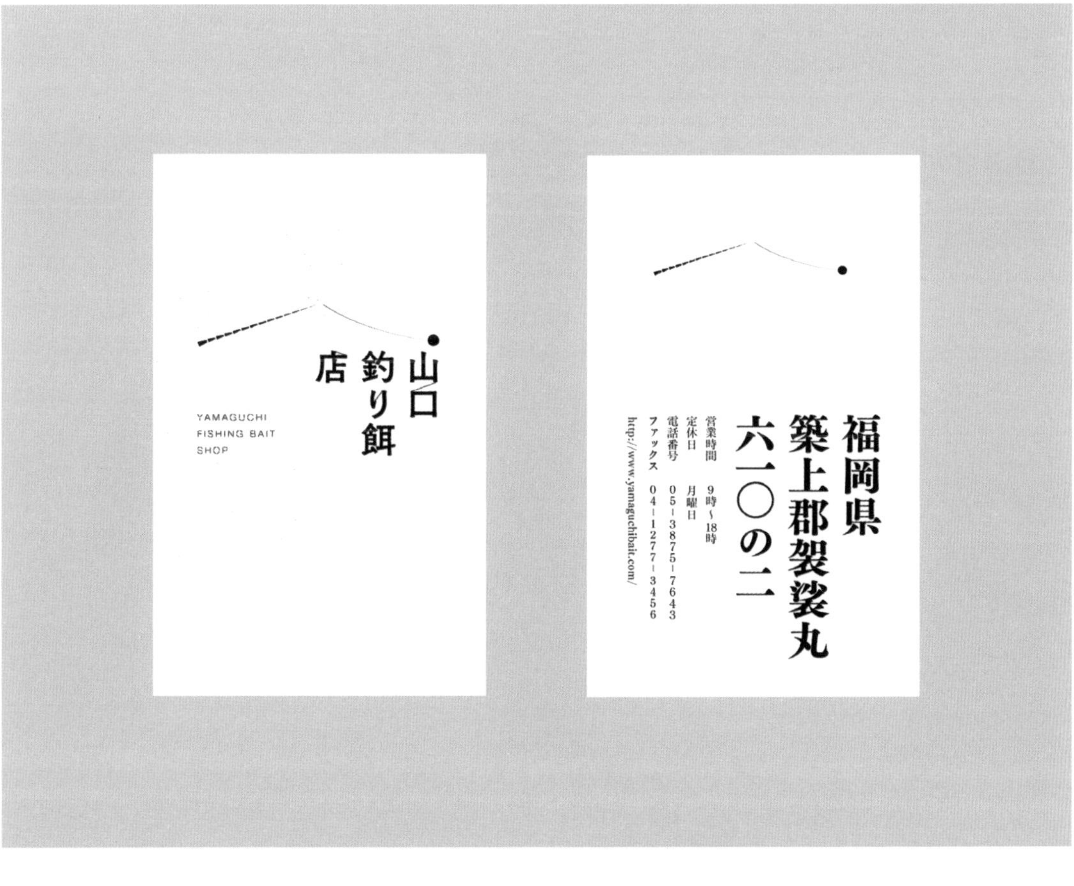

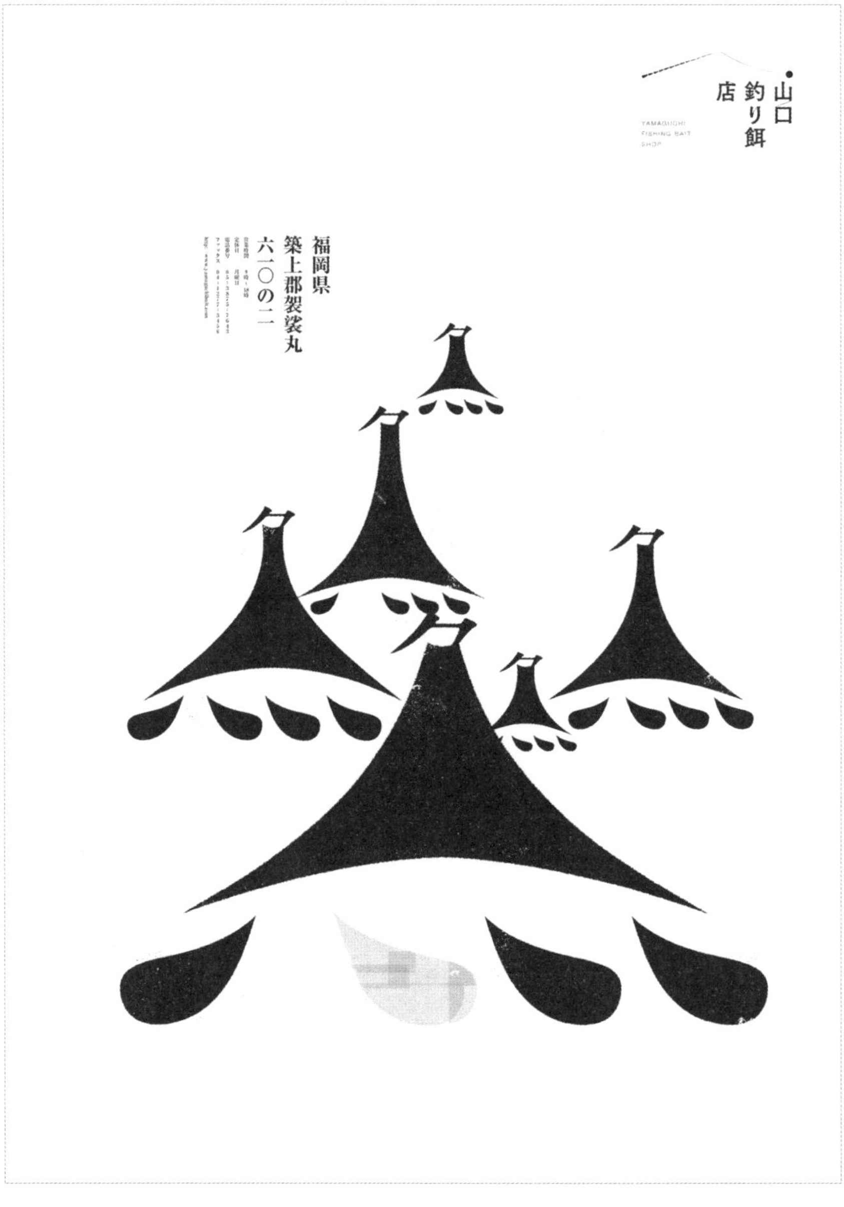

山口釣り餌店
YAMAGUCHI
FISHING BAIT
SHOP
福岡県
築上郡製裟丸
六一〇の二

福岡県
築上郡製裟丸
六一〇の二

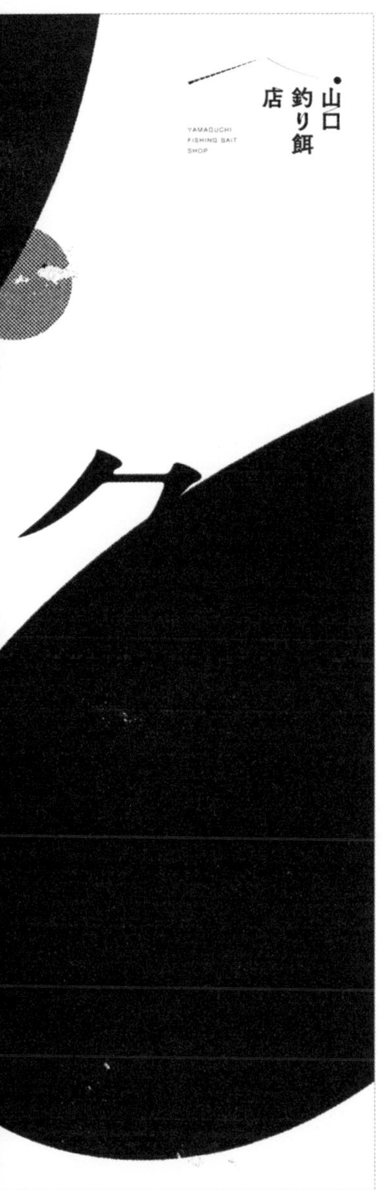

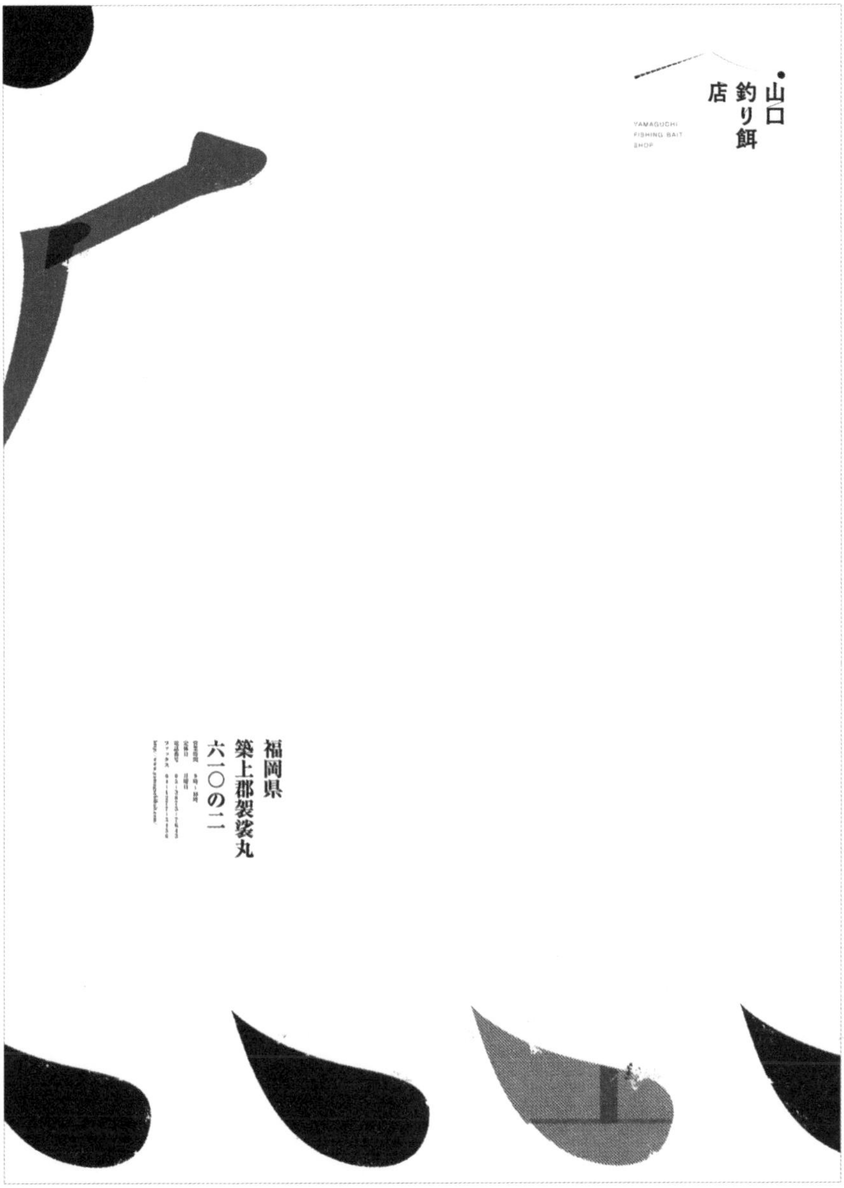

山口釣り餌店

YAMAGUCHI FISHING BAIT SHOP

福岡県
築上郡製裟丸
六一〇の二

営業時間
定休日　月曜日
電話番号
ファックス

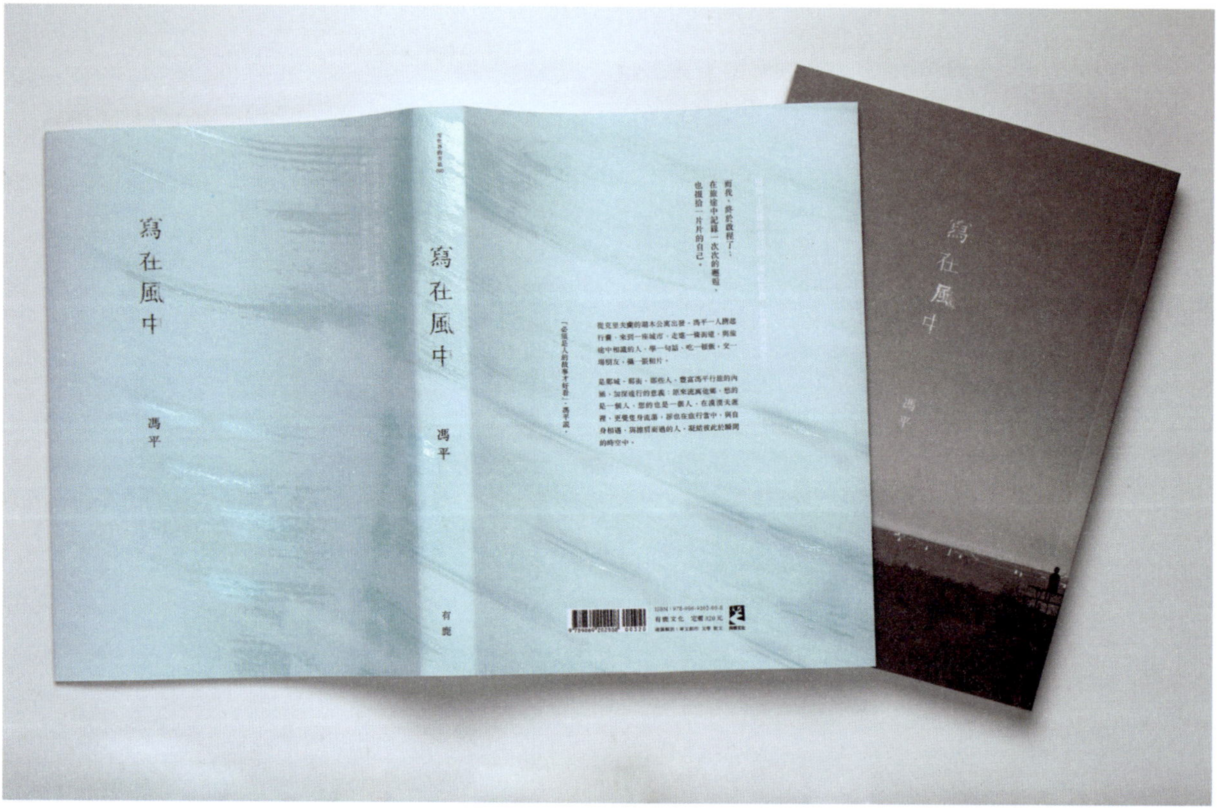

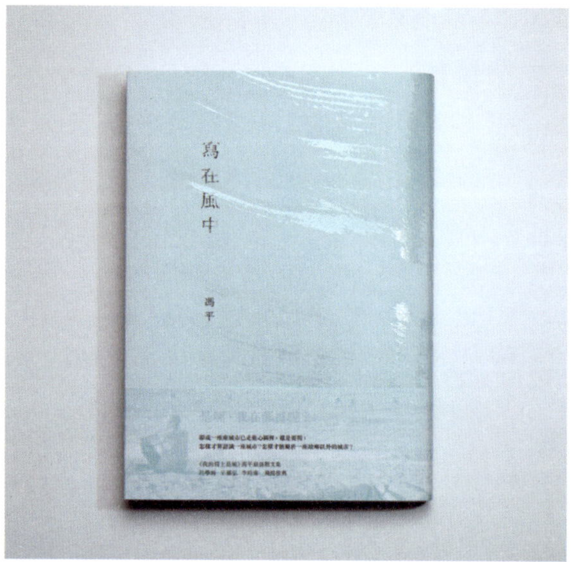

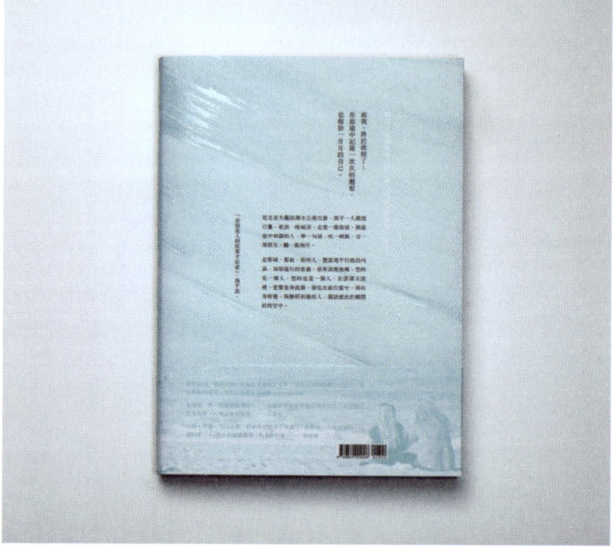

This is the book cover designed for *Xie-Zai-Feng-Zhong (writing in the wind)*, an anthology of travel writings, by writer Feng Ping. A special layer of reflective texture on the book jacket enriches both visual and tactile experience. Its tilting patterns mimic blowing wind, recalling those moments and memories captured in the writings. The typography of the book title incorporated the effect of wind erosion, as if it has been engraved on something or it is a mark left by time. The inside cover expresses one's smallness against the universe's vastness.

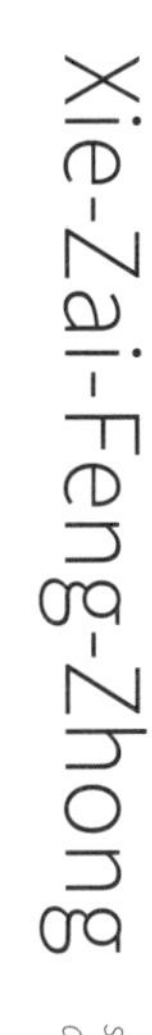

Xie-Zai-Feng-Zhong

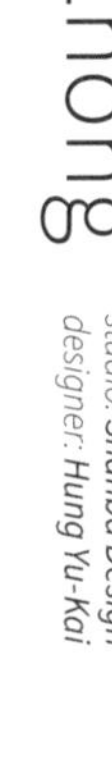

studio: ***Shanba Design***
designer: ***Hung Yu-Kai***

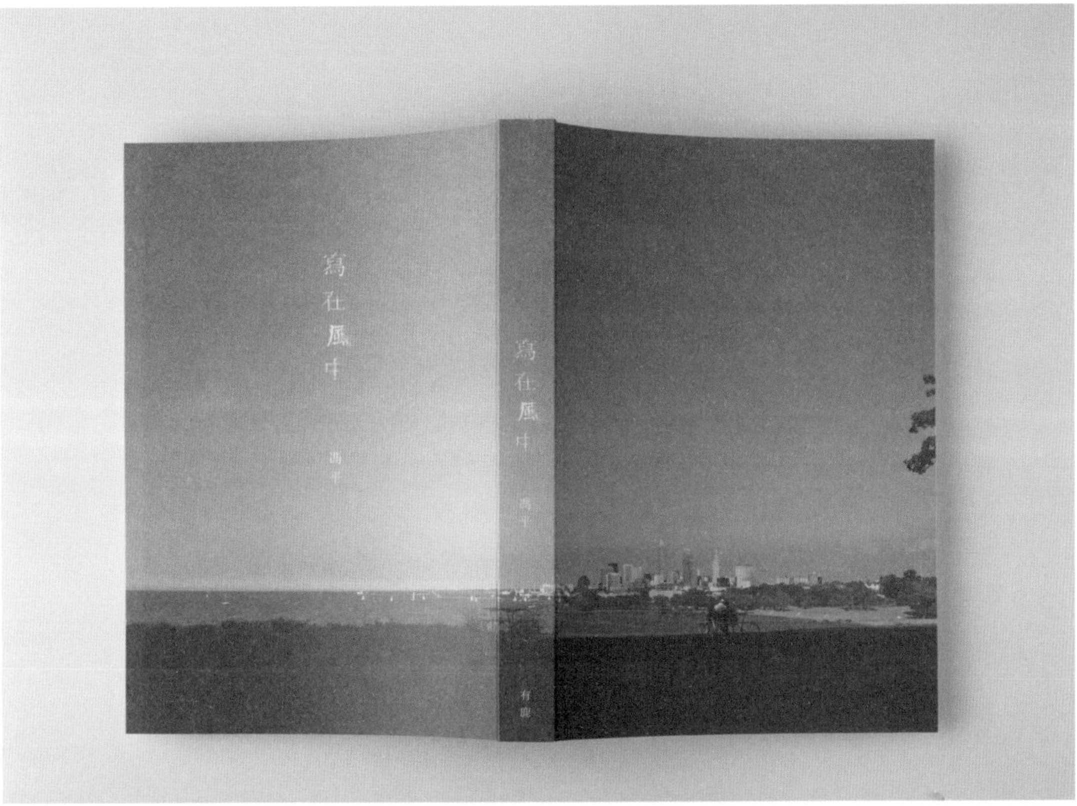

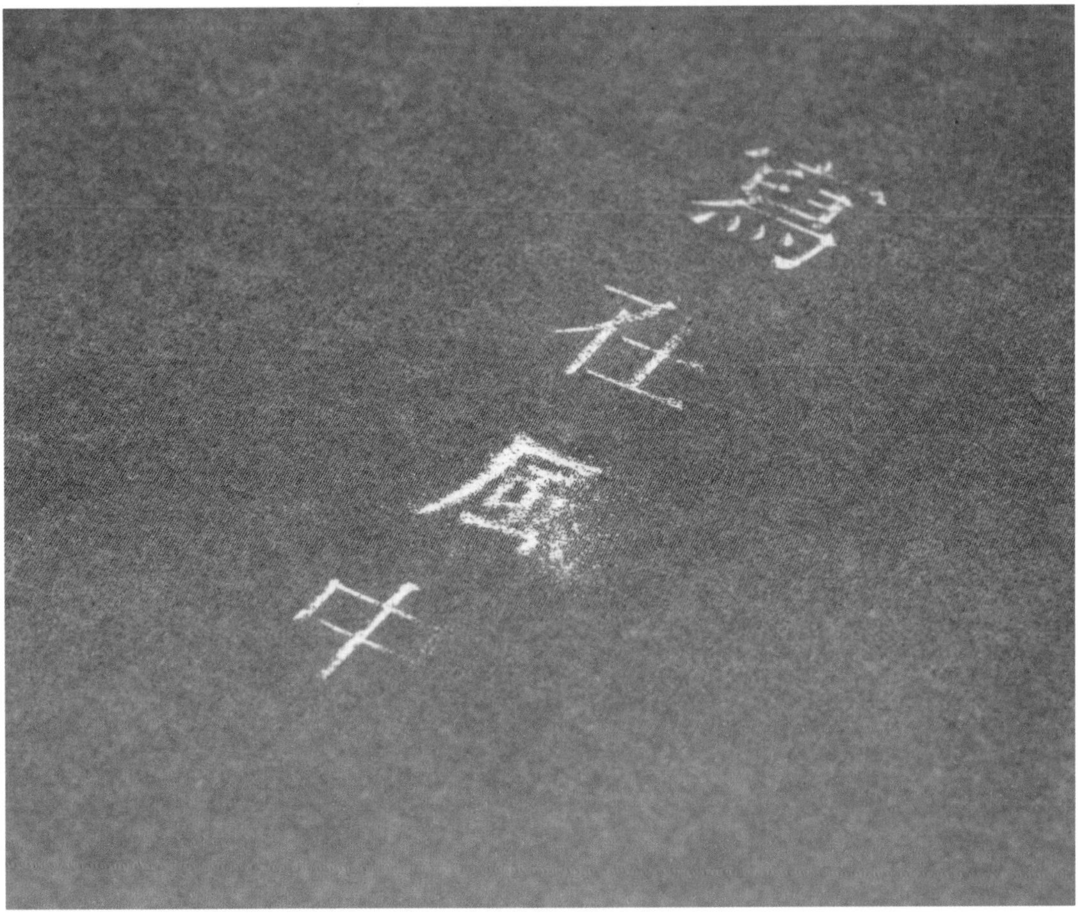

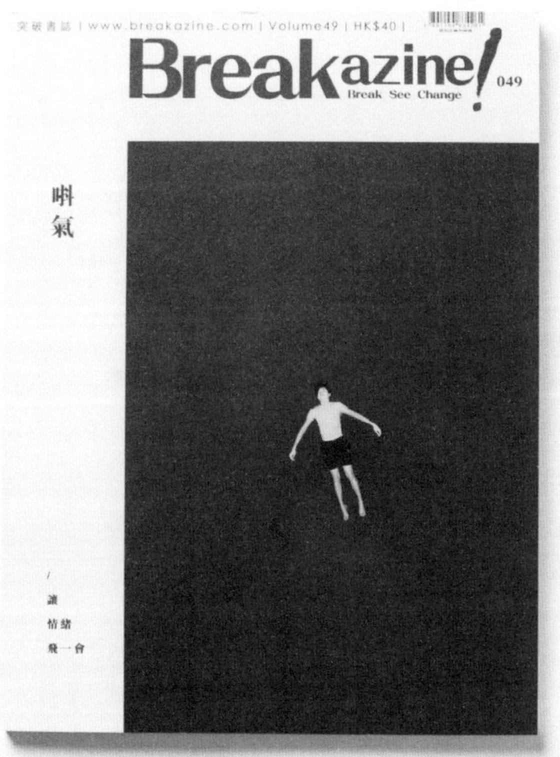

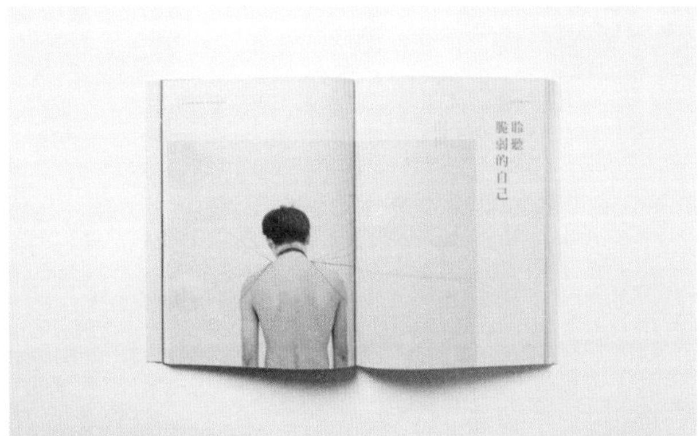

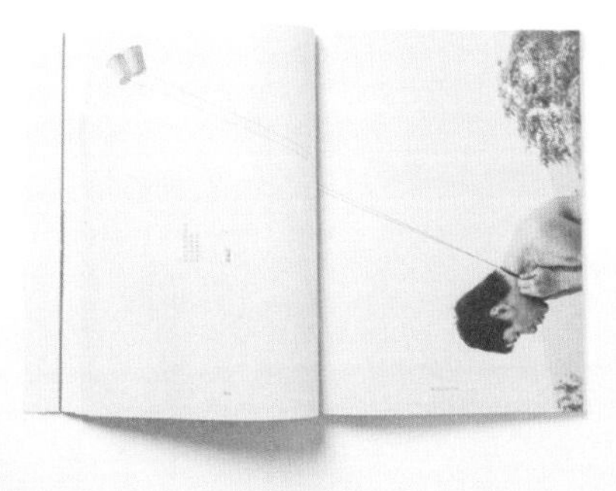

Orange Chan Design was invited to provide creative and design services for volume 49 of *Breakazine!*, a Hong Kong bimonthly cultural magazine. The topic of this volume is "Emotion". The designers redesigned the layout for the magazine, keeping more extensity and slowing the pace of reading through kerning, line spacing and grid system, in order to tie in with the heavy theme. For the cover, whose title is a Cantonese phrase "唞气" meaning "pause for breath", the designers chose a photo of a boy floating up to the surface, which also looks like someone flying in the blue sky or a dead body floating on the sea. Accompanied is the editorial theme text: let the mood fly for a while.

Breakazine! volume 049

studio: *ORANGE CHAN DESIGN*
designer: *Orange Chan, Ming Leung*

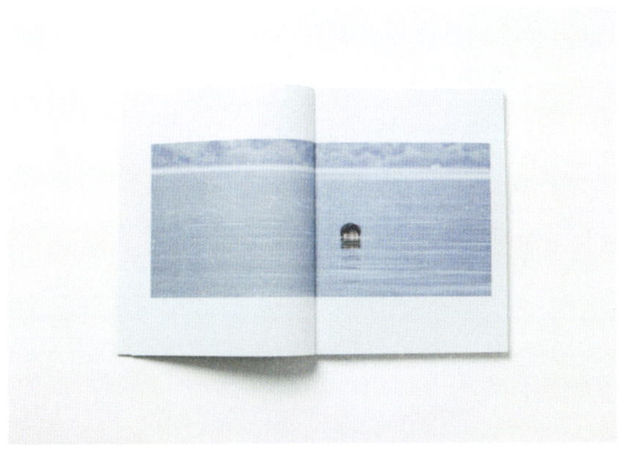

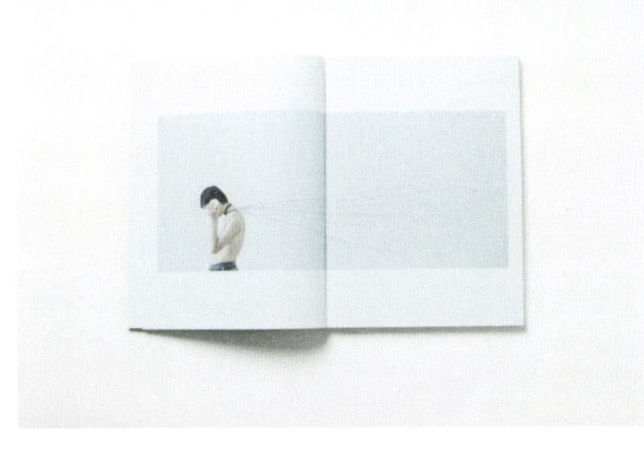

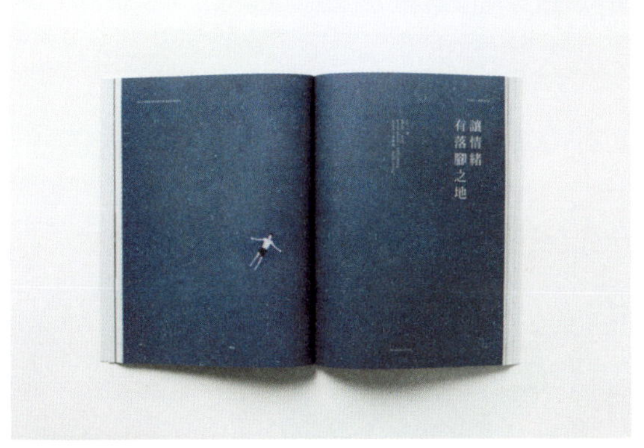

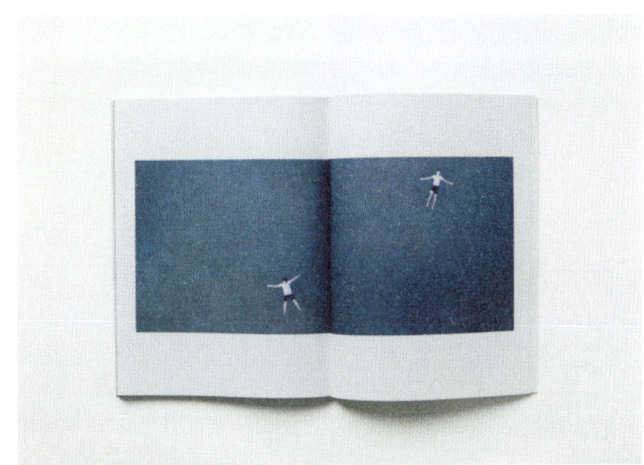

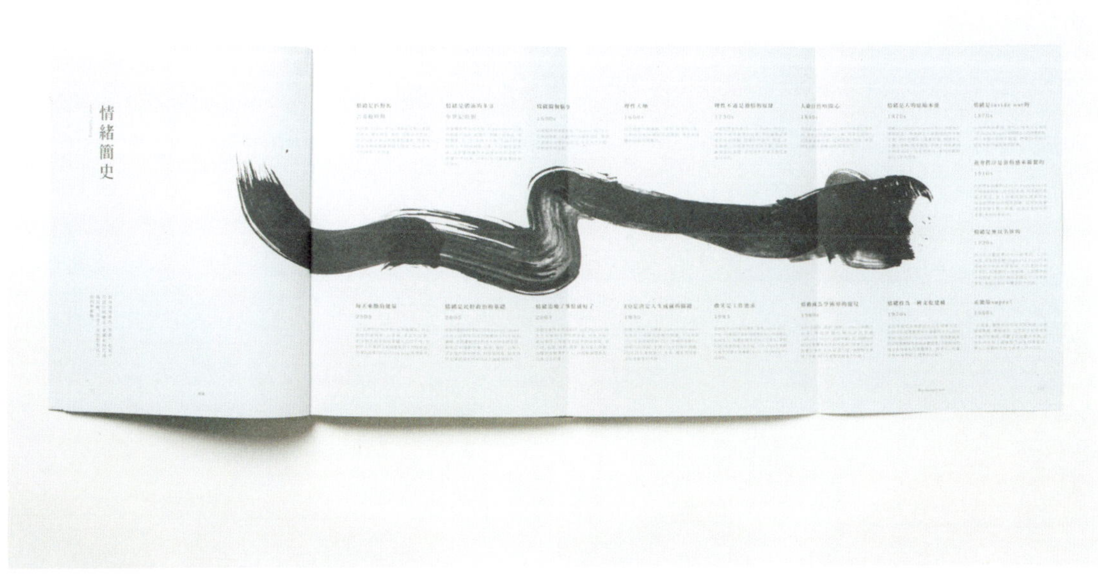

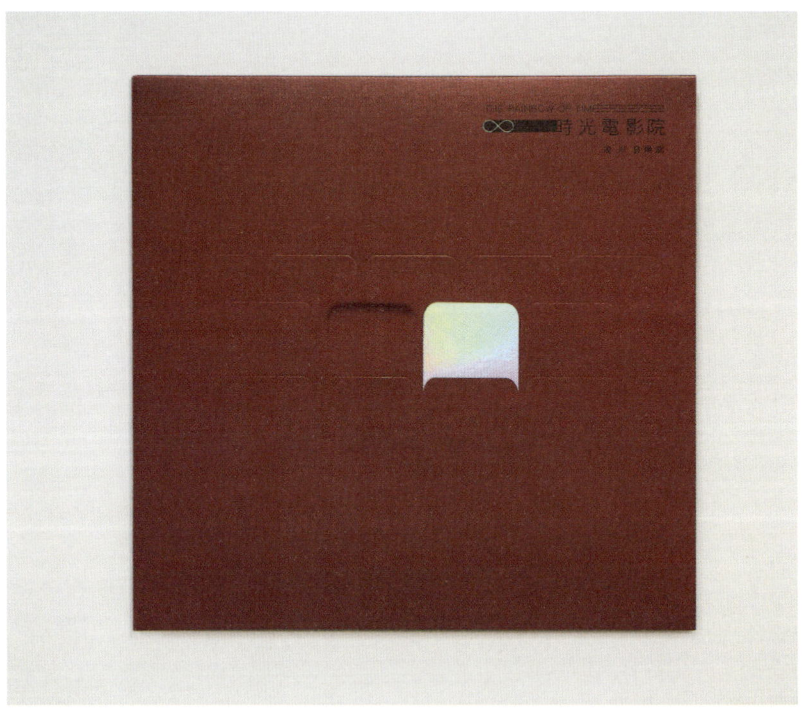

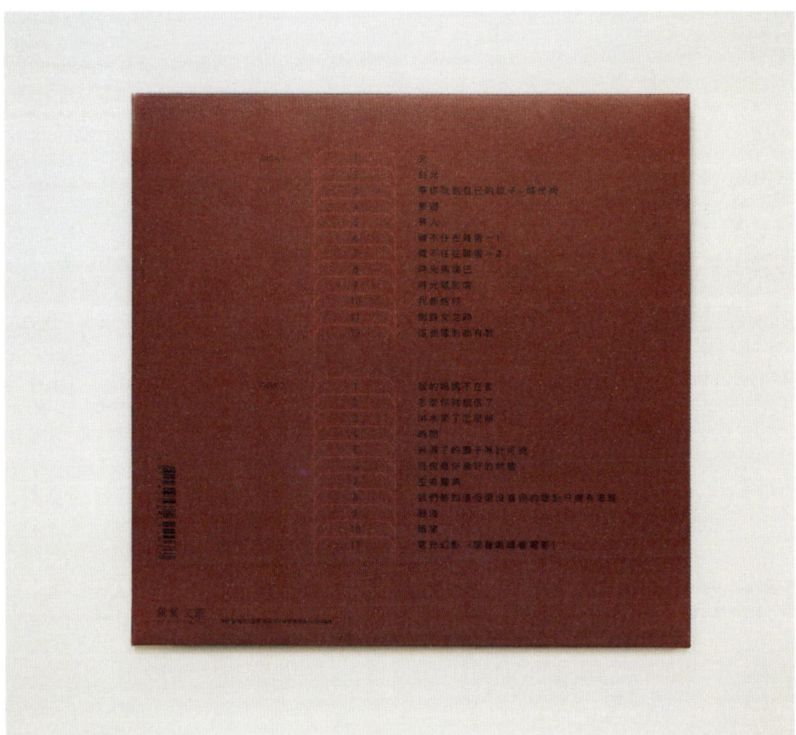

This is packaging for music CD *The Rainbow of Time* based on a novel of the same name by famous illustrator Jimmy Liao.

Everyone's memory is a movie theater,
Someone came into play, the movie started; when the play is over, where did they go?
Who promised to come but left empty seats?
Now, who is by your side?

The Rainbow Of Time

studio:
Shu yu Tsai

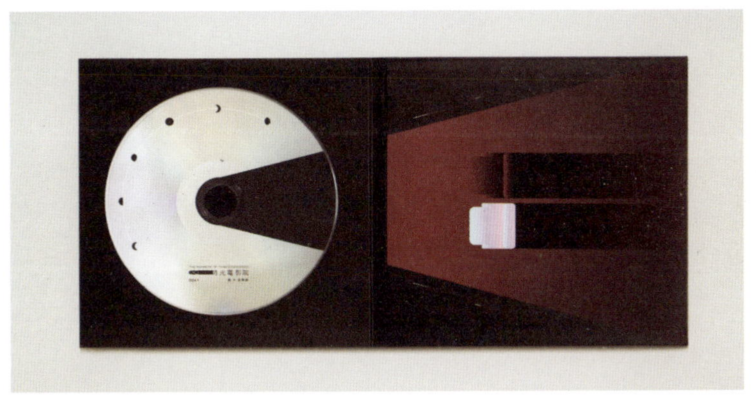

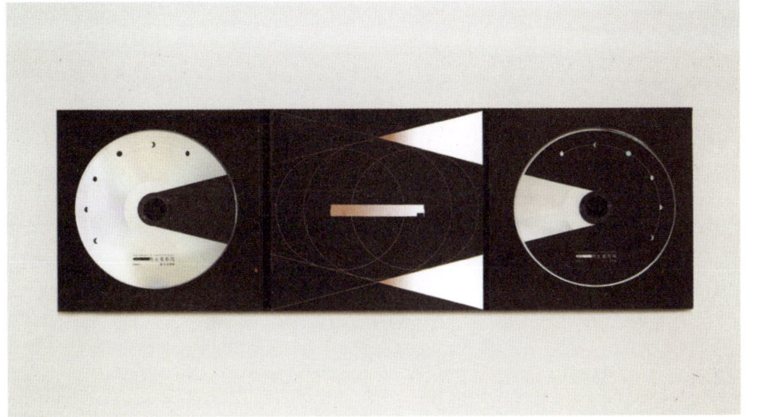

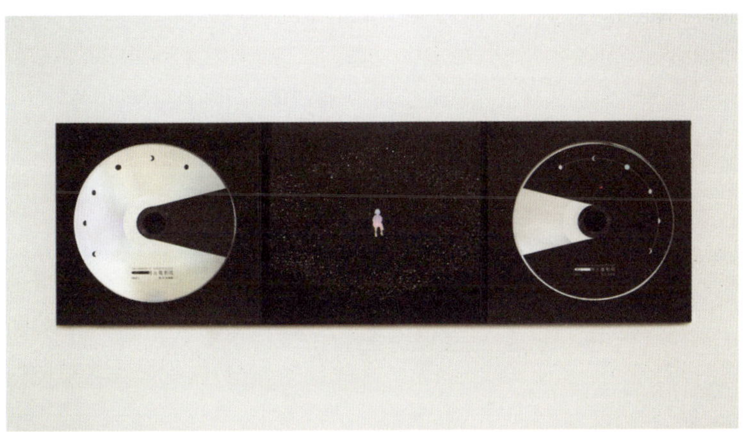

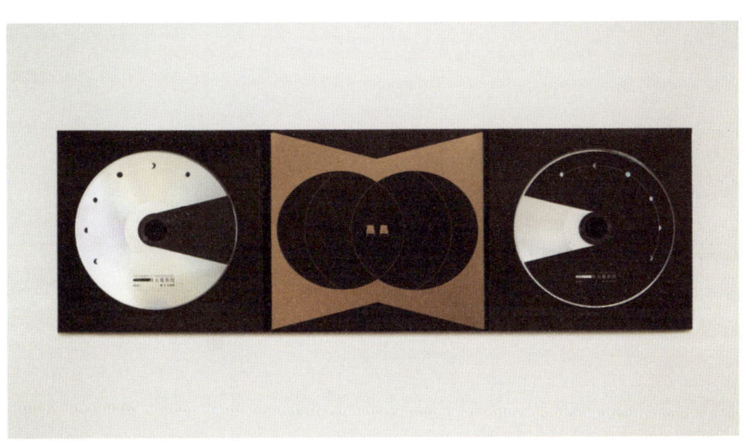

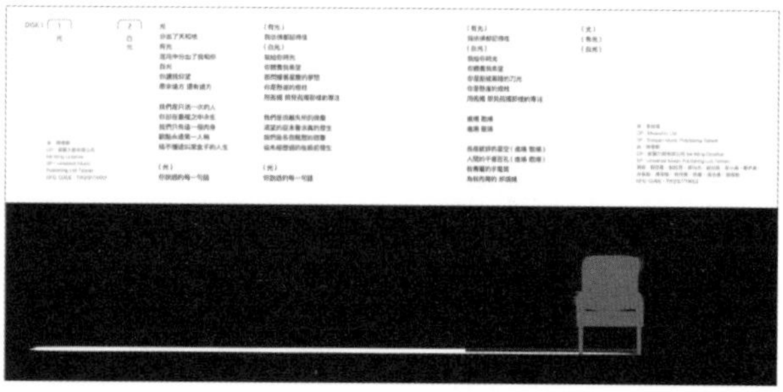

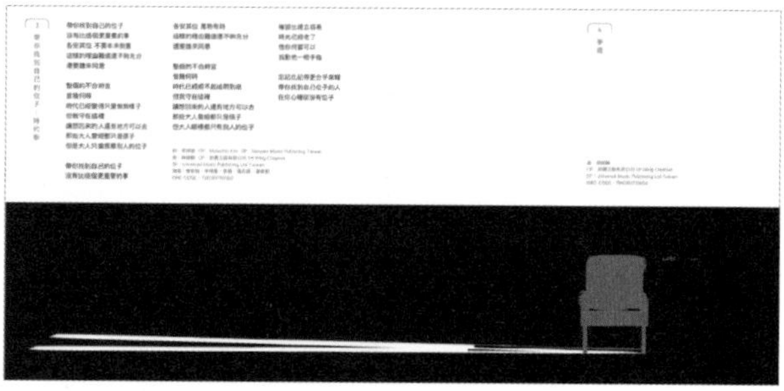

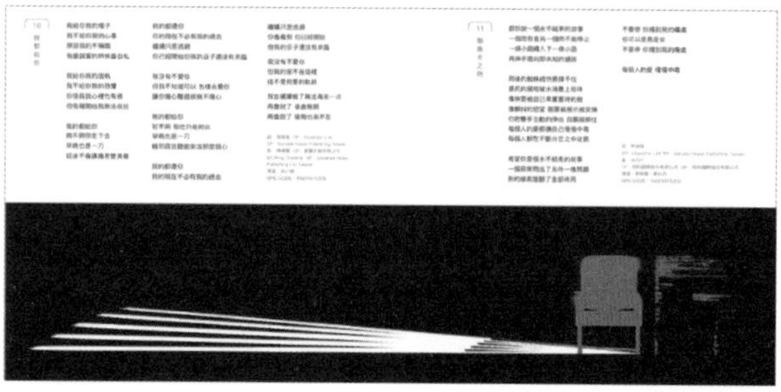

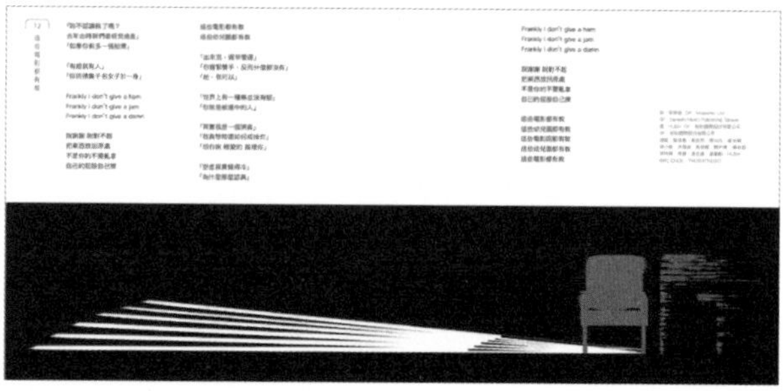

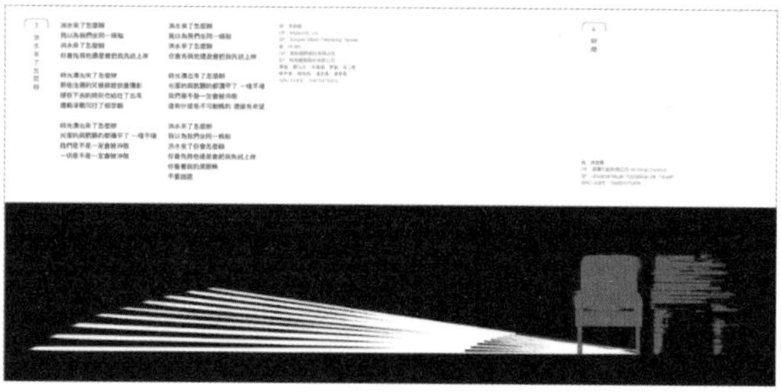

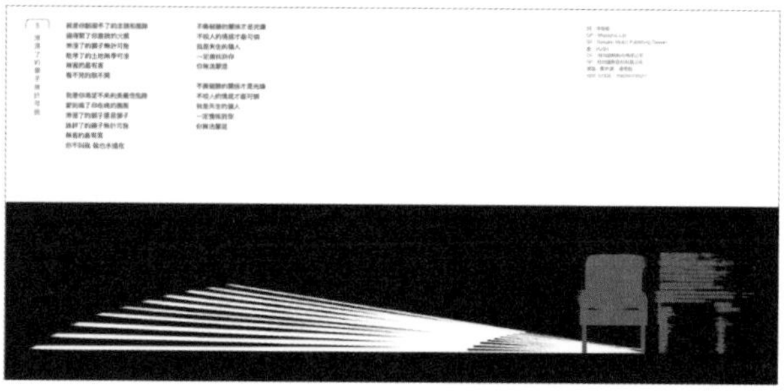

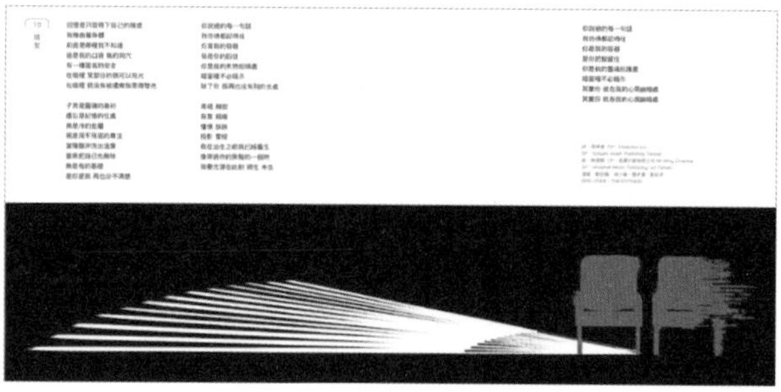

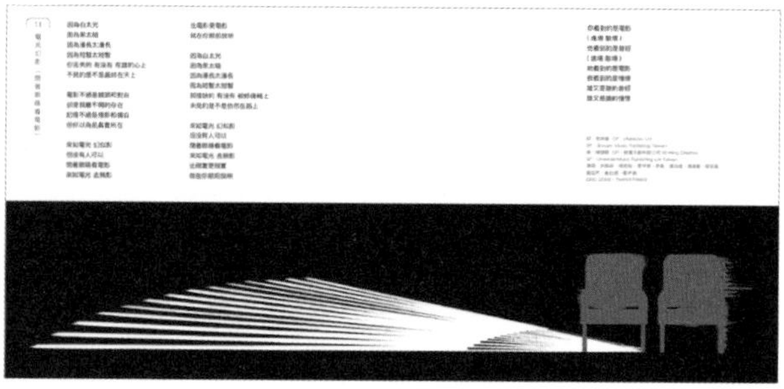

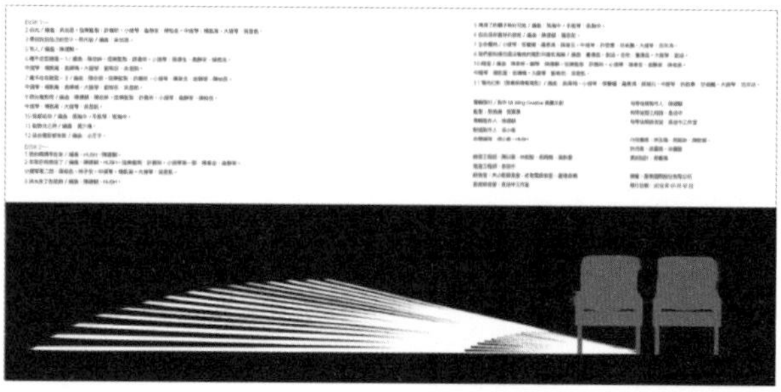

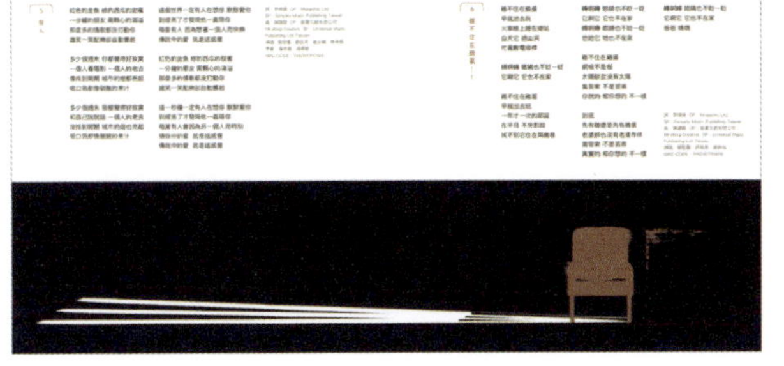
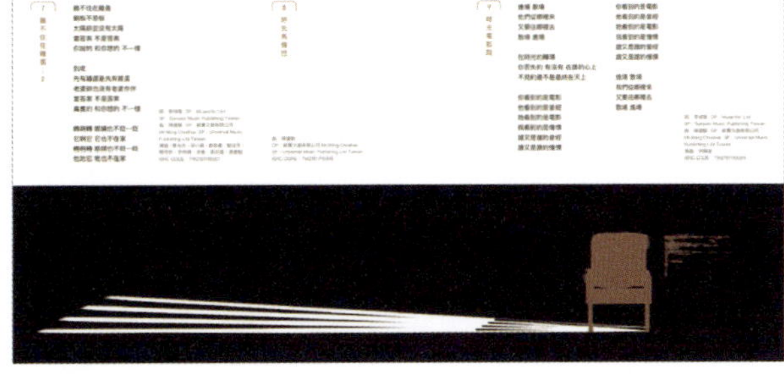
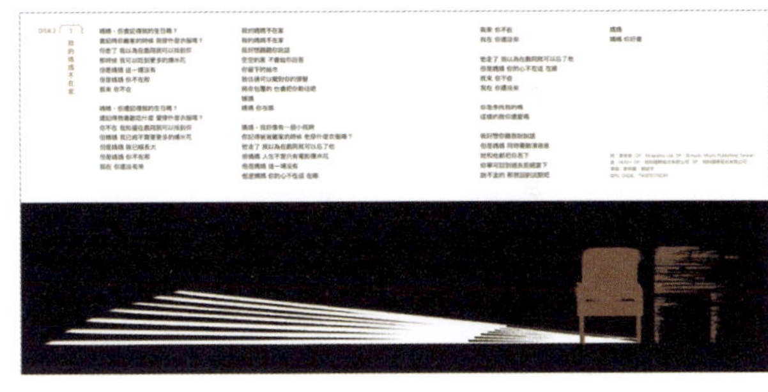
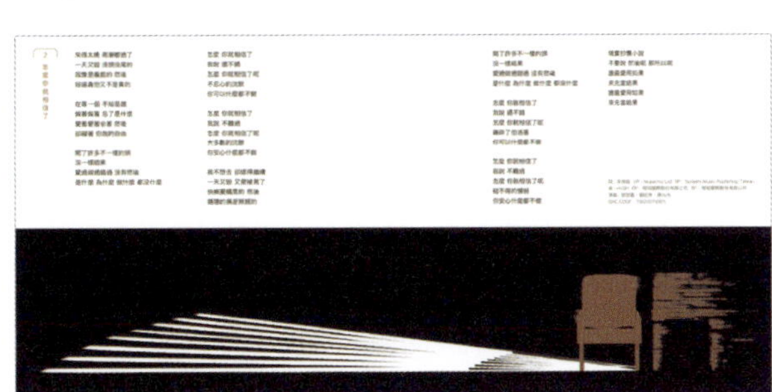
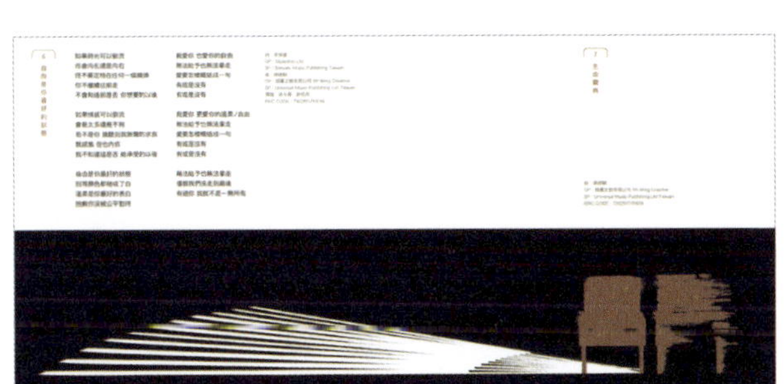
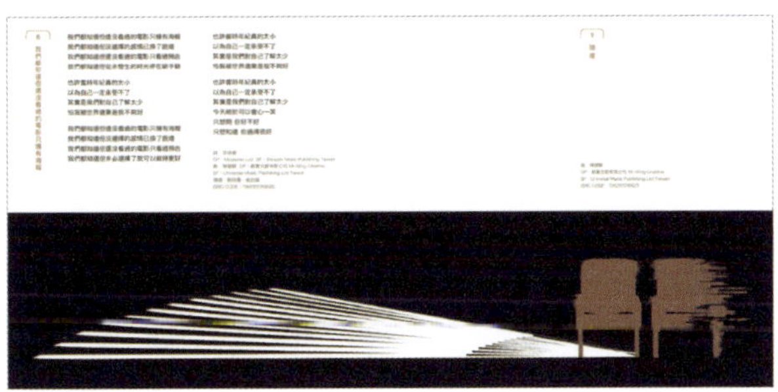

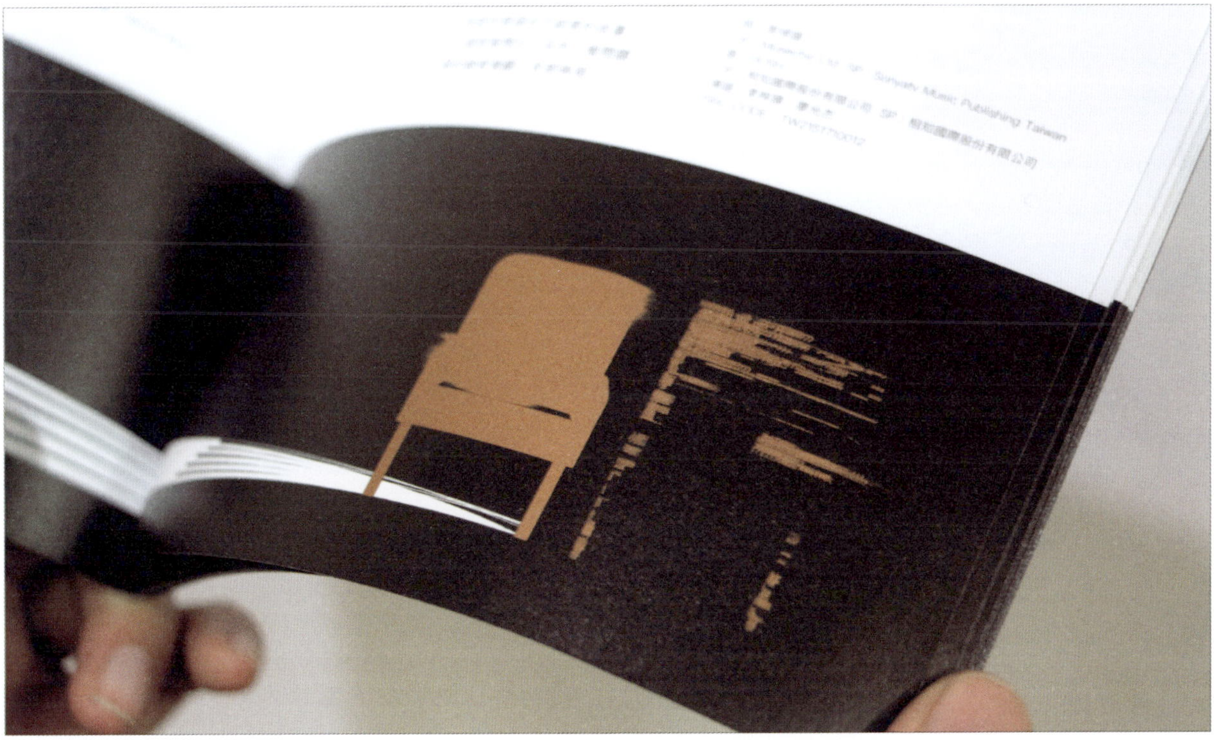

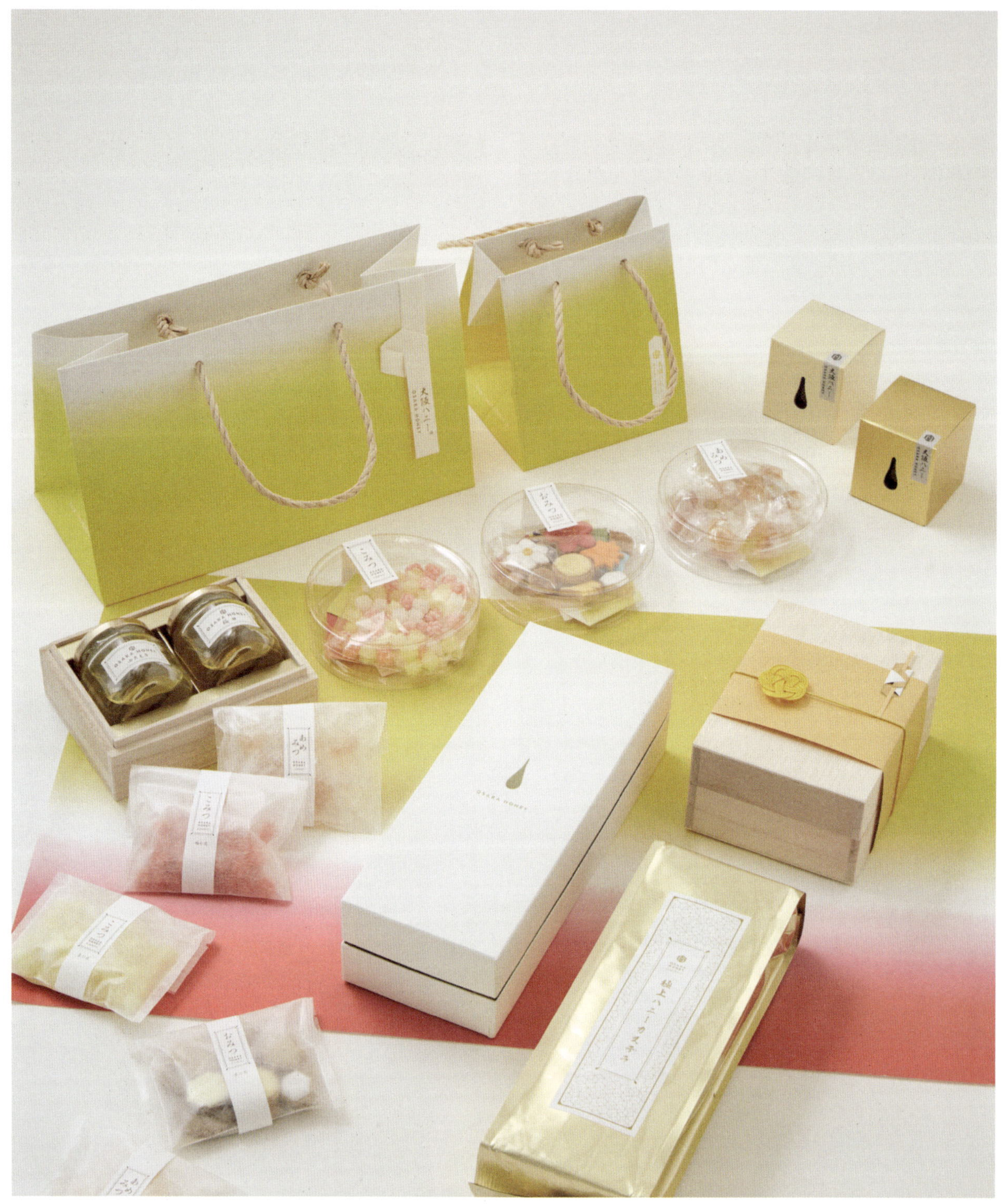

The designer has devised various packages for the products of raw honey—meaningful gifts for the significant others. In the design process, the designer was particular about details. High-quality materials were applied and Japanese traditional art of paper folding (origkata) was introduced in a way that fits for the modern age.

Osaka Honey

studio: *FROM GRAPHIC*
designer: *Yoko Maruyama*

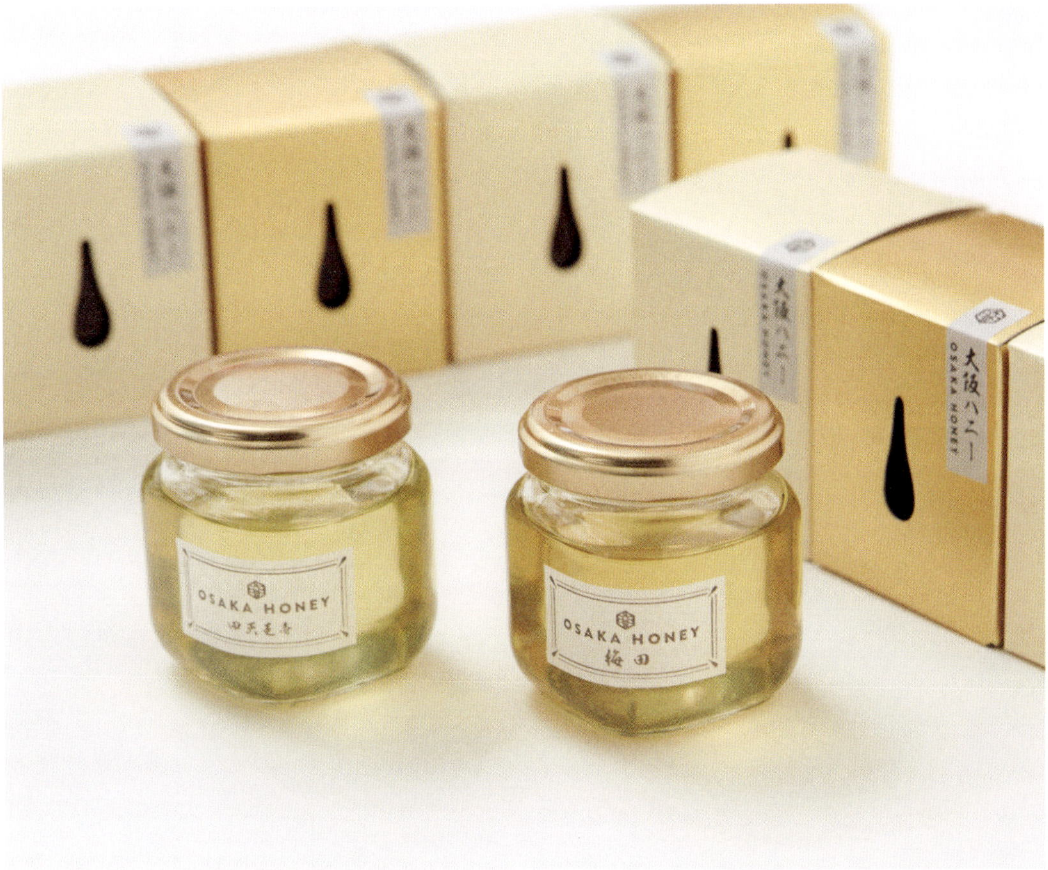

OSAKA HONEY

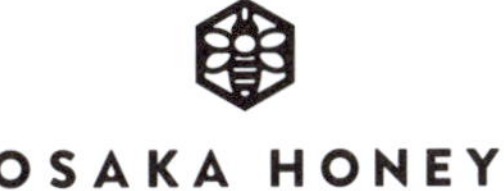

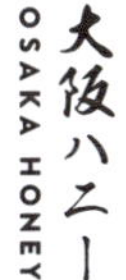

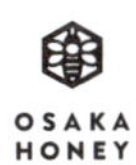

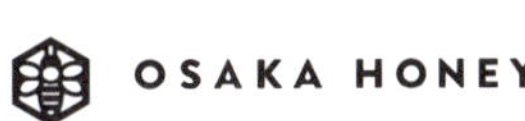

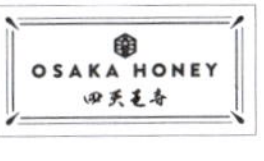

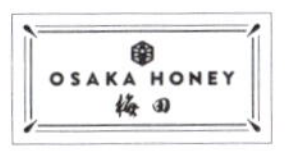

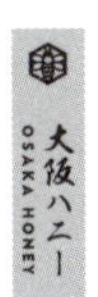

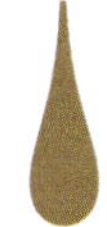

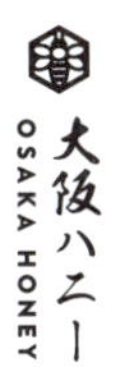

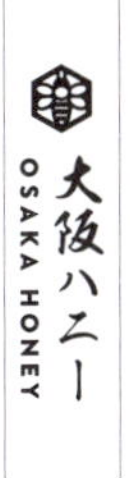

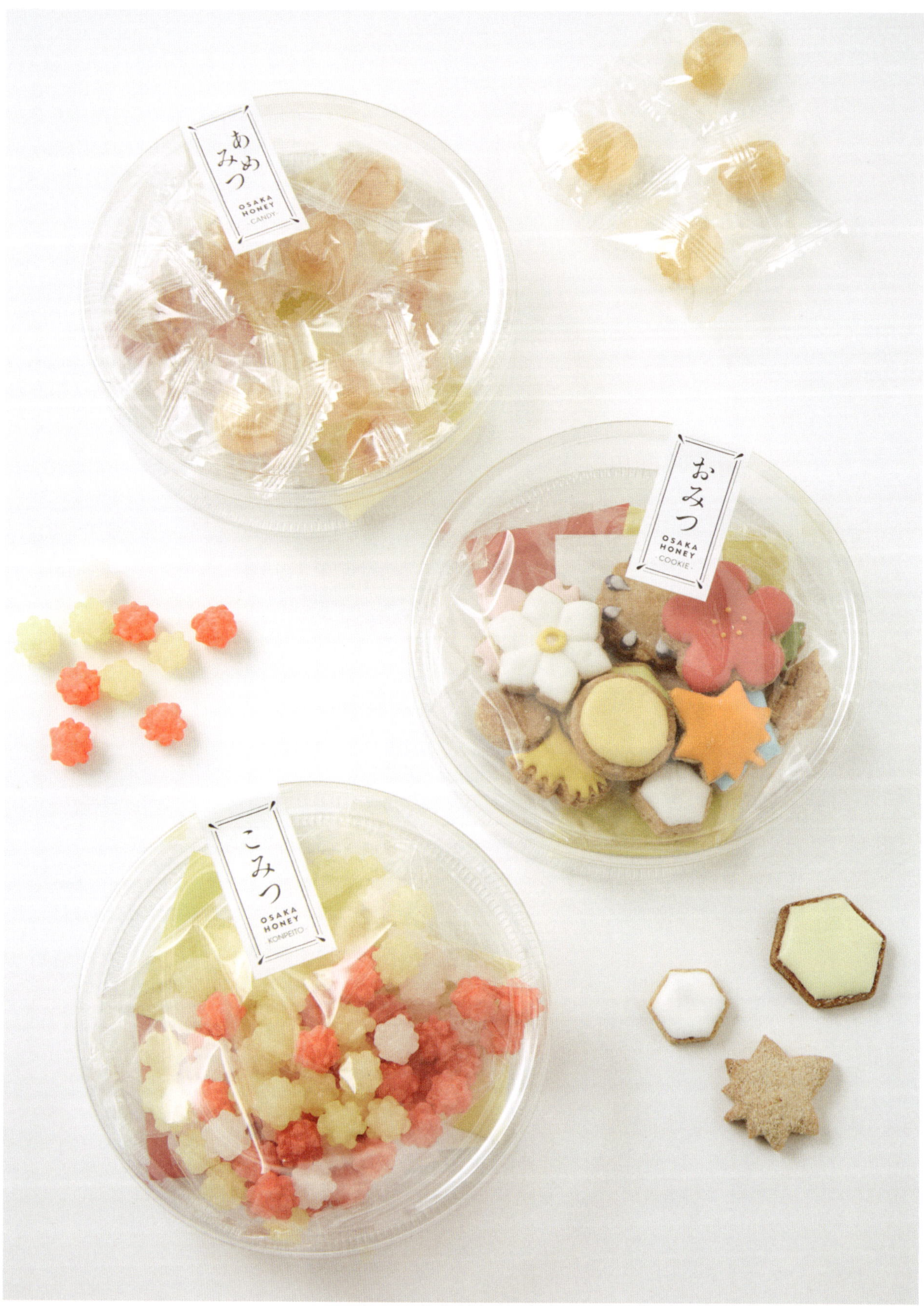
あめみつ
OSAKA HONEY
CANDY
おみつ
OSAKA HONEY
COOKIE
こみつ
OSAKA HONEY
KONPEITO

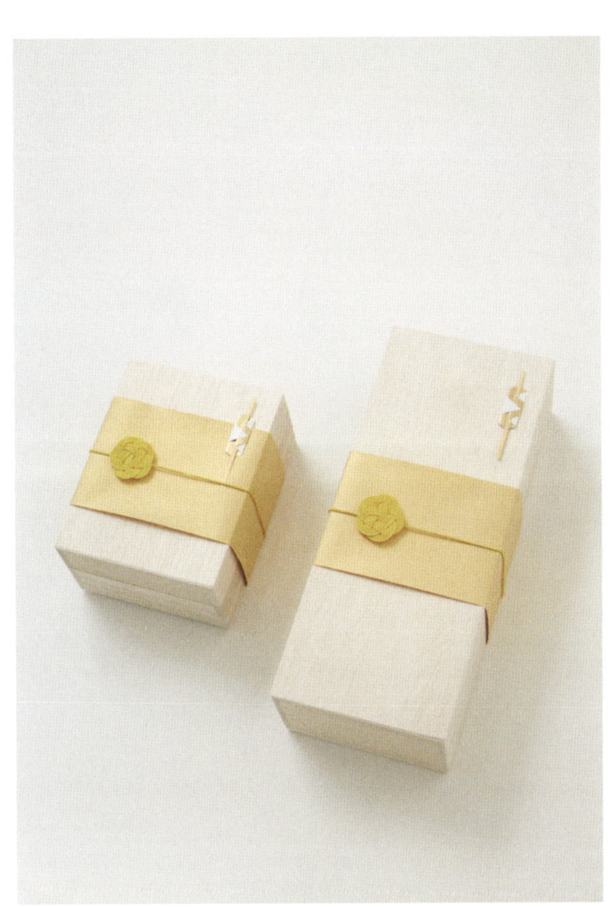

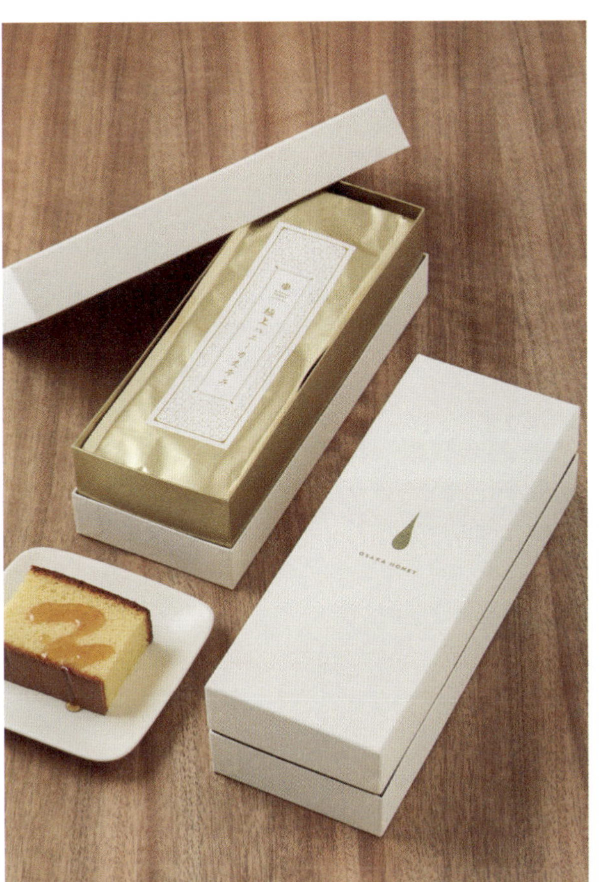

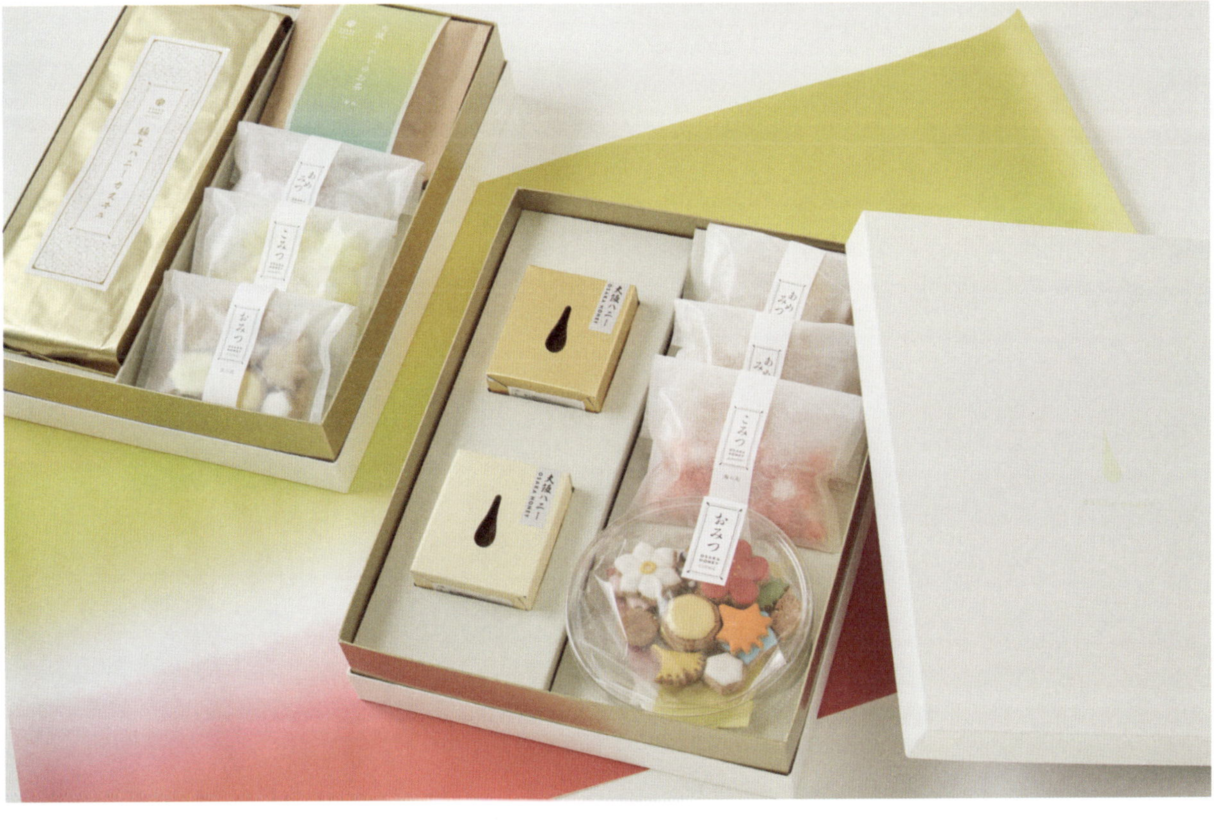

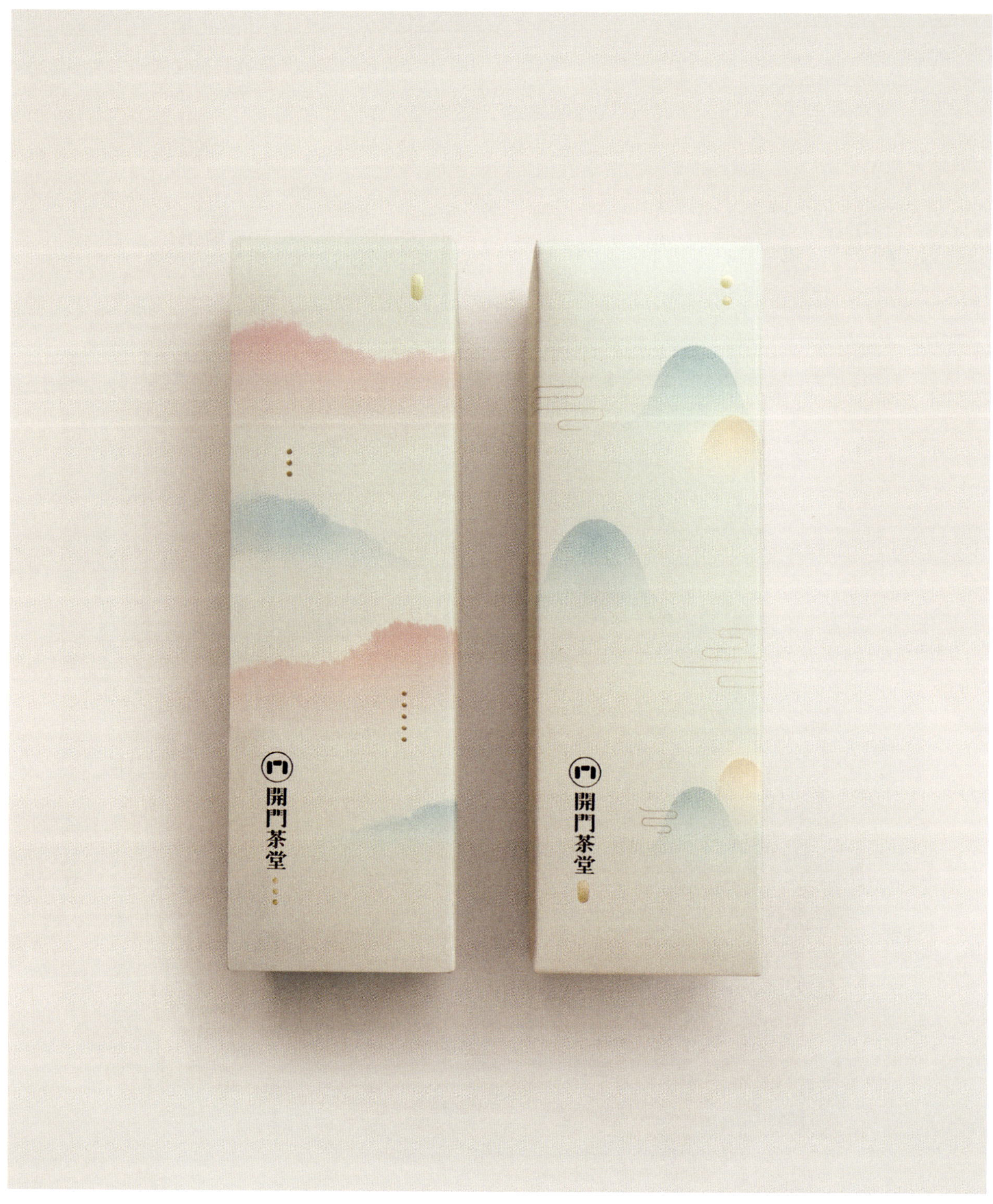

This packaging embodies a blessing to spring by Kaimon Tea House. It features clean geometric shapes with wash colors to represent the poetic fog of mountains, expressing a gratitude towards the fertile land for cultivating tea.

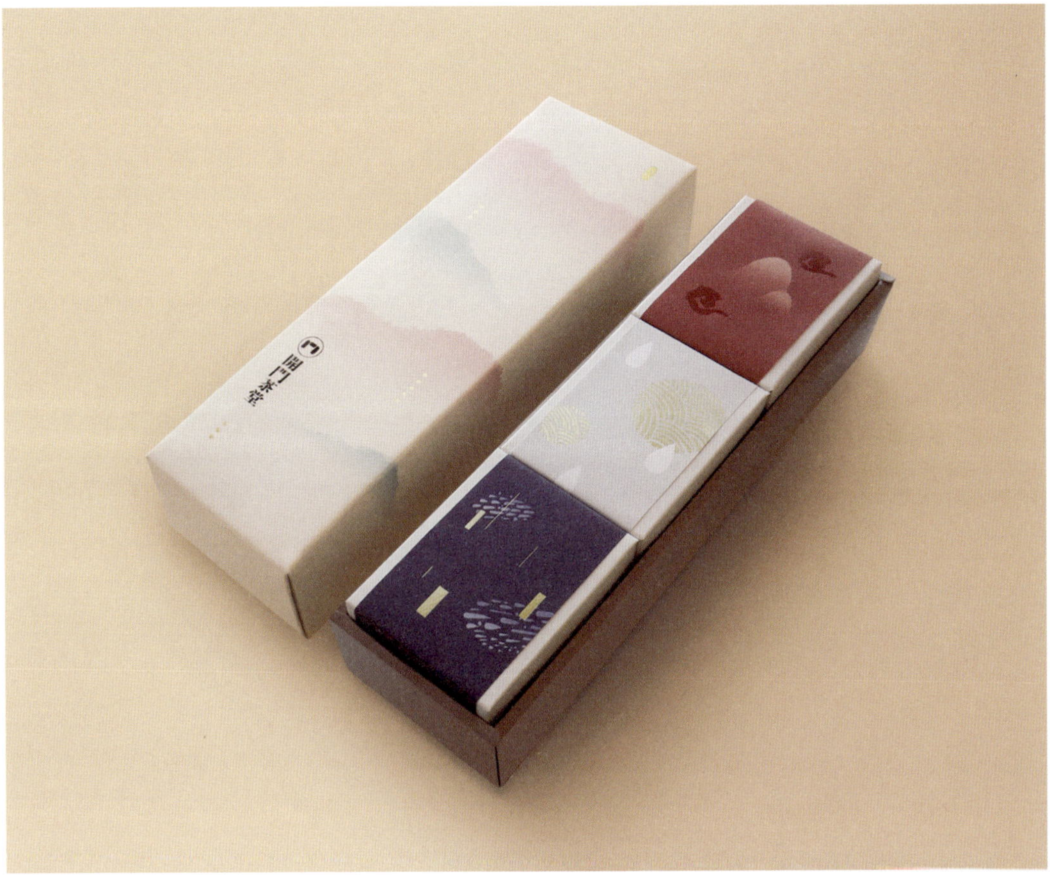

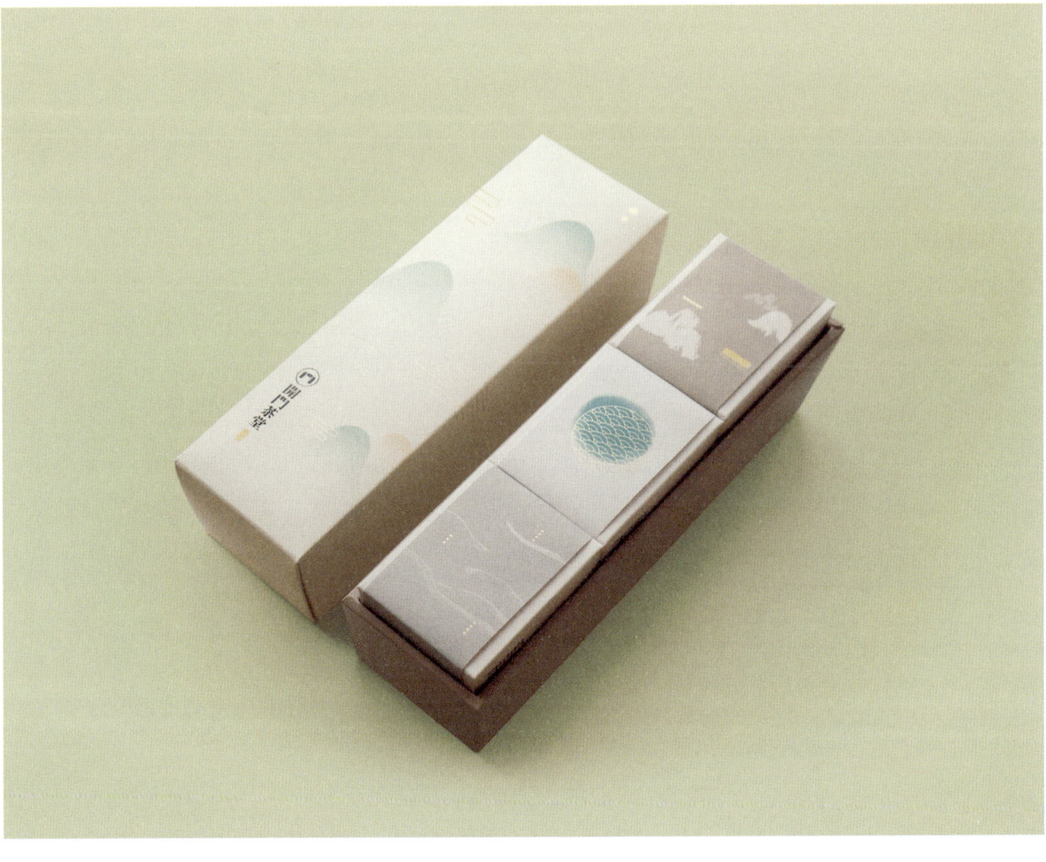

Kaimon | Tea House Spring Gift Box

designer:
Su Wan-Ling

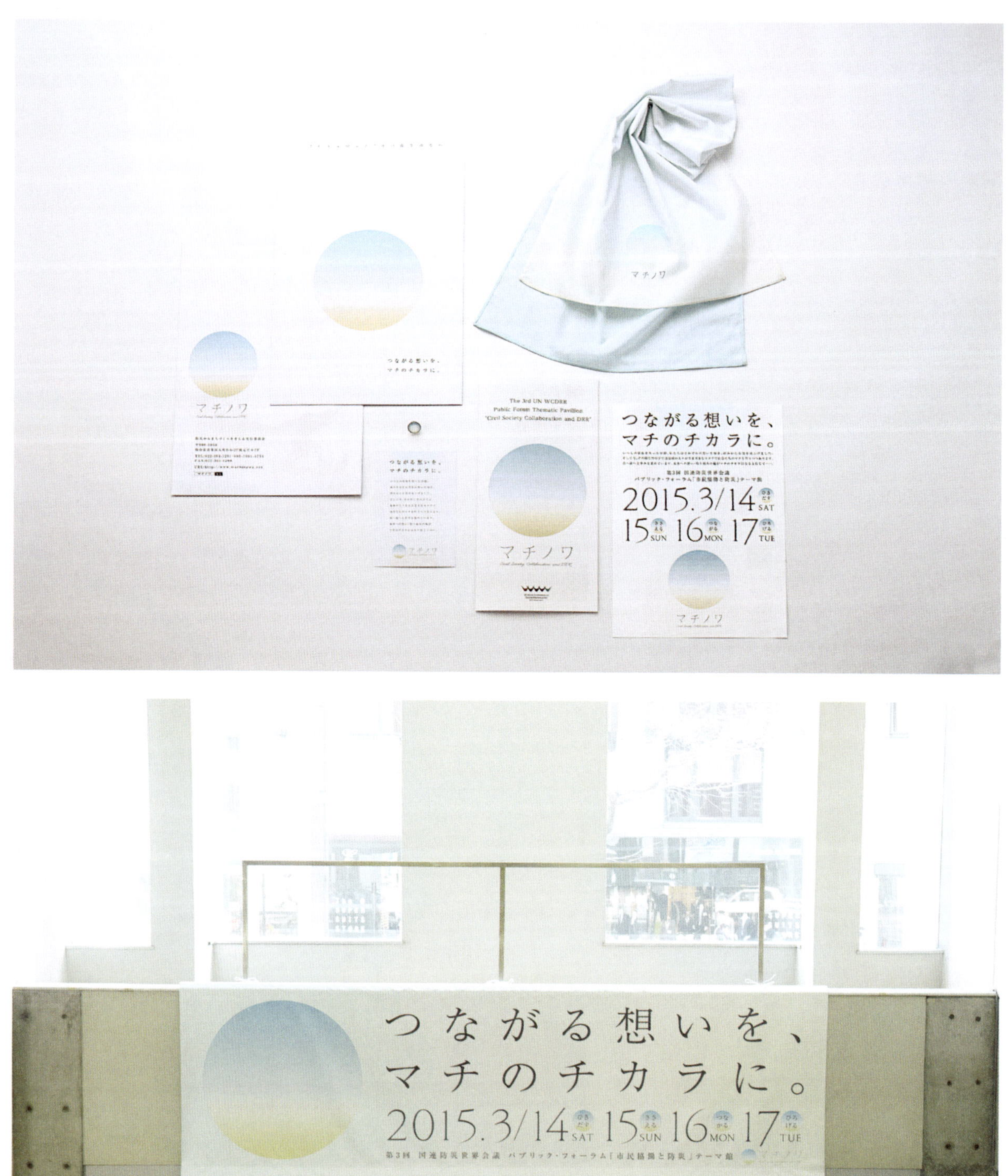

This is a visual identity for the thematic pavilion of "Civil Society Collaboration and DRR" as part of the public forum of the UN World Conference on Disaster Reduction. Based on the understanding of the reconstruction after earthquake, Luck Show created a special Japanese towel and many other promotional materials to frame the image of the pavilion, where discussions on disaster prevention would take place.

Thematic Pavilion "Civil Society Collaboration and DRR"

studio: LUCK SHOW

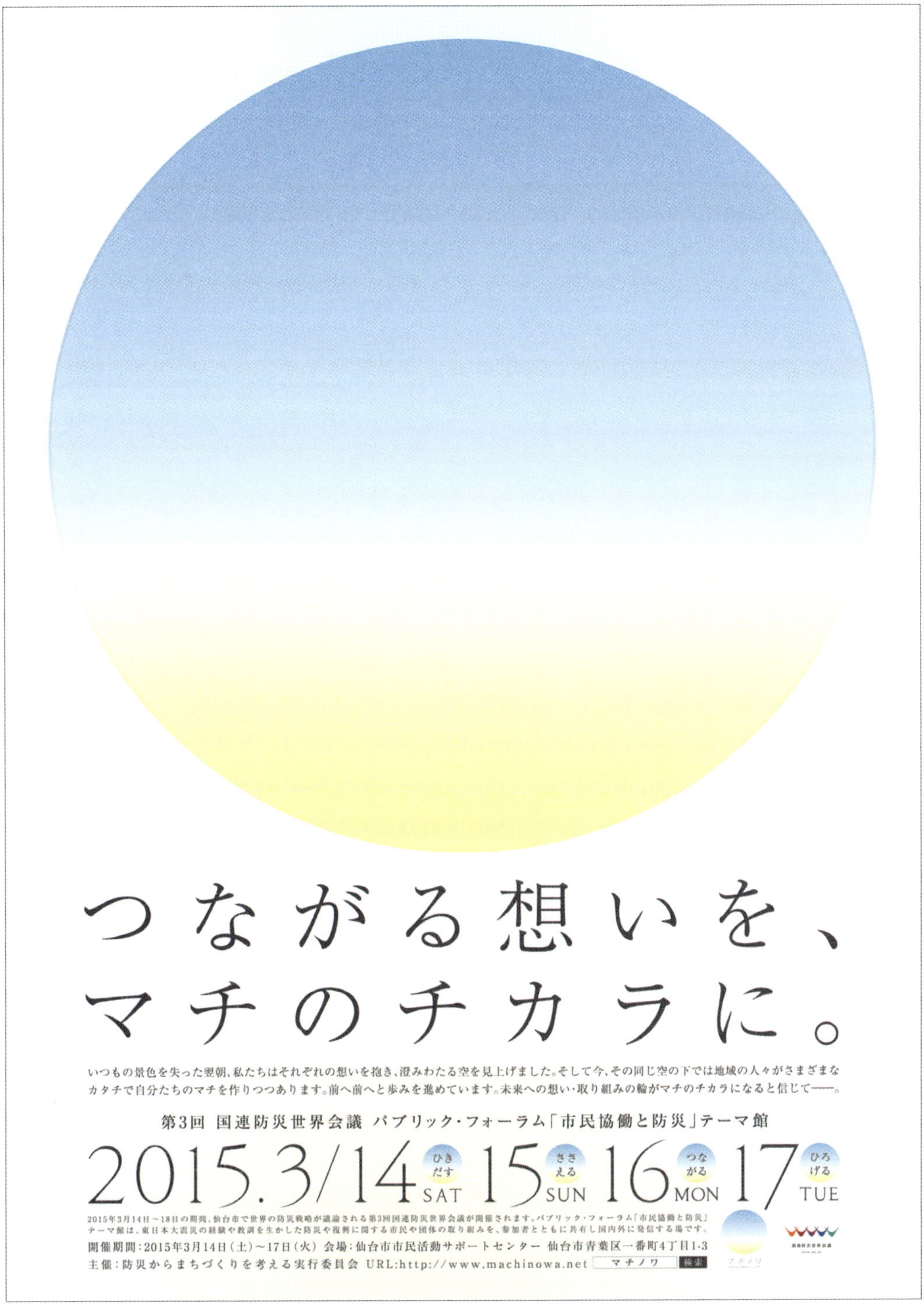

つながる想いを、
マチのチカラに。

いつもの景色を失った翌朝、私たちはそれぞれの想いを抱き、澄みわたる空を見上げました。そして今、その同じ空の下では地域の人々がさまざまなカタチで自分たちのマチを作りつつあります。前へ前へと歩みを進めています。未来への想い・取り組みの輪がマチのチカラになると信じて——。

第3回 国連防災世界会議 パブリック・フォーラム「市民協働と防災」テーマ館

2015.3/14 ひきだす SAT 15 ささえる SUN 16 つながる MON 17 ひろげる TUE

2015年3月14日～18日の期間、仙台市で世界の防災戦略が議論される第3回国連防災世界会議が開催されます。パブリック・フォーラム「市民協働と防災」テーマ館は、東日本大震災の経験や教訓を生かした防災や復興に関する市民や団体の取り組みを、参加者とともに共有し国内外に発信する場です。

開催期間：2015年3月14日（土）～17日（火） 会場：仙台市市民活動サポートセンター 仙台市青葉区一番町4丁目1-3

主催：防災からまちづくりを考える実行委員会 URL:http://www.machinowa.net マチノワ 検索

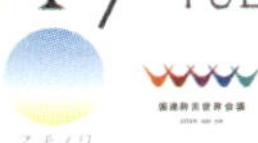

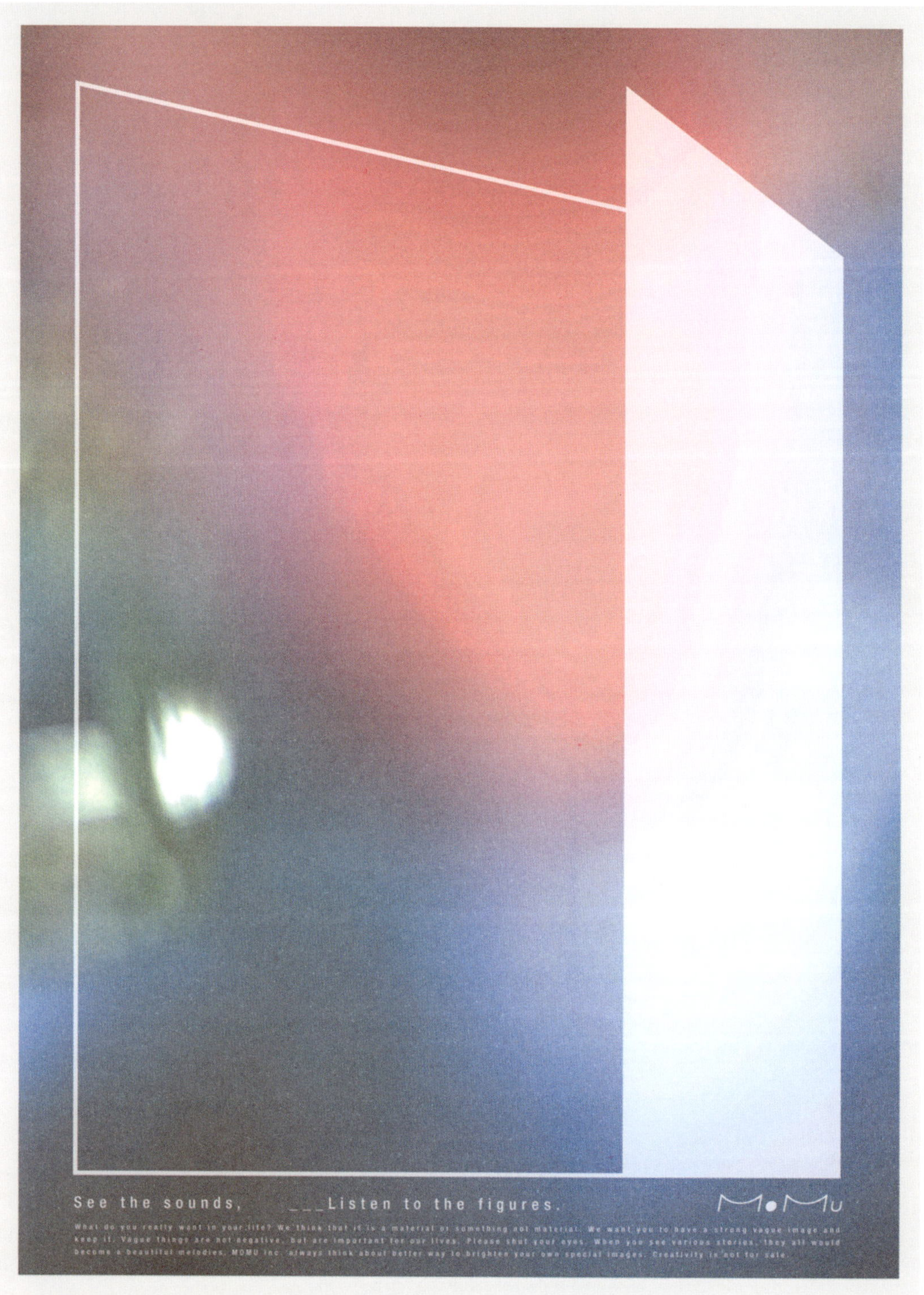

The designer placed transparent paper printed with typographic elements on highly chromatic photographs, the colors of which were tuned to a pale tone, to arrive at a vague impression desired by MO-MU. The abstract nature of sound and sight were expressed through the work.

See The Sounds, ___ Listen To The Figures

studio: **room-composite**
designer: ***Tomoya Kaishi*** photographer: ***Mina Imai***

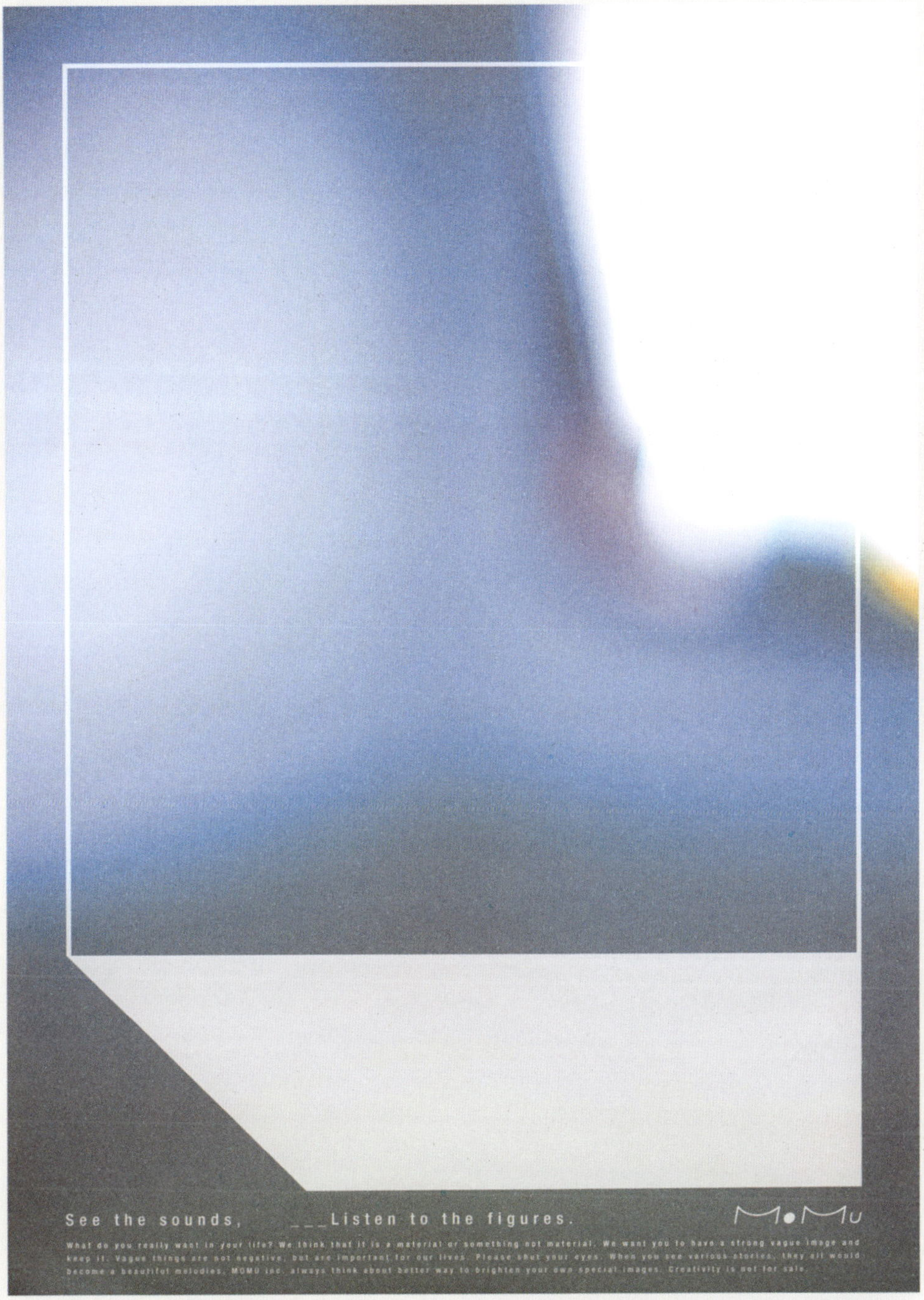

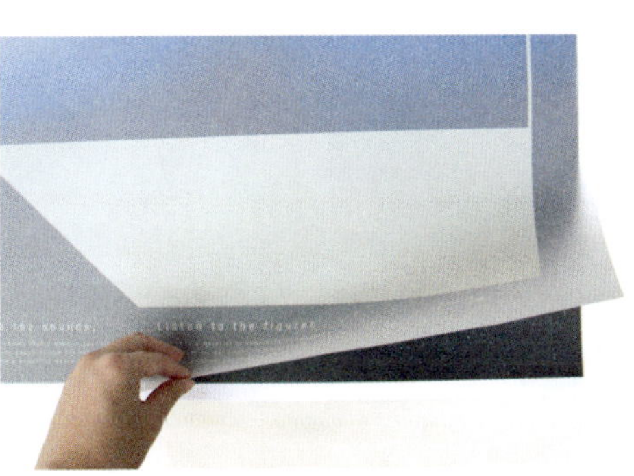

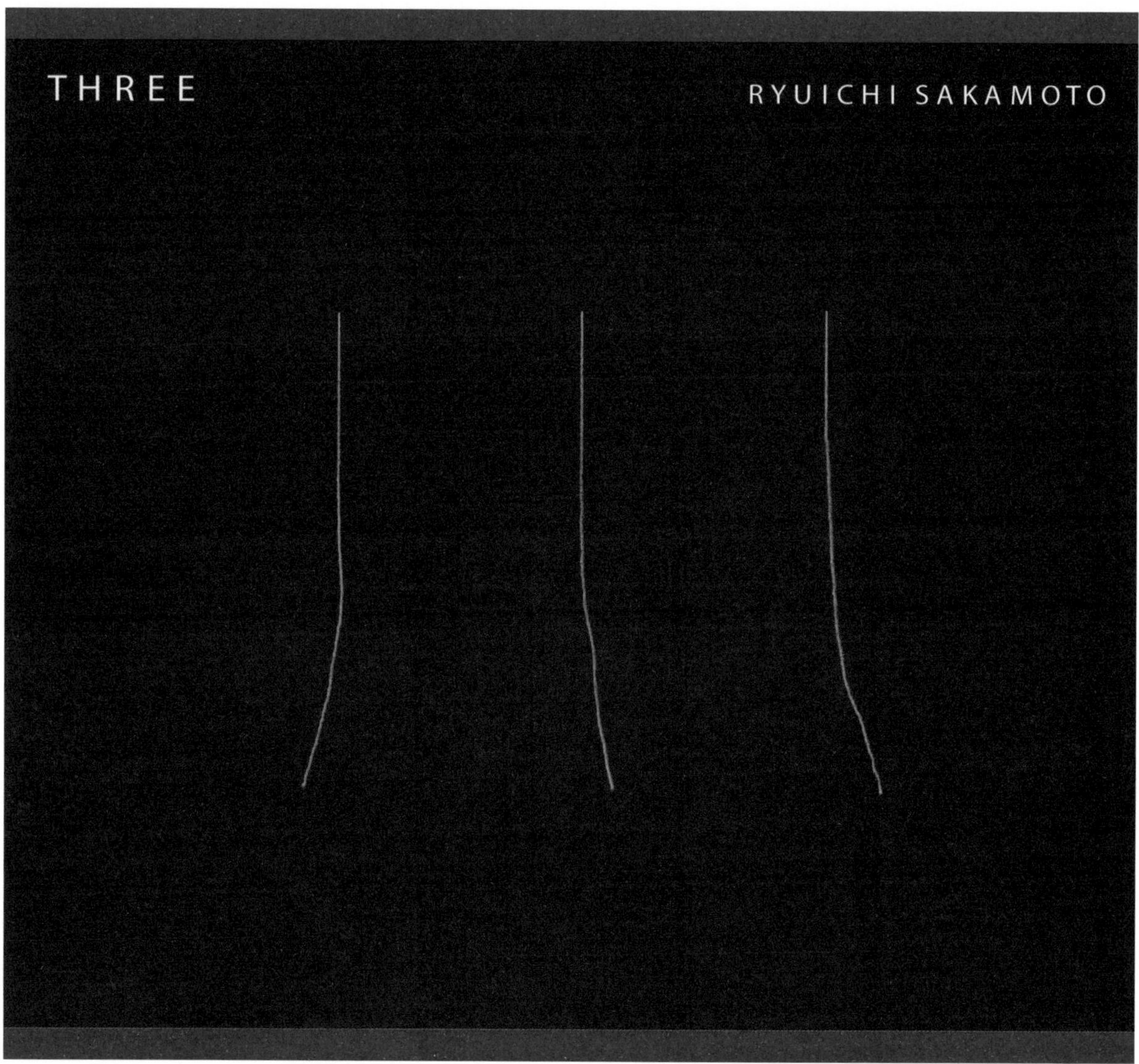

1

▲

This album cover was created for Ryuichi Sakamoto's album *Three*, which features the then new arrangements of Ryuichi's trio works in 2011. In the design, a combination of three lines were created to serve as an analogy to the trio performance by three artists. Since the word "three" is similar to "tree", the visual also resembles a tree growing from the ground.

1 Three

2 Playing The Orchestra 2013

studio: ***Nakajima Design***
designer: ***Hideki Nakajima***

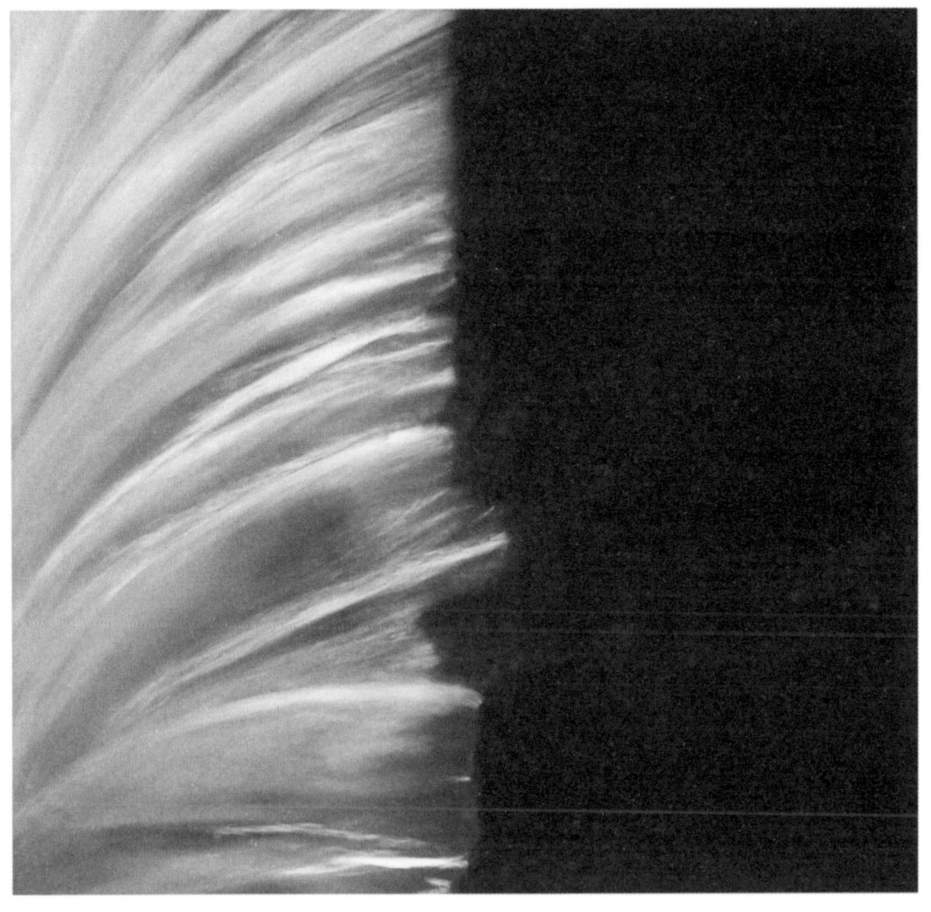

2

▲
This work is a CD cover designed for Ryuichi Sakamoto's album *Playing the Orchestra 2013*, which contains the best tracks selected from Ryuichi's performances of full orchestra. A view of looking down on a waterfall from the top was adopted, upon which the image of the orchestra was overlapped in a way that it produced music that also flow linearly just as water running down.

一〇五年
Poets of Tainan
十月十八

臺南詩展

詩星璀璨耀南瀛。

乙未改隸1895
二戰結束1945
疾走する別墅。
工場があるときはいつでも
私は震えるだろう
それが私たちのスレーブデンです
私たちを保護することはあ
搖仔搖 惜仔惜；
『構築蟻窩』
陳雷台語文學選 台灣
《風車》詩刊

終戰1945
至1959年
屬於「戰後嬰兒潮」世代

才黃昏哪。
張敬忠 走方郎中
骨歸塵 塵歸土
土歸石 石歸骨
我知道那必然是你
我認得你對我依戀不捨得目光
縱使匆忙
但總是拖得細細長長的

六〇年代1960
介系詞 代名詞
副詞
過去式 現在式
未來進行式

英國王子來投胎
鴻鴻《與我無關的東西》
鐵窗邊一枝柑仔樹葉尾溜
垂吊一粒必痕的娘仔豆

I was sitting up here all that time trying to
Figure out if I was
-
Brokeback Mountain

指導單位

文化部

主辦單位
國立台灣文學館
National Museum of Taiwan Literature
臺南市政府文化局

Exhibition of Tainan's Poems by Qi-Dong Poetry Salon

studio: ***archicake*** *designer: Tung Yi-Ching*
art direction: Chung Ping-Hung

終戰1945
至1959年
屬於「戰後嬰兒潮」世代

才黃昏哪。
張敬忠 走方郎中

骨歸塵 塵歸土
土歸石 石歸骨
我知道那必然是你
我認得你對我依戀不捨得目光
縱使匆忙
但總是拖得細細長長的

六〇年代1960
介系詞 代名詞
副詞
過去式 現在式
未來進行式

英國王子來投胎
鴻鴻《與我無關的東西》
鐵窗邊一枝柑仔樹葉尾溜
垂吊一粒必痕的娘仔豆

For those whose impressions of Tainan were confined to Chihkan Tower or Tainan Confucian Temple in Hú-siânn (the old capital city), poems by Tainan poets will offer pieces of a broader picture of the vicissitudes of Tainan in the history, in addition to its diverse natural landscapes and the dynamism of its people. This poster was created for Qi-Dong Poetry Salon's exhibition of Tainan's poems. Graphic representations of the Salt Mountain and red bricks were depicted to symbolize labor and the development of political culture. Beautiful excerpts from poetry by Tainan poets in different languages are displayed alongside to reflect the change of time and culture.

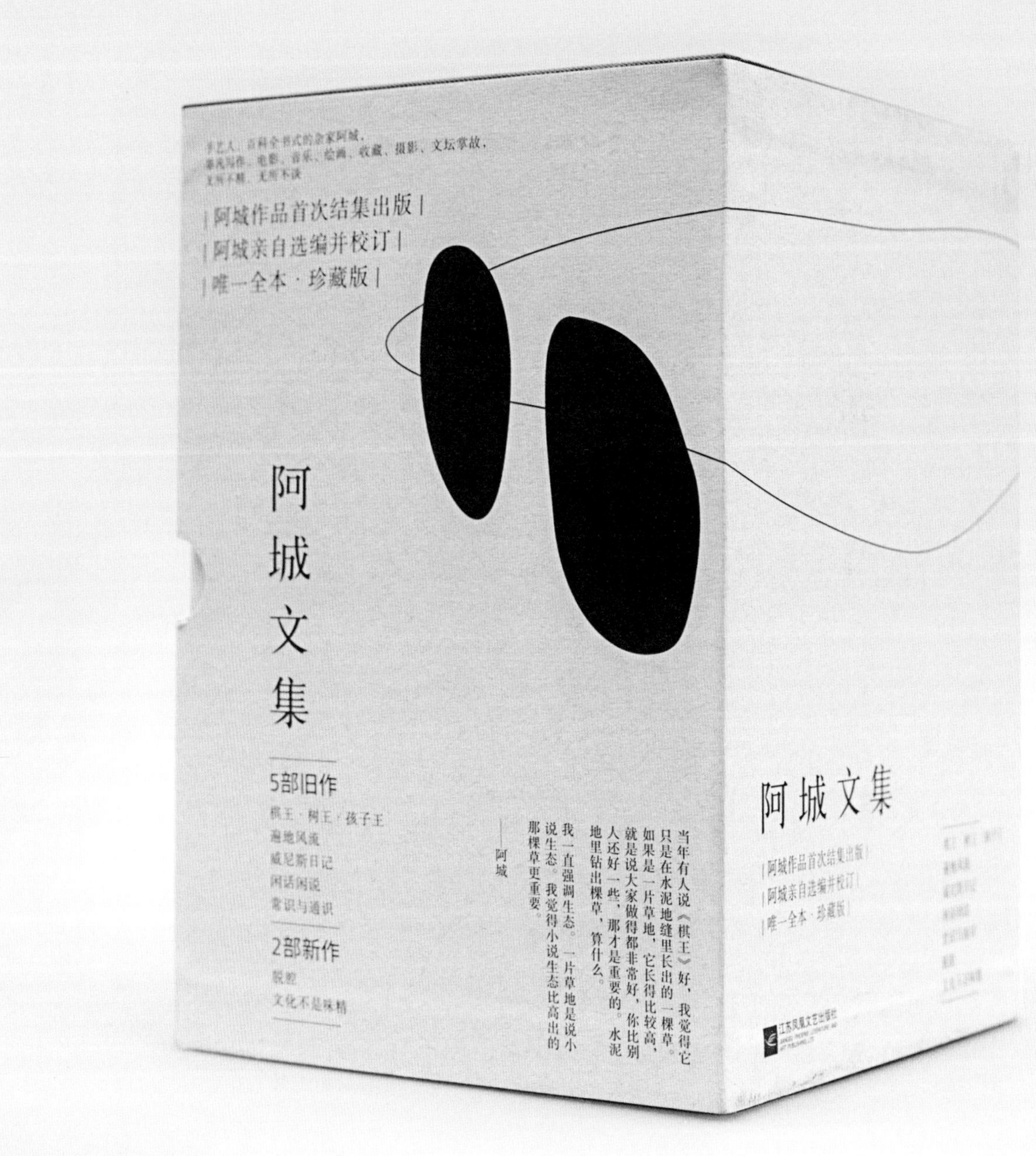

For the visual design for the new edition of *Collected Works of A Cheng*, the studio created a set of printing archaize font as the main visual element. The font helps maintain consistency through the whole collection and highlights the blankness in the composition. This seemingly effortless visual expression coincides with A Cheng's literature style.

A Cheng

阿城文集

studio: ***1000 Times Studio***
designer: ***Zhu Sha***

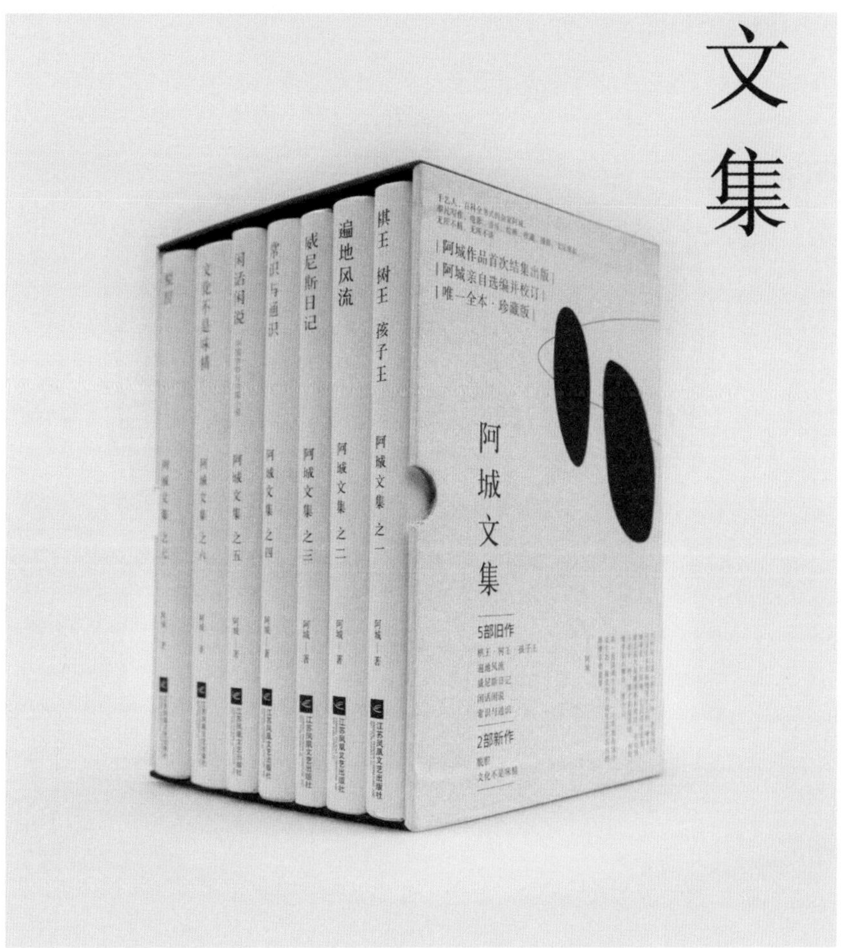

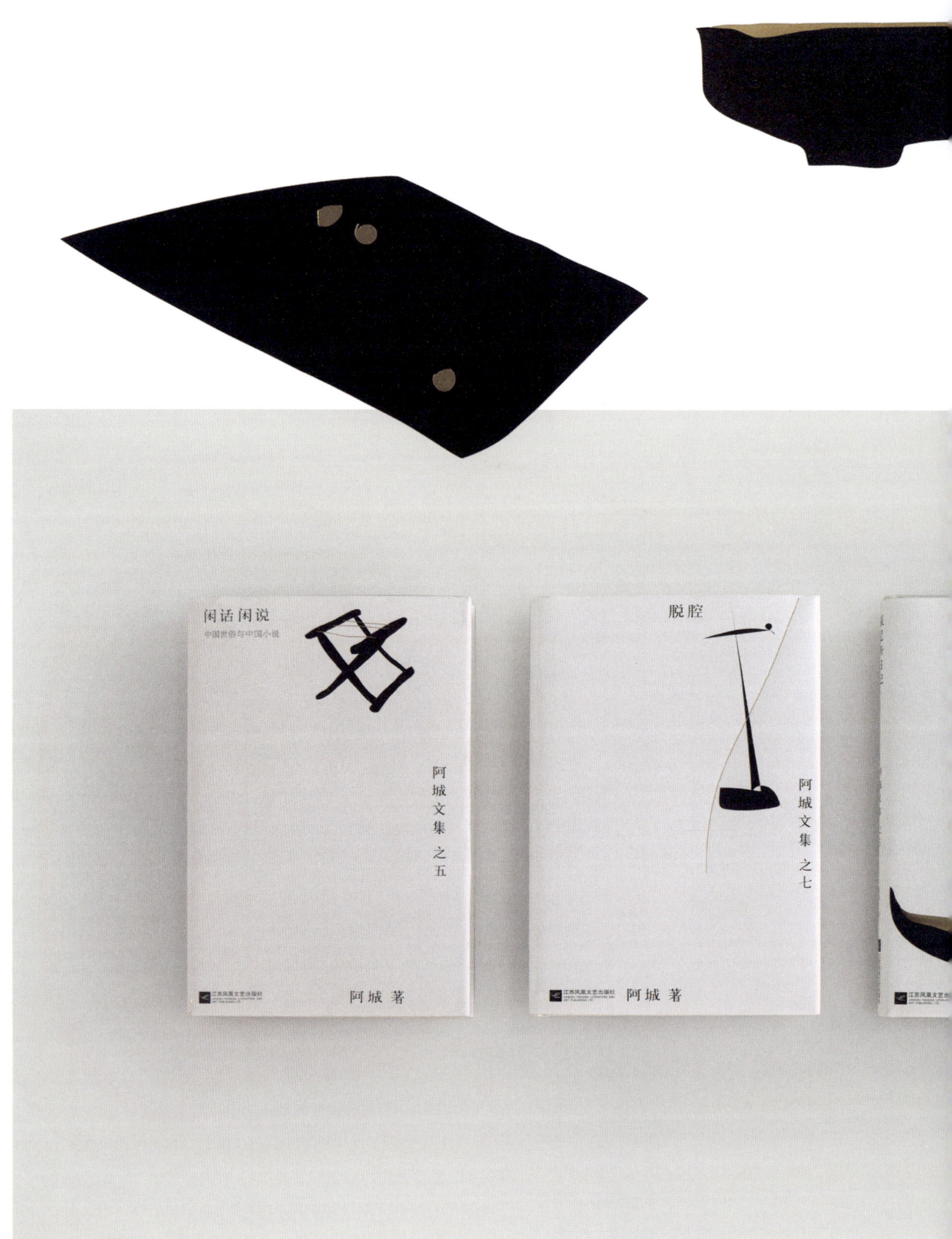
闲话闲说
中国世俗与中国小说
阿城文集 之五
江苏凤凰文艺出版社
阿城 著
脱腔
阿城文集 之七
江苏凤凰文艺出版社
阿城 著

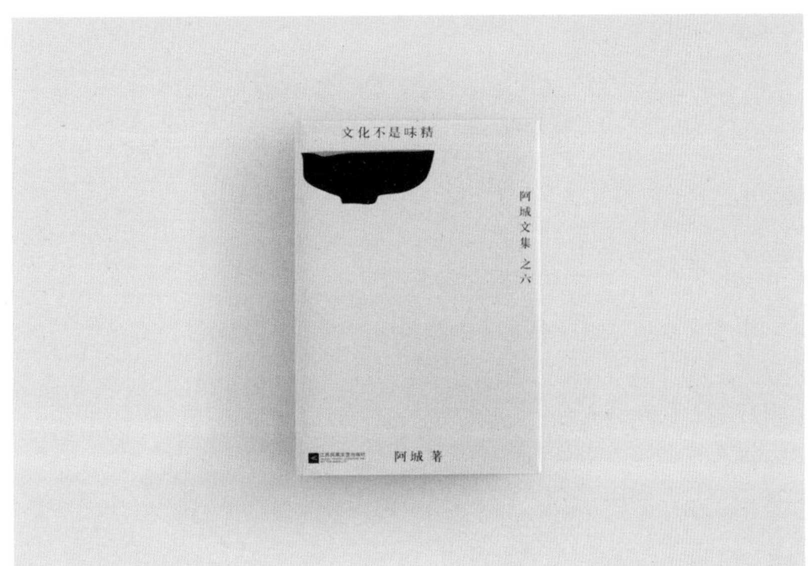
文化不是味精
阿城文集 之六
阿城 著

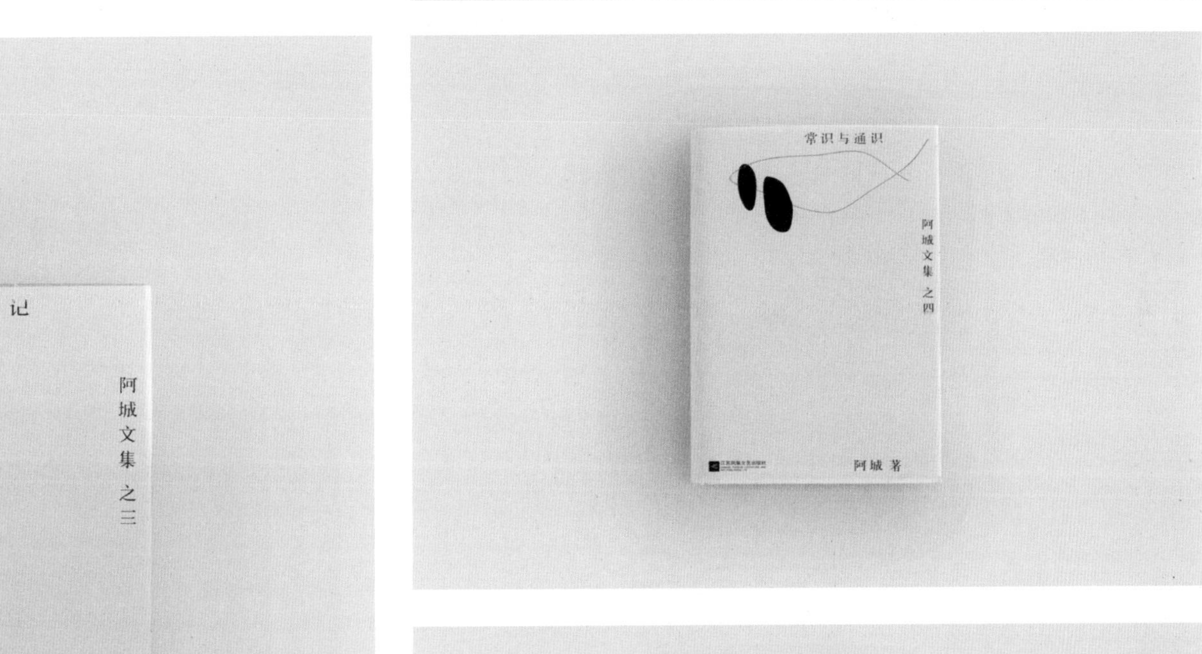
斯日记
阿城文集 之三
常识与通识
阿城文集 之四
阿城 著

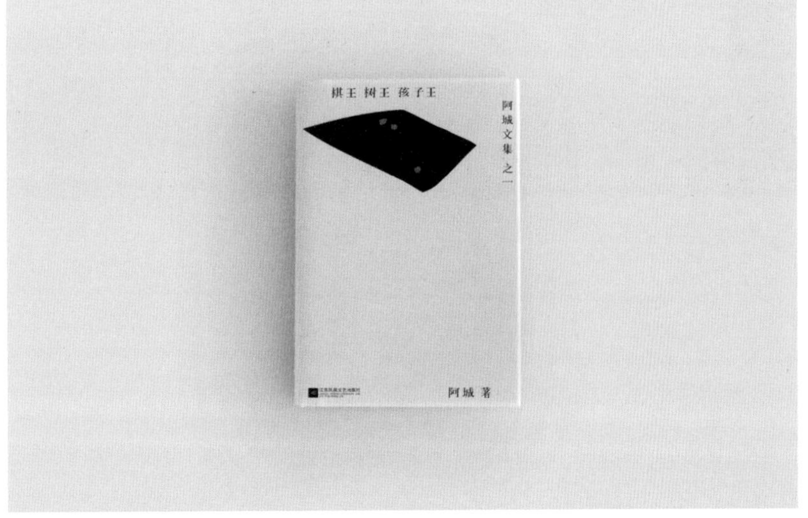
棋王 树王 孩子王
阿城文集 之一
阿城 著

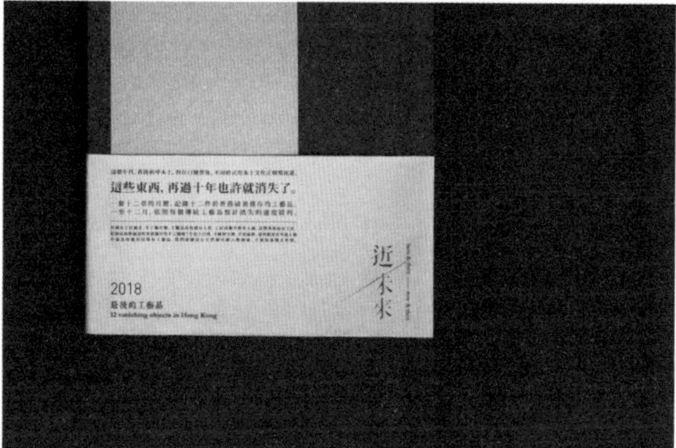

The Vanishing Object Calendar is one of the publication from the design project "here & there—now & then". 12 vanishing handicrafts in Hong Kong are recorded and displayed in the 12 chapters of the calendar in the order in which they are expected to disappear. By presenting the calendar in the form of a book with stories and introductions of each handicraft, the designer hoped to raise awareness of the importance of cherishing and appreciating these vanishing objects. After detailed research and analysis, the designer created images of color blending through silk screen with the corresponding sets of colors representative of each object. These and specific patterns were then applied in the graphics of the calendar.

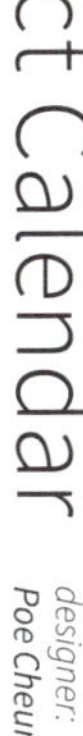

Vanishing Object Calendar

designer:
Poe Cheung

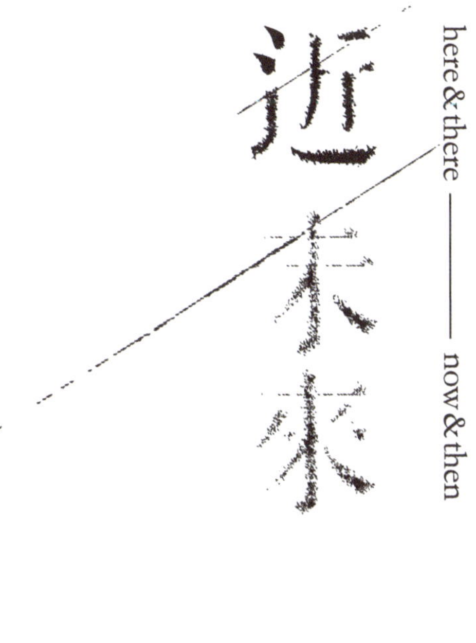

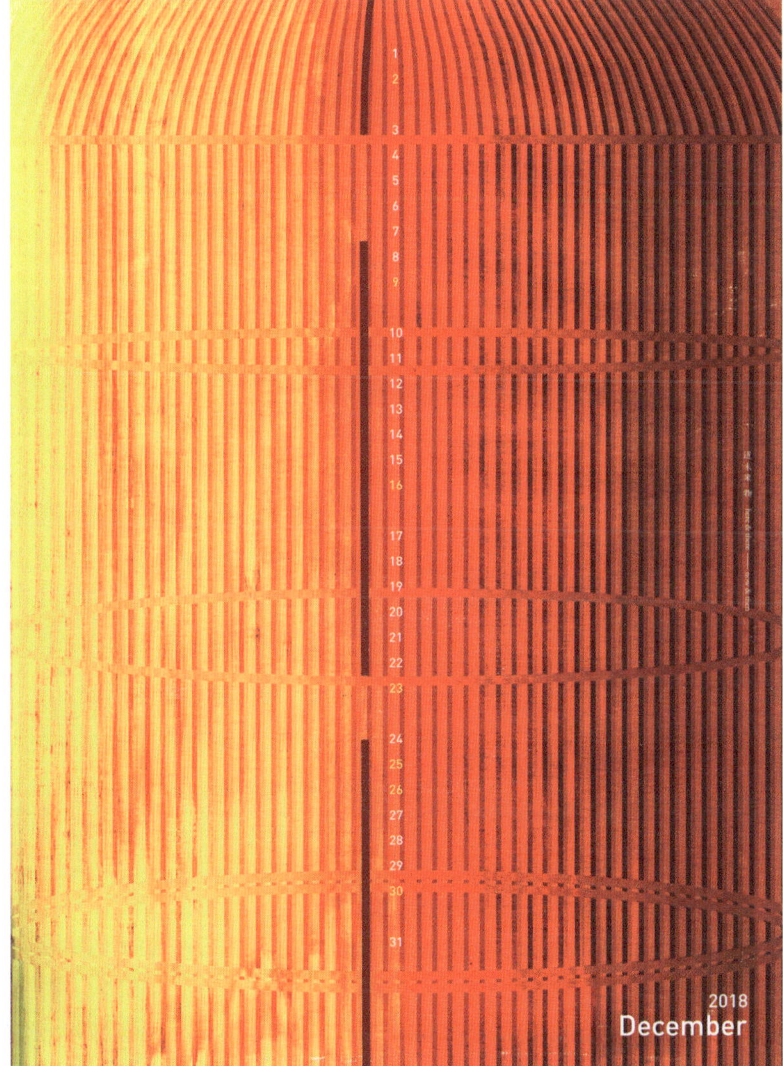

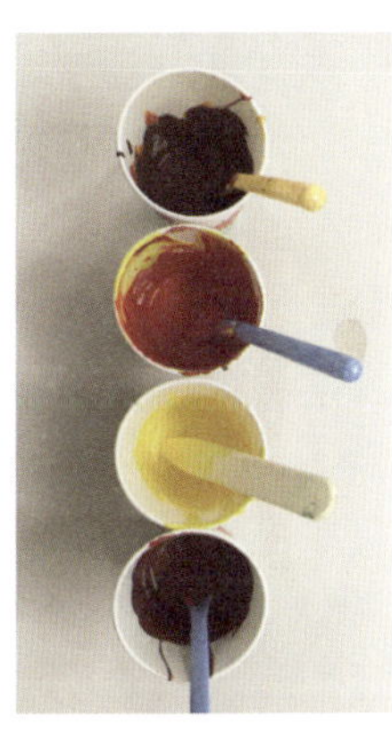

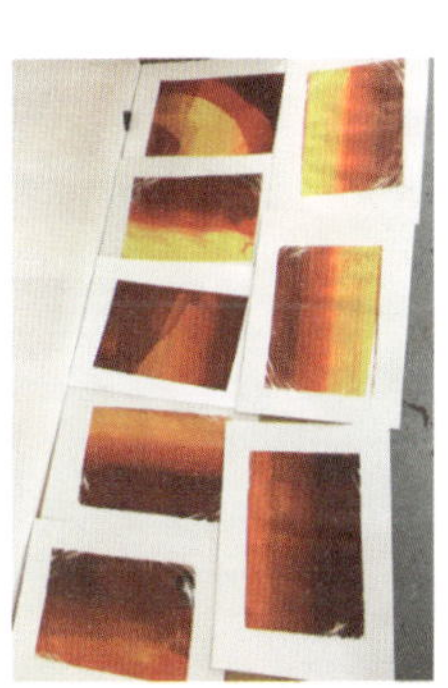

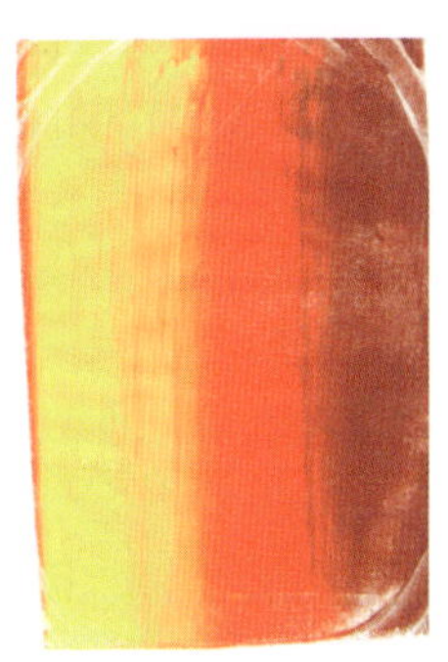

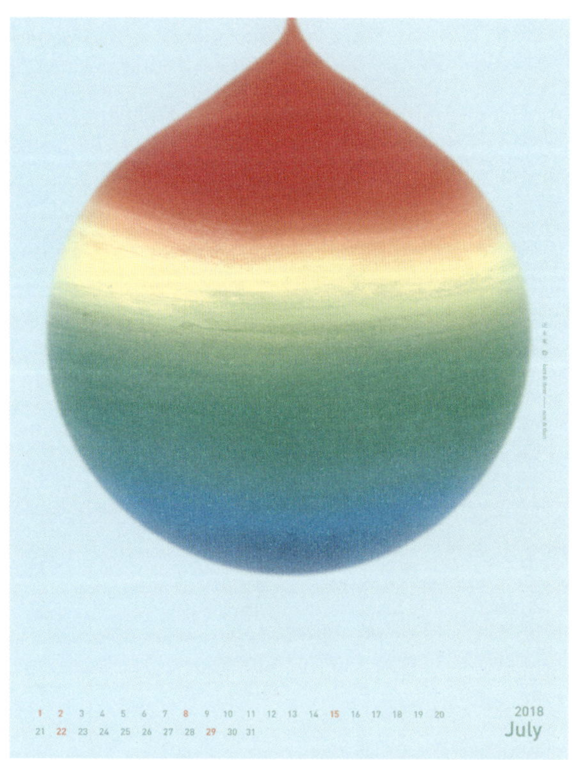
1 2 3 4 5 6 7 8 9 10 11 12 13 14 15 16 17 18 19 20
21 22 23 24 25 26 27 28 29 30 31
2018
July

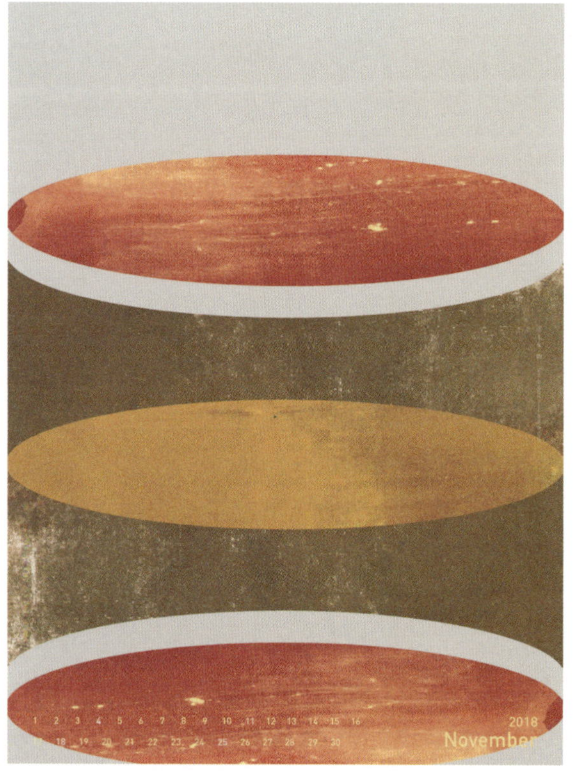
2018

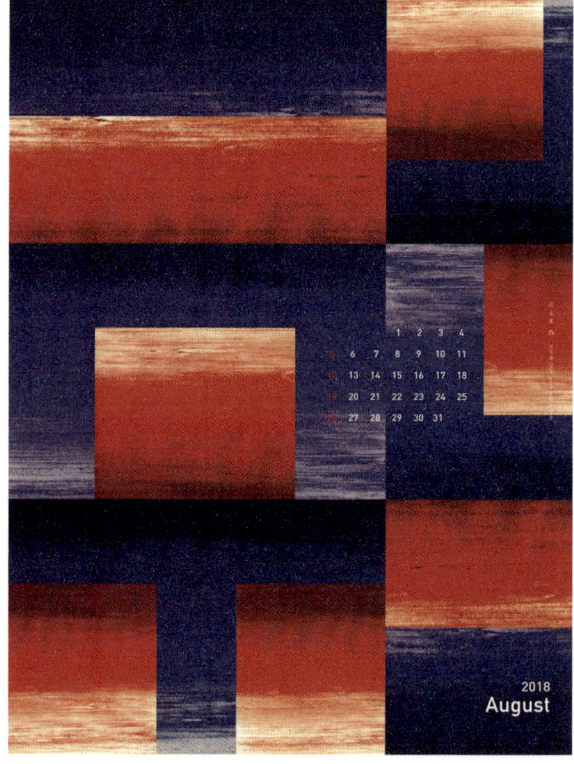
1 2 3 4
6 7 8 9 10 11
13 14 15 16 17 18
20 21 22 23 24 25
27 28 29 30 31
2018
August

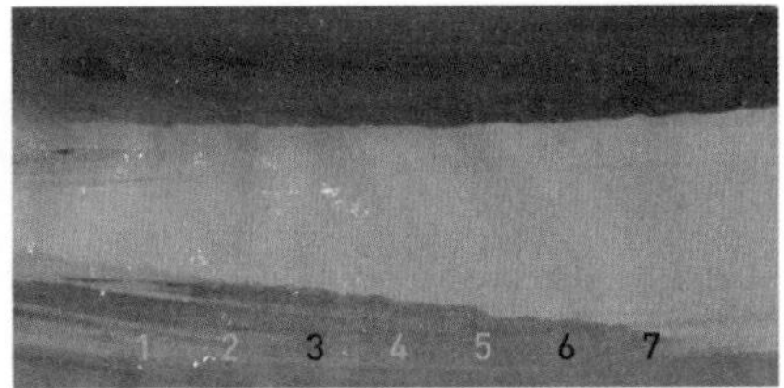

1	2	3	4	5	6	7
8	9	10	11	12	13	14
15	16	17	18	19	20	21
22	23	24	25	26	27	28
29	30					

近未来物 here & there —— now & then

2018
April

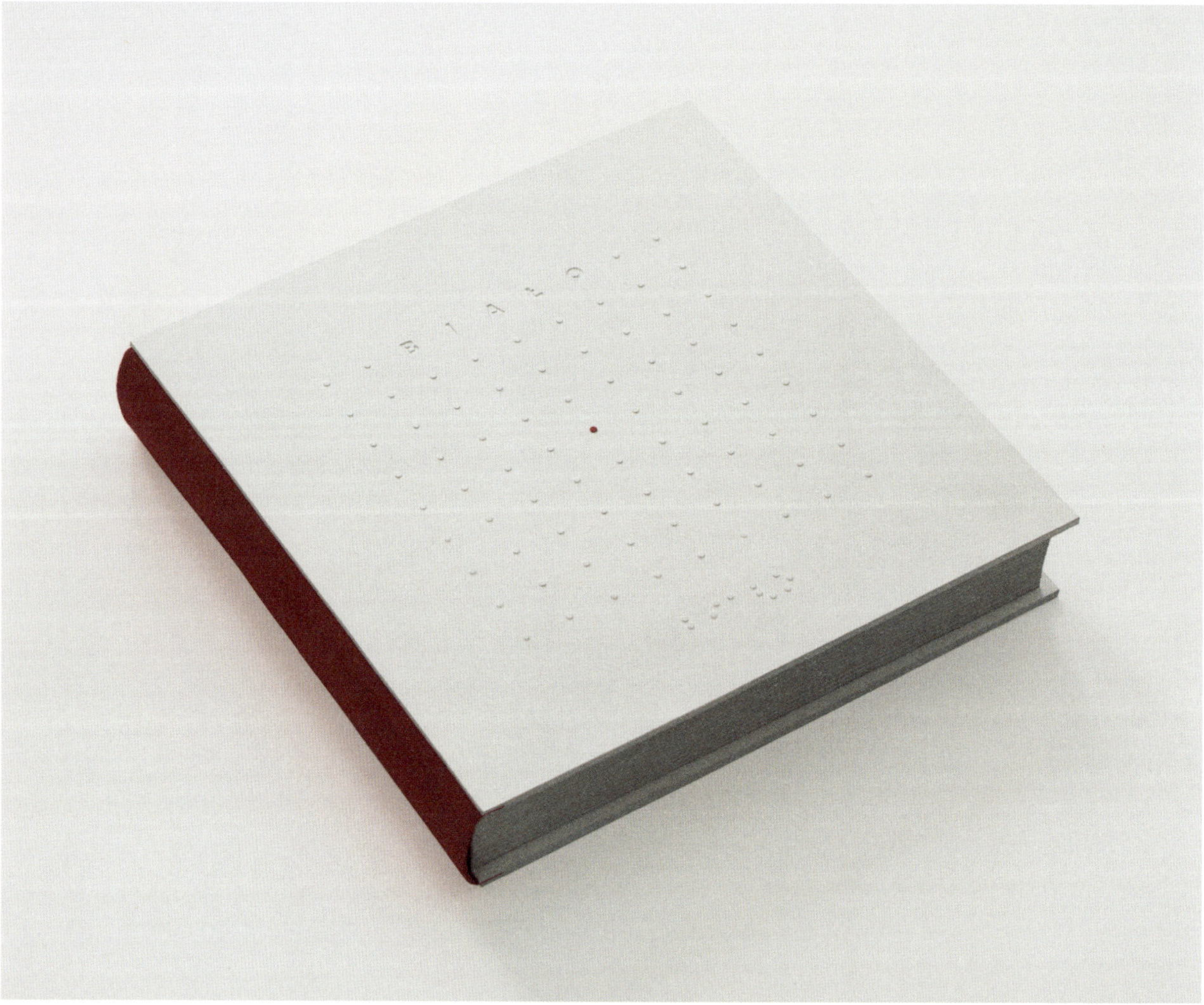

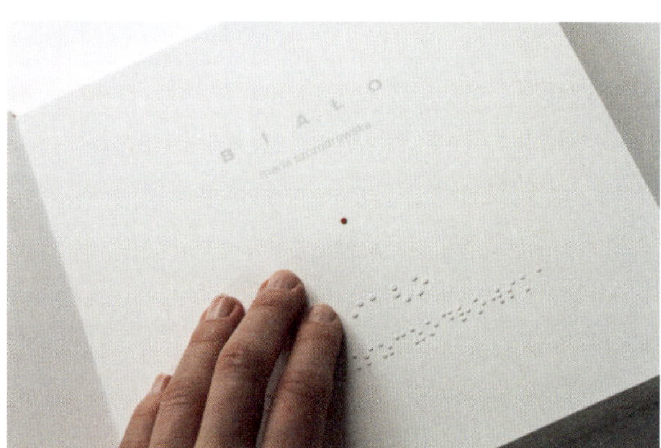

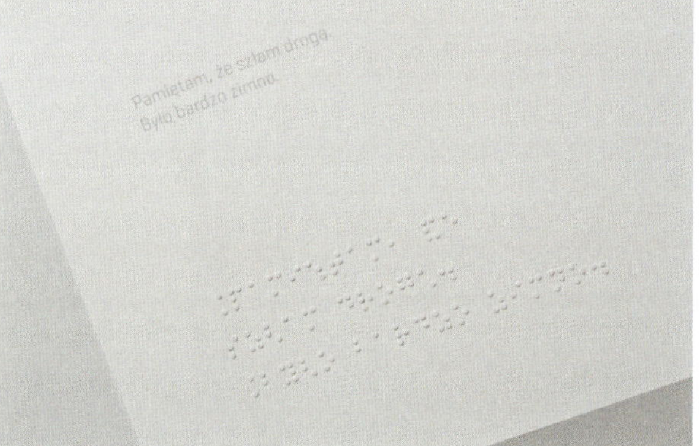

Based on the idea that book has been made to appeal to the sighted and the unsighted alike, the designer created a book that incorporated tactile pictures and traditionally printed and embossed Braille texts to broaden the reading experience to multisensory perception. In the short text, the topic of vision loss has been subtly developed, providing rationale for all formal procedures applied in this work.

Biało

designer:
Maria Szczodrowska

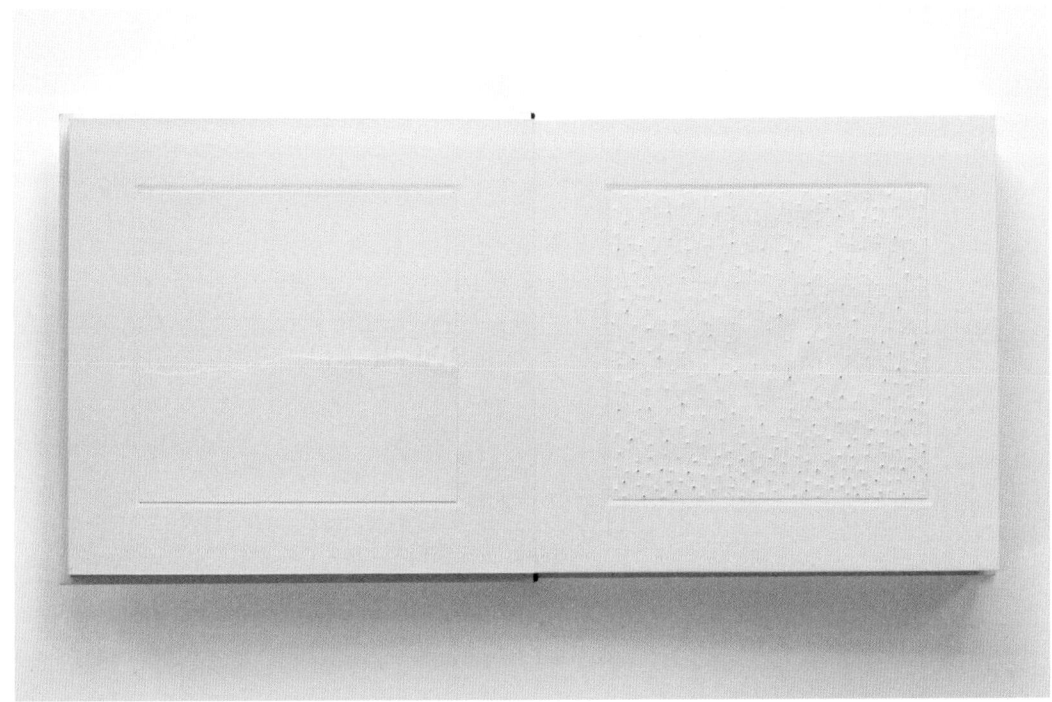

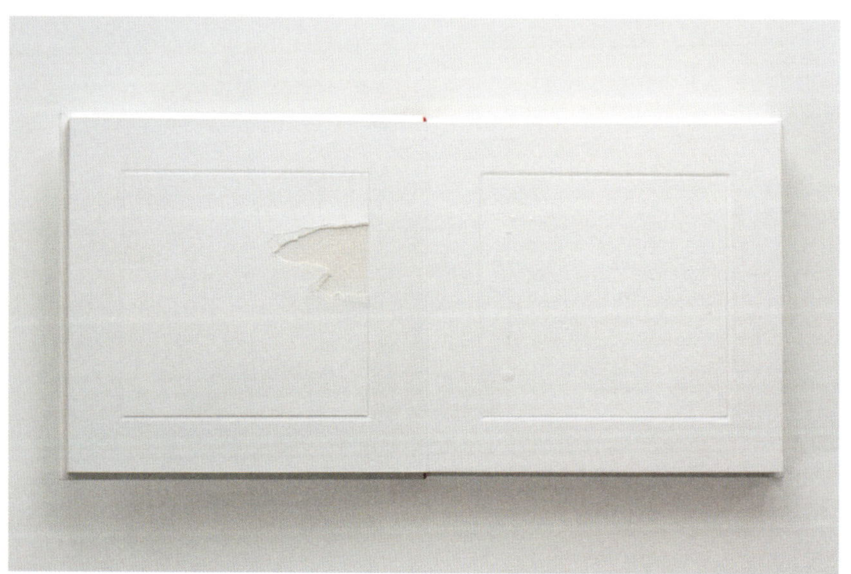

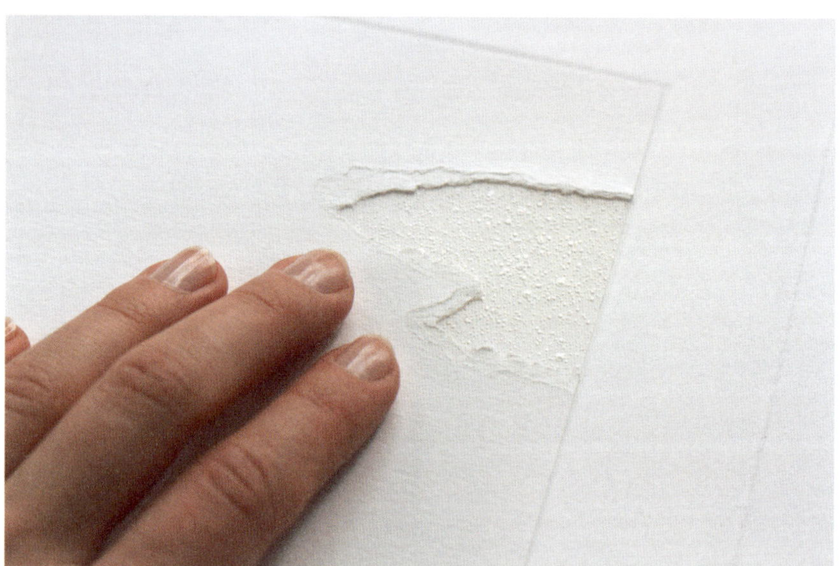

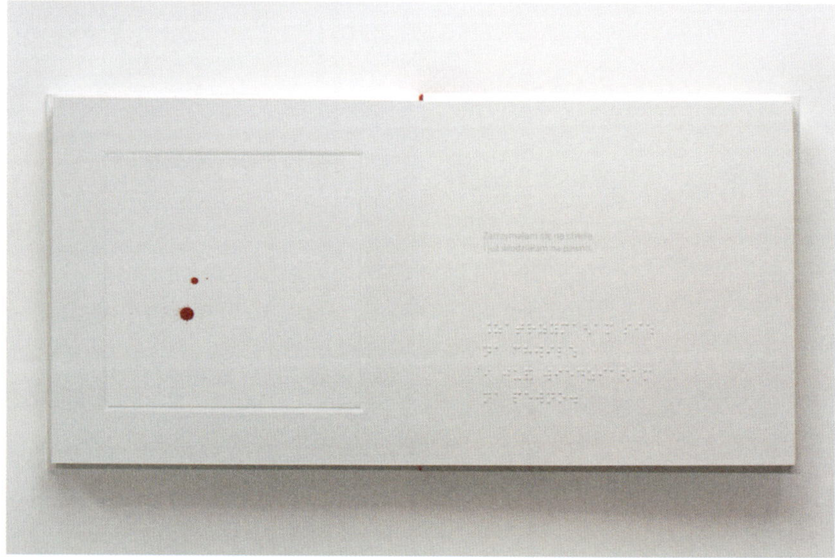

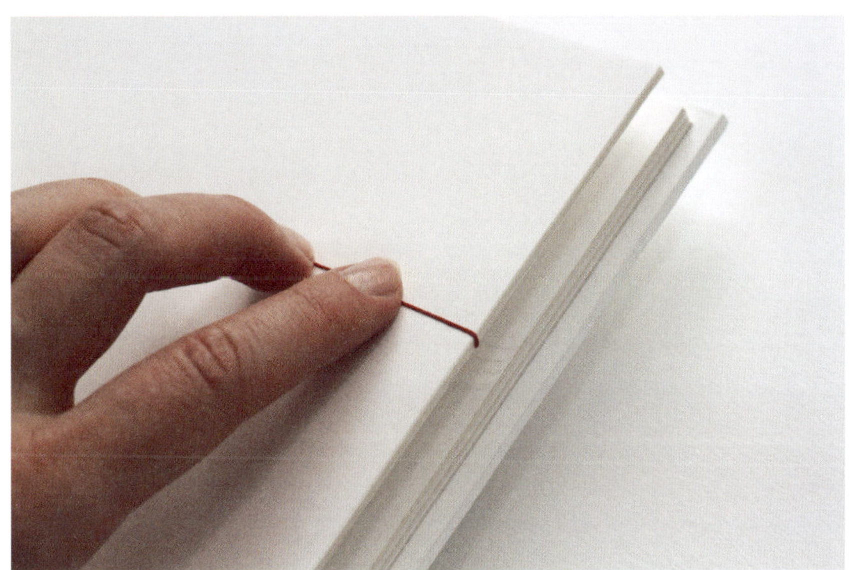

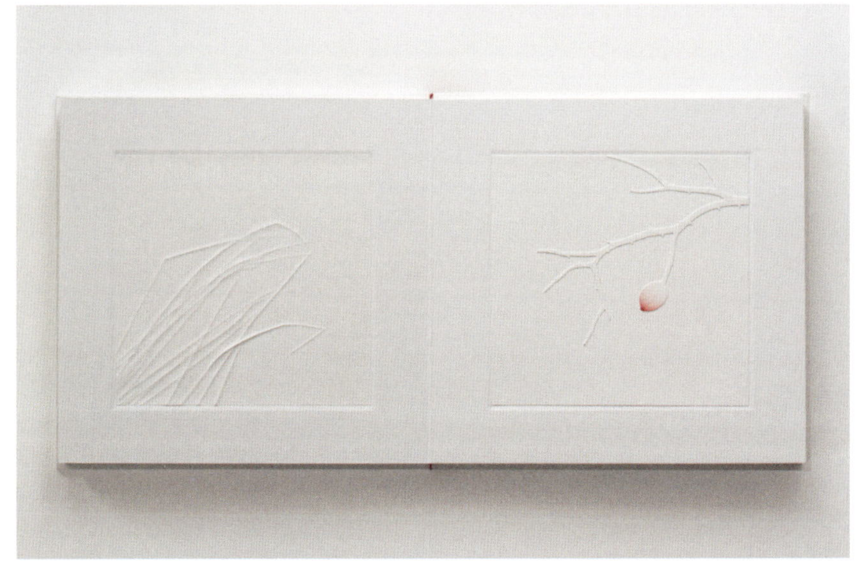

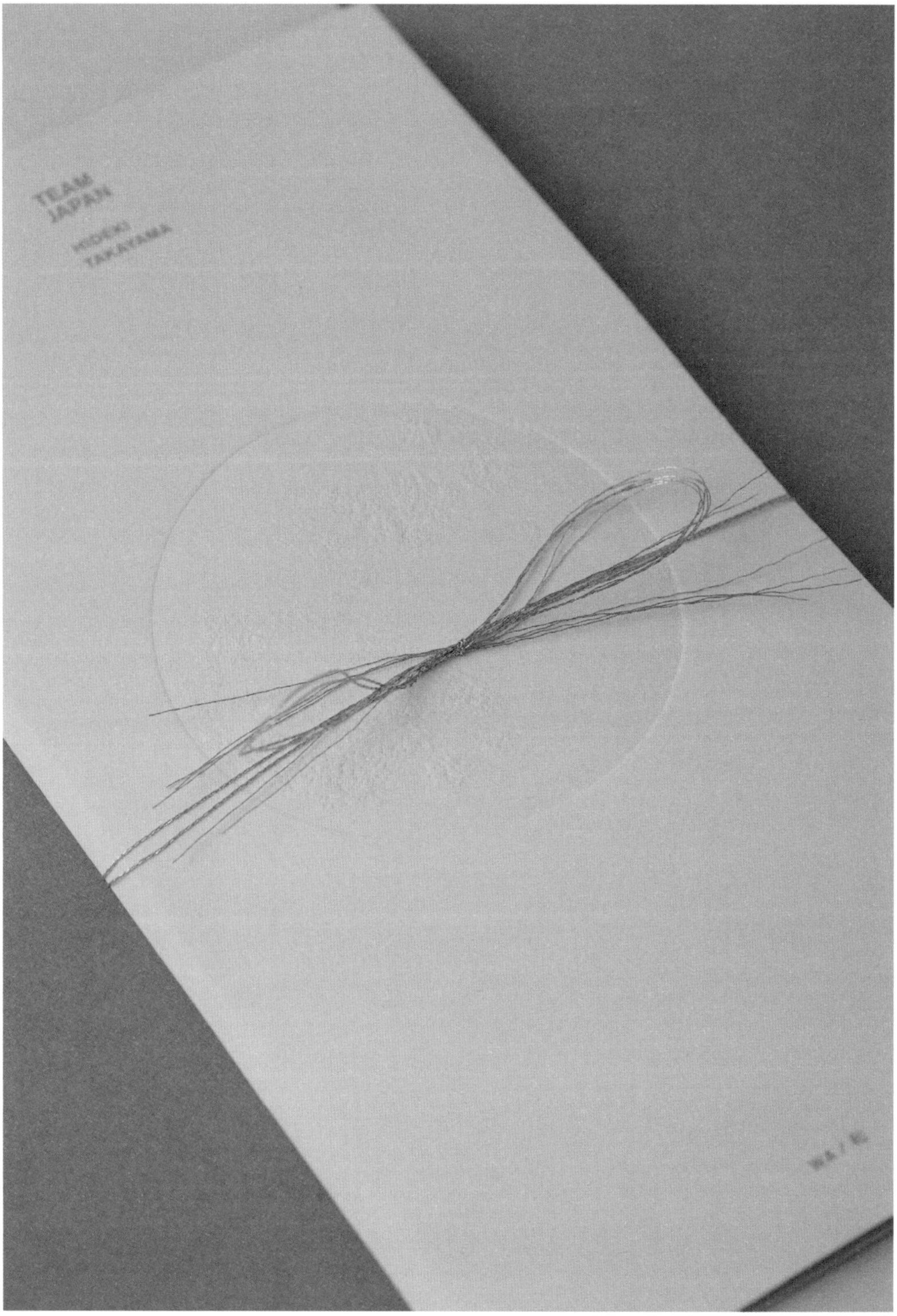

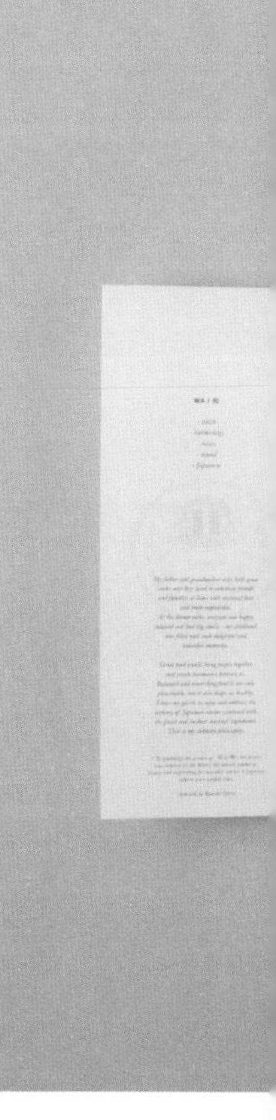

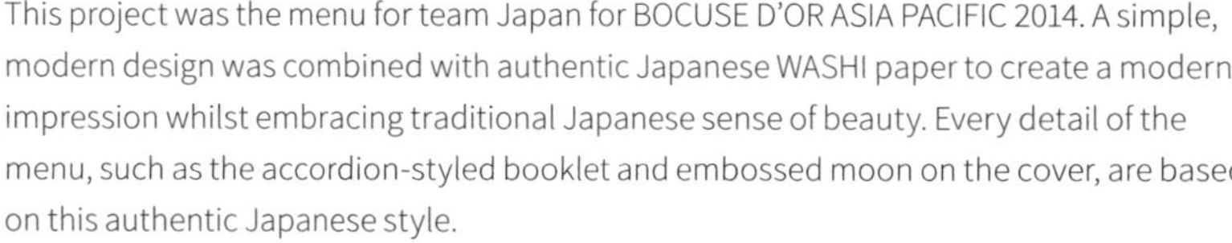

This project was the menu for team Japan for BOCUSE D'OR ASIA PACIFIC 2014. A simple, modern design was combined with authentic Japanese WASHI paper to create a modern impression whilst embracing traditional Japanese sense of beauty. Every detail of the menu, such as the accordion-styled booklet and embossed moon on the cover, are based on this authentic Japanese style.

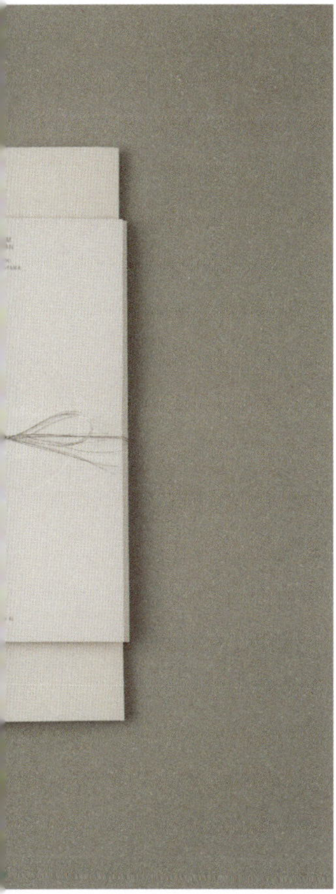

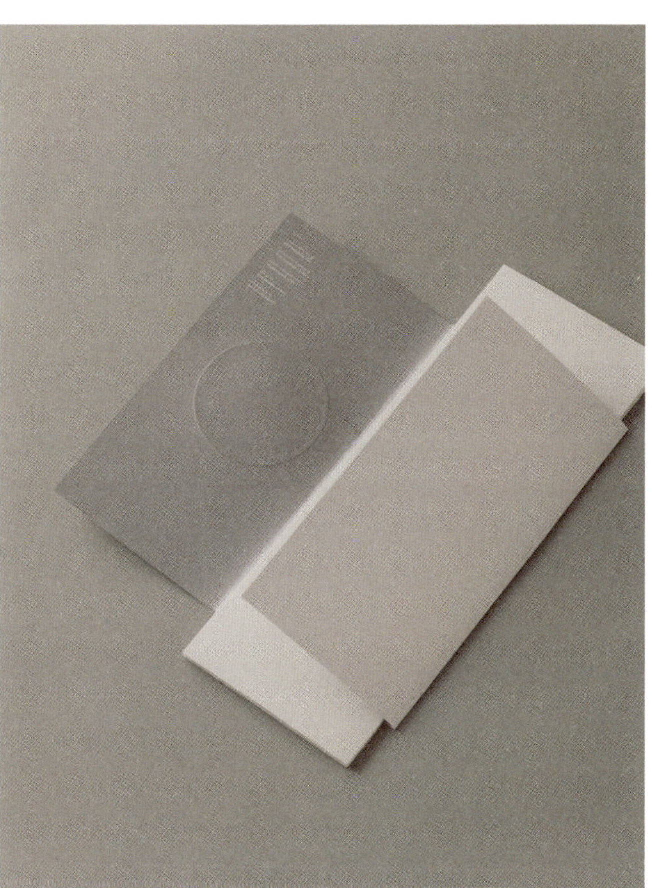

Menu for Team Japan for Bocuse D'or

studio: ***artless Inc*** *art director:* ***shun kawakami***
designer: ***nao nozawa***

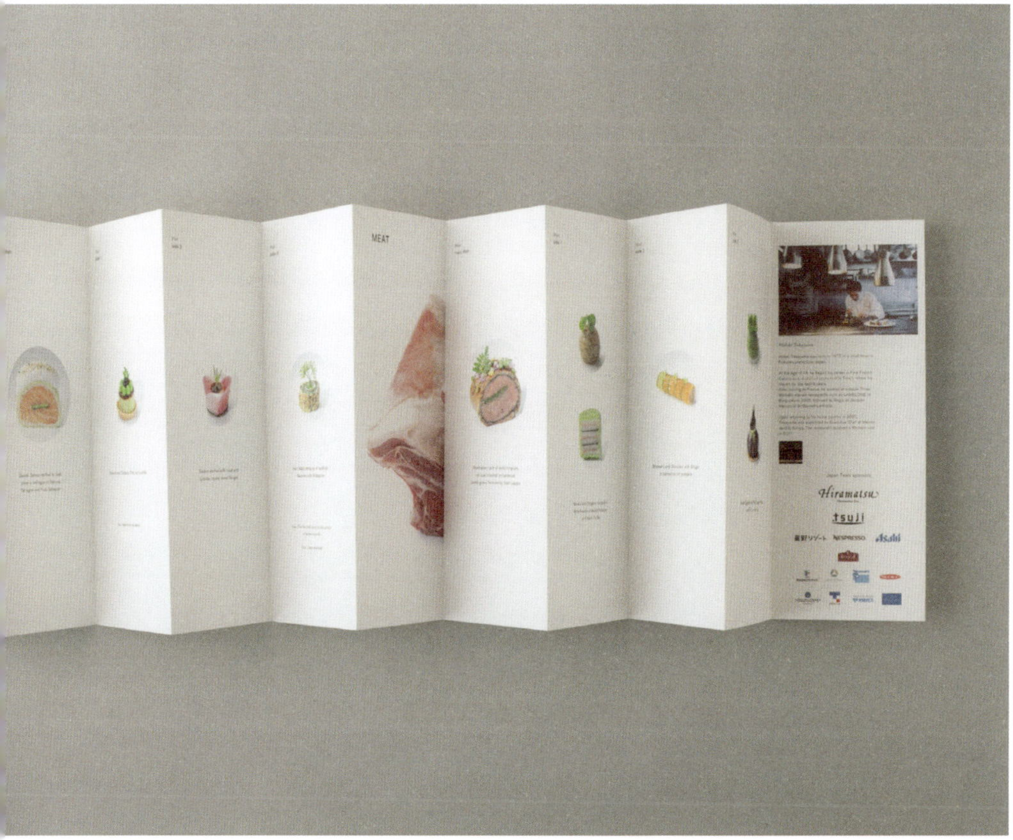

リンゴ酸の奏でる、爽やかな余韻

可愛くて飲みやすい、でも本格派。
”日本酒”の新しい可能性を広げていく
カジュアルスタイルの純米吟醸酒。
白ワインに多く含まれるリンゴ酸が奏でる
奥ゆかしい香り、甘みと酸味の調和、爽やかな余韻。
軽快な後味は、冷やすことでより一層
美味しくお飲みいただけます。
日本酒に馴染みのない方にも新しい味わいと喜びを
そんな想いから生まれたのが「きのえねアップル」です。

日本酒の世界は、もっと広がっていく

Junmai Ginjo

Kinoene Apple

An amiable yet authentic image was created for Kinoene Apple, a seasonal premium sake with malic acid which brings forth a refreshing aroma. The apple-shaped bottle necker was devised to increase recognition. The brand name is written in Kanji to maintain its bond with traditional Japanese sake. The long and narrow label made up of Japanese paper arrives at a light expression soothing for summer, just like the sake.

Kinoene Apple

studio: **tegusu Inc**
designer: **Masaomi Fujita**

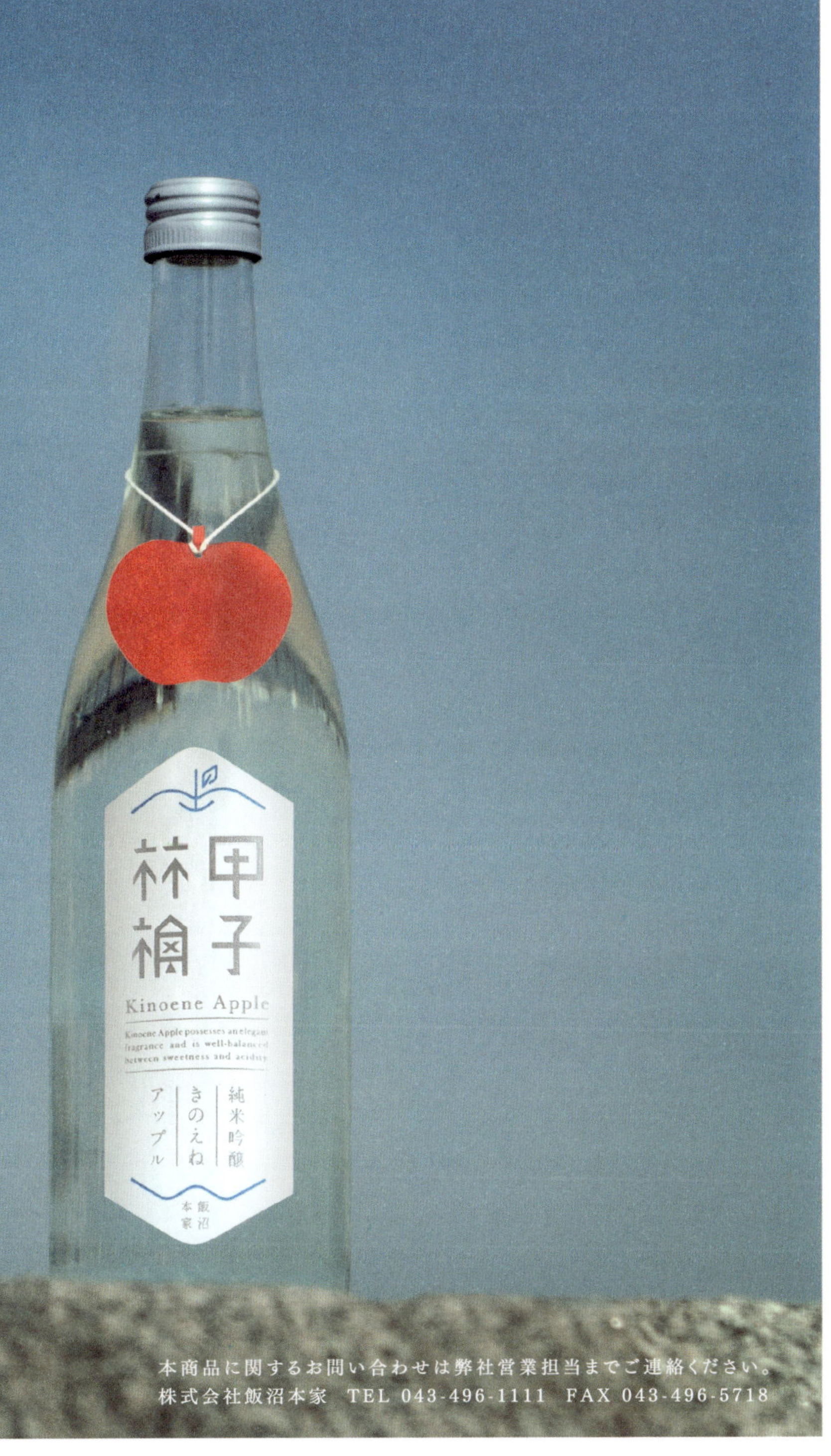

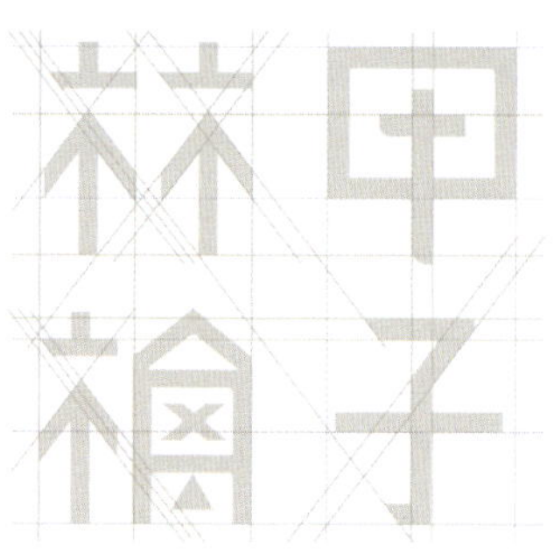

Kinoene Apple

Kinoene Apple possesses an elegant fragrance and is well-balanced between sweetness and acidity.

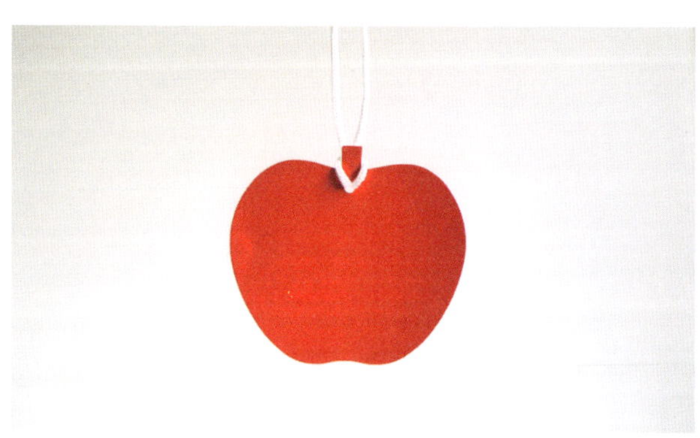

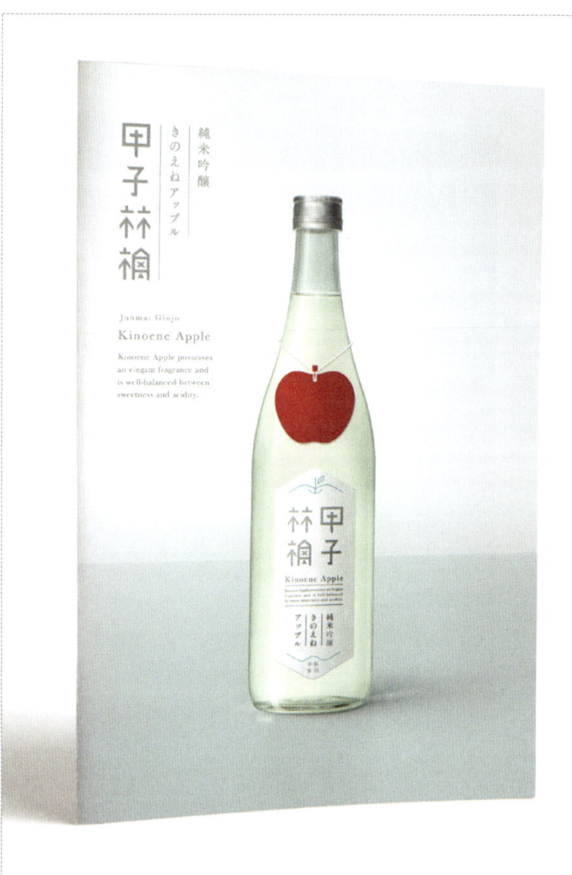

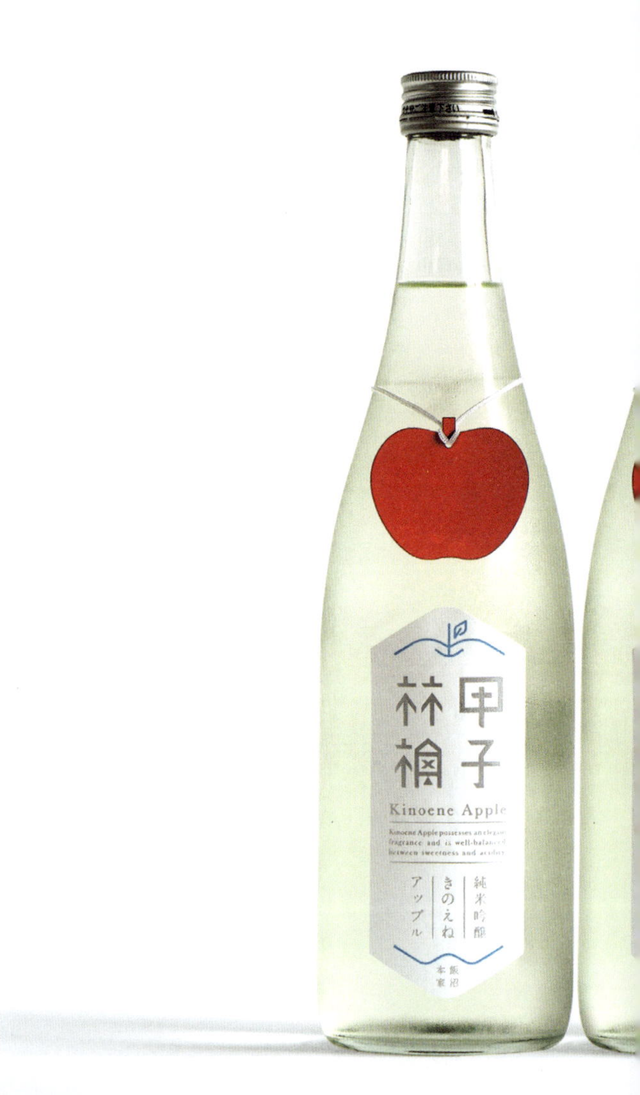

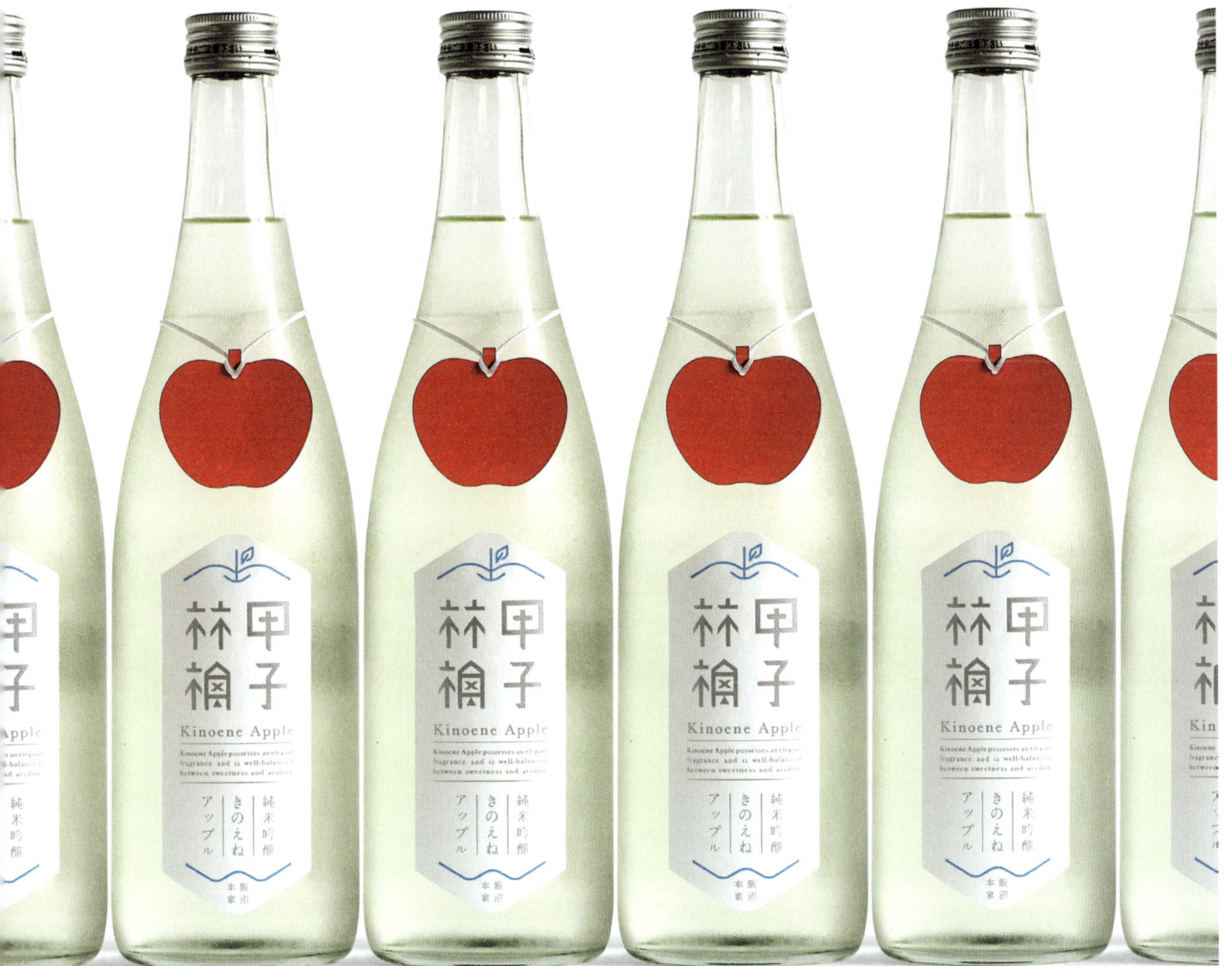
甲子
林檎
Kinoene Apple
純米吟醸
きのえね
アップル
飯沼
本家

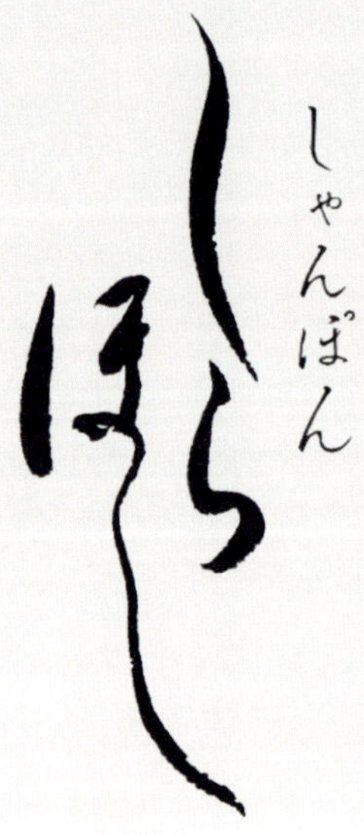

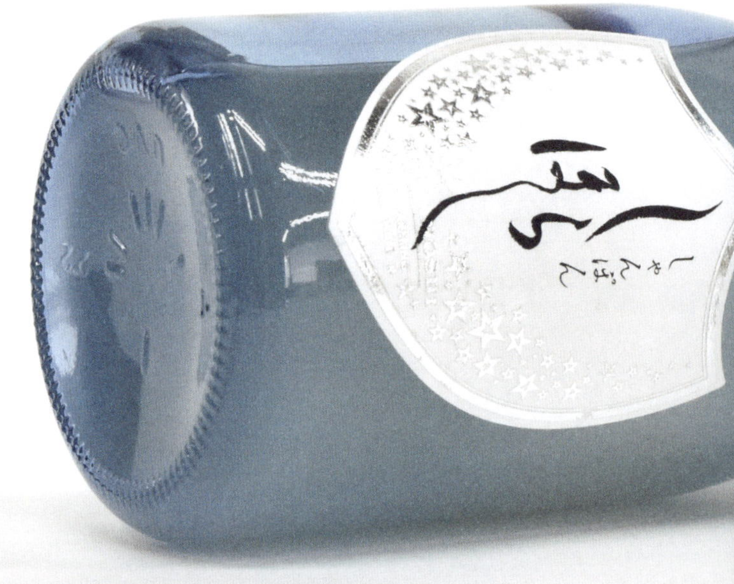

This is a packaging design for the sparkling Japanese sake SHIRAHOSHI, a collaboration product of Imayotsukasa Sake Brewery and professional baseball team Yokohama DeNA BayStars. It exhibits a fusion of Japanese and Western features—a label suitable for champagne combined with Japanese calligraphy. Star motifs symbolizing the baseball team are scattered around the edge of the label, mimicking the dispersal of carbonation and evoking the impression of champagne.

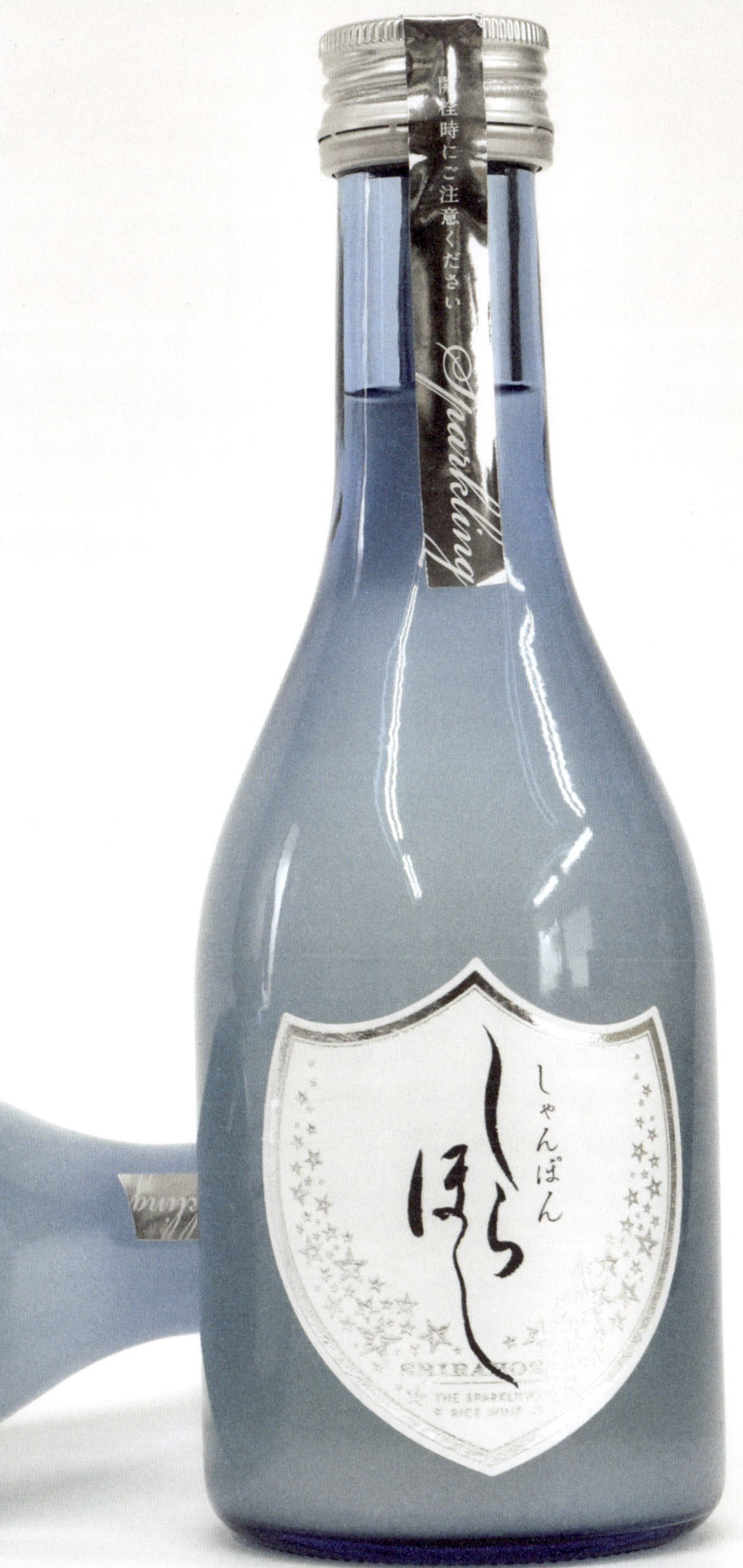

Shirahoshi

studio: **BULLET Inc.**
designer: ***Aya Codama***

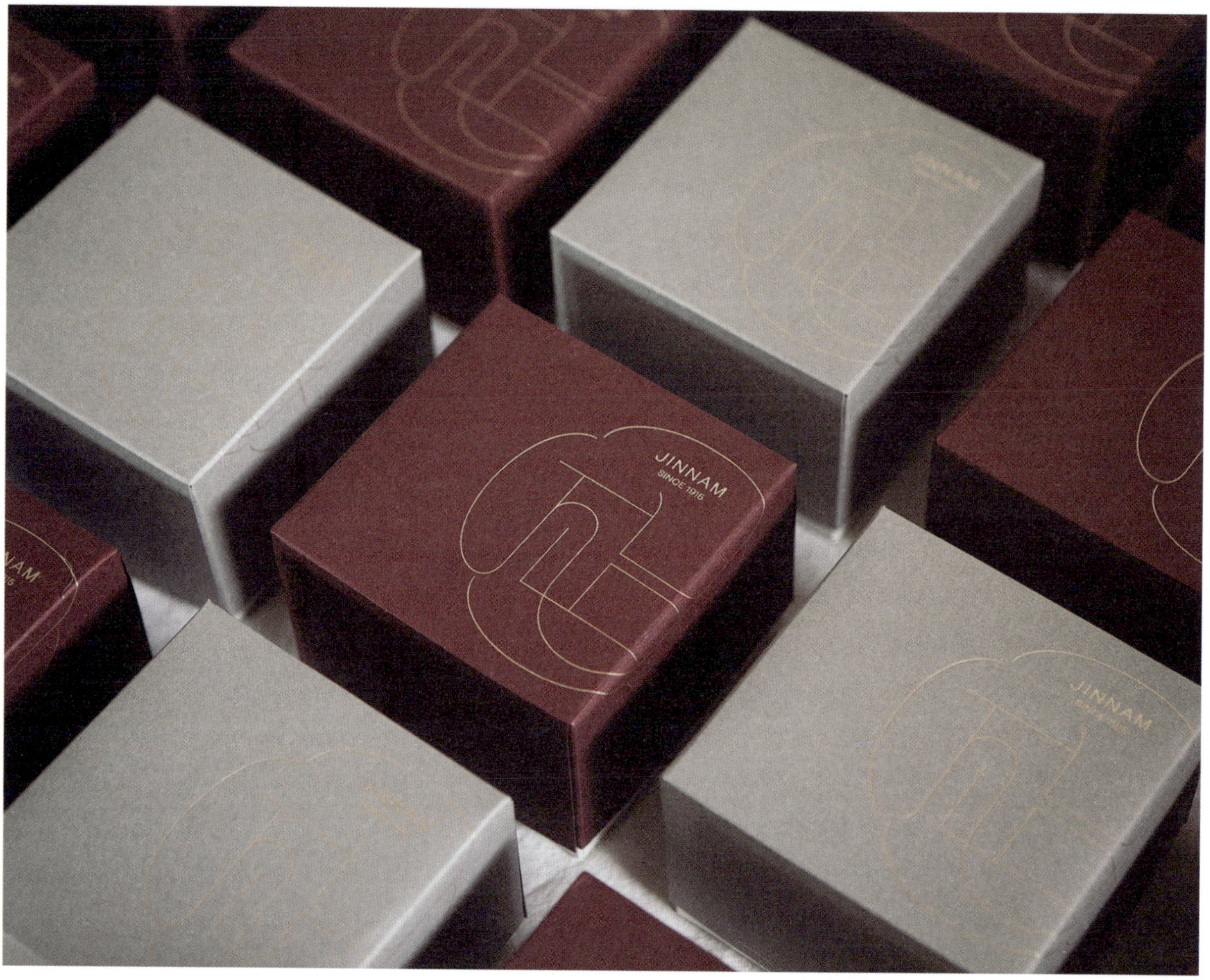

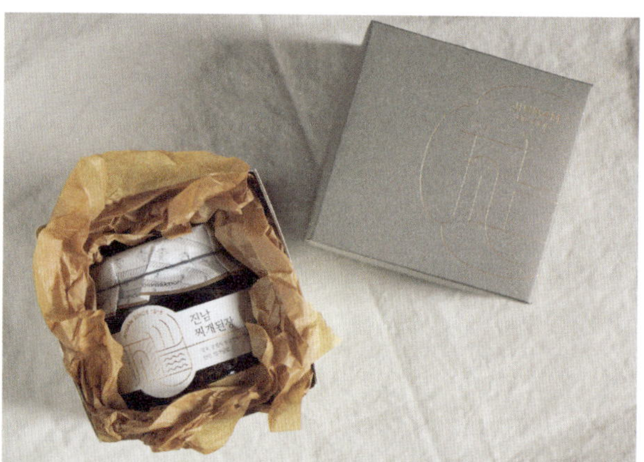

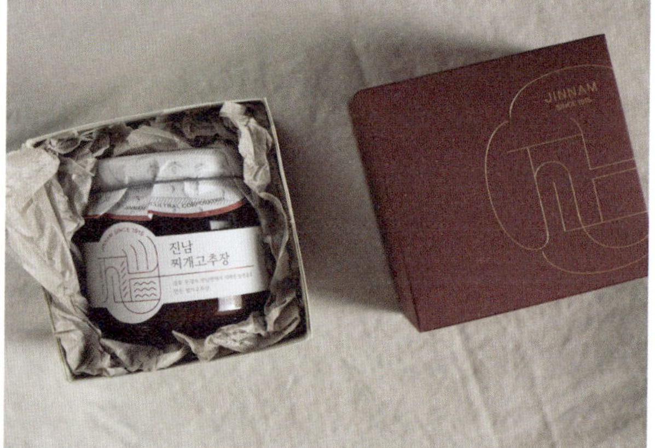

This work is a branding for Jinnam Agricultural Corporation, which has been producing high-quality fermented food since 1915. Based on two Korean letters "Jin" and "Nam" and the local scenery, the designers created different graphics to represent the Jinnam village where fresh ingredients were harvested, hoping to engage intimate communications between the brand and viewers.

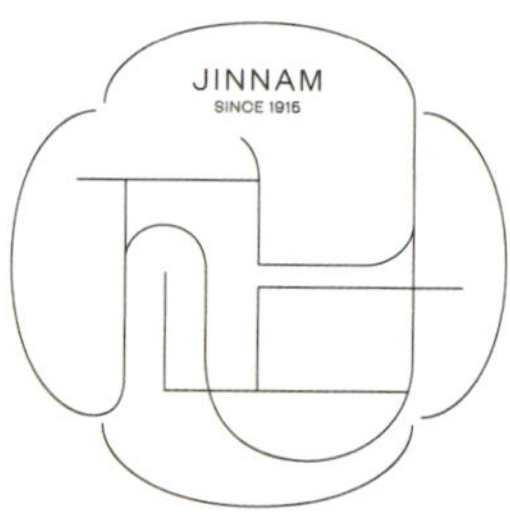

Jinnam

studio:
CFC Studio

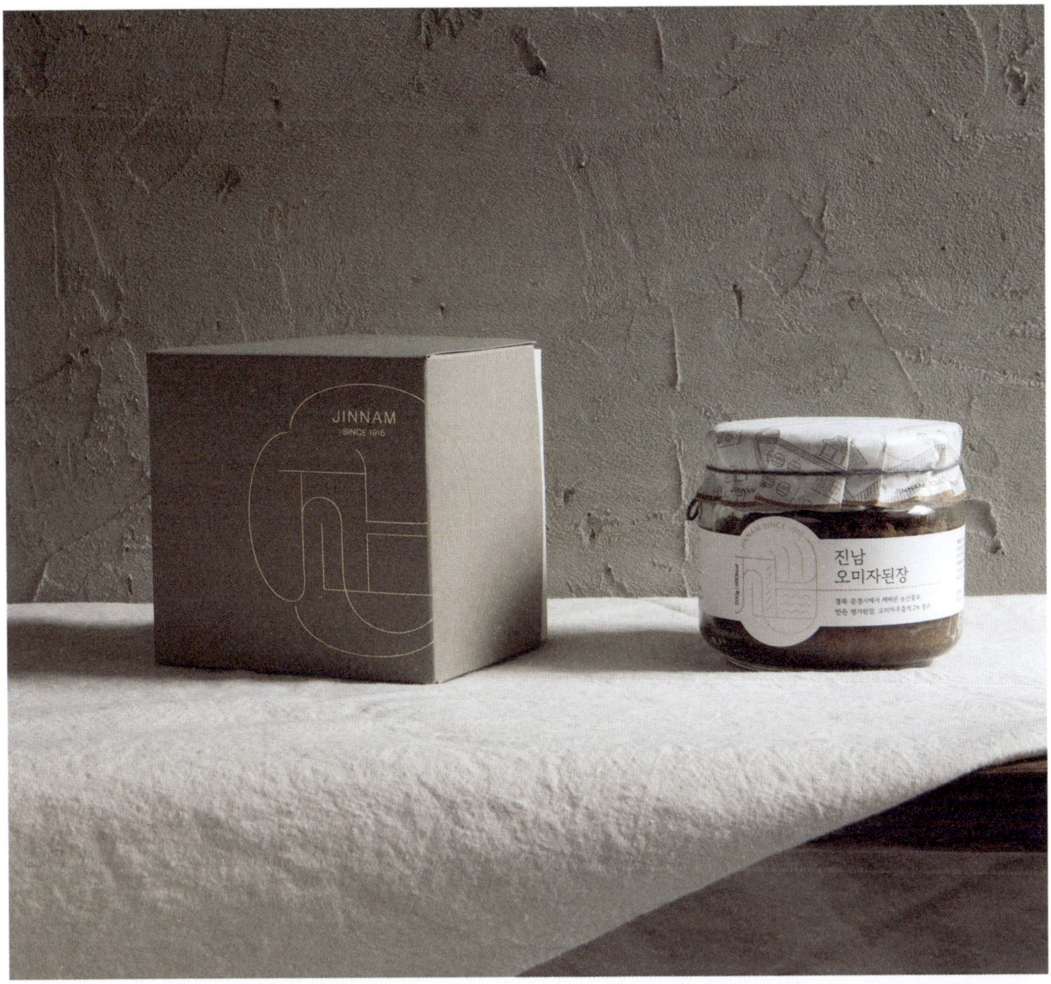

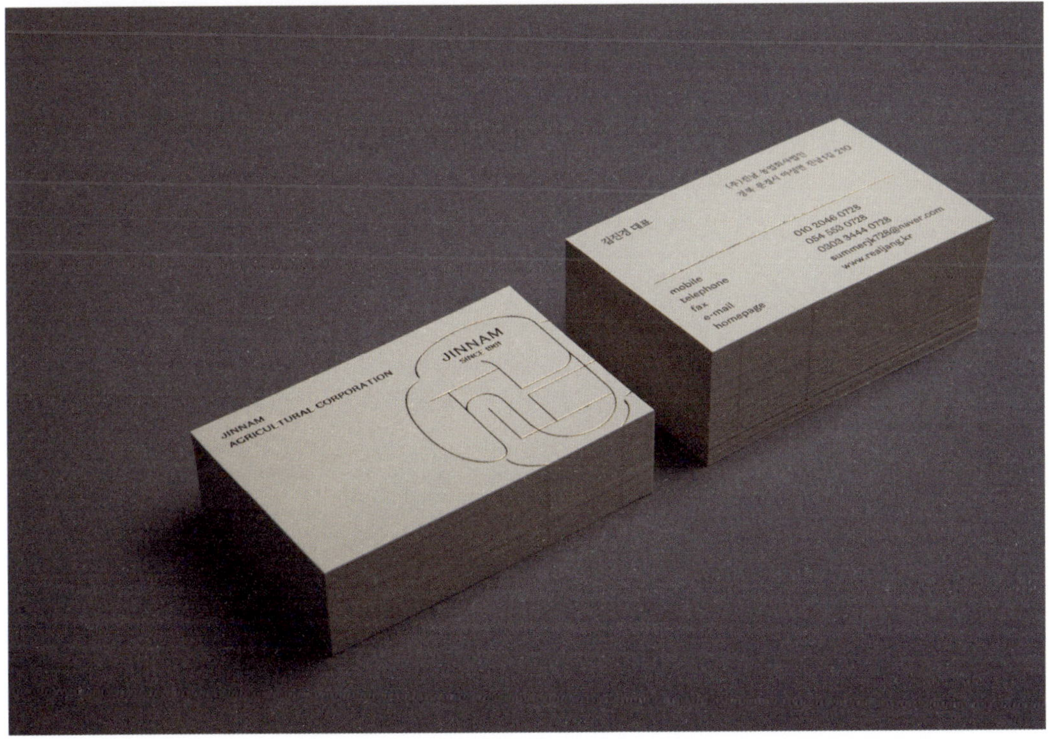

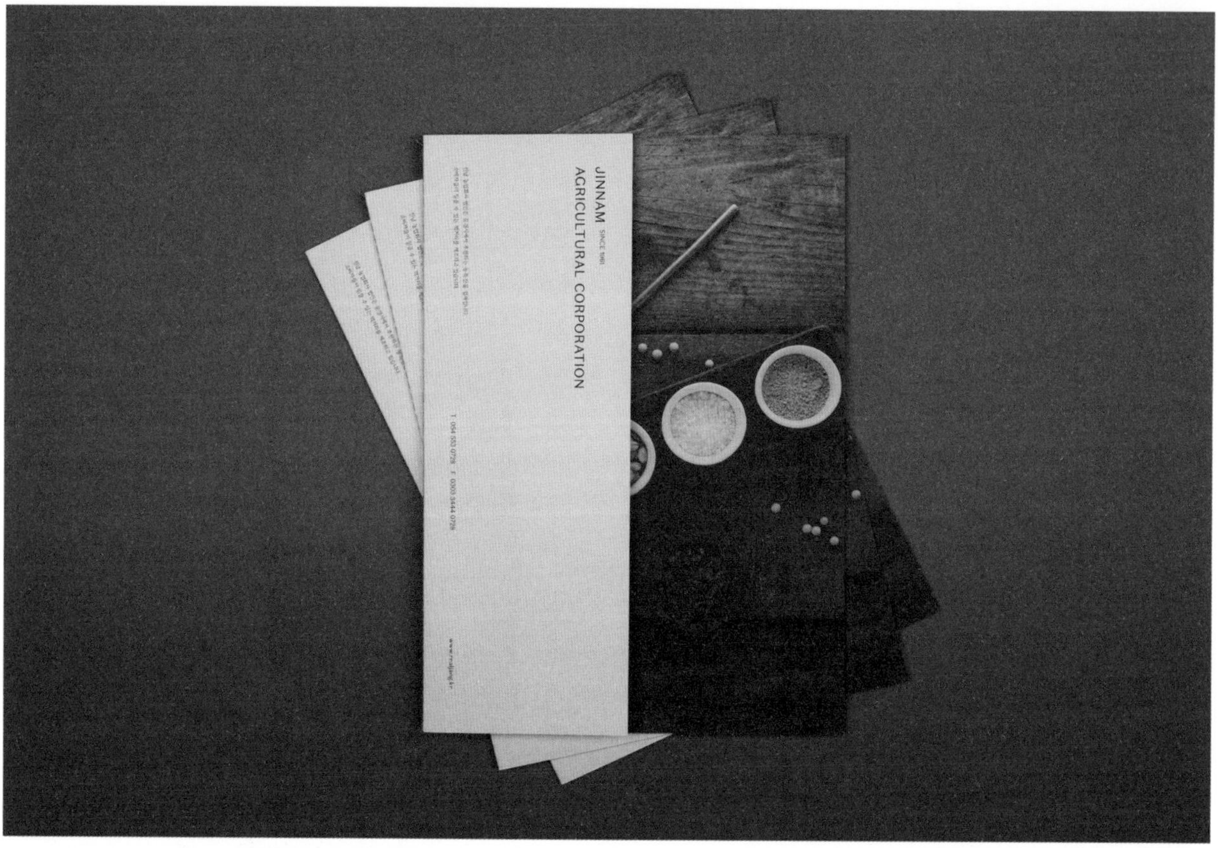
JINNAM SINCE 1980
AGRICULTURAL CORPORATION

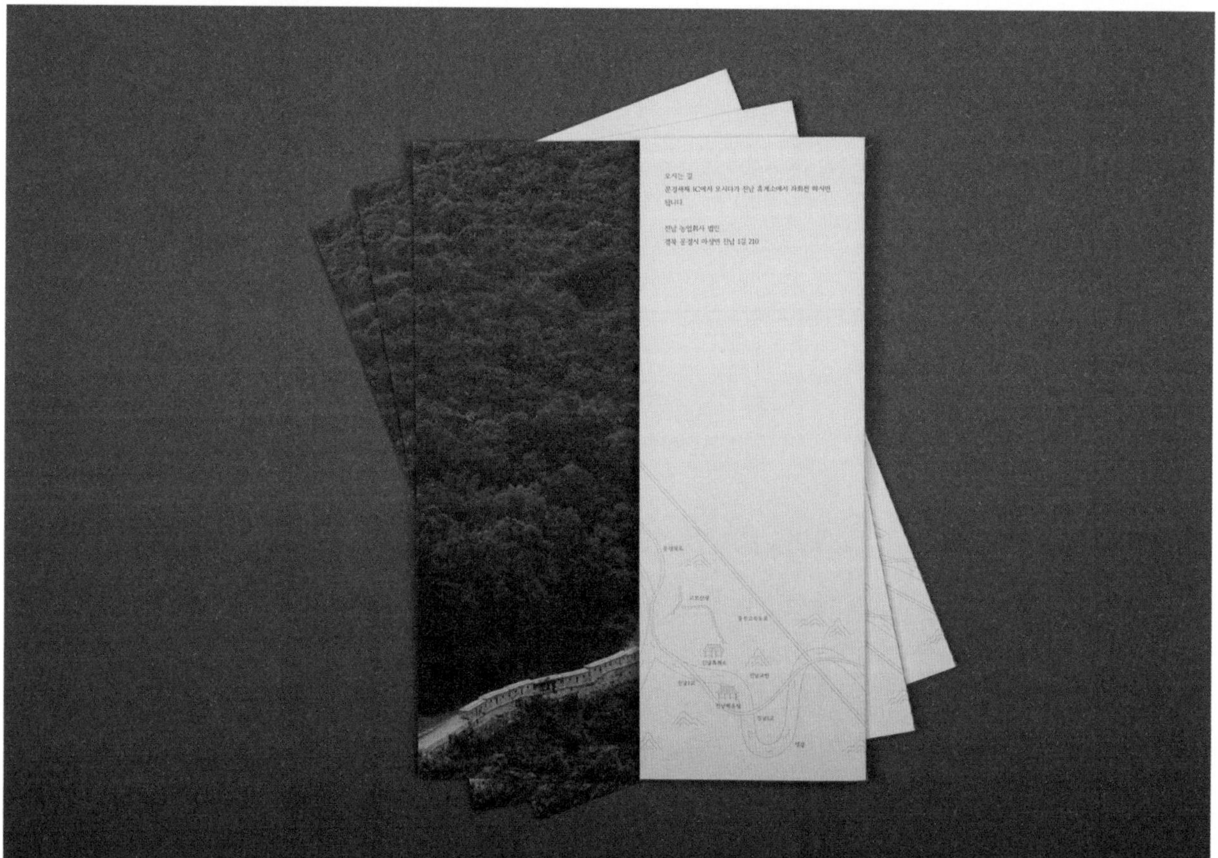
오시는 길
문경새재 IC에서 오시다가 진남 휴게소에서 좌회전 하시면
됩니다.
진남 농업회사 법인
경북 문경시 마성면 진남 1길 210

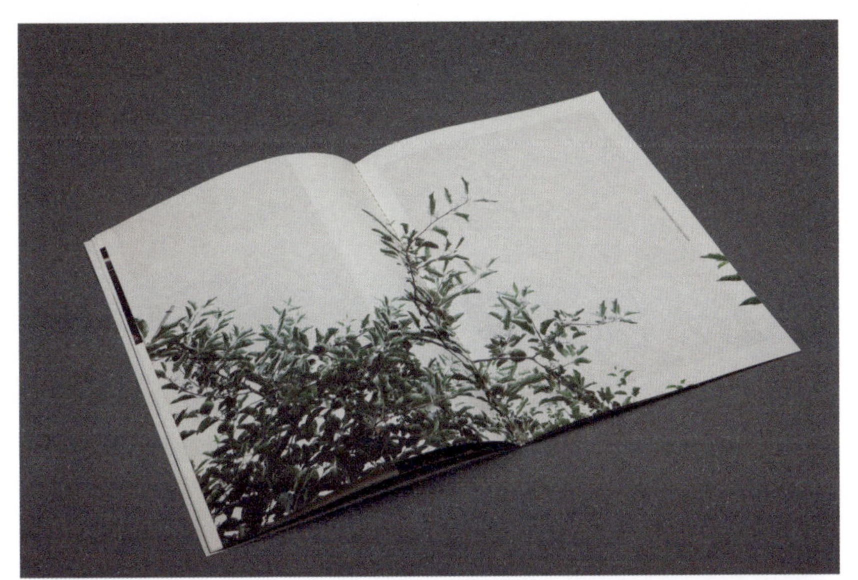

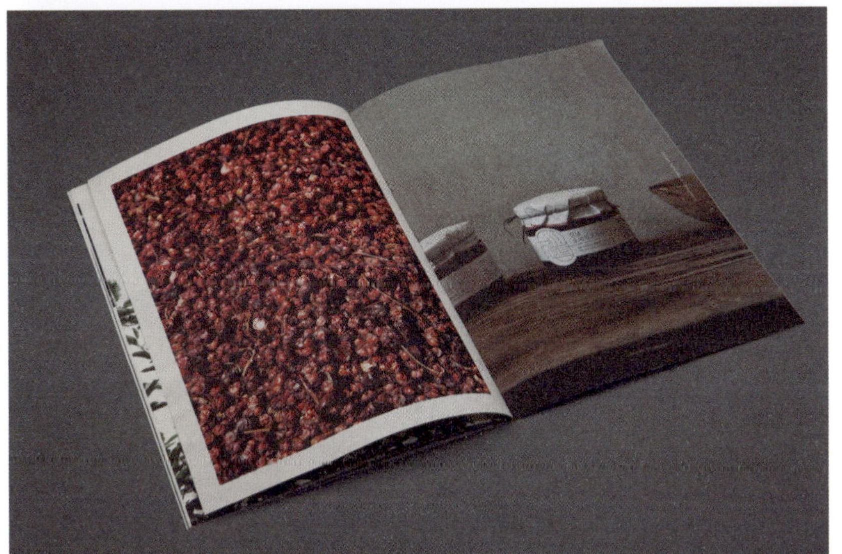

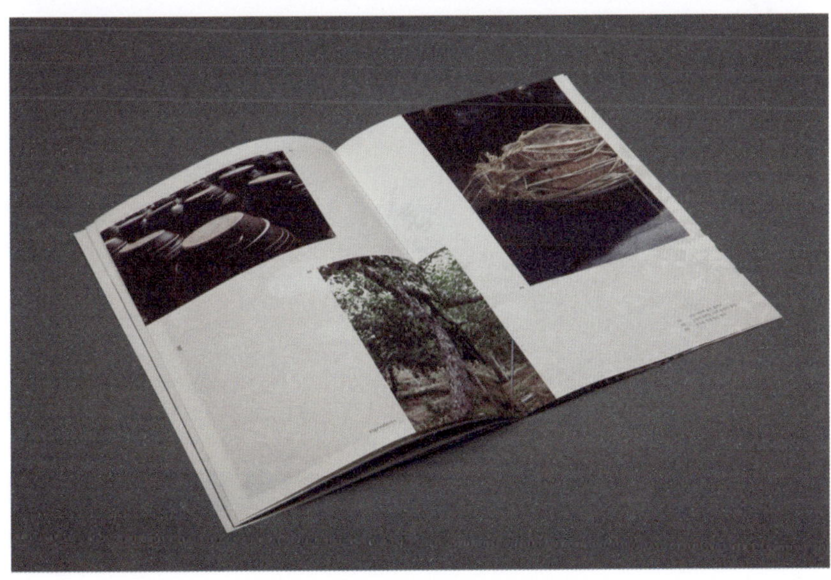

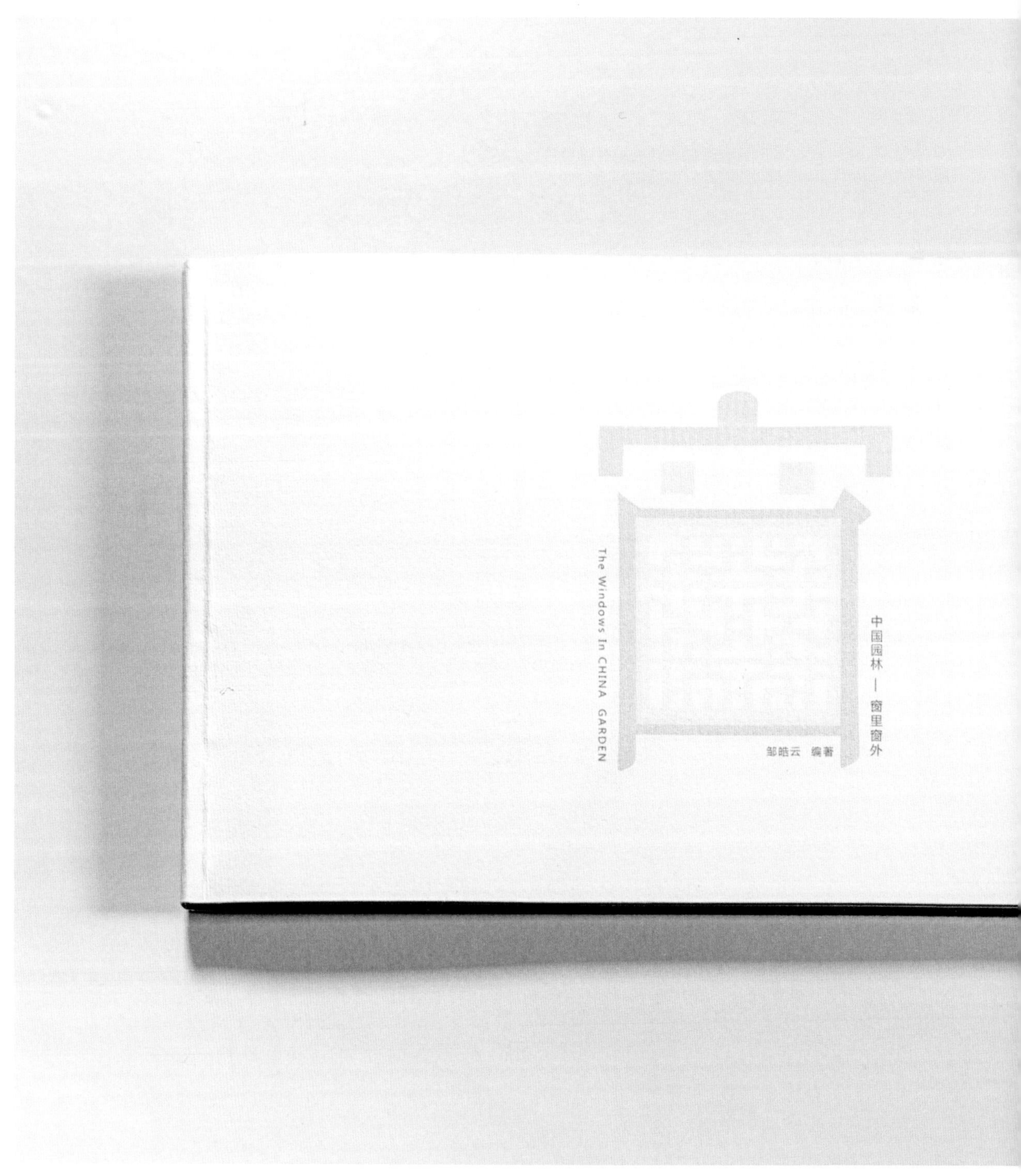

Intrigued by the unique lattice windows embellishing traditional Chinese gardens, the designer created this book to explore their patterns and stories to communicate a multisensory message of the Chinese philosophy of life. Soft watercolor paper was used for the cover to reproduce the expression of white walls dabbed with black tiles. Inside the book displays outlined profiles of traditional windows with hollow carved design, through which hand drawn scenes and the typography could be peeked.

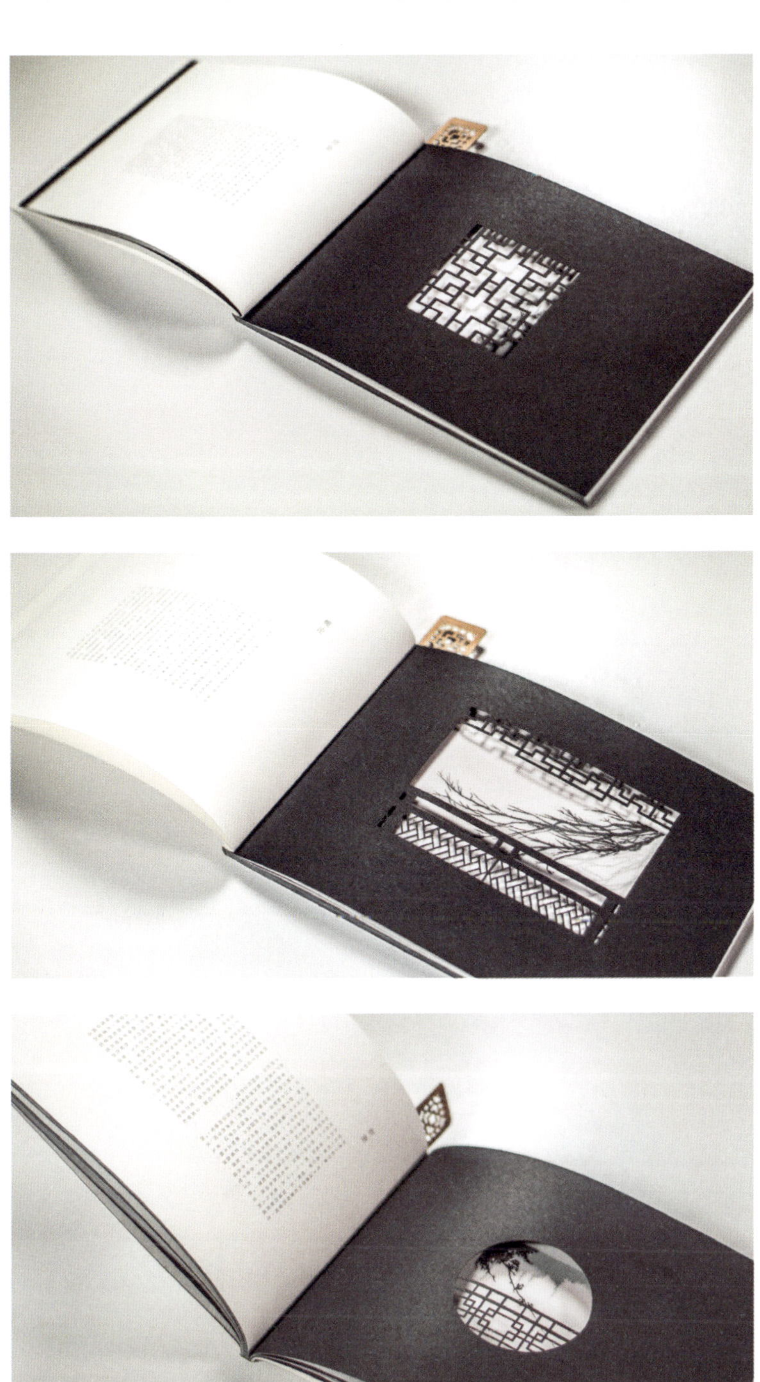

The Windows in Chinese Garden

designer:
Zou Haoyun

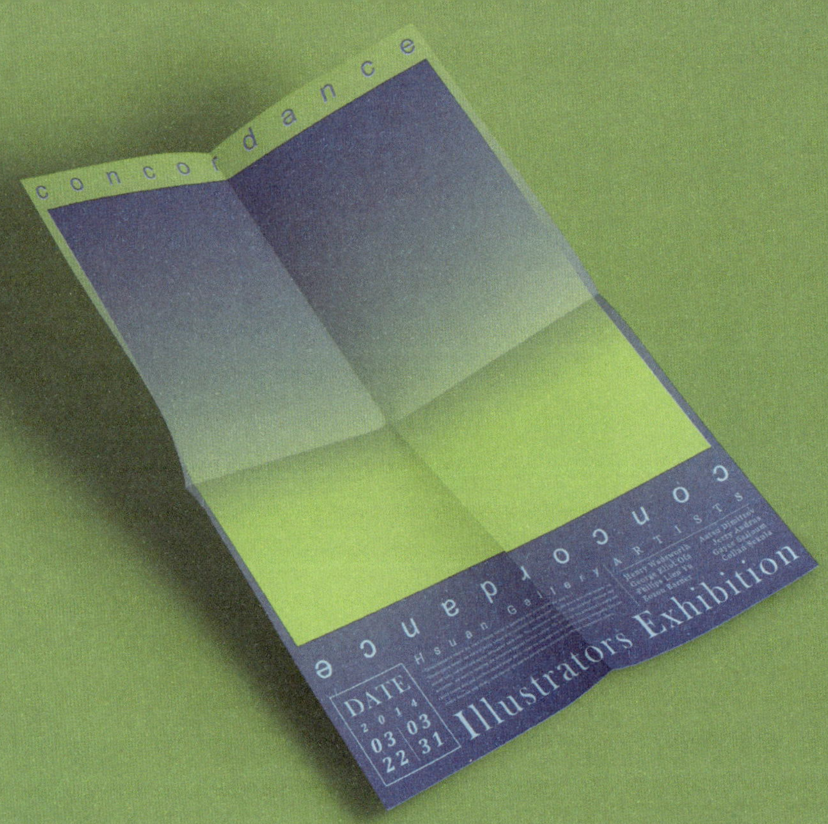

The posters for exhibition "Concordance", a word indicating the state of being similar to or consistent with each other, feature two vivid colors gradually becoming one in the squares to represent the gradual acceptance to and concordance with life in different environments. Through the exhibition, the designer wants to describe the difference between various cultures.

Concordance

studio: Yi-Hsuan LI_Studio Pros
designer: Yi-Hsuan LI

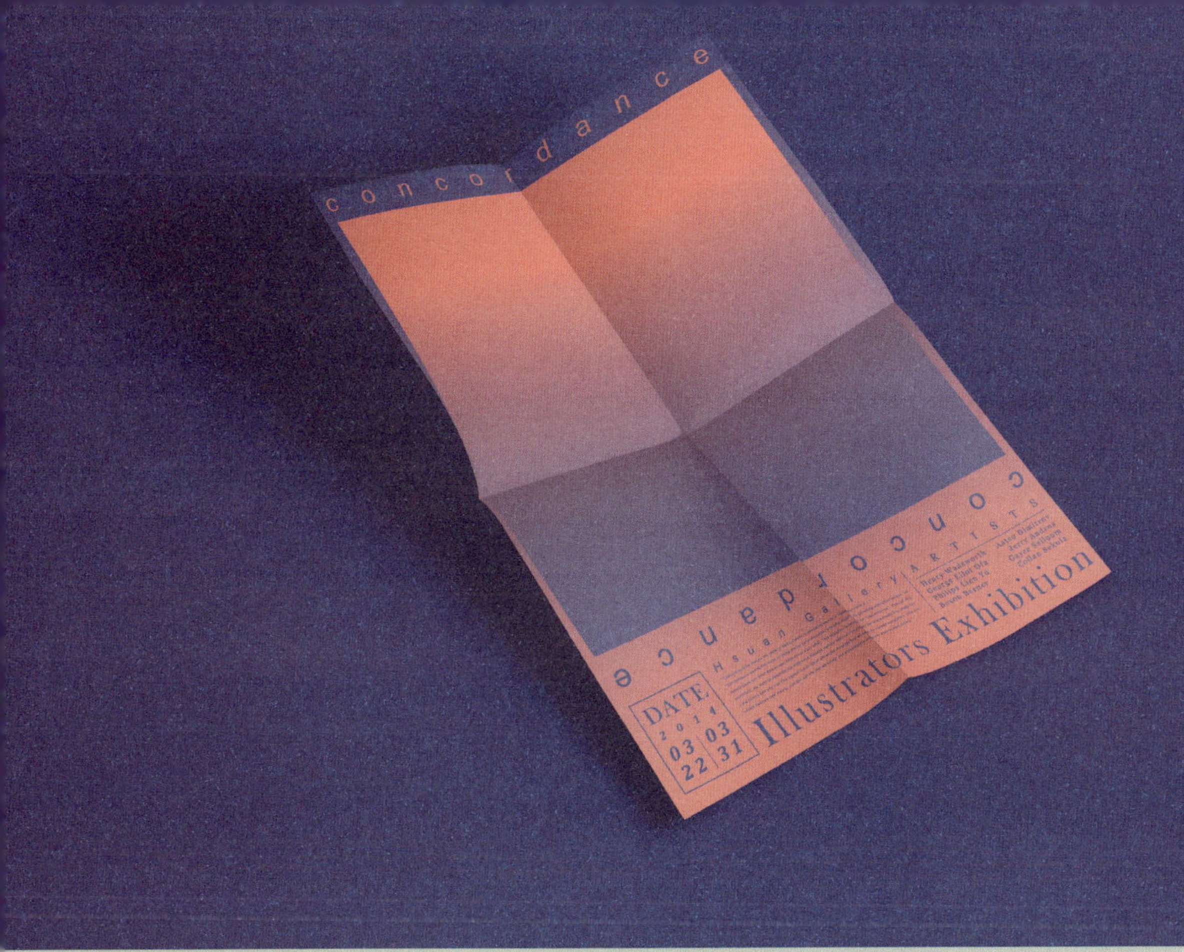

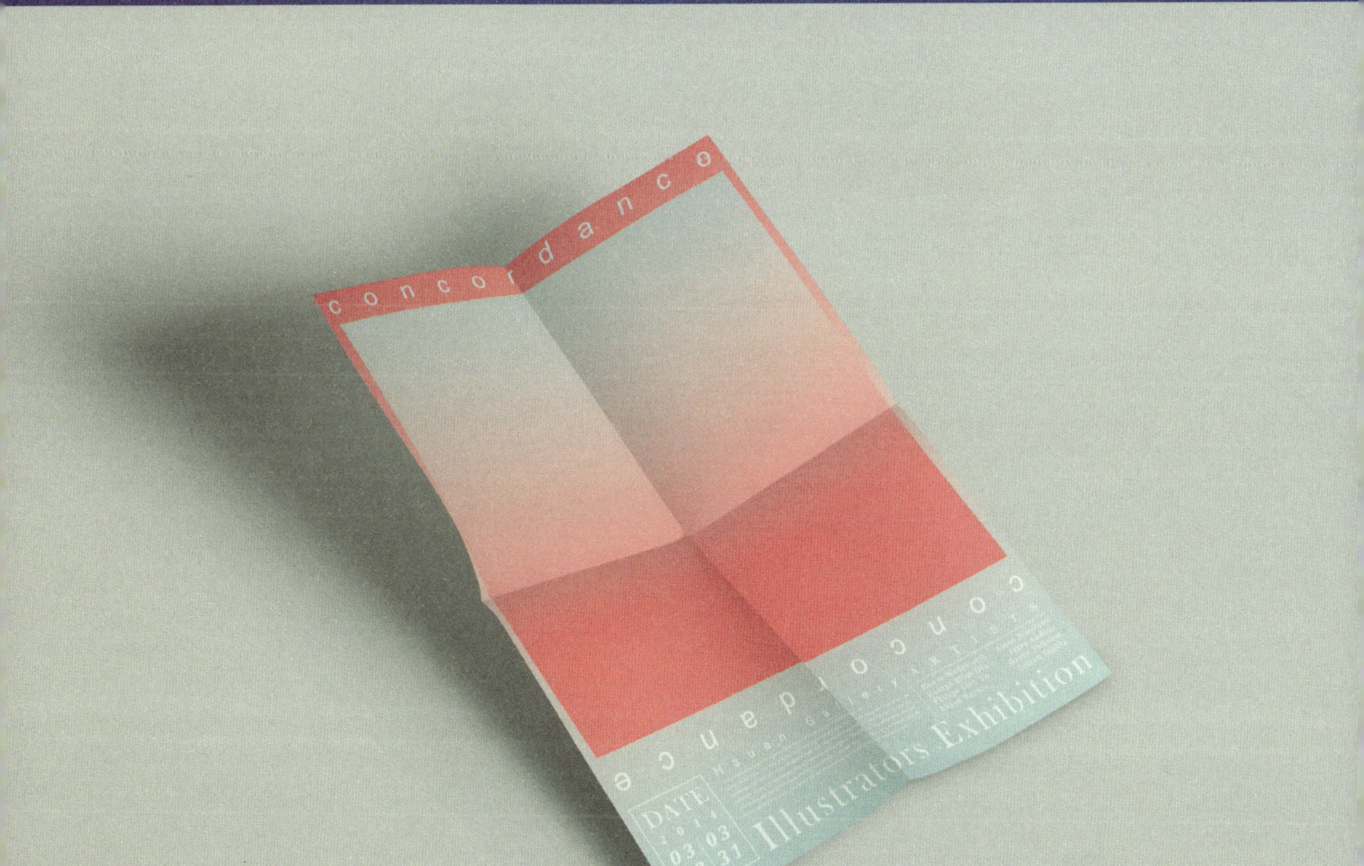

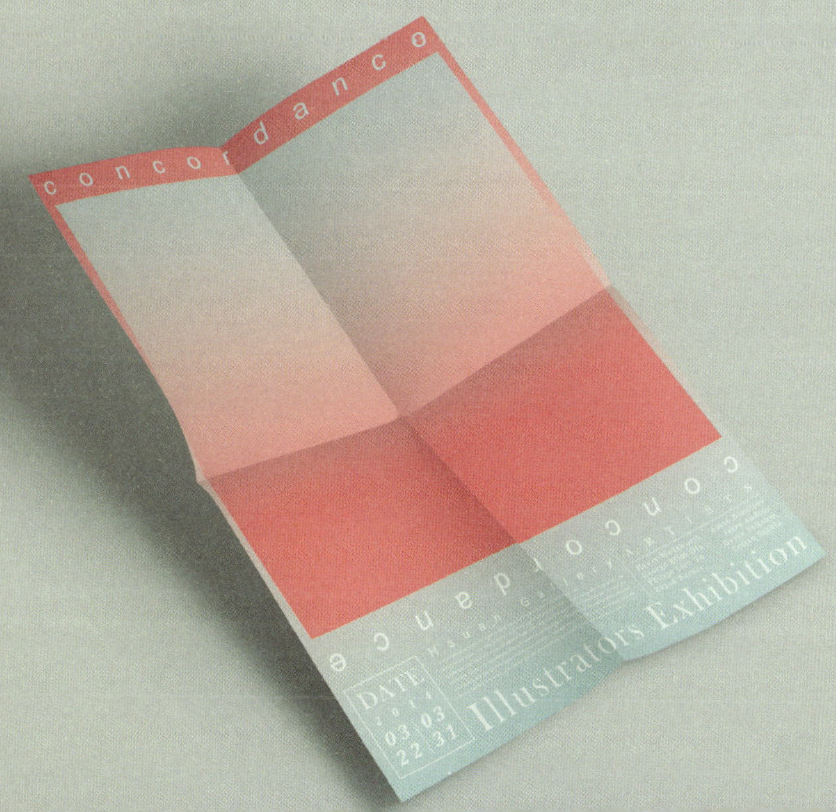

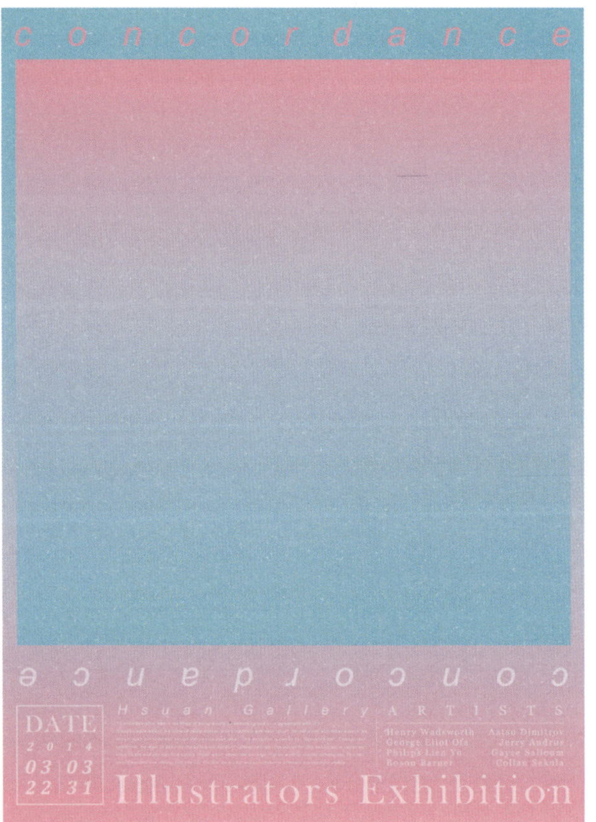
c o n c o r d a n c e
Hsuan Gallery
ARTISTS
Henry Wadsworth
Aatso Dimitrov
George Eliot Ofa
Jerry Andrus
Philips Lien Yu
Gayce Salloum
Boson Barner
Collan Sekula
DATE
2 0 1 4
03 03
22 31
Illustrators Exhibition

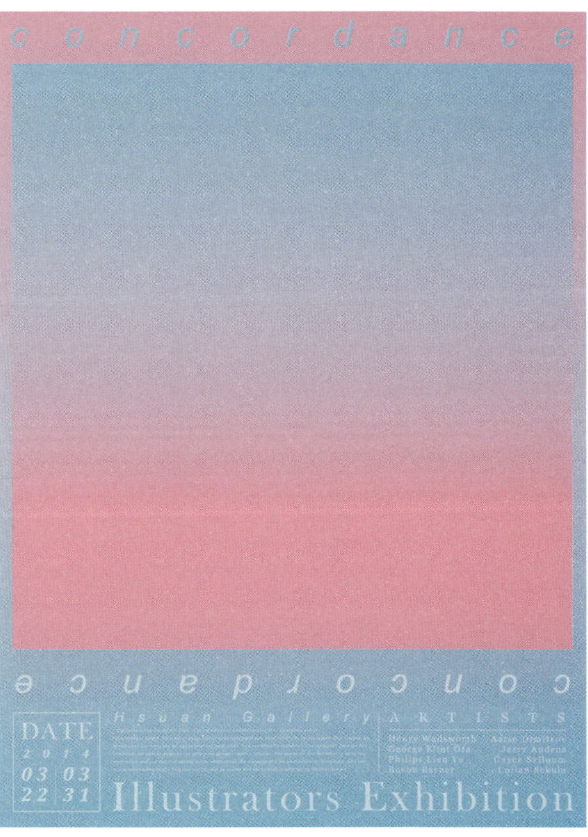
c o n c o r d a n c e
Hsuan Gallery
ARTISTS
Henry Wadsworth
Aatso Dimitrov
George Eliot Ofa
Jerry Andrus
Philips Lien Yu
Gayce Salloum
Boson Barner
Collan Sekula
DATE
2 0 1 4
03 03
22 31
Illustrators Exhibition

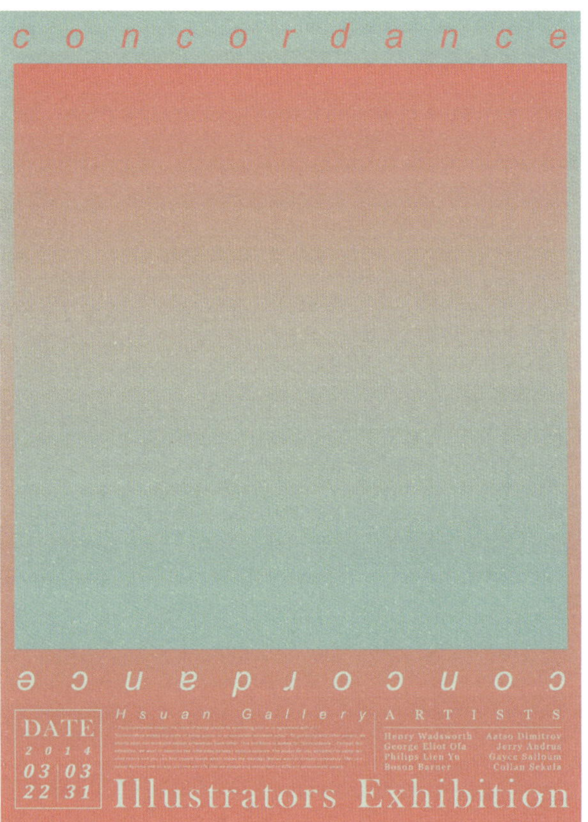
c o n c o r d a n c e
Hsuan Gallery
ARTISTS
Henry Wadsworth
Aatso Dimitrov
George Eliot Ofa
Jerry Andrus
Philips Lien Yu
Gayce Salloum
Boson Barner
Collan Sekula
DATE
2 0 1 4
03 03
22 31
Illustrators Exhibition

c o n c o r d a n c e
Hsuan Gallery
ARTISTS
Henry Wadsworth
Aatso Dimitrov
George Eliot Ofa
Jerry Andrus
Philips Lien Yu
Gayce Salloum
Boson Barner
Collan Sekula
DATE
2 0 1 4
03 03
22 31
Illustrators Exhibition

c o n c o r d a n c e
Hsuan Gallery
ARTISTS
Henry Wadsworth
George Eliot Ofa
Philips Lien Yu
Boson Barner
Aatso Dimitrov
Jerry Andrus
Gayce Salloum
Collan Sekula
DATE
2014
03 03
22 31
Illustrators Exhibition

c o n c o r d a n c e
Hsuan Gallery
ARTISTS
Henry Wadsworth
George Eliot Ofa
Philips Lien Yu
Boson Barner
Aatso Dimitrov
Jerry Andrus
Gayce Salloum
Collan Sekula
DATE
2014
03 03
22 31
Illustrators Exhibition

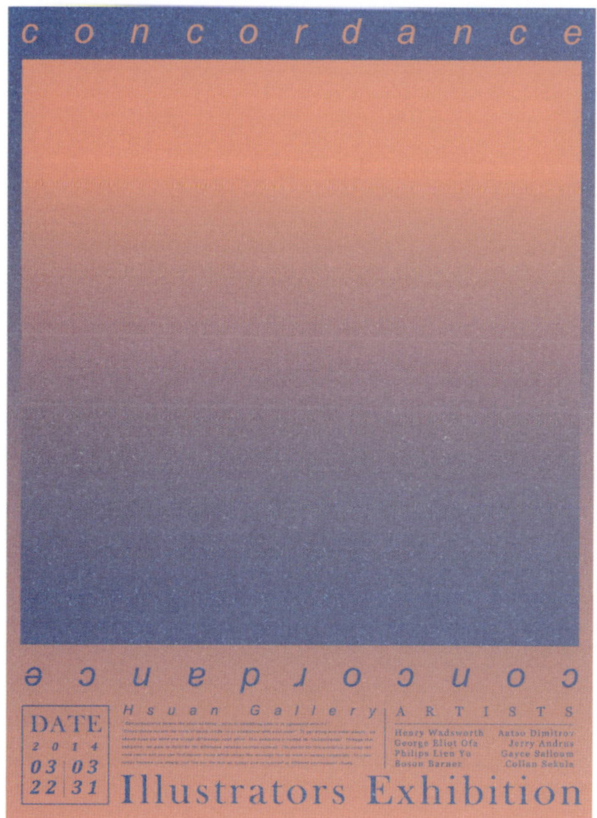
c o n c o r d a n c e
Hsuan Gallery
ARTISTS
Henry Wadsworth
George Eliot Ofa
Philips Lien Yu
Boson Barner
Aatso Dimitrov
Jerry Andrus
Gayce Salloum
Collan Sekula
DATE
2014
03 03
22 31
Illustrators Exhibition

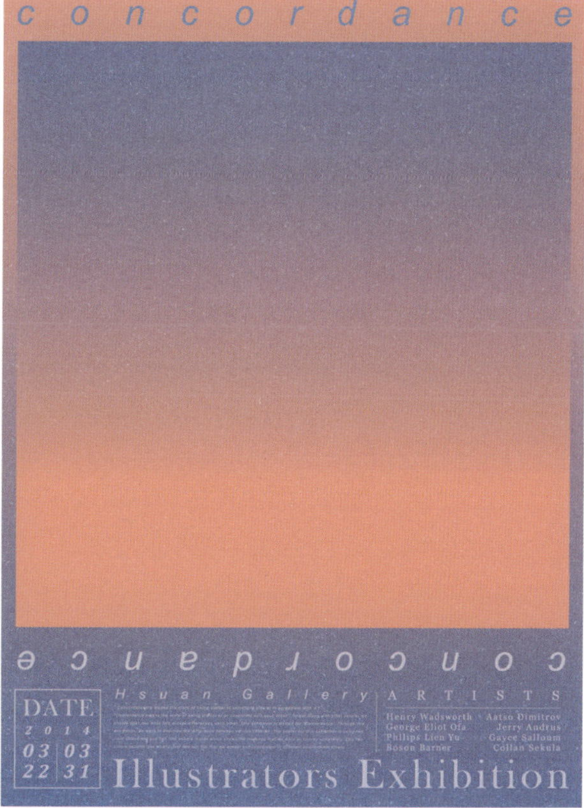
c o n c o r d a n c e
Hsuan Gallery
ARTISTS
Henry Wadsworth
George Eliot Ofa
Philips Lien Yu
Boson Barner
Aatso Dimitrov
Jerry Andrus
Gayce Salloum
Collan Sekula
DATE
2014
03 03
22 31
Illustrators Exhibition

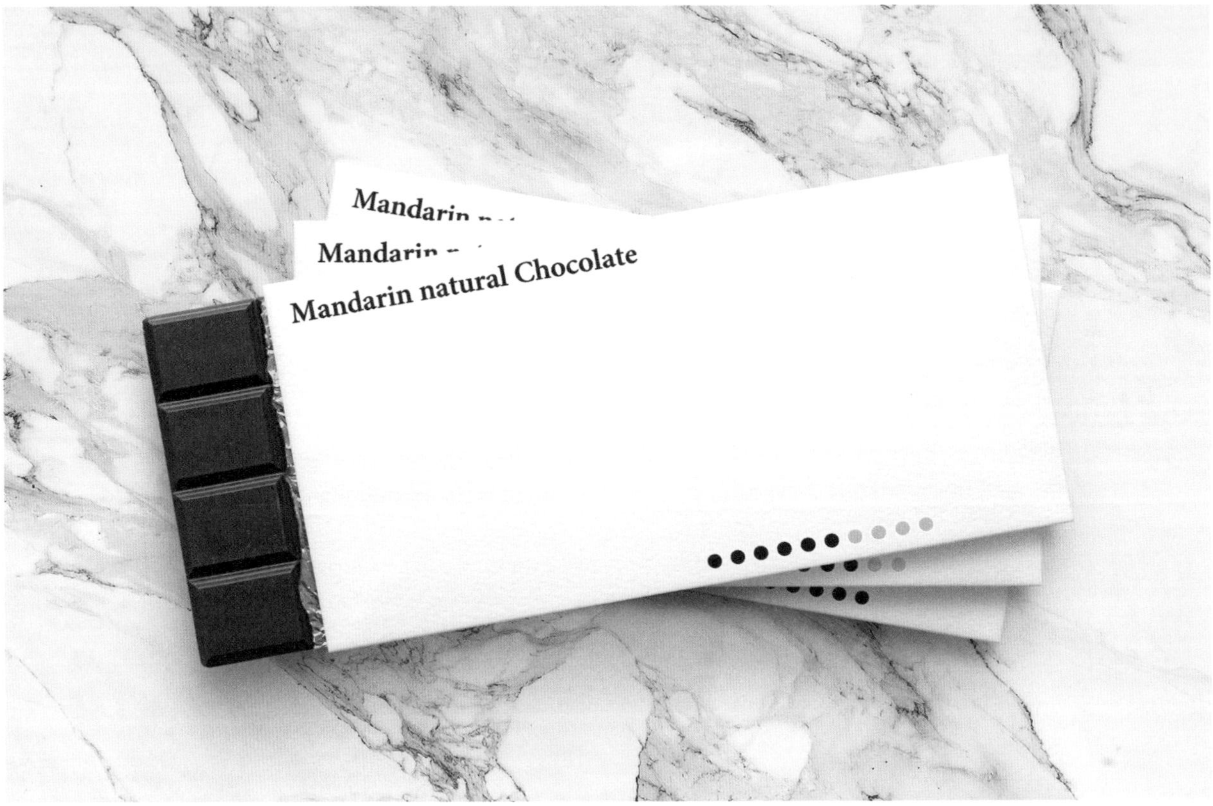

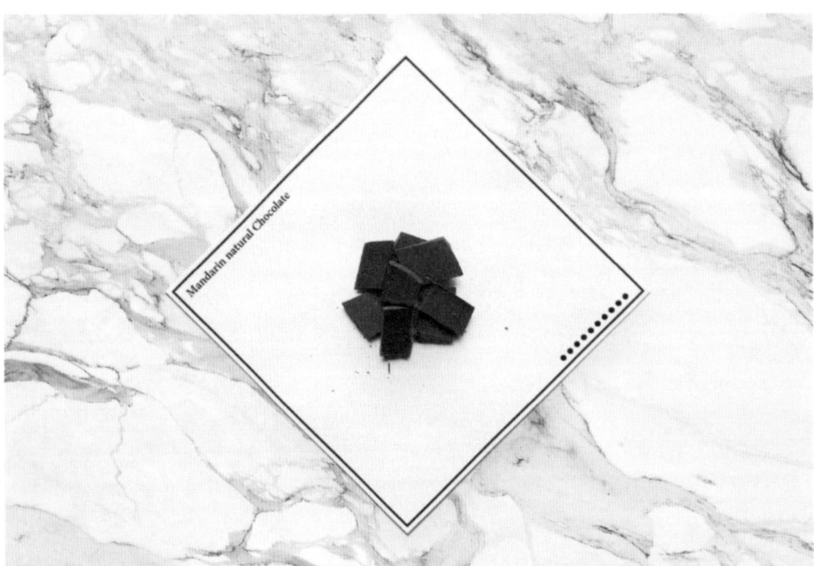

The quality chocolate brand who is dedicated to improving the quality of people's lives expresses itself through a modernistic graphic system characteristic by stunning white. The distinct identity integrates a minimalistic elegance with a contemporary impression, bringing out a lovely and novel image. An array of dots on the packaging subtly indicates the chocolate's intensity, ranging from 60%, 80% to 100%.

Mandarin Natural Chocolate

designer:
Yuta Takahashi

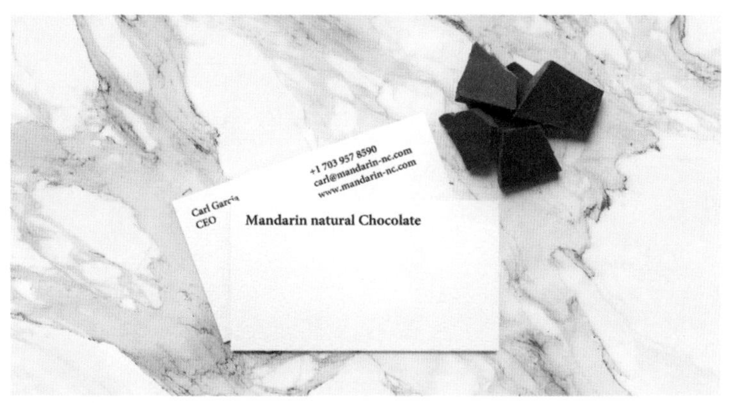

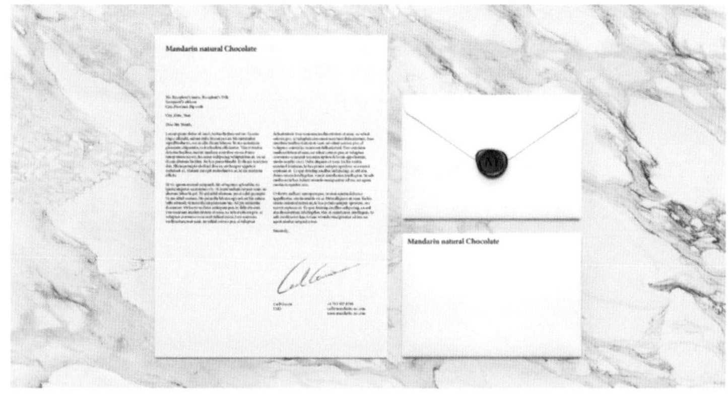

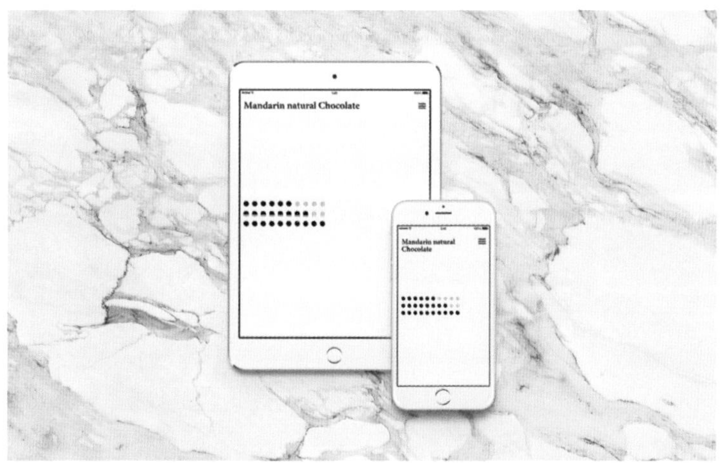

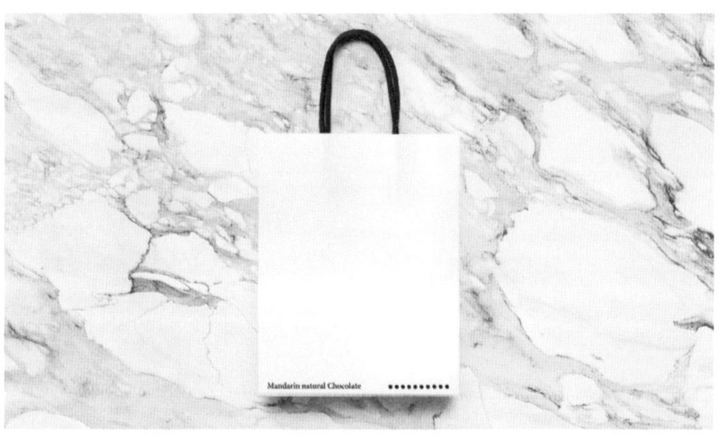

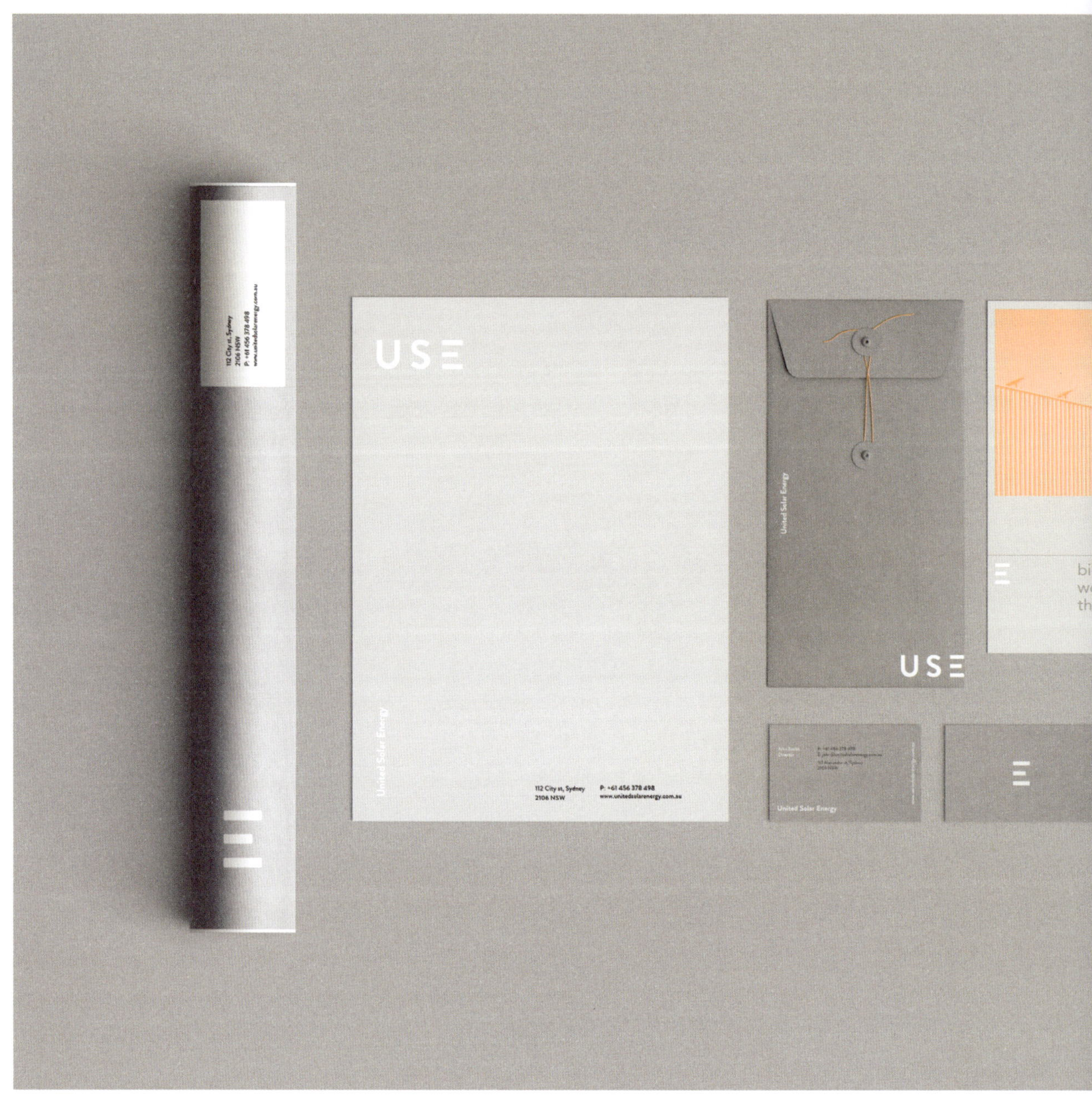

A new brand identity was created for United Solar Energy highlighting its beliefs in cost-effectiveness and its supply of solar panels and installation. The designer stuck to a minimal, grey toned color palette with hints of orange to bring vibrancy to the collaterals and to indicate the power generated. The "E" in "USE" acts as three panels, becoming a unique mark for the brand across all collateral items.

U-S-E

designer:
Madelyn Bilsborough

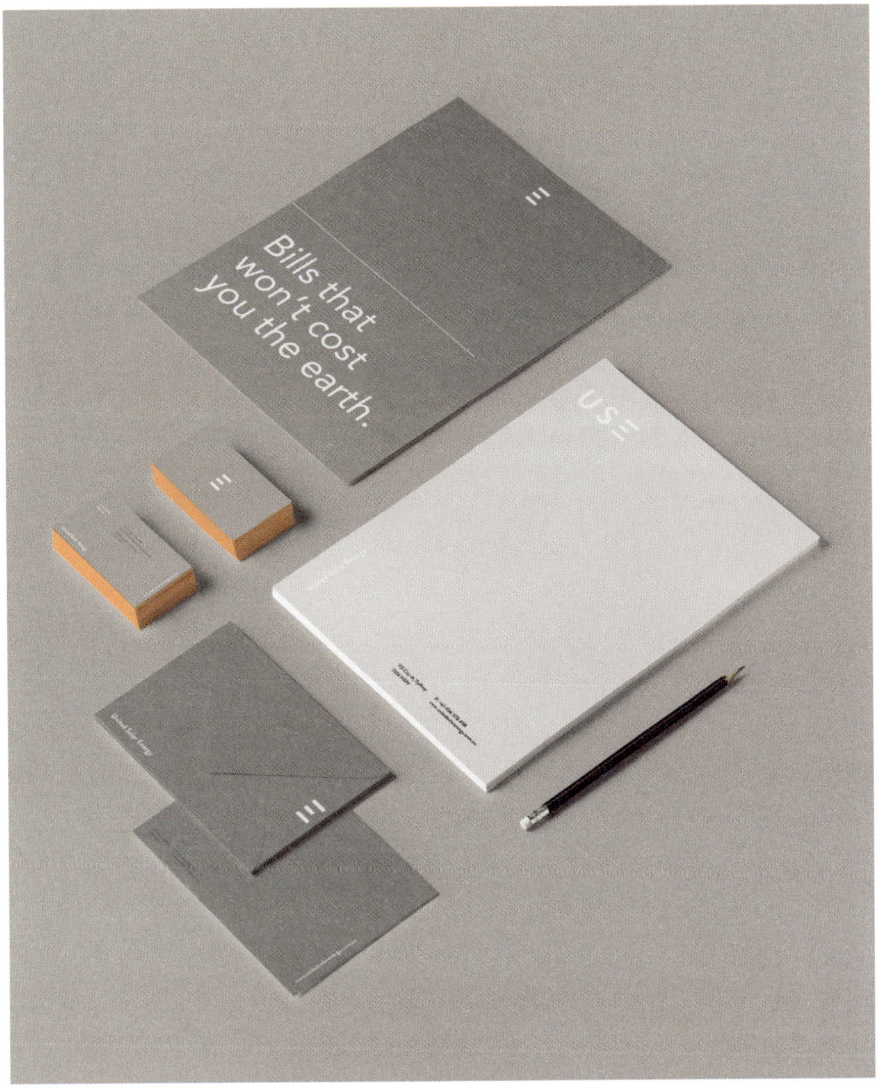

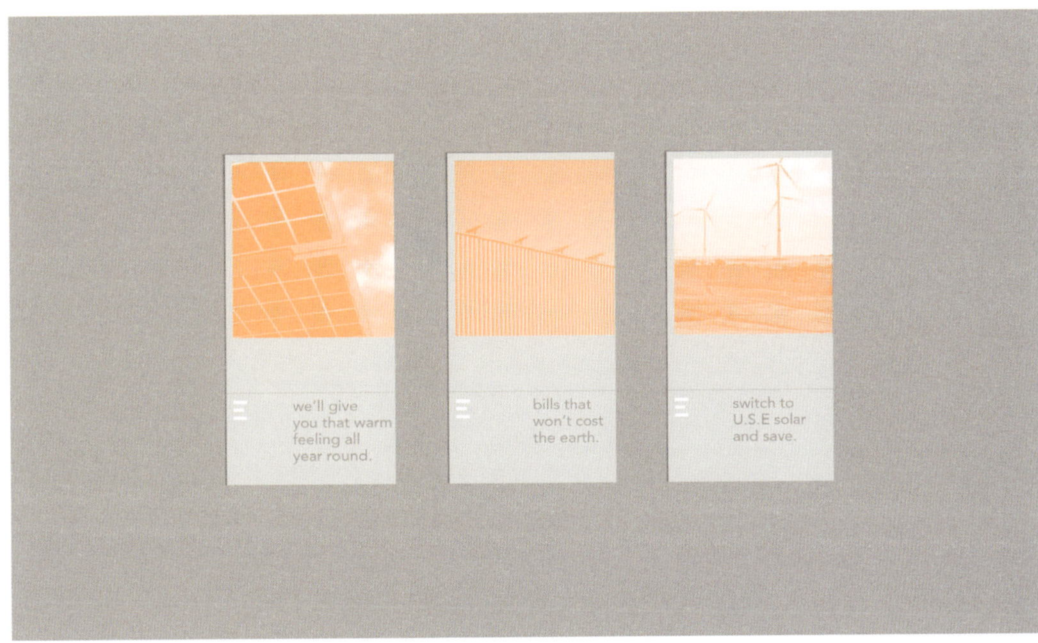

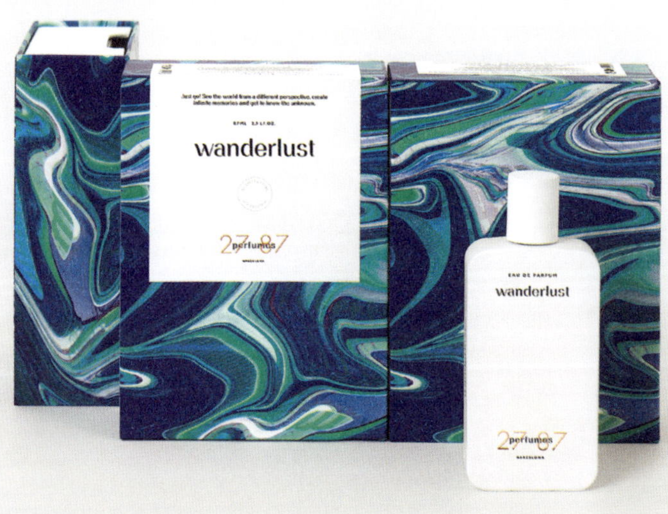

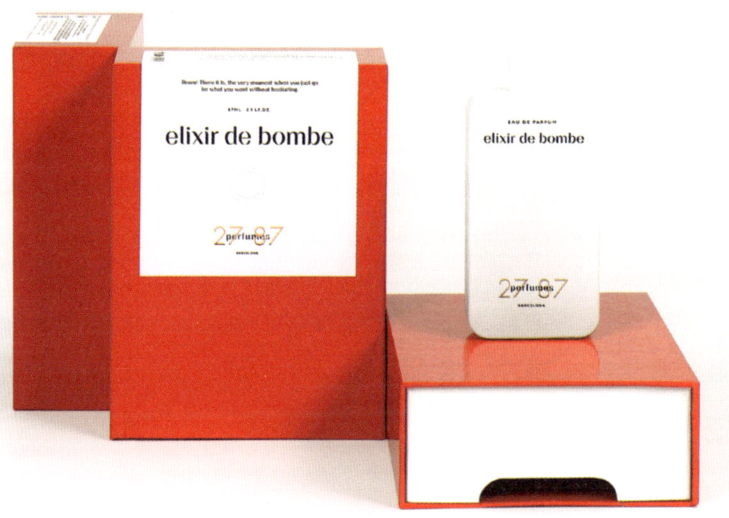

Inspired by the present generation, a bottle with blunted rectangle shape that characterizes technological devices was created. Since a constantly changing generation needs naive design, the graphics for the entire collection featured blank canvas for projecting individual's unrestricted imagination while the packaging is based on concepts of each scent. The unconventional opaque bottle invites people to experience the scent with the most important sense: smell.

27-87-Perfumes

studio: ***Ingrid Picanyol Studio***
designer: ***Ingrid Picanyol***

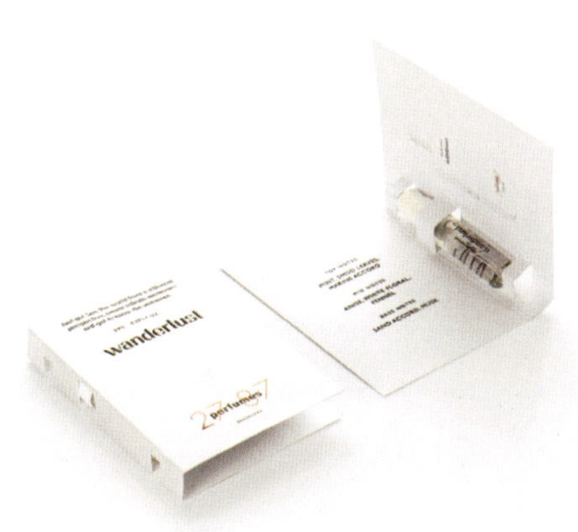

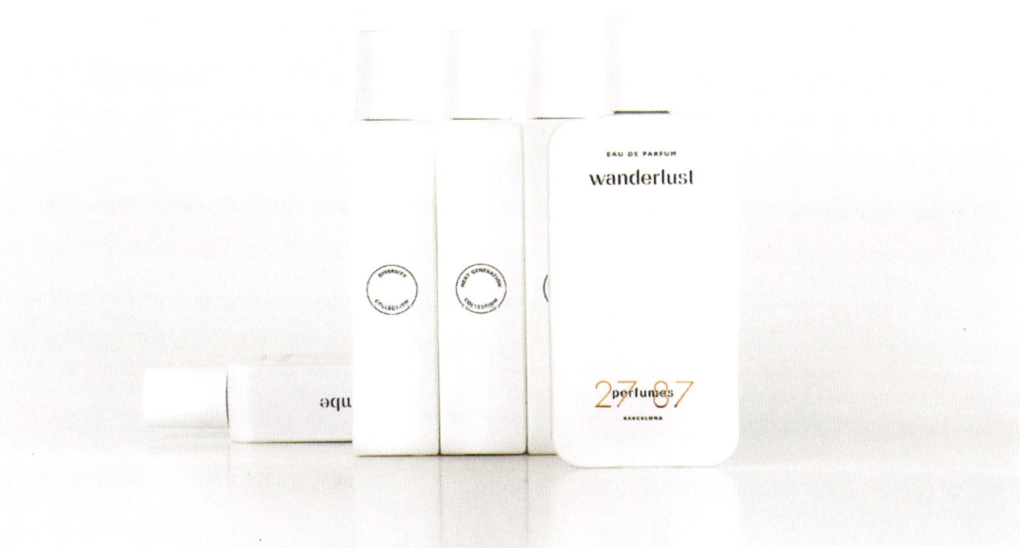

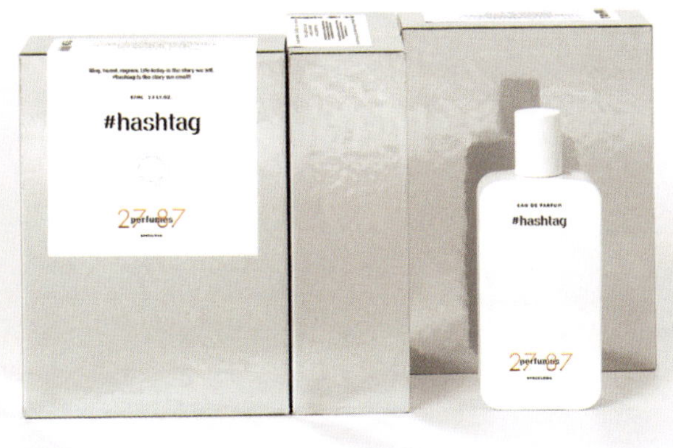

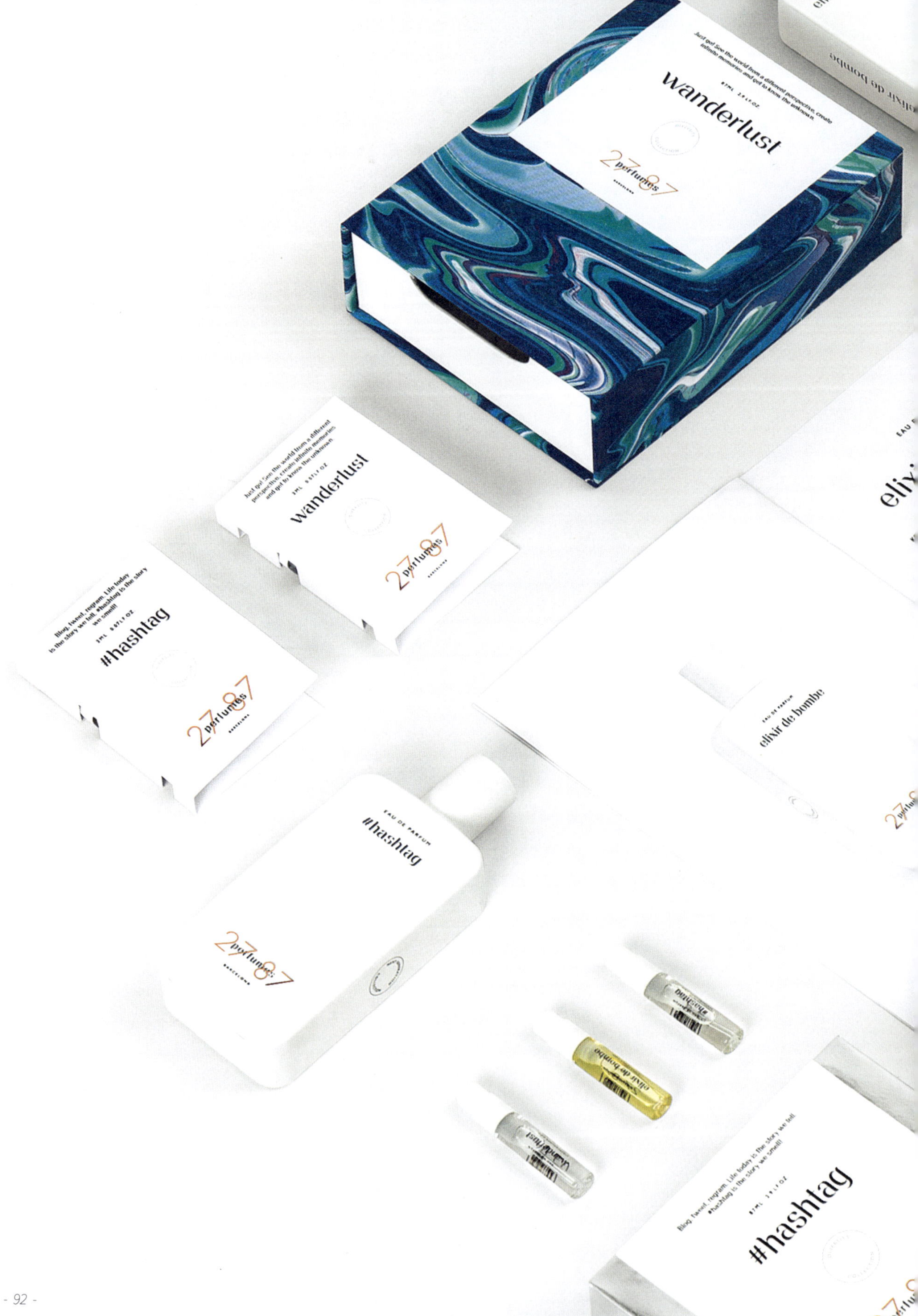
wanderlust
Just go! See the world from a different perspective, create infinite memories and get to know the unknown.
27 87 perfumes
BARCELONA
#hashtag
Blog, tweet, regram. Life today is the story we tell. #hashtag is the story we smell!
EAU DE PARFUM
elixir de bombe

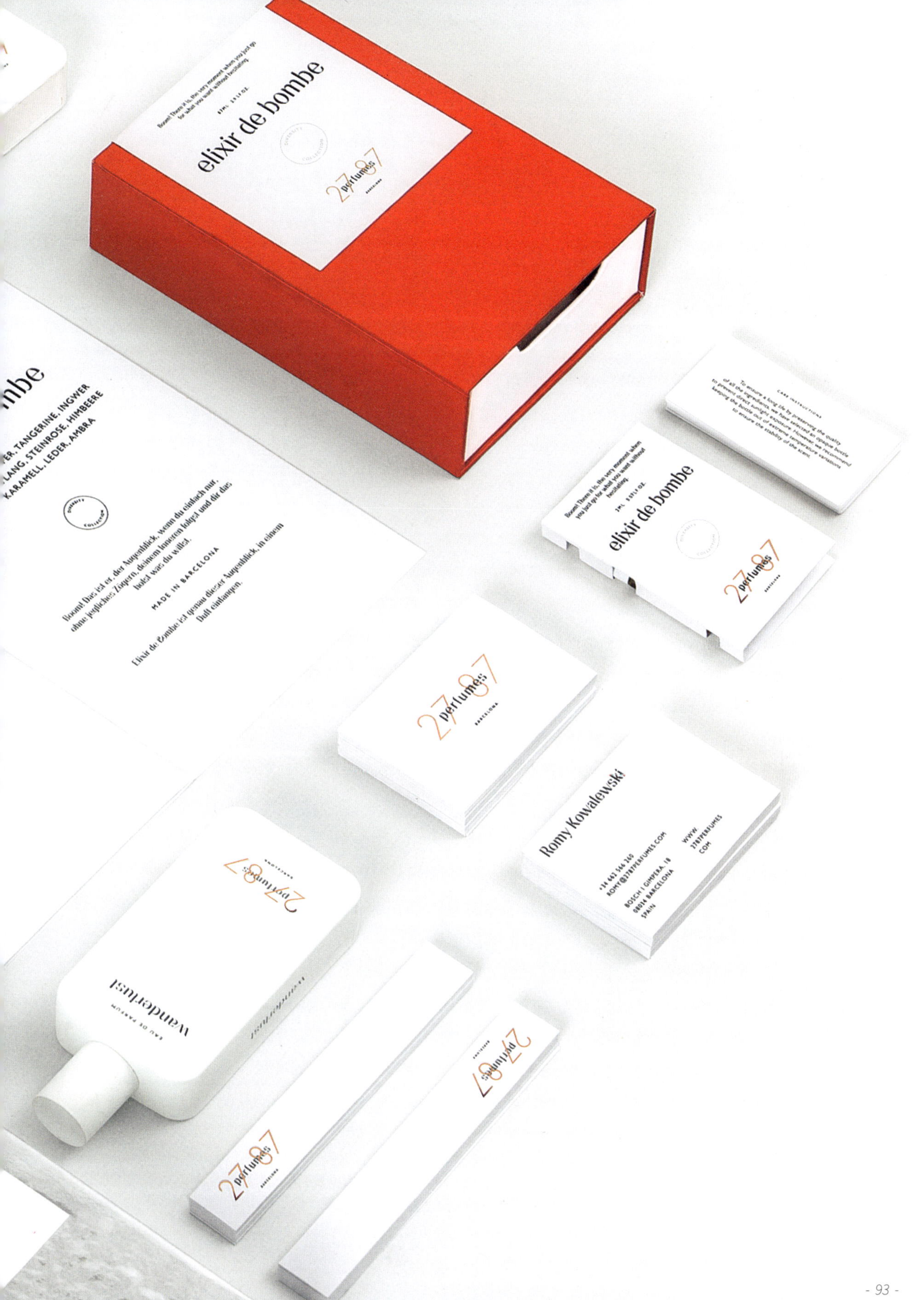
elixir de bombe
Boom! There it is, the very moment when you just go for what you want without hesitating.
27 87 perfumes
BARCELONA
Boom! Das ist er, der Augenblick, wenn du einfach nur, ohne jegliches Zögern, deinem Inneren folgst und dir das holst was du willst.
MADE IN BARCELONA
Elixir de Bombe ist genau dieser Augenblick, in einem Duft einfangen.
Romy Kowalewski
+34 662 566 260
ROMY@2787PERFUMES.COM
BOSCH I GIMPERA, 18
08034 BARCELONA
SPAIN
WWW.
2787PERFUMES
.COM
wanderlust
EAU DE PARFUM

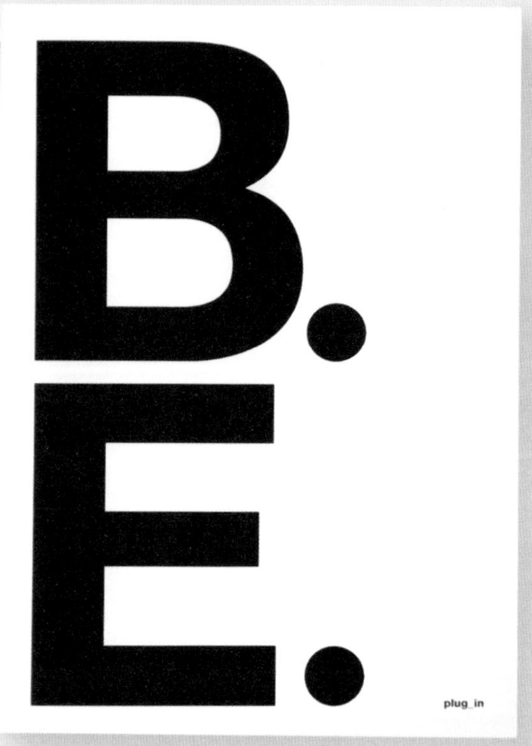

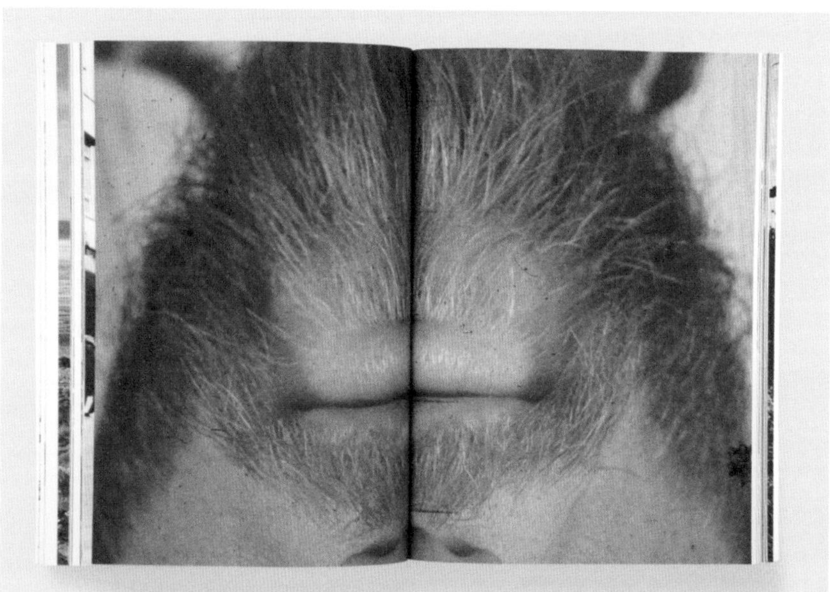

All the superfluous elements have been cleared for the second reprint of Beyond Environment, expectantly a homage to extraordinary artist Magdalo Mussio. The focus is on the only protagonists, the letters B and E, short for Beyond Environment. All of the contents are organized following a strict grid system.

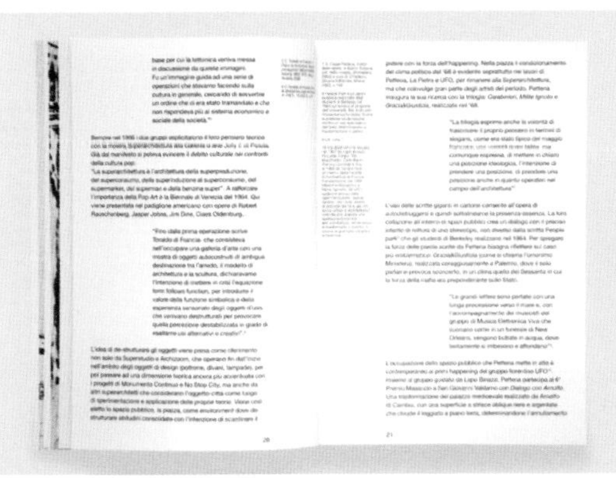

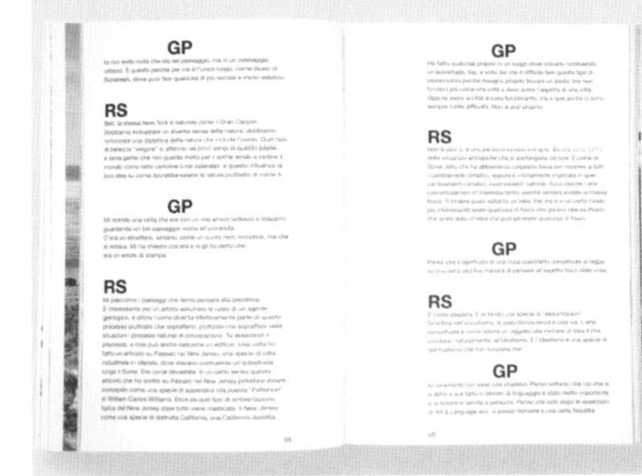

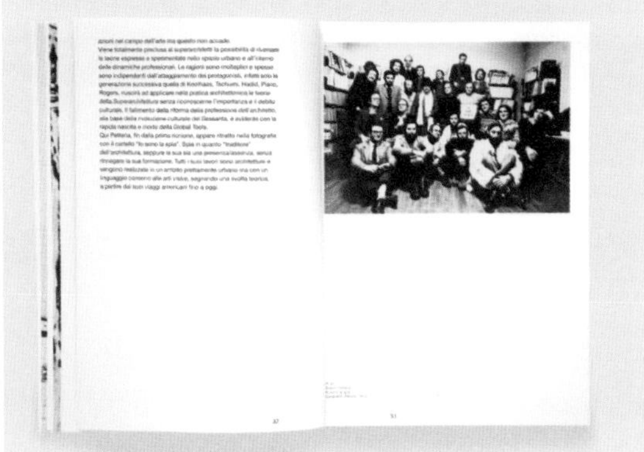

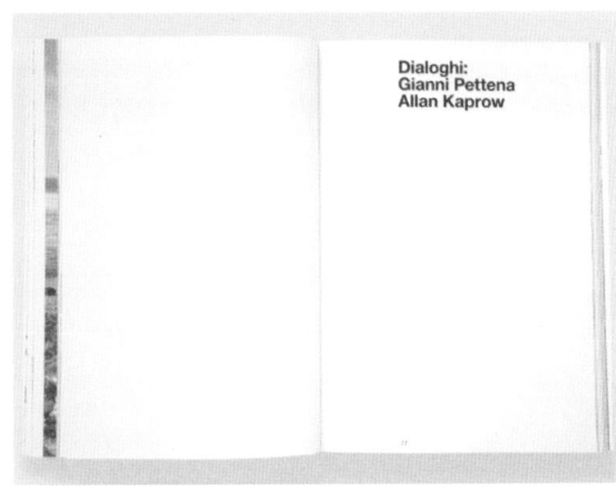

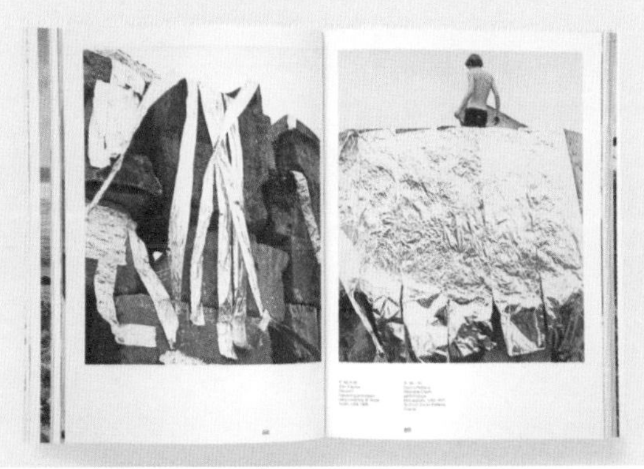

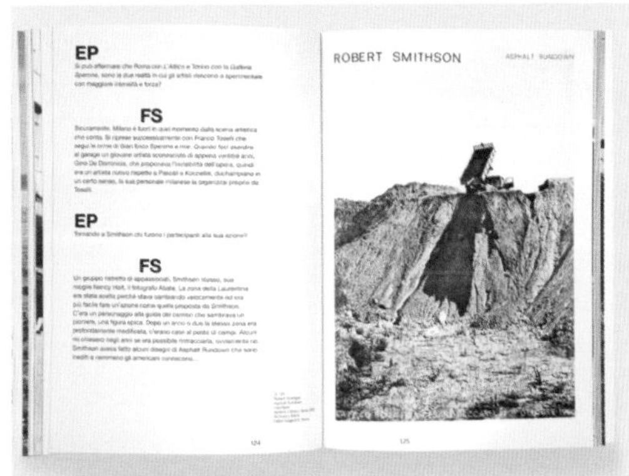

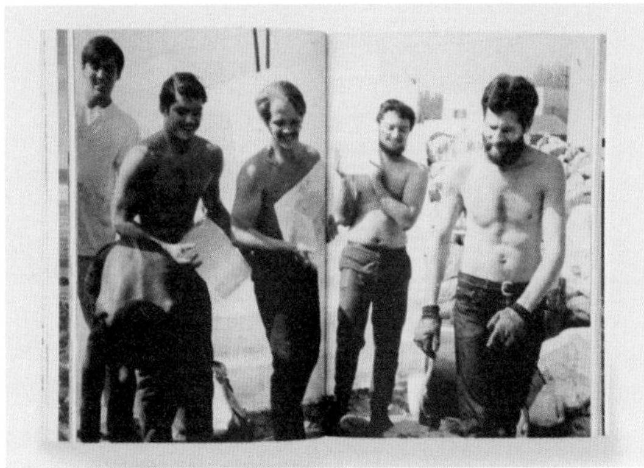

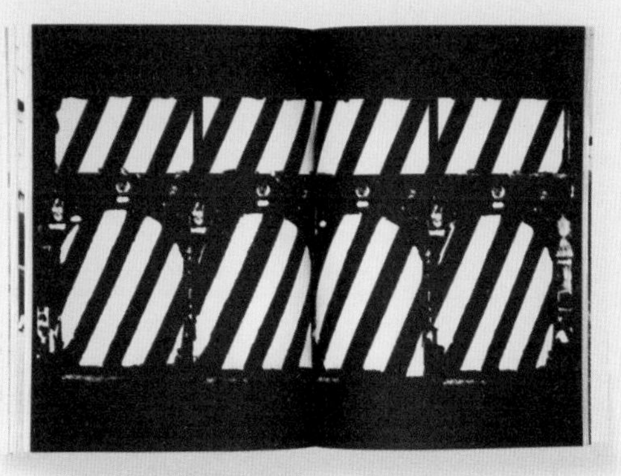

Beyond Environment

studio: *ARTIVA Design*
designer: *Daniele De Batté, Davide Sossi*

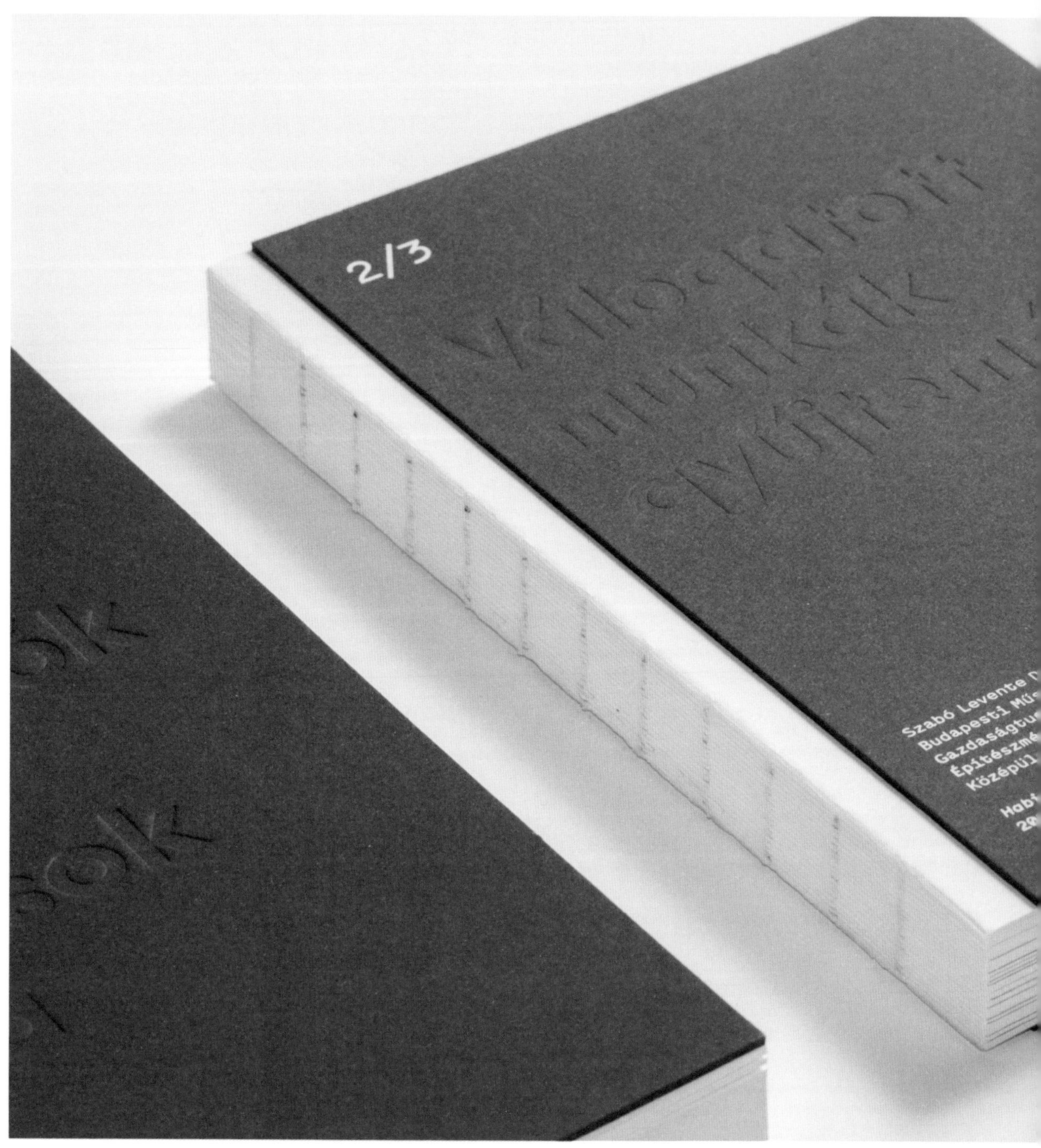

This habilitation thesis of architect Levente Szabó DLA in 3 volumes were bound by hand with the spines exposed. Their covers were letterpress-printed by a Heidelberg windmill. The original content and the secondary content were printed on different kinds of paper to signal the variation.

The Spatial Beauty of Memory

designer:
Ákos Polgárdi

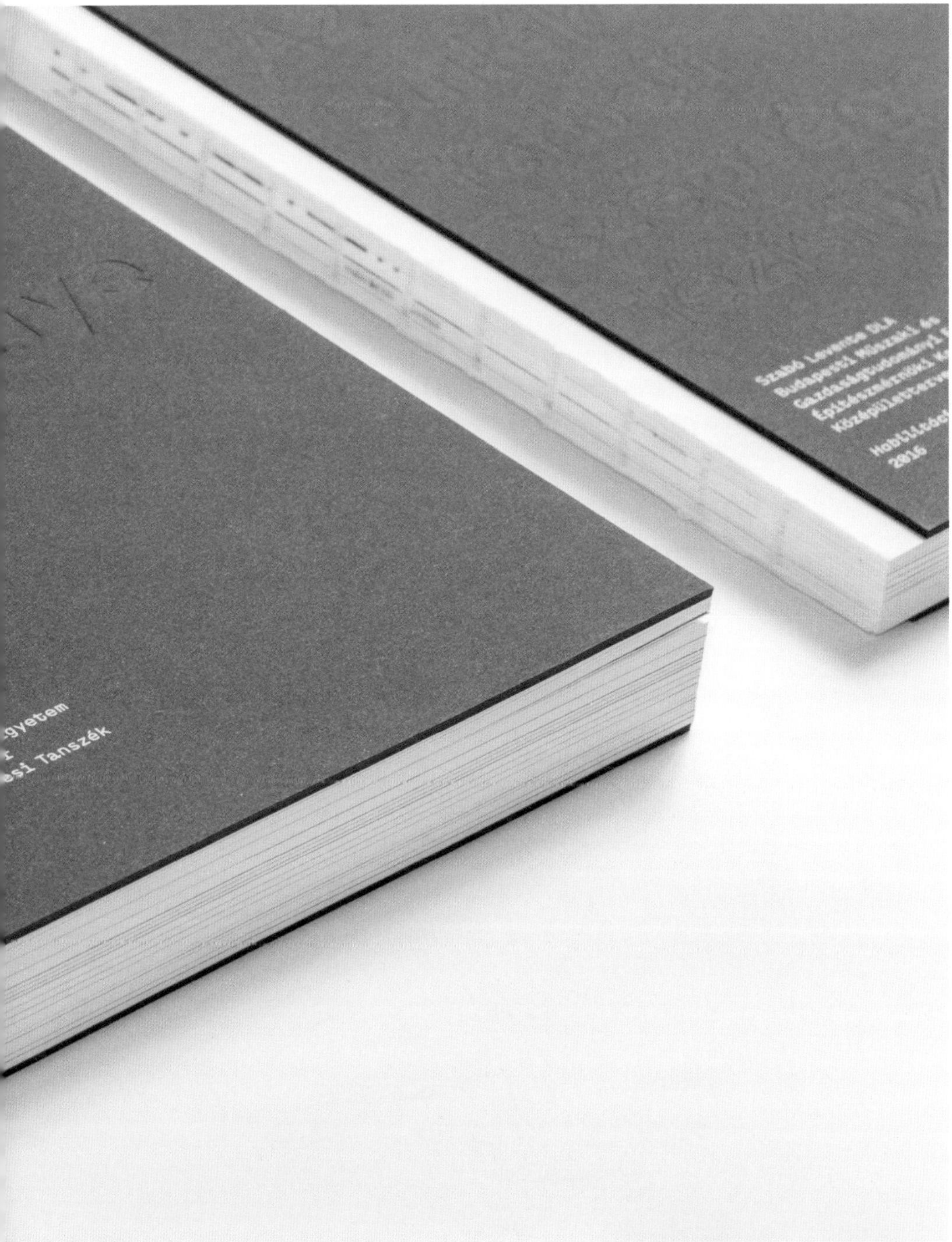

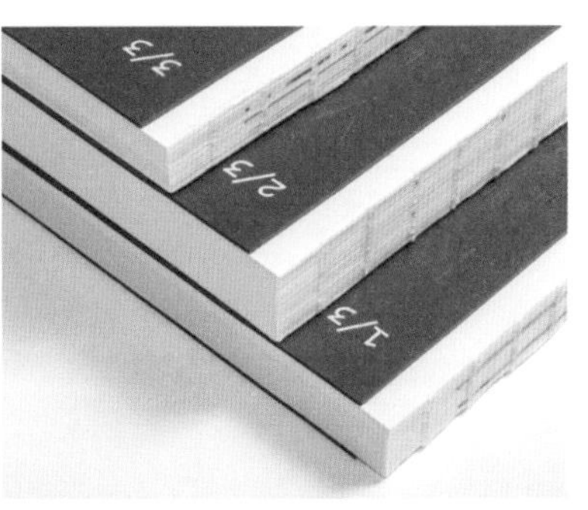

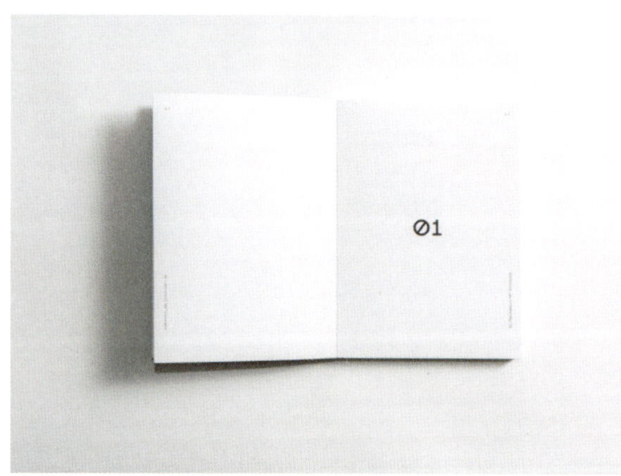

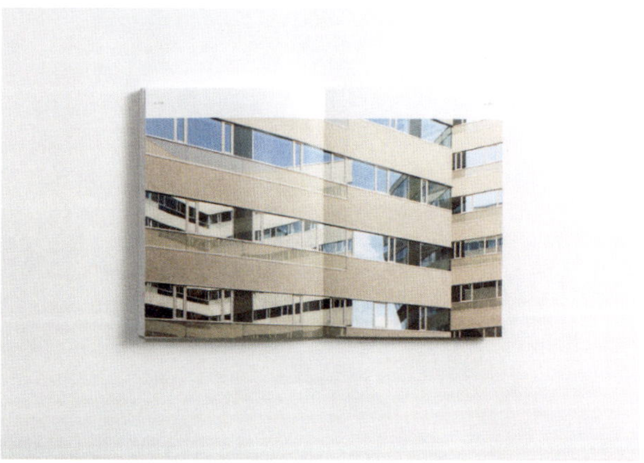

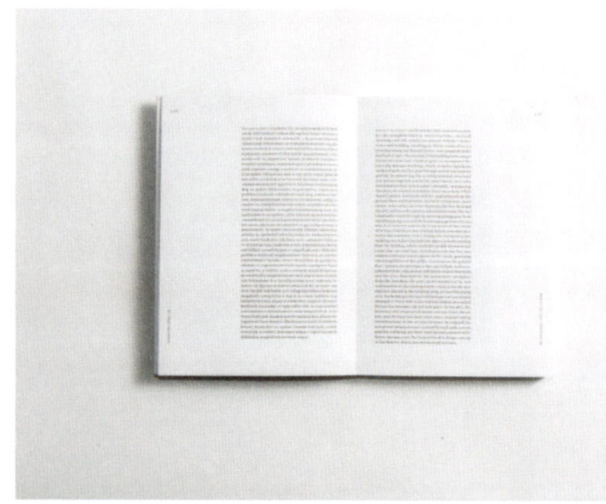

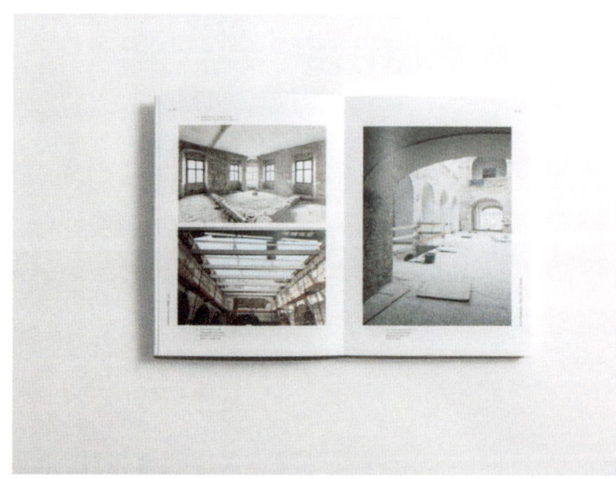

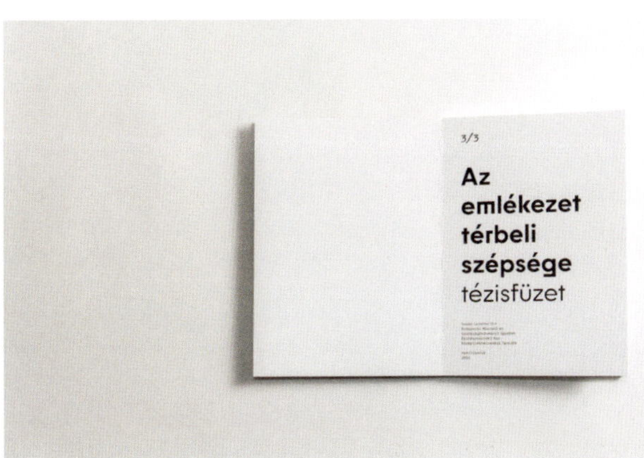
3/3
Az
emlékezet
térbeli
szépsége
tézisfüzet

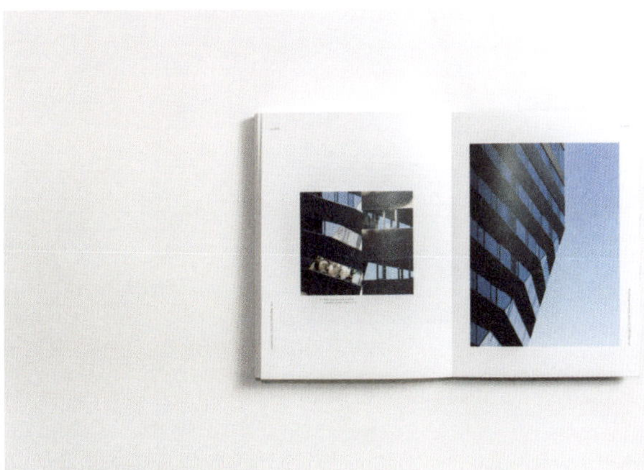

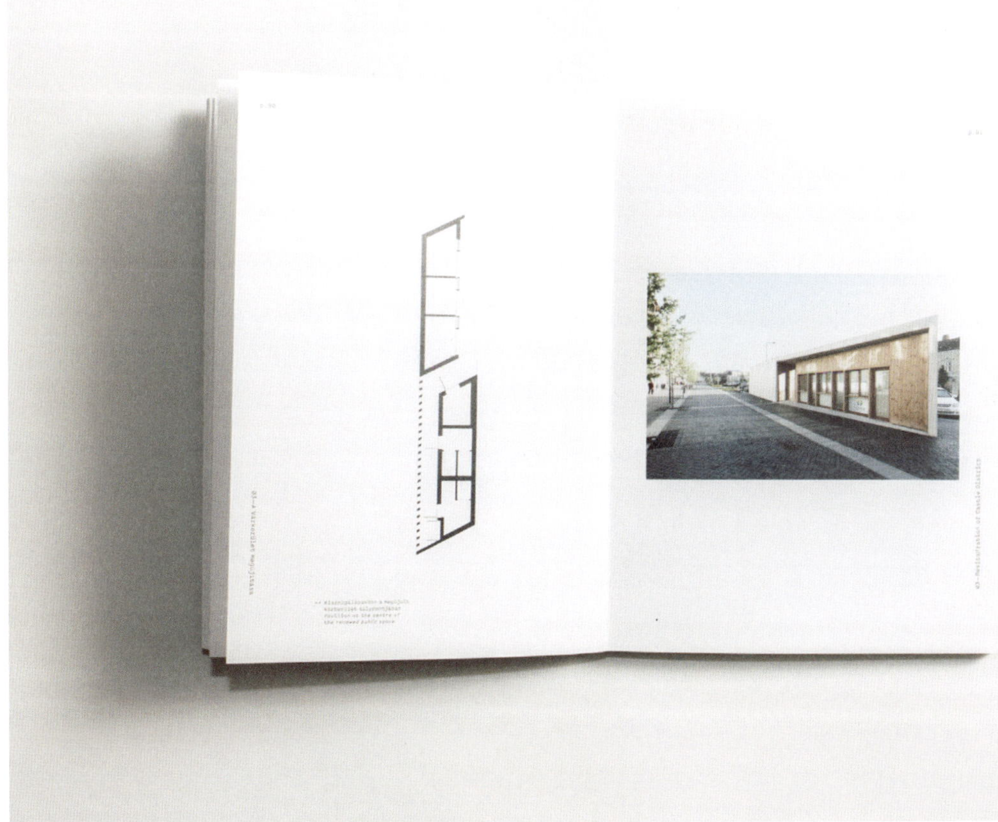

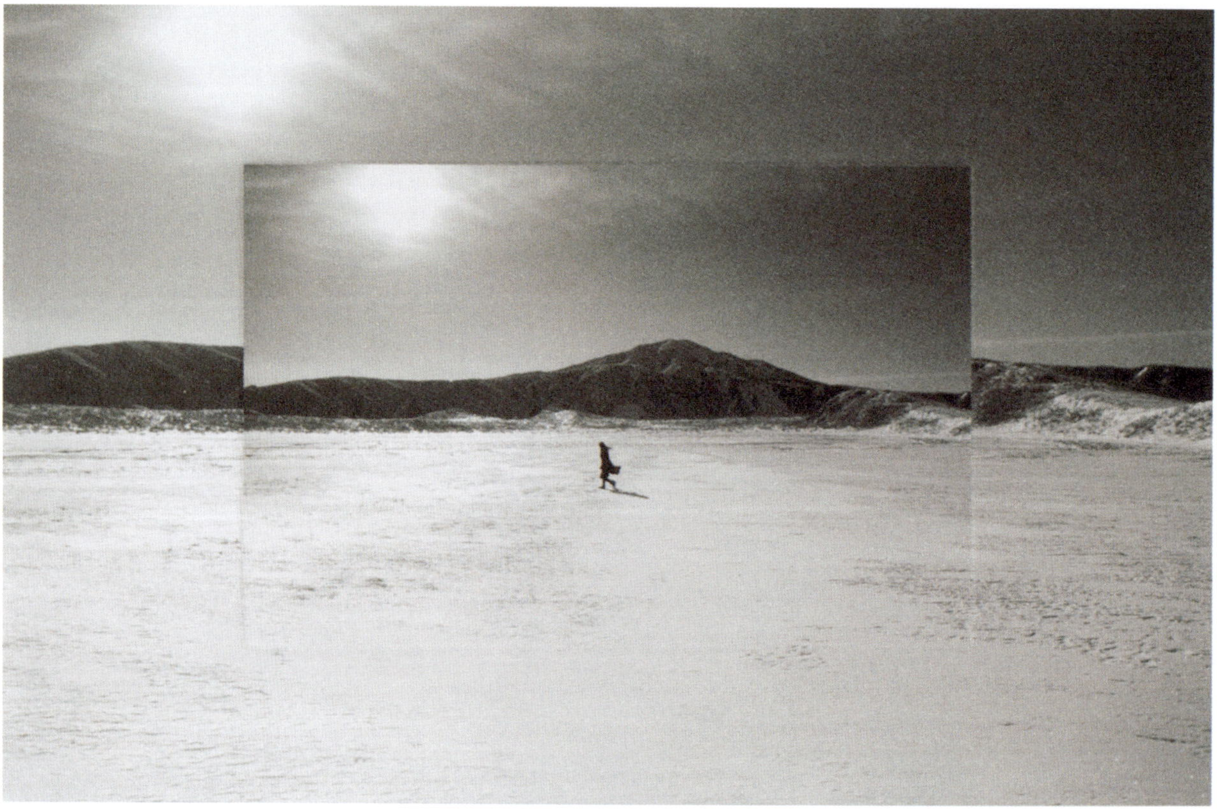

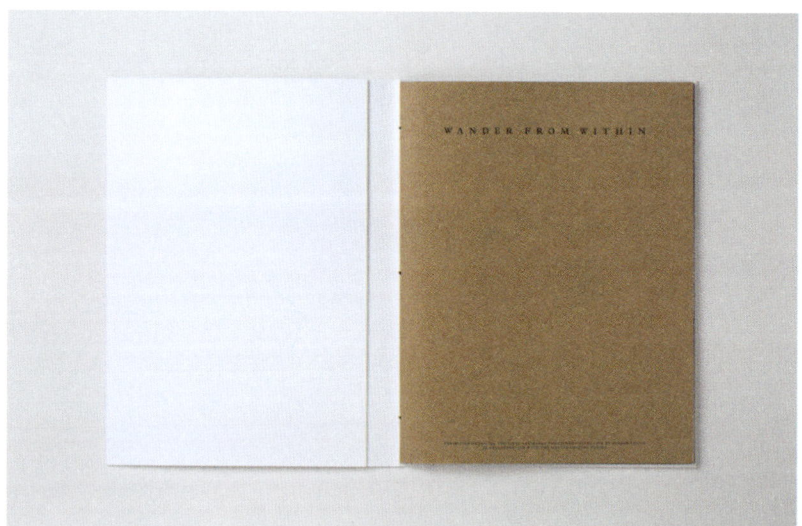

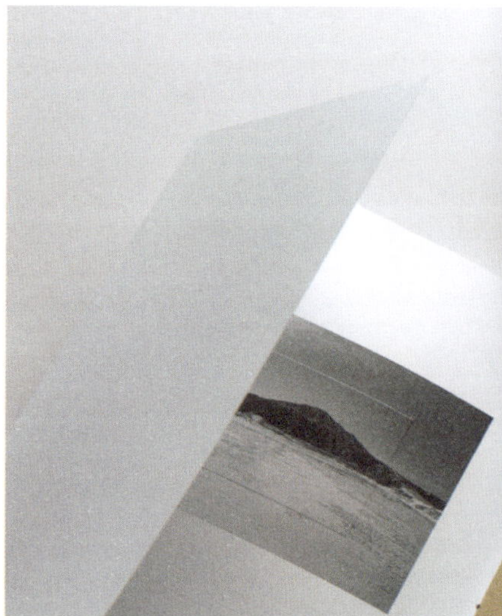

This is an event identity and catalogue created for an exhibition that unveiled Khora's artisanal furniture collection. To reflect the concept of Khora, a philosophical space between being and non-being, physical and non-physical, a resized key image is superimposed on the original to create a frame as a dimension to a metaphysical world that transcends the reality. Printed on the finest Japanese paper, the catalogue was hand sewn to resemble the artisanal craftsmanship.

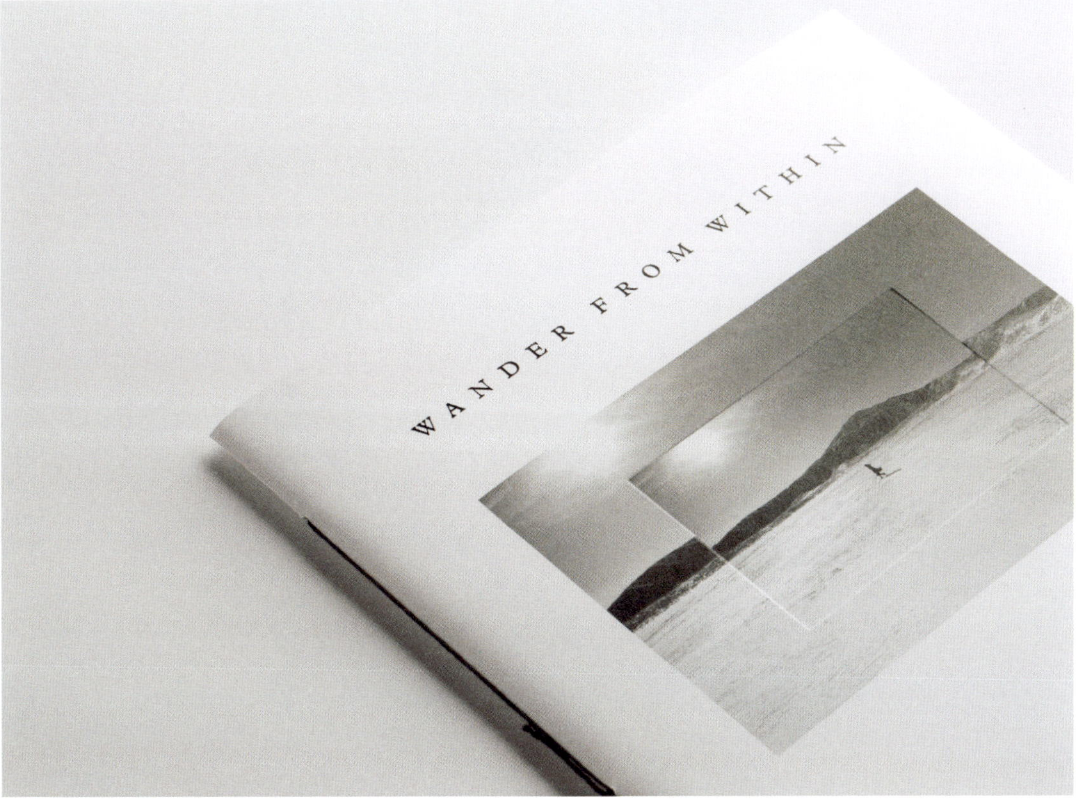

Wander from Within

studio: Toby Ng Design
designer: Toby Ng, Ronald Cheung

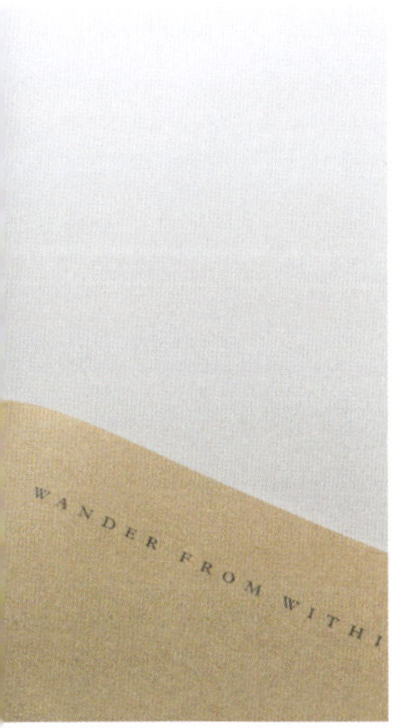

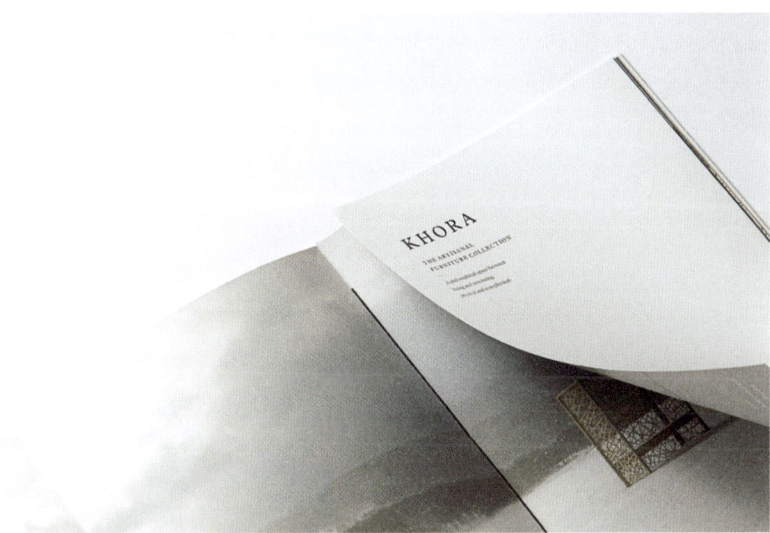

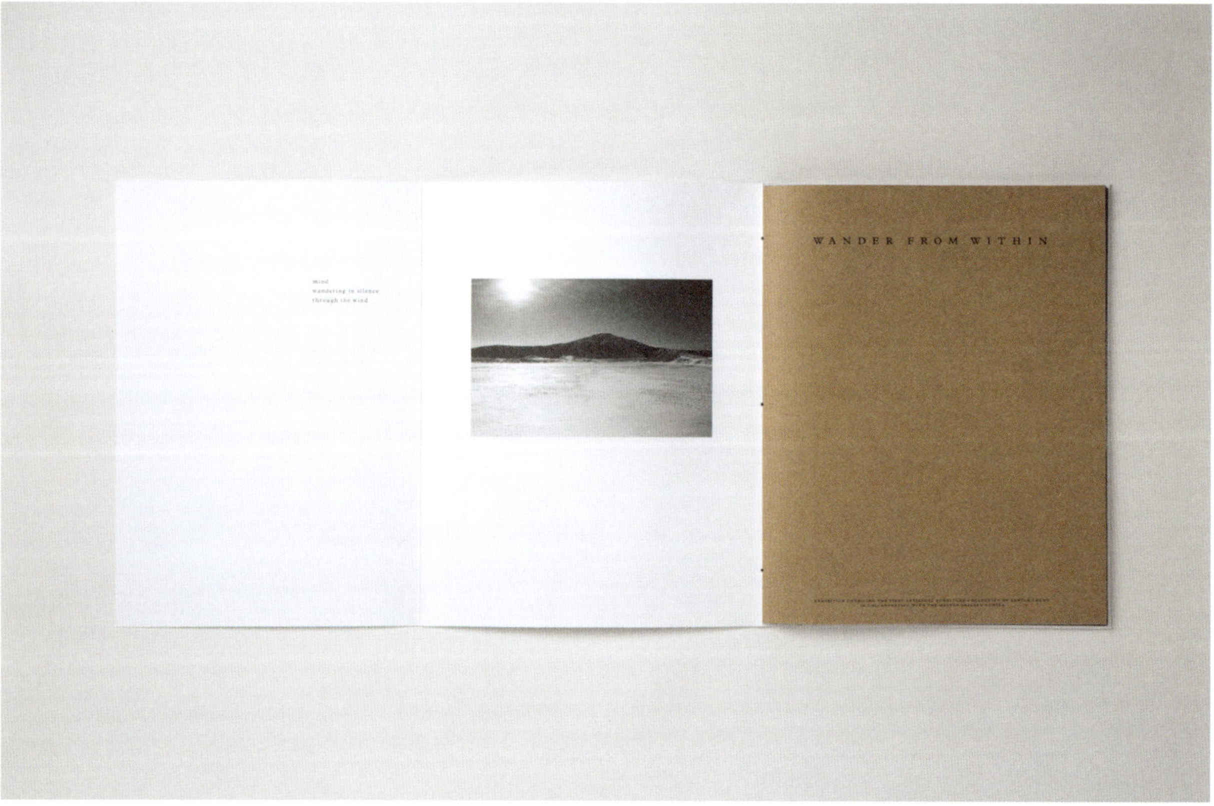

mind
wandering in silence
through the wind

WANDER FROM WITHIN

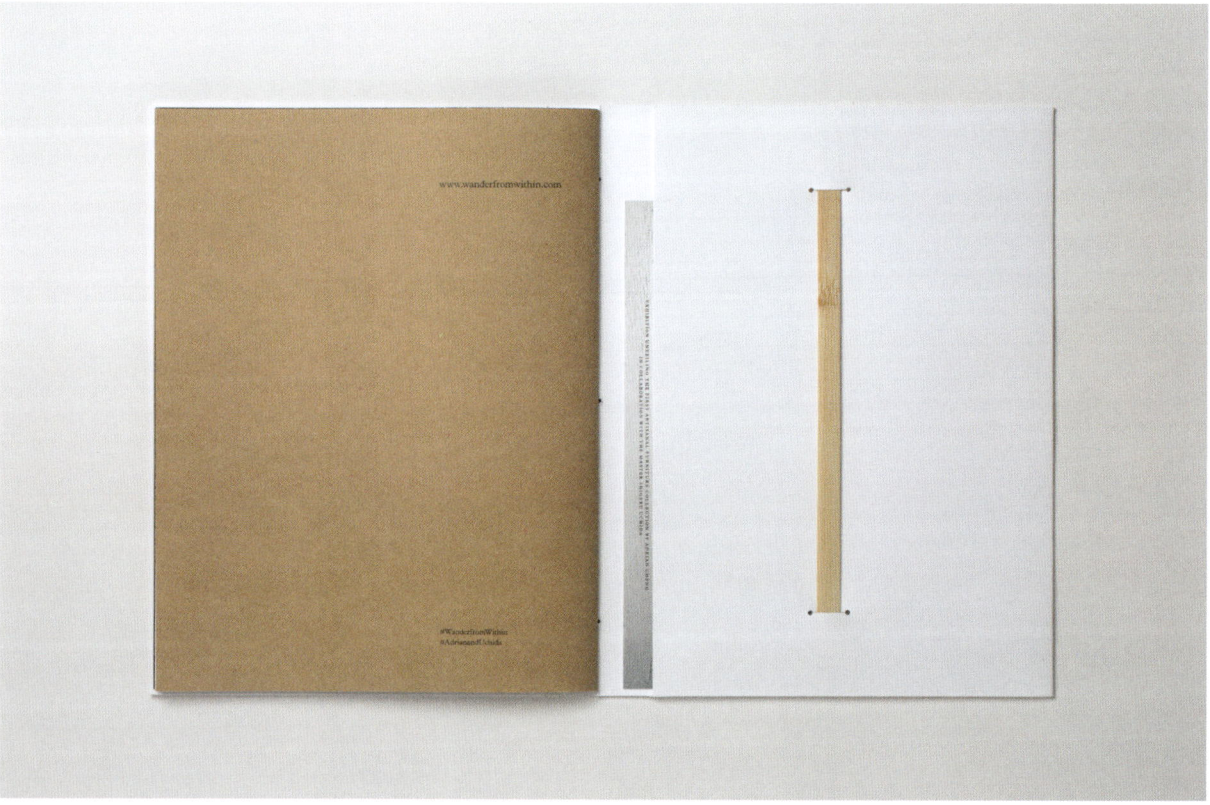

www.wanderfromwithin.com

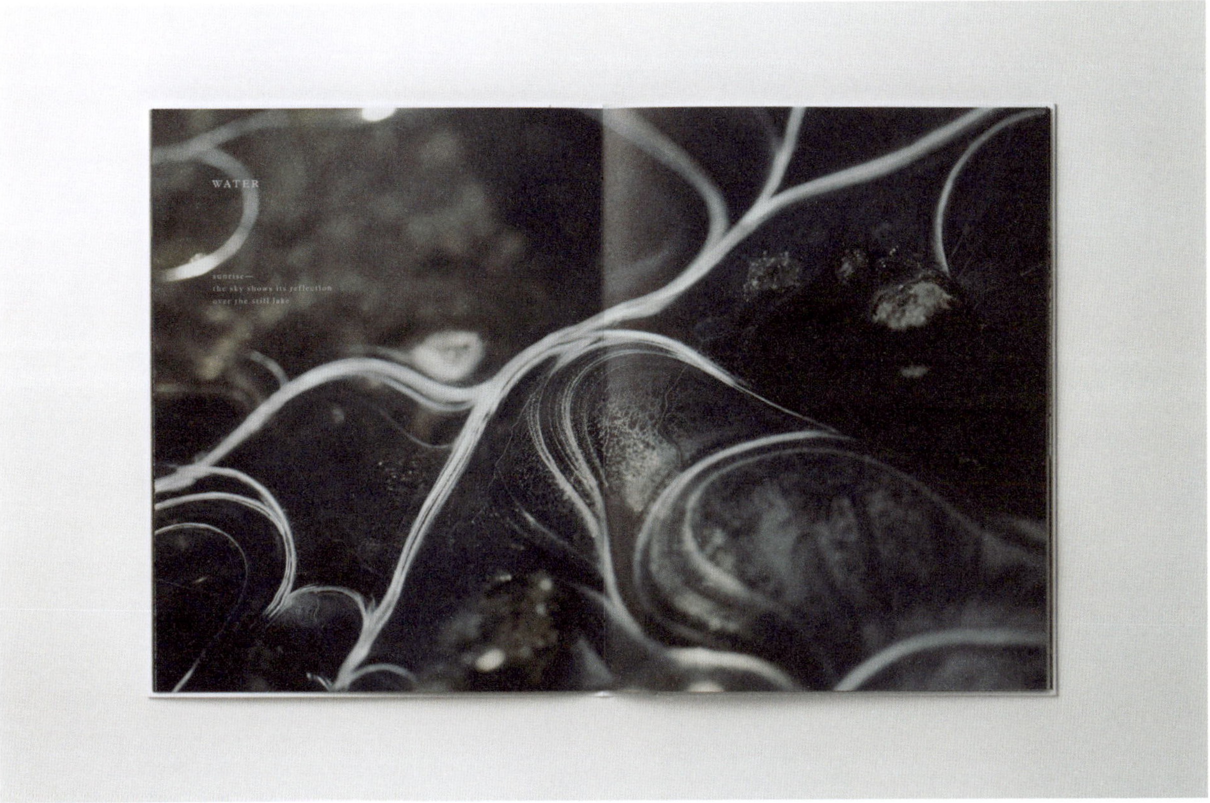

WATER

sunrise—
the sky shows its reflection
over the still lake

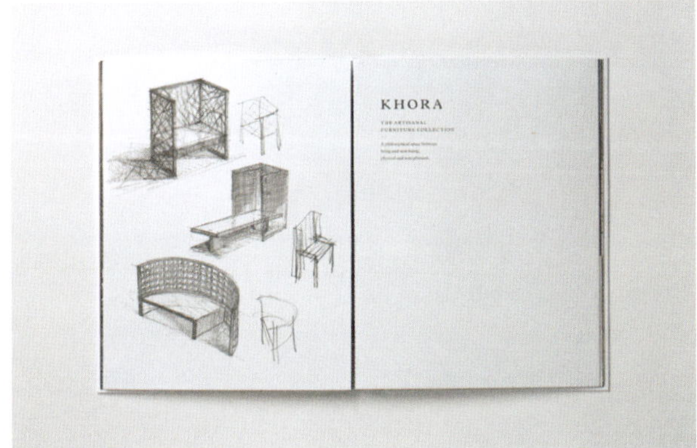

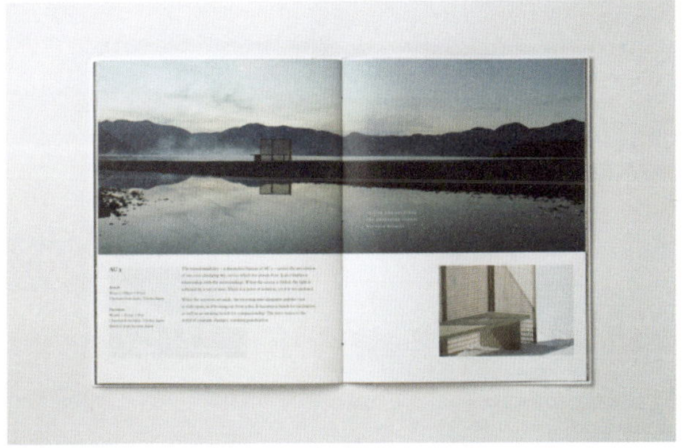

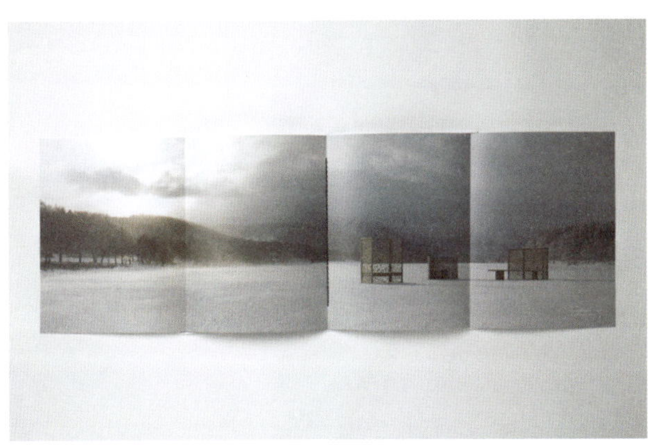

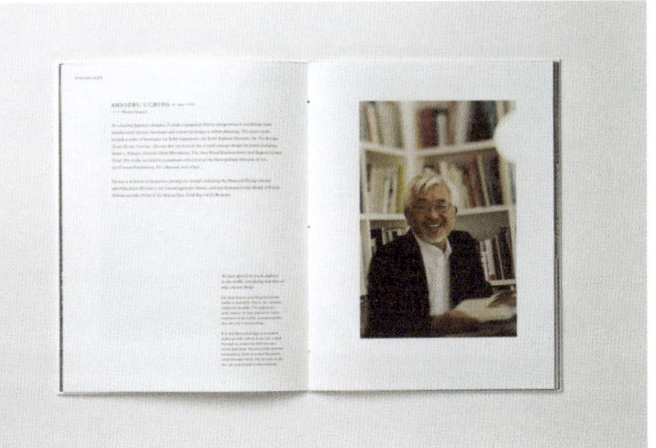

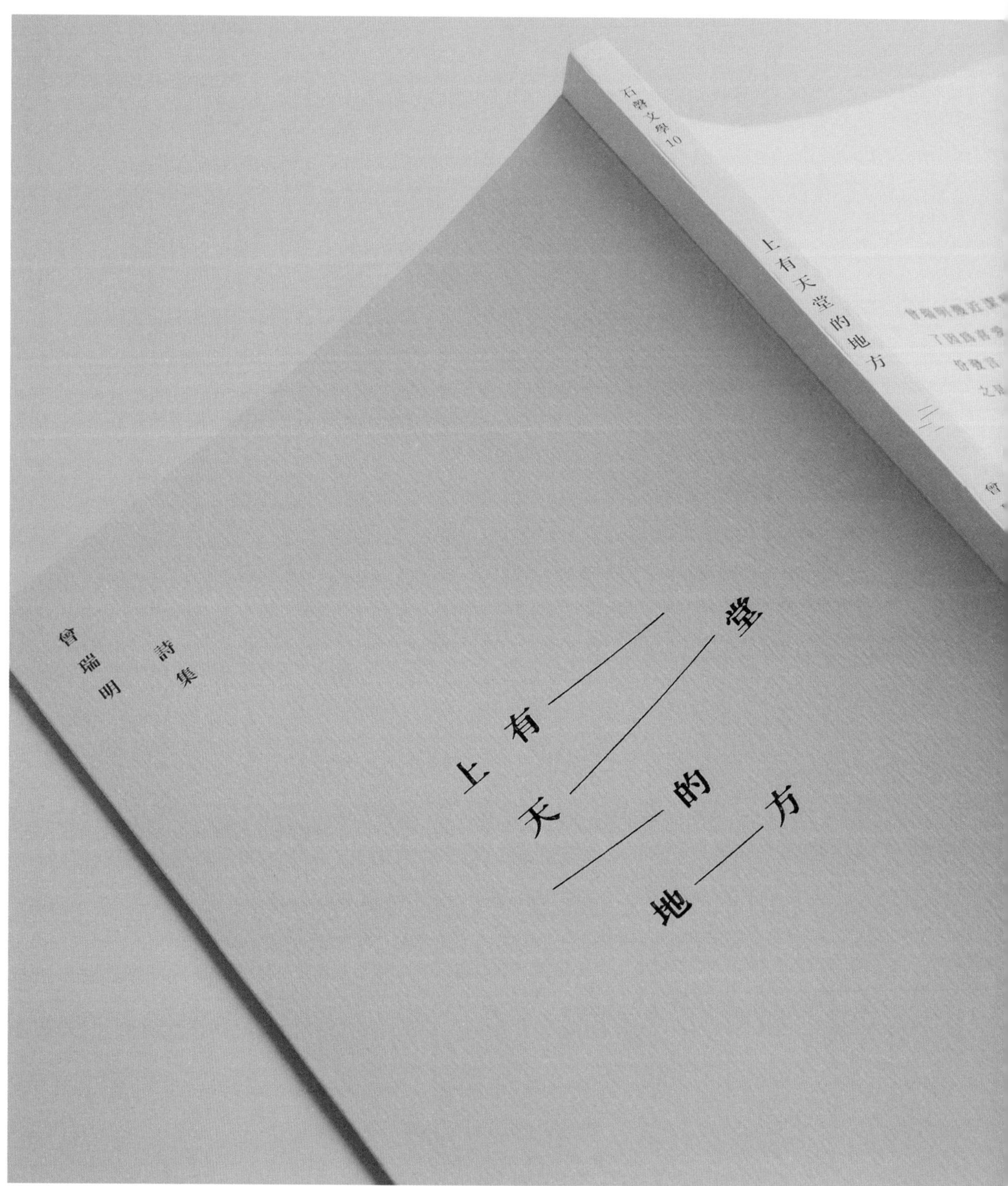

A bespoke visual tone of simplicity and emptiness was set to echo with this poetry collection's imperturbable and subtle writing on contemporary everyday life. The seemingly arbitrary lines and disordered characters form a ladder that metaphorically lead to somewhere beyond heaven.

Somewhere beyond Heaven

studio: ***ACST Design***
designer: ***Albert Cheng-Syun Tang***

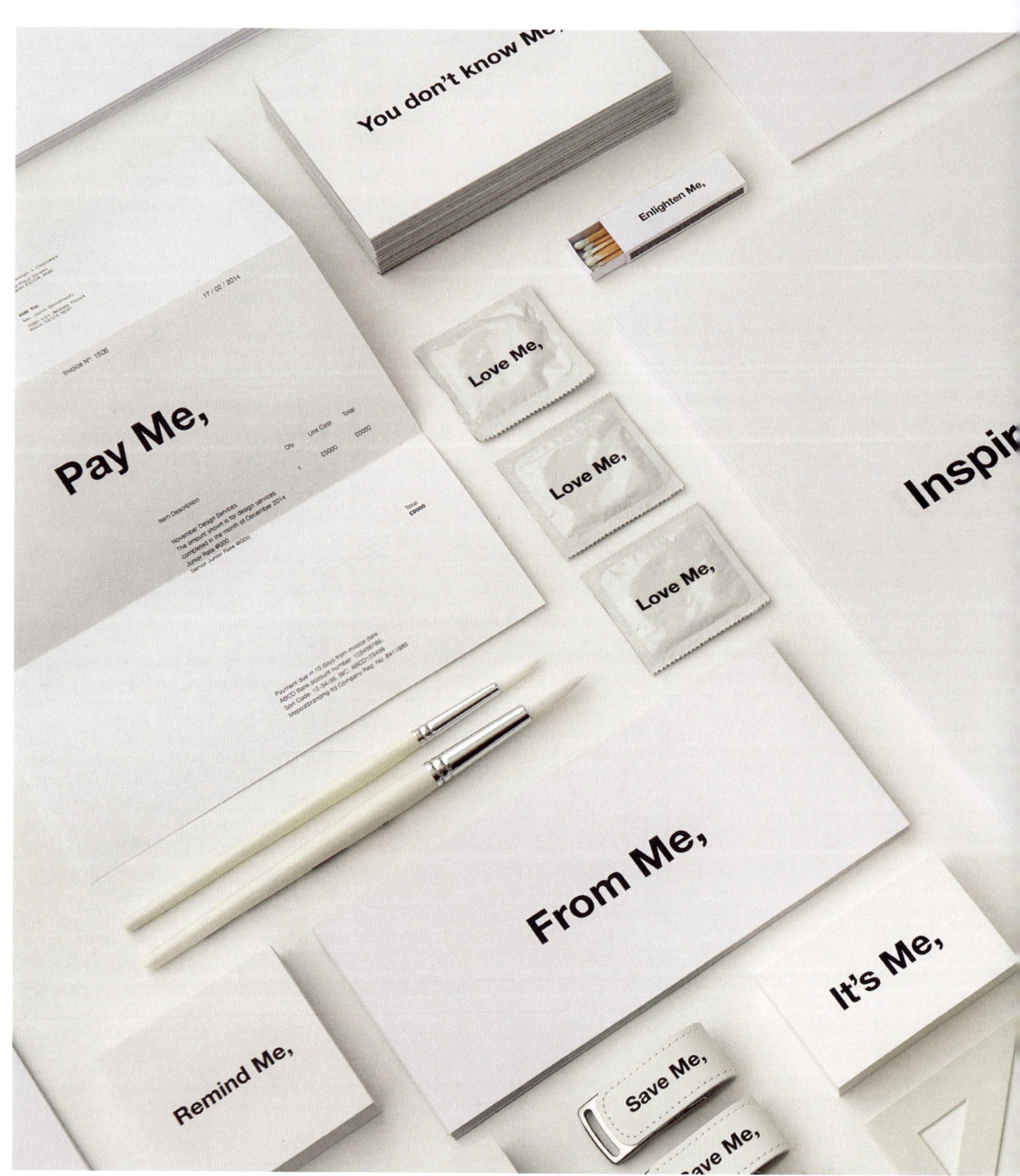

"Me," represents the union of the initials of the co-founders of the multi-disciplinary studio while the coma reflects the narrative process of their practice. For its promotional material, a selection of unconventional objects is branded with simple and bold phrases incorporating the "Me," theme to create a message that not only highlights the nature of the product but also creates an emotional link between people and "Me,".

Brand Me,

studio: Me, Postbranding LTD
designer: Mirco Colonna, Eva Miguel

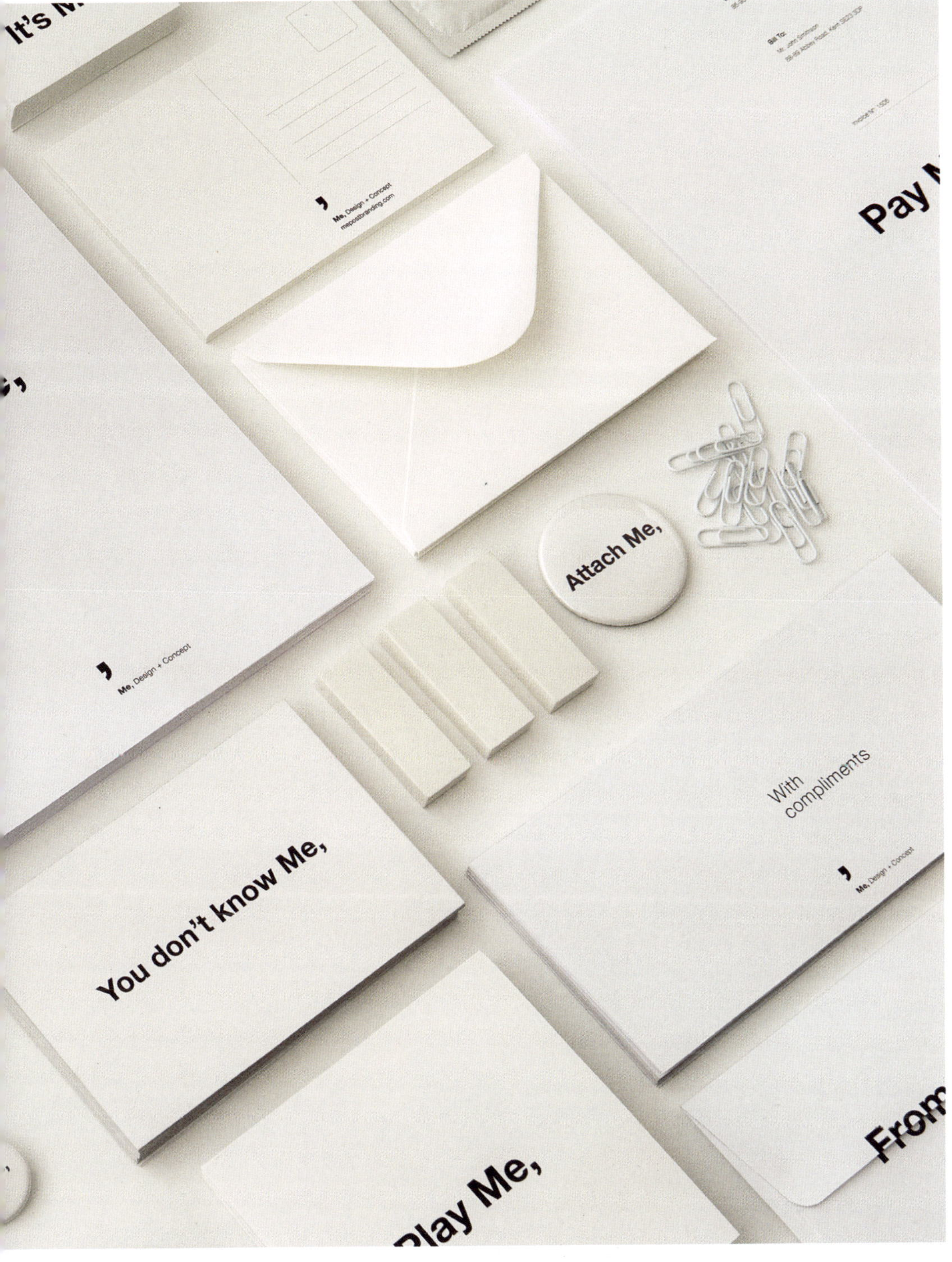

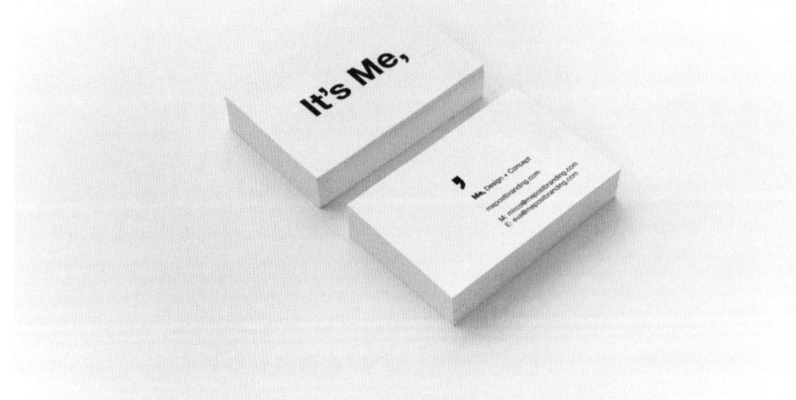
It's Me,
Me, Design + Concept

Pay Me,

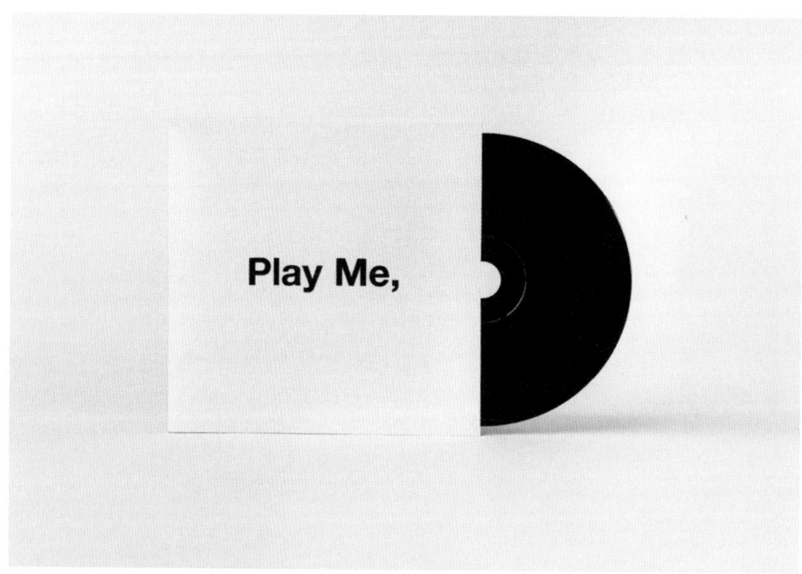
Play Me,

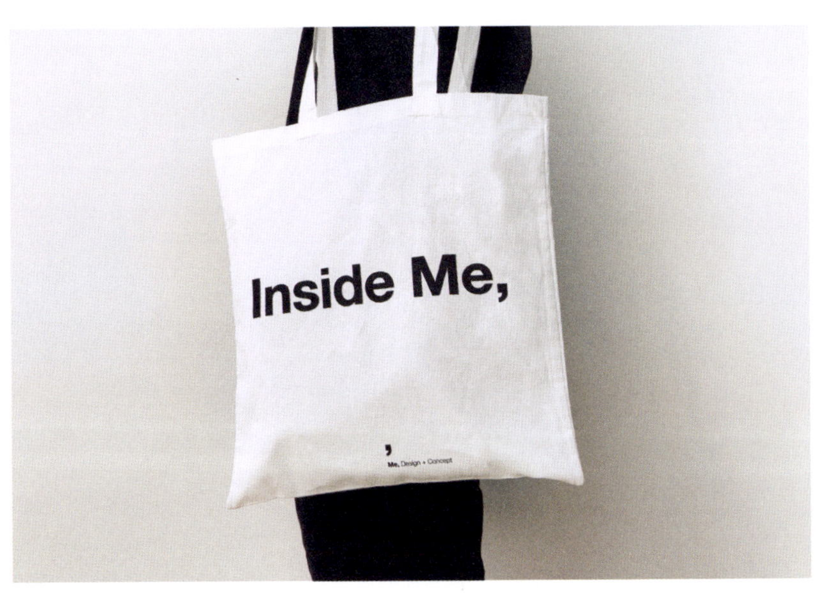
Inside Me,
Me, Design + Concept

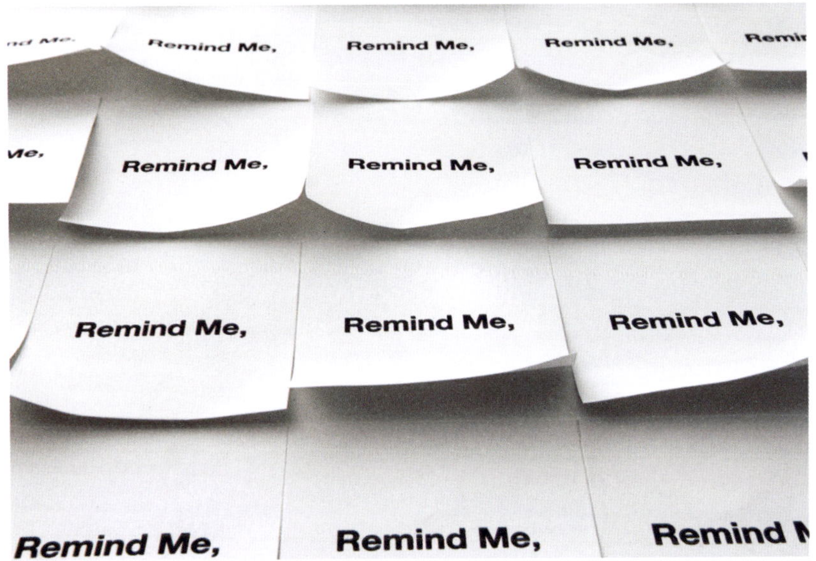
Remind Me,
Remind Me,
Remind Me,
Remind Me,
Remind Me,
Remind Me,
Remind Me,
Remind Me,
Remind Me,
Remind Me,
Remind Me,

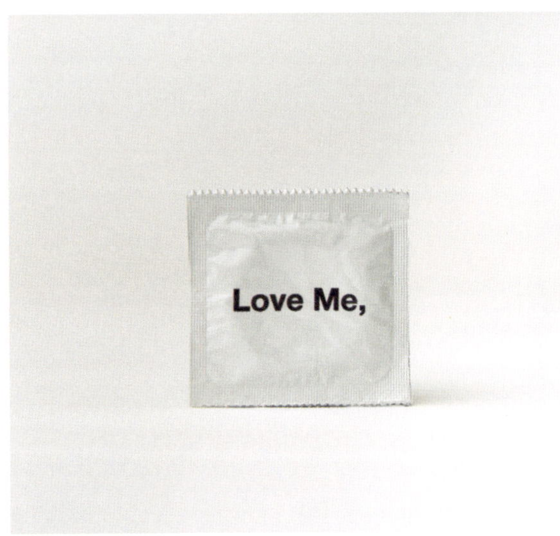
Love Me,

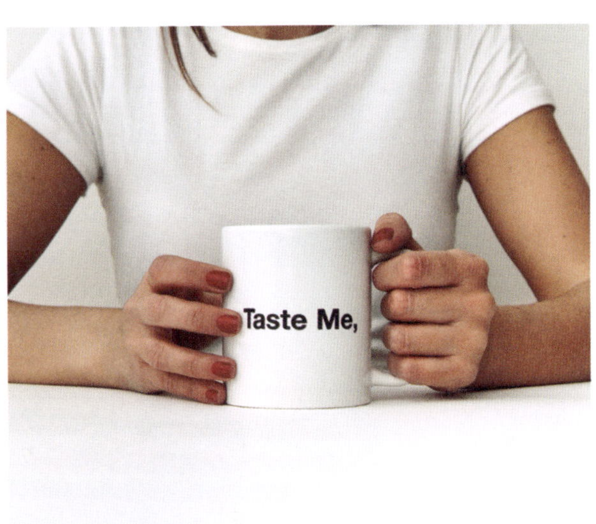
Taste Me,

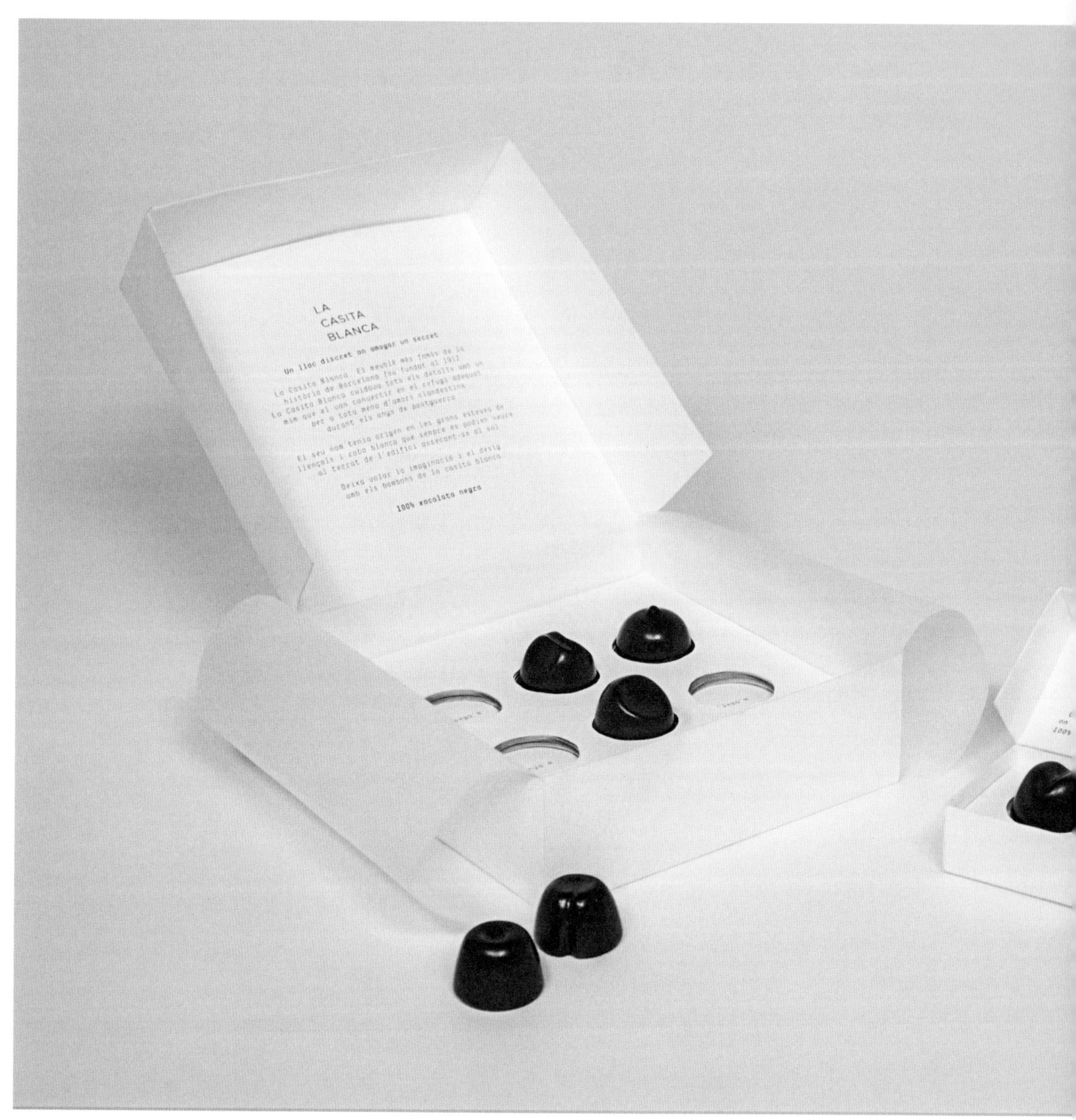

The mysterious, elegant and impressive chocolate and its packaging were inspired by the famous Meublé in the history of Barcelona, a building with white linen stretches on the roof and whose attention to details once made it the perfect shelter for clandestine love. Against the white packaging, the rich brown chocolates stand out boldly. The brand name will be revealed by pulling the small tab attached.

La Casita Blanca

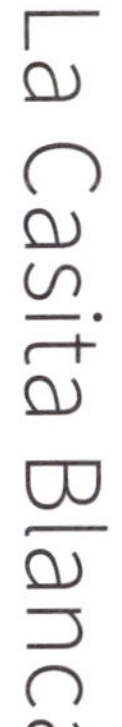

studio: ***Students, ELISAVA***
designer: ***Laura de Miguel, Cristian Varela, Maria Romero***

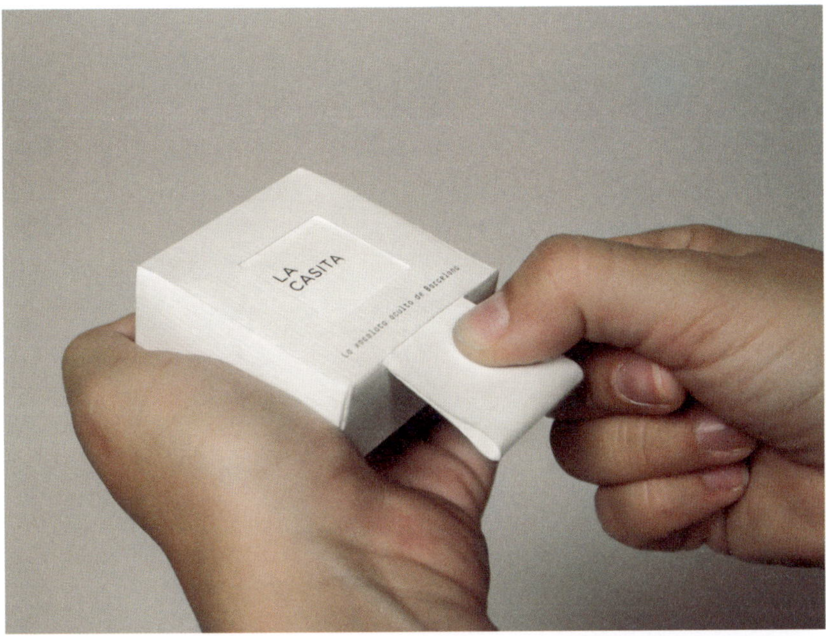

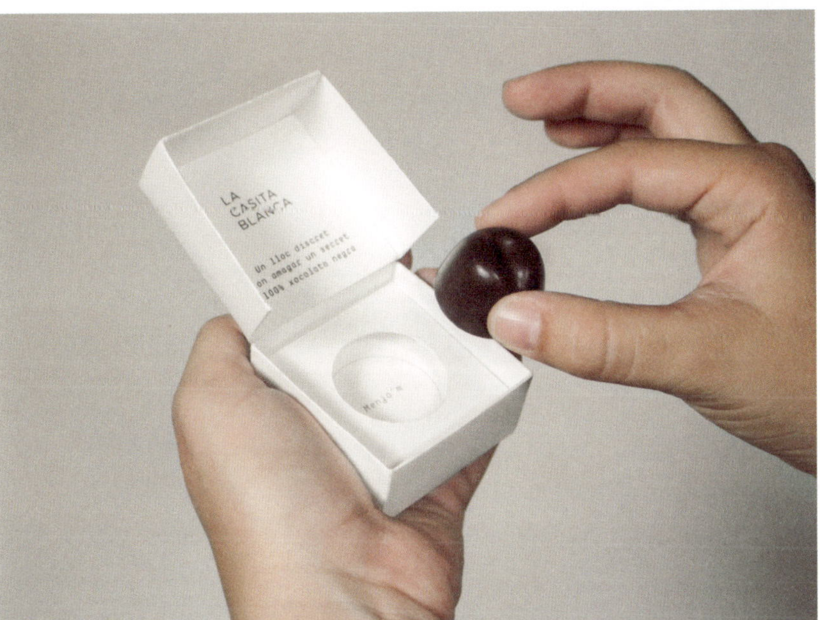

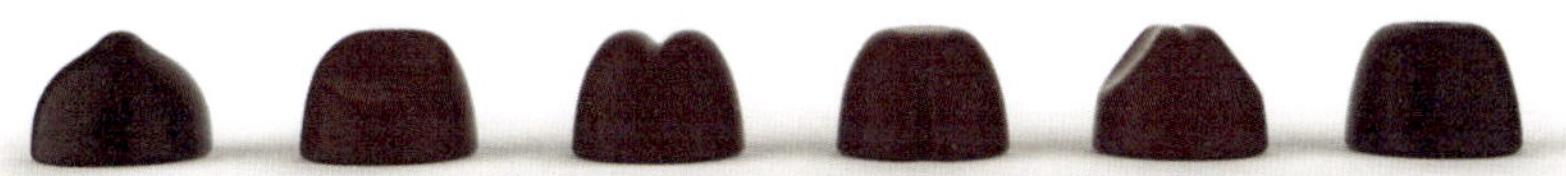

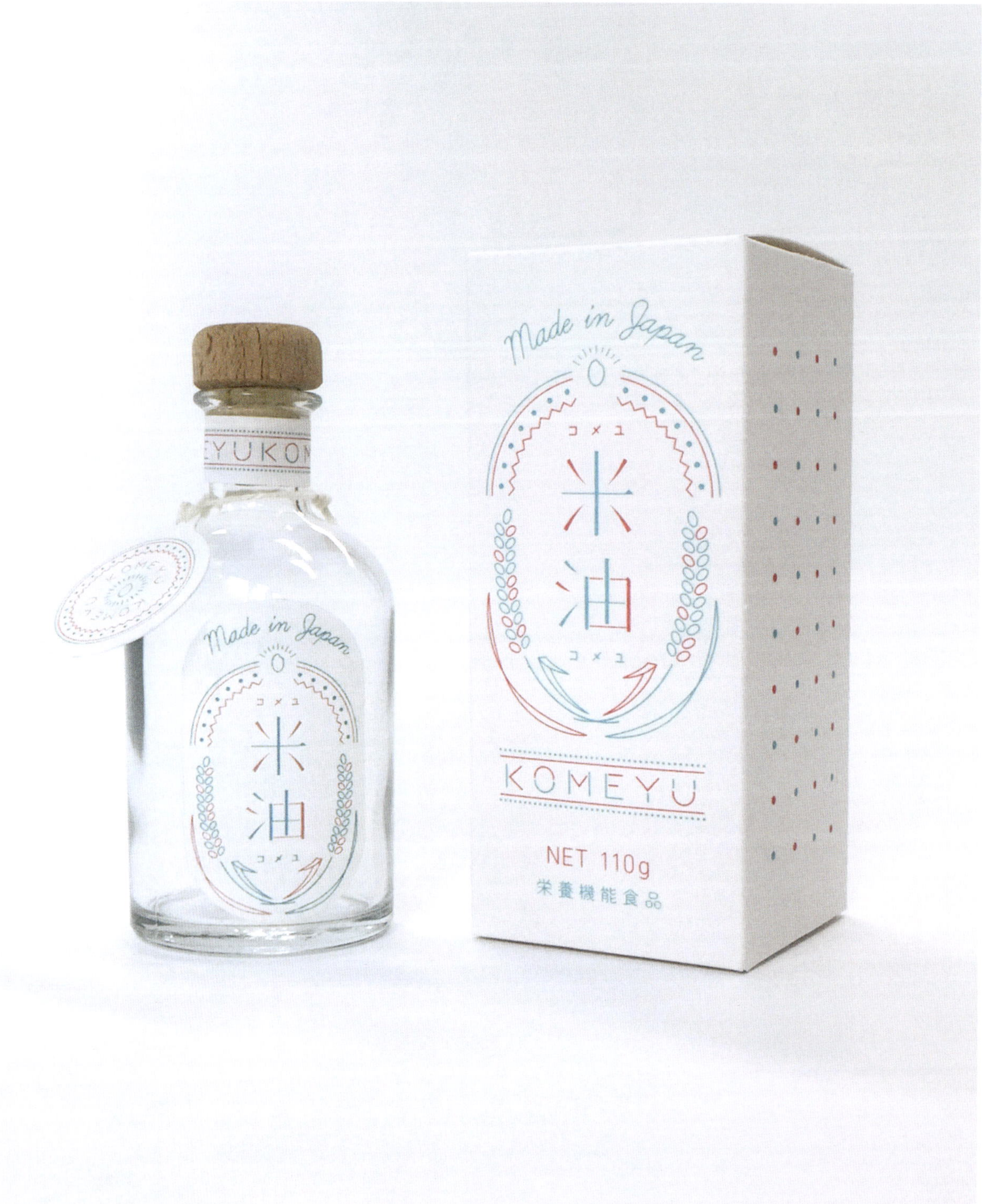

This packaging was designed to promote the rice bran oil to more young people. To make the product suited for shelves of stores with a rich array of knick-knacks, a soft and pale expression was chosen with a sense of whiteness.

Komeyu

studio: **ARROMATA.LLC**
designer: **Shunsuke Aoki**

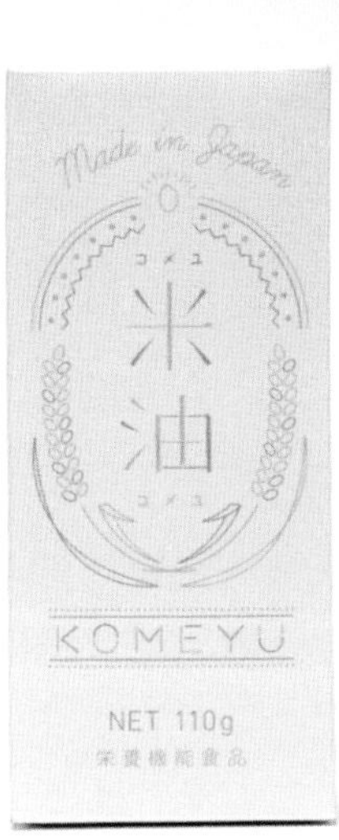

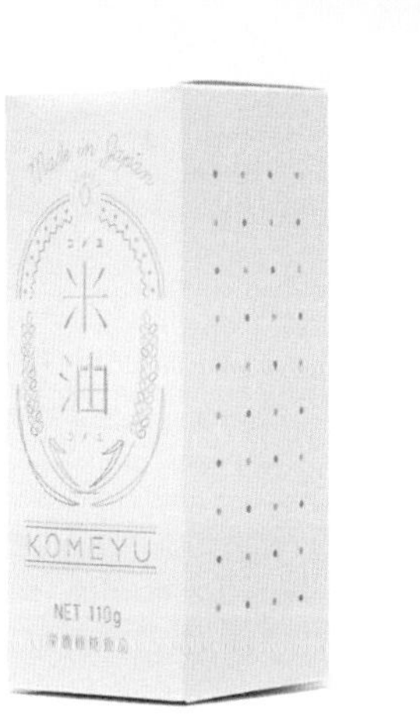

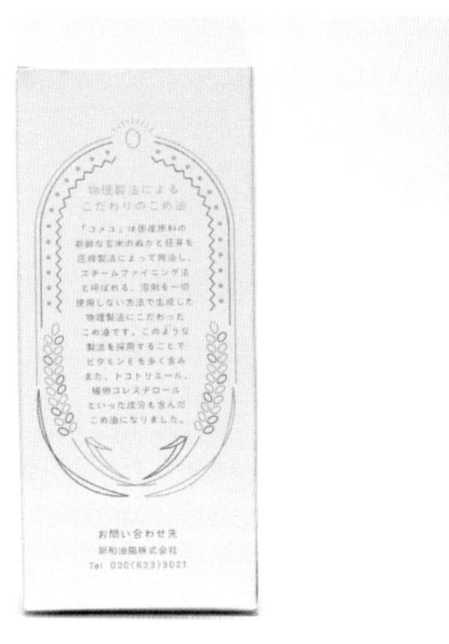

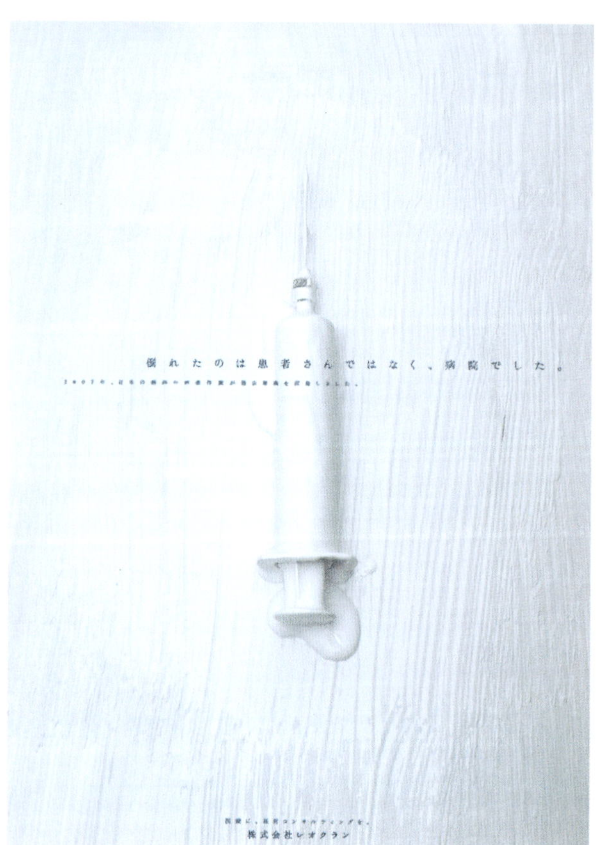

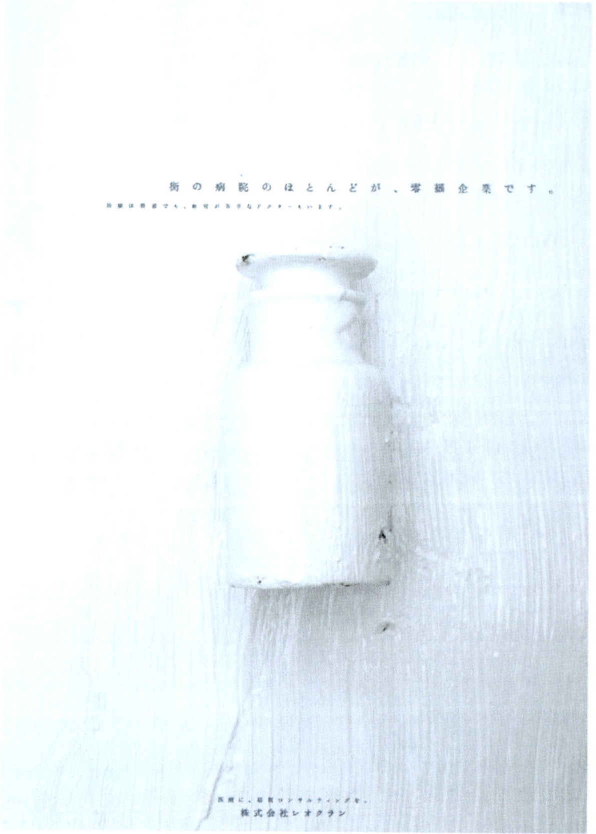

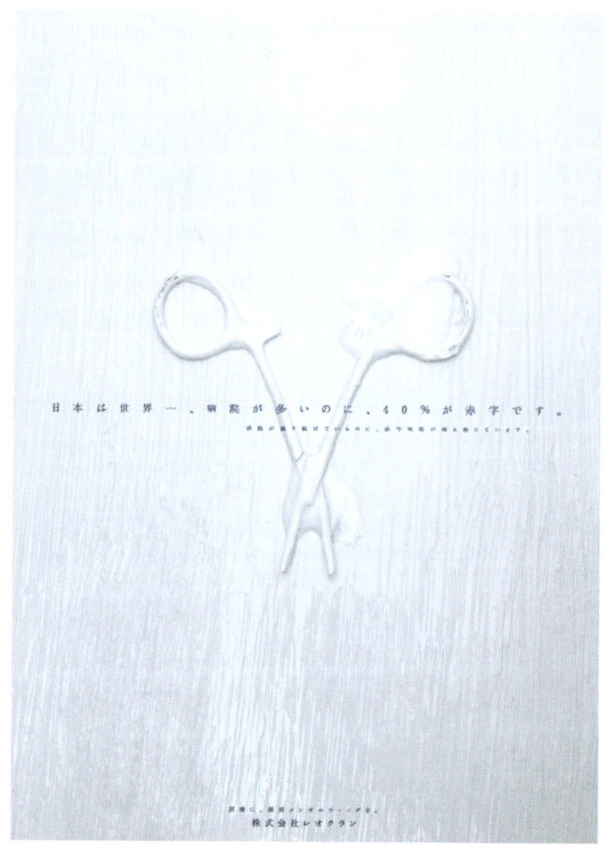

This series of posters belongs to a corporate advertisement for LEOCLAN, a management consulting company focusing on medical institutions. For creating a sense of crisis for the medical institutions with poor management, visuals depicting decayed medcal tools were created.

Branding Posters For Leoclan

designer: Daisaku Ono
studio: Creative Company GIFT

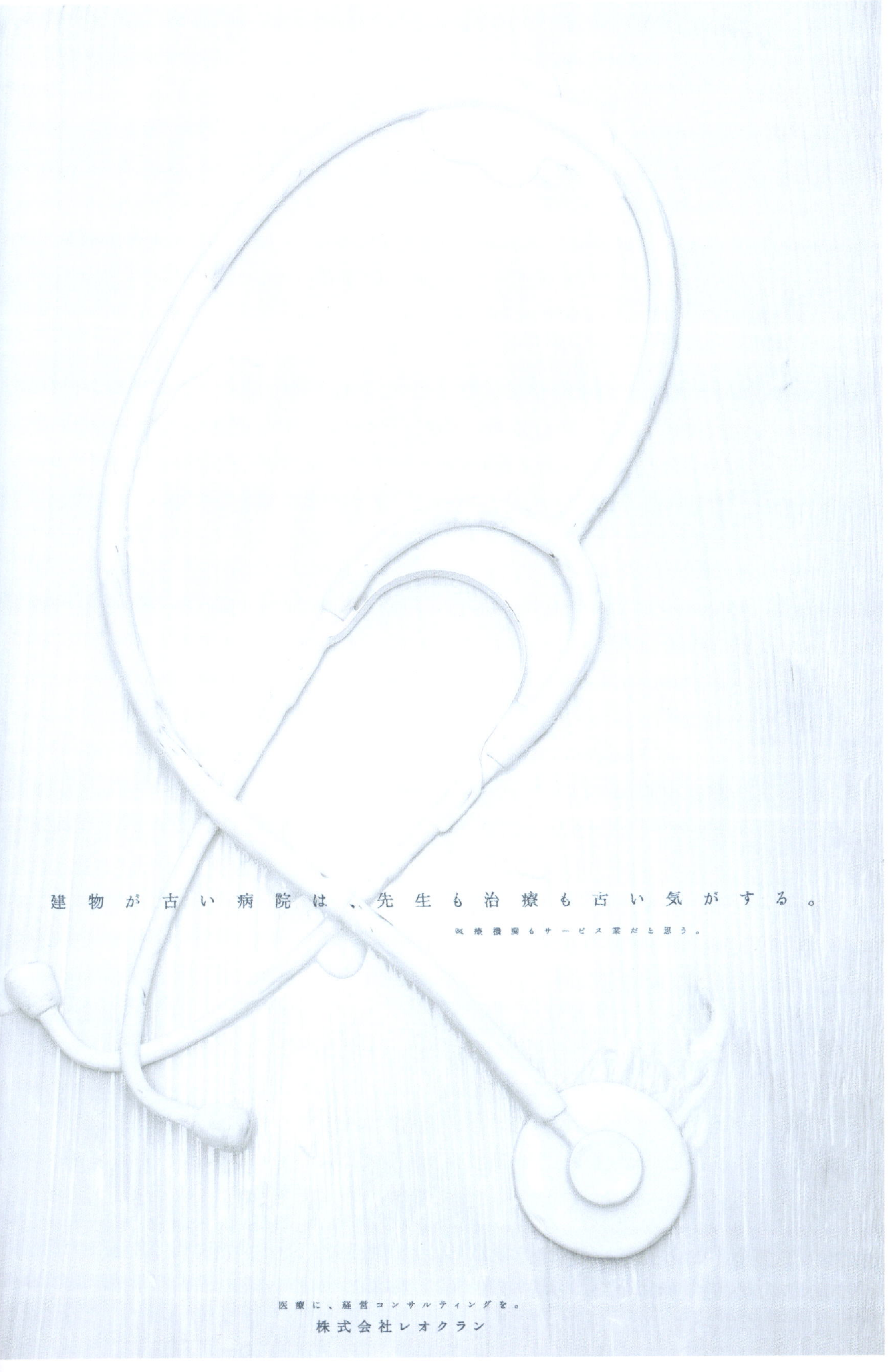

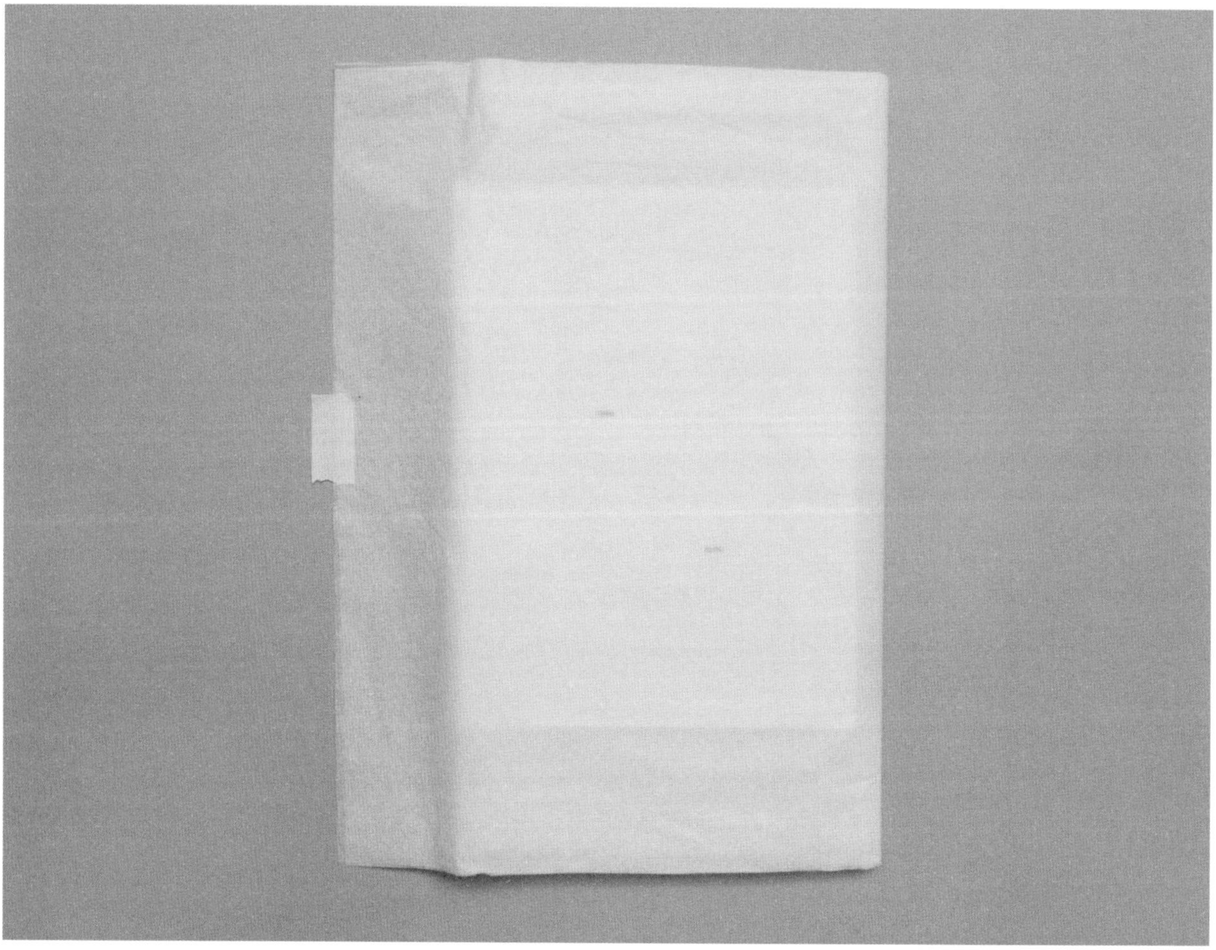

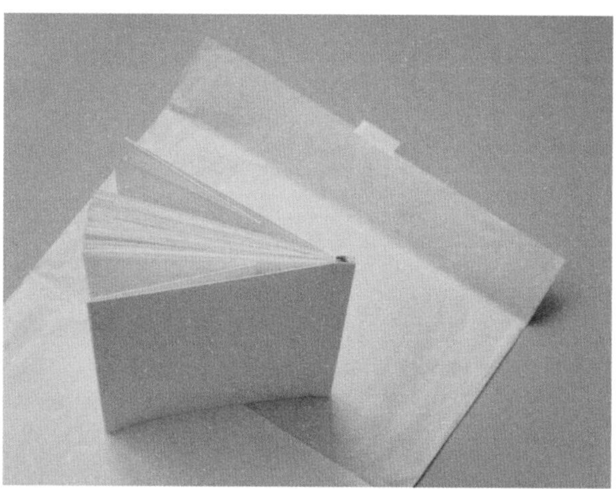

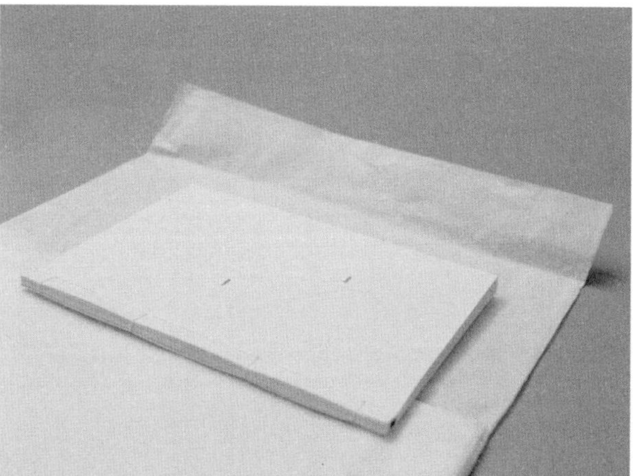

Come Home is a delicate book containing articles on missing persons from 1995 to 2005, extracted from *The Sydney Morning Herald*. The articles are chronologically ordered, starting with the most recent.

As one flips through the pages, the article slowly fades away, just like the hope that dwindles with every passing day. Only the darker words "come" and "home" resonate through the pages, whispering, crying. For the people involved, each day can feel like a hopeless eternity as they soon come to realise that their loved ones are never coming home.

Come Home

designer:
Ebony Goh

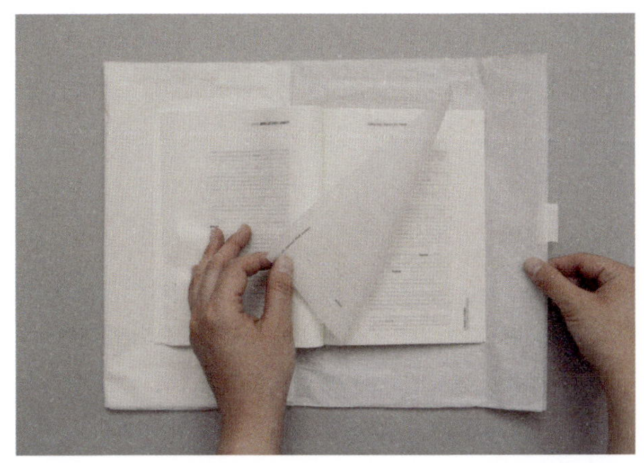

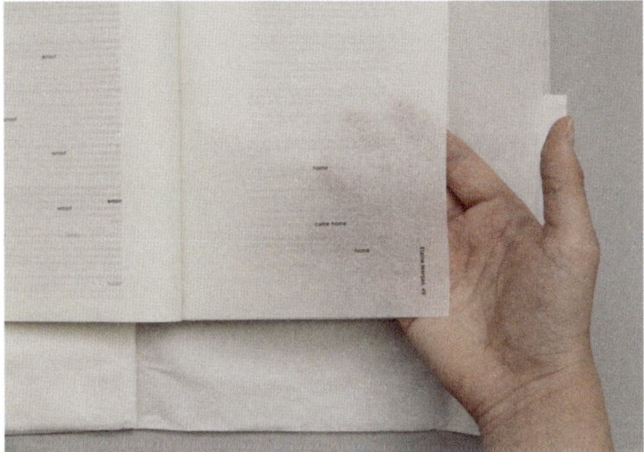

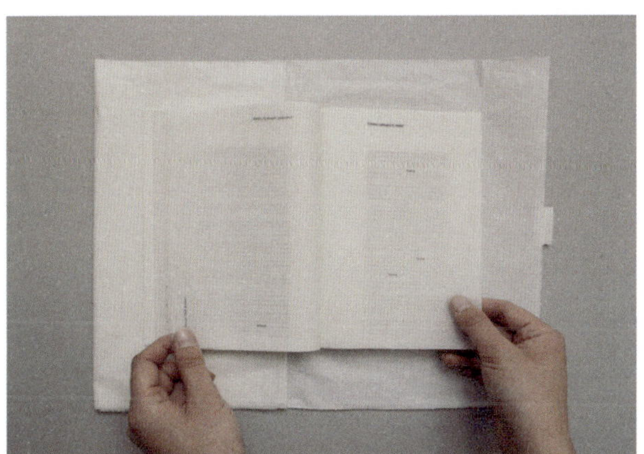

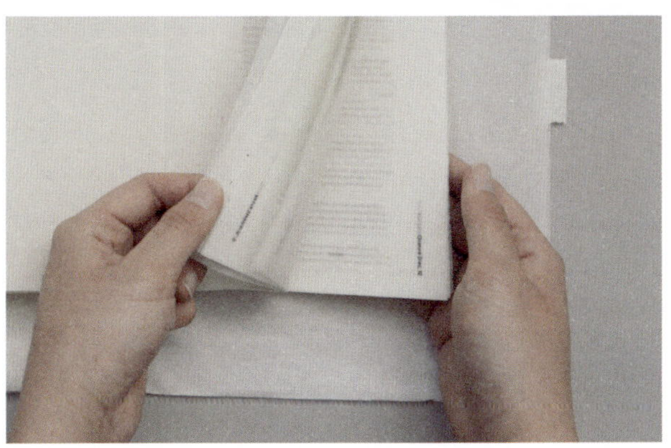

Aphrodite

WWW.APHRODITE.CO
INFO@APHRODITE.COM
+01 2148 604 004

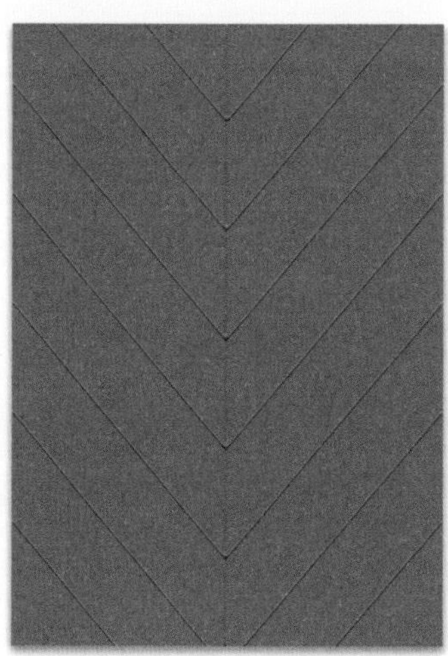

Aphrodite offers a wide range of wedding dresses featuring a romantic, fresh and pure style that grace every bride. For the brand identity, deep green was used as the main color to make it as pure as nature. The visual system evokes a different but familiar sense.

Aphrodite

designer:
Eldur Ta

Aphrodite

From	Mr. Eldur Ta
To	Mrs. Huy
Code	#304514
Date	17/04/2017

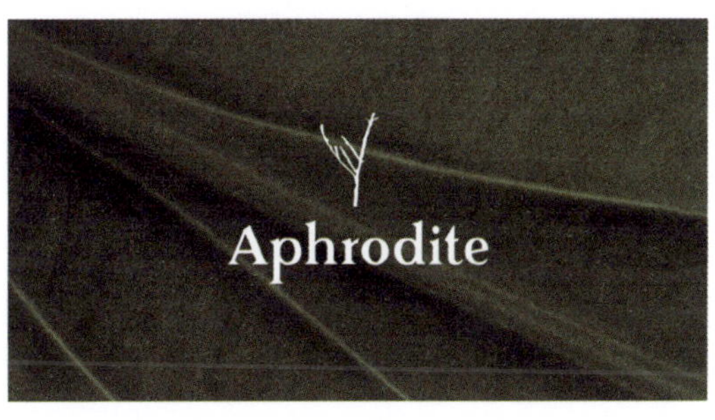

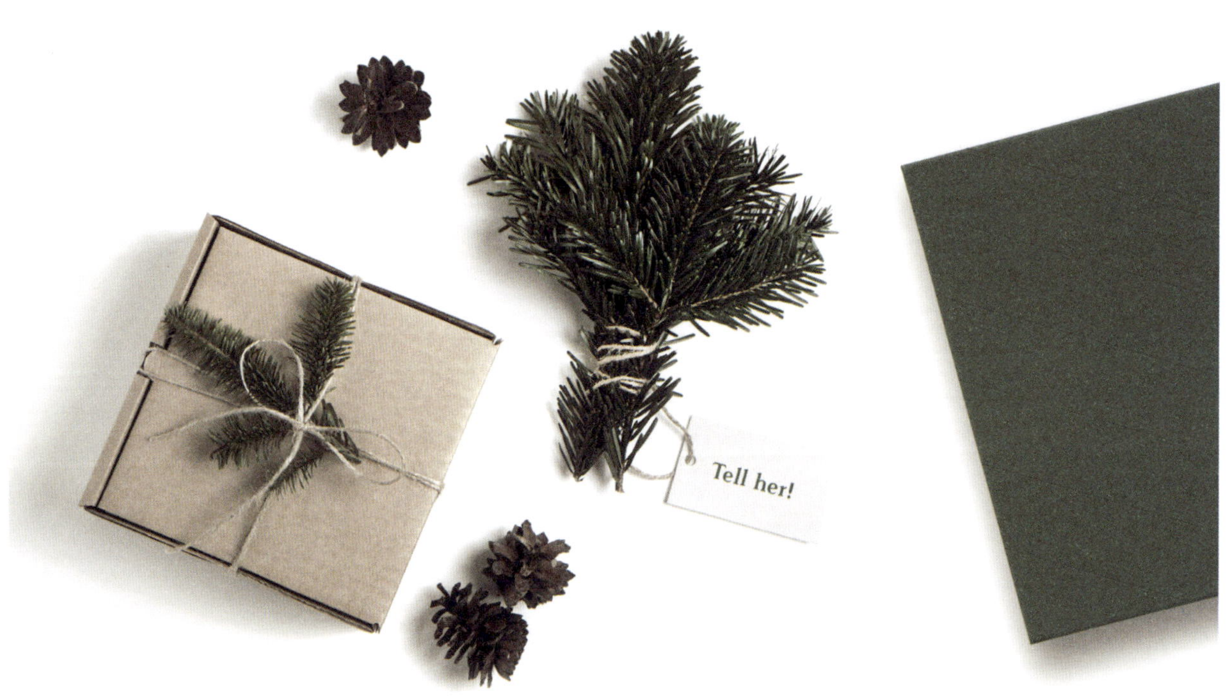
Tell her!

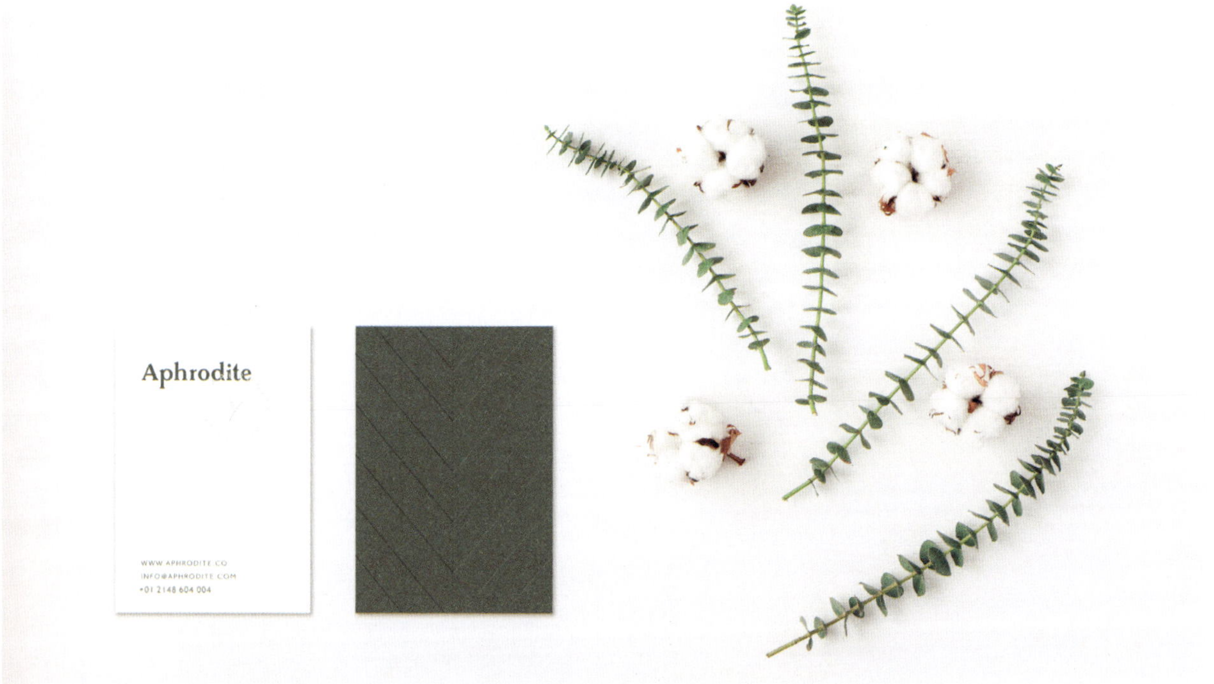

Aphrodite
WWW.APHRODITE.CO
INFO@APHRODITE.COM
+01 2148 604 004

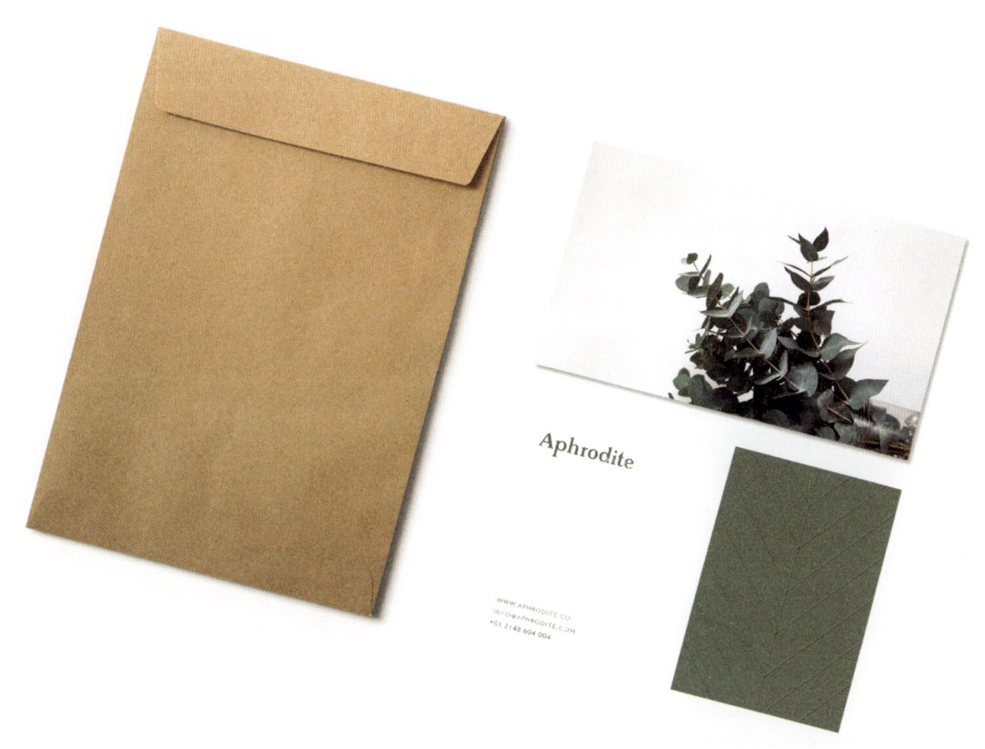
Aphrodite
WWW.APHRODITE.CO
INFO@APHRODITE.COM
+01 2148 604 004

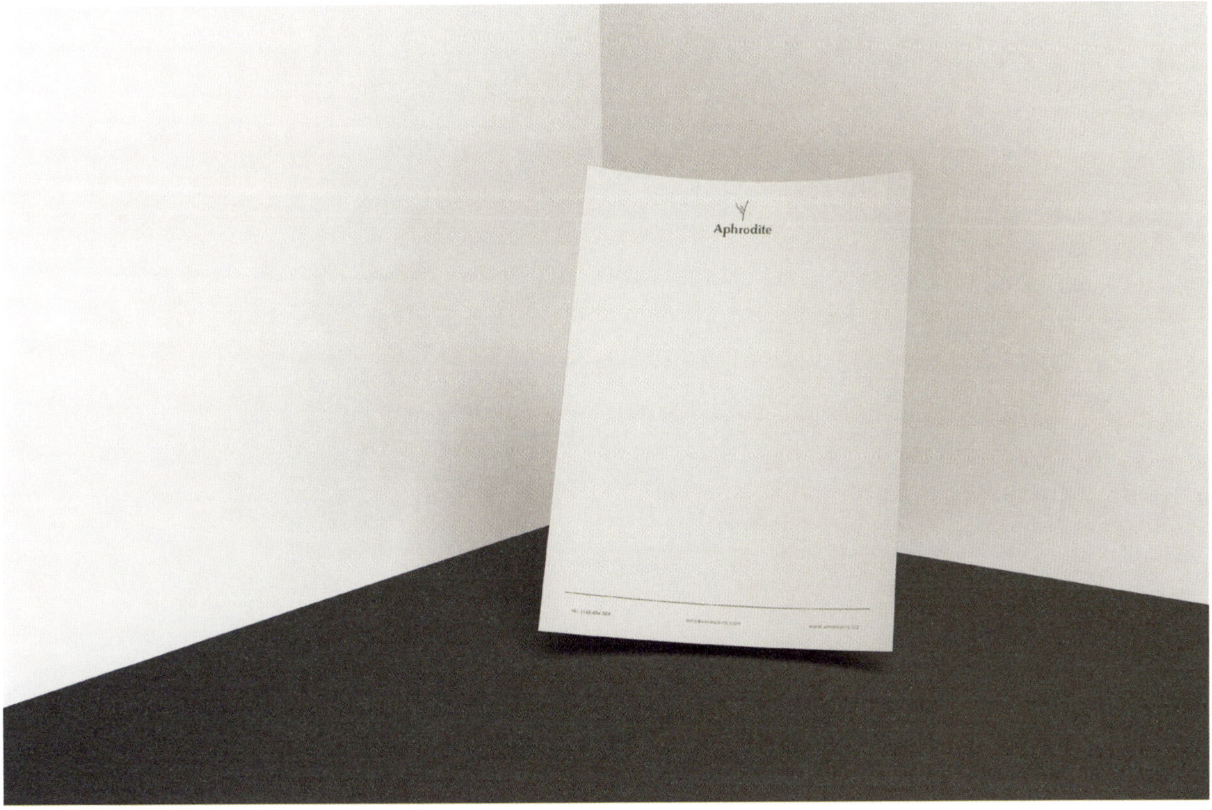

DIGITAL RELEASE
SESSION (MIXTAPE)
D-Ribeiro—
No. 39
Specs
Hour 0
Minute 58
Second 52
Release
November
20th
Midlight.nl
Copyright #3276

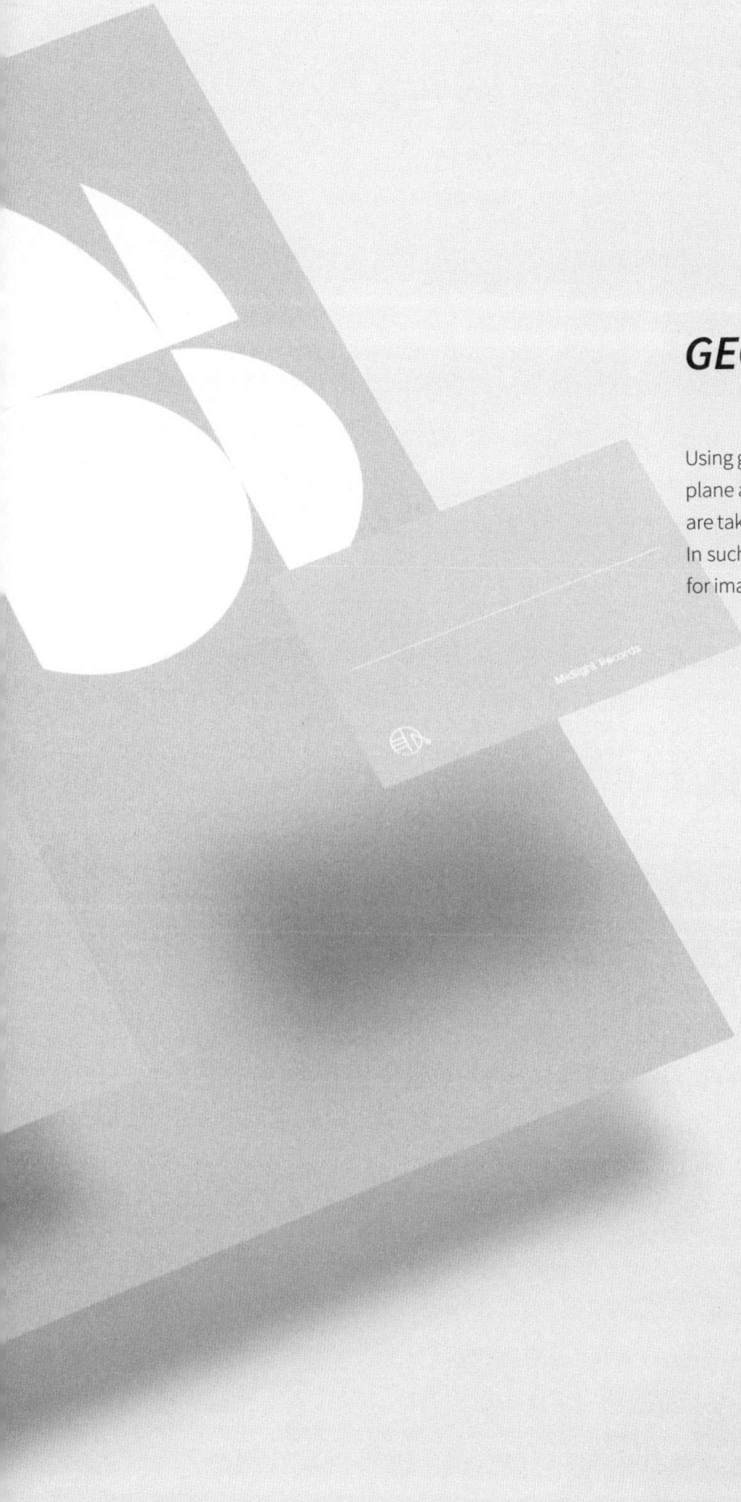

GEOMETRIZATION

Using geometric shapes or those derived from dot, line and plane as design elements, the superfluous embellishments are taken away and the most essential form is retained. In such a way of abstracting the design image, more space for imagination is possible.

image © Studio Naam

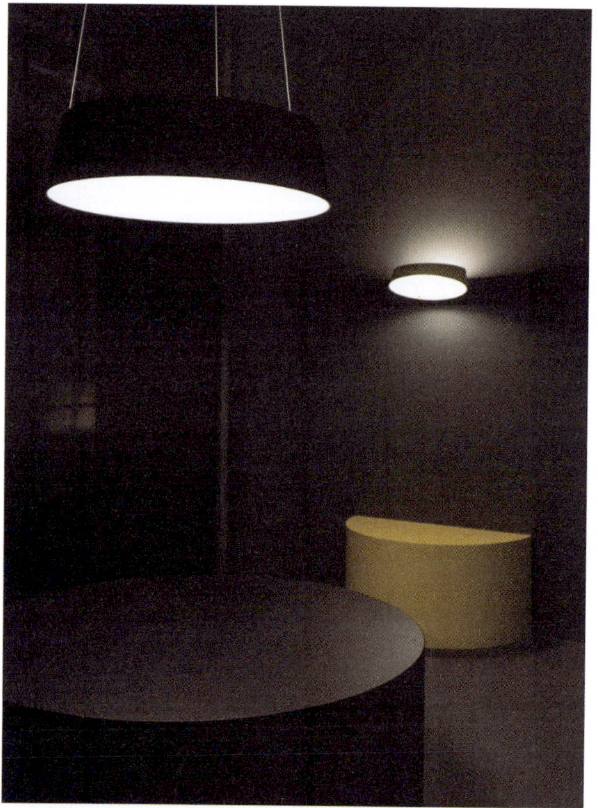

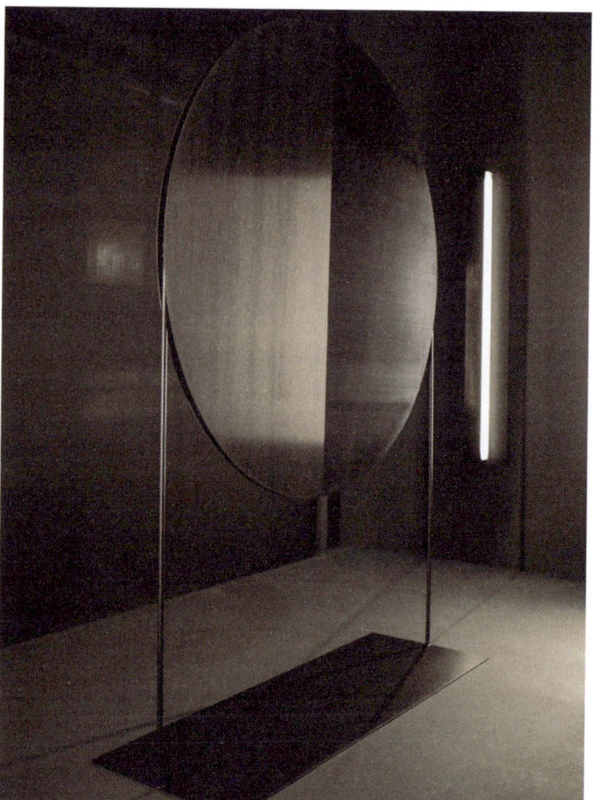

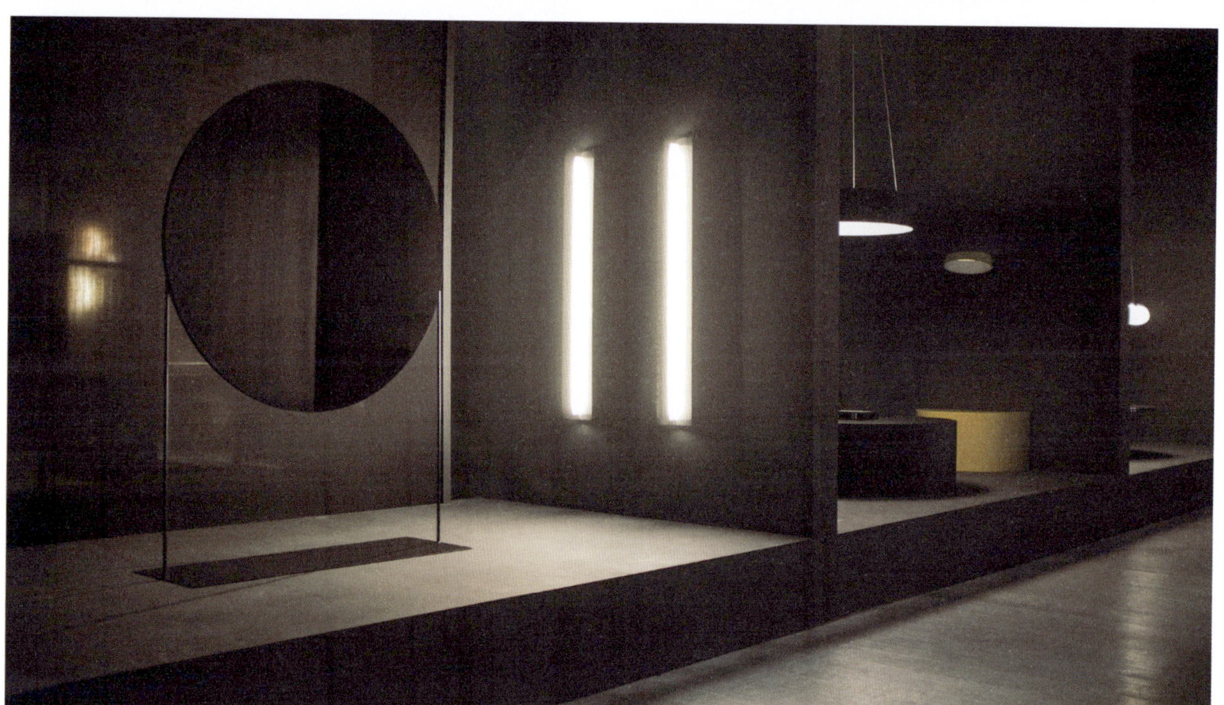

- *Studio:* ***makethatstudio***
- *Designer:* ***Dea Sgarbossa, Nicola Russo***

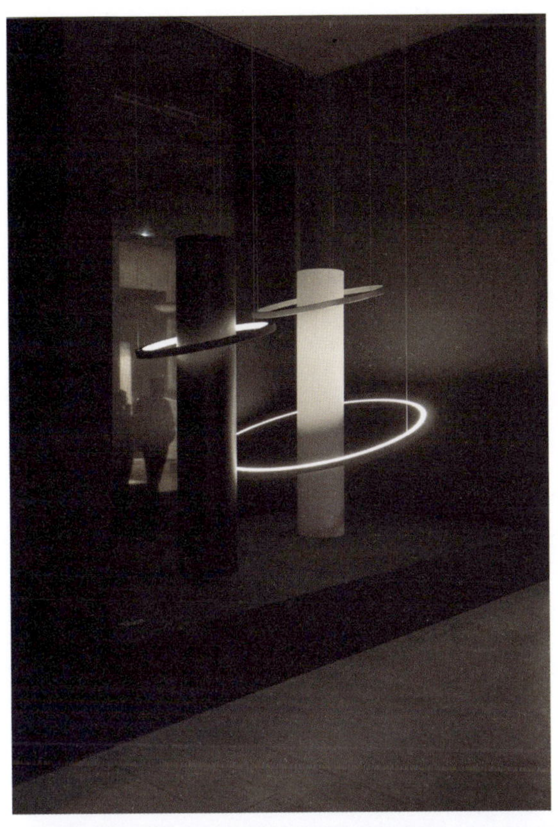

The studio has curated the entire concept and the visual communication project for Linea Light Group during Euroluce 2017. The lighting installation has been imagined as a museum where six settings tell the brand products and their features:

- The impalpable becomes matter.
- Pure and static forms, sturdy overtime.
- Lively and dynamic lights, that breathe and project themselves into the future.

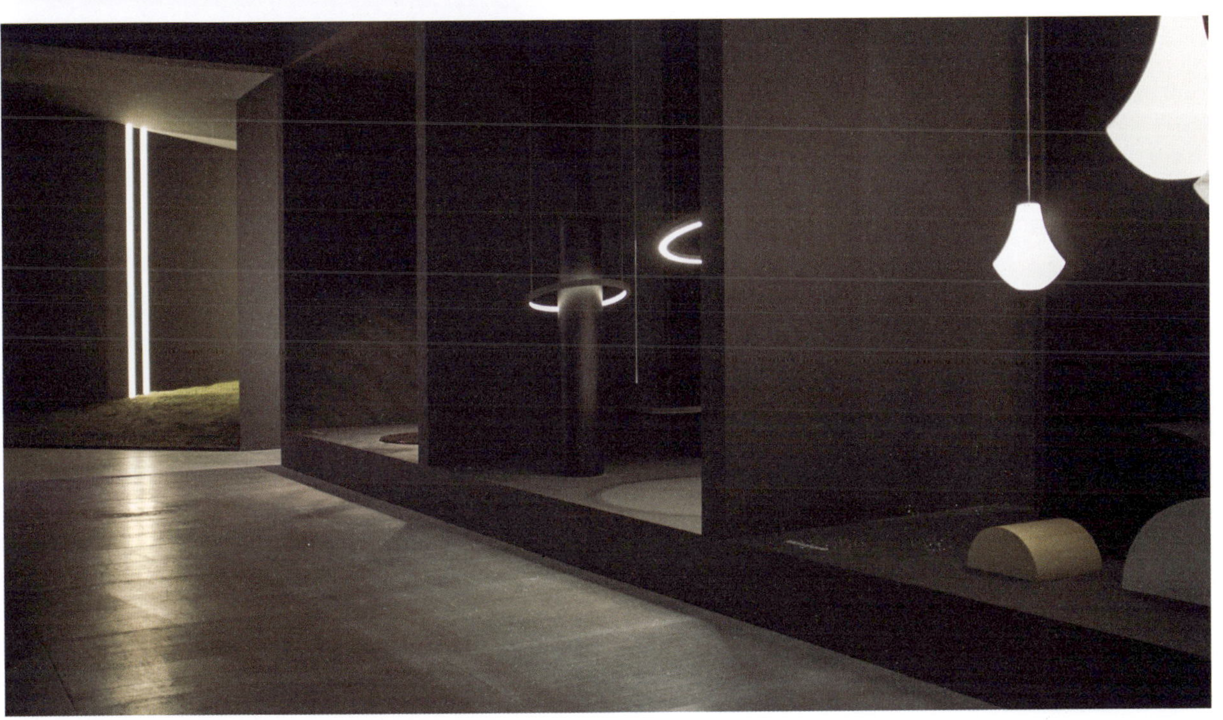

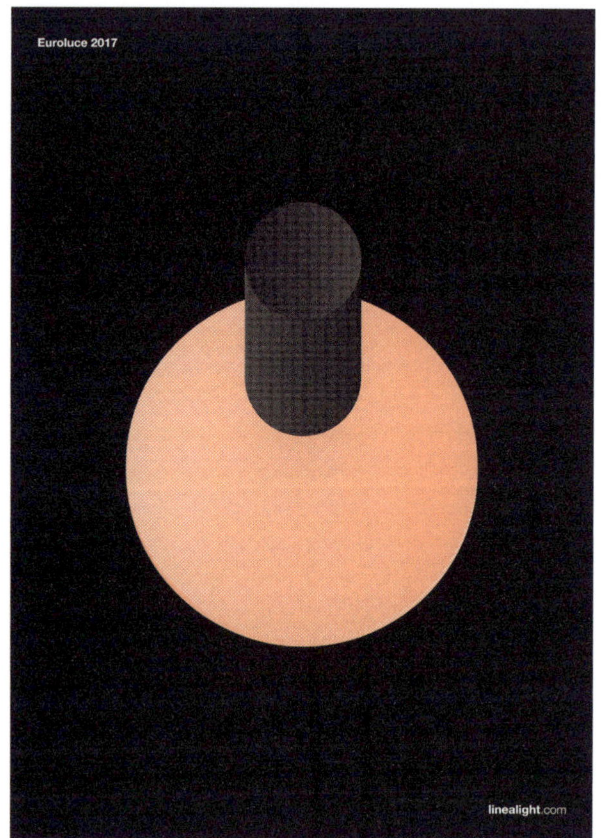
Euroluce 2017
linealight.com

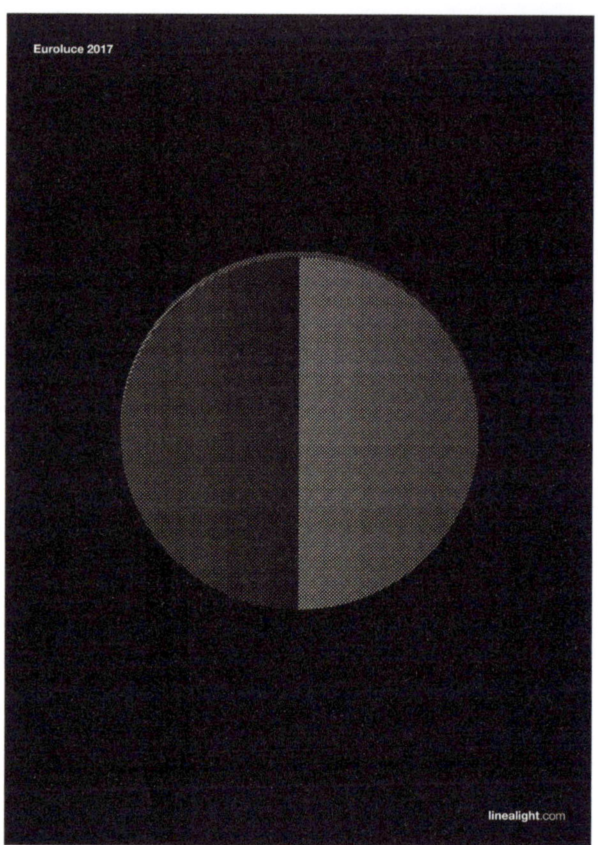
Euroluce 2017
linealight.com

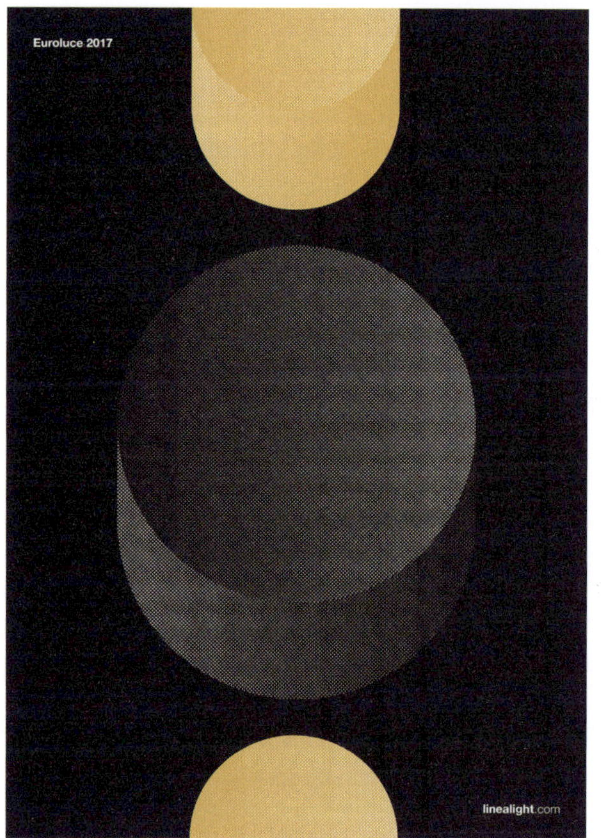
Euroluce 2017
linealight.com

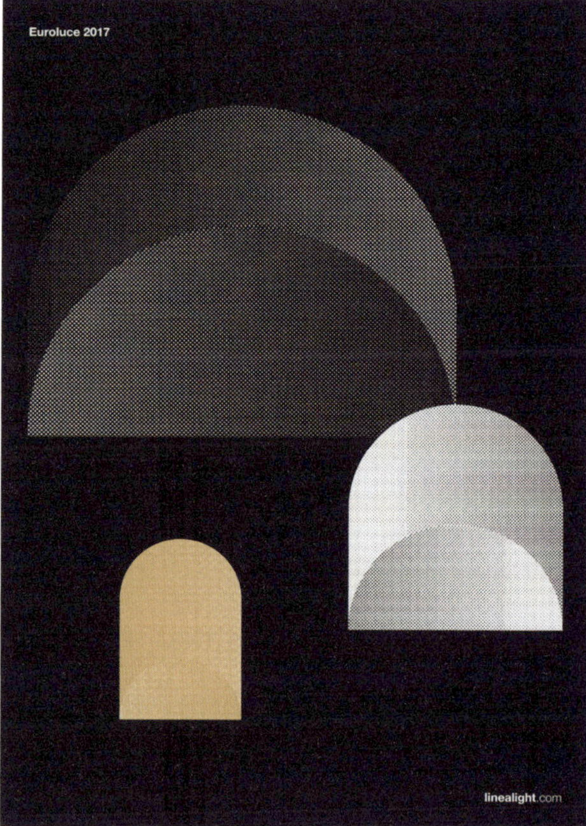
Euroluce 2017
linealight.com

Interview

- As a kind of visual experience, what do you think about the "voidness" in graphic design?

- We believe that voidness is an essential element in graphic design because it serves to focus on subjects, words, and images. It also serves to give order and hierarchy. Voidness is the distance between one object and another, and is the matter that weighs as much as other contents to create visual harmony. It has the same weight as words or any other elements.

- What are your common approaches to produce a VOID visual effect?

- To produce the void, we usually start with a deep synthesis process, which begins with locating the most important elements in a hierarchical system, erasing what is superfluous to us.

In the case of graphic design, we leave only the basic elements that deeply represent the concept we are designing. In set design, instead, we can choose to subtract the props or we can work on those elements, shaping their appearance to produce, for example, pure shapes, as in the case of Euroluce project for Linea Light Group.

In all cases, void remains a very important and fundamental element in our design toolkit.

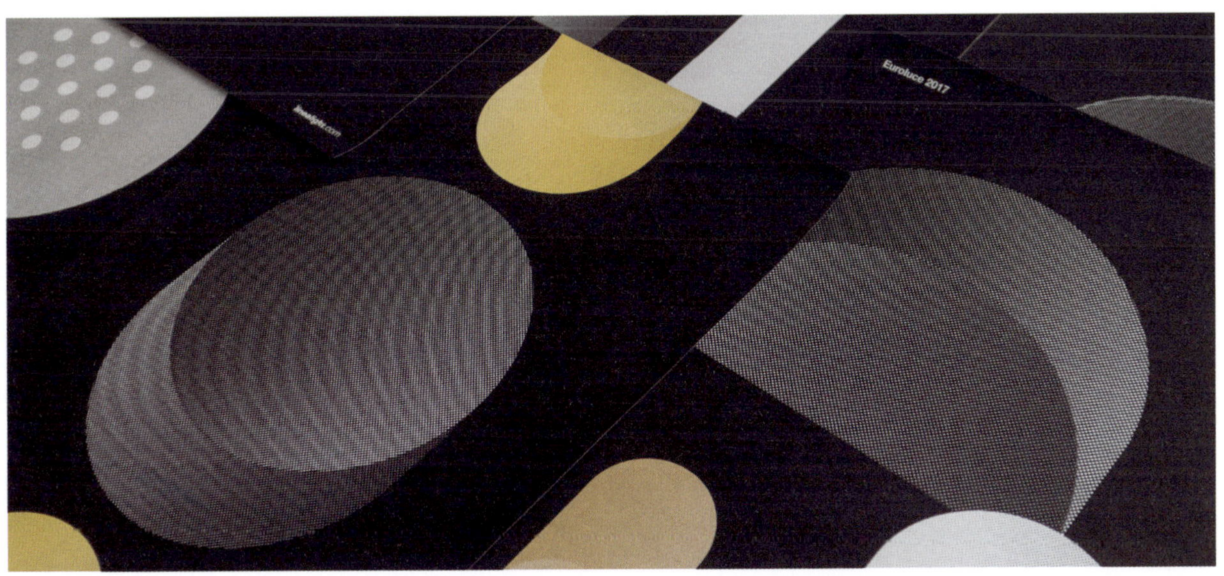

MIDLIGHT

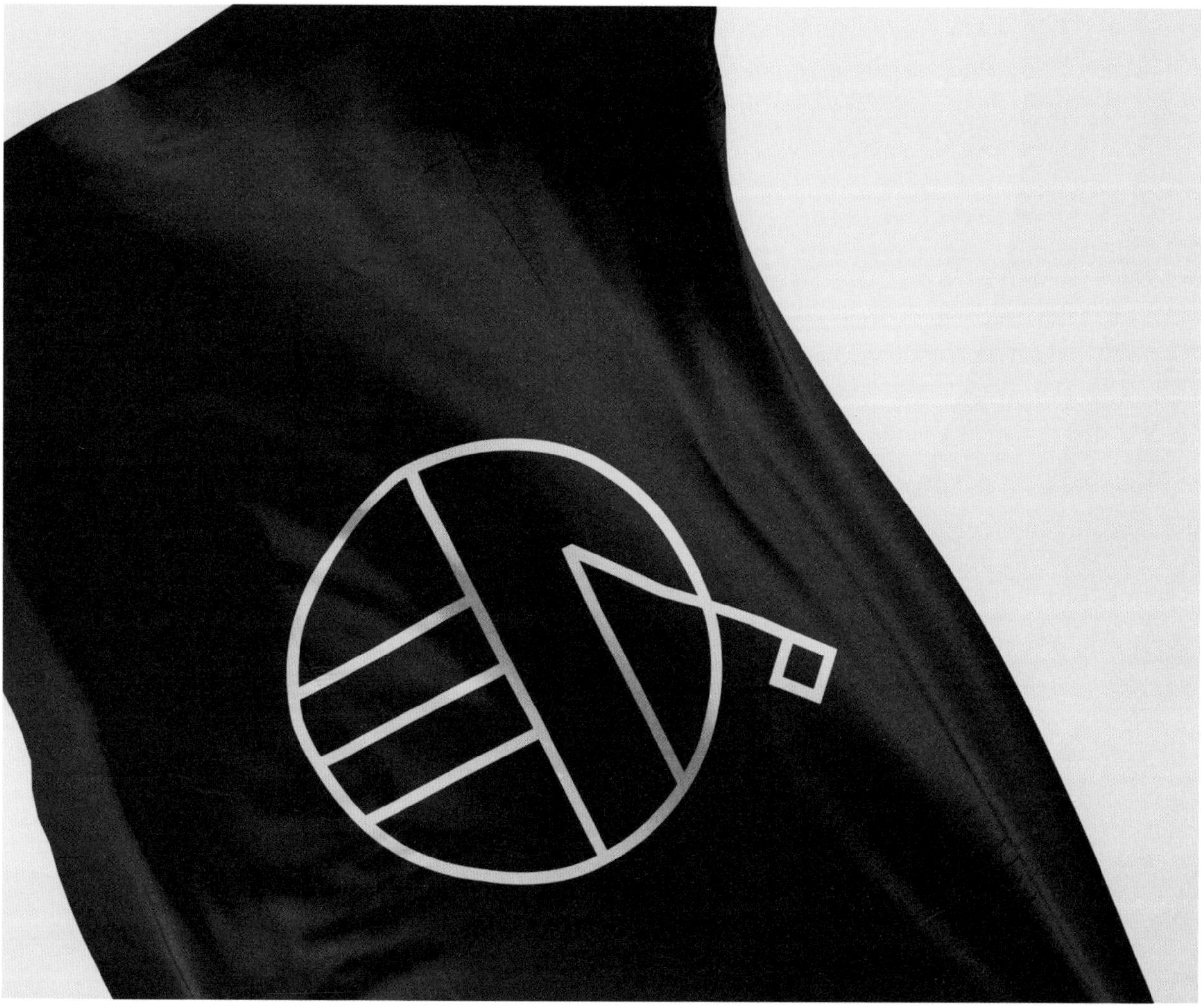

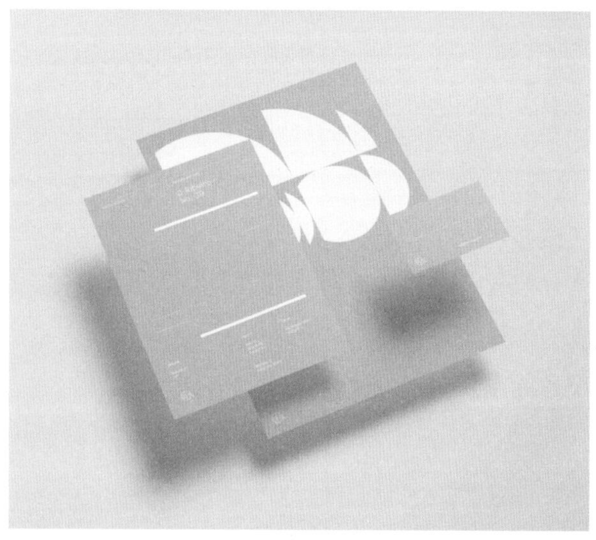

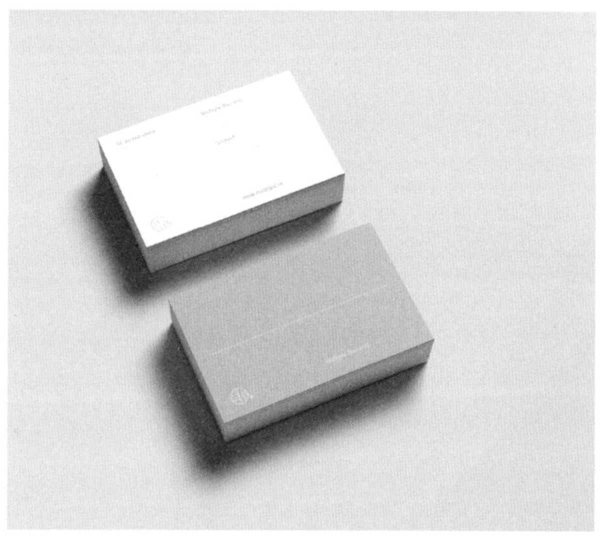

- *Studio:* **Studio Naam**

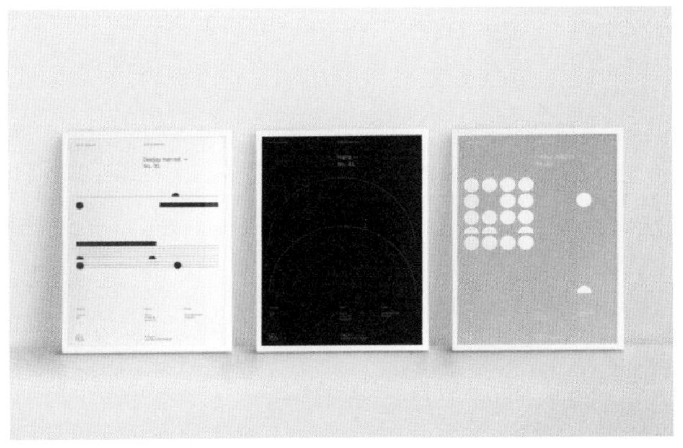

Midlight Records is a Dutch label and platform that releases hot tracks, hosts smooth radio shows, dandy events, and curates mesmerizing mixtapes. Studio Naam has been working with Midlight since the very beginning with outspoken, methodic, clear and effective solutions to arrive at a balance between usability, beauty and innovation.

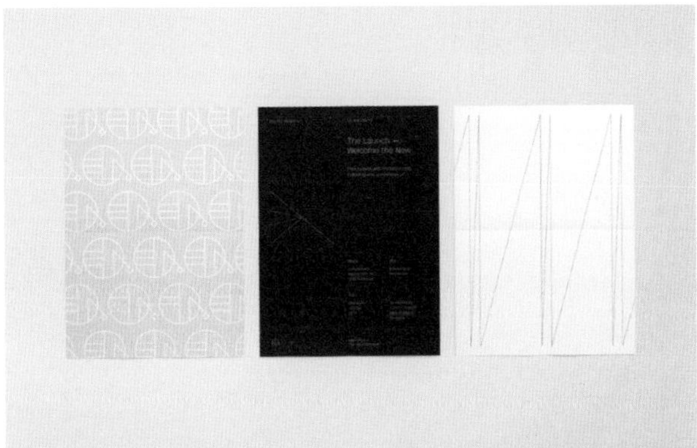

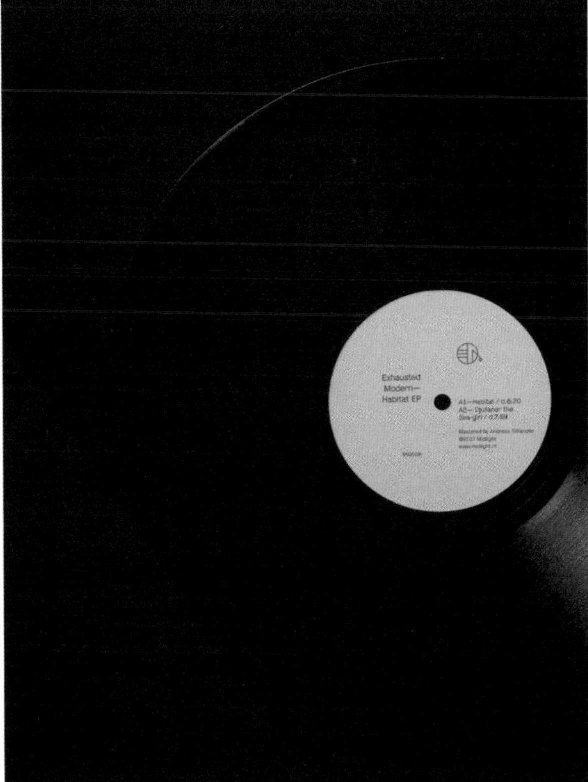

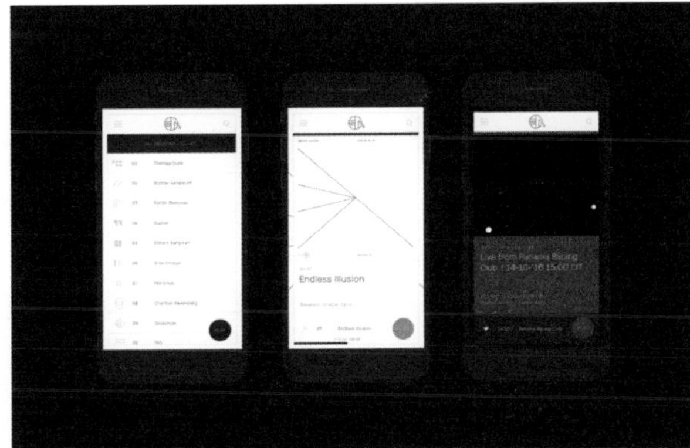

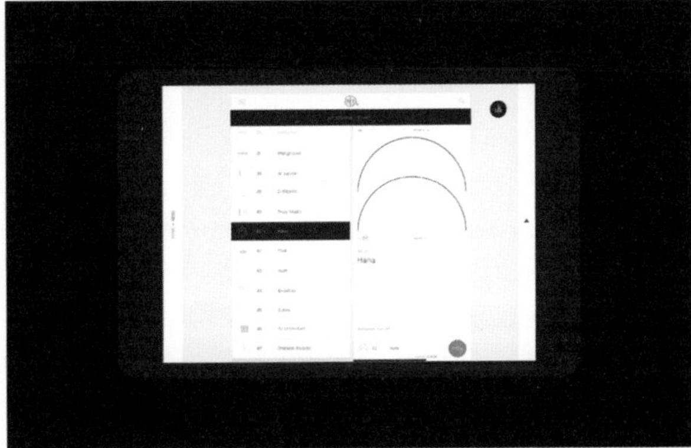

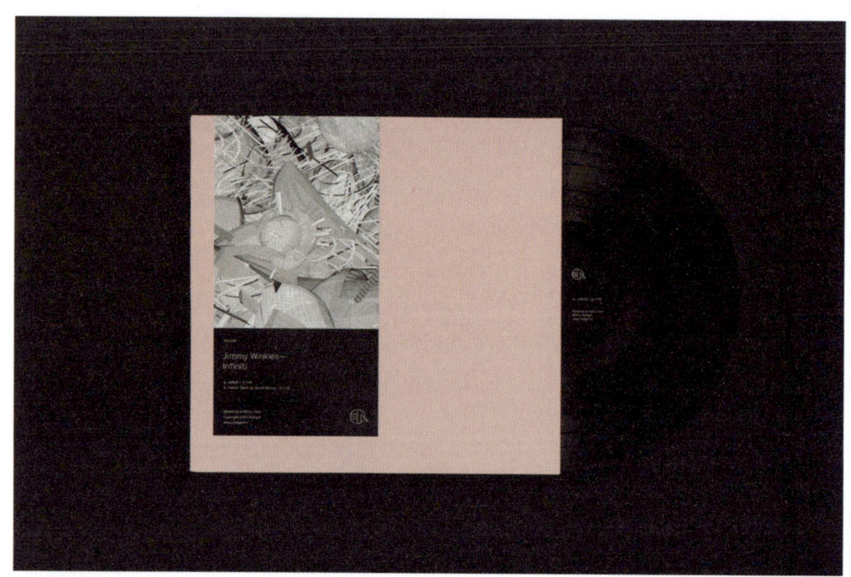
Jimmy Winkles —
Infiniti

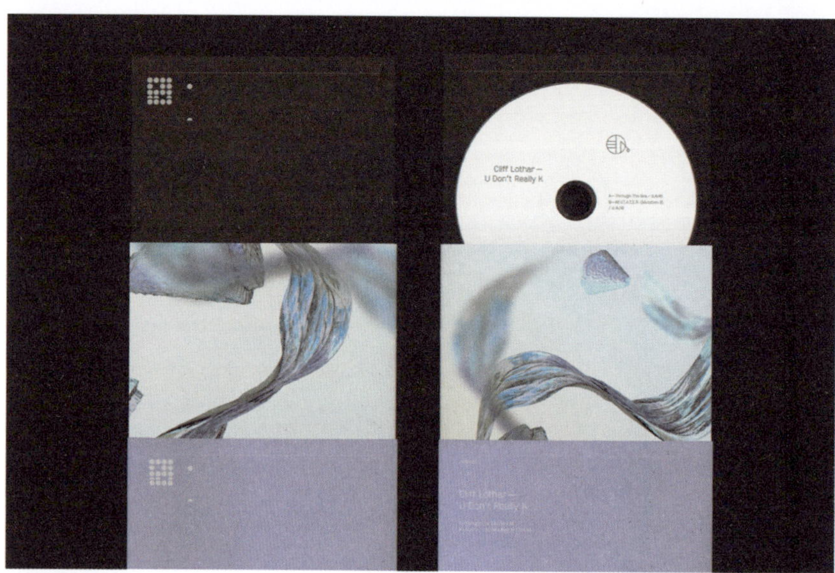
Cliff Lothar —
U Don't Really K

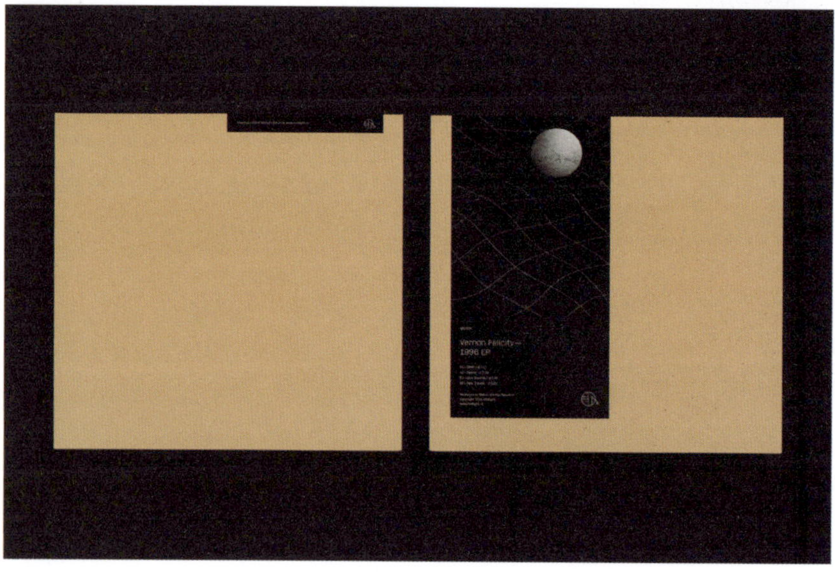
Vernon Felicity —
1998 EP

Interview

- As a kind of visual experience, what do you think about the "voidness" in graphic design?

- Using space and objects in a minimal, thoughtful way creates room for interpretation and rest for the viewers. It provides tension and at the same time a feeling of control and focus in the things we design. It is one of the most important visual ingredients we use in our work.

Much like using silence when telling a story to create tension, using void spaces in visual design creates the same effect. It puts users on the edge of their seat and draws their eyes, setting their imaginations free to explore and discover what lies beyond.

- What are your common approaches to produce a VOID visual effect?

- We approach all of our projects with a "less is more" attitude, answering complex questions with understandable, simple solutions. All of this sounds a lot easier than it is. We found that simple design solutions are often the hardest to find, since the details are no longer just details. Every object or solution within the design is there for a reason, whether it be functional, emotional or both.

When we start a project we always design more. Too much, actually. This process is essential for us to decide which elements are really necessary to tell an effective story. From there on we start improving the hierarchy, grid-system, usability and graphical elements into one cohesive design solution.

One of the most important things that the "minimal" design philosophy has taught us is a great respect for the process of thoughtful decision-making.

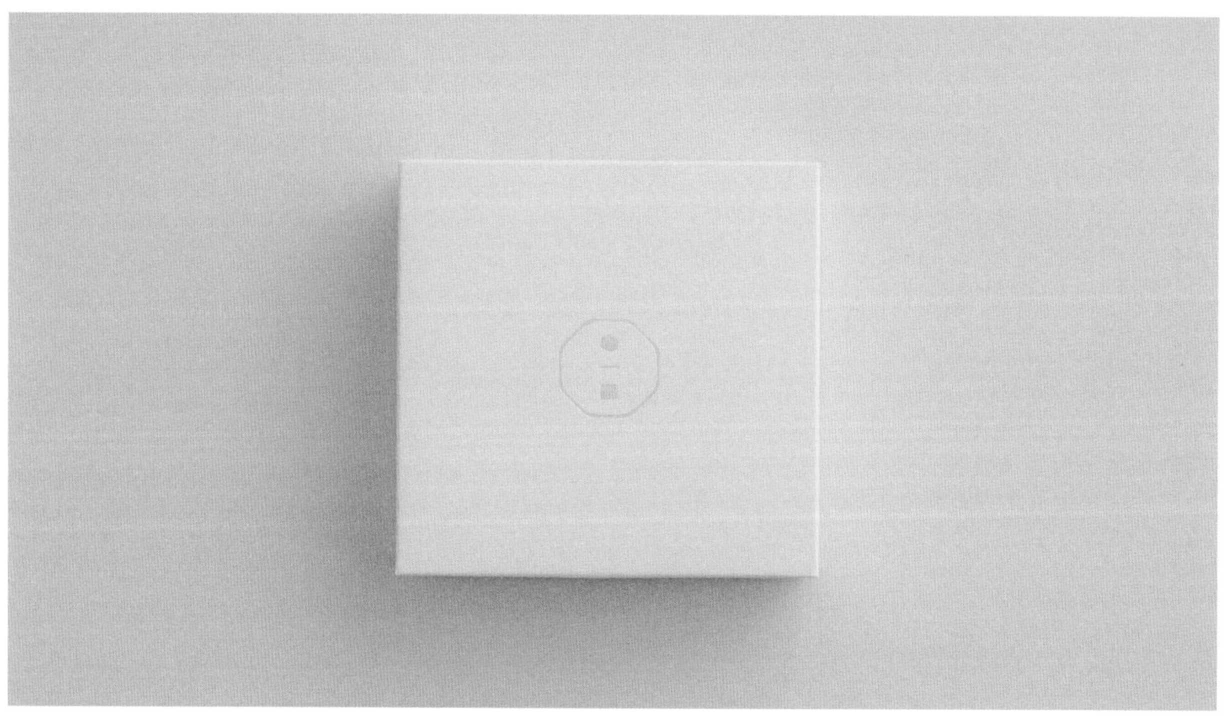

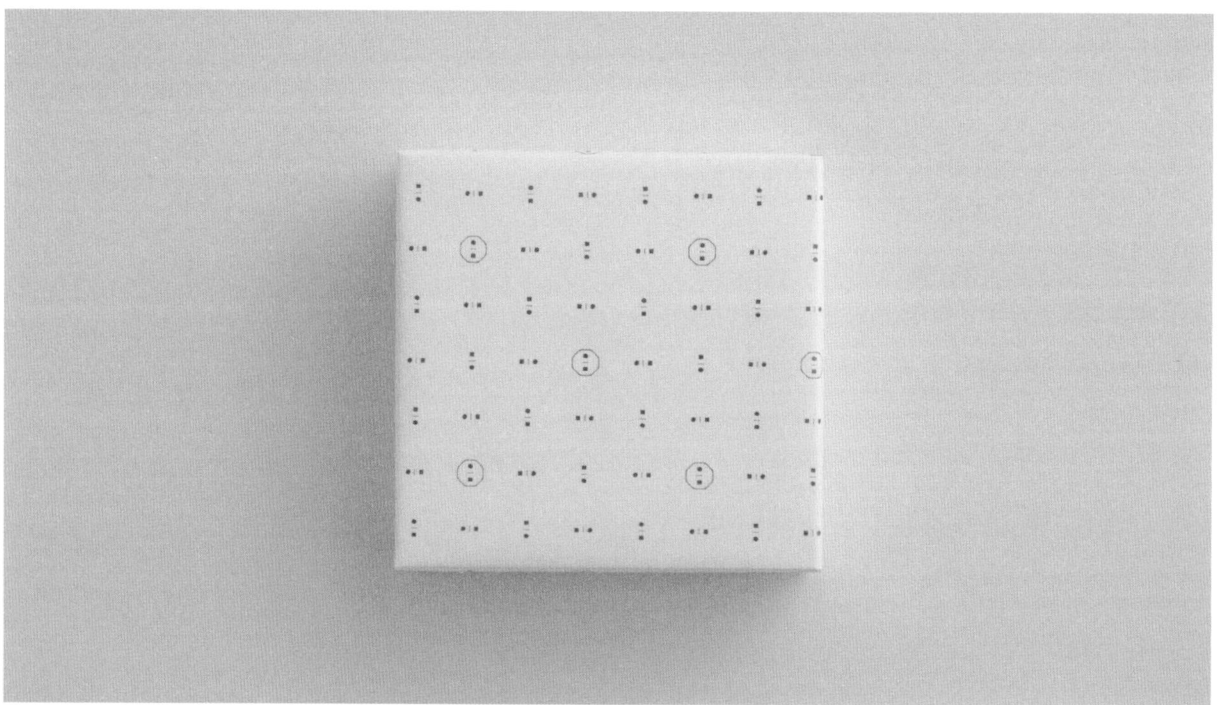

Tsurutama is a new brand of Tsurunotamago Honpo, a time-honored Japanese shop which created the special Japanese marshmallow confectionery about 120 years ago by enveloping Anko (traditional Japanese red bean paste) with marshmallow from Western culture. This innovative Japanese sweet, with a round shape like eggs and a fluffy texture, became a confectionery representative of Okayama. Nuttuo Inc. was in charge of not only establishing the new brand and product development, but also handling the web design, package design and interior design.

Tsurutama Branding

studio: **nottuo Inc.**
designer: **Kouhei Suzuki**

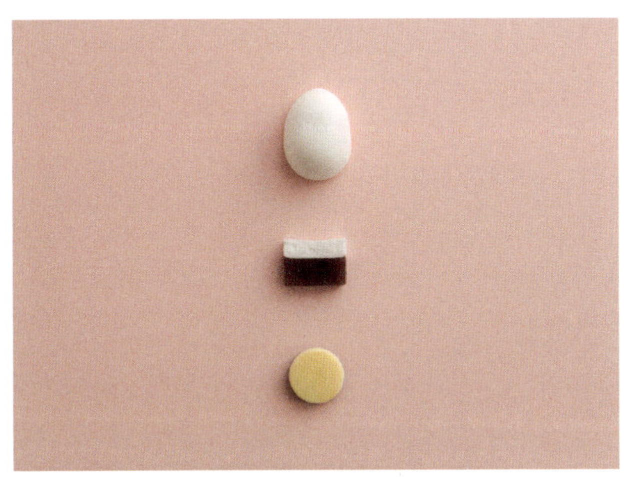

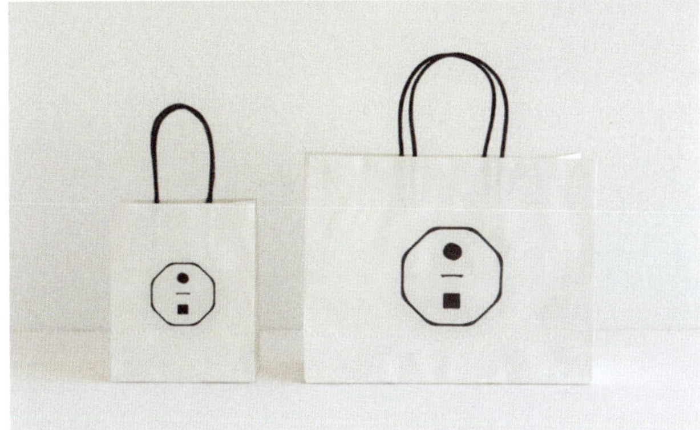

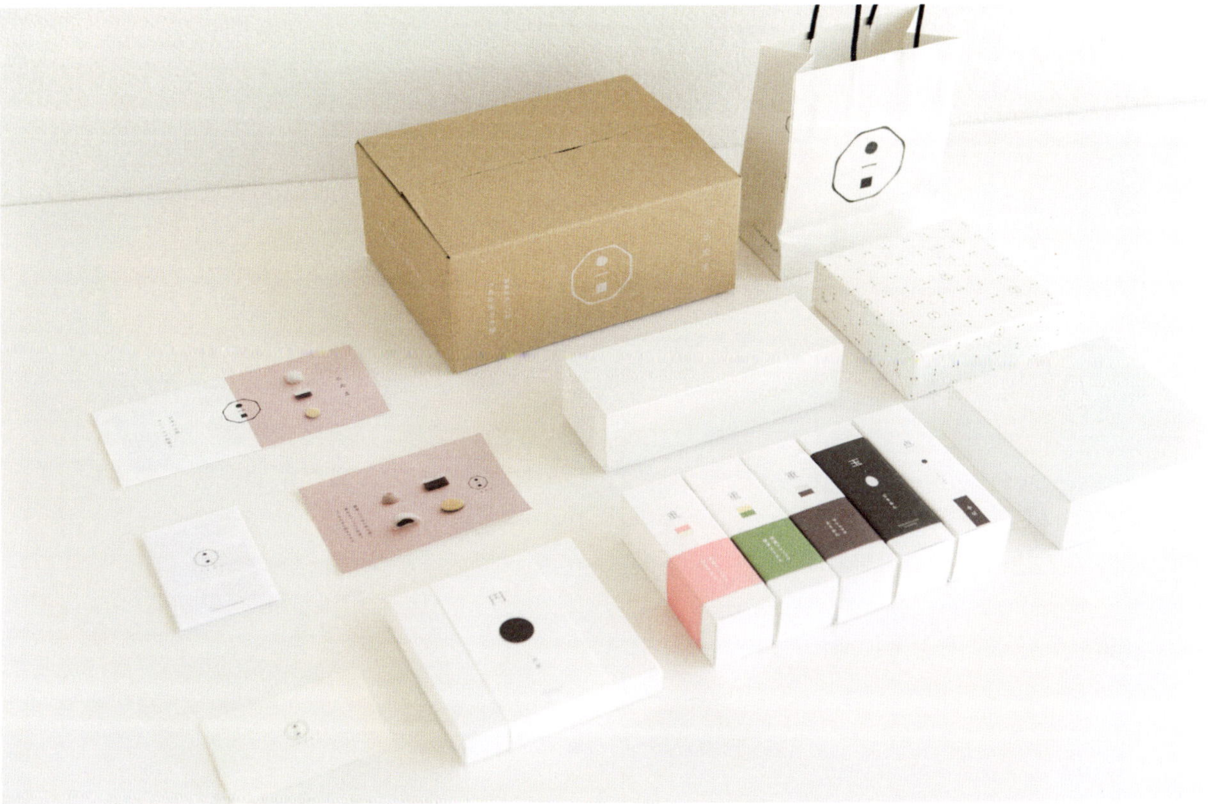

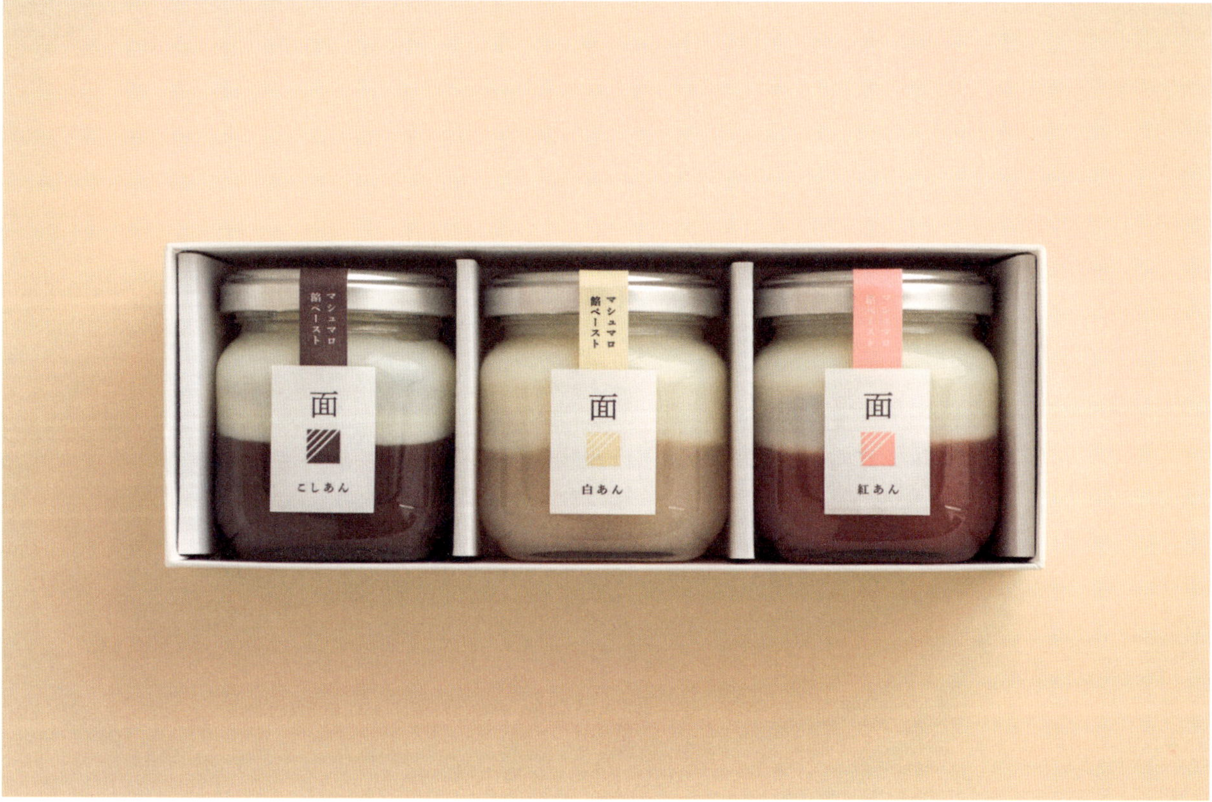

マシュマロ
餡ペースト
面
こしあん

マシュマロ
餡ペースト
面
白あん

面
紅あん

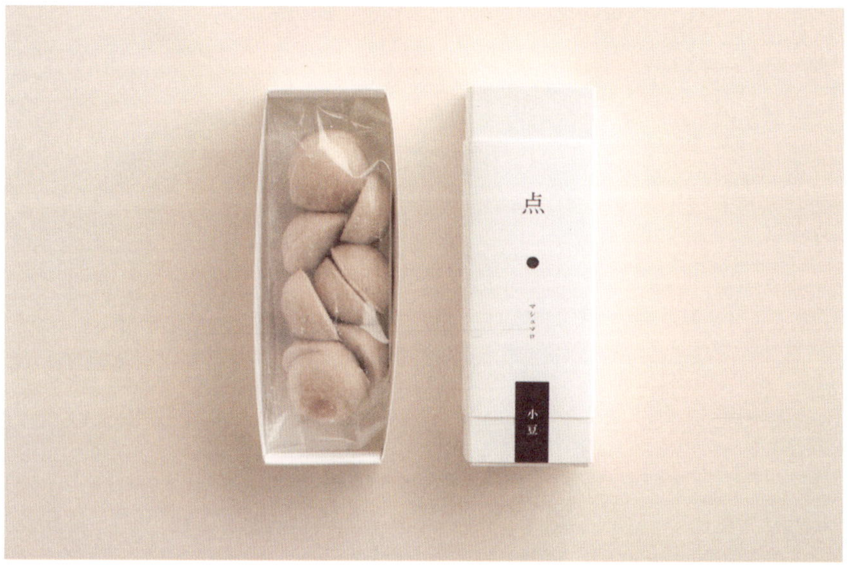

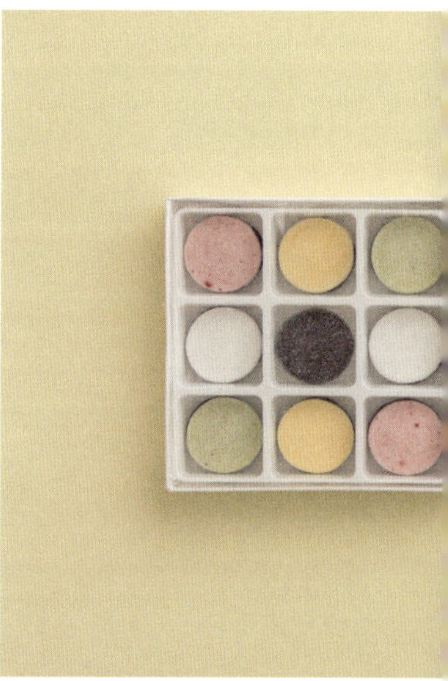

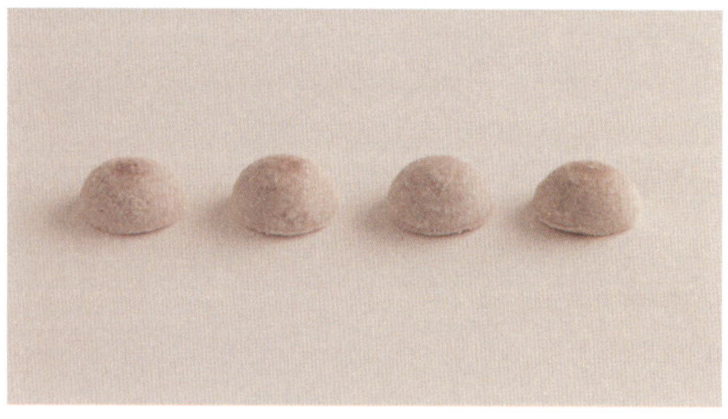

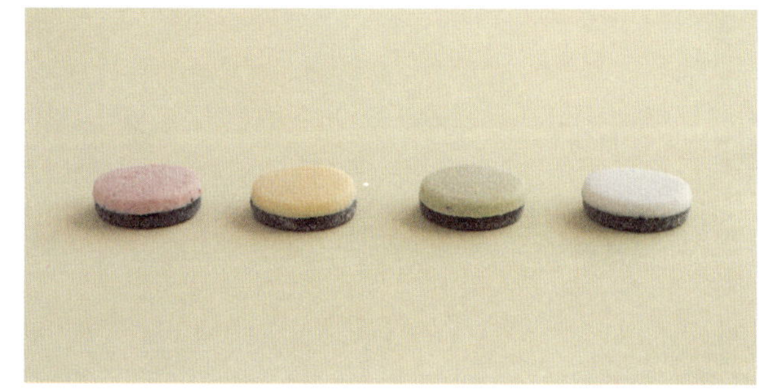

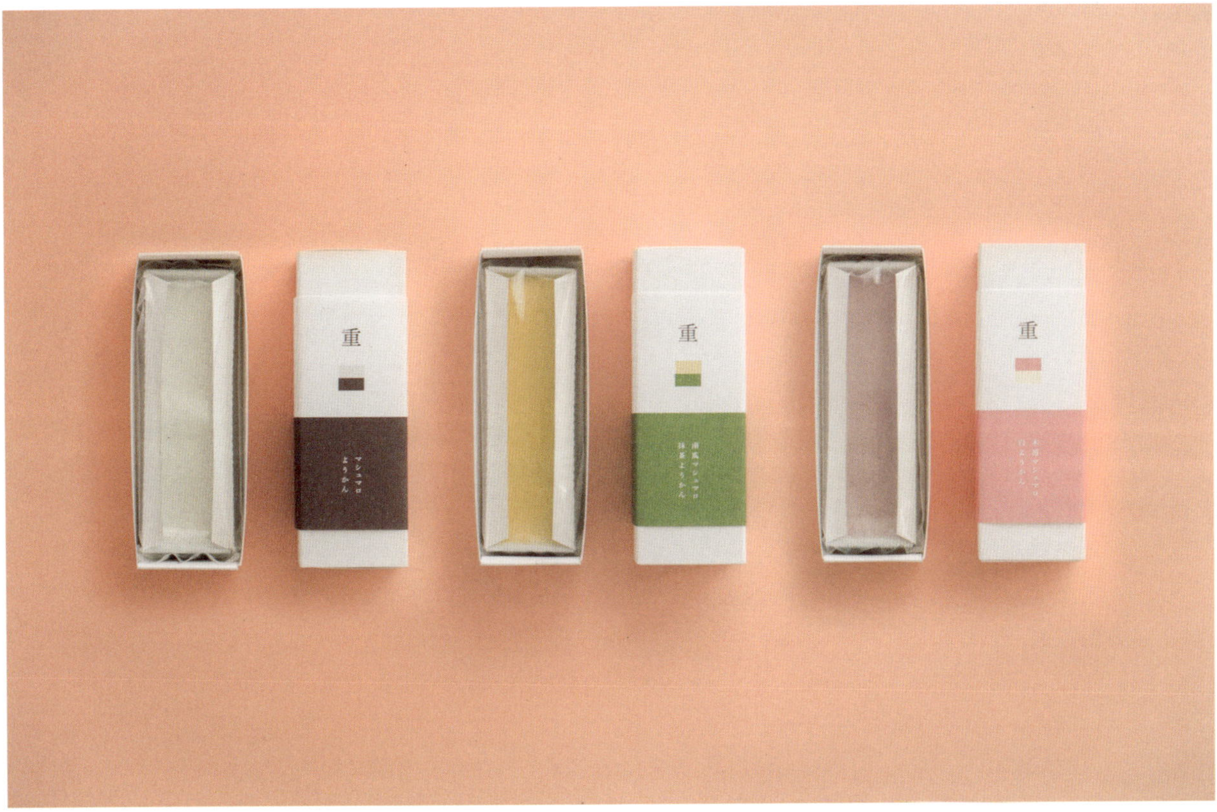

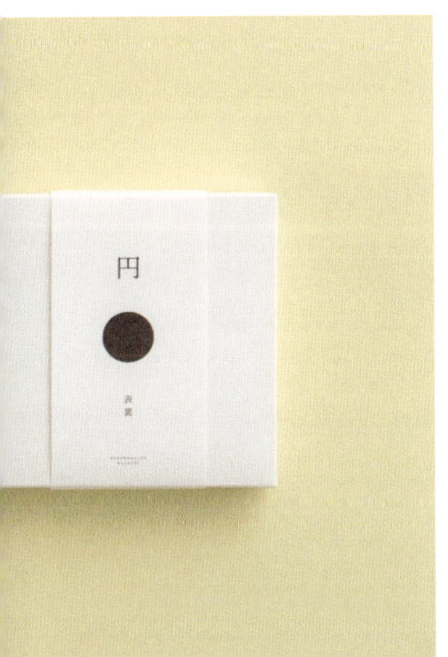
円

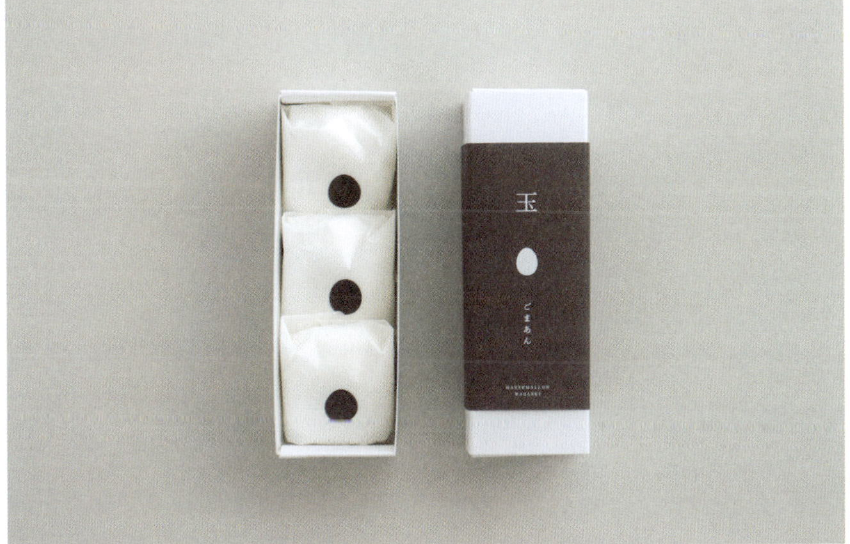
玉
ごまあん

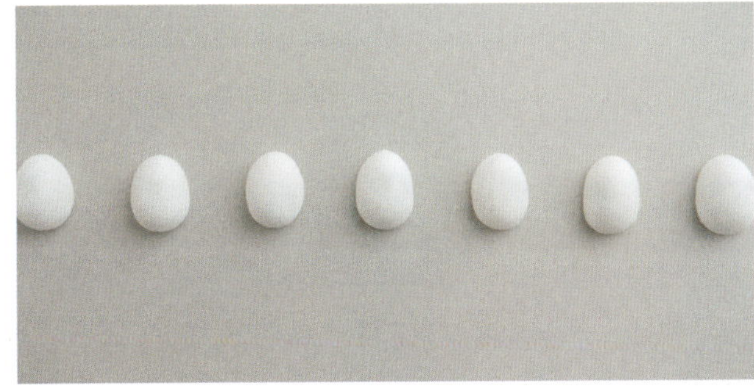

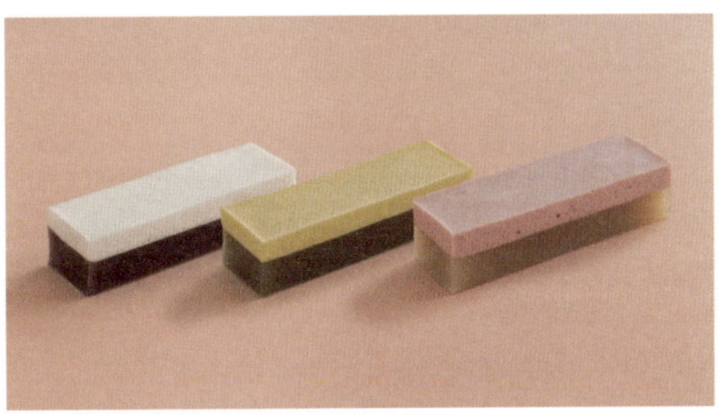

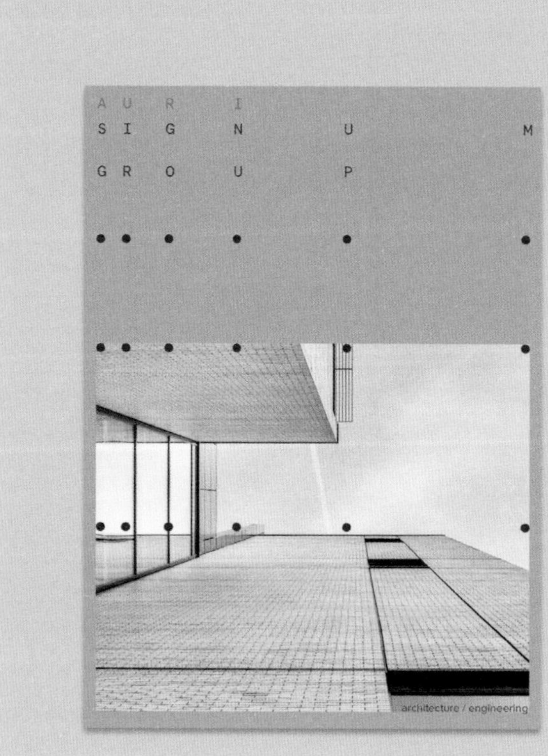

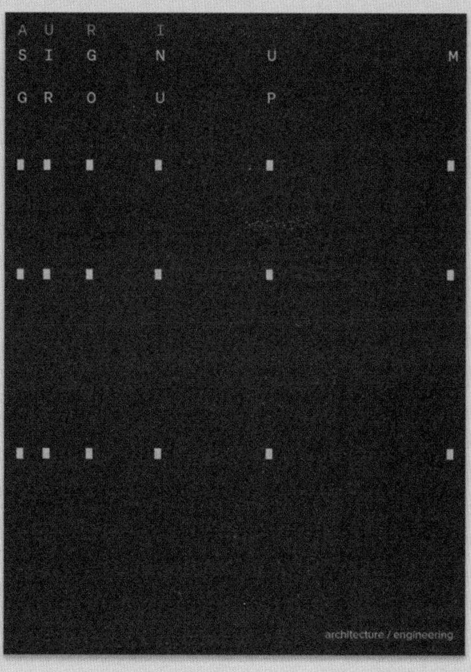

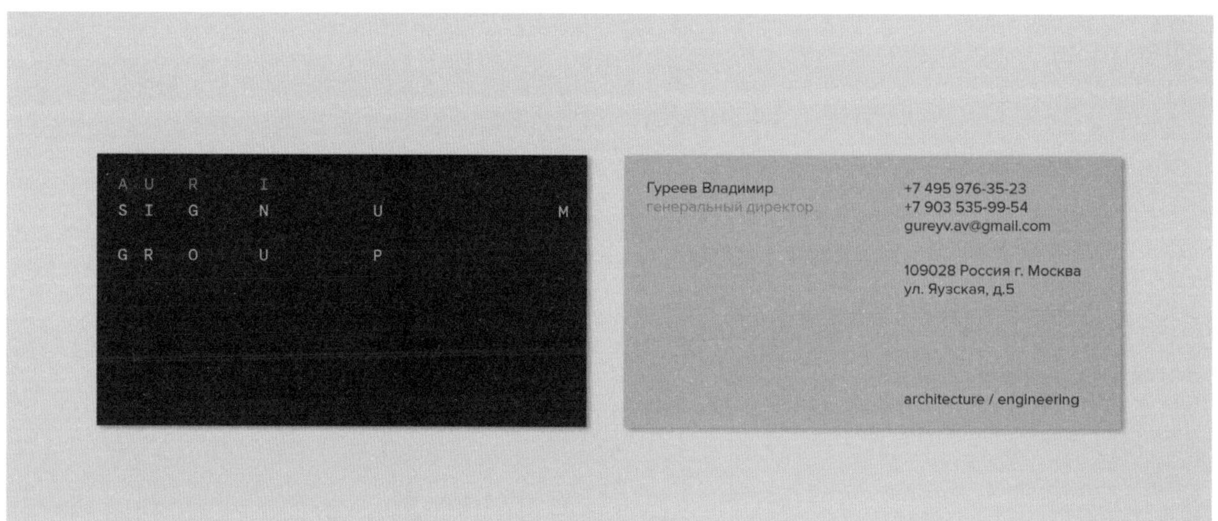

Auri Signum means "golden standard" in Latin, signifying the supreme quality, which, in the context of architecture, refers to golden ratio. In the branding for the architectural studio Auri Signum Group, both the horizontal and vertical distances between letters and words are designed in strict accordance with the proportions of the golden ratio.

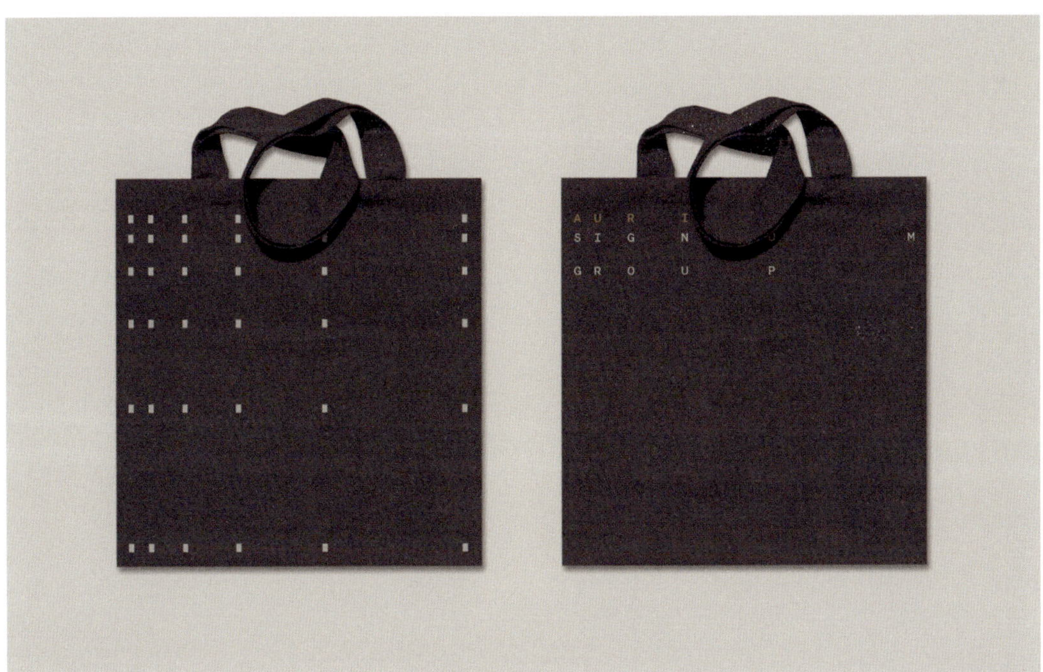

Auri Signum Group

studio: **omsky studio**
designer: **Oksana Paley, Alice Retunsky**

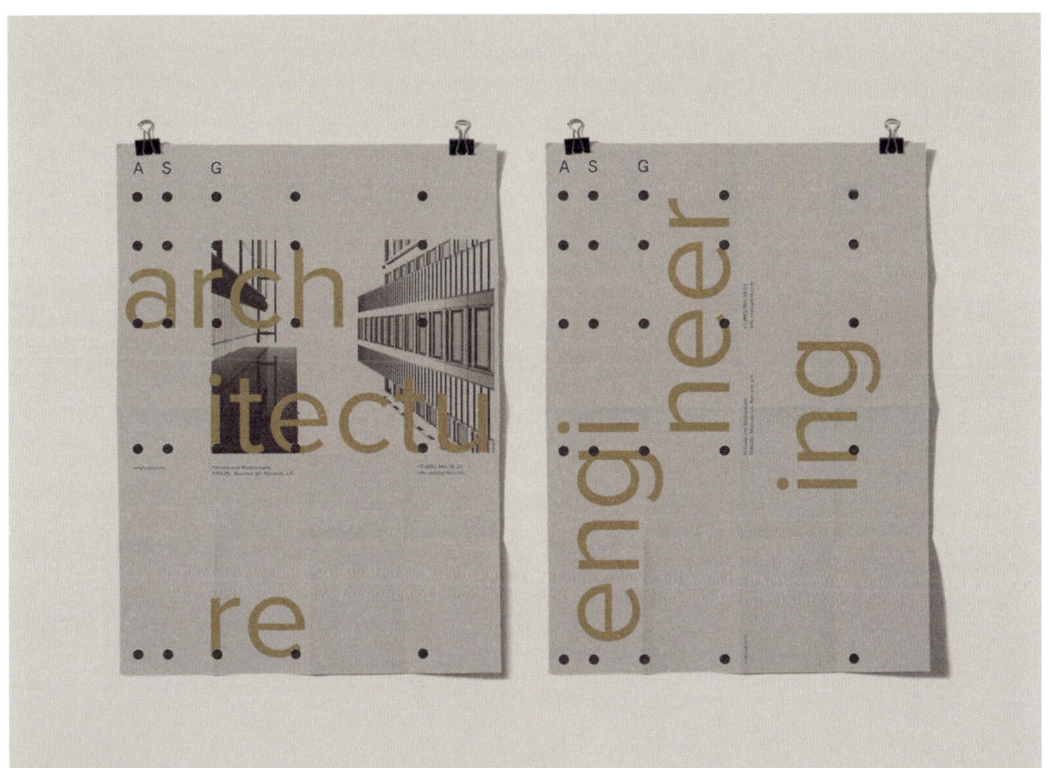

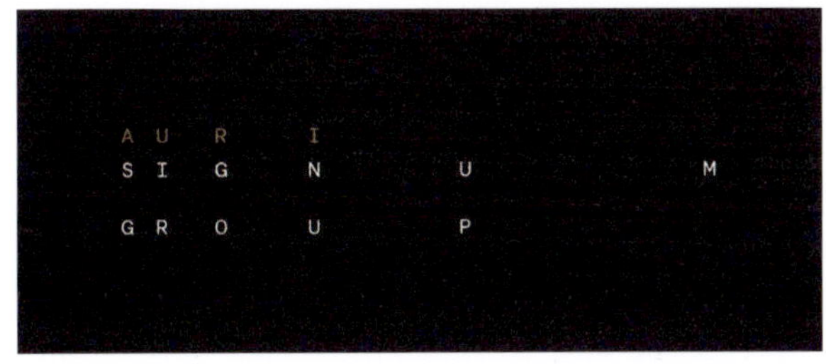

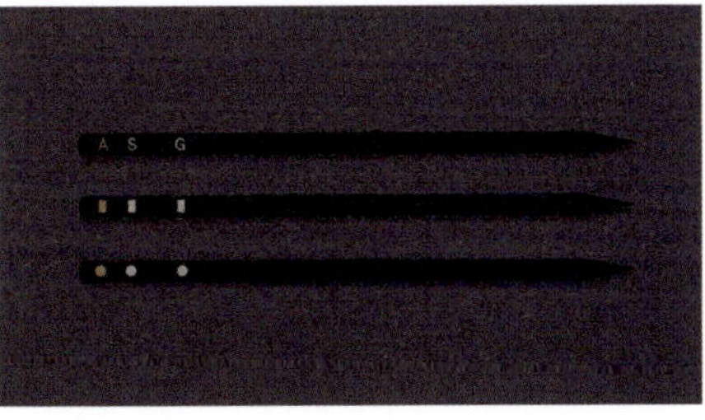

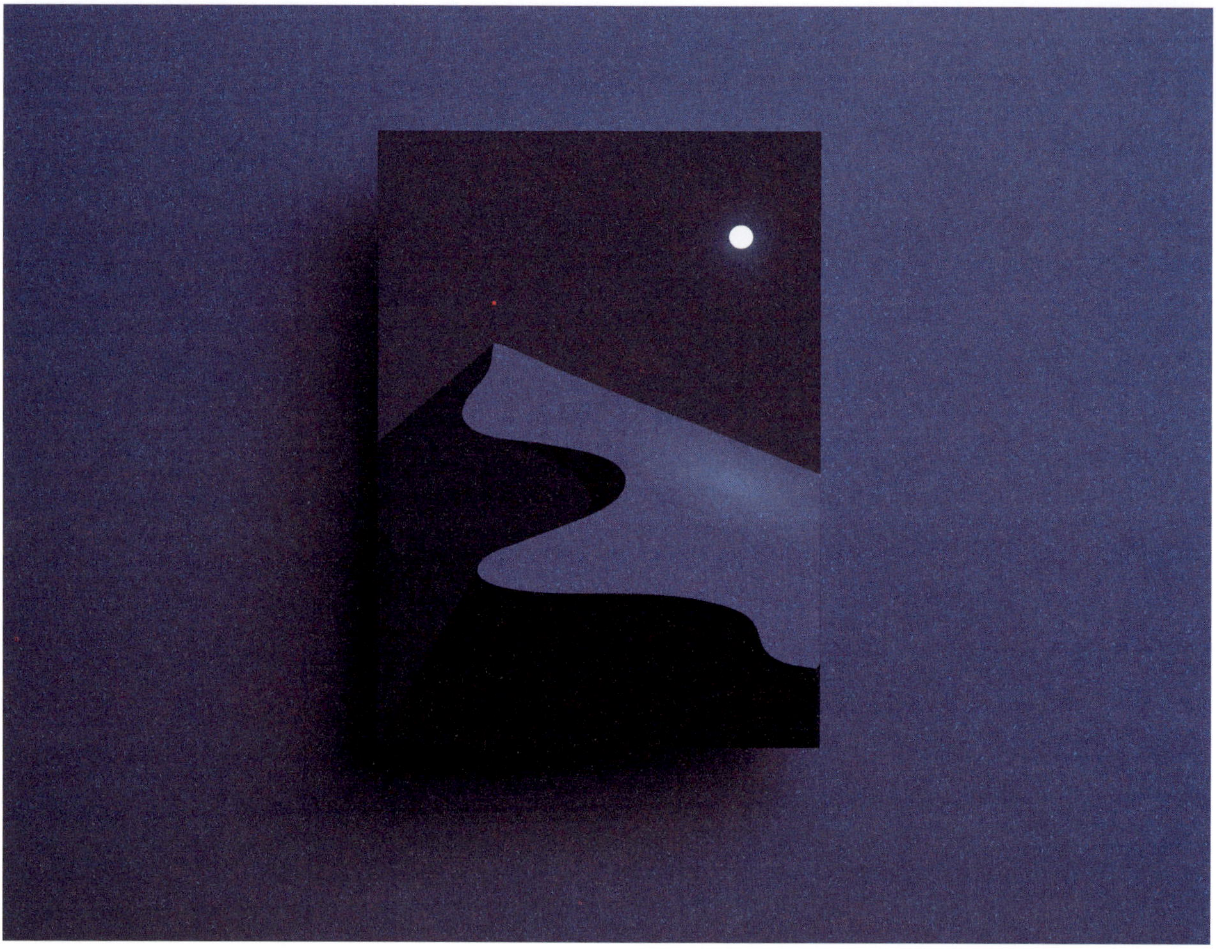

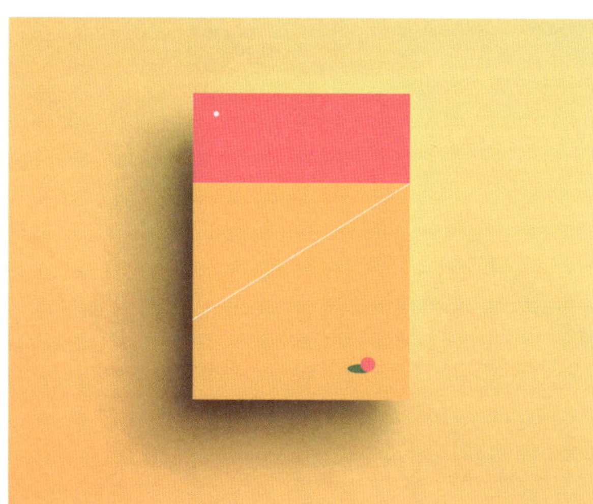

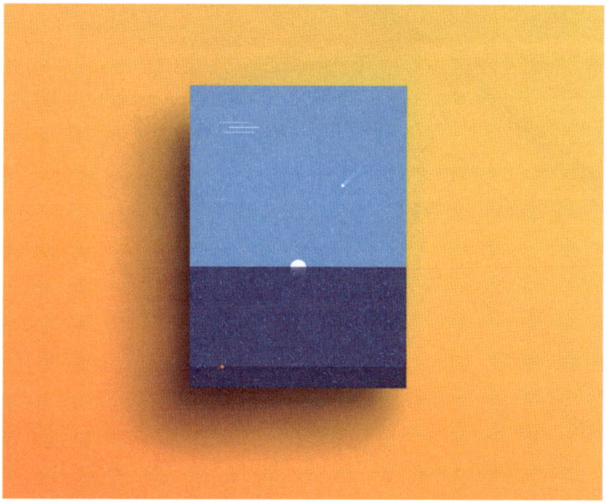

A Geometry A Day is a personal visual diary. The designer transformed everything that happens in her unique and unforgettable every day into graphic. The project was born in the Valentine's Day 2015, and continues every day since then. Her style and her works are simple and are inspired by humanity as well as nature and the city around us.

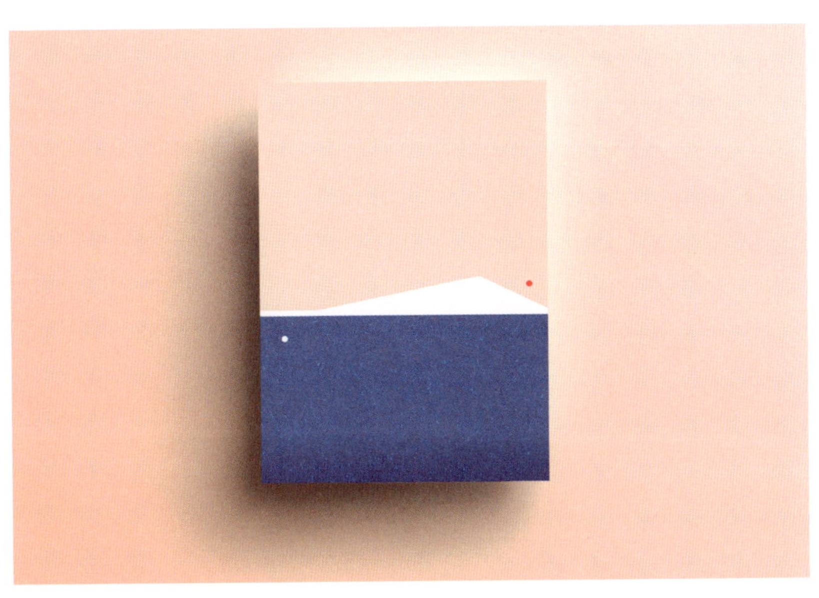

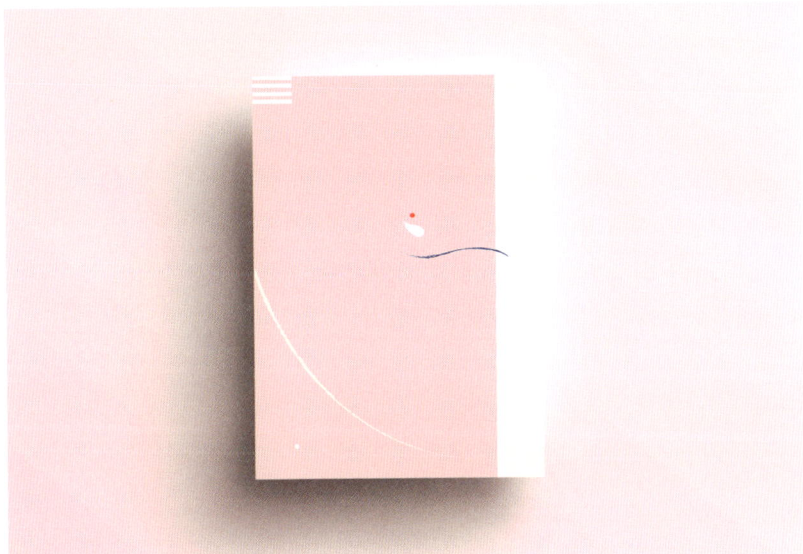

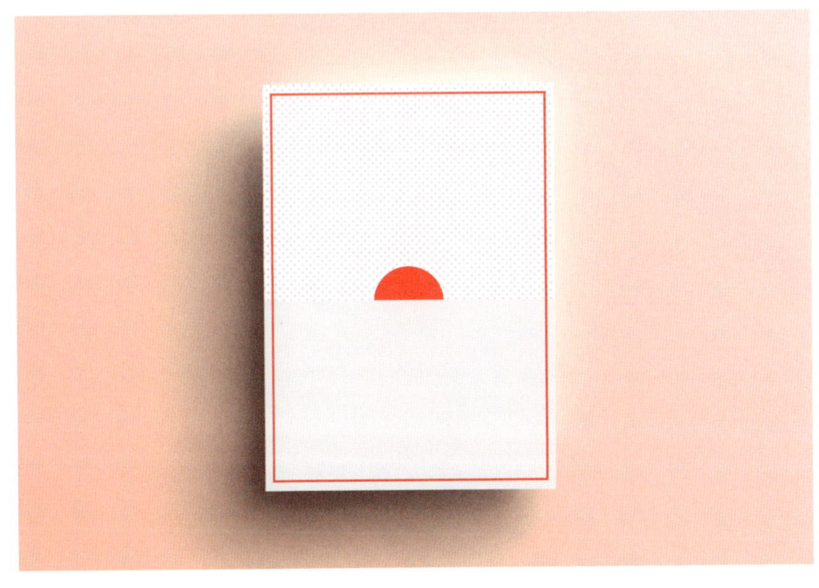

A Geo A Day

designer:
Isabella Conticello

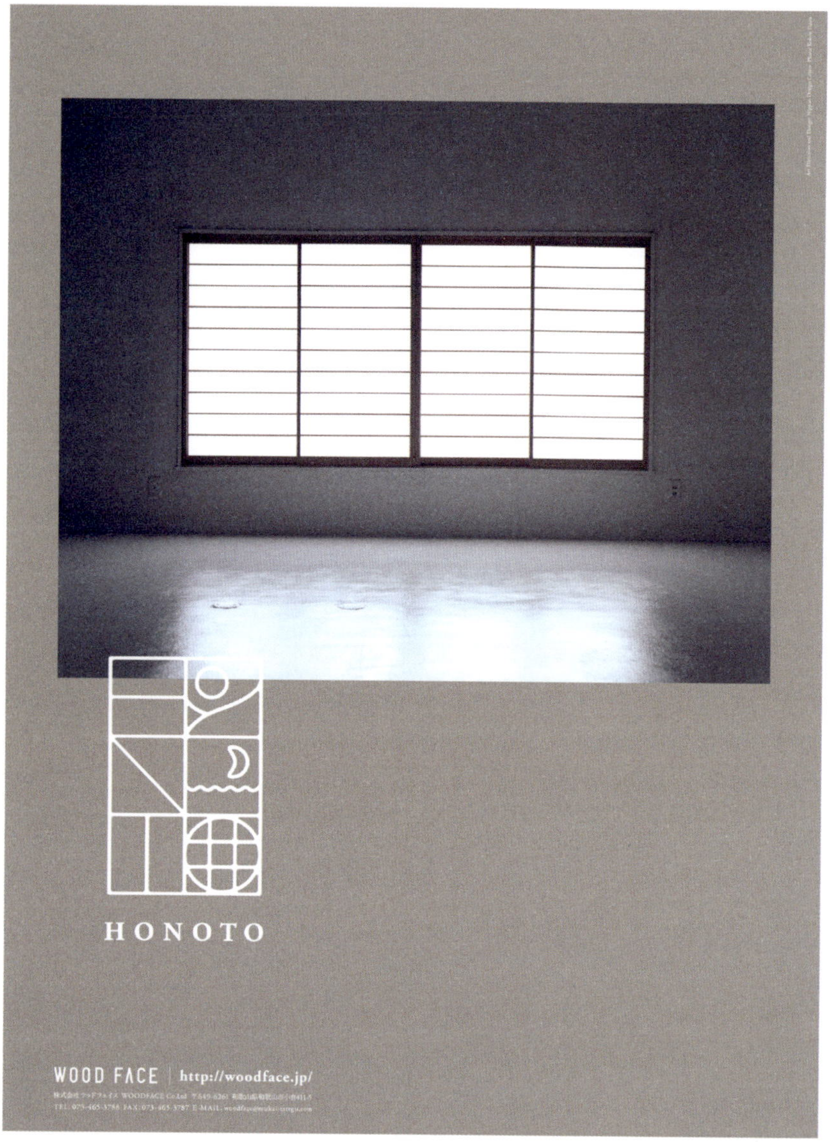

HONOTO

WOOD FACE | http://woodface.jp/

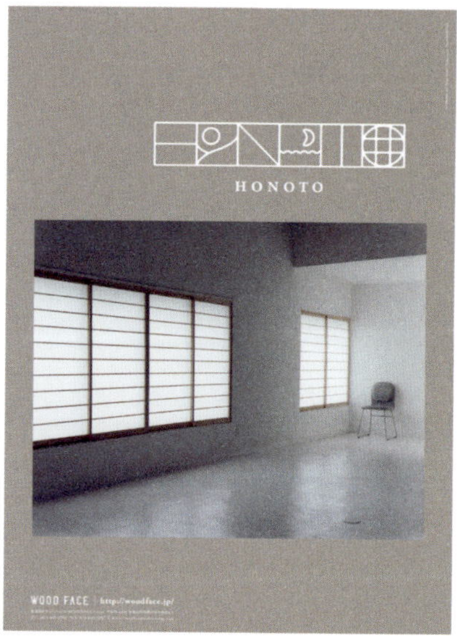

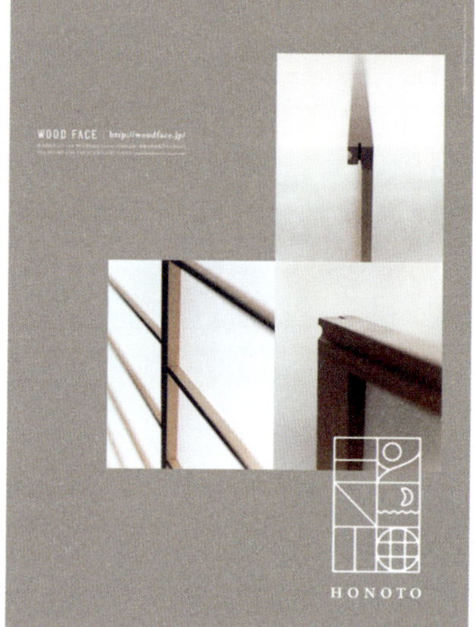

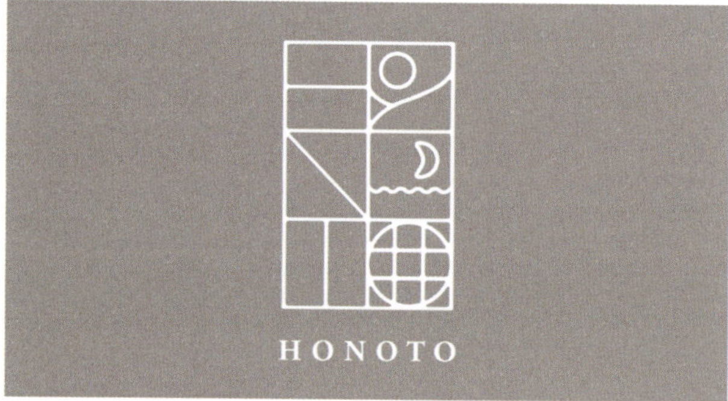

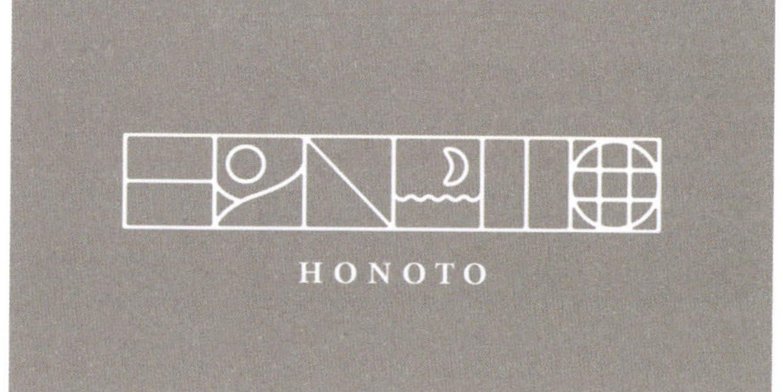

This visual identity for shoji brand "HONOTO" aimed at promoting shoji for a comfortable modern life. It consists of a new logo and new communication and promotion materials such as the catalog and the website. The logo incorporates features of shoji and can be adjusted into different forms, just like sliding doors. The key visuals focus on the soft light provided by shoji.

Honoto

studio: *Nippon Design Center, Inc. / Junya MAEJIMA*
designer: *Junya MAEJIMA*

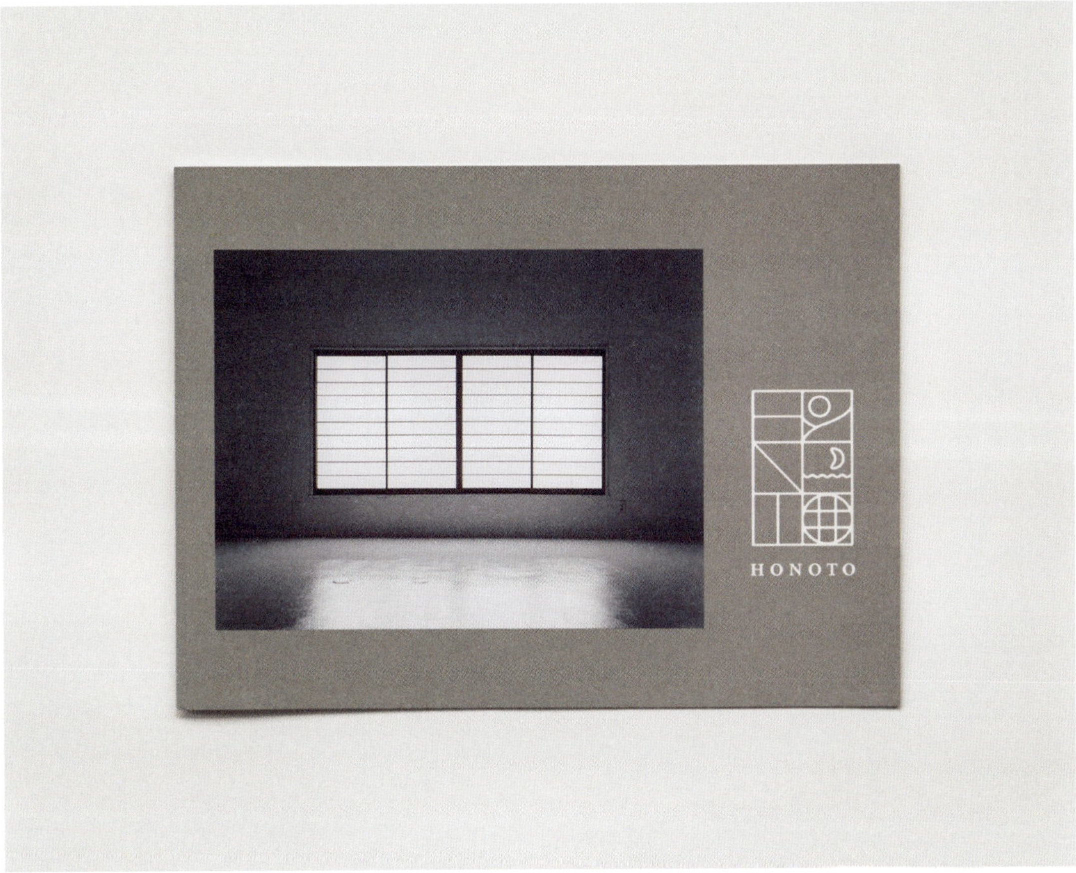

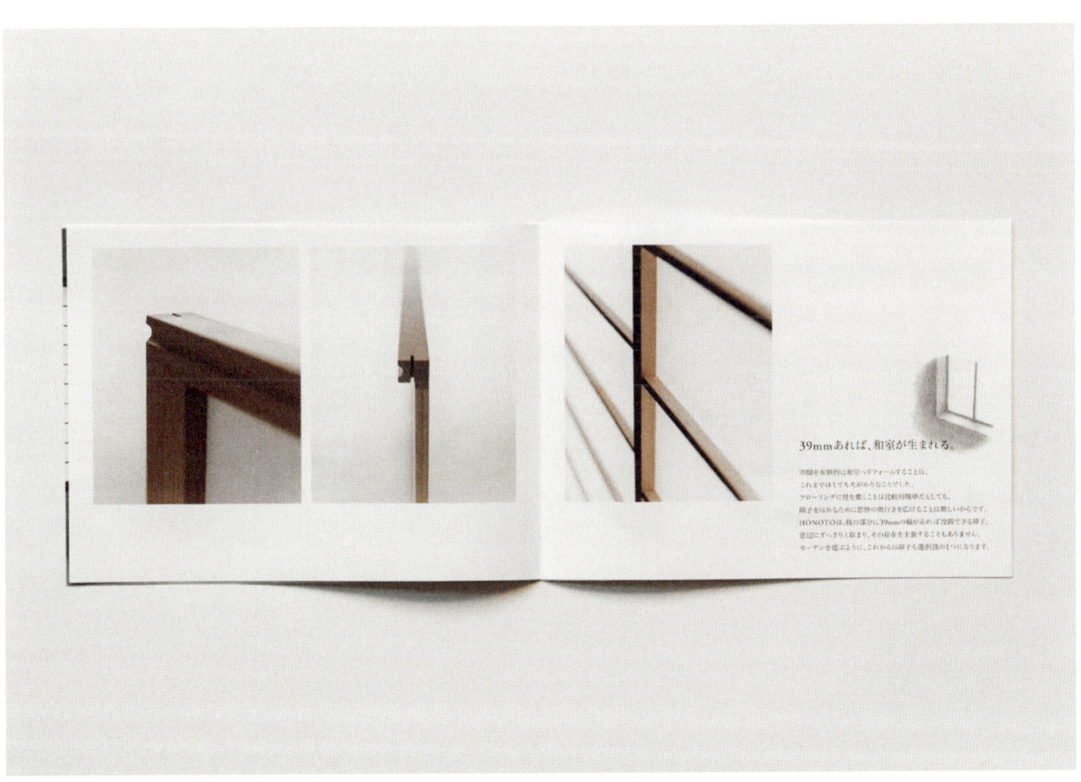

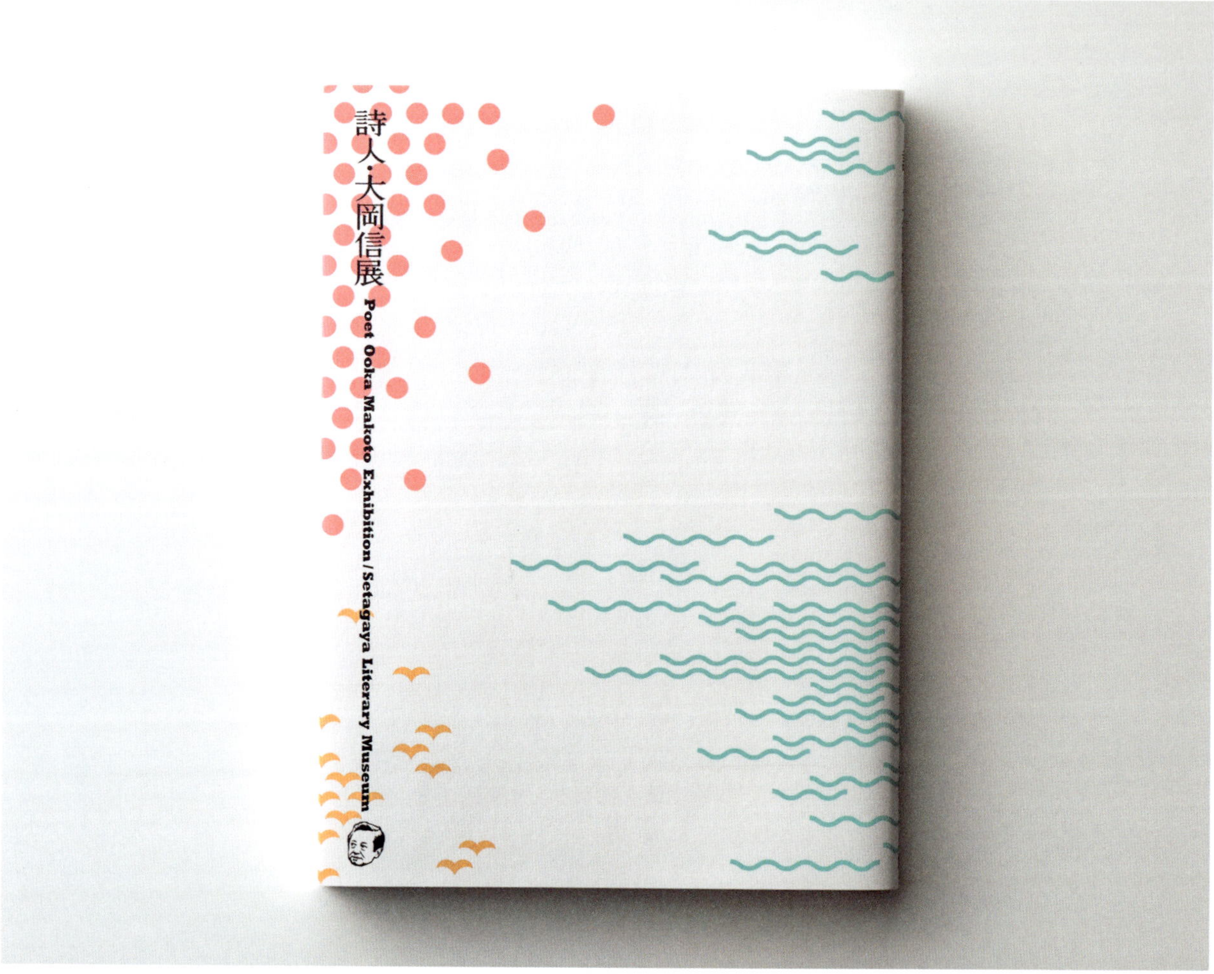

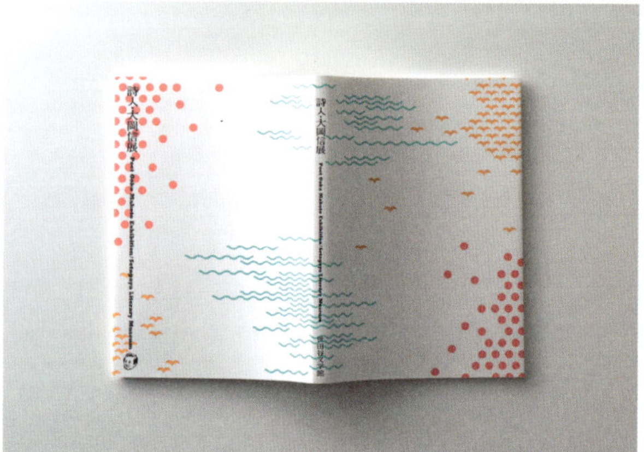

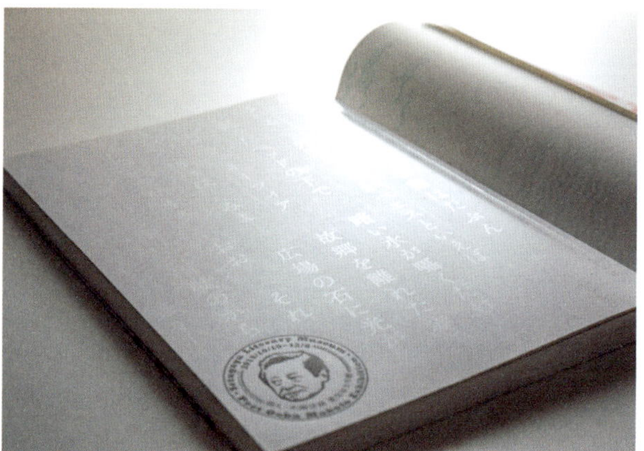

The advertising materials were created for an exhibition held for the great Japanese poet Makoto Ooka. To accentuate Makoto Ooka's lyrical world, the posters and flyers were designed with minimum materials. A bold and fascinating typography was chosen for the advertising while the finishes resemble that of letterpress printing. On the cover of the book a poetry printed with varnish will reveal itself when being viewed with certain lighting.

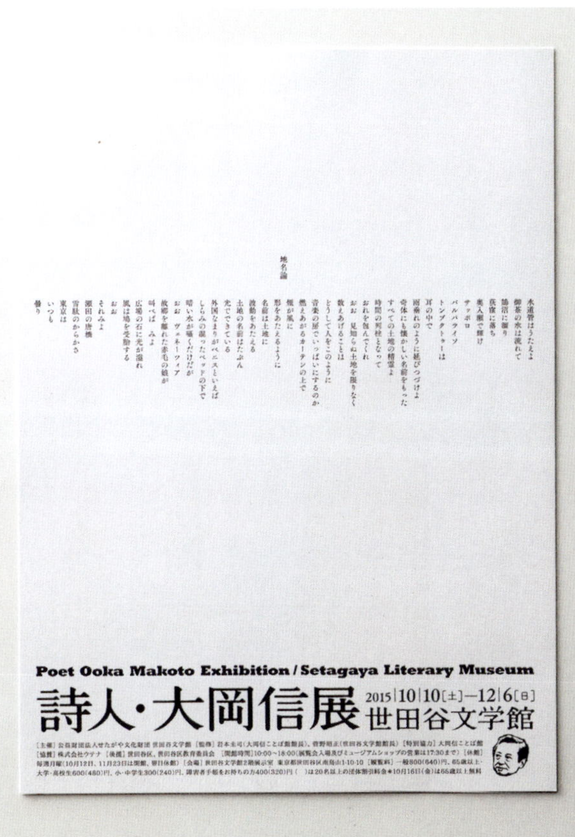

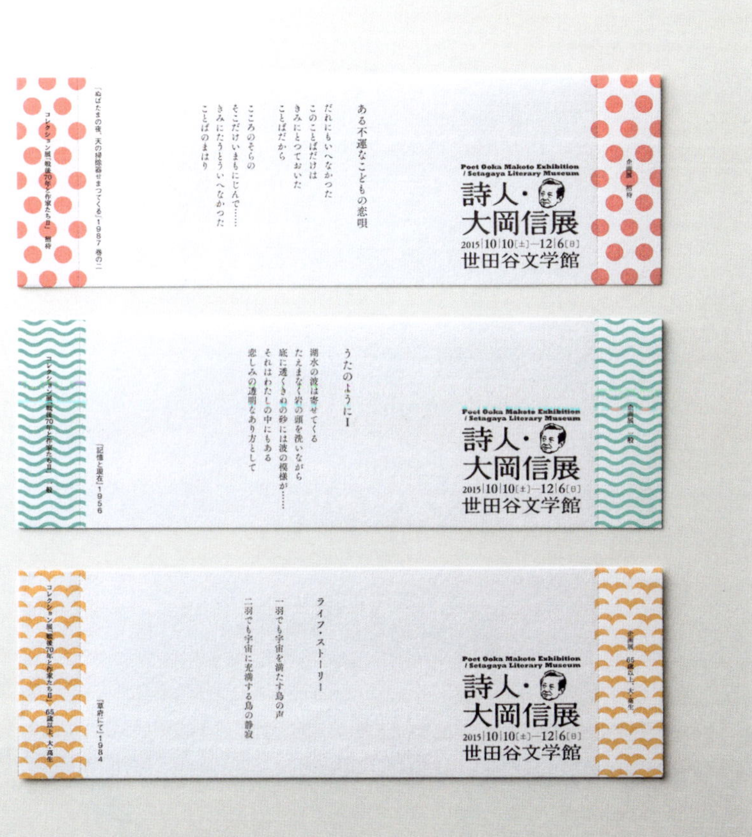

Poet Ooka Makoto Exhibition

studio: ABEKINO DESIGN
designer: Hirokazu Abeki Photographer: Katsushi Takakura

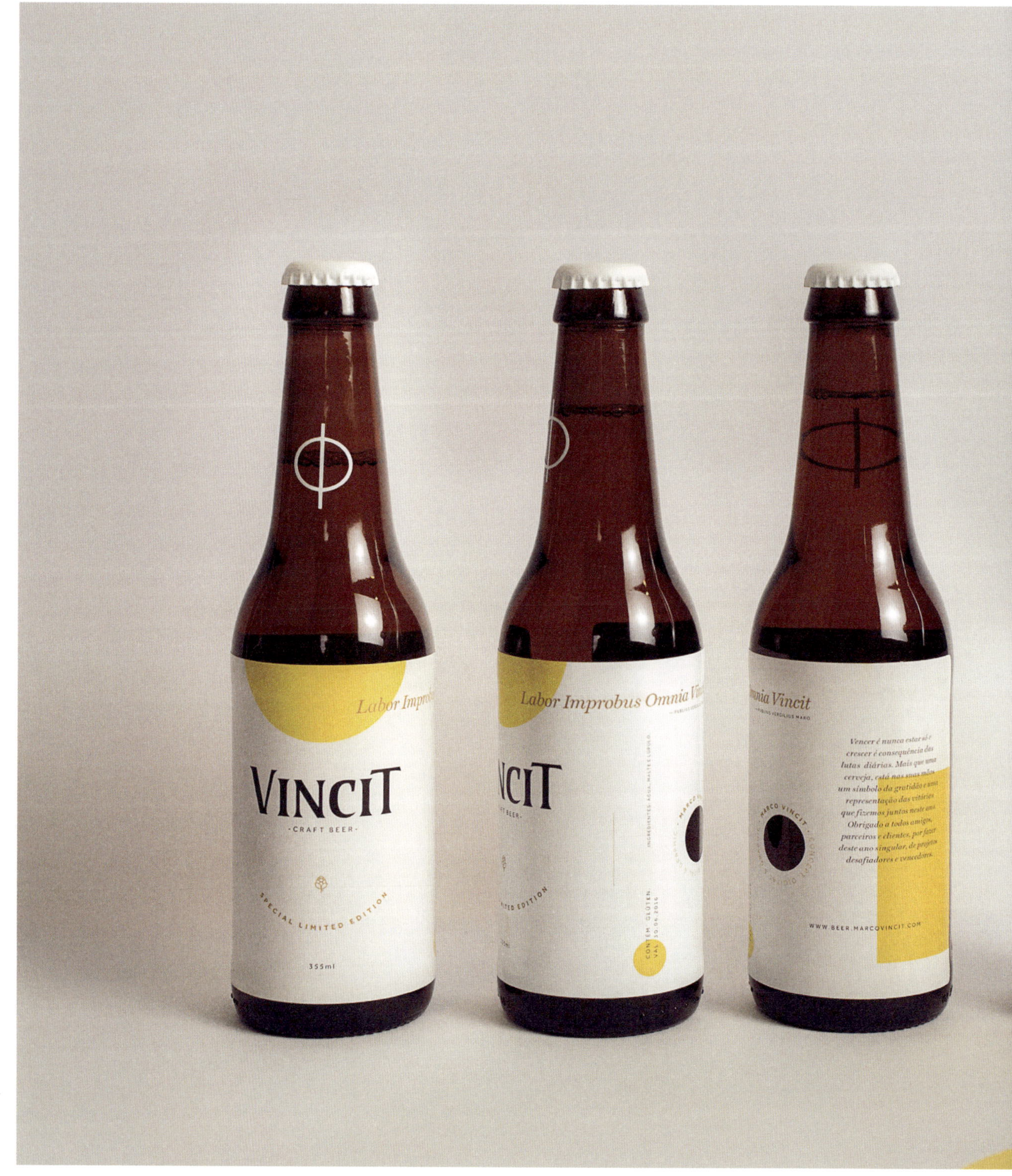

Vincit Beer is a new year gift for the designer's customers, partners and friends. It carries his best wishes to people by his side every day for learning and achieving amazing things together. The work is also a tribute to the poet Publius Virgilius Maro.

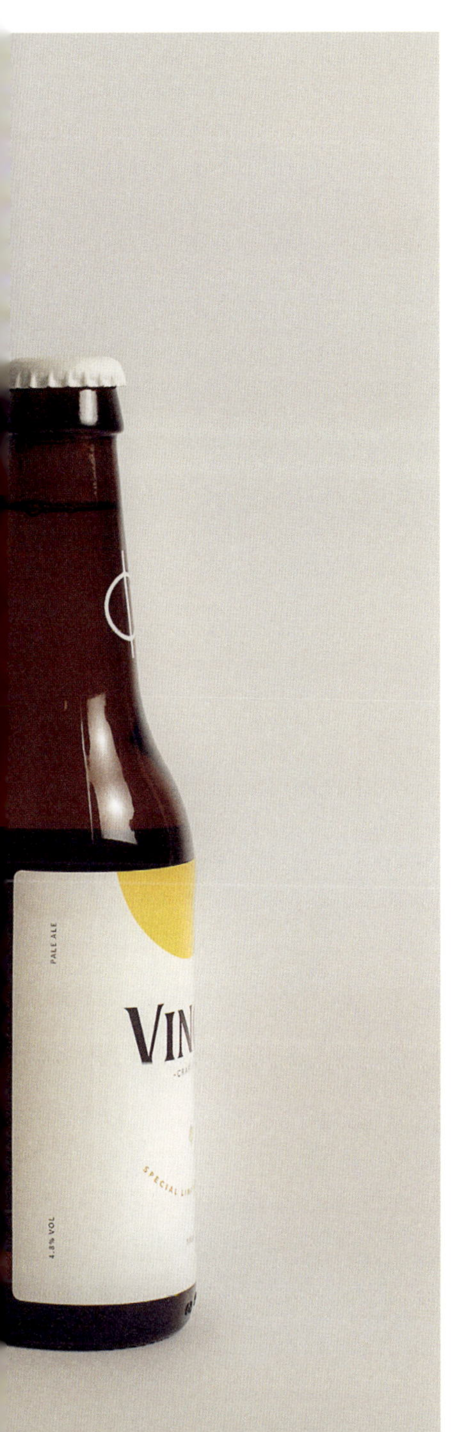

Vincit Beer

designer:
Marco Vincit

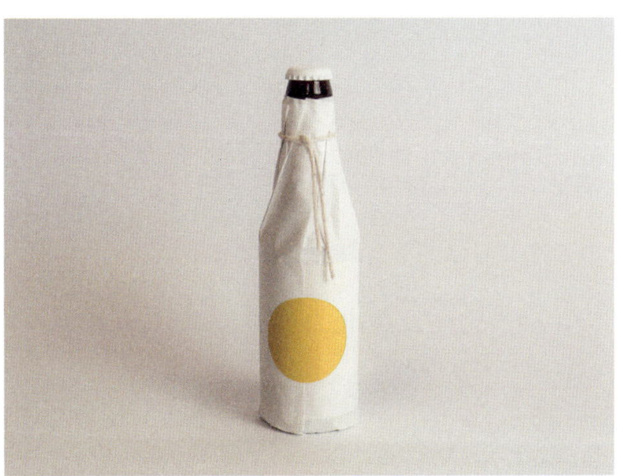

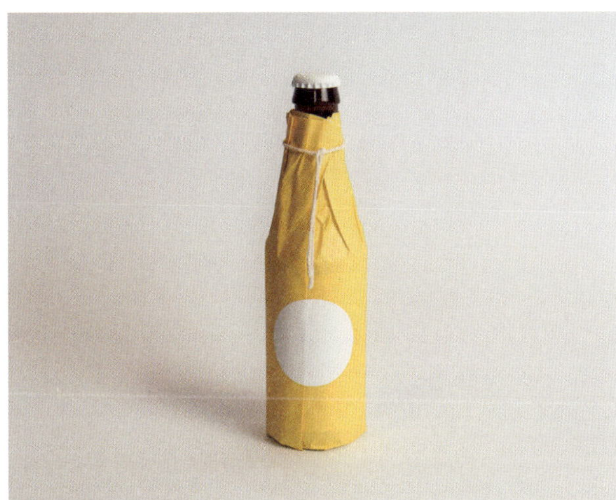

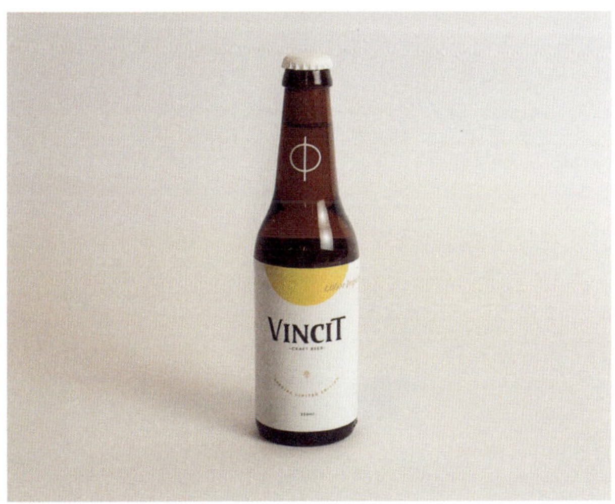

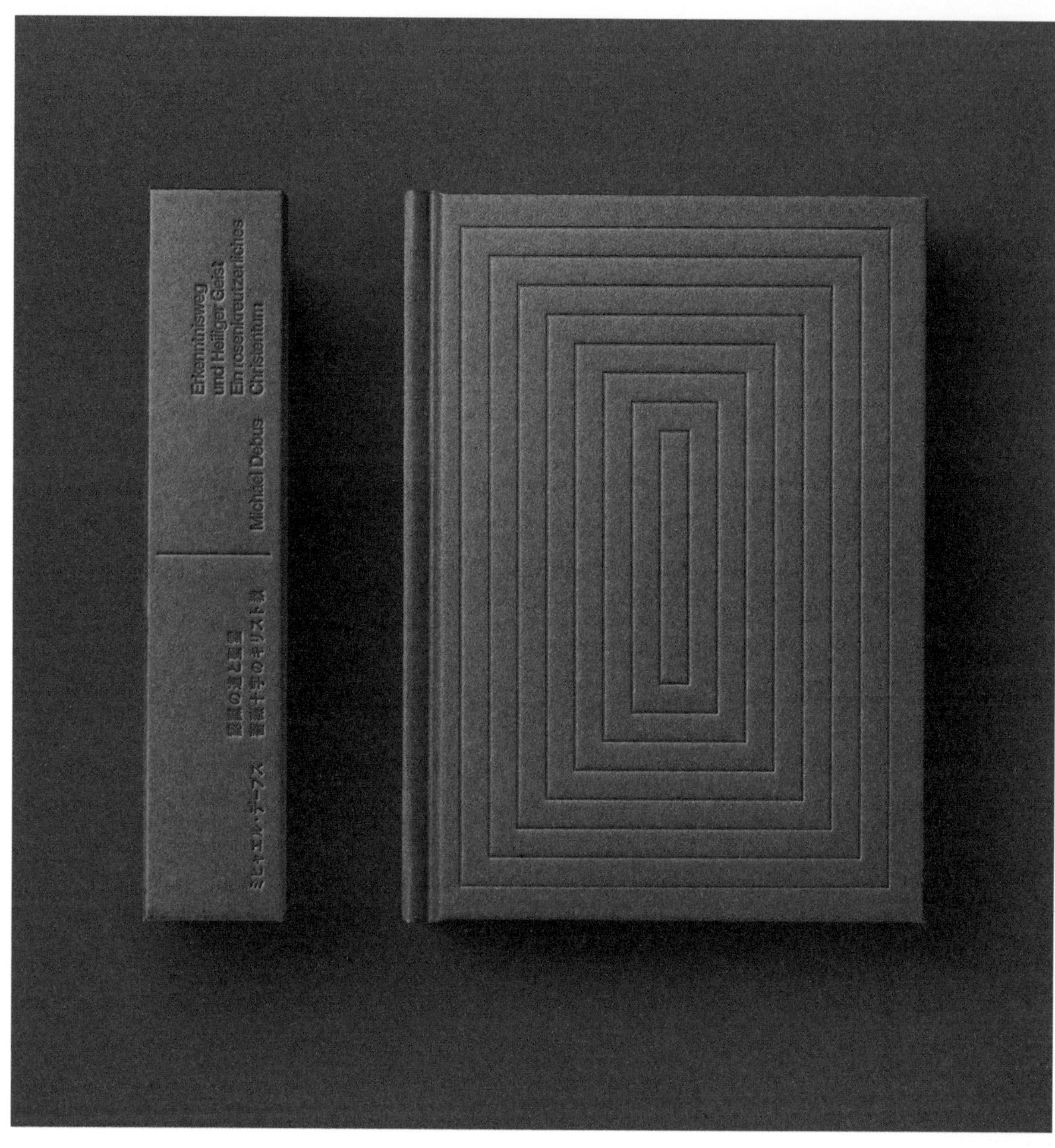

The book unraveling wisdom under the veil of myths and legends features a unique design that combined modernity and minimalism. The cover presents the idea of a corridor of doors of knowledge appearing and being opened by thought, at the end of which emerges the letter I. Through the use of neutral colors between light and shadow, the transition of reader's awareness from darkness to daylight is captured. The entire system is a reminiscent of the cloister in church.

Erkenntnisweg und Heiliger Geist

designer:
Yuta Takahashi

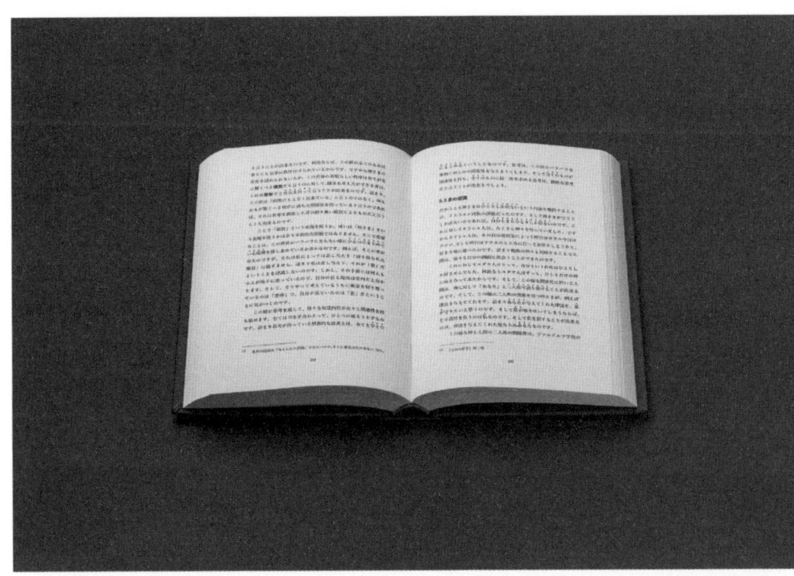

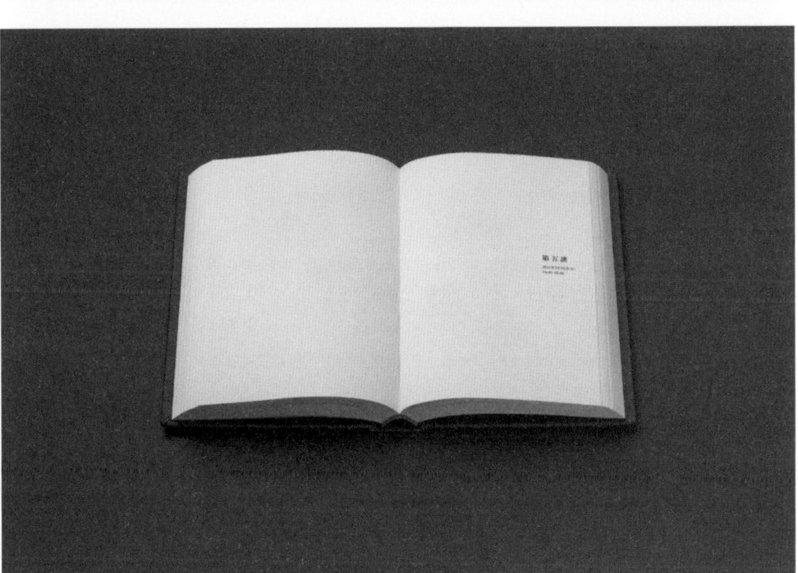

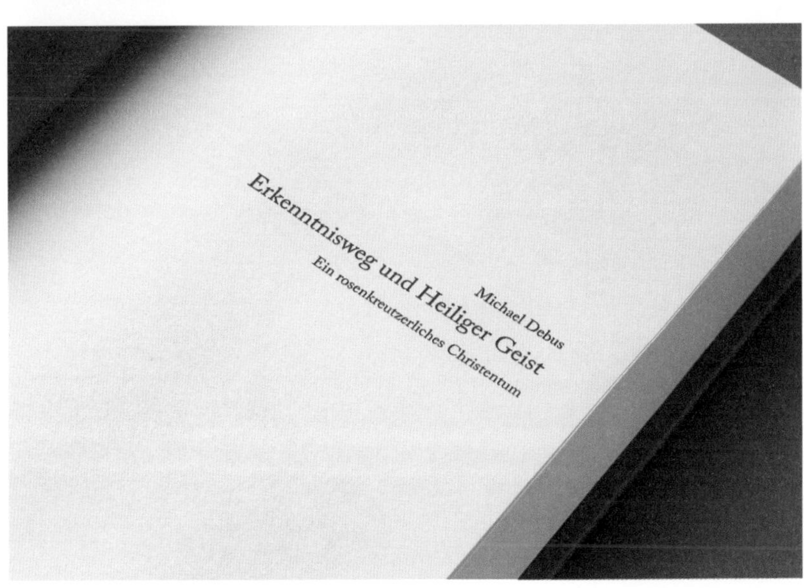

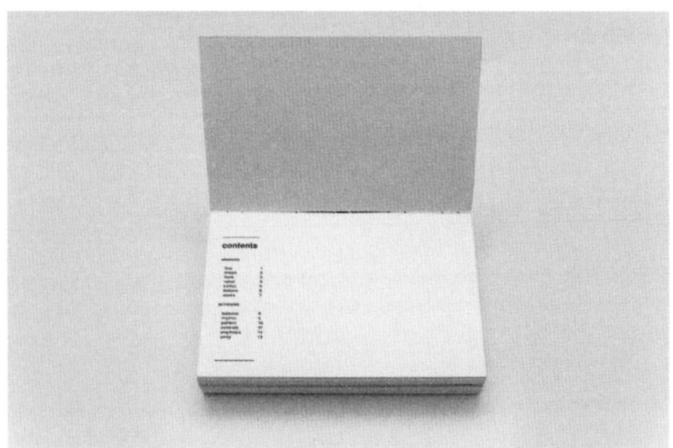

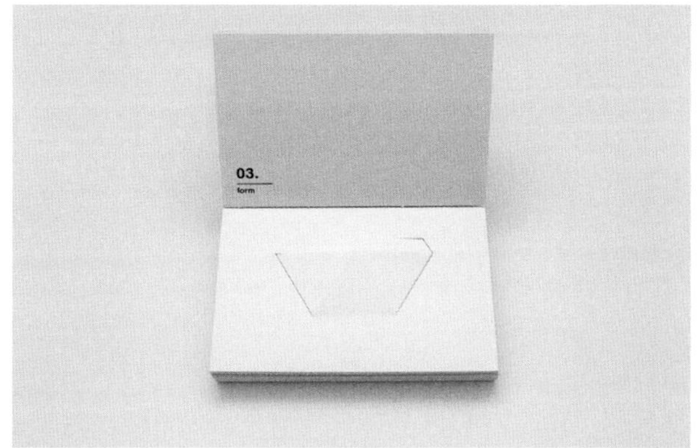

Visual Language explores the founding principles and elements of design in an interactive and tactile hand-bound book. The project approaches each element and principle through a restricted palette while limiting the visual expression to elementary shapes and forms. Through die-cut designs that introduce tangible and dimensional elements, the book invites hands-on reading participation and interaction.

Visual Language

designer:
Jiani Lu

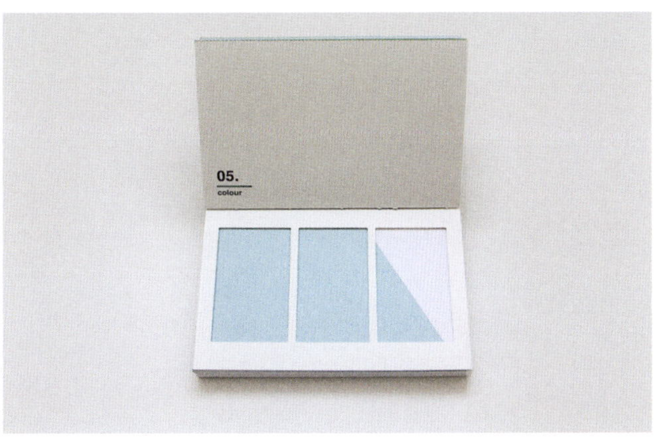

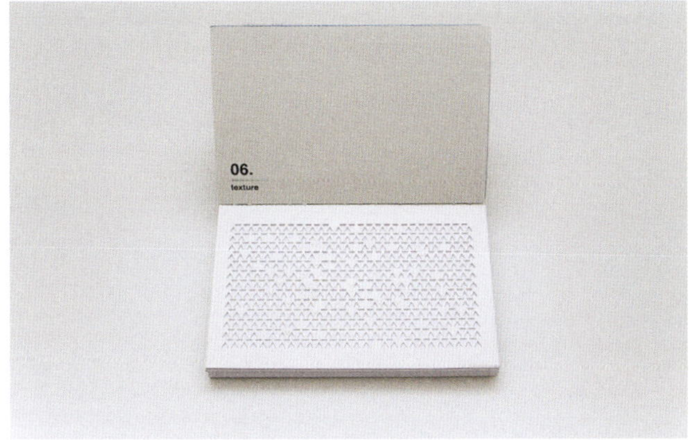

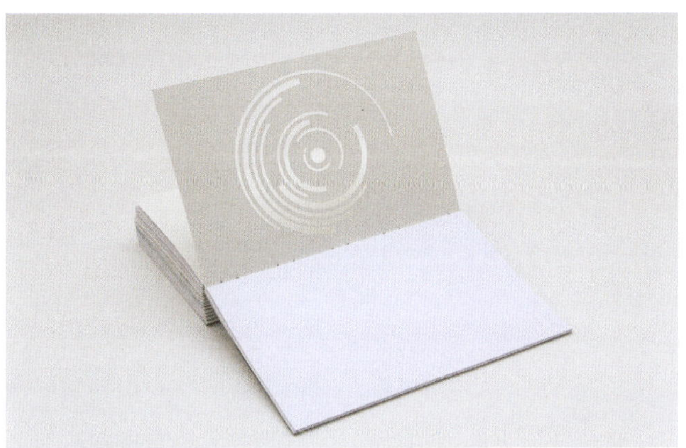

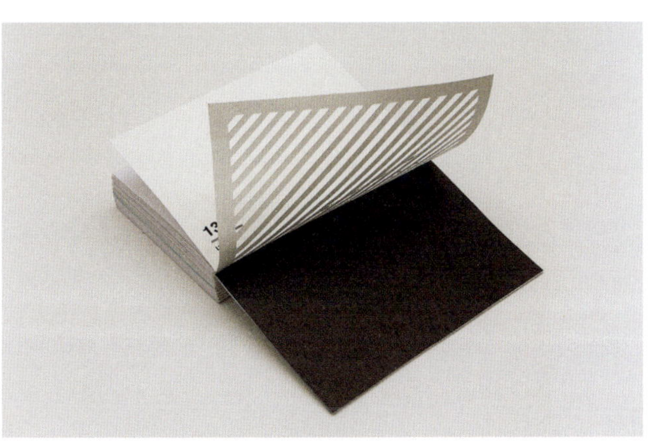

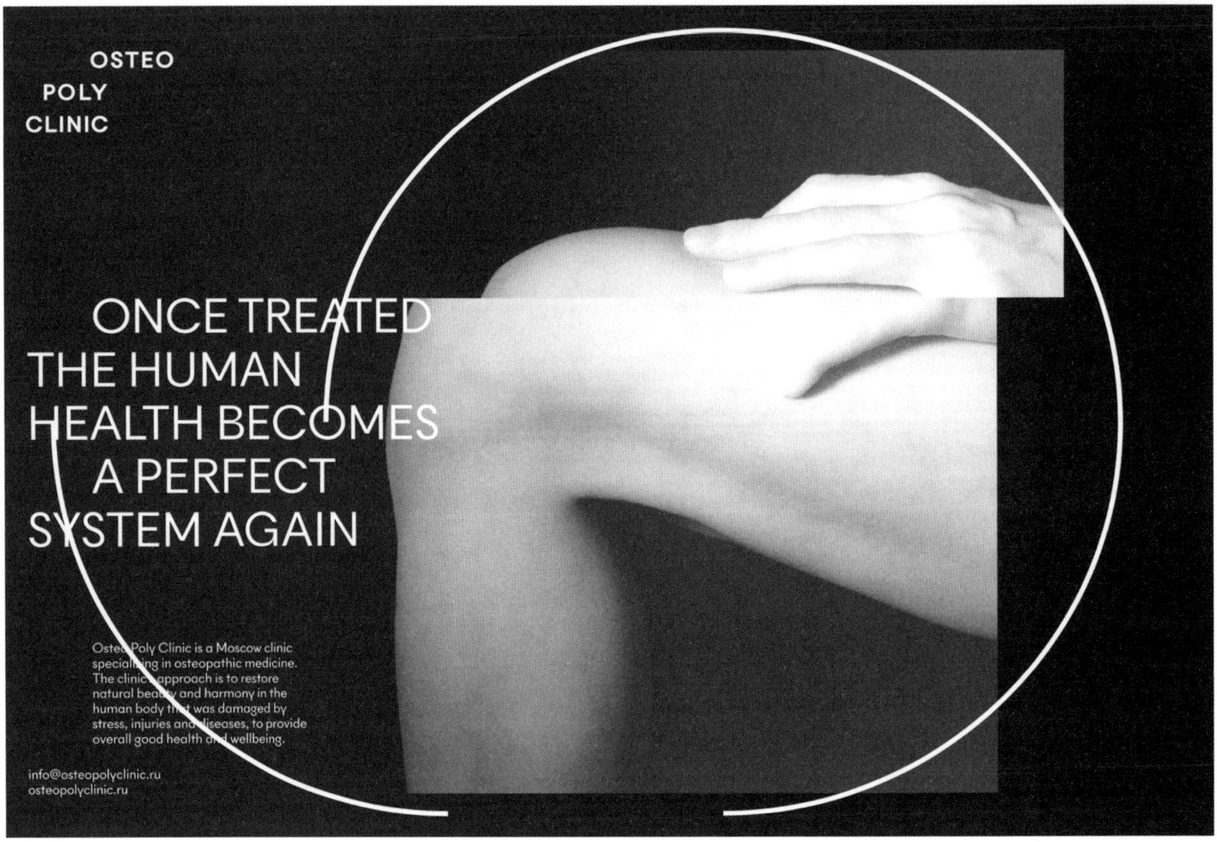

OSTEO
POLY
CLINIC

ONCE TREATED
THE HUMAN
HEALTH BECOMES
A PERFECT
SYSTEM AGAIN

Osteo Poly Clinic is a Moscow clinic specializing in osteopathic medicine. The clinic's approach is to restore natural beauty and harmony in the human body that was damaged by stress, injuries and diseases, to provide overall good health and wellbeing.

info@osteopolyclinic.ru
osteopolyclinic.ru

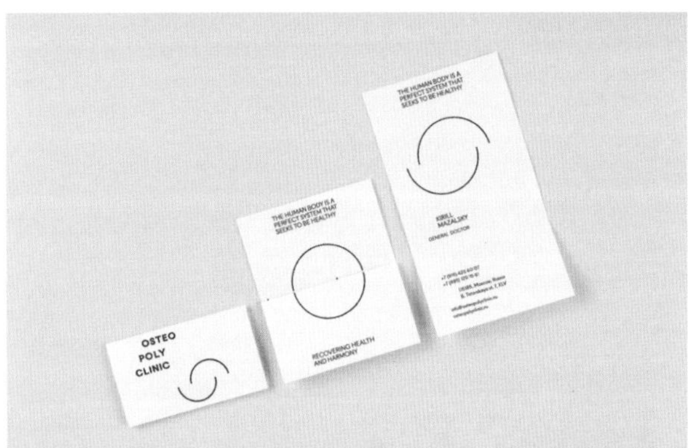

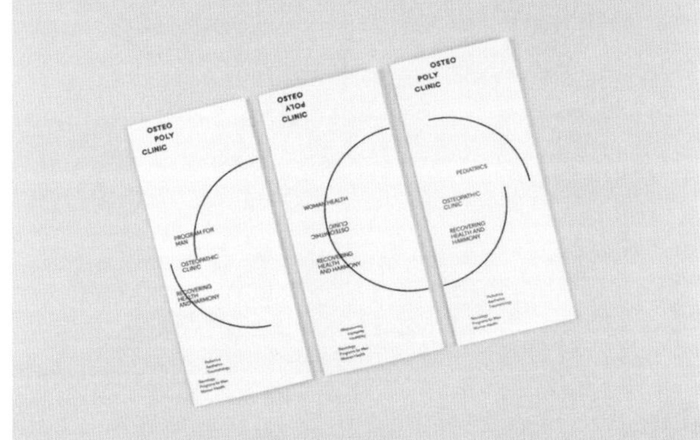

Based on osteopathy, this brand identity features a complete circle that symbolizes perfect health and a broken circle that indicates problematic health. All visual elements work in connection with the logo. If the circle deforms, other elements change accordingly, just like the mechanism of the human body.

Osteo Poly Clinic

studio : Ermolaev Bureau
designer: Vlad Ermolaev, Eline Van Der Ploeg, Anastasia Tolstokorova

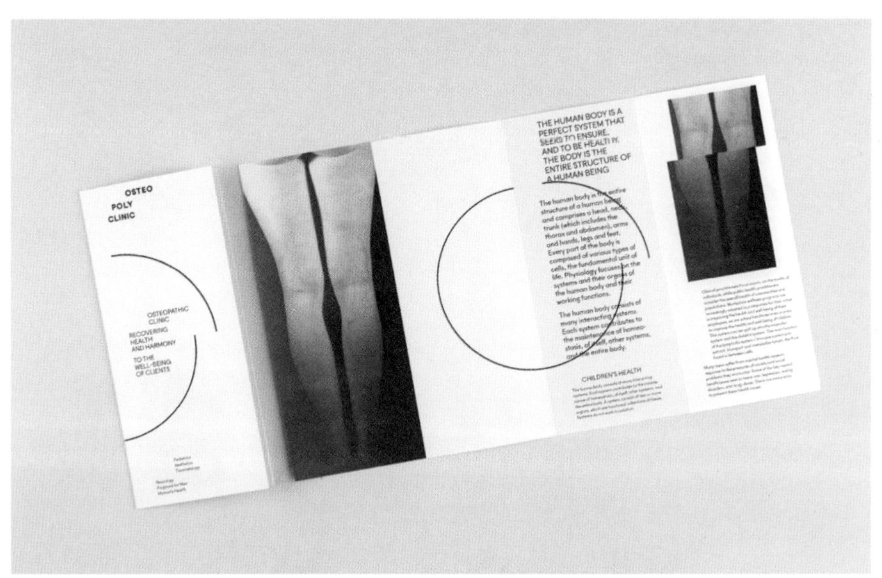

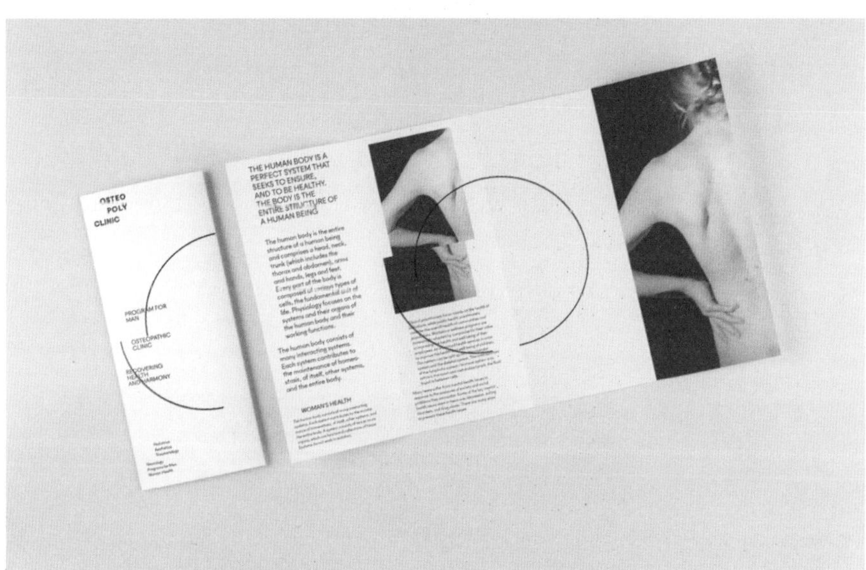

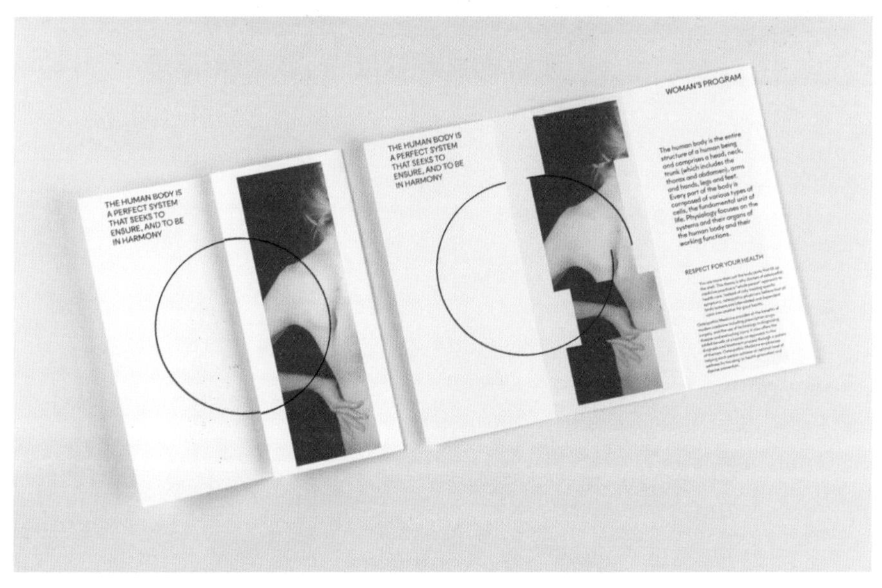

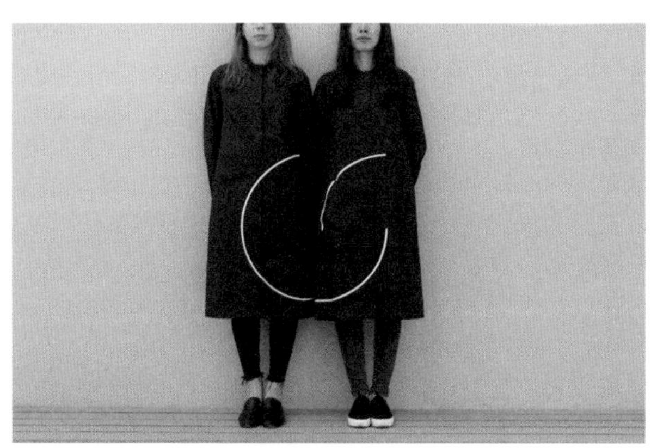

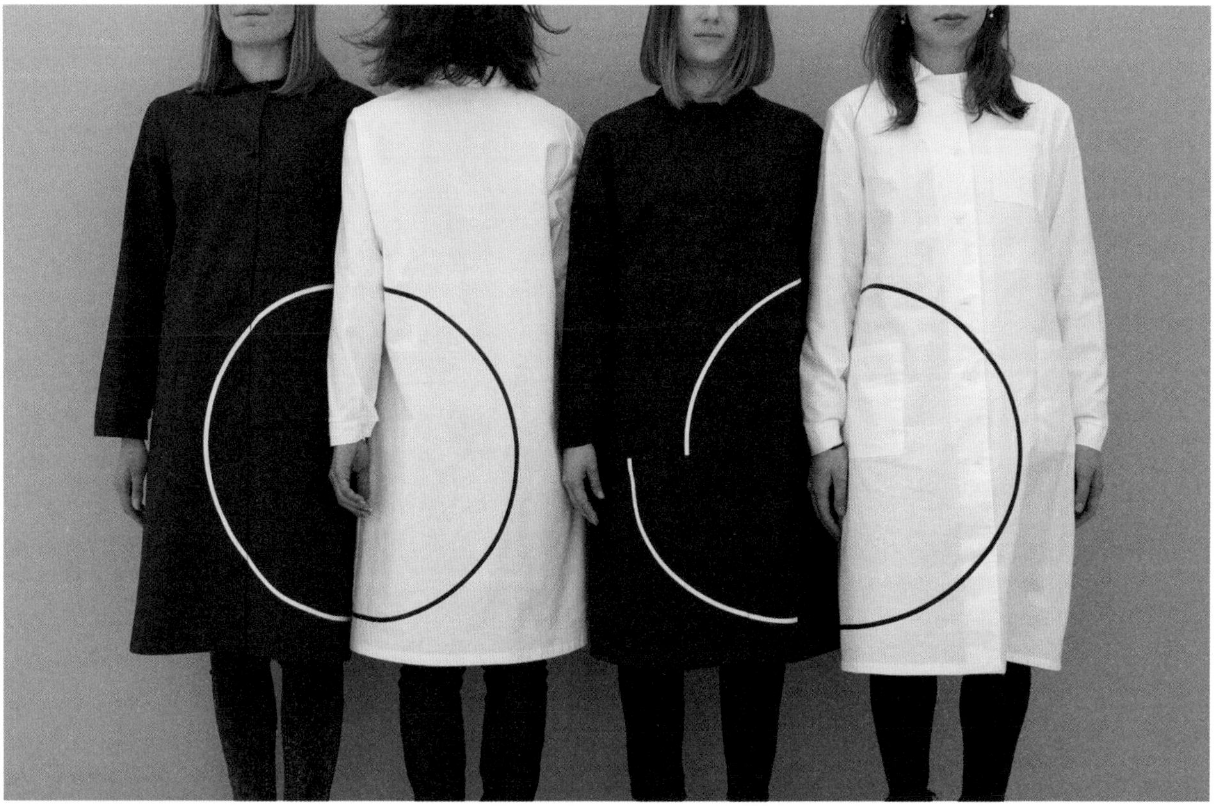

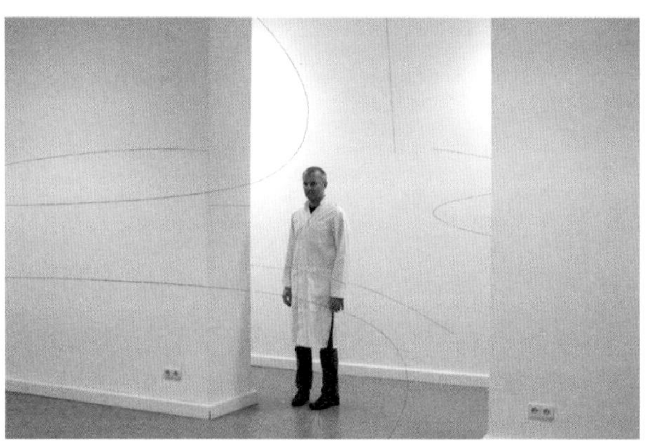

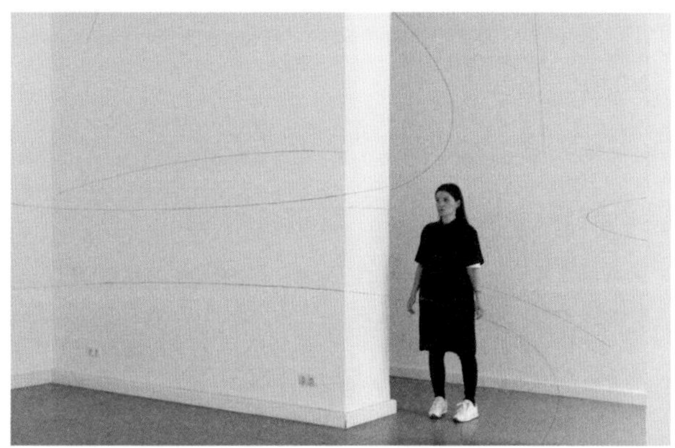

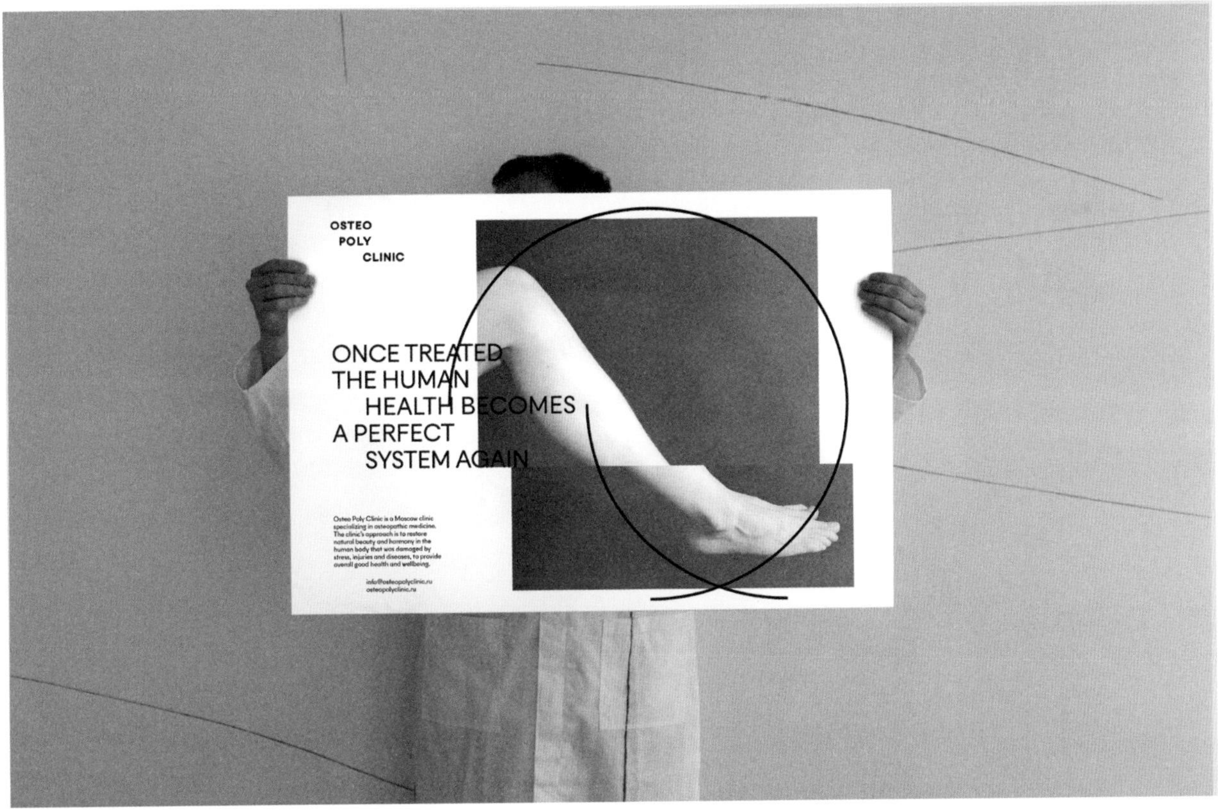

OSTEO
POLY
CLINIC
ONCE TREATED
THE HUMAN
HEALTH BECOMES
A PERFECT
SYSTEM AGAIN
Osteo Poly Clinic is a Moscow clinic specializing in osteopathic medicine. The clinic's approach is to restore natural beauty and harmony in the human body that was damaged by stress, injuries and diseases, to provide overall good health and wellbeing.
info@osteopolyclinic.ru
osteopolyclinic.ru

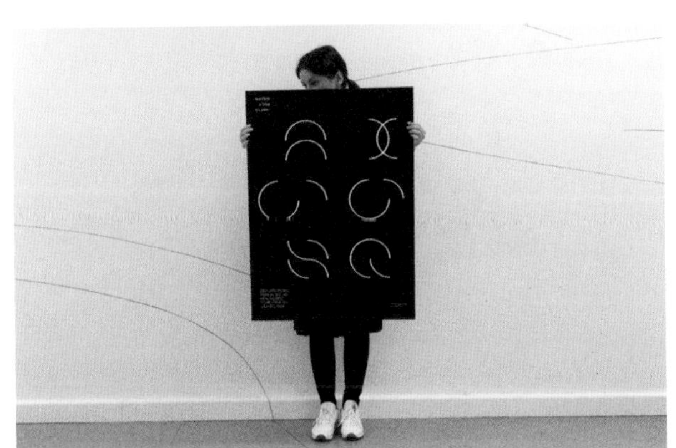

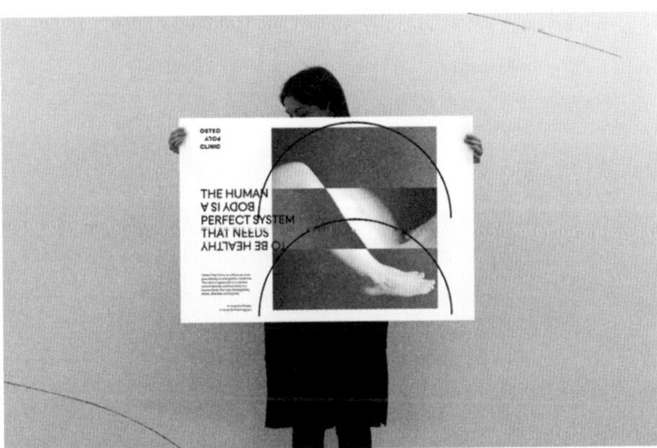
OSTEO
CLINIC
THE HUMAN
PERFECT SYSTEM
THAT NEEDS

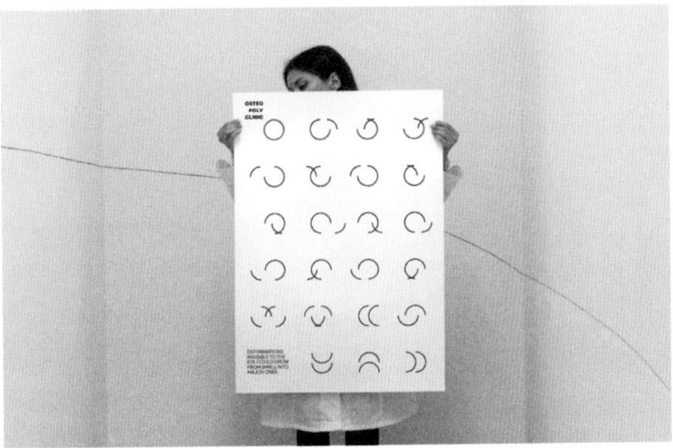
OSTEO
POLY
CLINIC

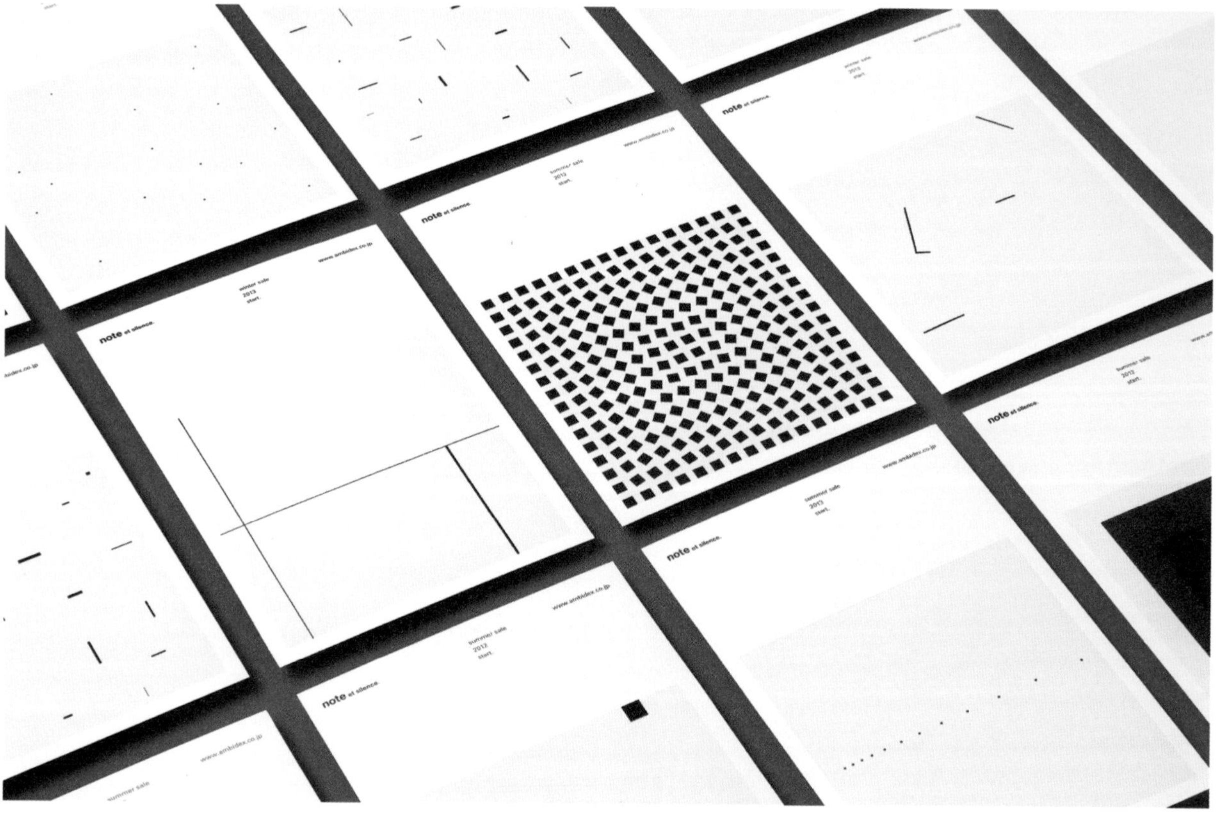

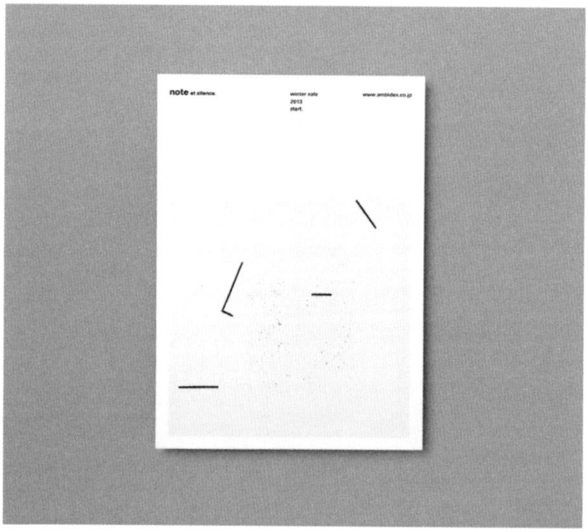

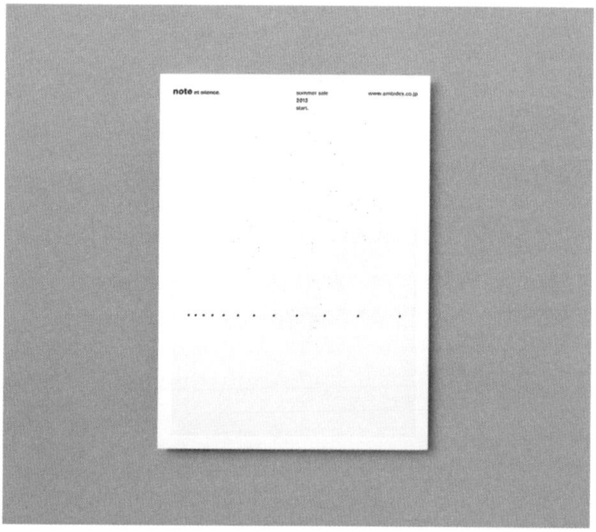

Points, lines and planes—the basic elements of graphics—are employed to arrive at visuals expressing the fashion brand's concept: change due to a combination of universal things. To highlight the shape, no colors were used in this series of monotone, attaining a sense of unity throughout the season. These printed objects are also a tribute to predecessors' experimental planar compositions.

Note et Silence

studio: ***KAMIMURA & Co.***
designer: ***Makoto Kamimura***

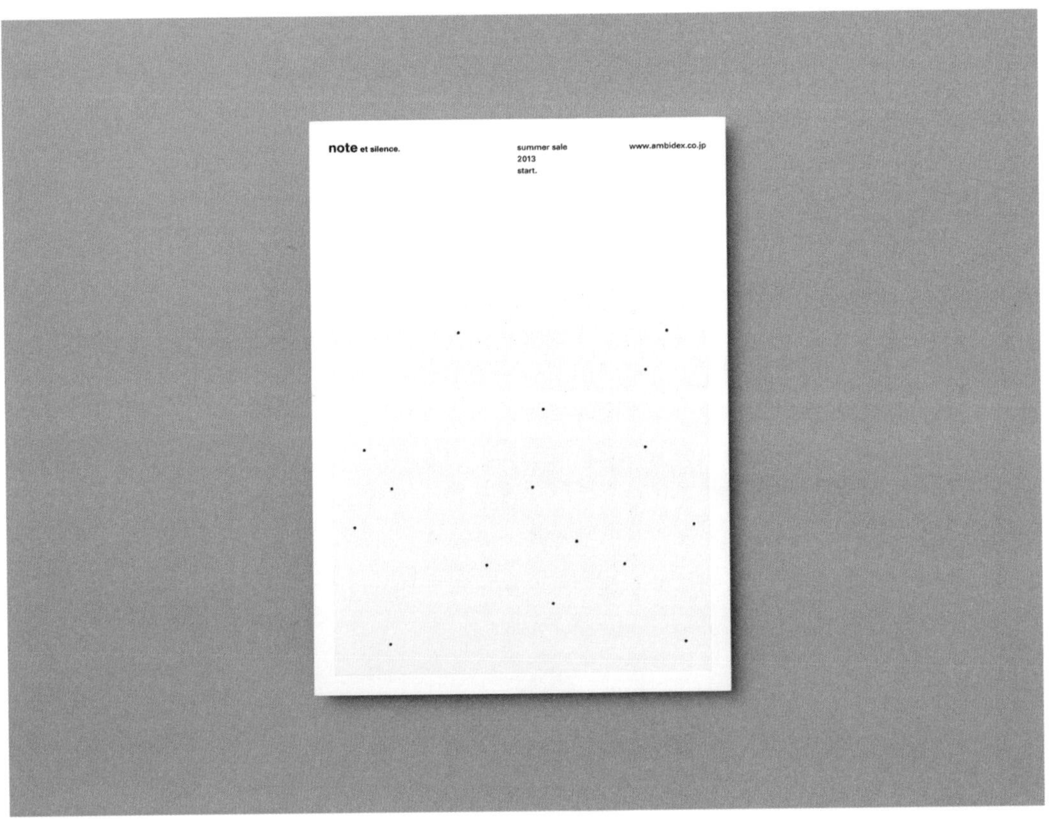

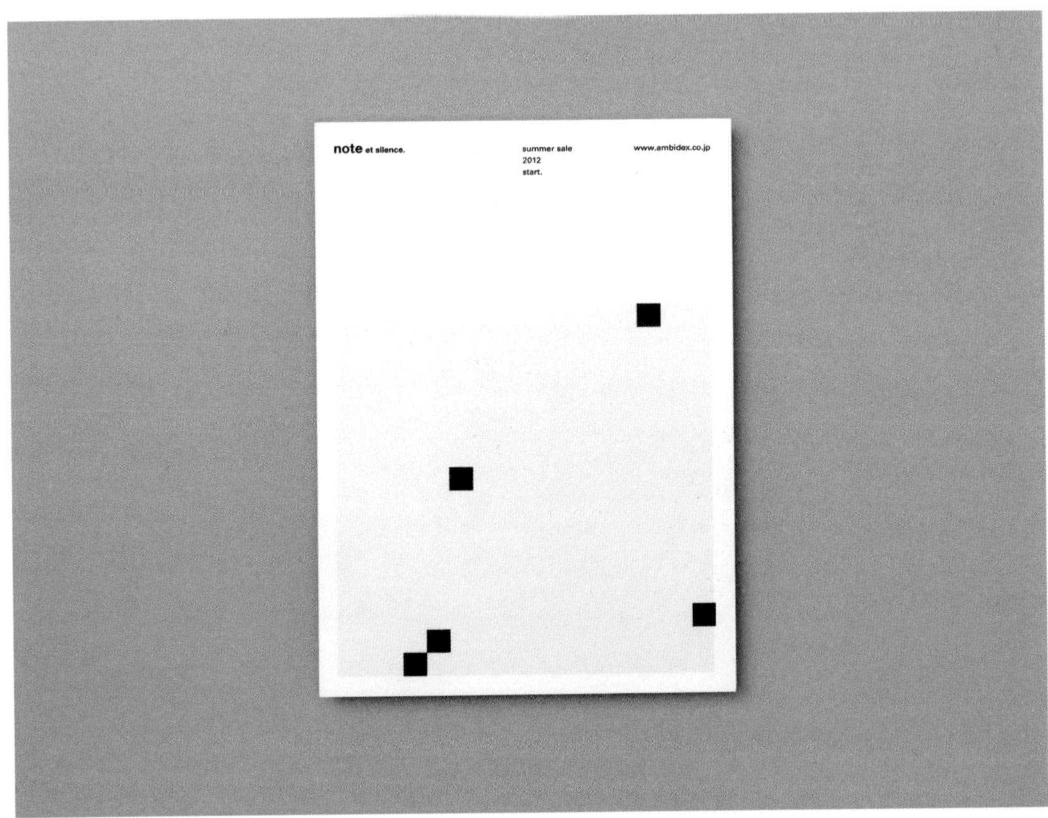

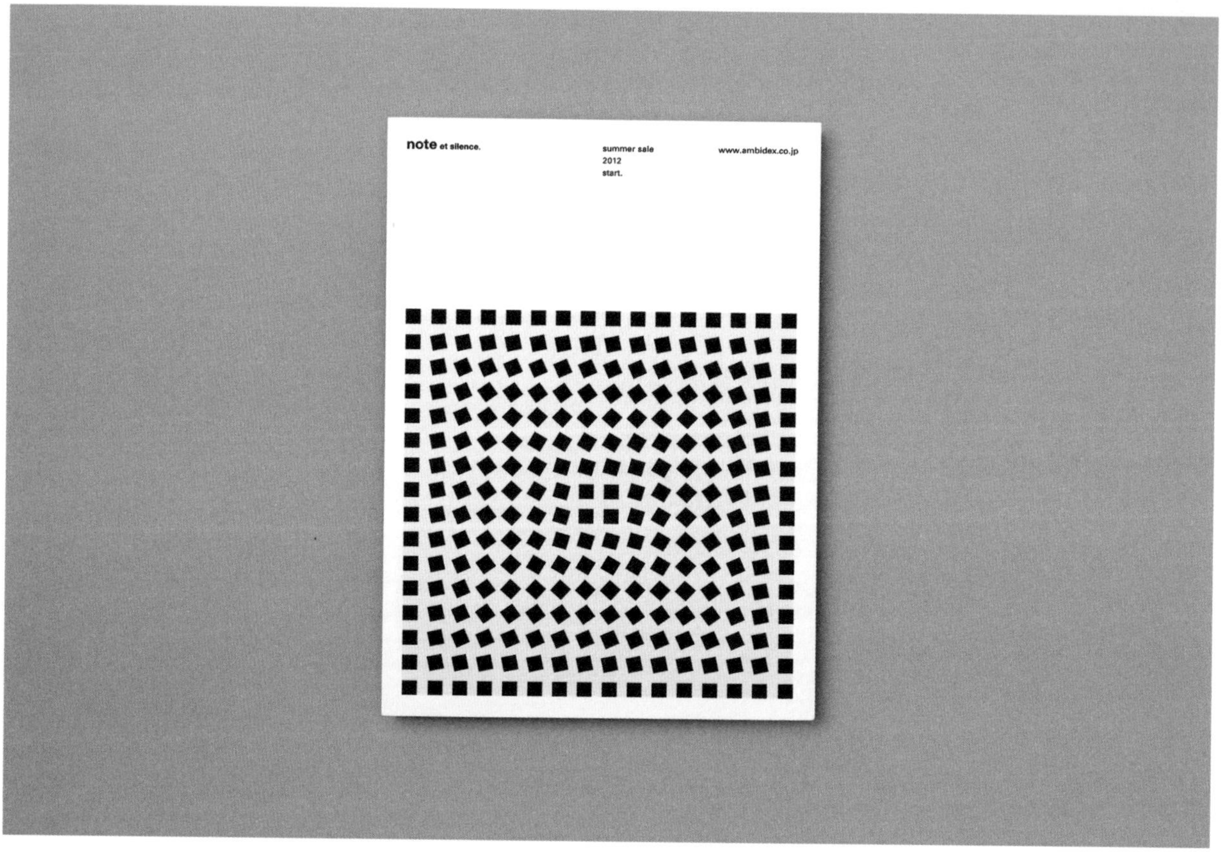

note et silence.
summer sale
2012
start.
www.ambidex.co.jp

note et silence.
summer sale
2012
start.
www.ambidex.co.jp

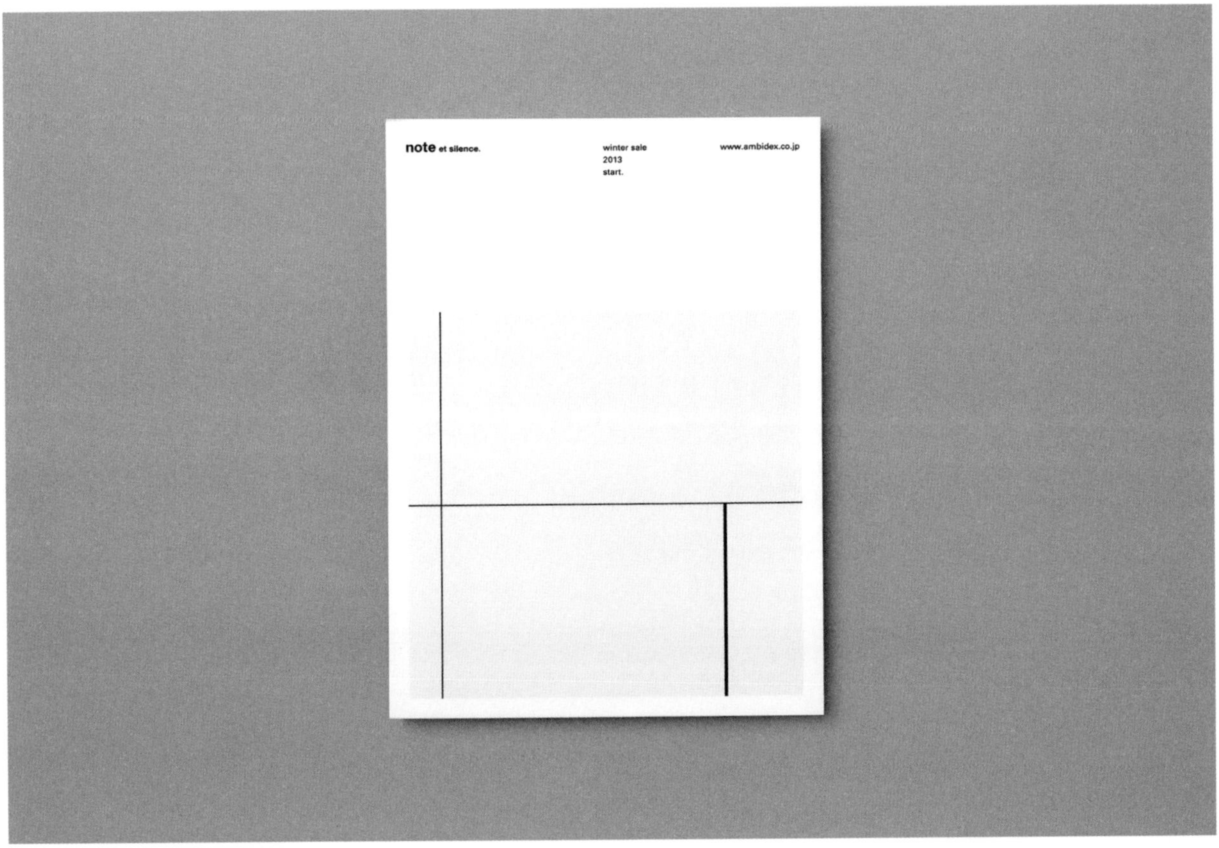

note et silence.

winter sale
2013
start.

www.ambidex.co.jp

note et silence.

summer sale
2013
start.

www.ambidex.co.jp

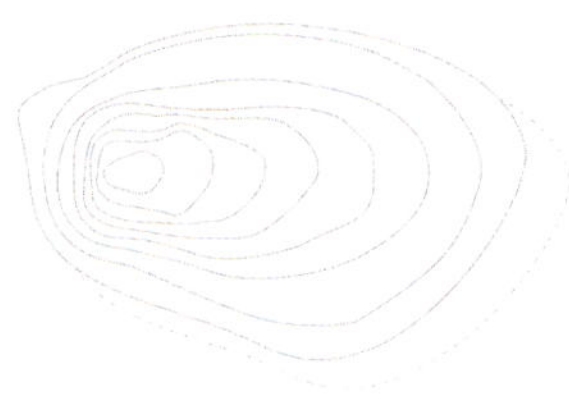

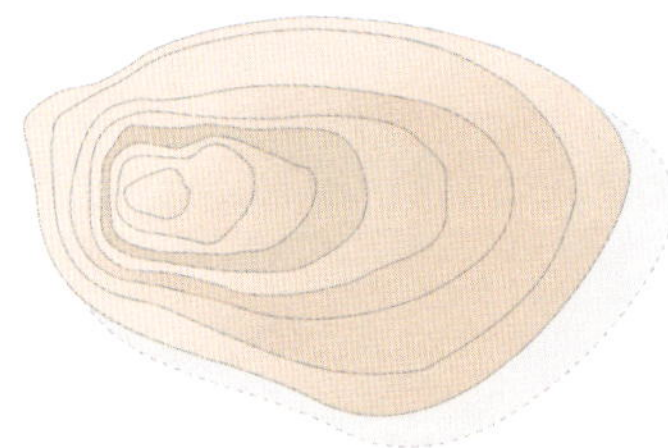

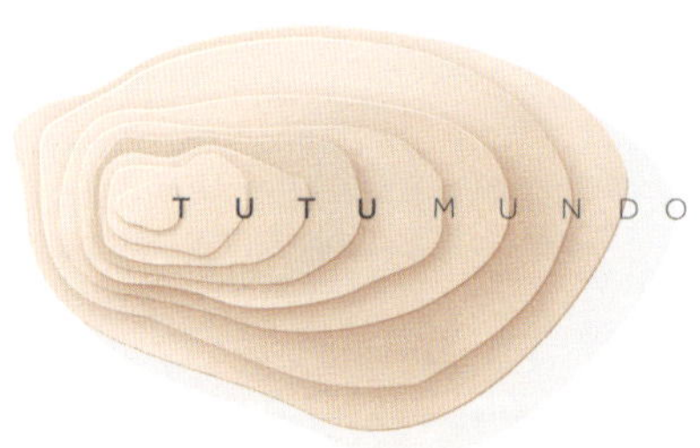

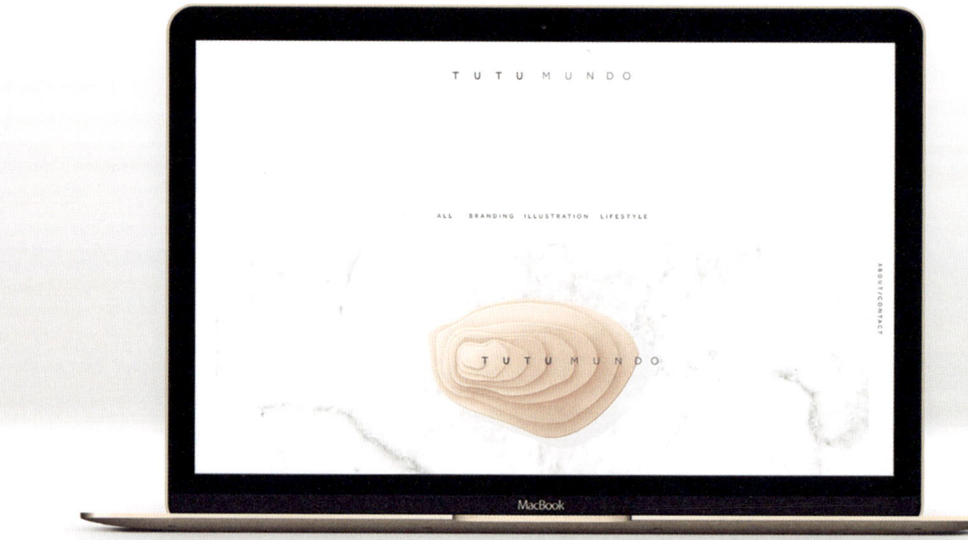

This is a brand identity for the designer's personal brand Tutu Mundo which specializes in branding, identity, advertising, packaging, print, apparel and more. The identity features a logo that consists of clean sans serif typeface and a pearl oyster, the brand's icon. It is a symbol of simplicity, boldness and purity, representing both pearl oyster and design.

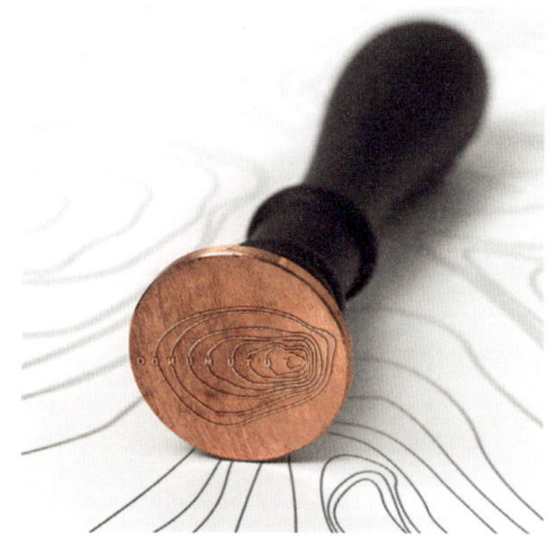

Tutu Mundo

studio: ***Tutu Mundo***
designer: ***Tuğba Özcan***

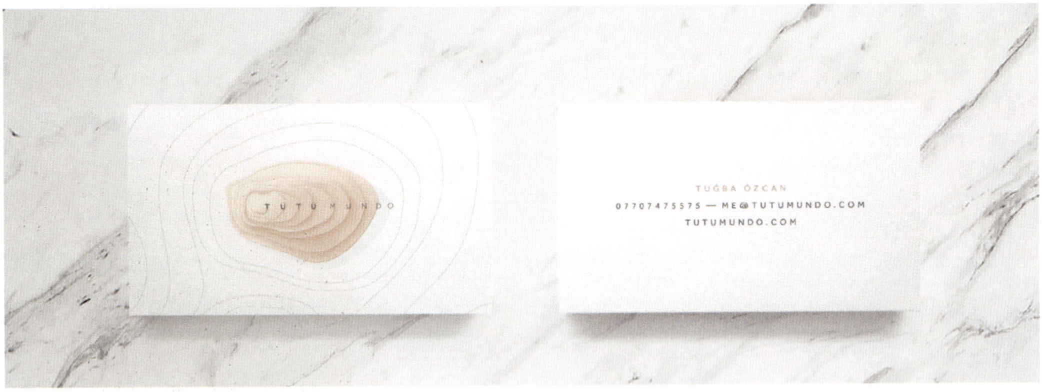

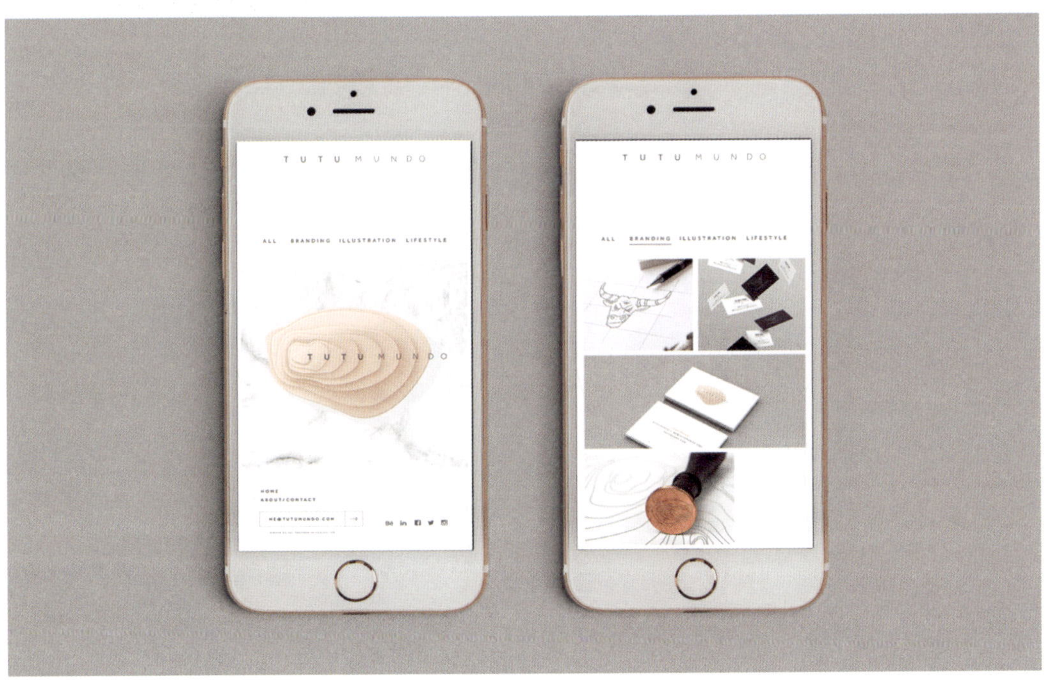

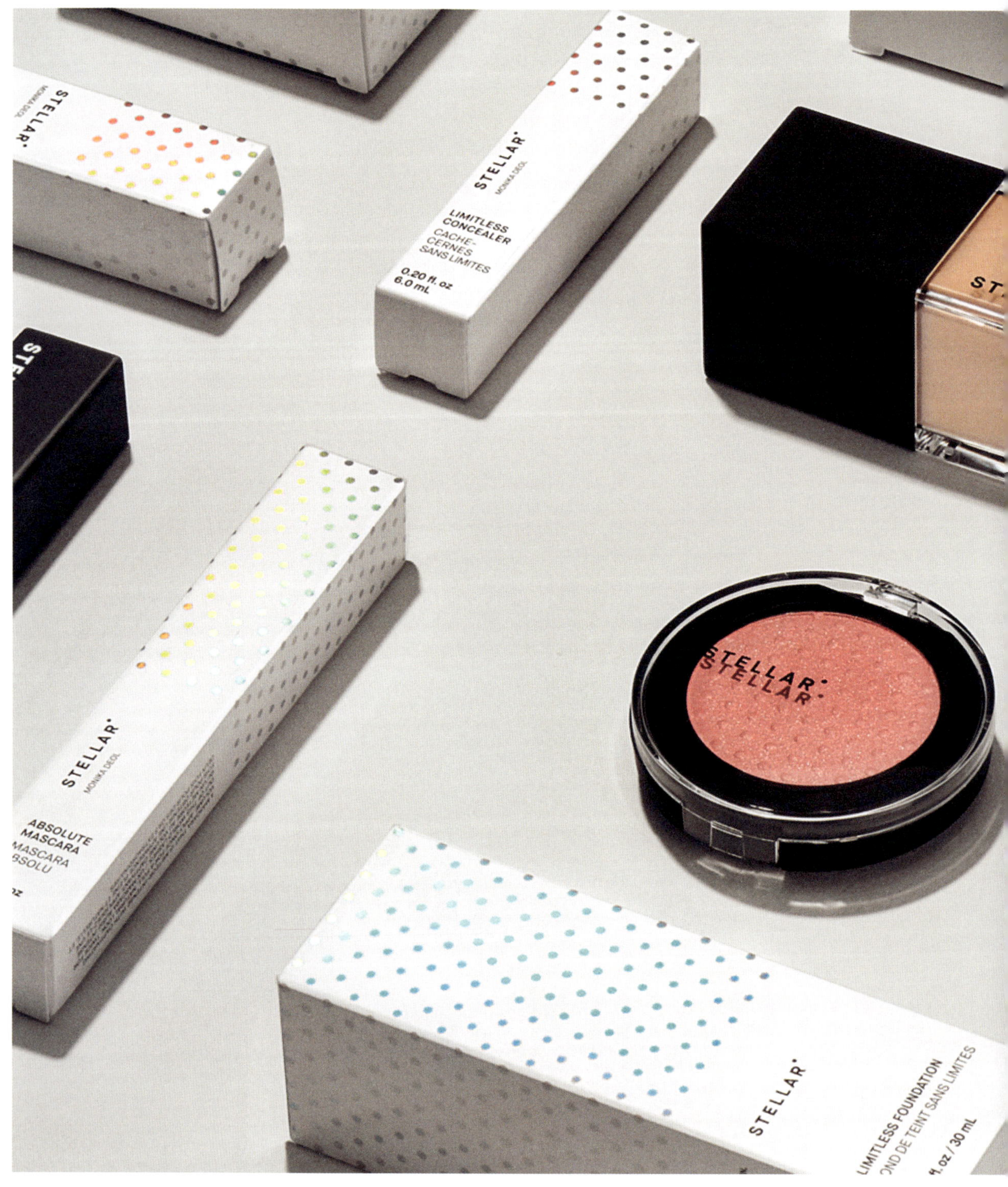

Inspired by the cosmos, the brand identity and name allude to starry constellations. The black and white represent night and day while a secondary opalescent palette vibrates across the full spectrum of light, reflecting the inclusive nature of the brand. Guidelines ensure all graphic elements reverberate the effortless, confident, and bold brand ethos of Stellar.

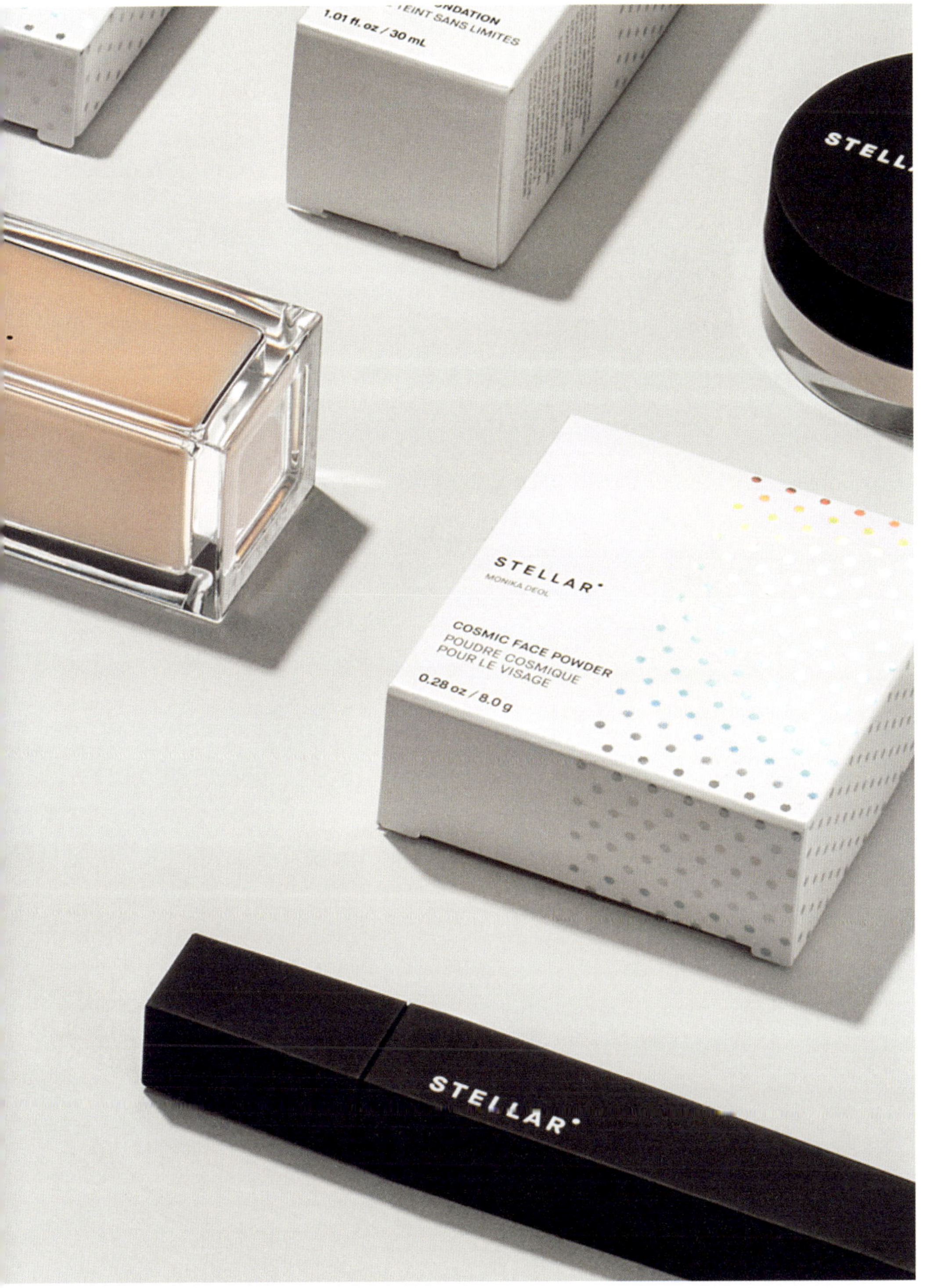

Stellar

studio: **Bruce Mau Design**
designer: **Luis Coderque**

STELLAR

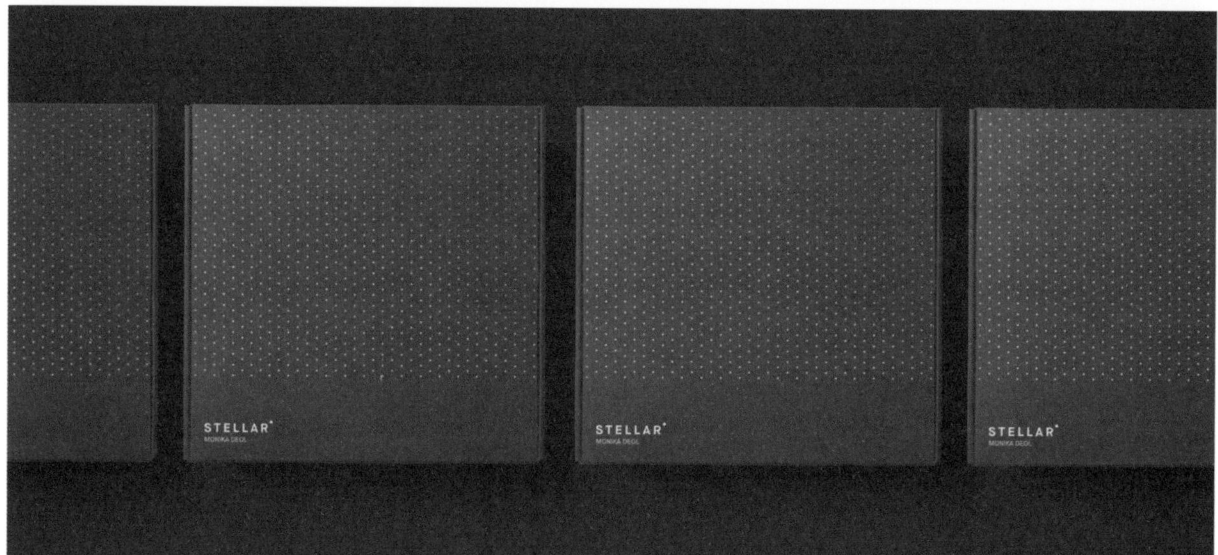
STELLAR
STELLAR
STELLAR

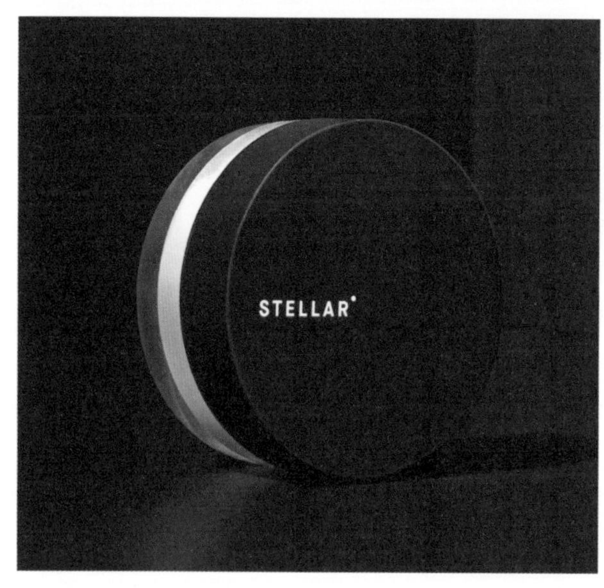
STELLAR

STELLAR

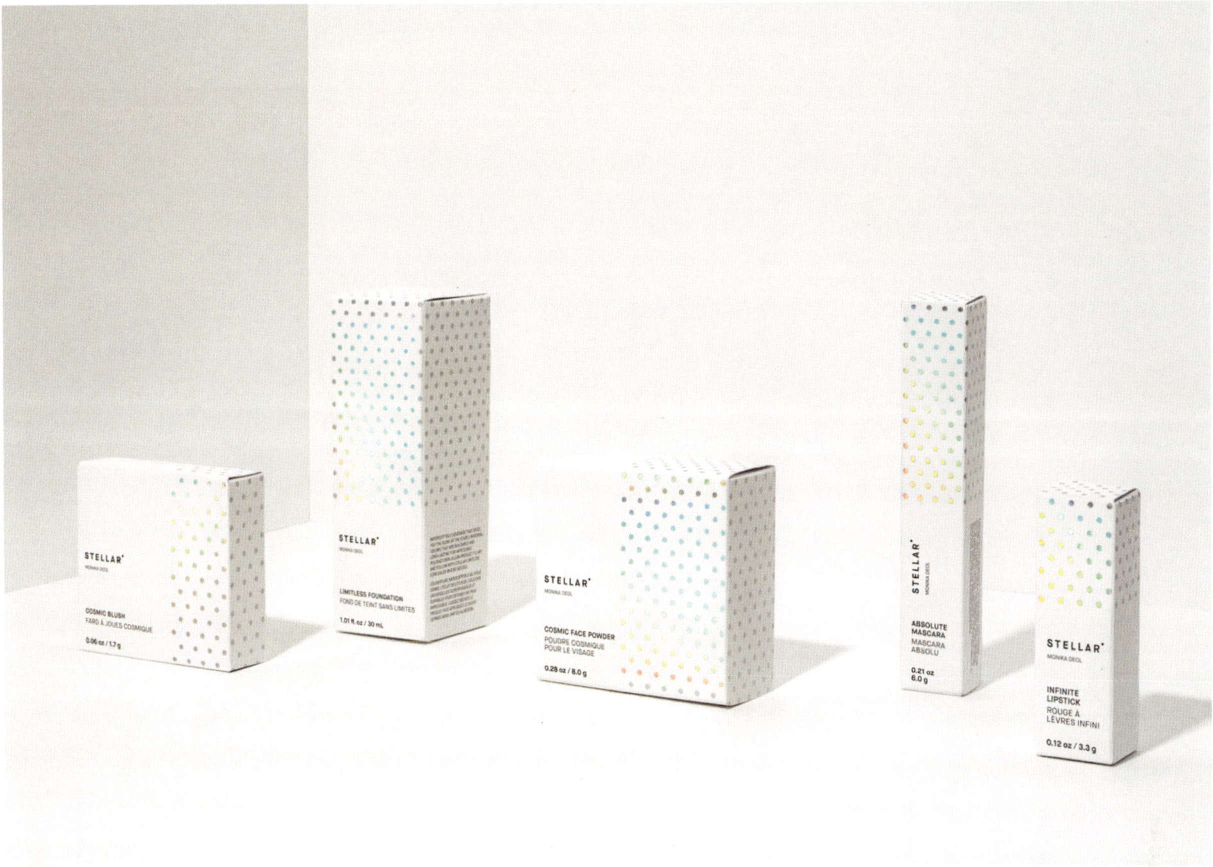

SHOP ON SEPHORA

STELLAR

MONIKA DEOL

Infinite Lipstick

DESCRIPTION / DETAILS / TIPS

STELLAR Infinite Lipstick is a luxurious, full coverage, creamy lipstick that glides on like silk. With a single stroke, your lips will be left with beautiful long-lasting color. Buildable coverage allows you to decide what look you want – natural and luminous or an intense illusion of fullness. Thoughtfully curated shades offer each complexion a customized look.

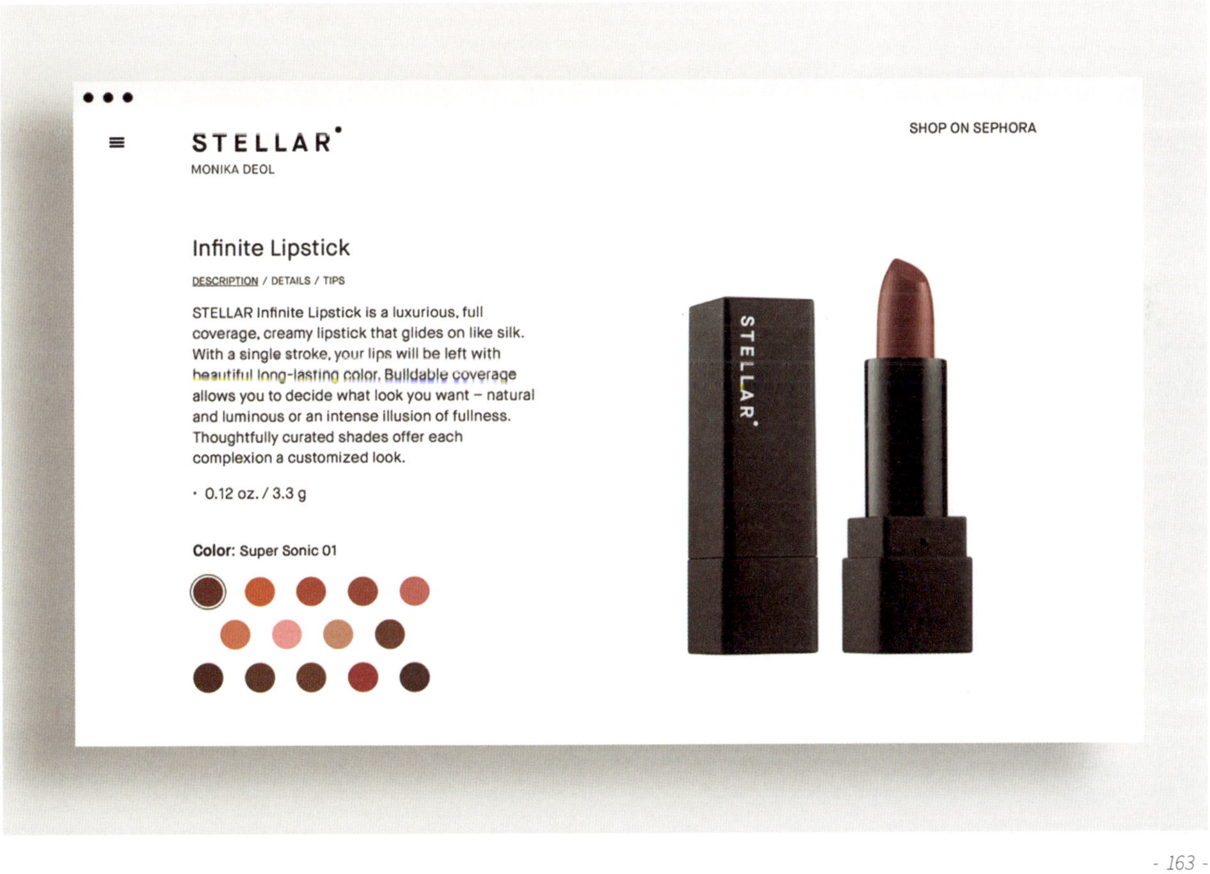

- 0.12 oz. / 3.3 g

Color: Super Sonic 01

STELLAR

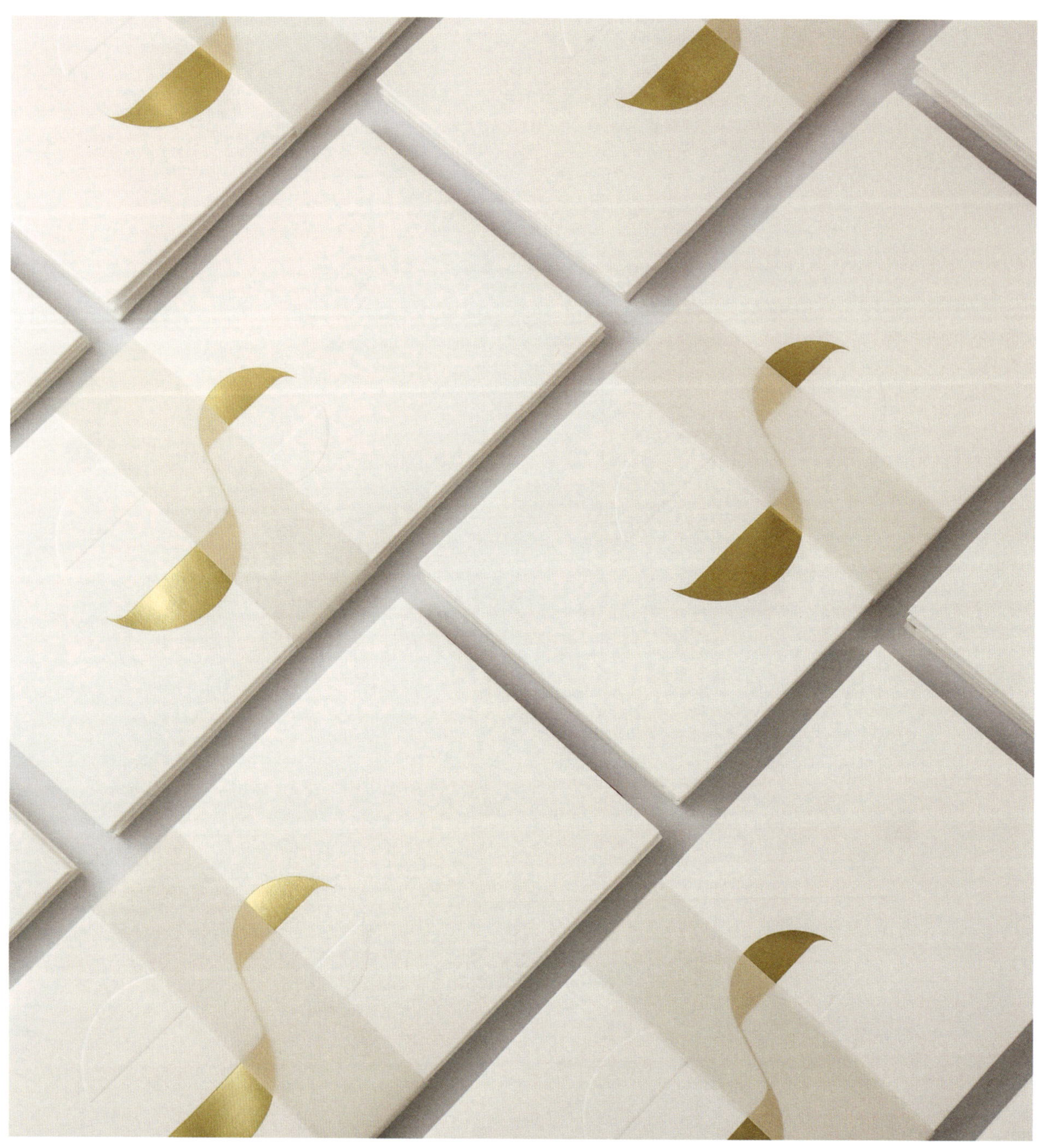

Number 8 is believed to be auspicious in Chinese culture as it rhymes with the word "Fa" that means wealth, lending its frequent presence in festive greetings. The horizontal 8 is similar to the infinity symbol. This design marries the two concepts to signify a continuous cycle of fortune unfolding a year of longevity with prosperity.

Minimalist Red Packets I

studio: *Kong Studio*
designer: *Kevin He* copywriter: *Mel Mohd*

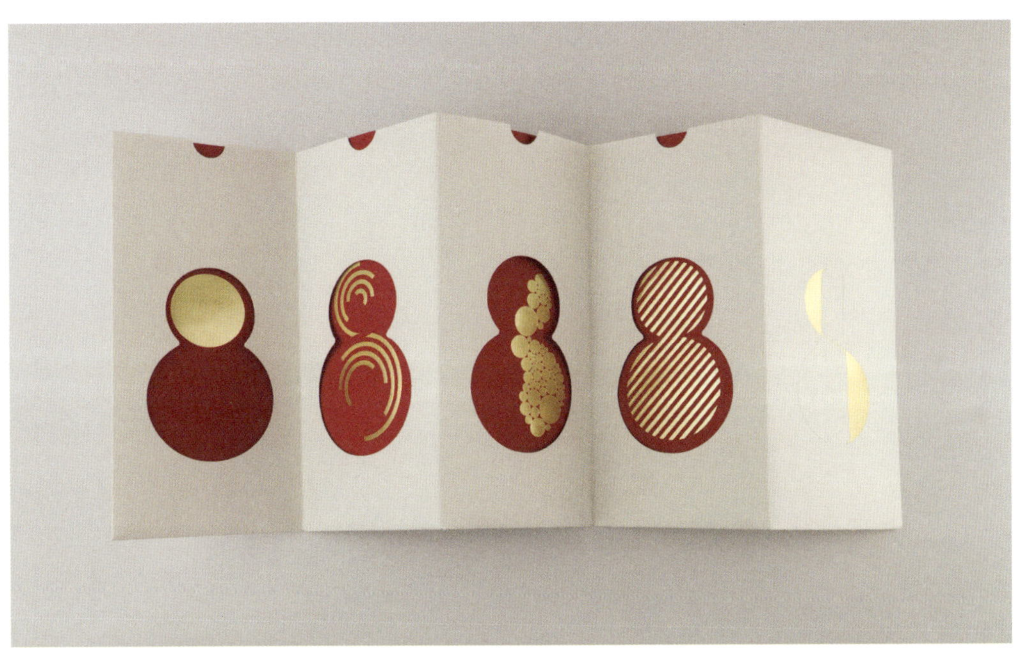

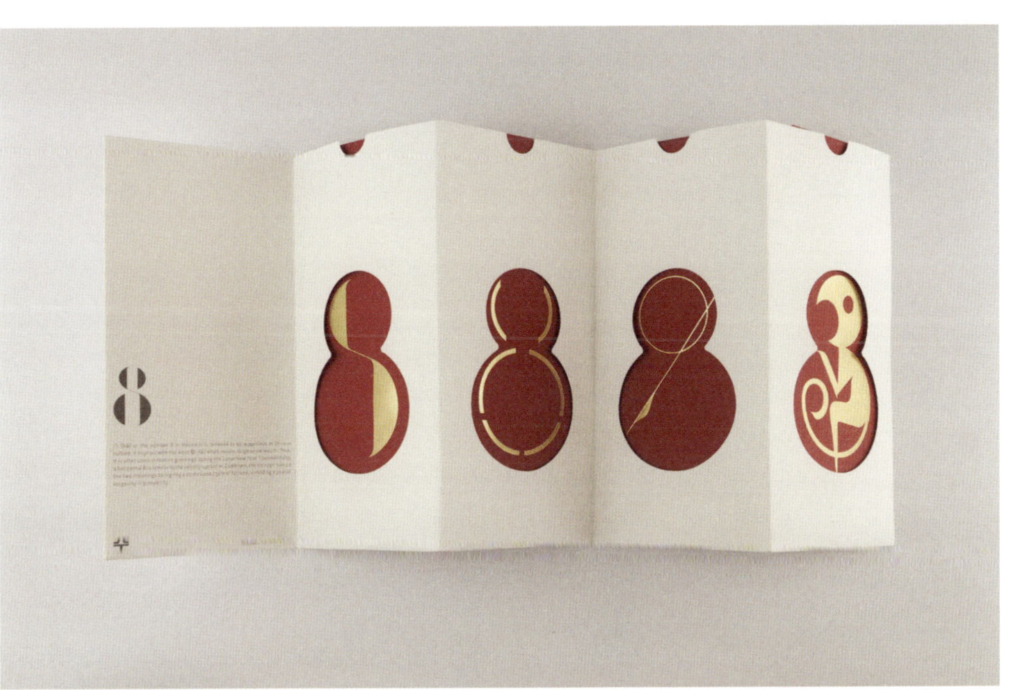

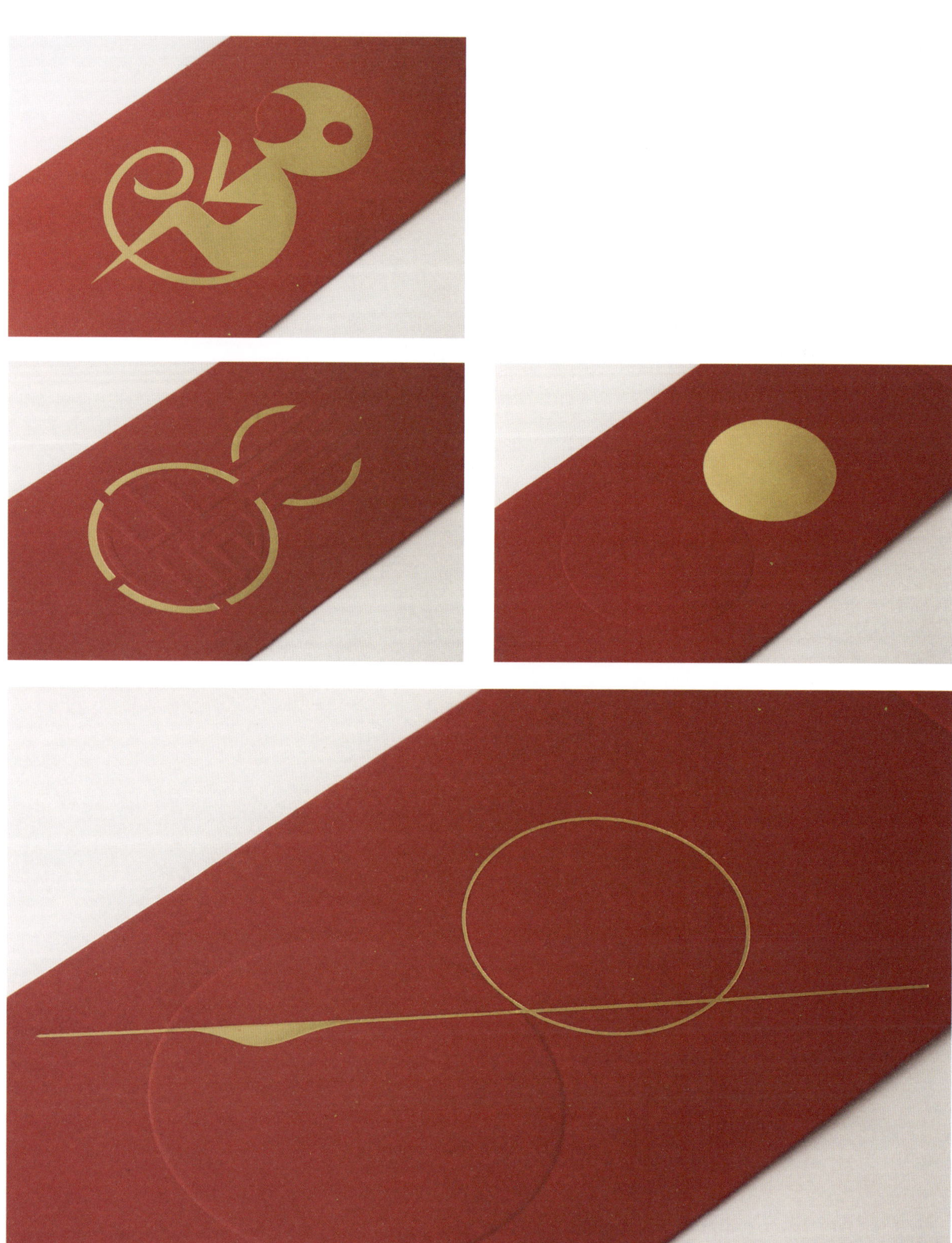

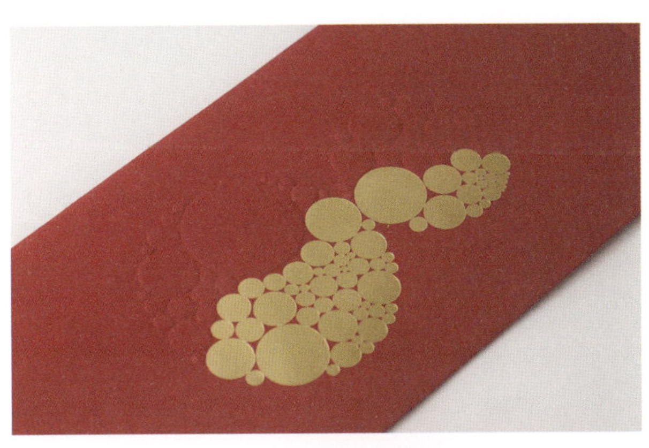

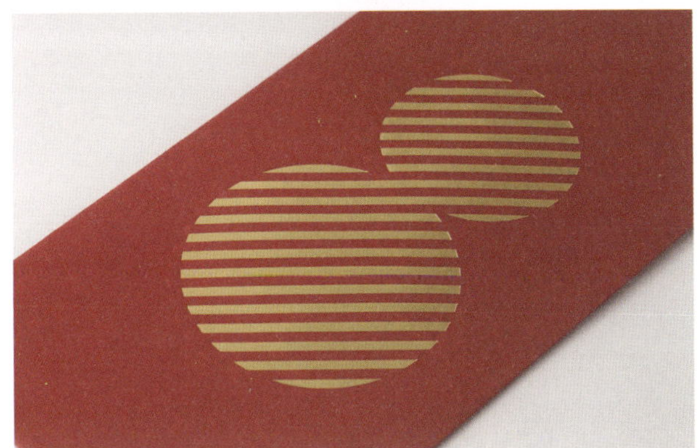

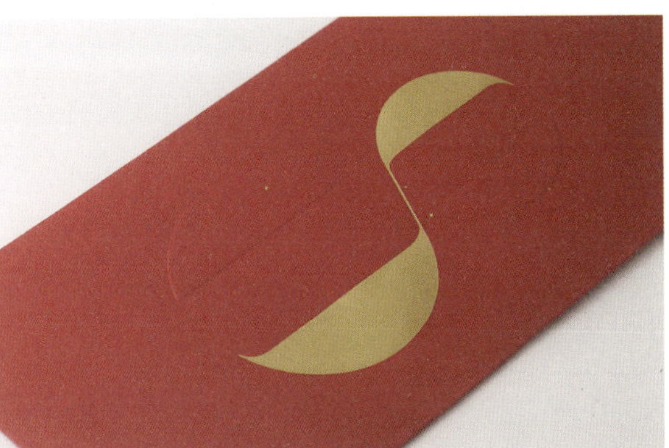

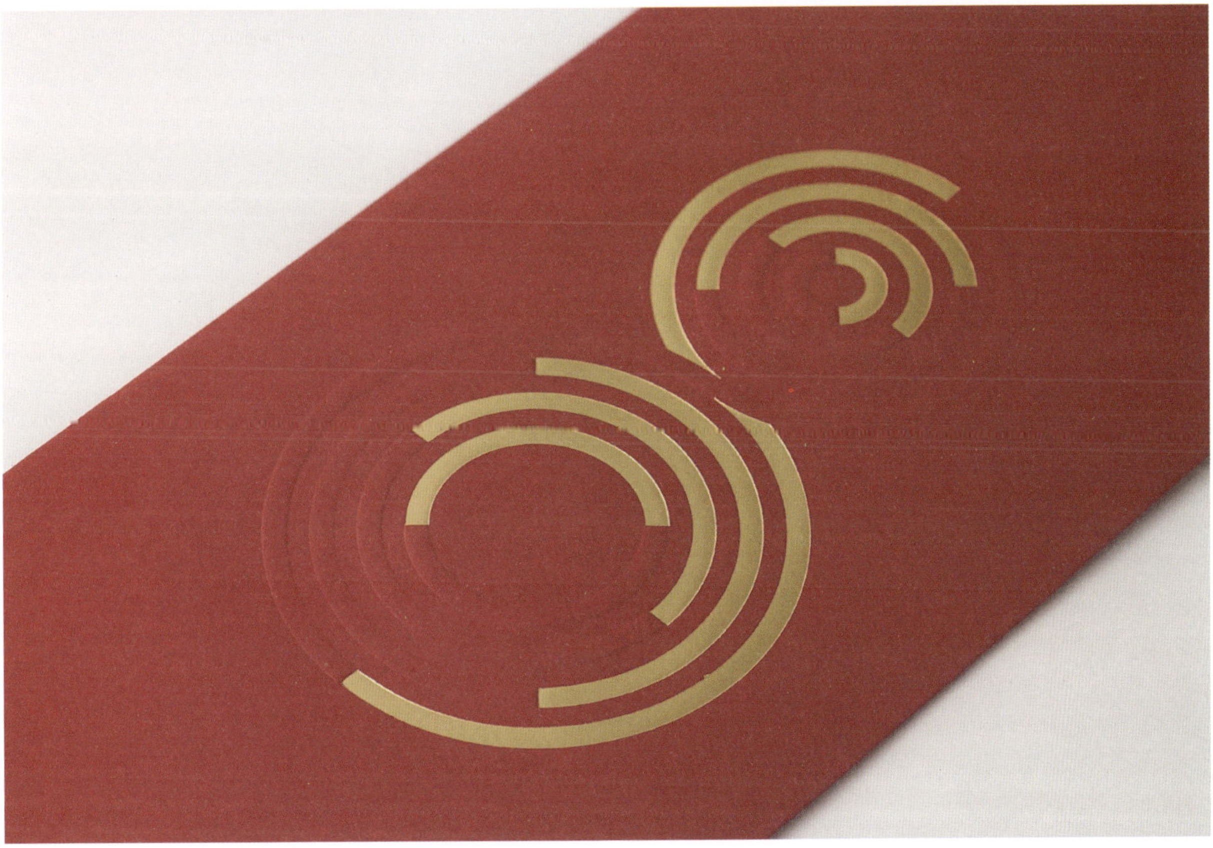

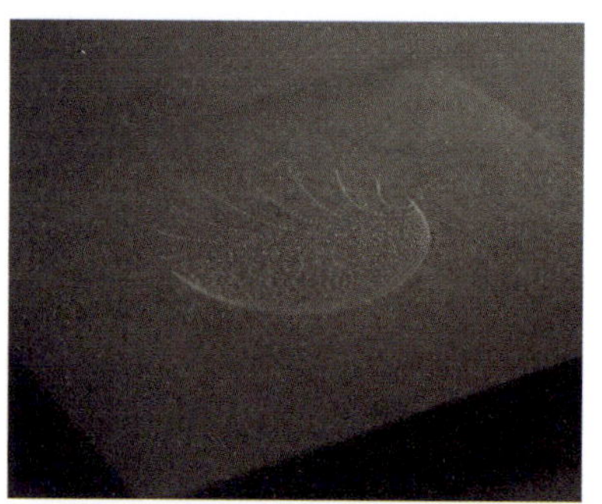

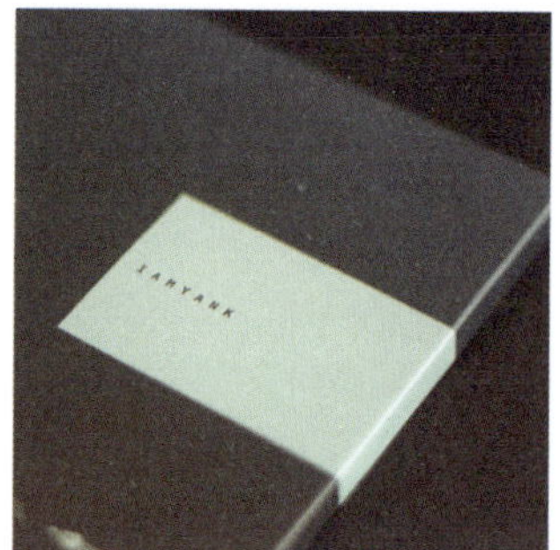

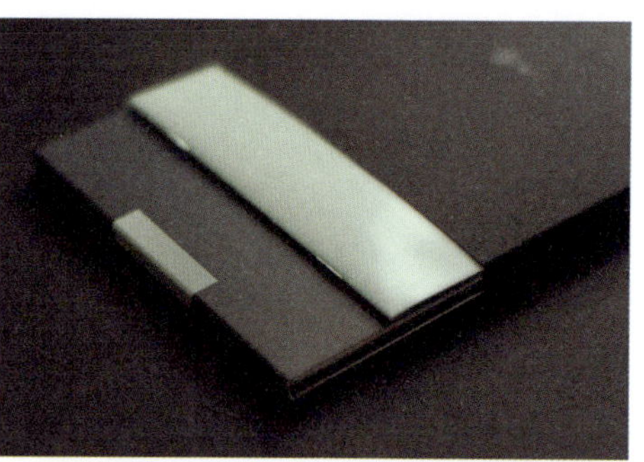

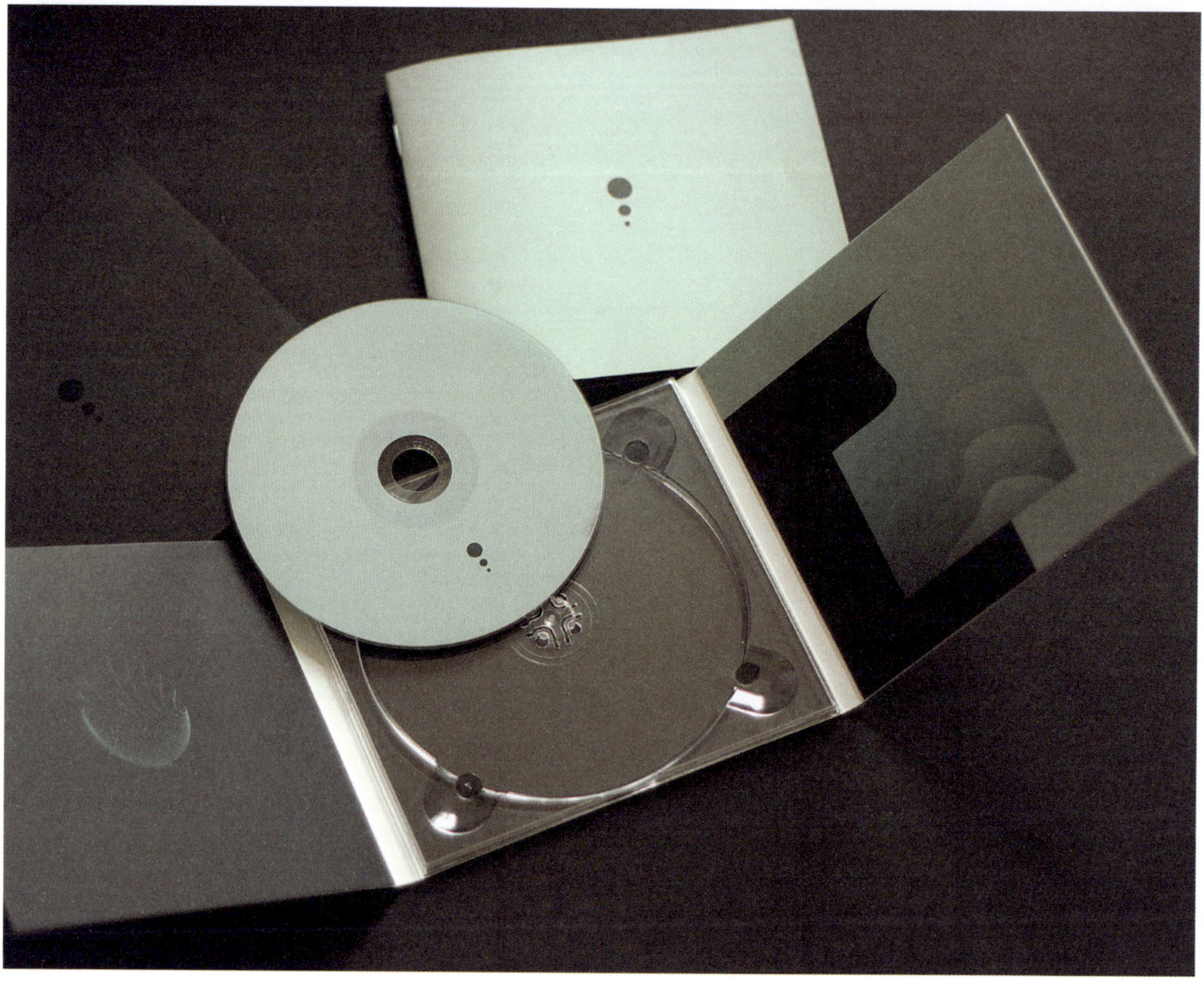

The identity design and art direction for the first IAMYANK LP, "HIRAETH" is to reflect the dreamy, magical music in this album, which collects all the influences that inspired the multi-instrumentalist producer and songwriter. It renders dark places, weird sounds mixed with peaceful soundscapes into a melancholic journey.

Iamyank - Hiraeth LP

designer:
Tamas Birinyi

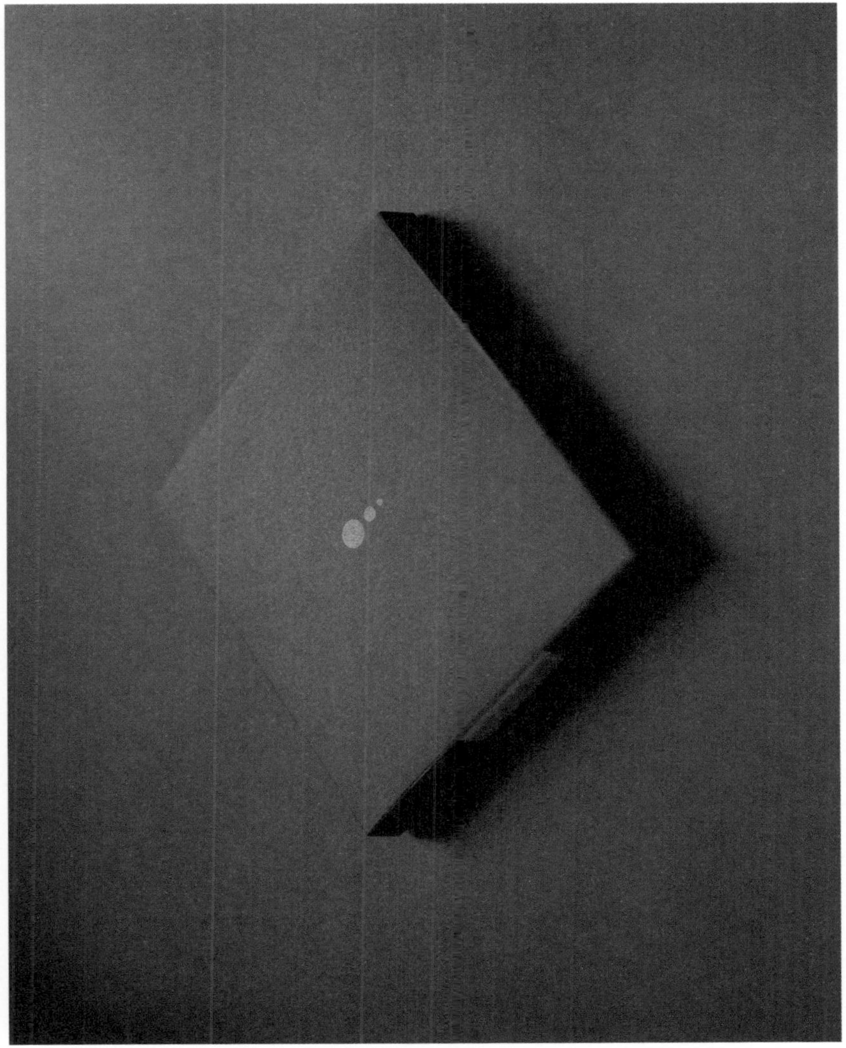

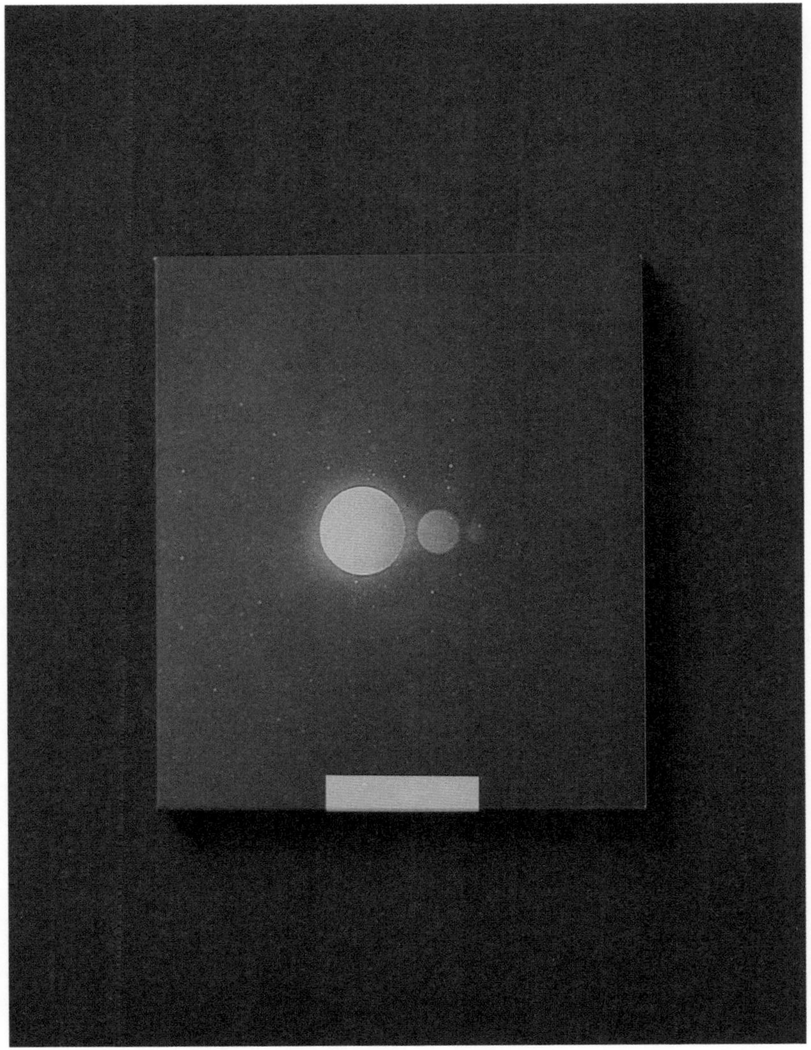

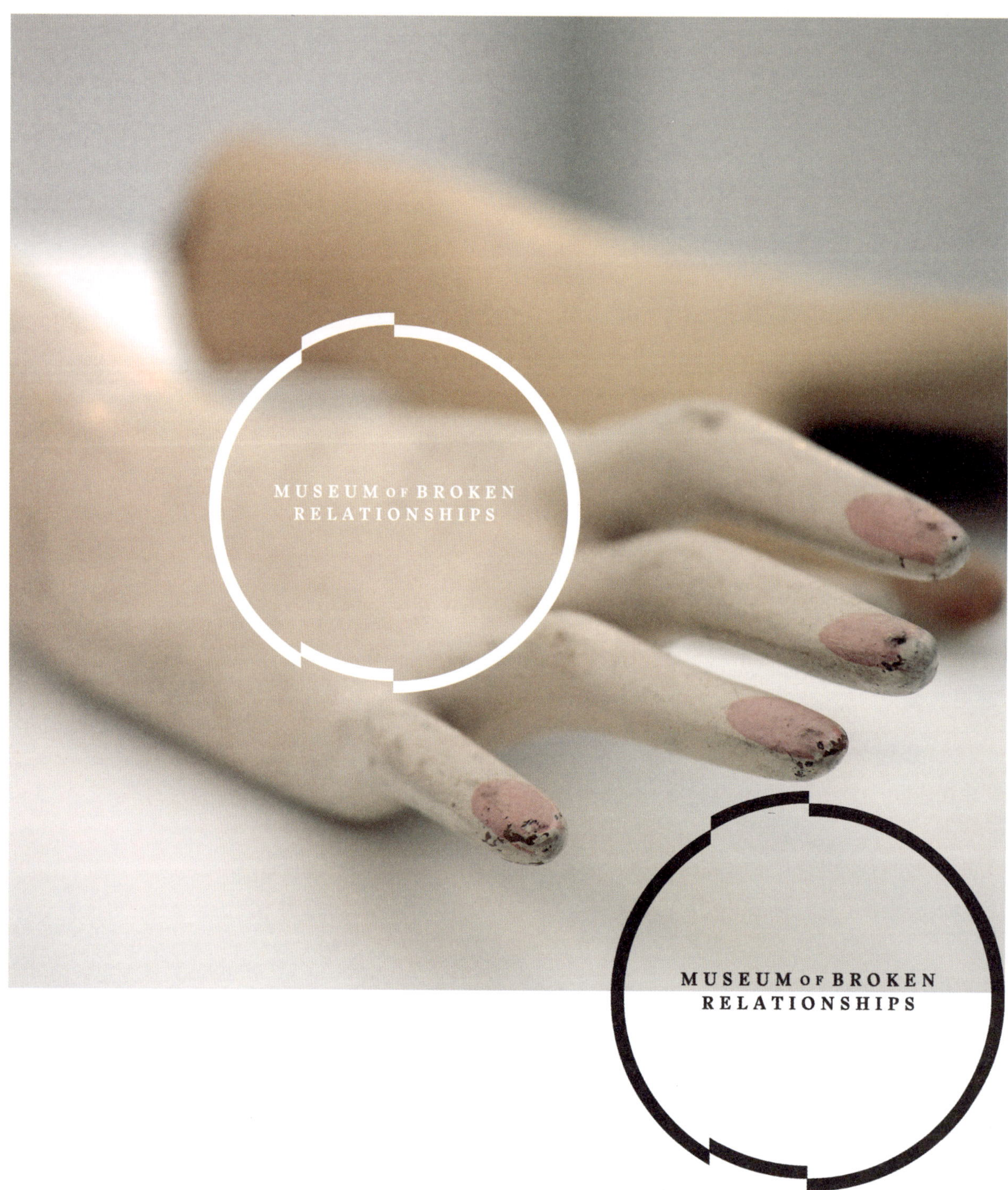

Based on familiarity, basic emotions and high aesthetic value, the rebranding for the Museum of Broken Relationships employs a logotype of a broken cycle to express simply and abstractly the feeling of being broken and out of place. The printed materials, with desaturated color palettes and selected typography, convey a sense of nostalgia and intimacy that roils the viewer, provoking empathy and a feeling of intrusiveness.

Museum Of Broken Relationships

studio:
Savvy Studio

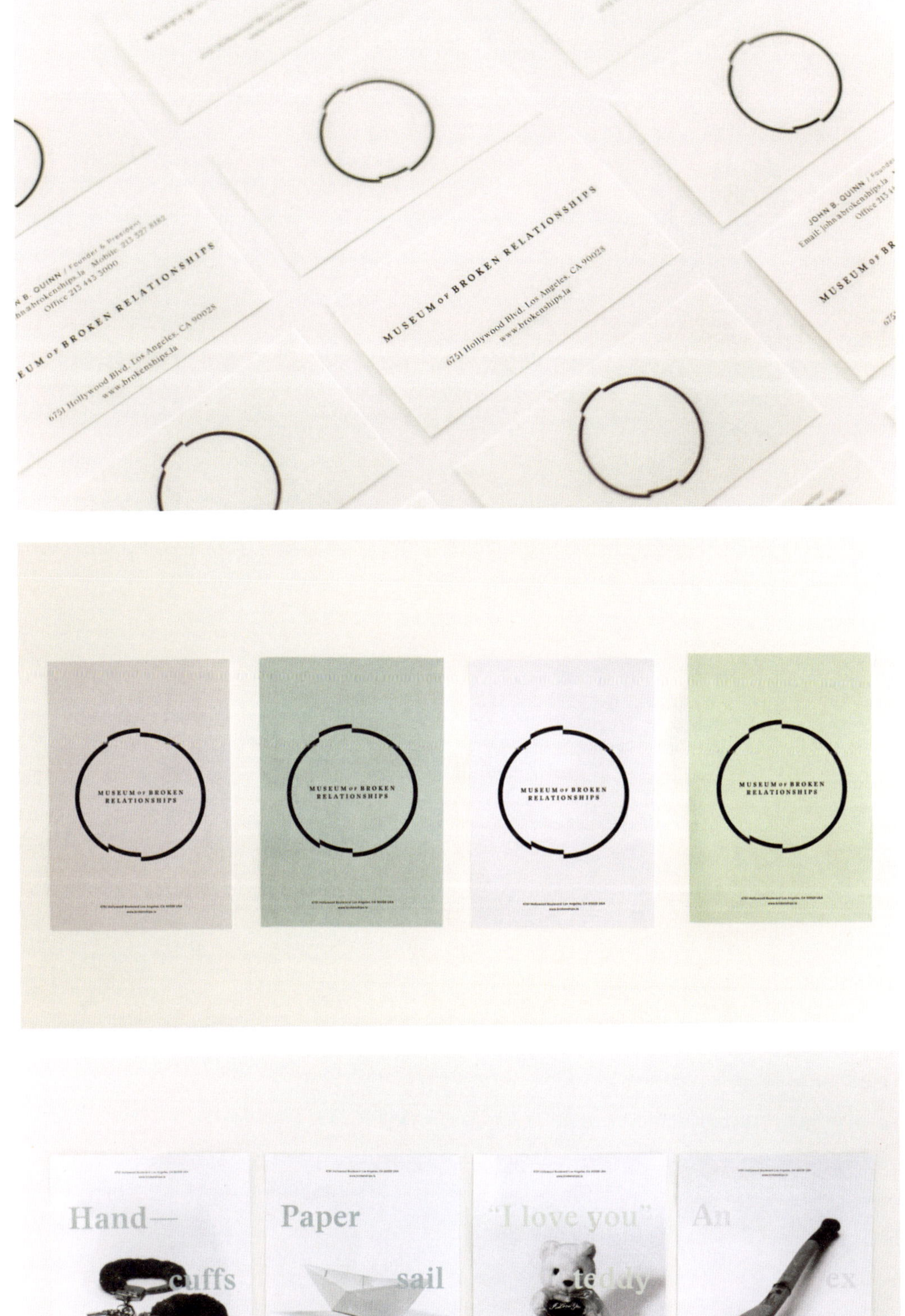

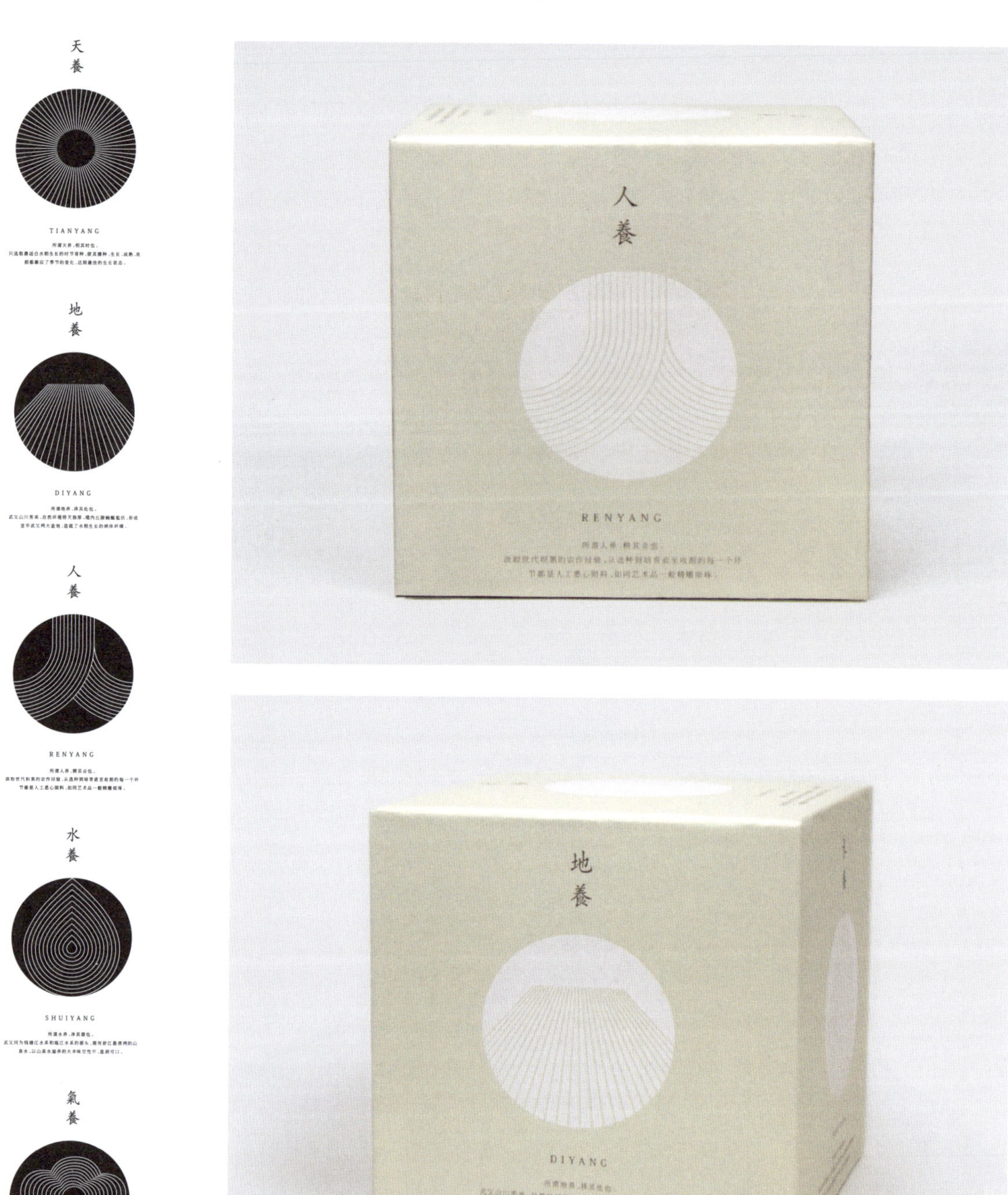

This is a packaging design for the organic rice produced by an ecological agricultural brand. The designer has devised five simple but quintessential symbols to visualize the product's five concepts of health preserving—celestial, earth, human, water and qi. The plain color is a reminder of the nature and purity of organic rice.

Wu Yang Xin Mi

studio:
Tang Shipeng

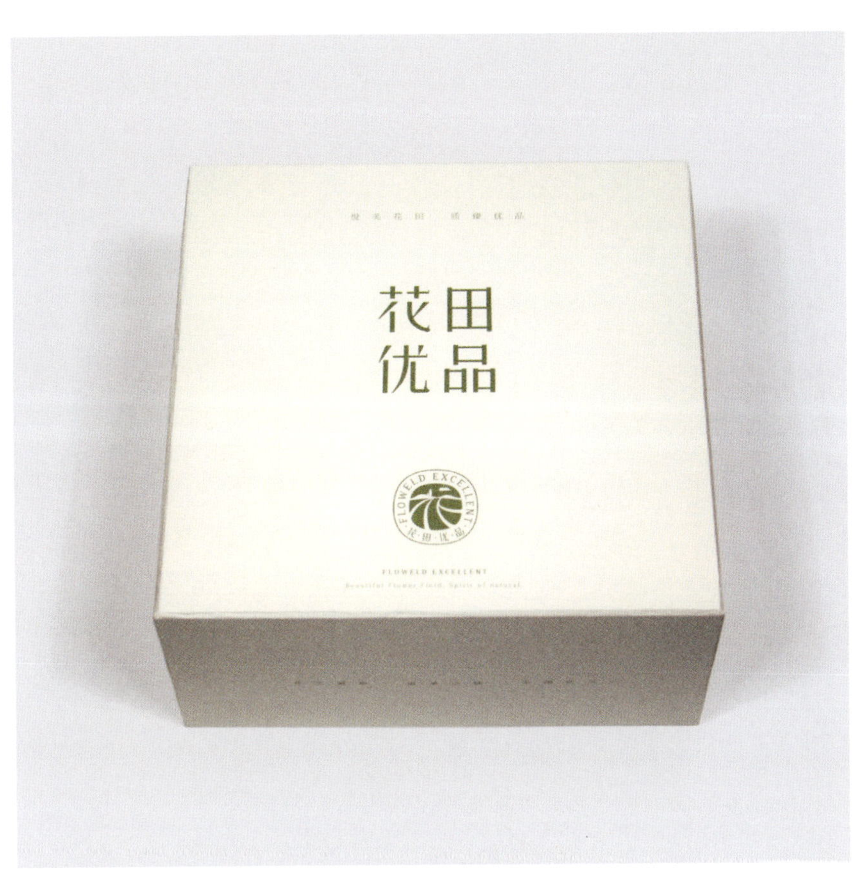

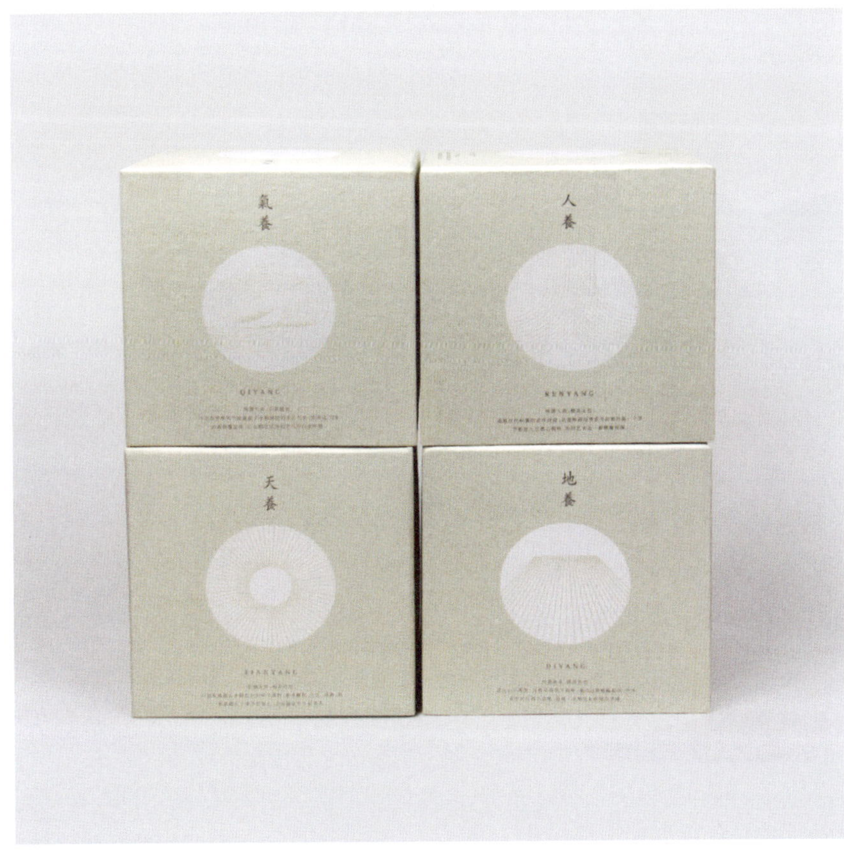

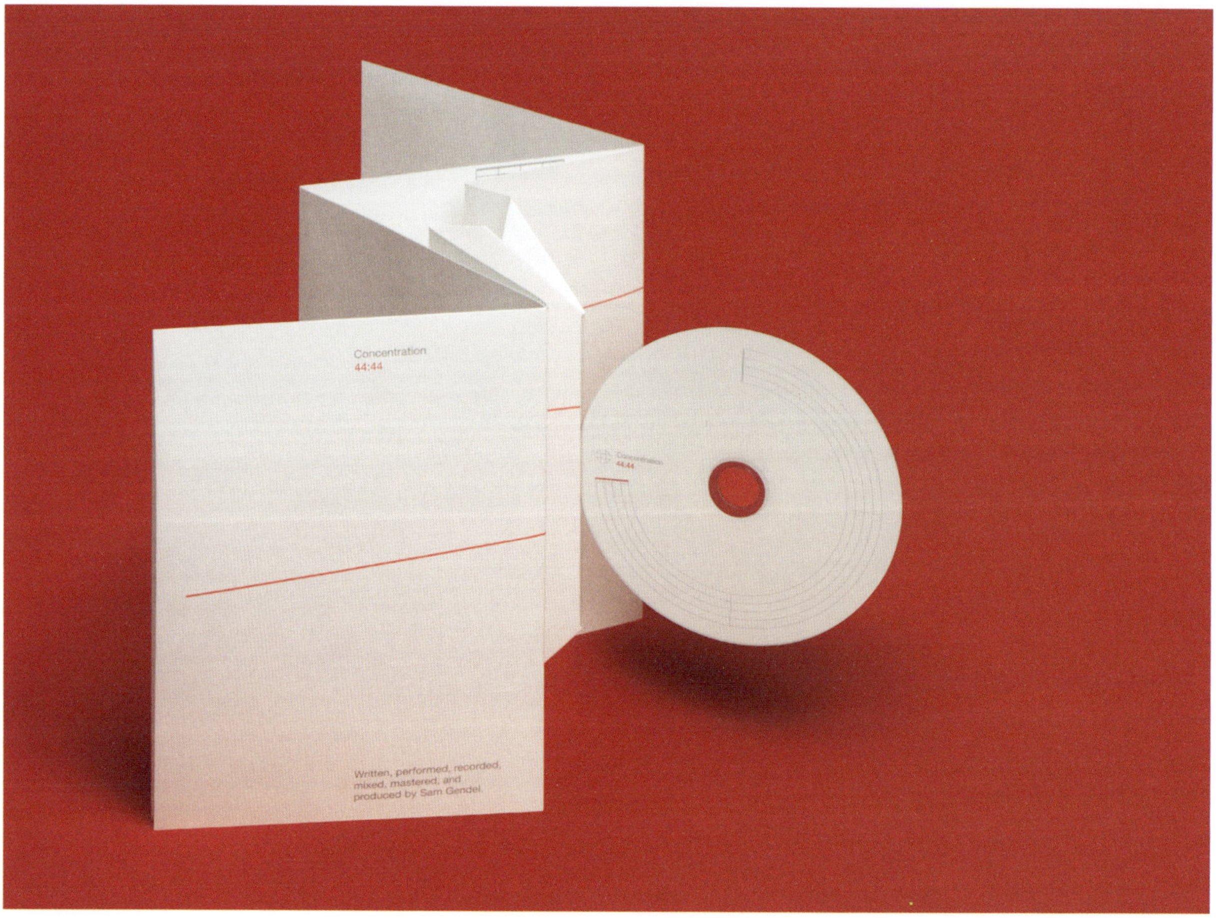

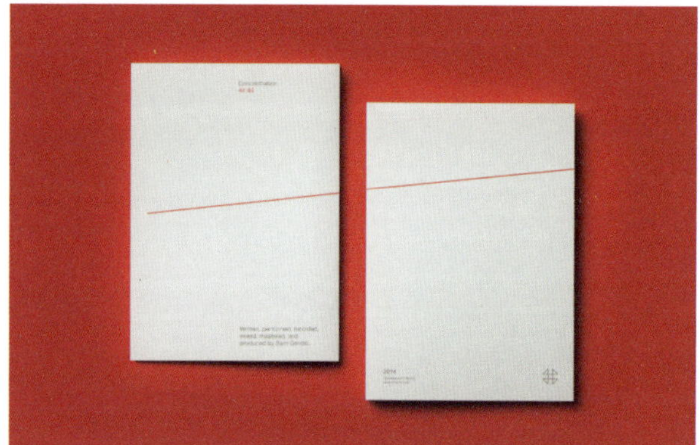

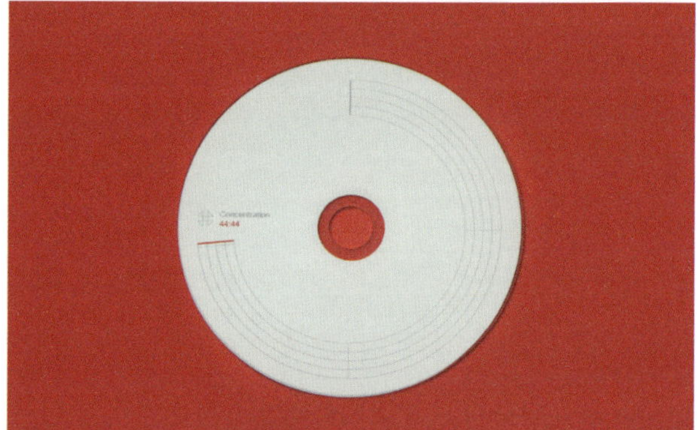

This is a limited edition CD and CD packaging for Sam Gendel, a professional saxophonist based in LA. As an art piece to celebrate a new beginning before his next album, he has produced 44 minutes and 44 seconds of complete silence, entitled Concentration. The CD design and its packaging, which could be unfolded to become a poster, represent the notion of time, music and silence.

Concentration

studio:
MUCHO

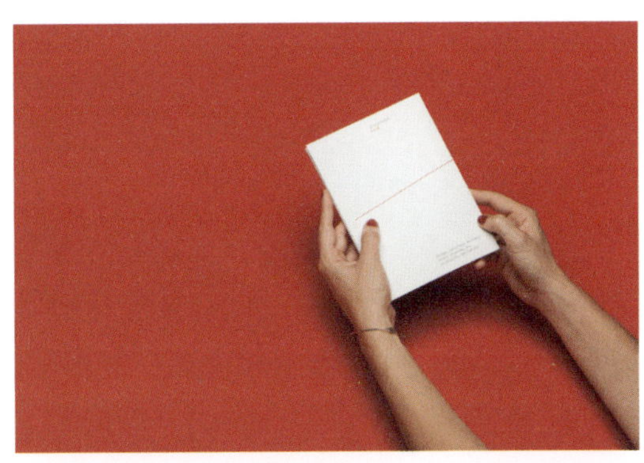

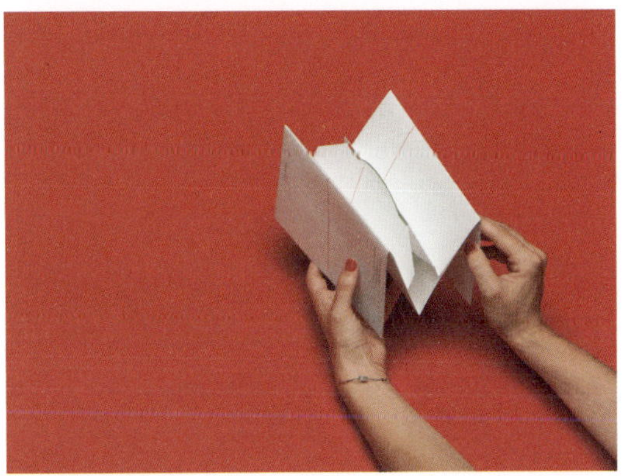

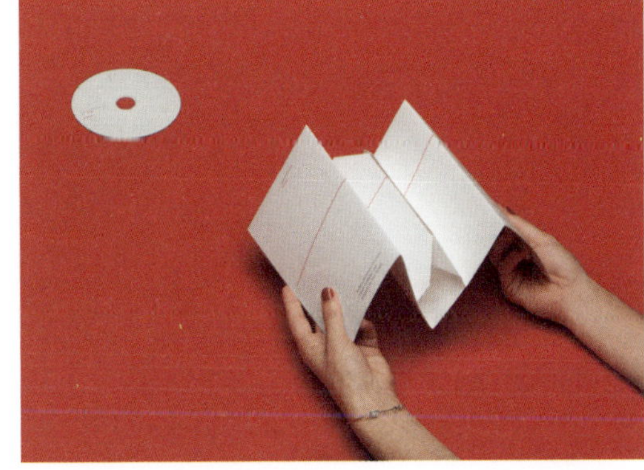

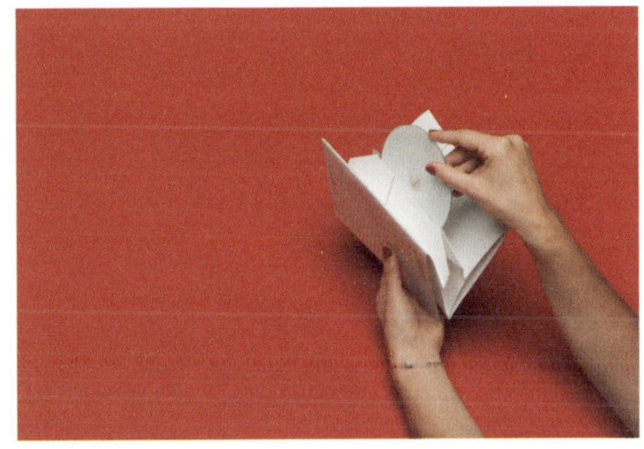

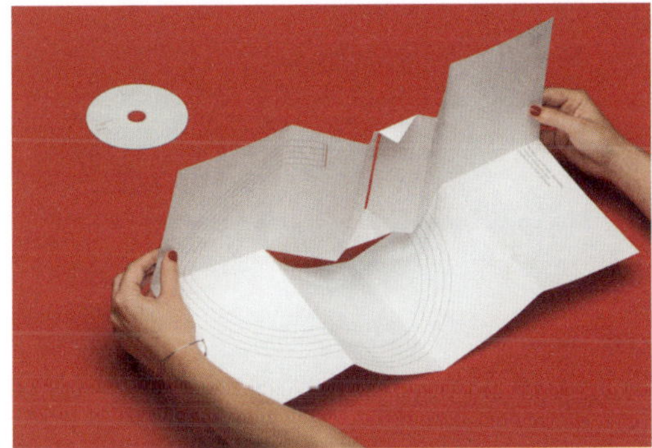

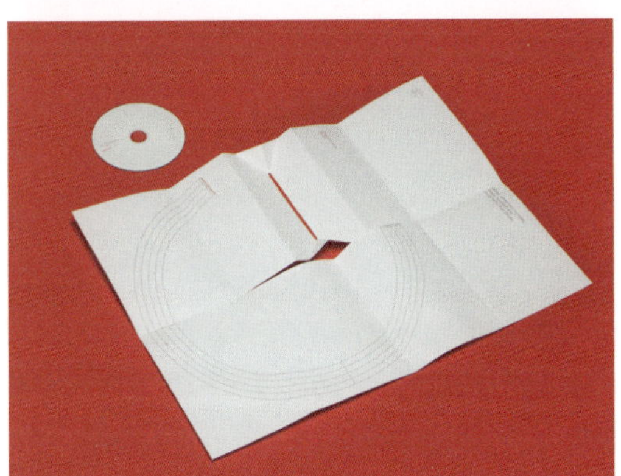

MONOCHROME

Whether it would be black, white and gray or other colors, the quantity and variance of the color used are minimized to generate an immersive mood. It gives consistency to the design, while establishing emotional connection with the viewer.

image ***© Fagerström Studio***

MT ARQUITECTOS

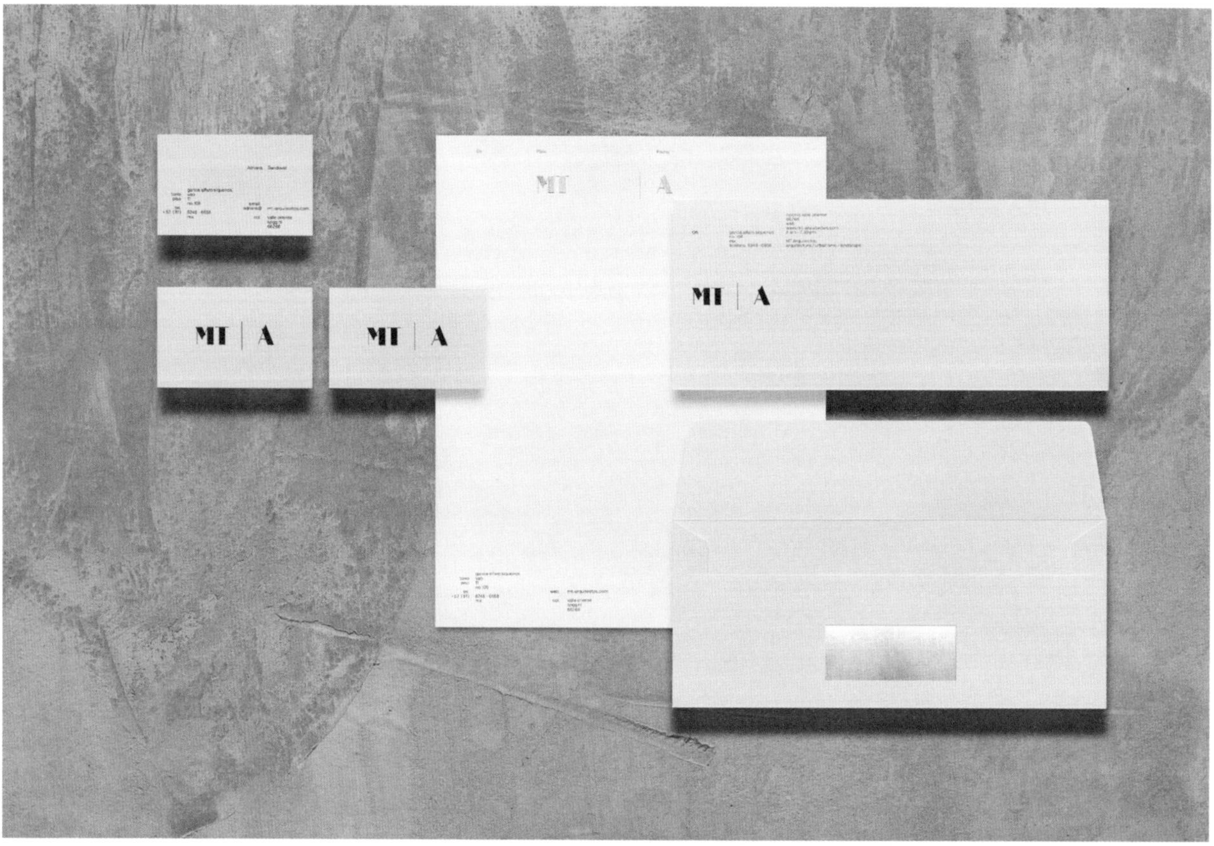

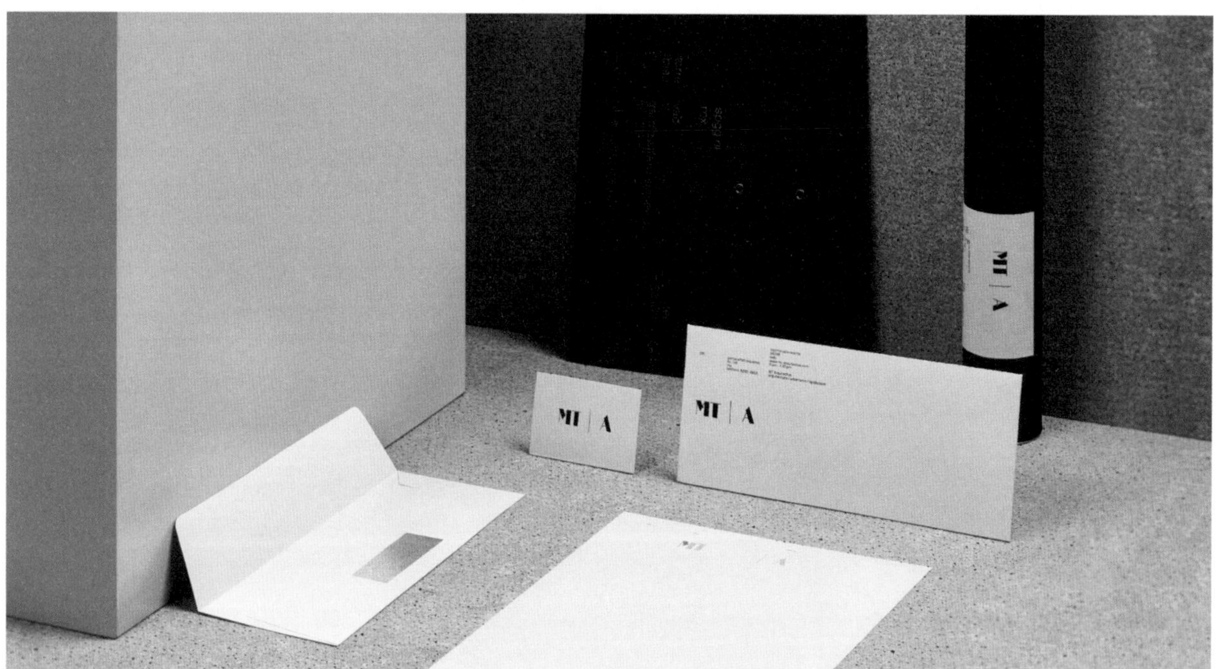

- Studio: **Anagrama**

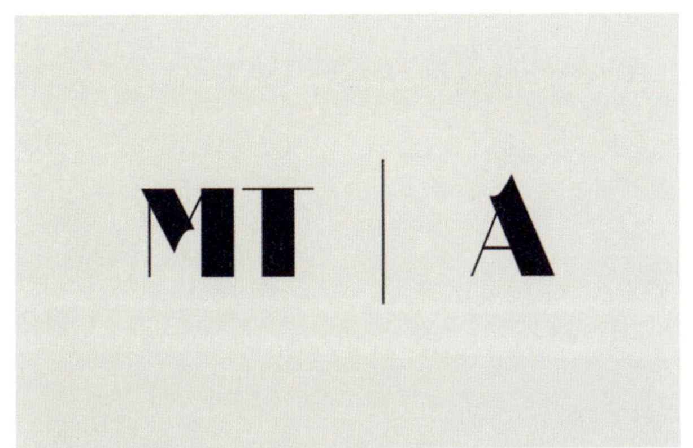

For the MTA's rebranding, Anagrama created a new identity based on the reflection on the brand's evolution. Efforts were centered on designing a typographical logo inspired by the architectural supporting elements from previous projects accentuating bold features to highlight the brand's personality in line with a clean and elegant identity.

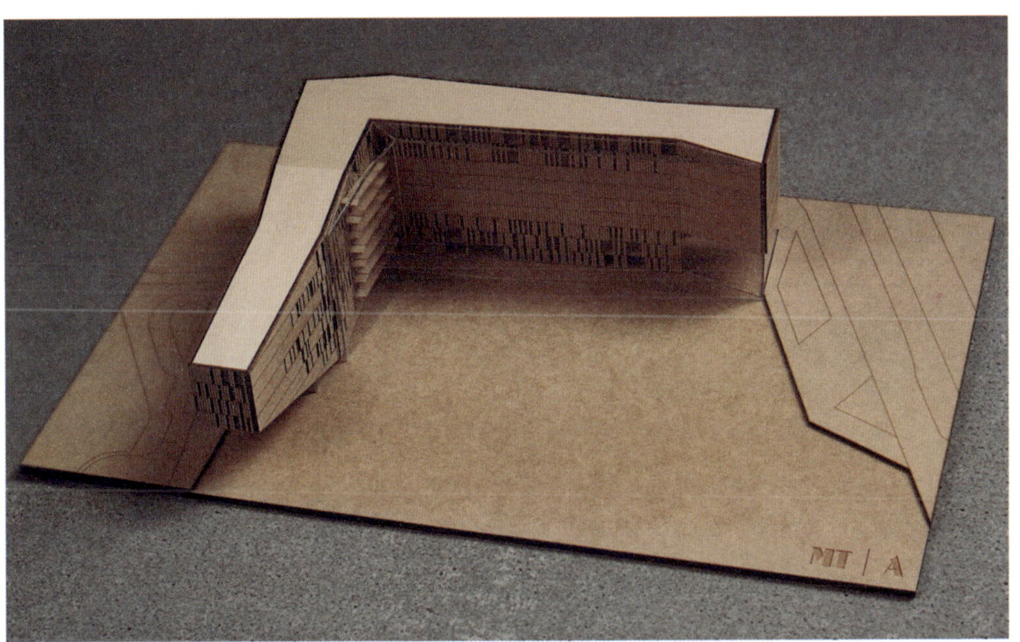

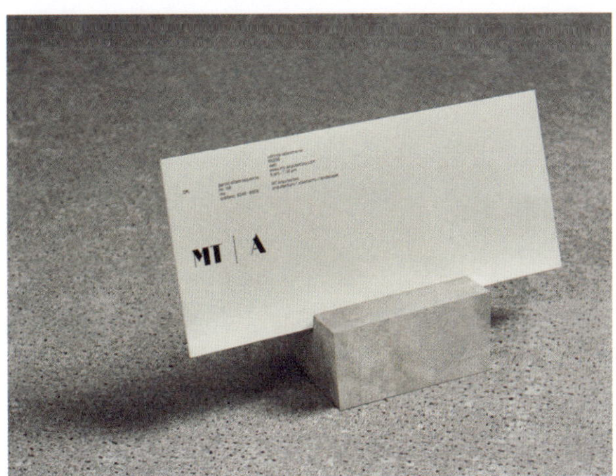

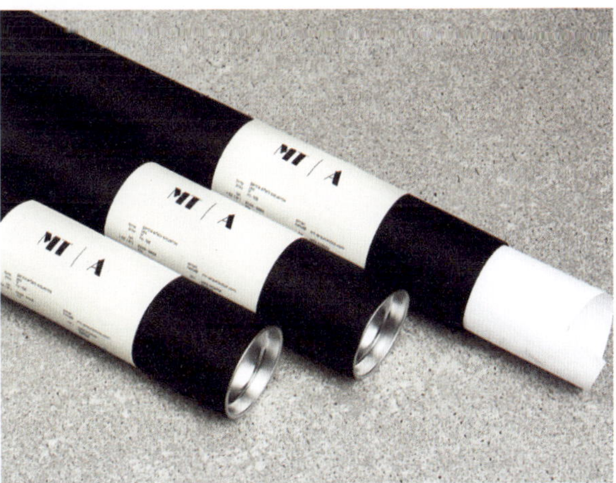

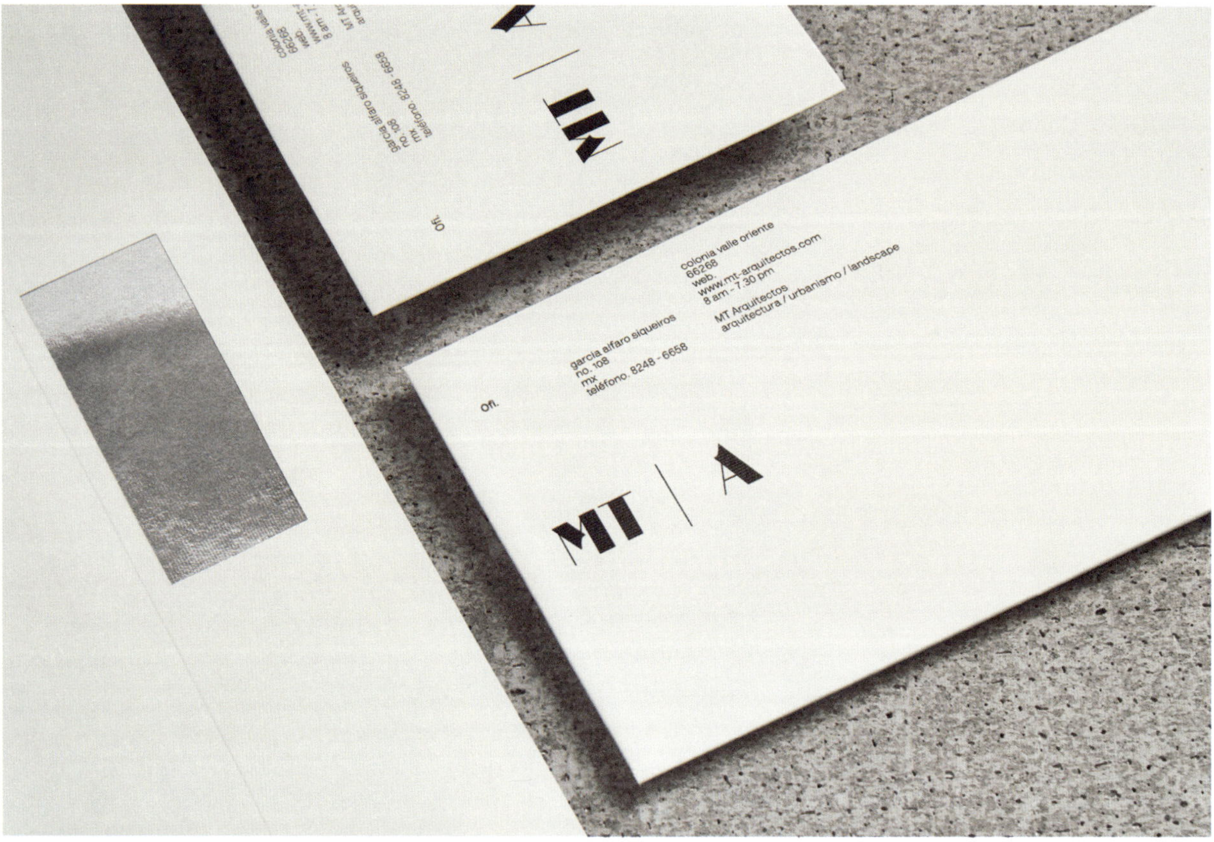
MT | A
ofi.
garcía alfaro siqueiros
no. 108
mx
teléfono. 8248 - 6658
colonia valle oriente
66268
web.
www.mt-arquitectos.com
8 am - 7.30 pm
MT Arquitectos
arquitectura / urbanismo / landscape

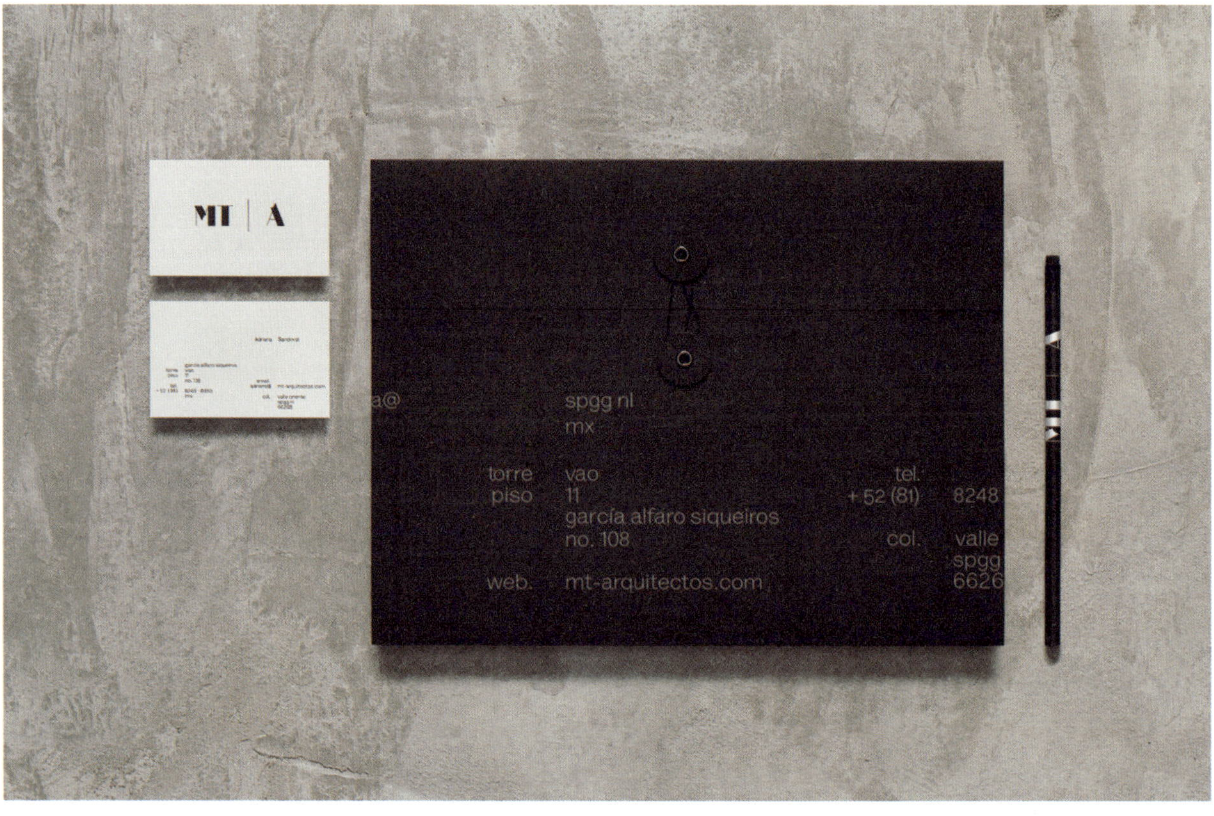
MT | A
spgg nl
mx
torre vao
piso 11
garcía alfaro siqueiros
no. 108
web. mt-arquitectos.com
tel.
+52 (81) 8248
col. valle
spgg
6626

Interview

- As a kind of visual experience, what do you think about the "voidness" in graphic design?

- To decide what kind of voidness we would employ, it's important to understand the objective, to figure out what we want to communicate through the project, and what is the best for the graphic identity. A perfectly executed and constructed minimal design should stem from an aesthetic decision supported by solid grounds.

- What are your common approaches to produce a VOID visual effect?

- We are grid lovers. First of all we would decide and establish a grid to work, while always thinking what is the message and information that belong to the design. This will create a system that can be repeated on the whole branding system.

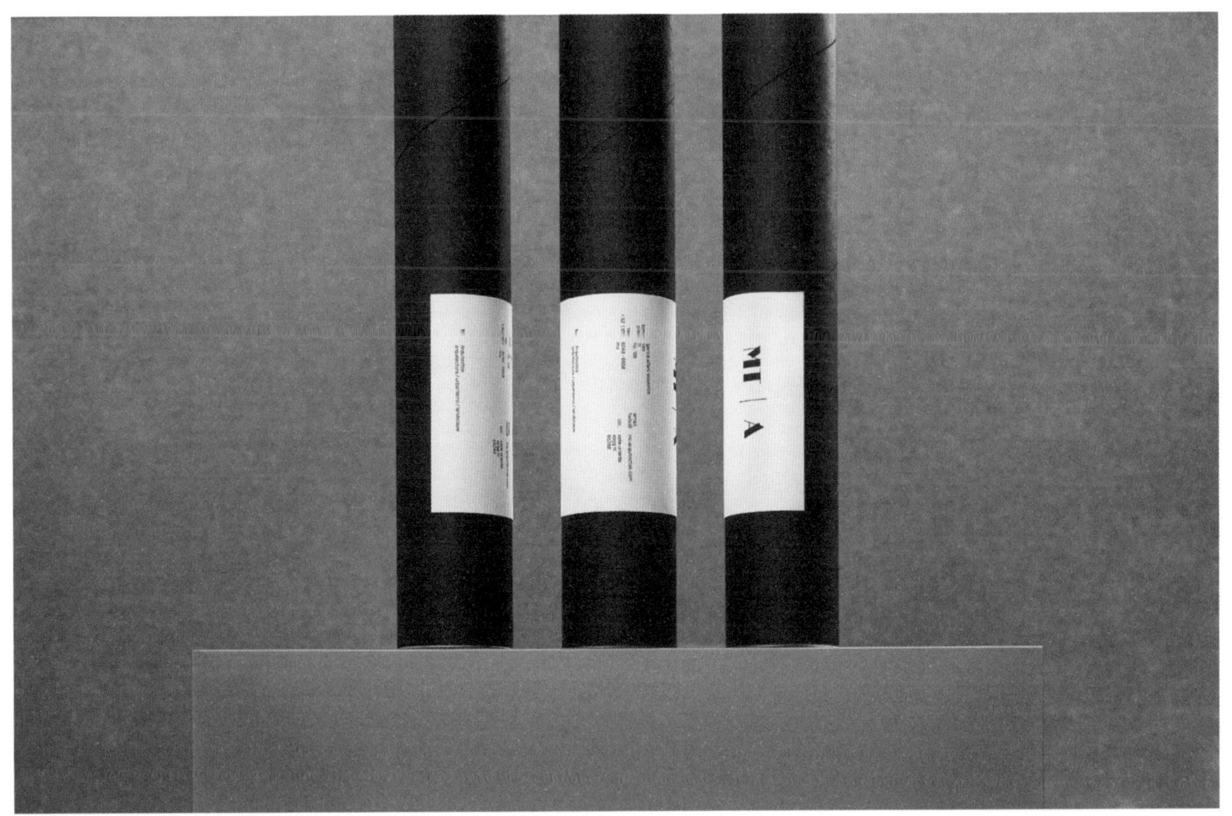

HIKESHI

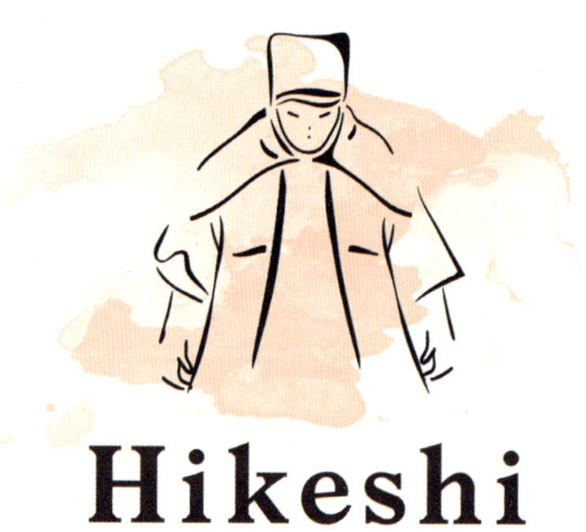

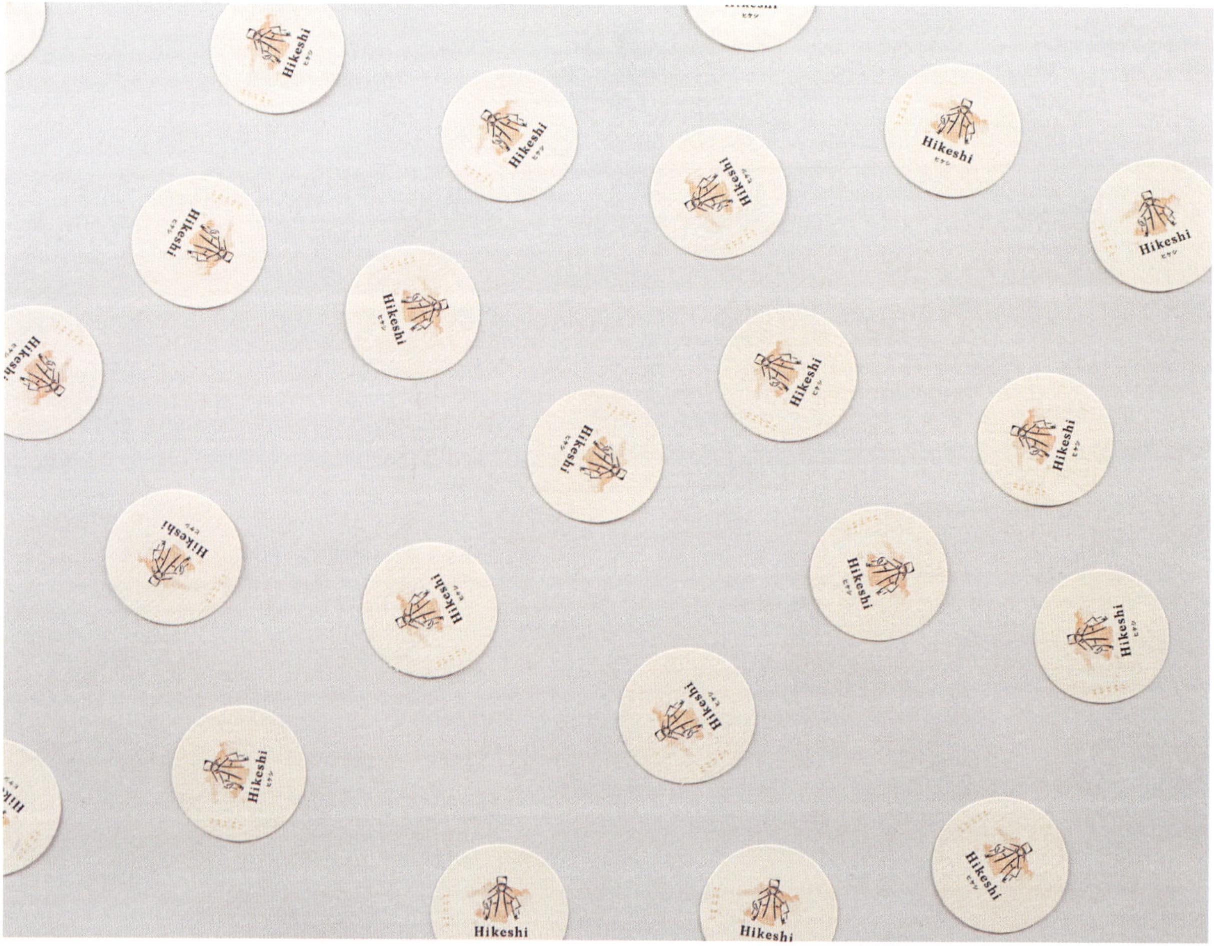

- Studio: ***Futura***

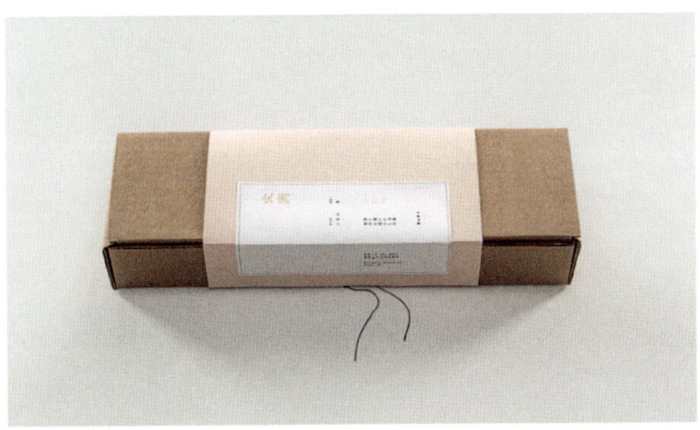

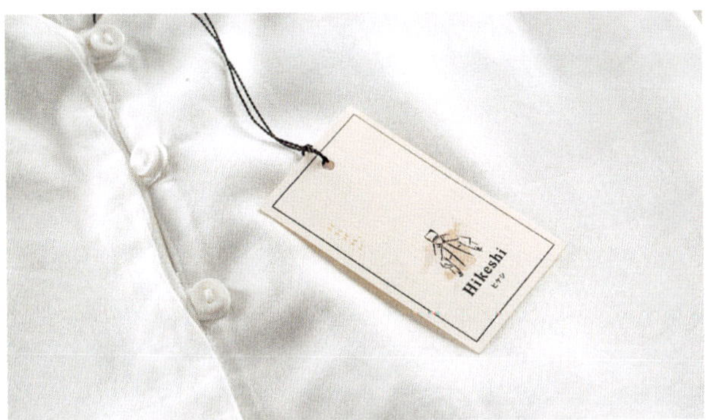

For the branding for Hikeshi, a high quality clothing line that belongs to the Japanese brand Resquad, the general concept was inspired by the Edo Period in Japanese history. Futura designed a series of illustrations featuring fire fighters from this period, who are considered as high ranked as samurais. The typographic selection and color palette turn the brand into something modern, while the material, the composition and the combination of elements altogether make Hikeshi a timeless brand.

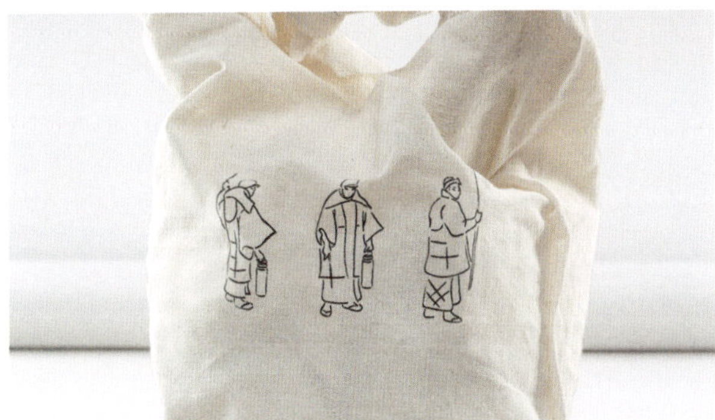

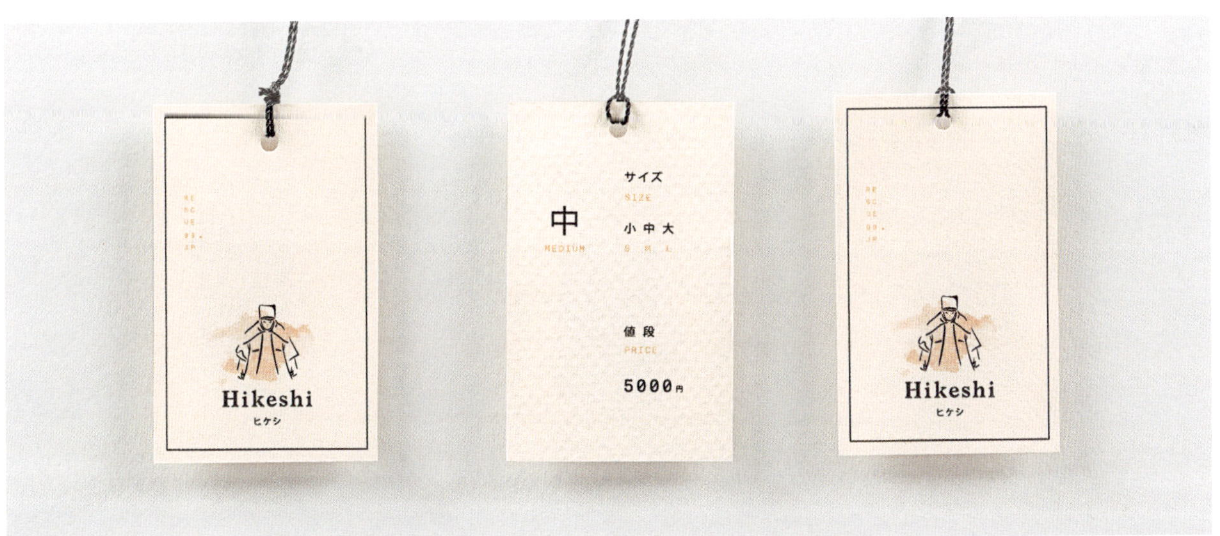

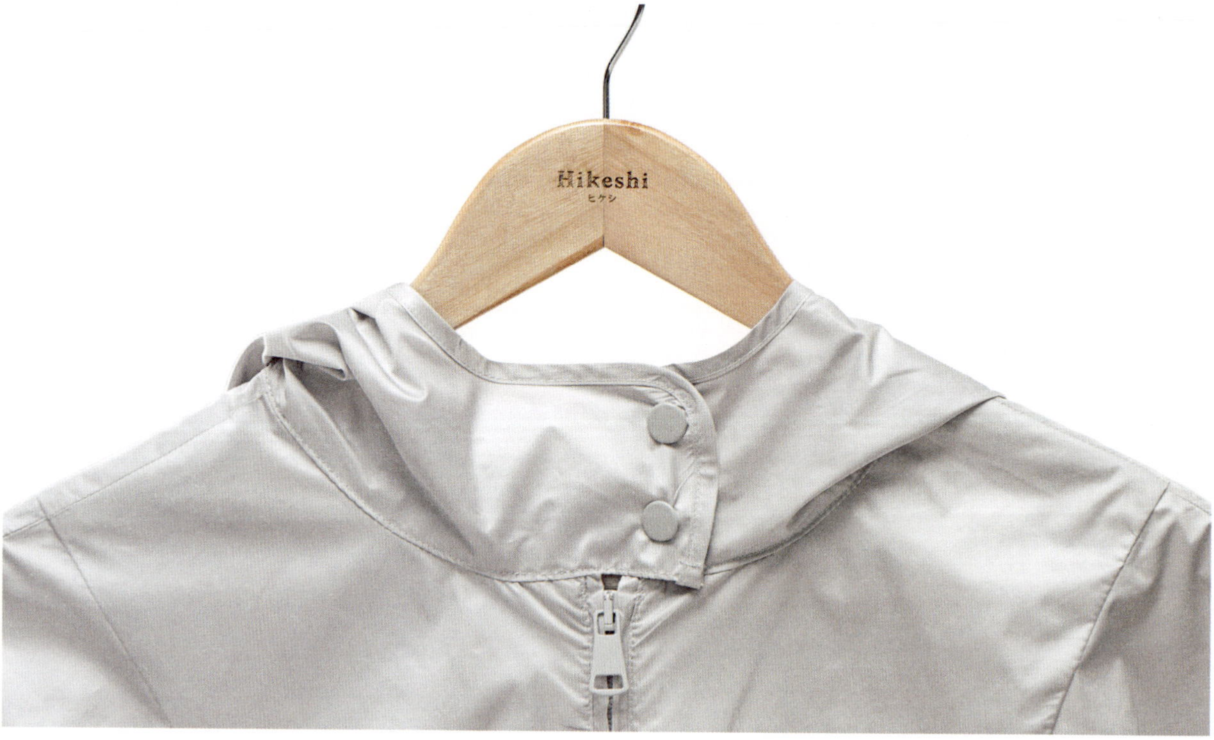

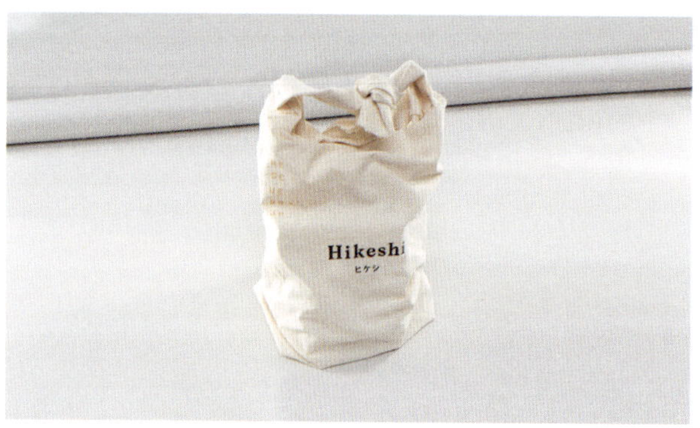

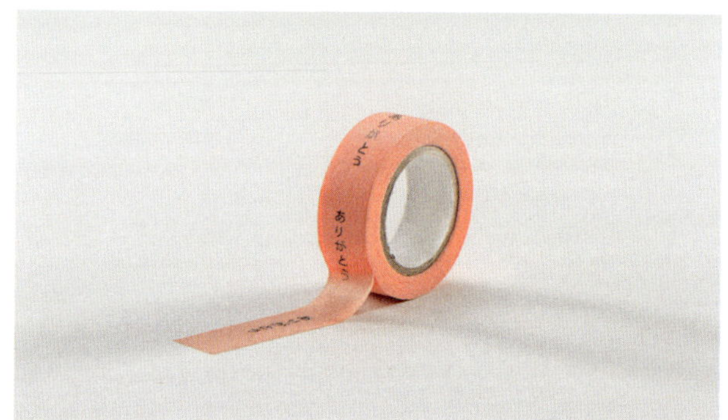

Interview

- As a kind of visual experience, what do you think about the "voidness" in graphic design?

-Even though we would try with different elements to make recognizable brands, there are some attributes of the product itself that could better speak for the identity. In some occasions, it is better to reduce as much as possible the final elements, to remove unnecessary visual stimulations and distractions. The voidness means going back to the basics and creating a legible and even "transparent" product. It means function before form.

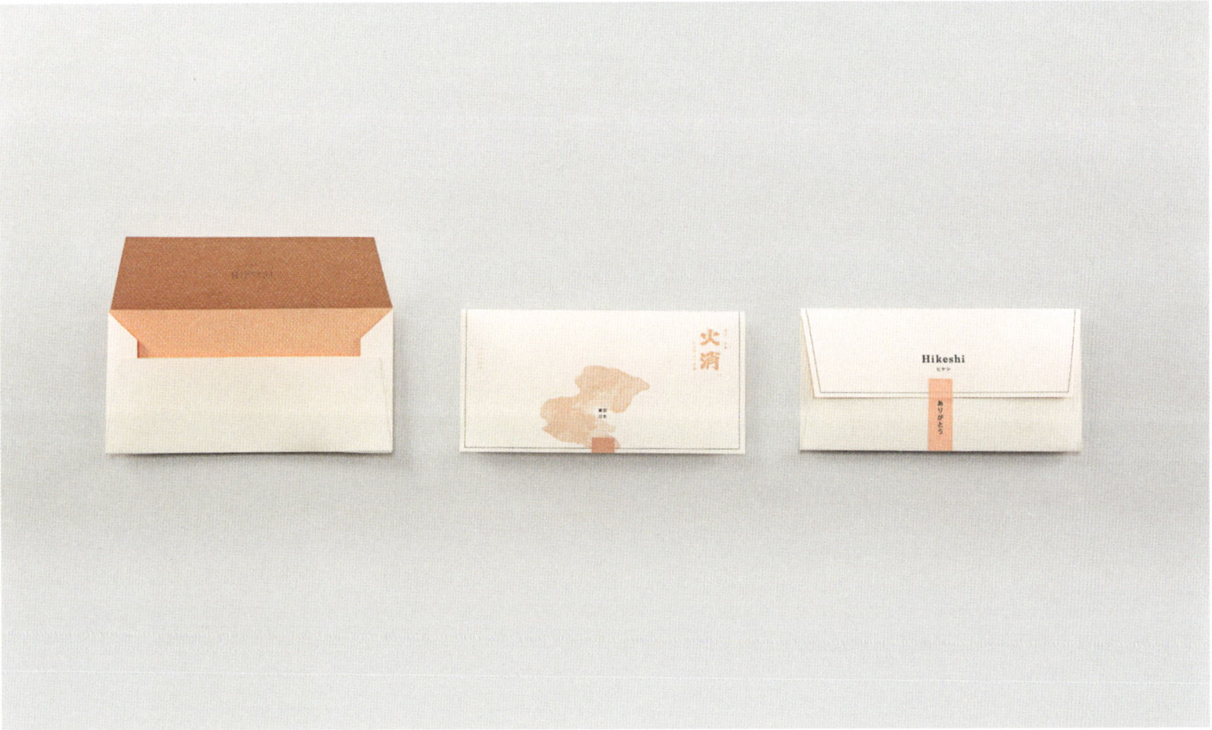

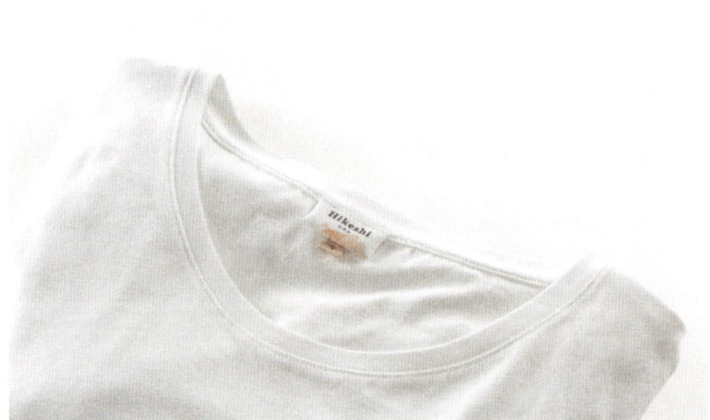

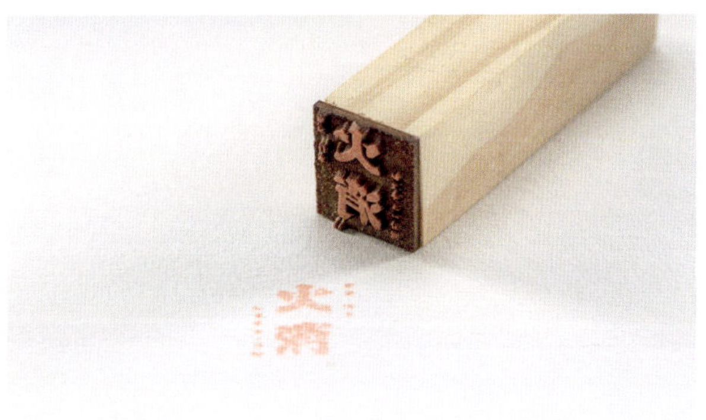

- What are your common approaches to produce a VOID visual effect?

-Voidness plays an important role in creating brands that are clear and direct. It helps to achieve 100% functional, consistent and informative designs. When conceiving designs for brands, we would move away the unnecessary ornamentation, and focus attentively on giving a clear message. We would carefully choose and adopt some other elements in order to acquire recognition and consistency for the design, which are essential for any brand. It is a good practice of exercising the creativity.

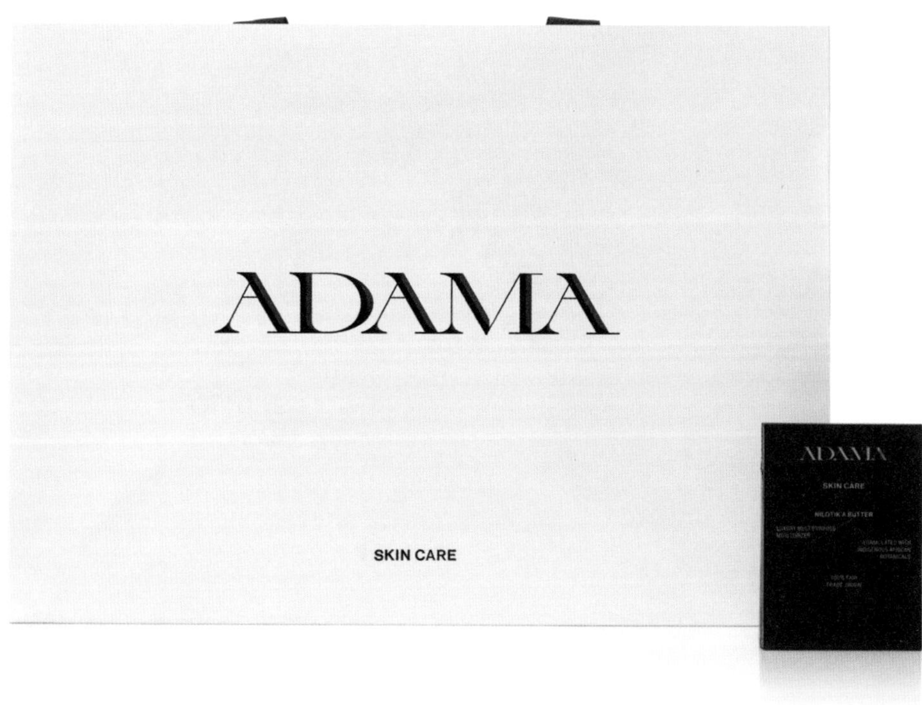

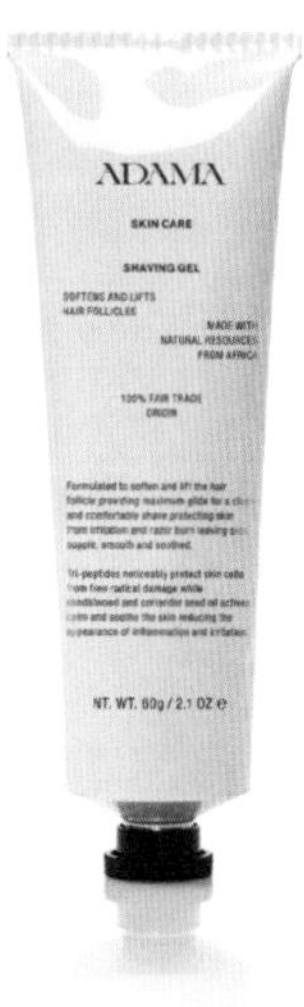

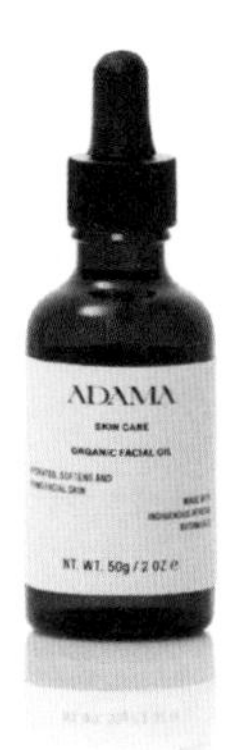

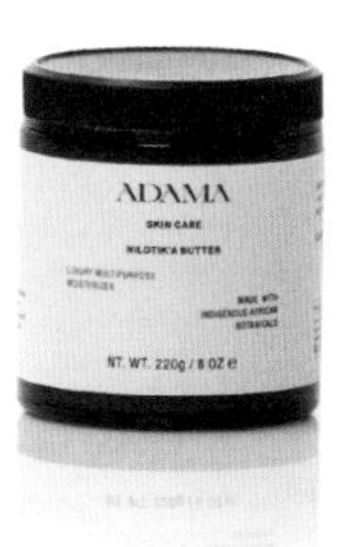

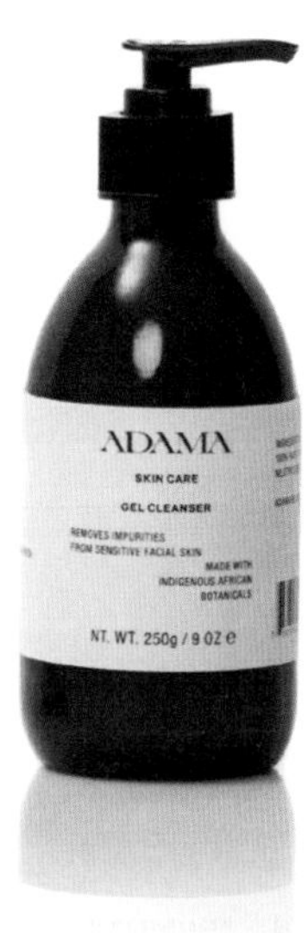

A delicate packaging featuring embossed roots was developed to enhance and compliment the healing attributes of Nilotik'a tree, the essential ingredient of the products. Black and white colors were employed to reflect Adama's elegance and purity while details in gold emphasizes the superiority of its botanical products.

Adama

studio:
Anagrama

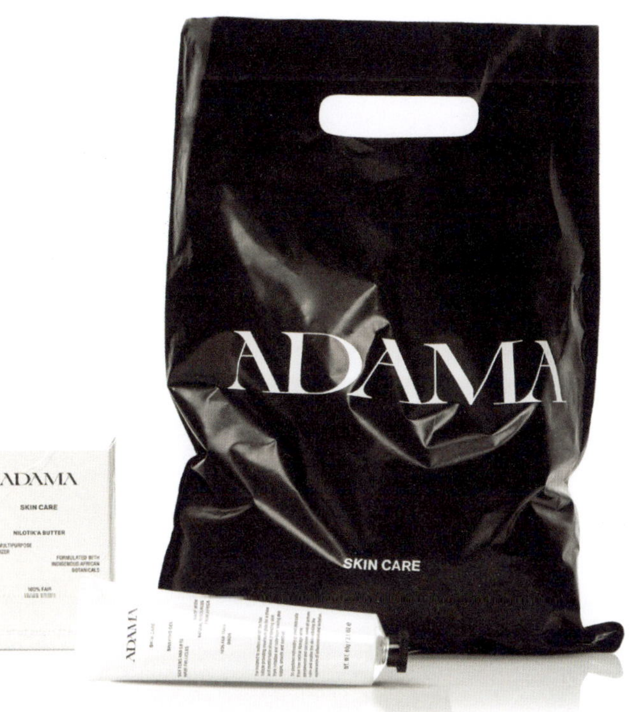

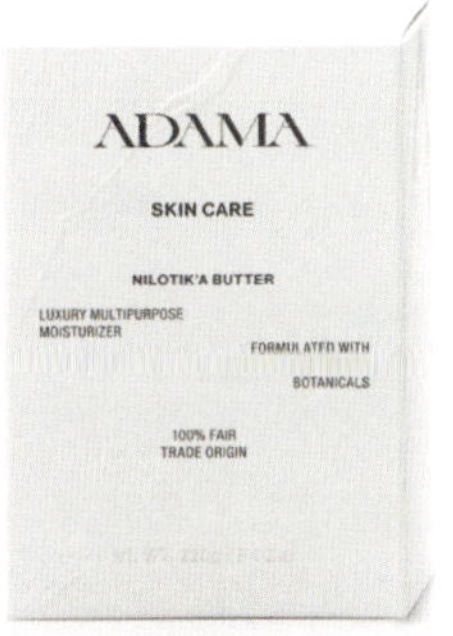

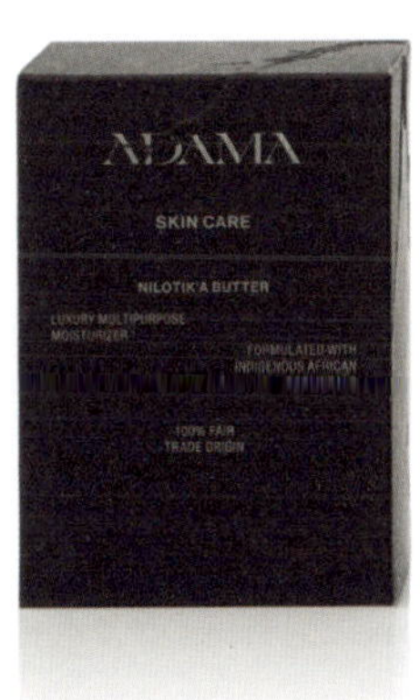

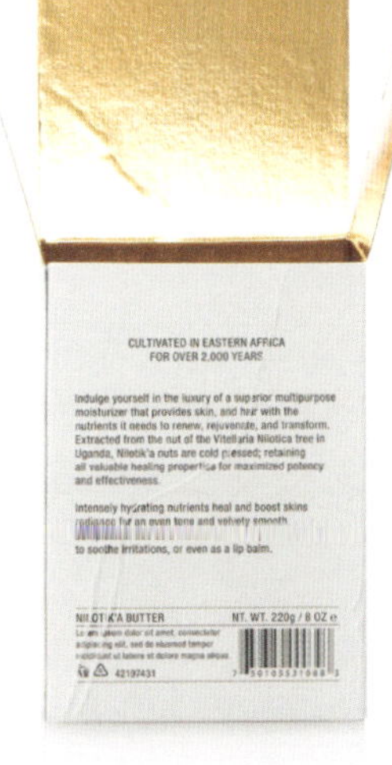

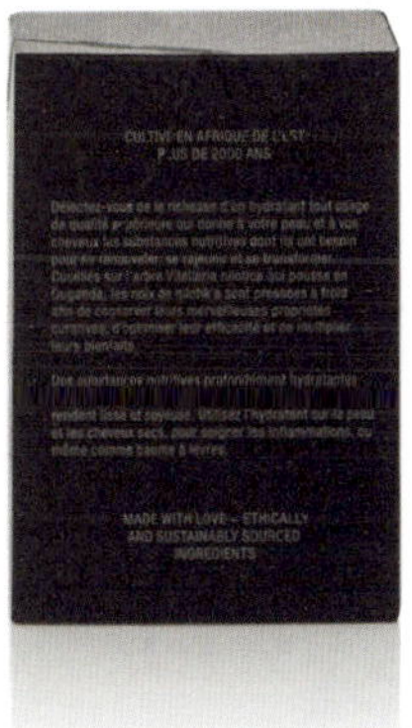

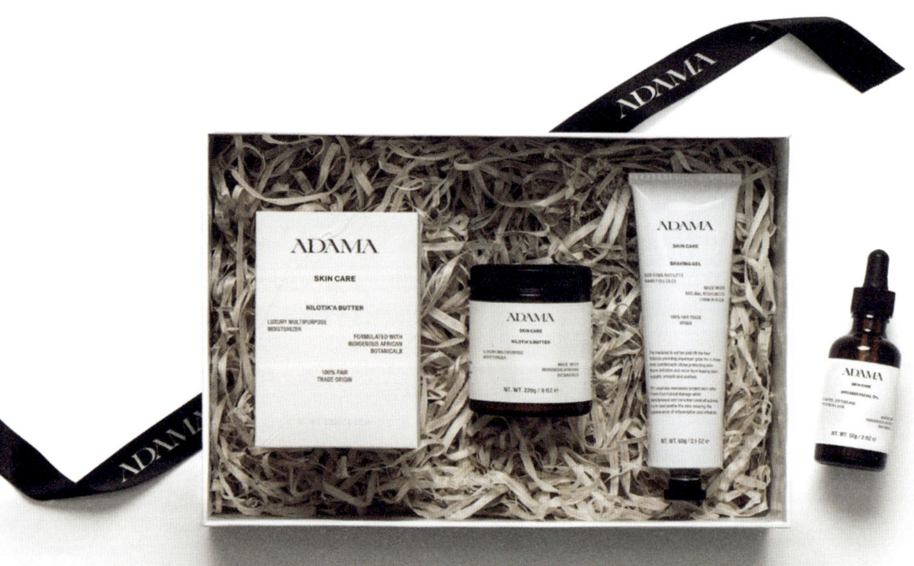
ADAMA
ADAMA
SKIN CARE
NILOTIK'A BUTTER
LUXURY MULTIPURPOSE MOISTURIZER
FORMULATED WITH INDIGENOUS AFRICAN BOTANICALS
100% FAIR TRADE ORIGIN
ADAMA
ADAMA
ADAMA

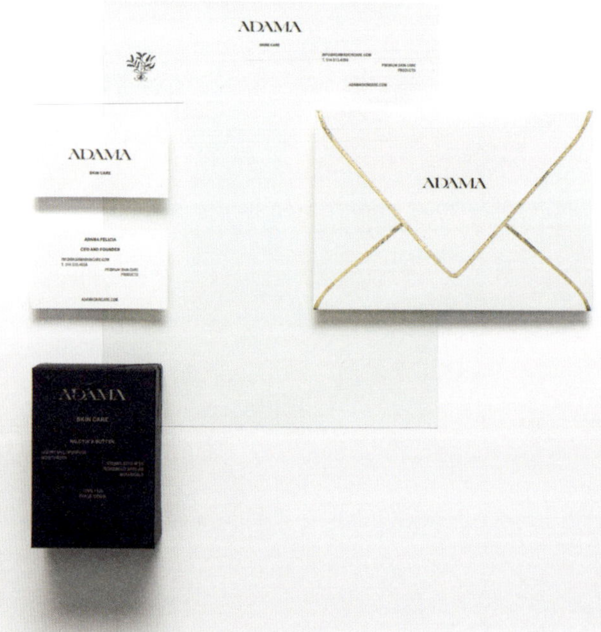
ADAMA
ADAMA
ADAMA
ADAMA

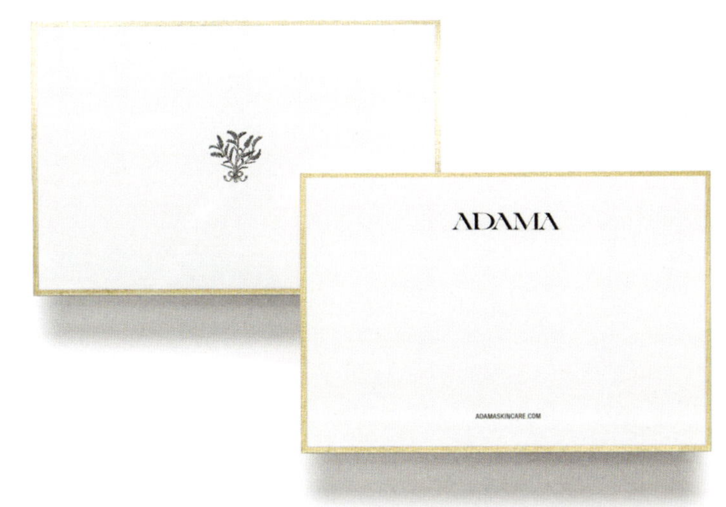
ADAMA
ADAMASKINCARE.COM

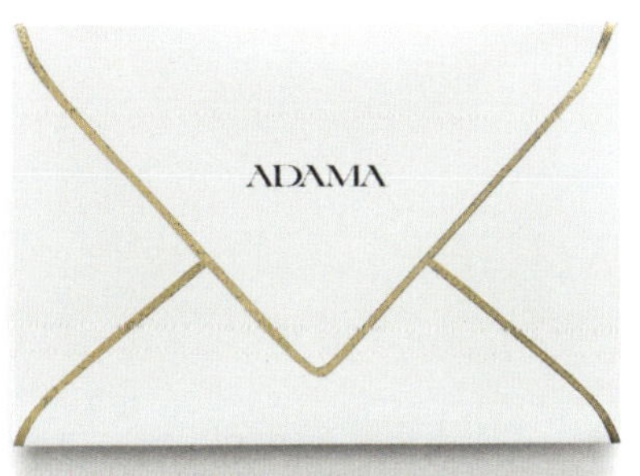
ADAMA

ADAMASKINCARE.COM

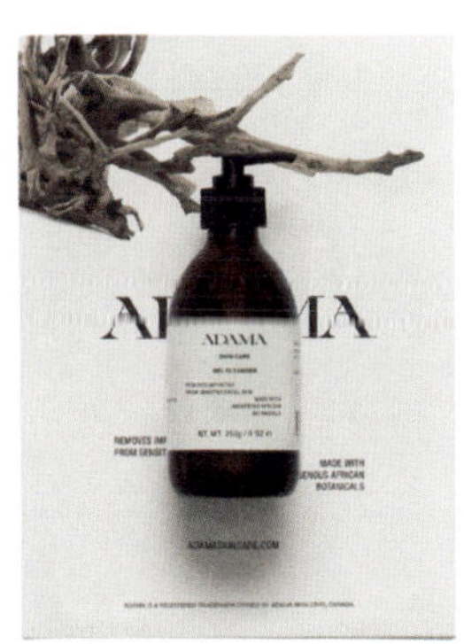

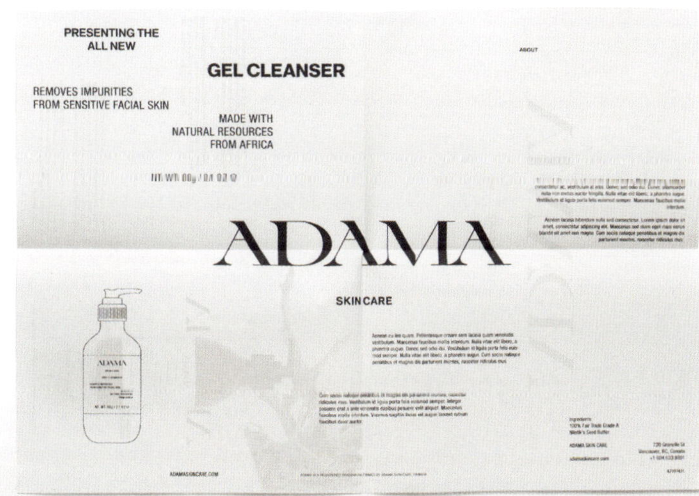
PRESENTING THE
ALL NEW
GEL CLEANSER
REMOVES IMPURITIES
FROM SENSITIVE FACIAL SKIN
MADE WITH
NATURAL RESOURCES
FROM AFRICA
ADAMA
SKIN CARE
ADAMASKINCARE.COM

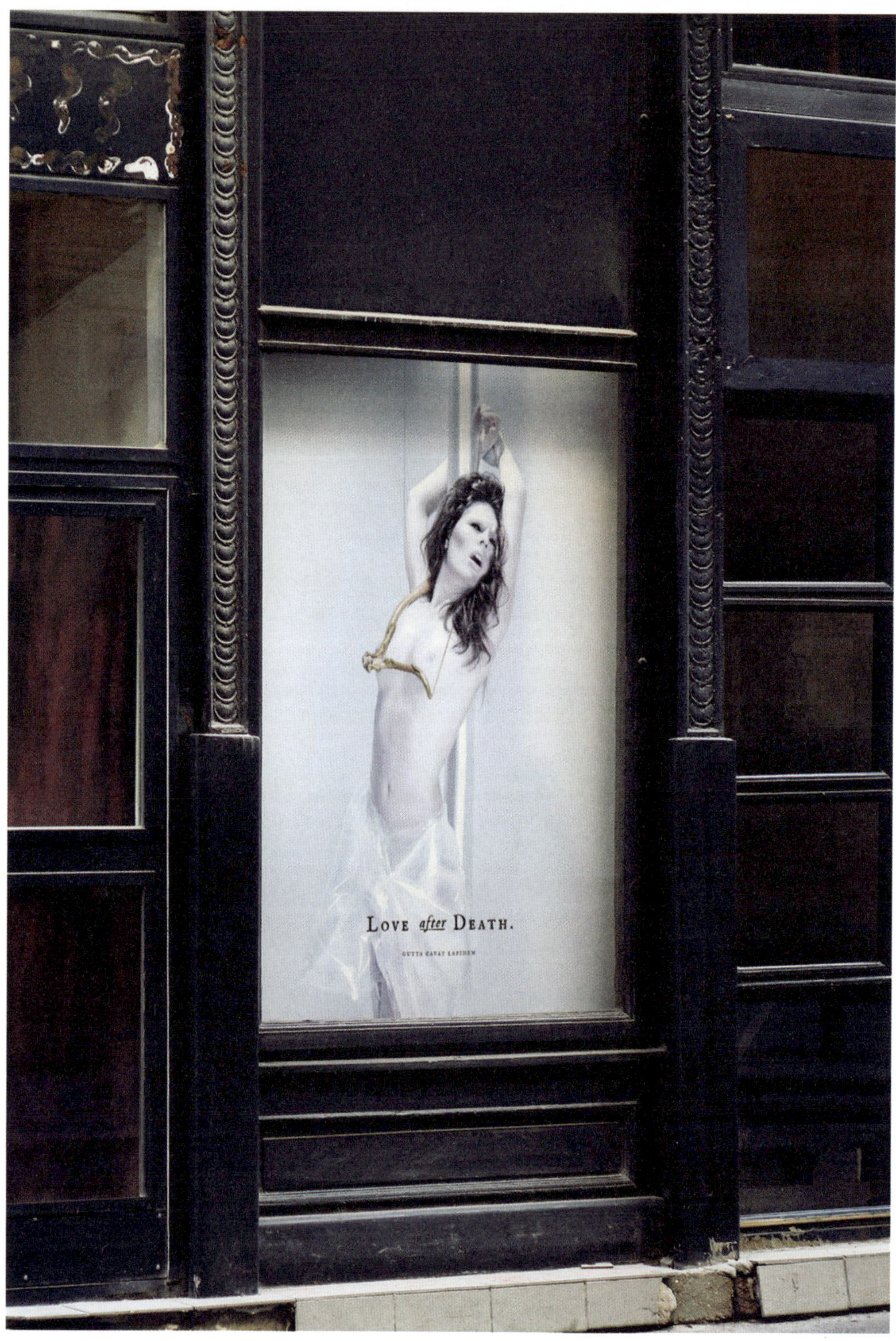

Love after Death is a jewelry brand by German fashion and jewelry designer Saskia Lubnow. The collection 13 features two main designs: In cauda venenum—a prehistoric jawbone coated with bronze and Gutta cavat lapidem—deer antlers covered with bronze.

LOVE *after* DEATH.

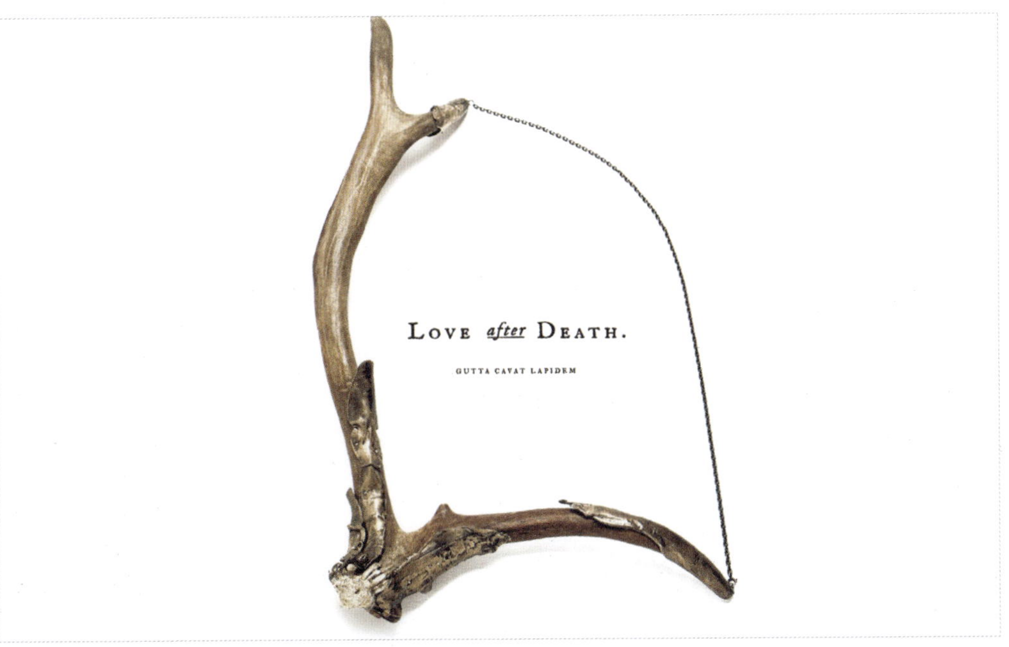

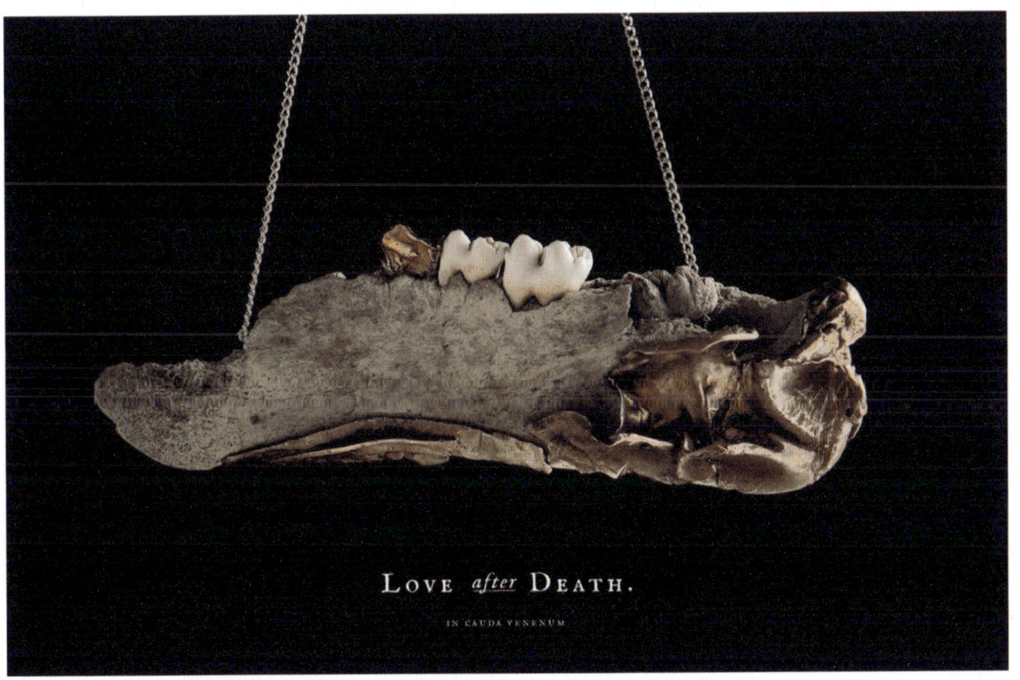

Love after Death

designer:
Daria Po

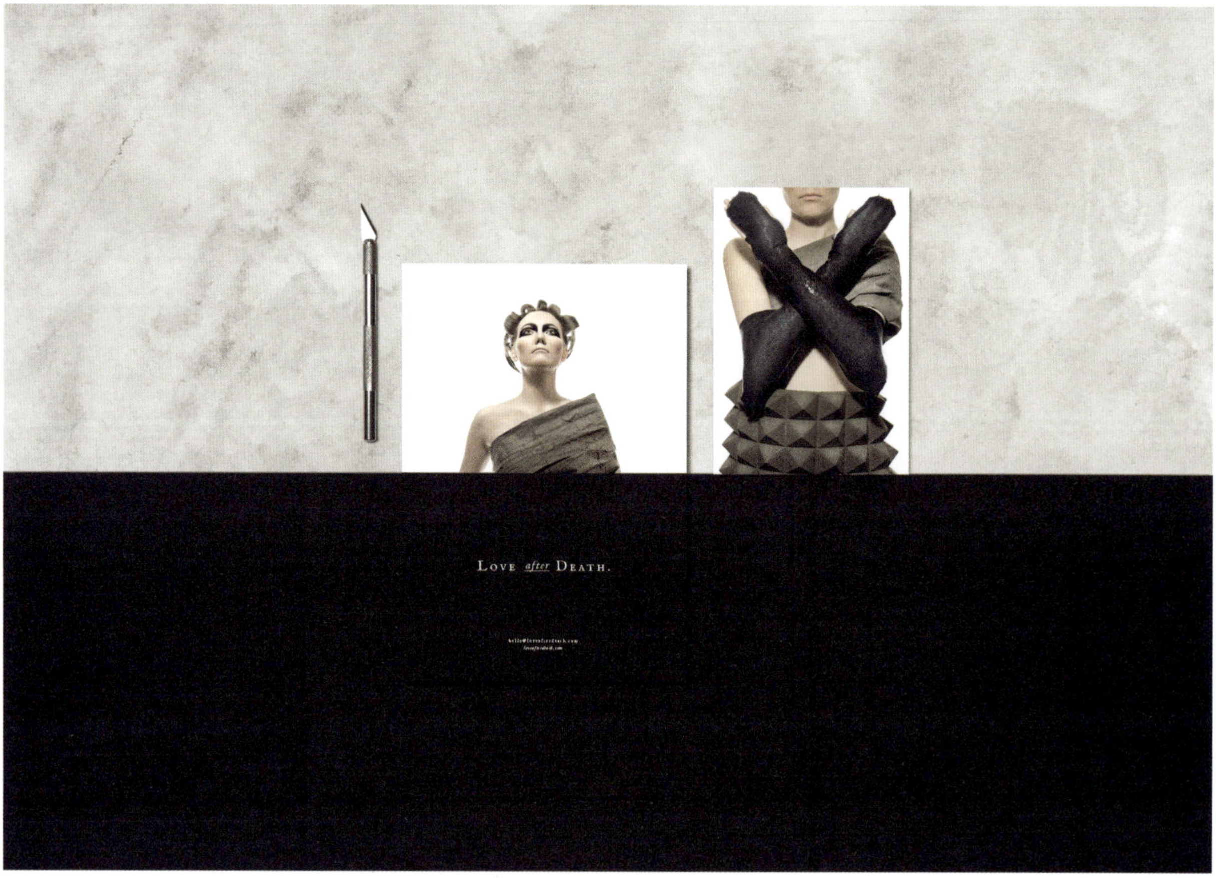

LOVE after DEATH.

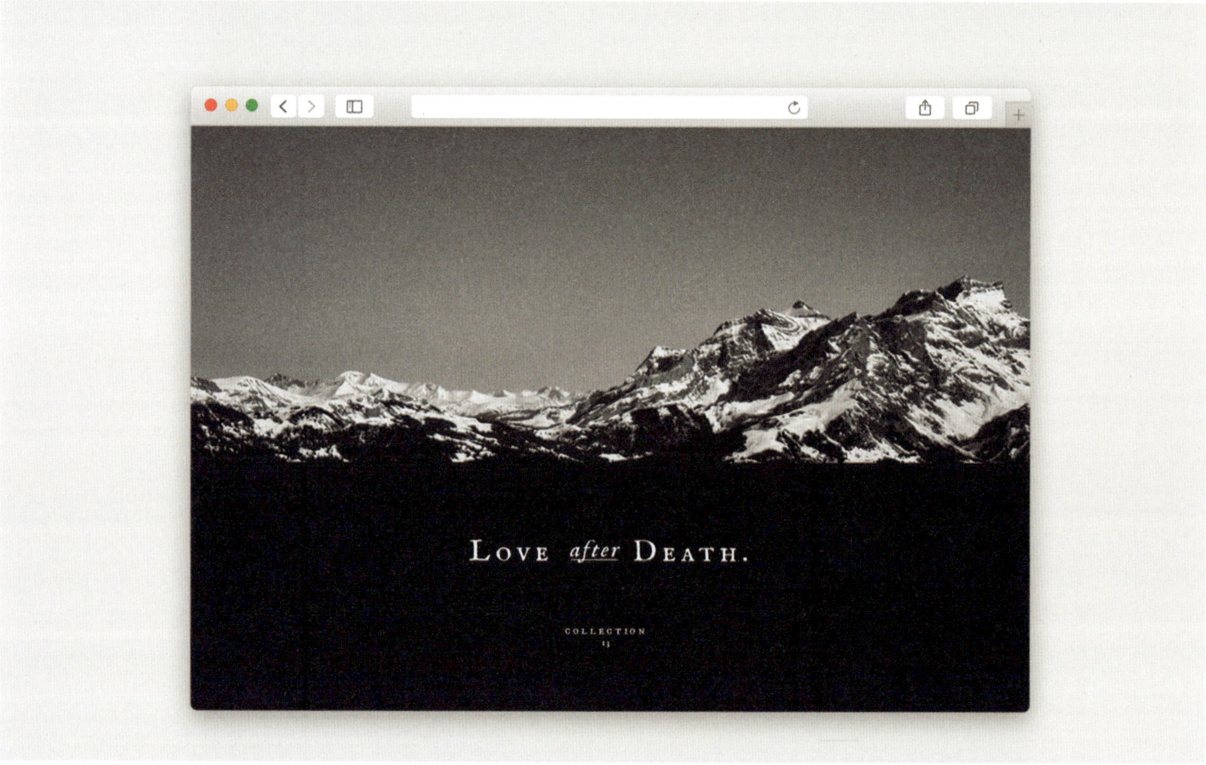

LOVE after DEATH.

COLLECTION

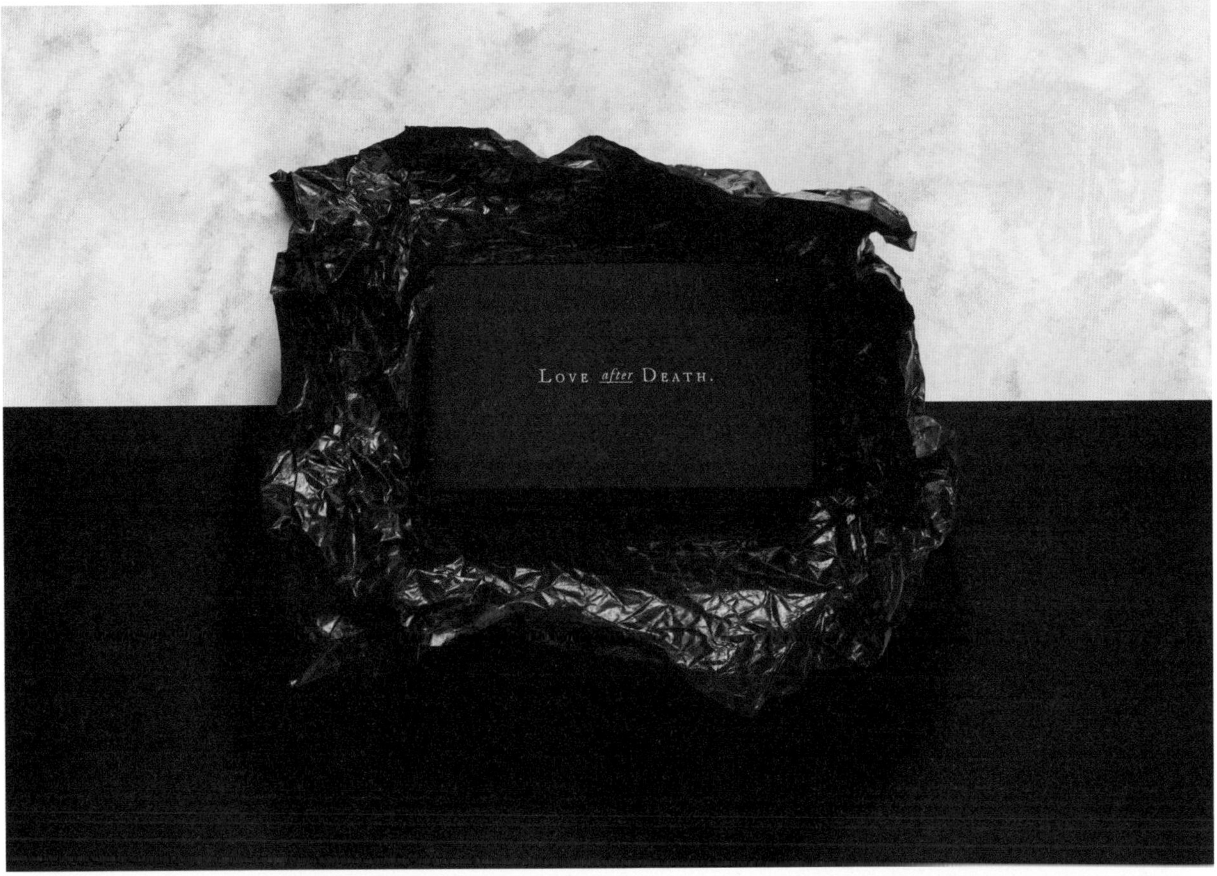
LOVE after DEATH.

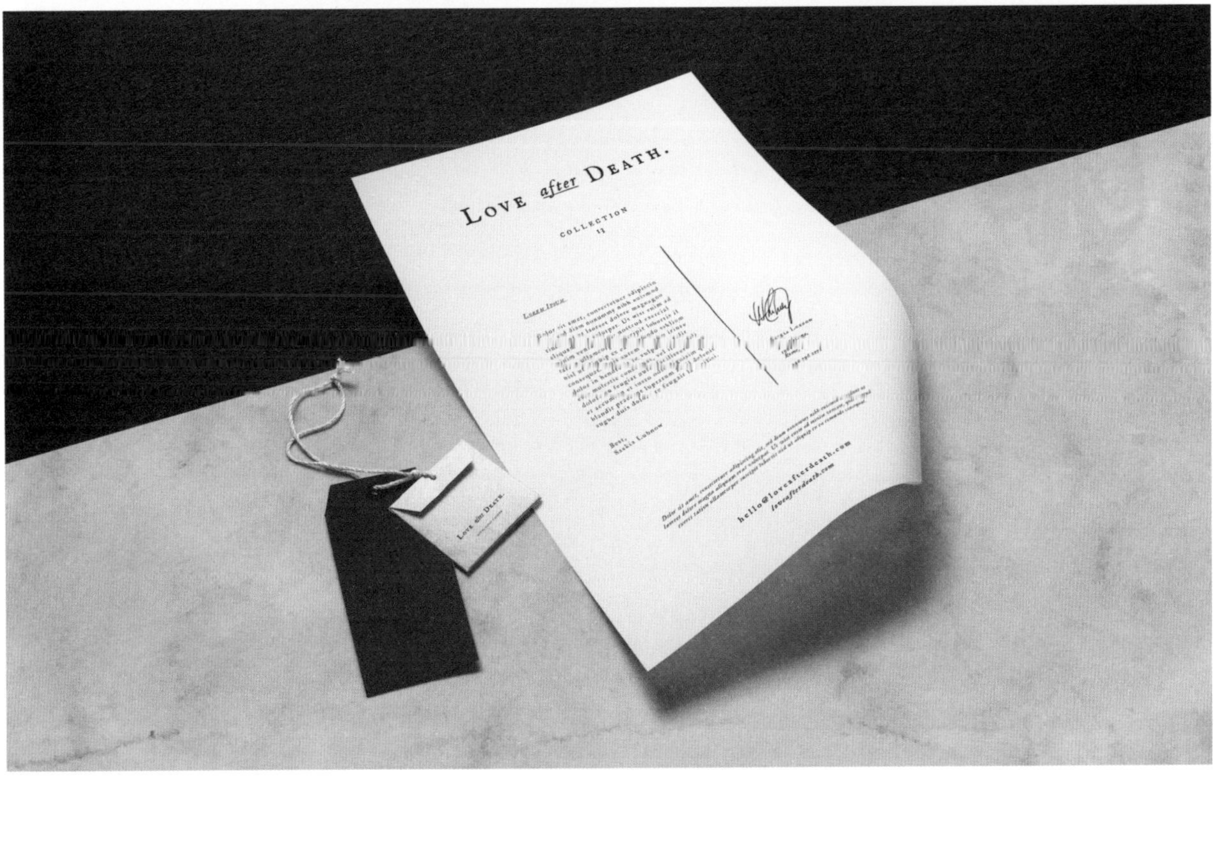
LOVE after DEATH.
COLLECTION
11
hello@loveafterdeath.com
loveafterdeath.com

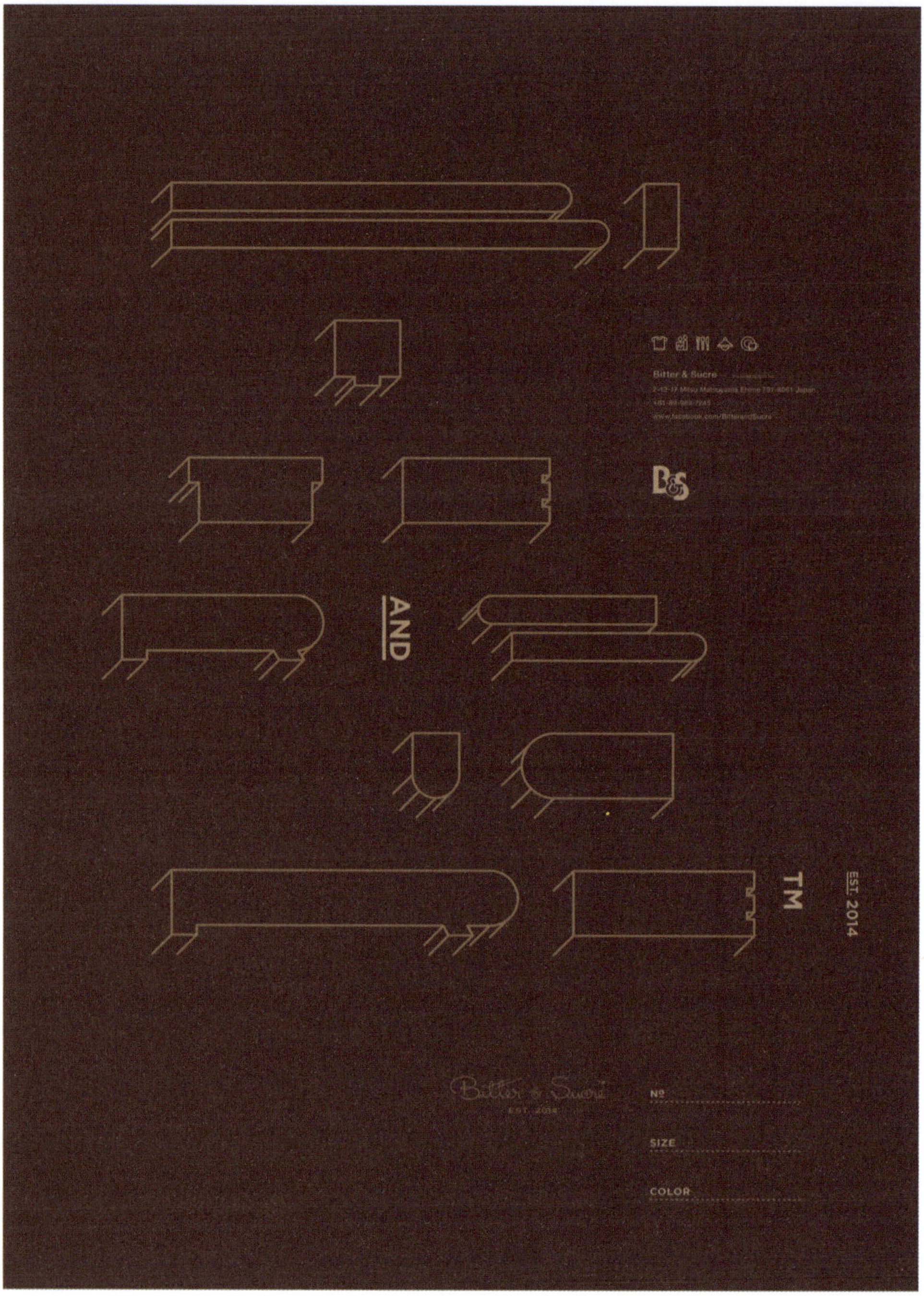

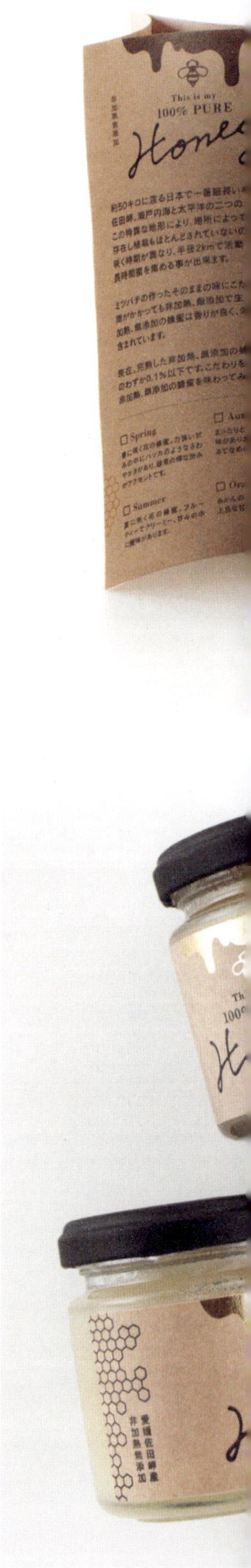

AND

TM

EST. 2014

Bitter & Sucre

Nº

SIZE

COLOR

This branding for a lifestyle shop in Japan features a rounded logo with an amiable character. The packaging for honey products shows honey dripping through gold foil stamping on craft paper. All are aimed to transmit a feeling of attentive craft of this brand.

Bitter & Sucre

studio: ***Grand Deluxe***
designer: ***Koji Matsumoto***

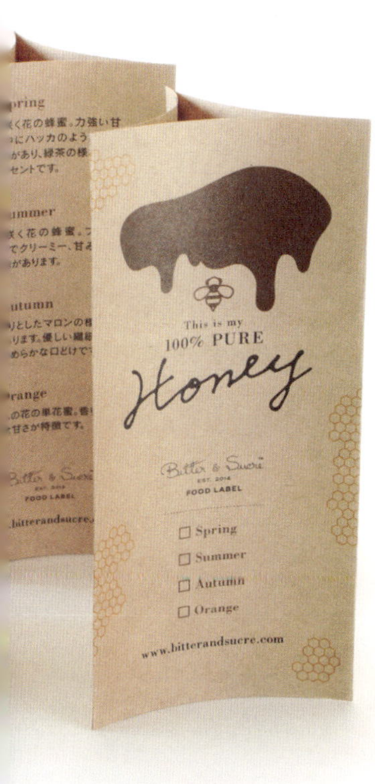

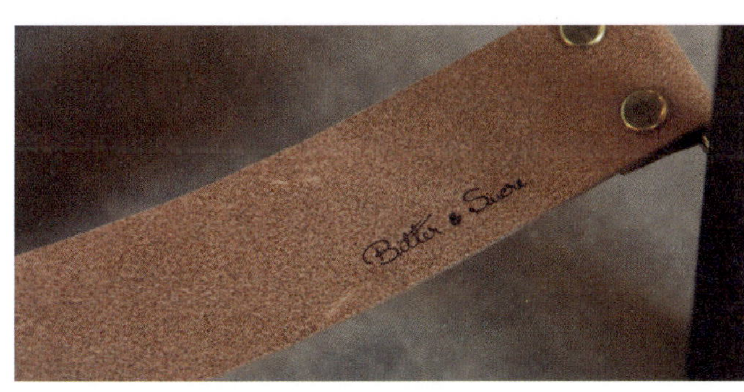

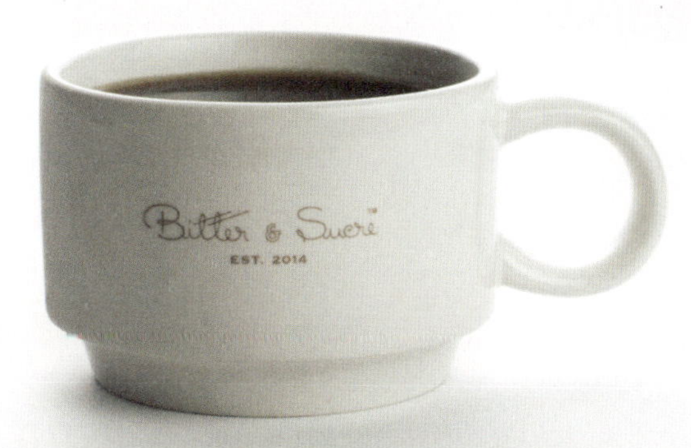

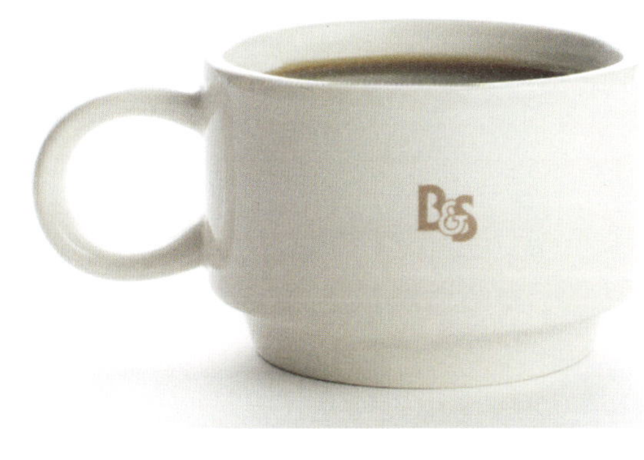

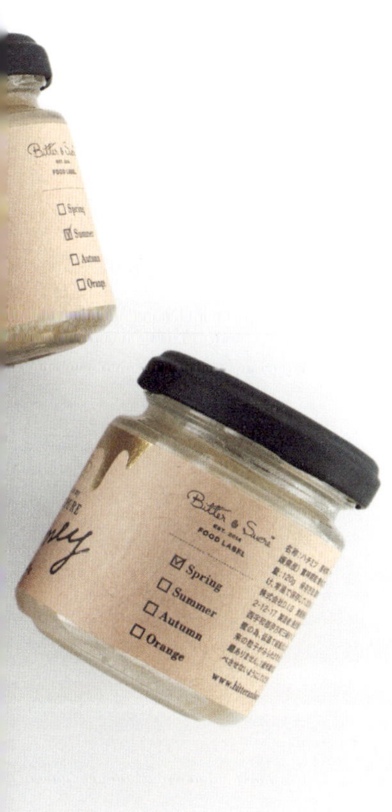

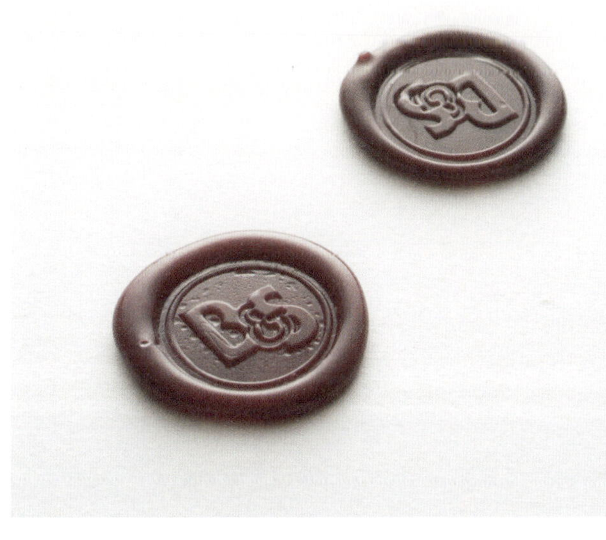

This work is a part of the new visual identity for an oil and gas company. Graphic compositions leading the visual identity system are based on the point, vertical and horizontal lines that embody the company's major businesses. Photos, toned to fit the company's signature color palette of navy blue, blue and red, are combined with graphic elements to discover the beautiful environment in which the field is located.

SNGP Annual Report

studio : **Ermolaev Bureau**
designer: **Vlad Ermolaev**

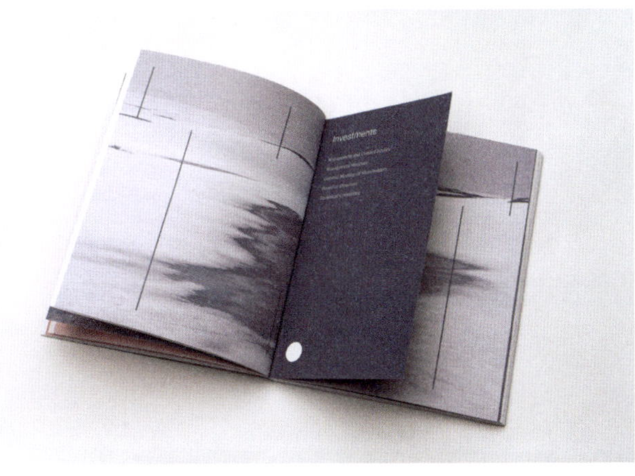

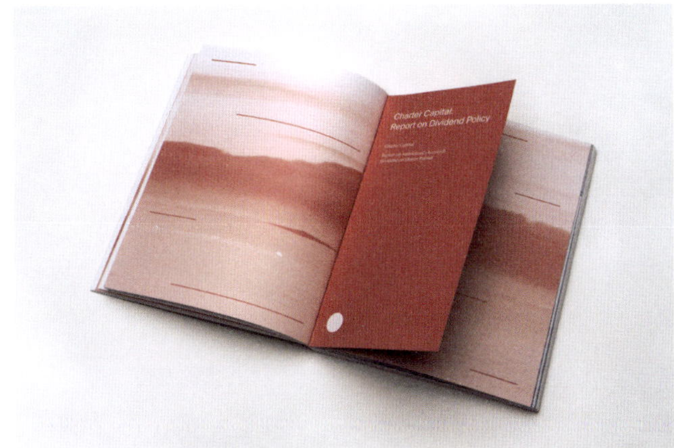

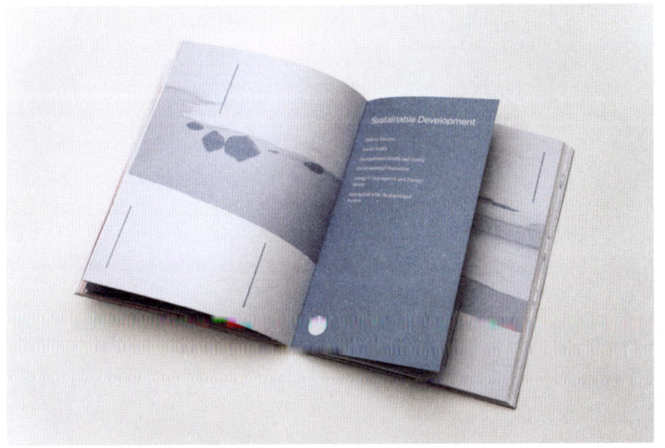

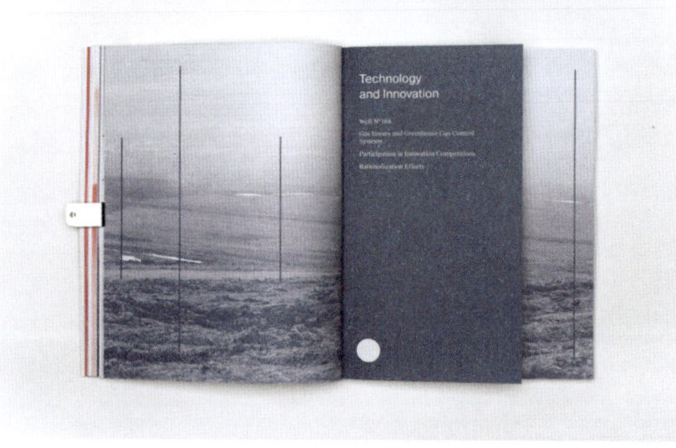
Technology
and Innovation

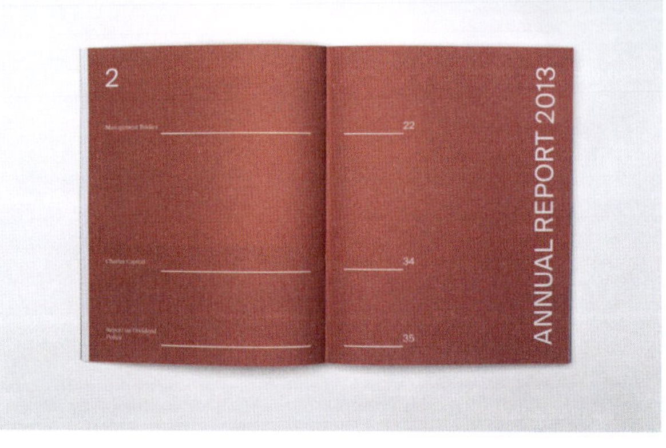
2
22
34
35
ANNUAL REPORT 2013

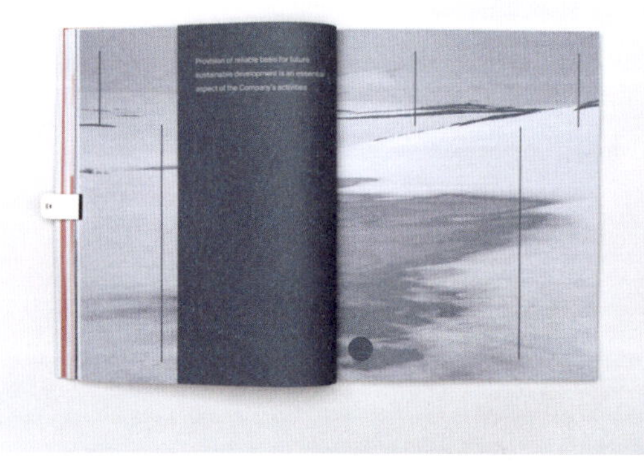
Provision of reliable basis for future sustainable development is an essential aspect of the Company's activities

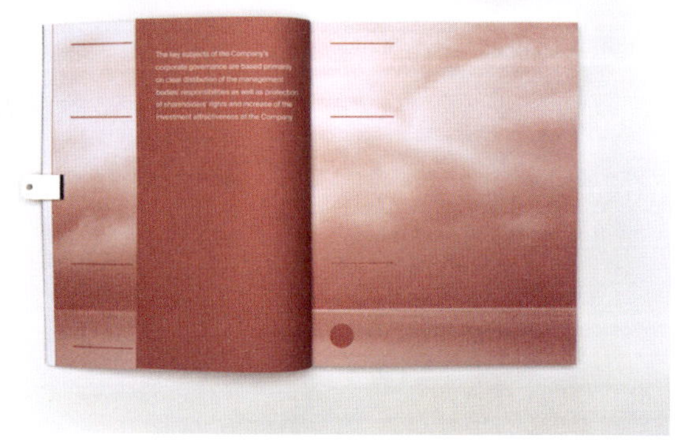
The key subjects of the Company's corporate governance are based primarily on clear distribution of the management bodies' responsibilities as well as protection of shareholders' rights and increase of the investment attractiveness of the Company

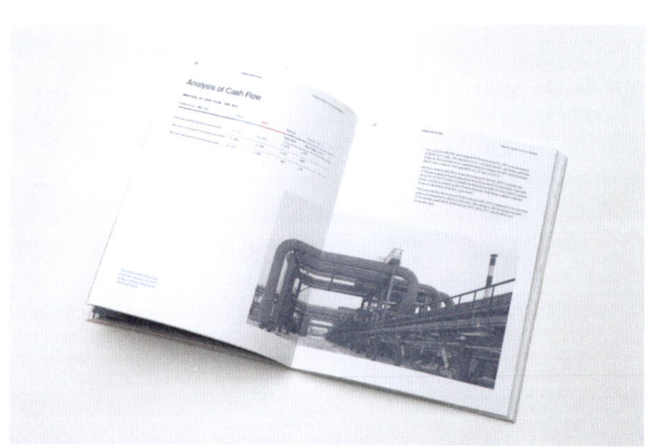
Analysis of Cash Flow

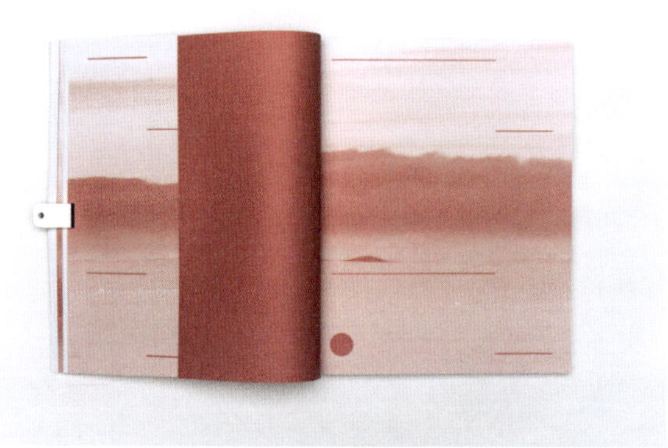

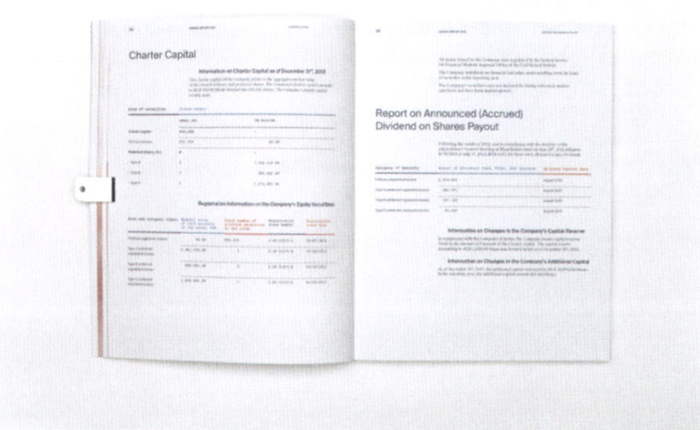
Charter Capital
Report on Announced (Accrued)
Dividend on Shares Payout

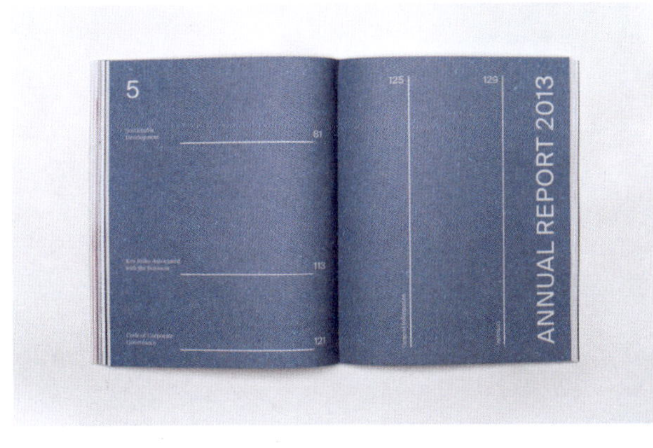
5
81
113
121
125
129
ANNUAL REPORT 2013

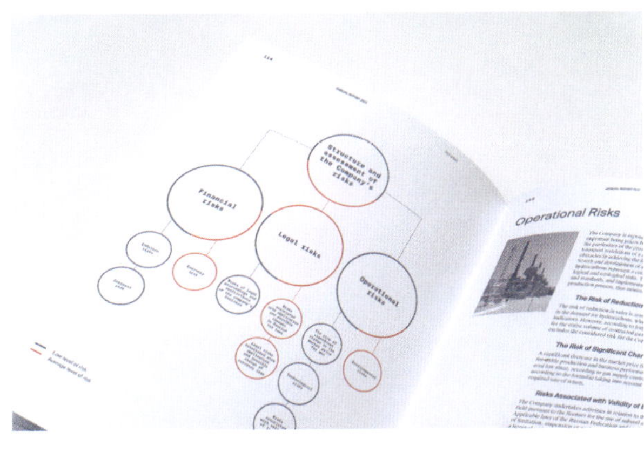
Financial risks
Legal risks
Operational risks
Operational Risks

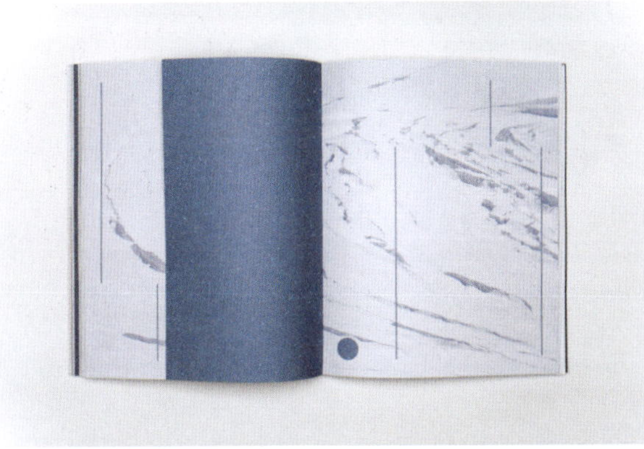

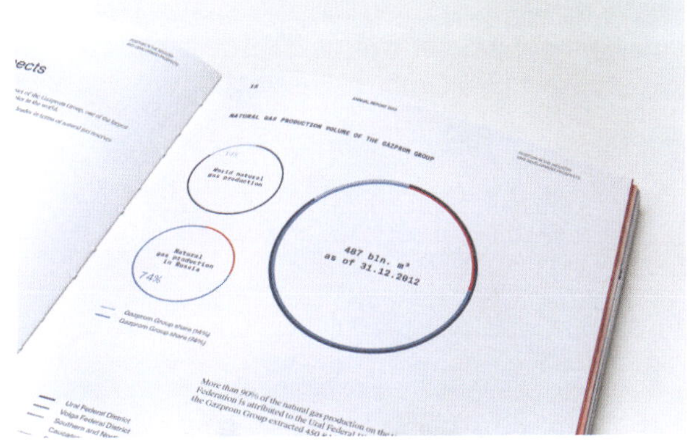
NATURAL GAS PRODUCTION VOLUME OF THE GAZPROM GROUP
487 bln. m³ as of 31.12.2012
74%

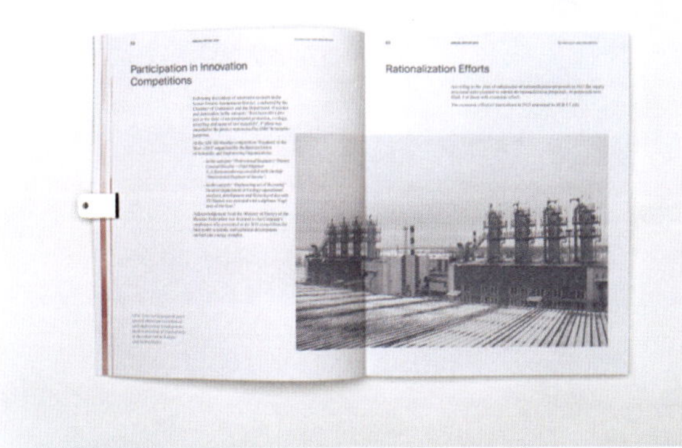
Participation in Innovation Competitions
Rationalization Efforts

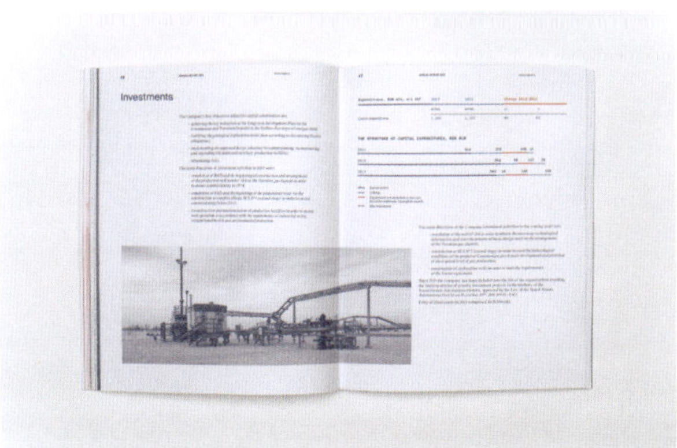
Investments

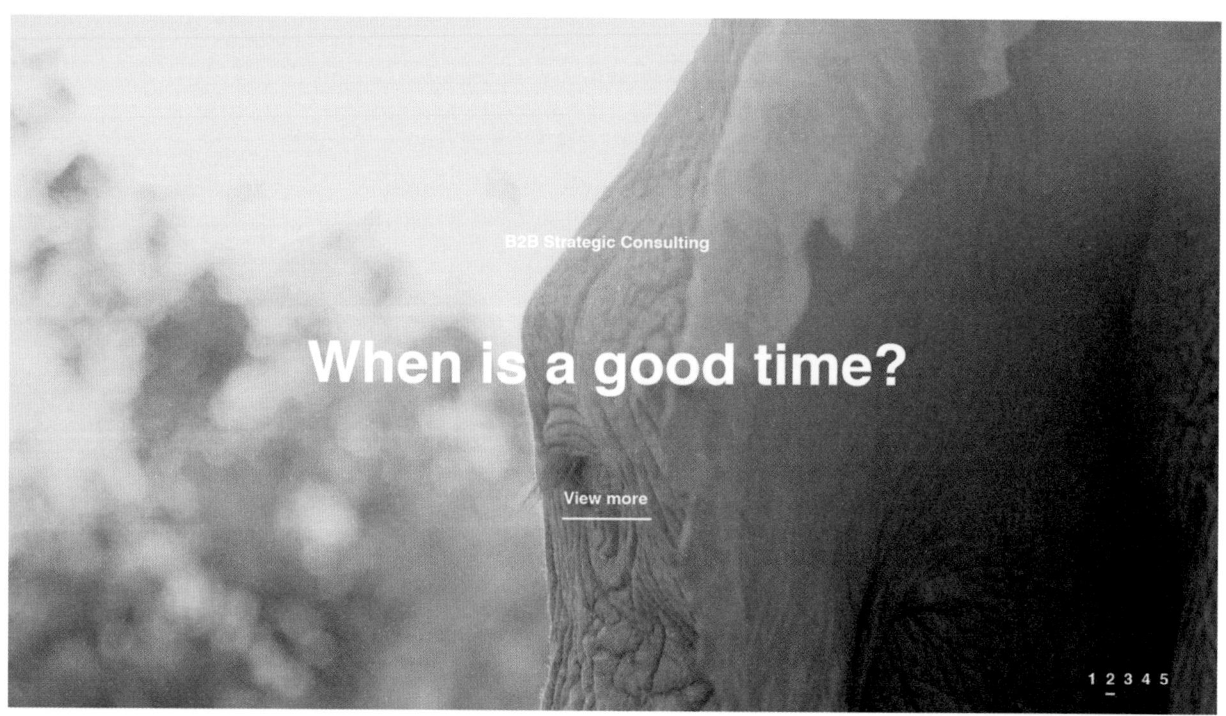

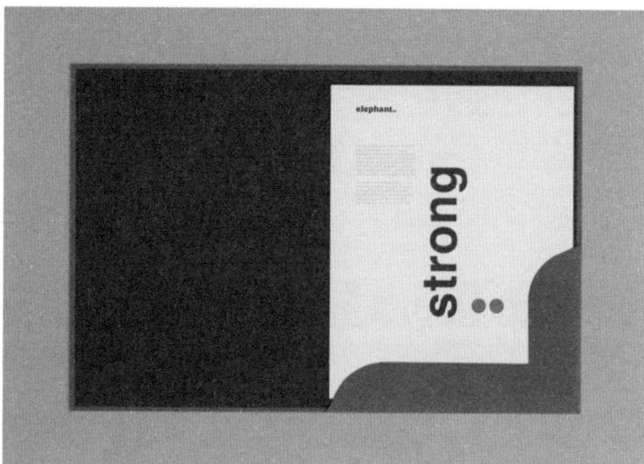

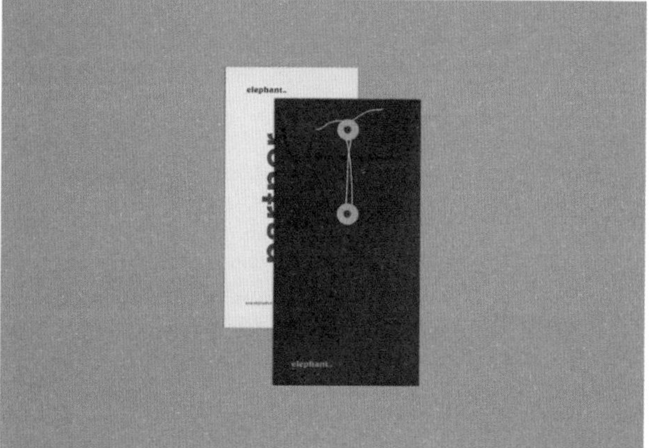

elephant..

This work is for a consulting agency specialized in developing marketing strategies for B2B companies. The naming and visual identity endows the brand with a unique personality and a set of values.

Elephant

studio: ***Fagerström Studio***
designer: ***Puli Arancibia***

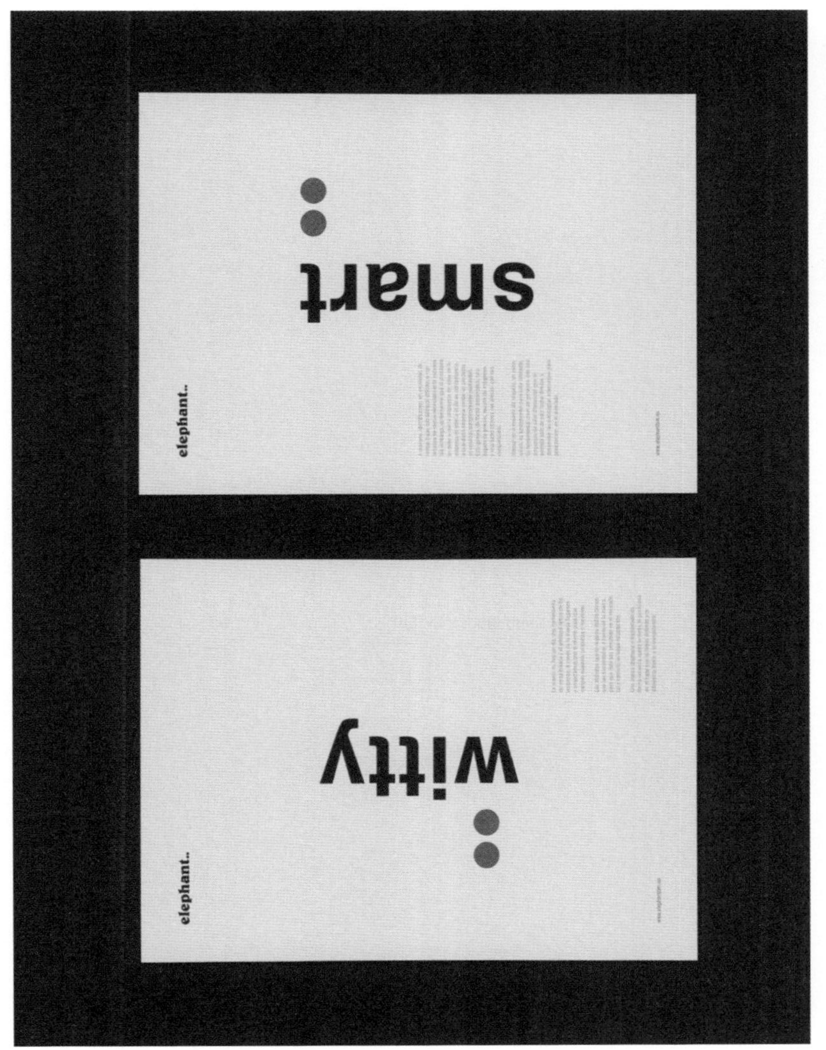

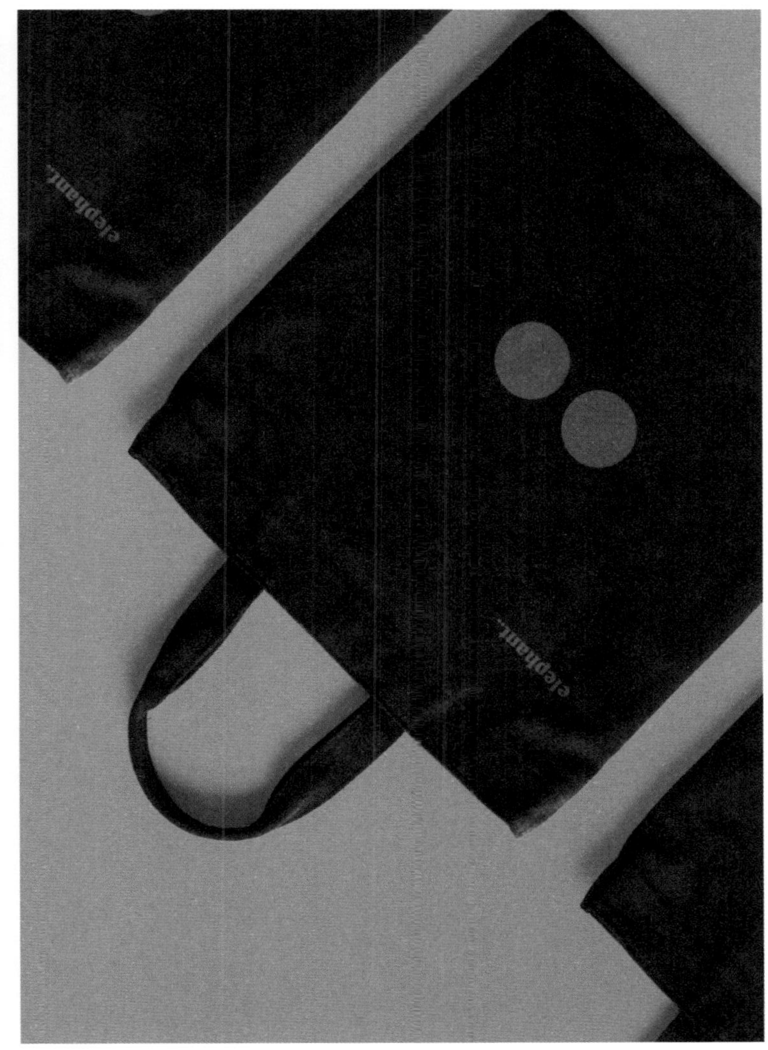

Combining meticulous and detailed work with a strong creative concept, a solid, recognizable and unique identity was created for Sara del Campo, an all-inclusive real estate rental system focused on the young public and offering service that goes beyond renting.

SDC

studio: *Fagerström Studio*
designer: *Puli Arancibia*

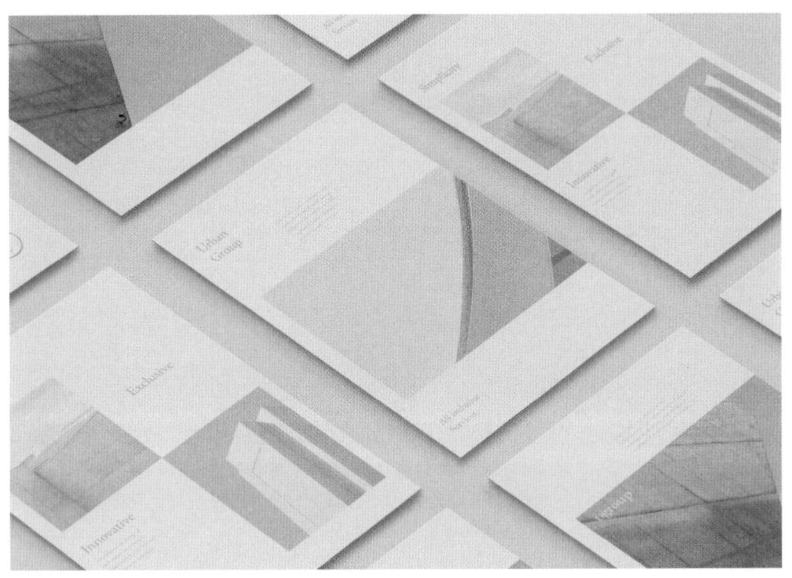

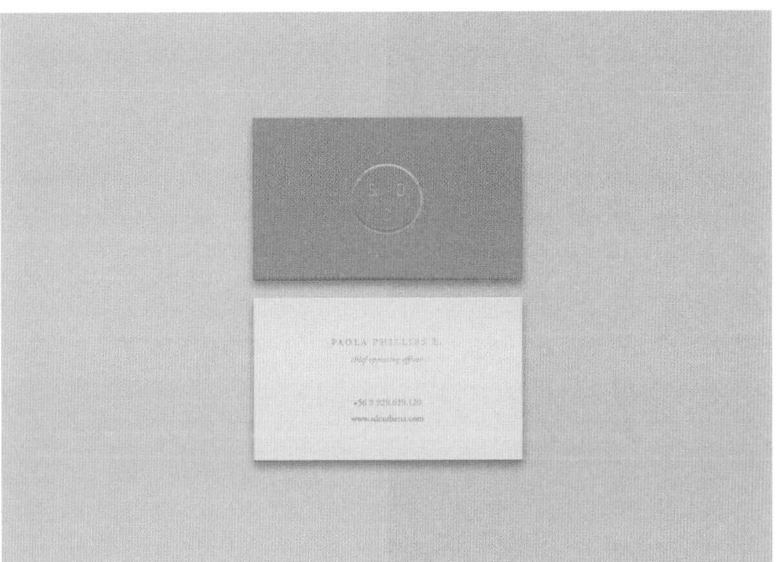

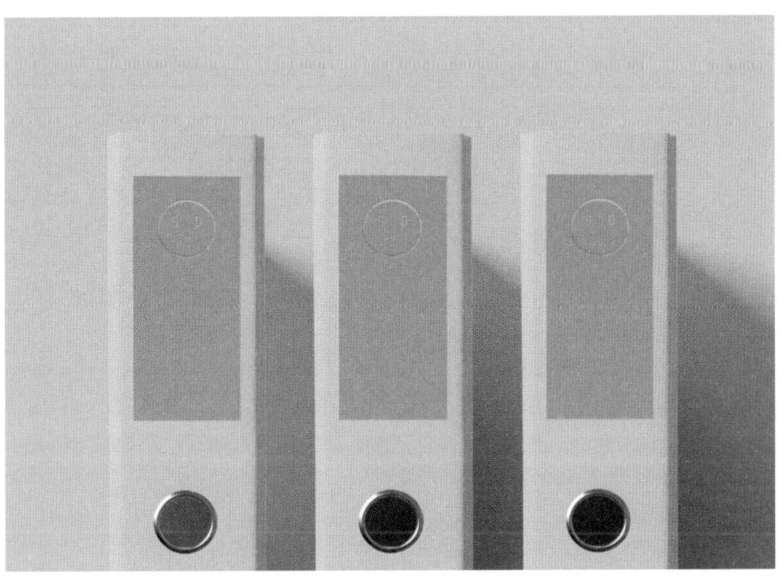

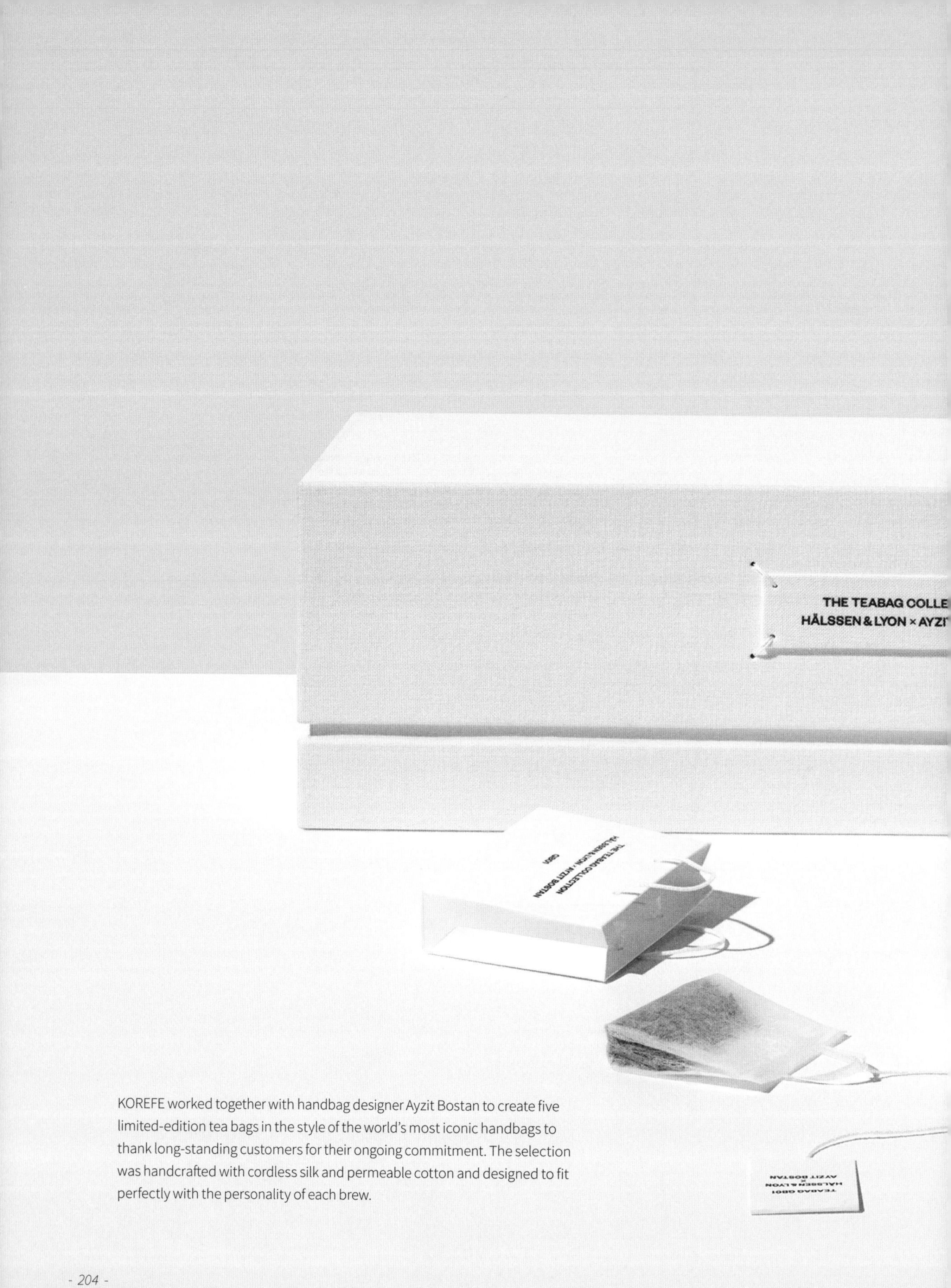

KOREFE worked together with handbag designer Ayzit Bostan to create five limited-edition tea bags in the style of the world's most iconic handbags to thank long-standing customers for their ongoing commitment. The selection was handcrafted with cordless silk and permeable cotton and designed to fit perfectly with the personality of each brew.

Hälssen & Lyon X Ayzit Bostan
The Teabag Collection

studio: ***KOREFE. Kolle Rebbe Form und Entwicklung***
concept & designer: ***Christian Doering*** *photographer:* ***Imke Jansen, Mitja Schneehage***

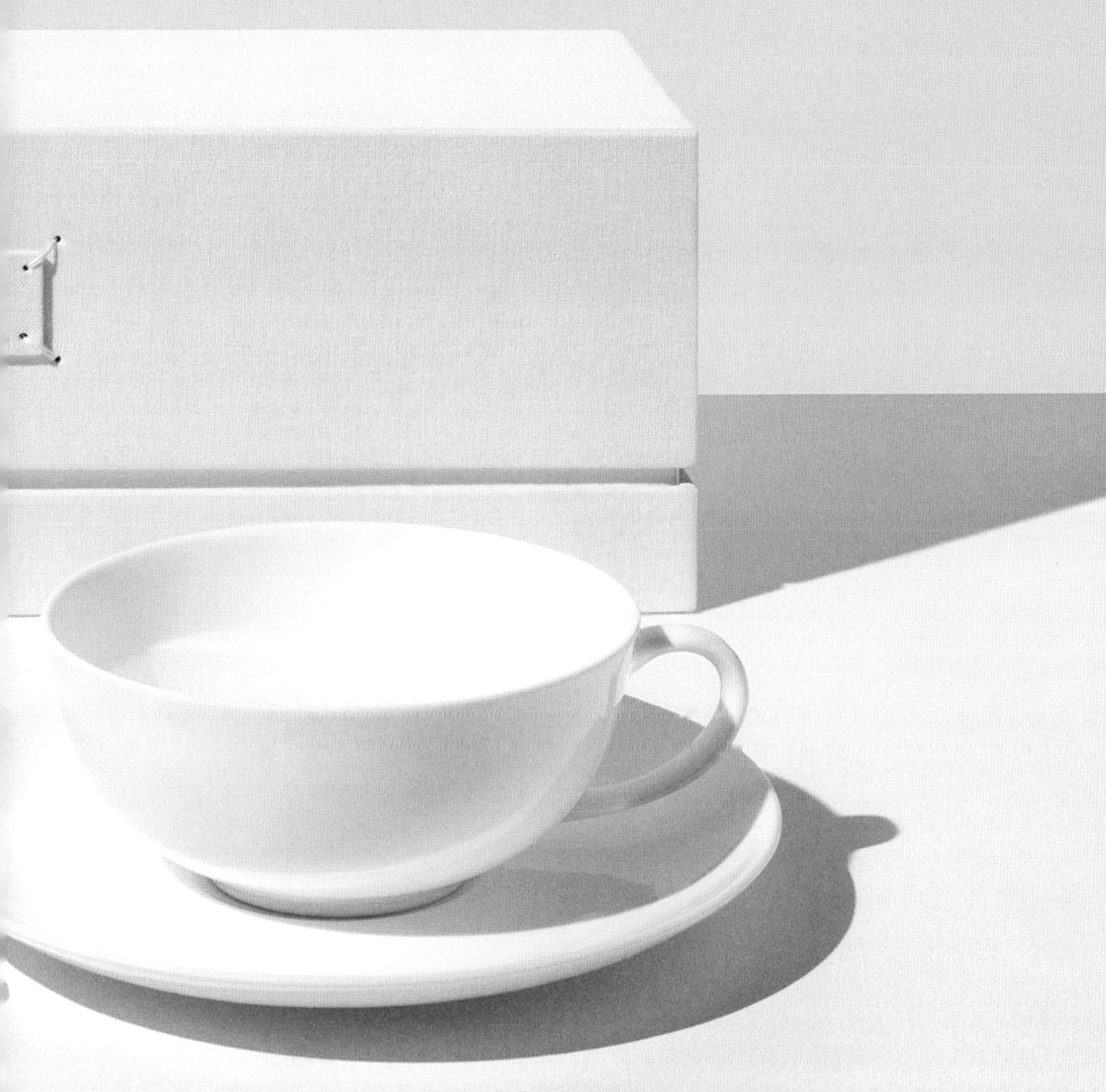

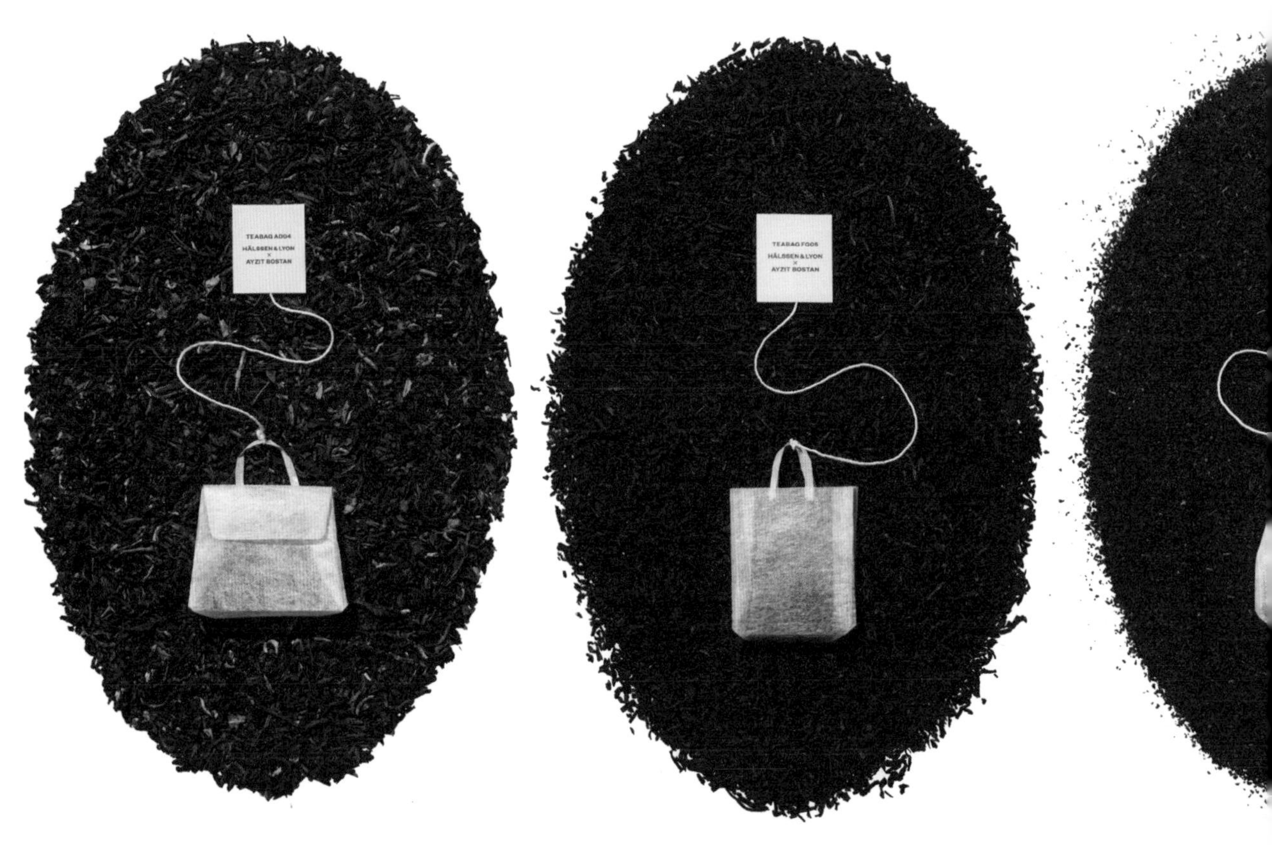
TEABAG A004
HÄLSSEN & LYON
×
AYZIT BOSTAN
TEABAG F005
HÄLSSEN & LYON
×
AYZIT BOSTAN

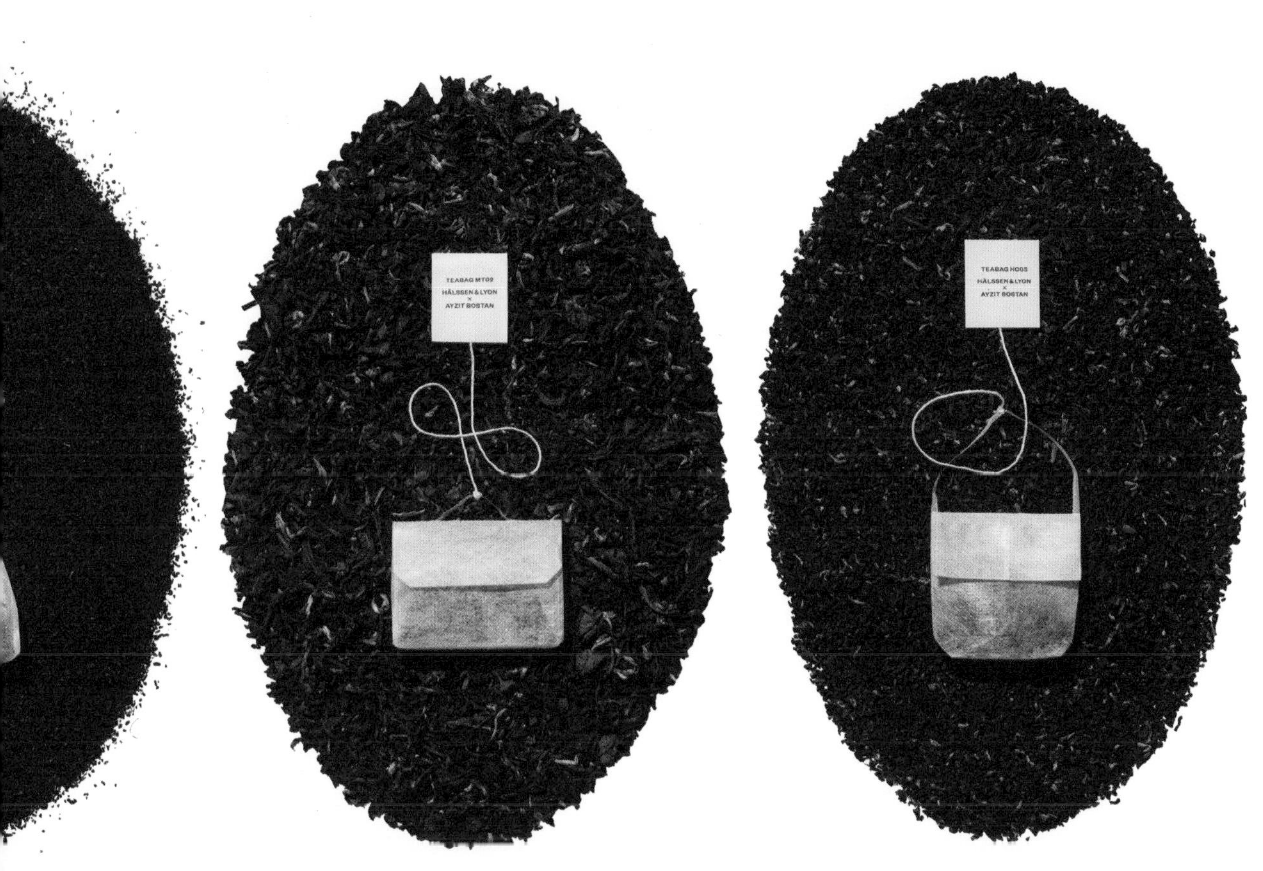
TEABAG MT02
HÄLSSEN & LYON
×
AYZIT BOSTAN
TEABAG HC03
HÄLSSEN & LYON
×
AYZIT BOSTAN

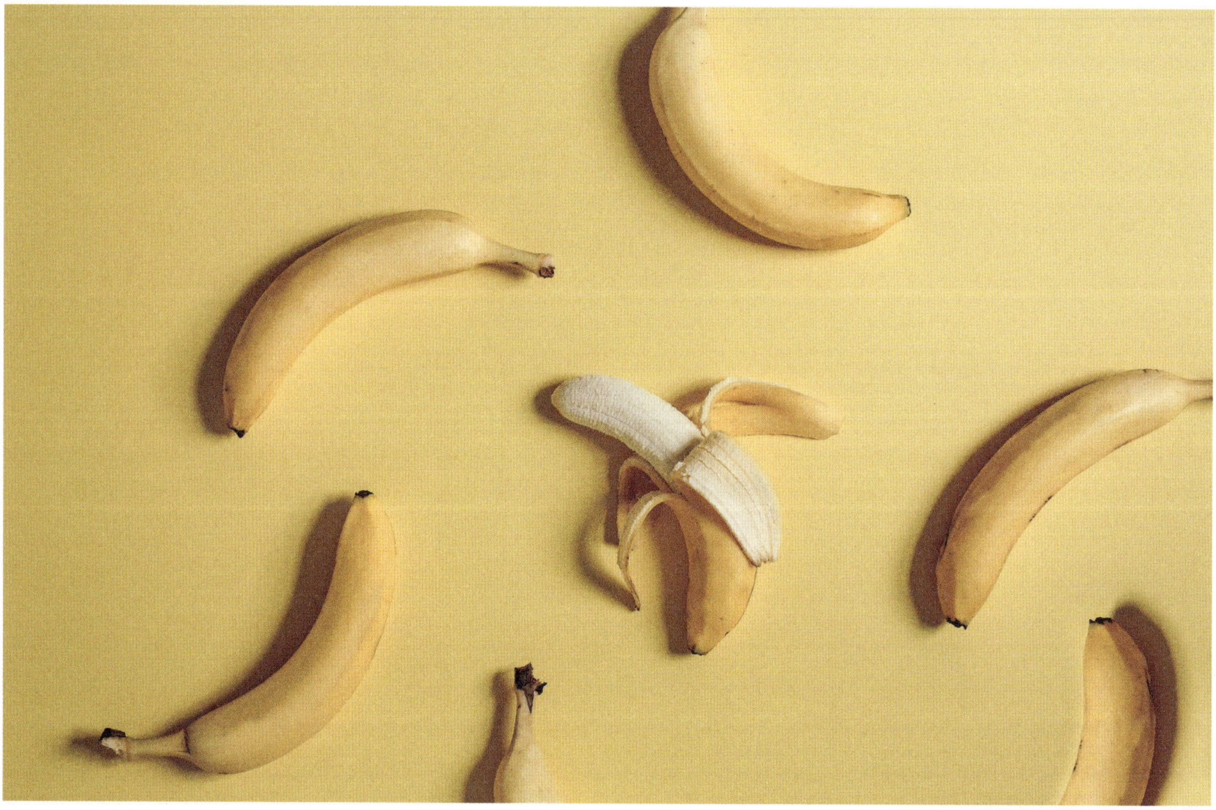

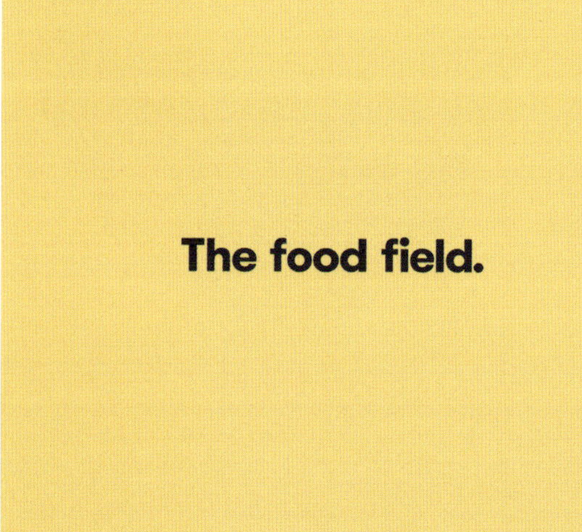

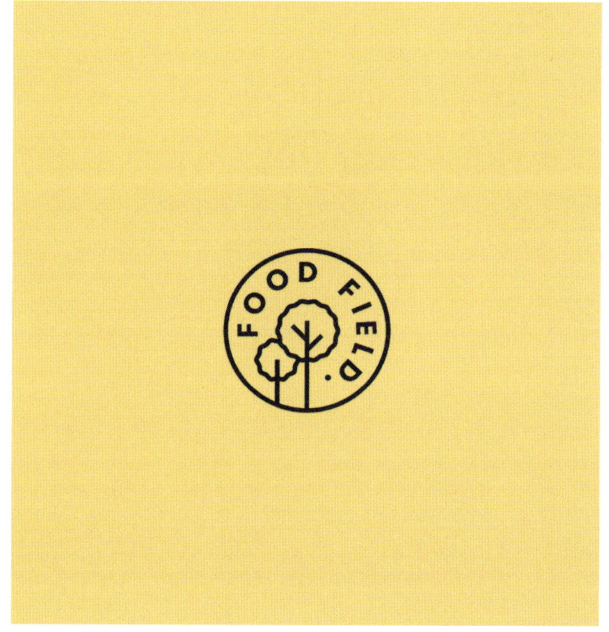

This comprehensive visual identity was created for an organic food store in México. To avoid an obvious green palette, a set of 3 different shades of yellow that symbolize the dawn and the start of a fresh new day was used. The logotype is accompanied by a simple geometric icon that can easily be used to mark their wide range of food products.

The Food Field

studio : *Parámetro Studio*
photographer: *Ana Hinojosa*

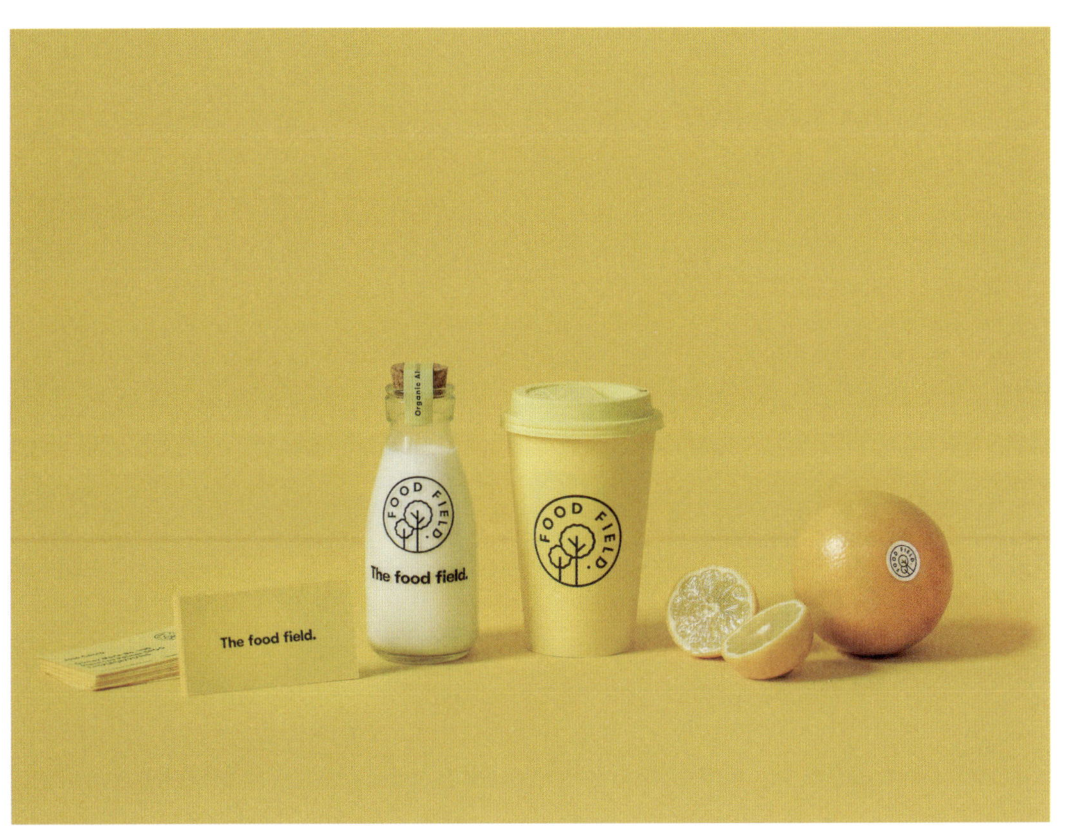

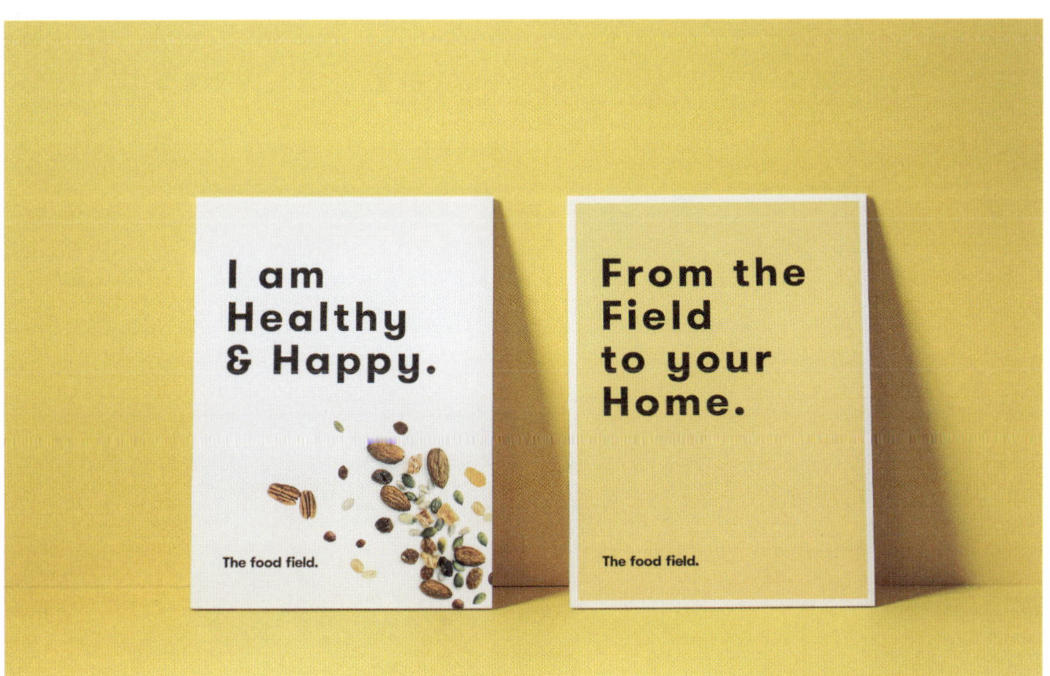

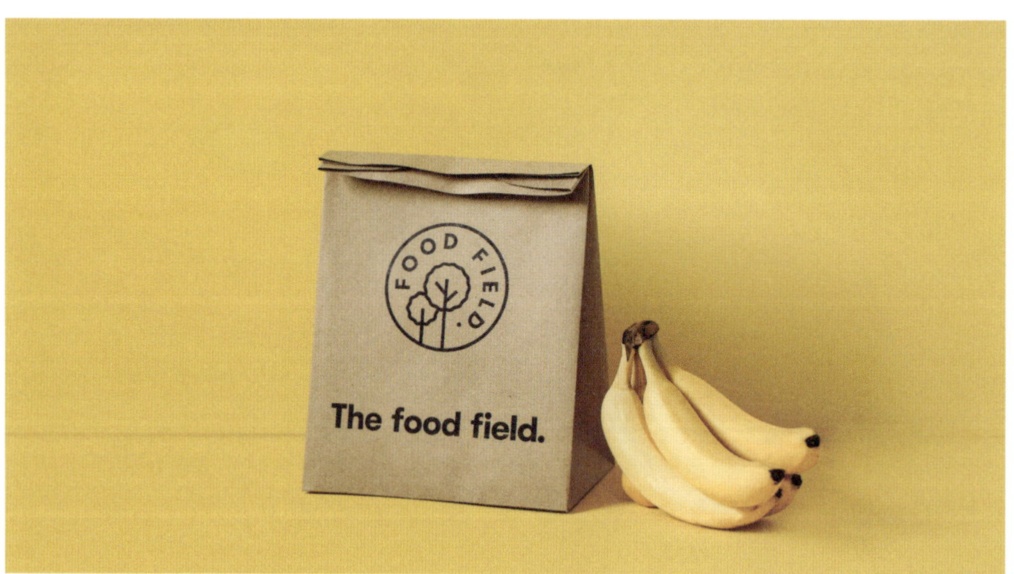
FOOD FIELD.
The food field.

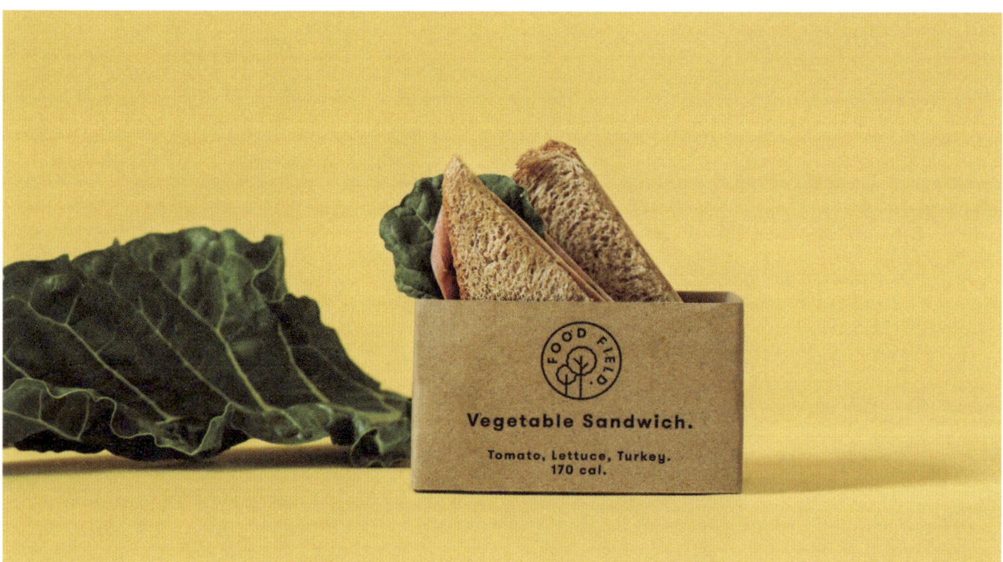
FOOD FIELD.
Vegetable Sandwich.
Tomato, Lettuce, Turkey.
170 cal.

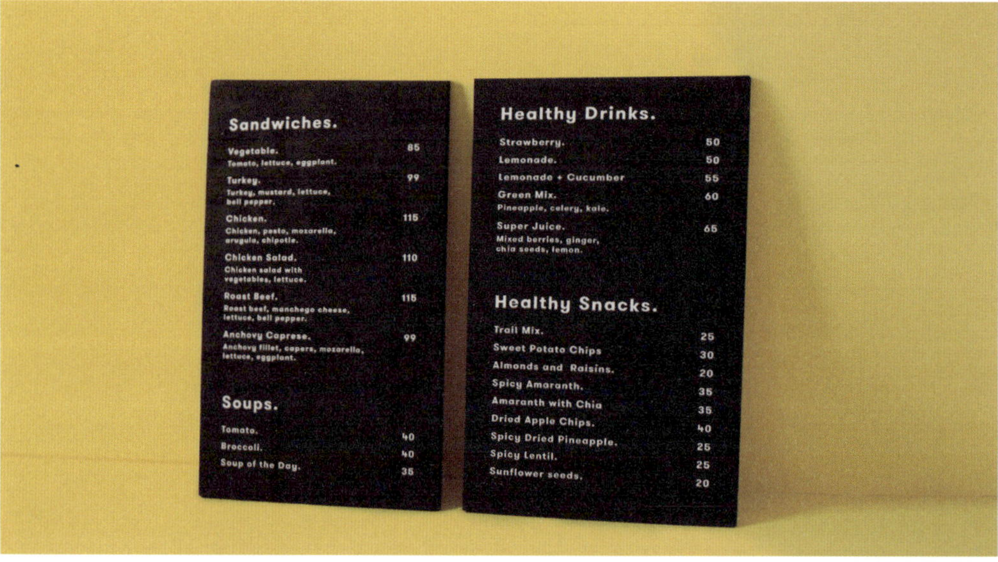
Sandwiches.
Vegetable. 85
Tomato, lettuce, eggplant.
Turkey. 99
Turkey, mustard, lettuce, bell pepper.
Chicken. 115
Chicken, pesto, mozarella, arugula, chipotle.
Chicken Salad. 110
Chicken salad with vegetables, lettuce.
Roast Beef. 115
Roast beef, manchego cheese, lettuce, bell pepper.
Anchovy Caprese. 99
Anchovy fillet, capers, mozarella, lettuce, eggplant.
Soups.
Tomato. 40
Broccoli. 40
Soup of the Day. 35
Healthy Drinks.
Strawberry. 50
Lemonade. 50
Lemonade + Cucumber 55
Green Mix. 60
Pineapple, celery, kale.
Super Juice. 65
Mixed berries, ginger, chia seeds, lemon.
Healthy Snacks.
Trail Mix. 25
Sweet Potato Chips 30
Almonds and Raisins. 20
Spicy Amaranth. 35
Amaranth with Chia 35
Dried Apple Chips. 40
Spicy Dried Pineapple. 25
Spicy Lentil. 25
Sunflower seeds. 20

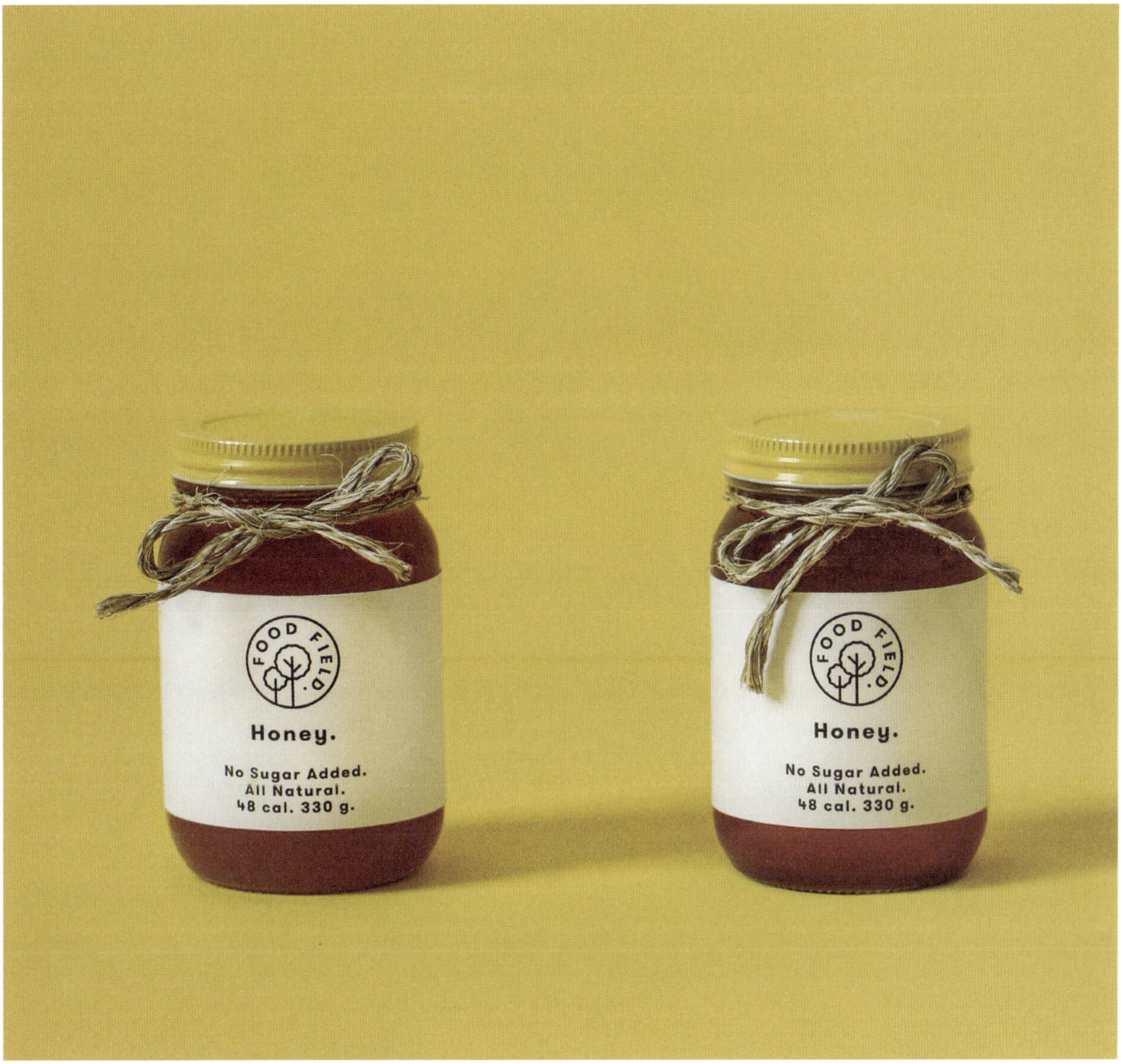

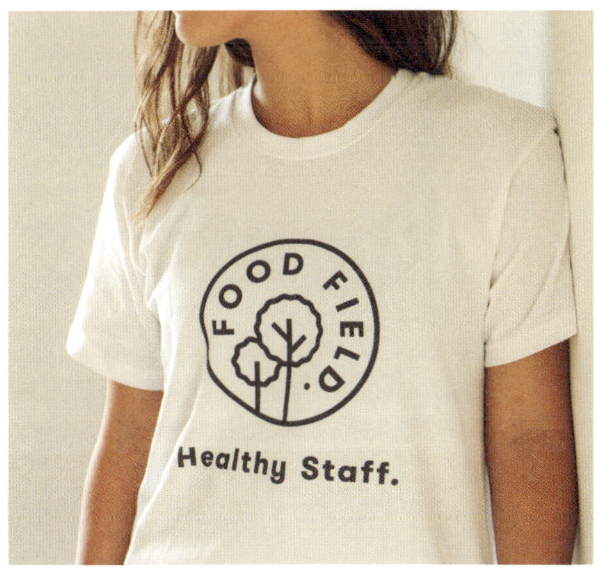
FOOD FIELD.
Healthy Staff.

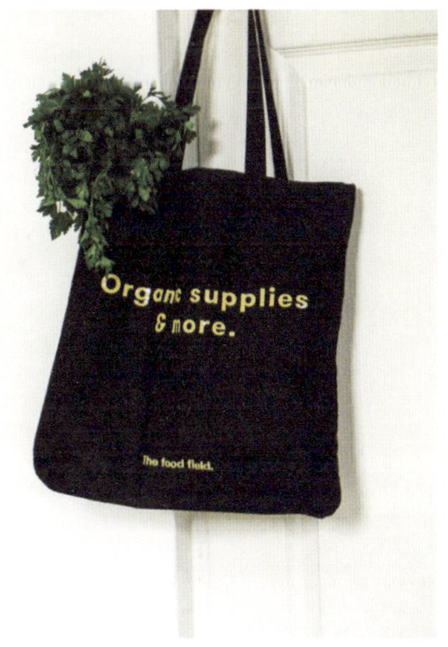
Organic supplies
& more.
The food field.

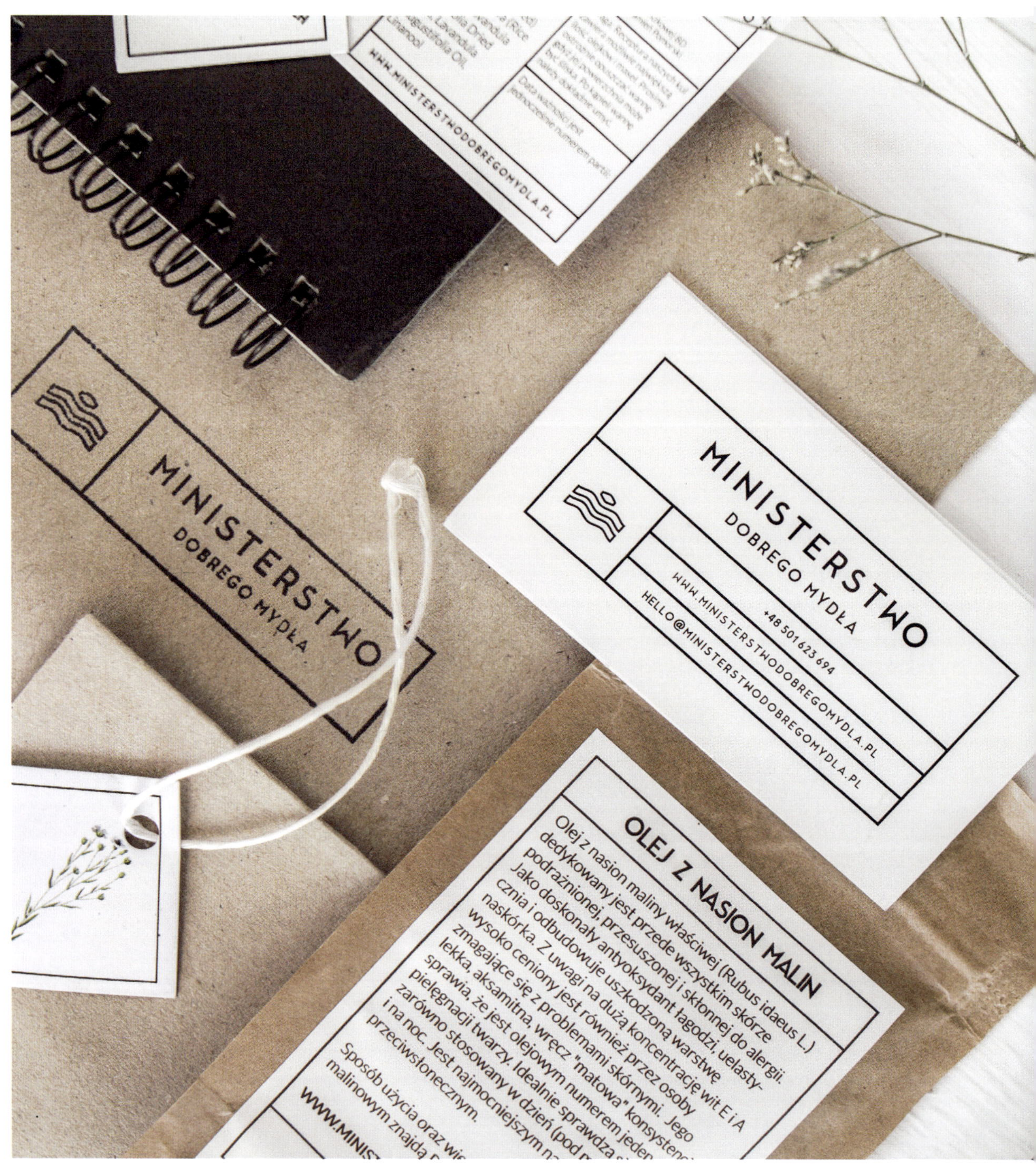

Ministerstwo Dobrego Mydła is a company that produces decent handmade soaps and cosmetics. The main idea of the branding was to design a functional and simple visual system using geometric shapes, combined with illustrations of soap ingredients in pharmacy style to reflect the recipe for the brand's success—good materials, good craftsmanship and hard work.

Ministerstwo Dobrego Mydła

studio: ***Paris+Hendzel Studio***
designer: ***Łukasz Hendzel***

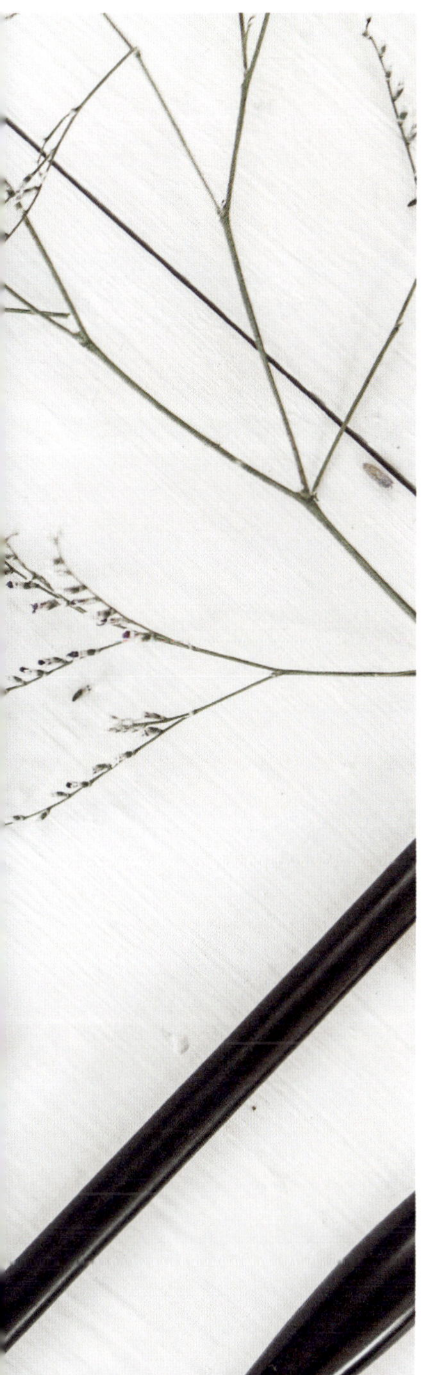

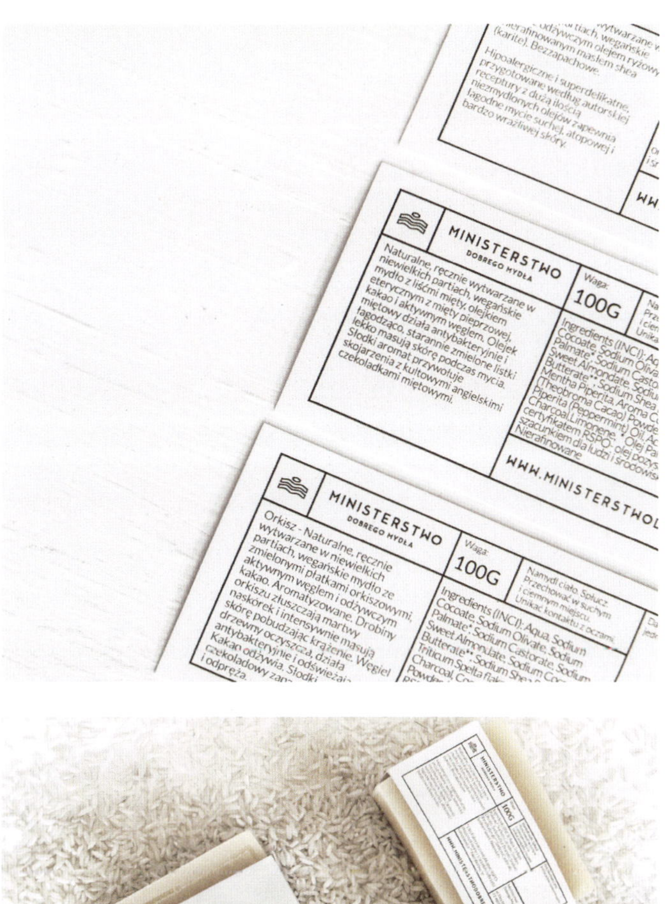

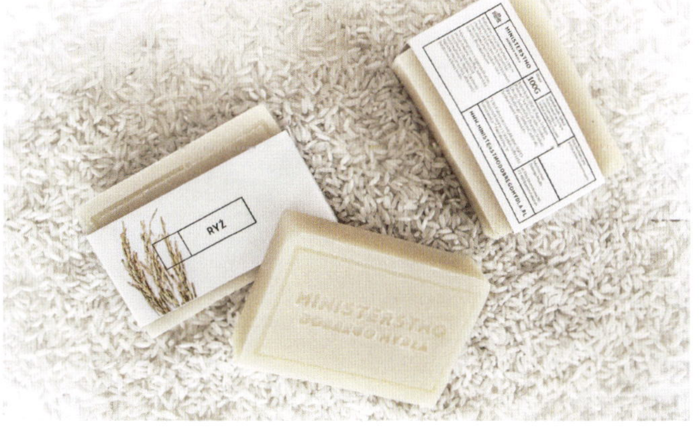

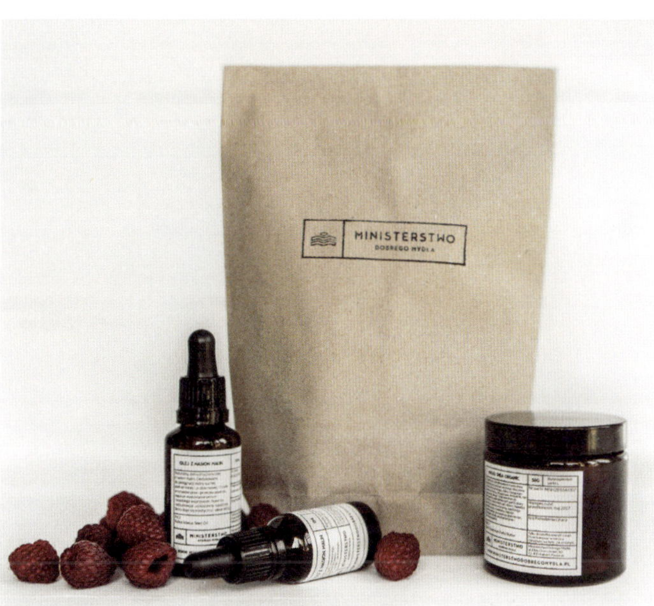

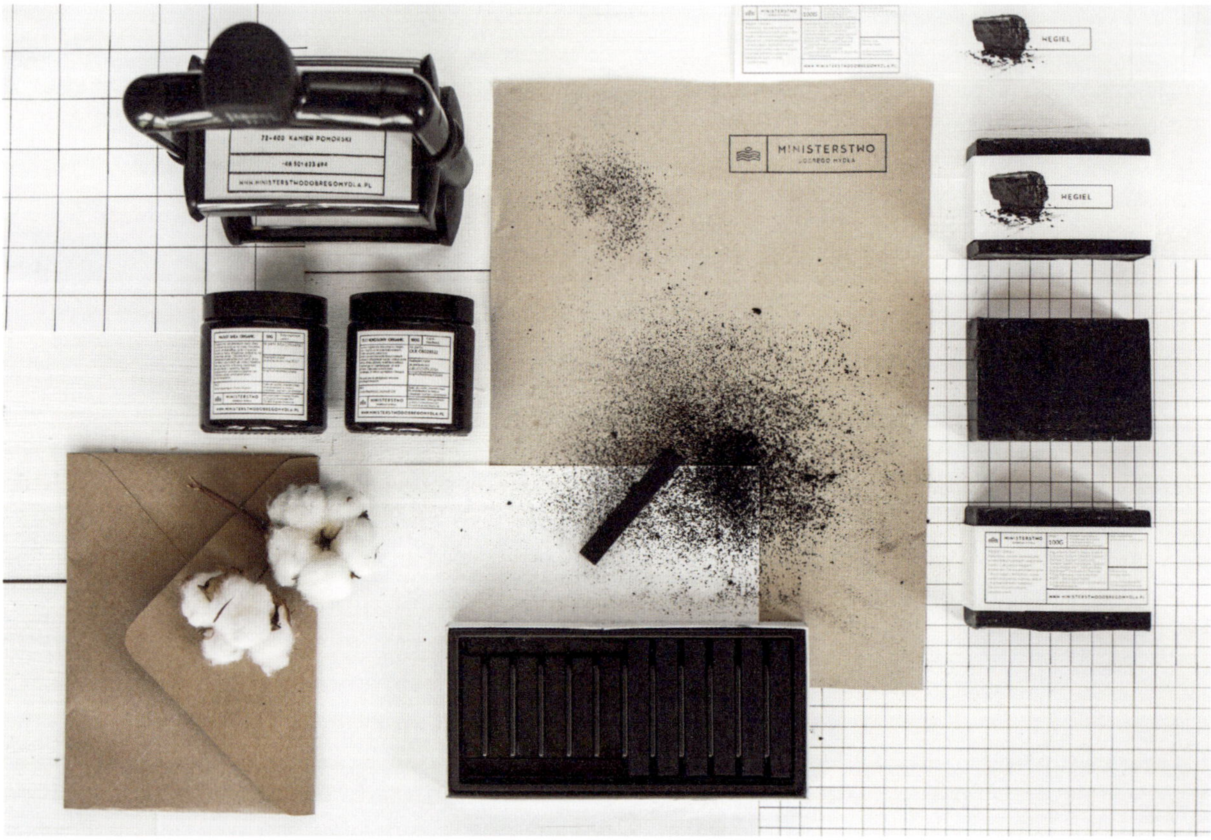
72-400 KAMIEN POMORSKI
WWW.MINISTERSTWODOBREGOMYDLA.PL
MINISTERSTWO
DOBREGO MYDŁA
WĘGIEL

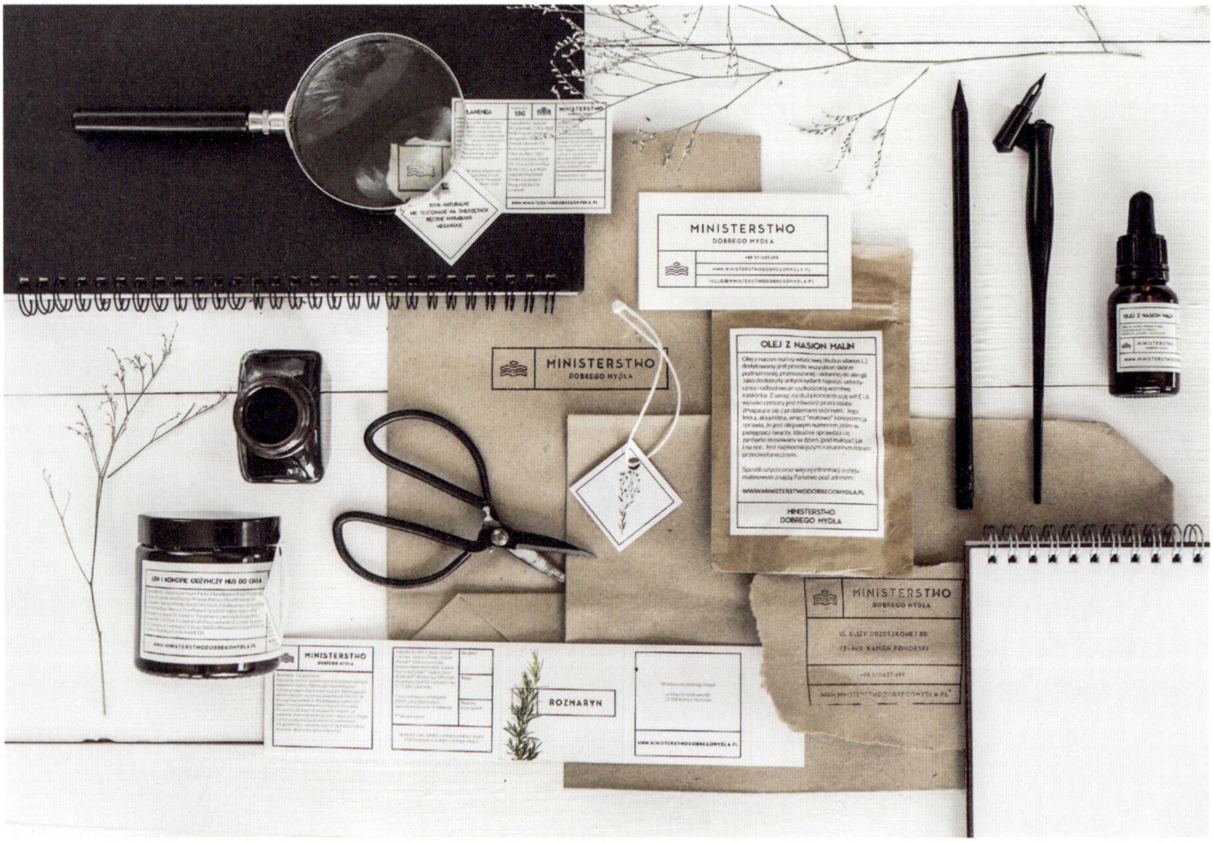
LAWENDA
100% NATURALNE
NIE TESTOWANE NA ZWIERZĘTACH
RĘCZNIE WYRABIANE
WEGAŃSKIE
MINISTERSTWO
DOBREGO MYDŁA
OLEJ Z NASION MALIN
WWW.MINISTERSTWODOBREGOMYDLA.PL
LEN I KONOPIE ODŻYWCZY MUS DO CIAŁA
ROZMARYN

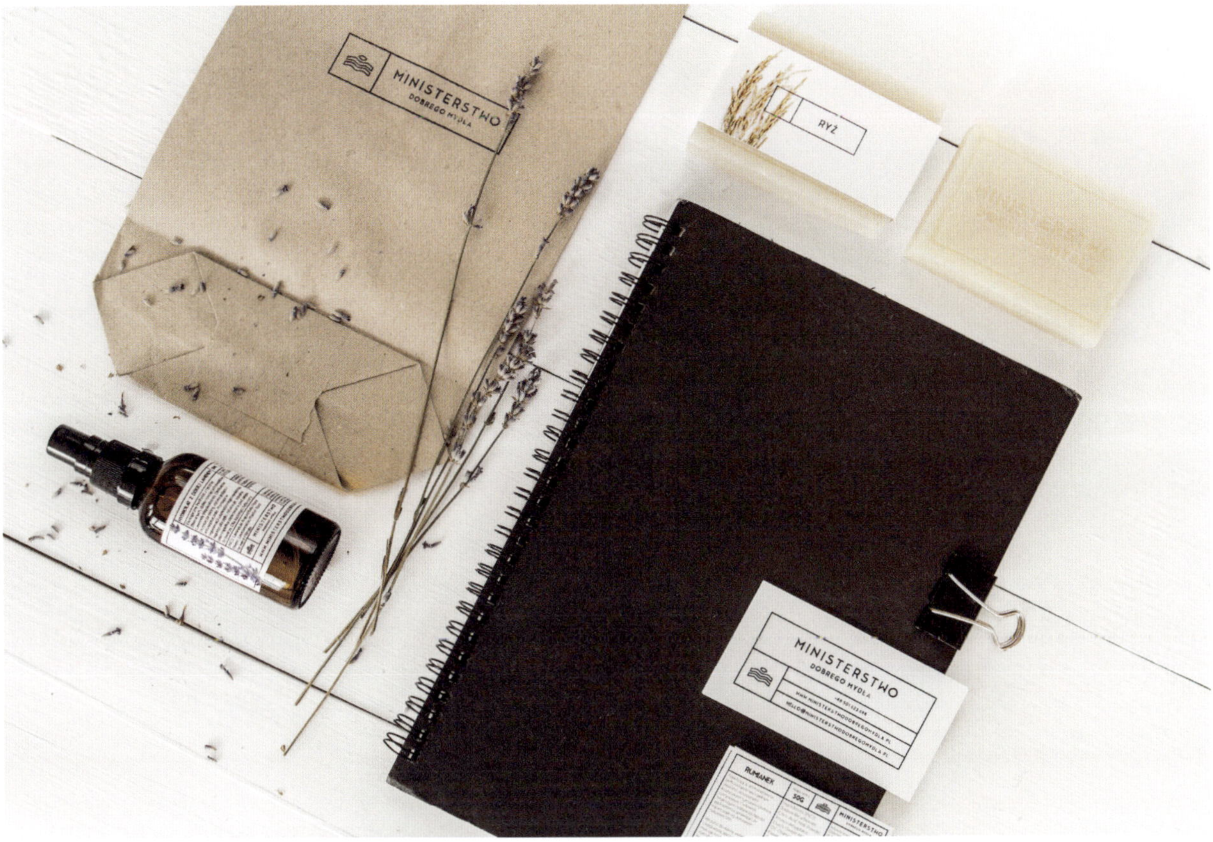
MINISTERSTWO
DOBREGO MYDŁA
RYŻ
MINISTERSTWO
DOBREGO MYDŁA
RUMIANEK
30G

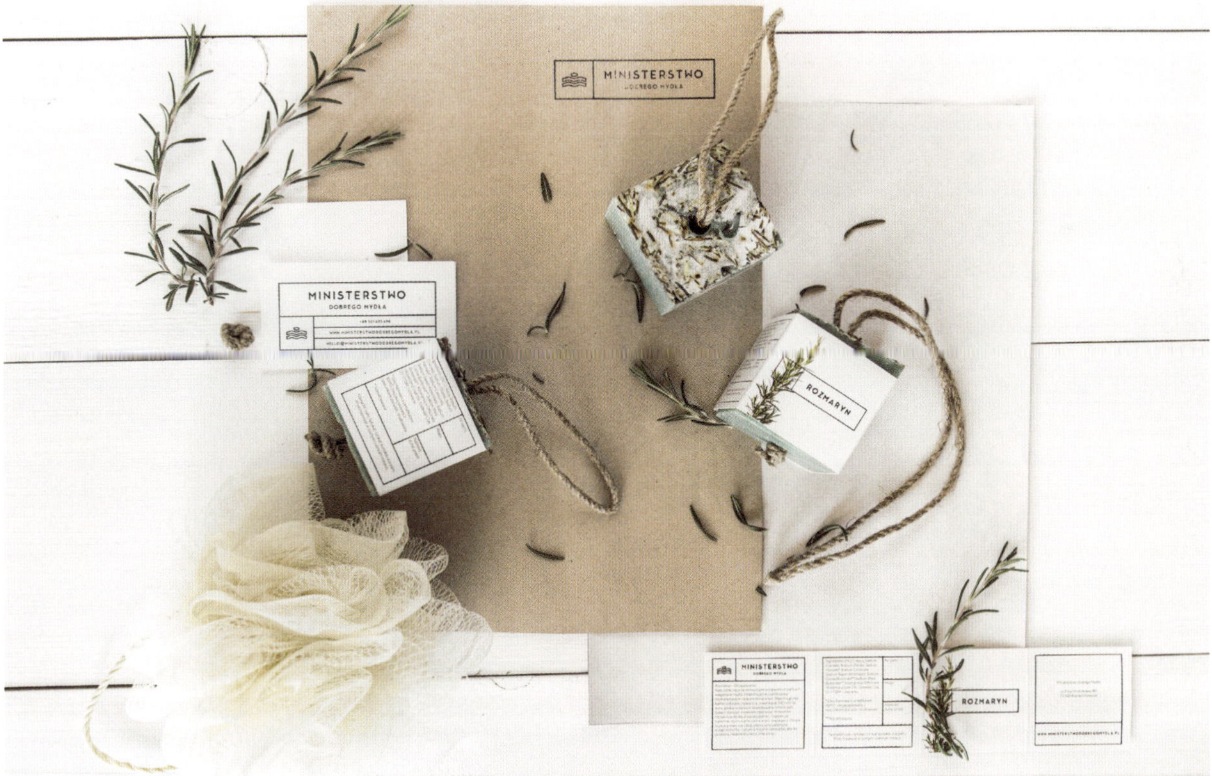
MINISTERSTWO
DOBREGO MYDŁA
MINISTERSTWO
DOBREGO MYDŁA
ROZMARYN
MINISTERSTWO
DOBREGO MYDŁA
ROZMARYN

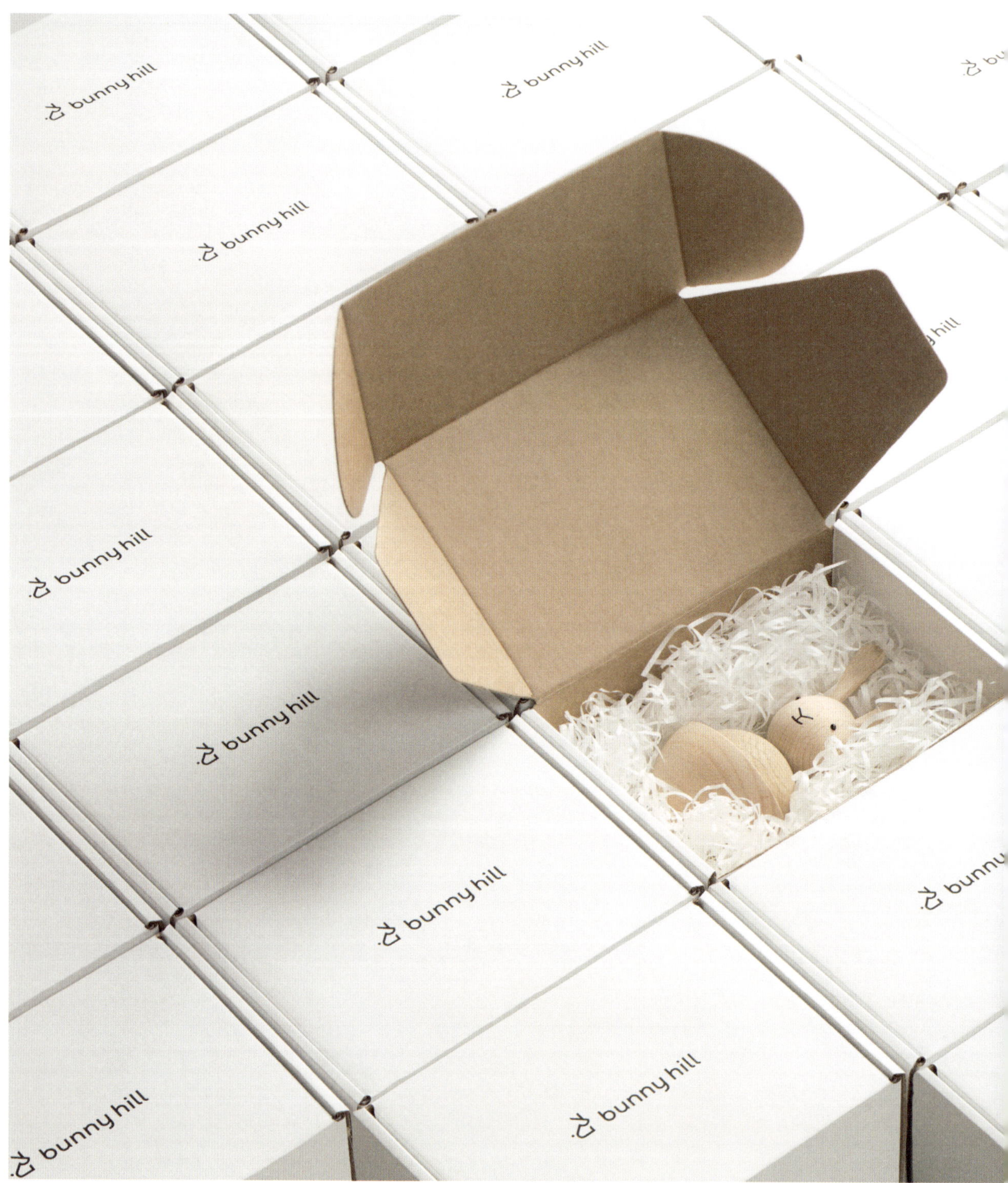

As the starting point for the brand identity design, a simple and clear logo featuring smooth and round shape was created for the loving and caring online shop Bunny Hill. The color white, inherent in the traditional Swedish design, imparts a shining, warm and friendly atmosphere. There are also a refreshing packaging concept and an official website.

Bunny Hill

studio: *Comence Studio*
designer: *Pavel Emelyanov*

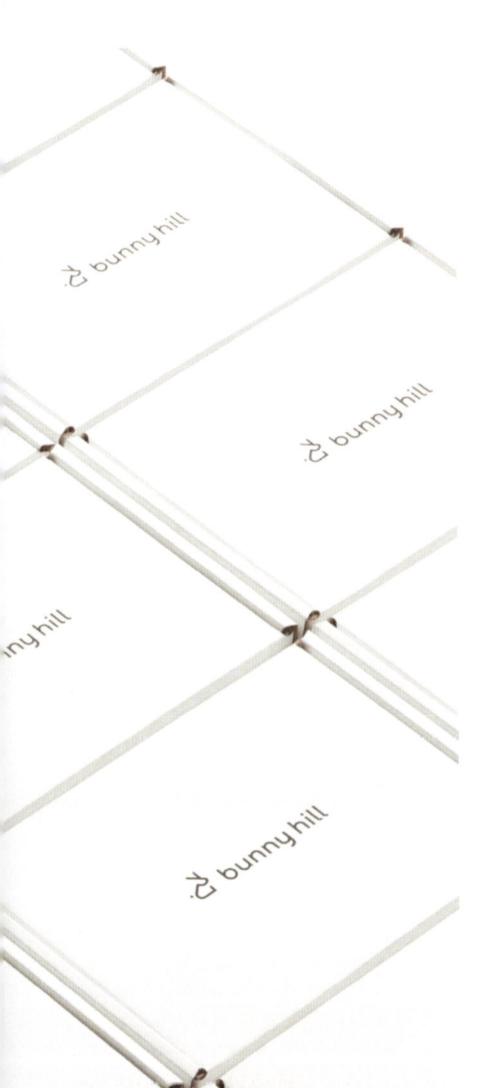

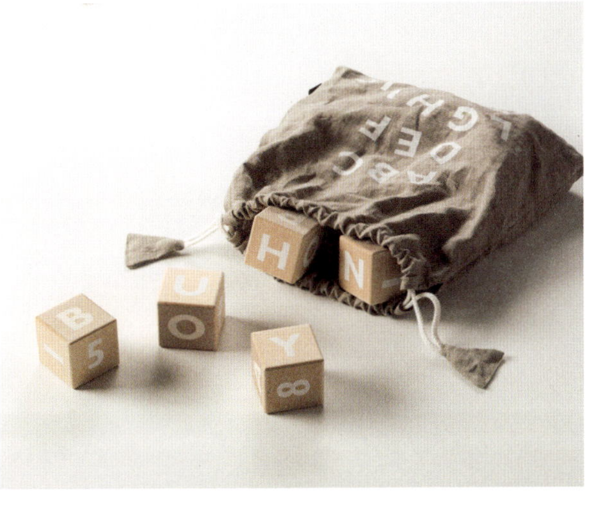

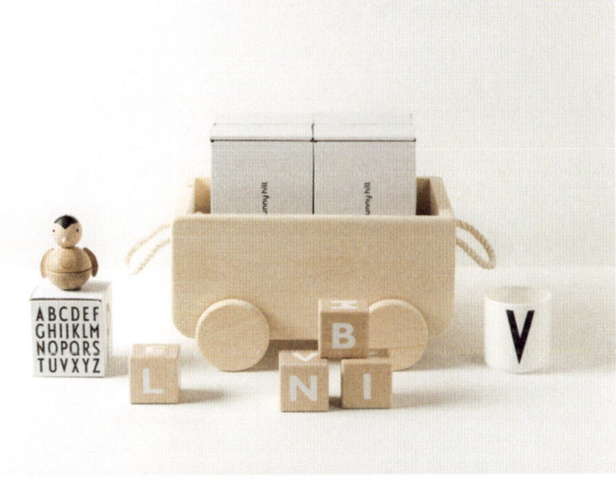

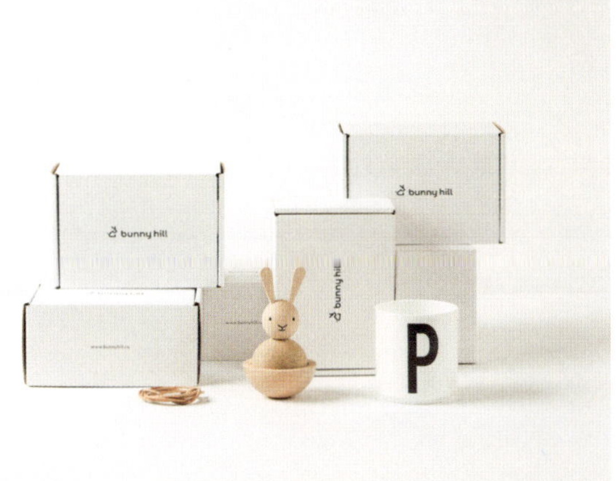

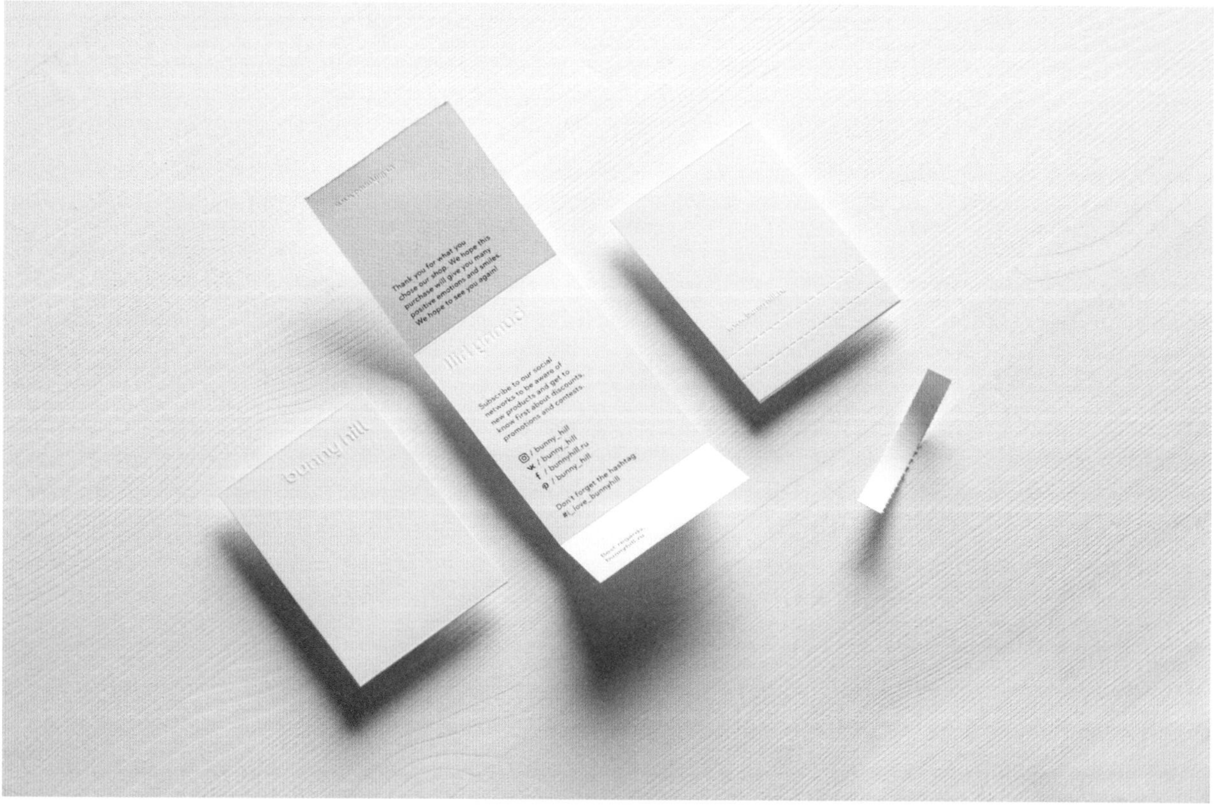

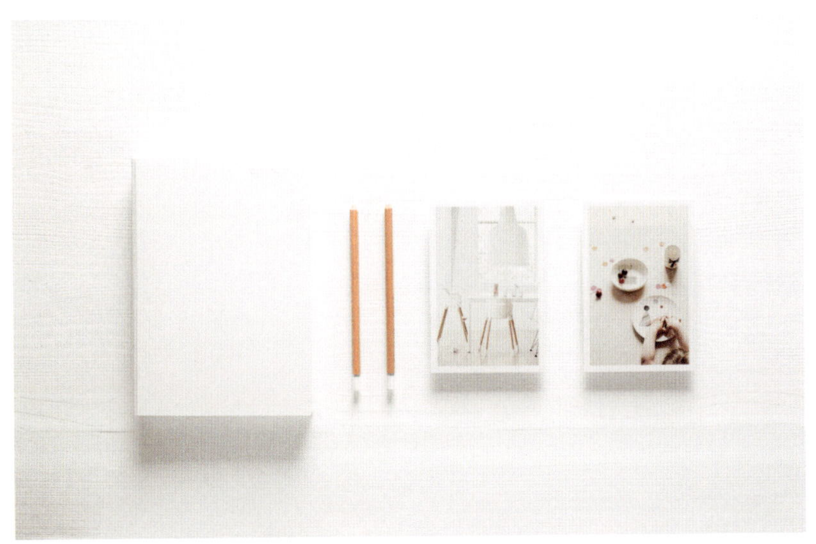

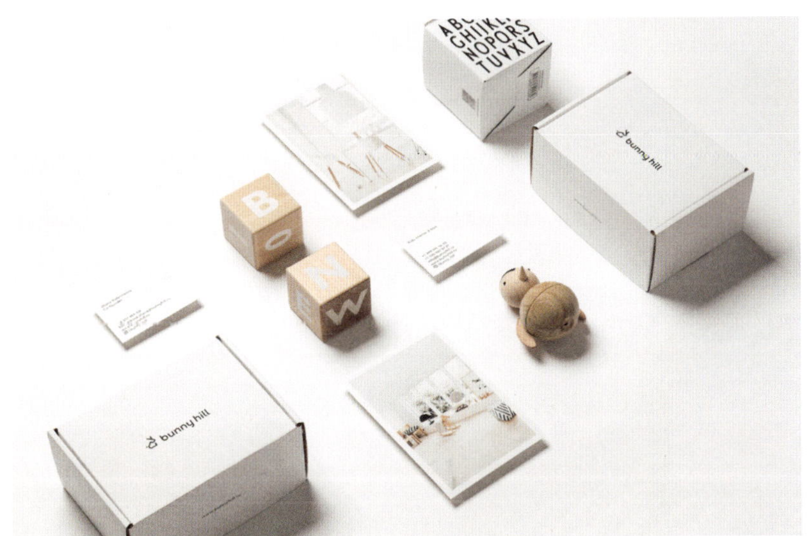
bunny hill
bunny hill

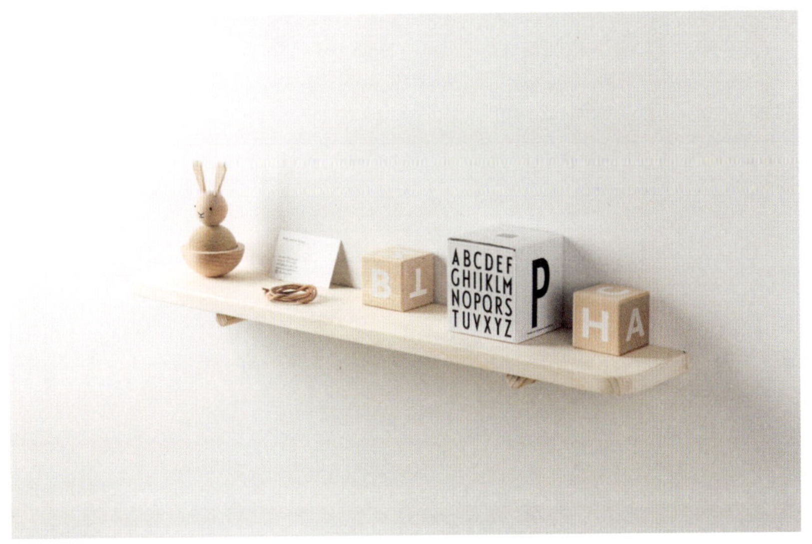
ABCDEF
GHIJKLM
NOPQRS
TUVXYZ
P

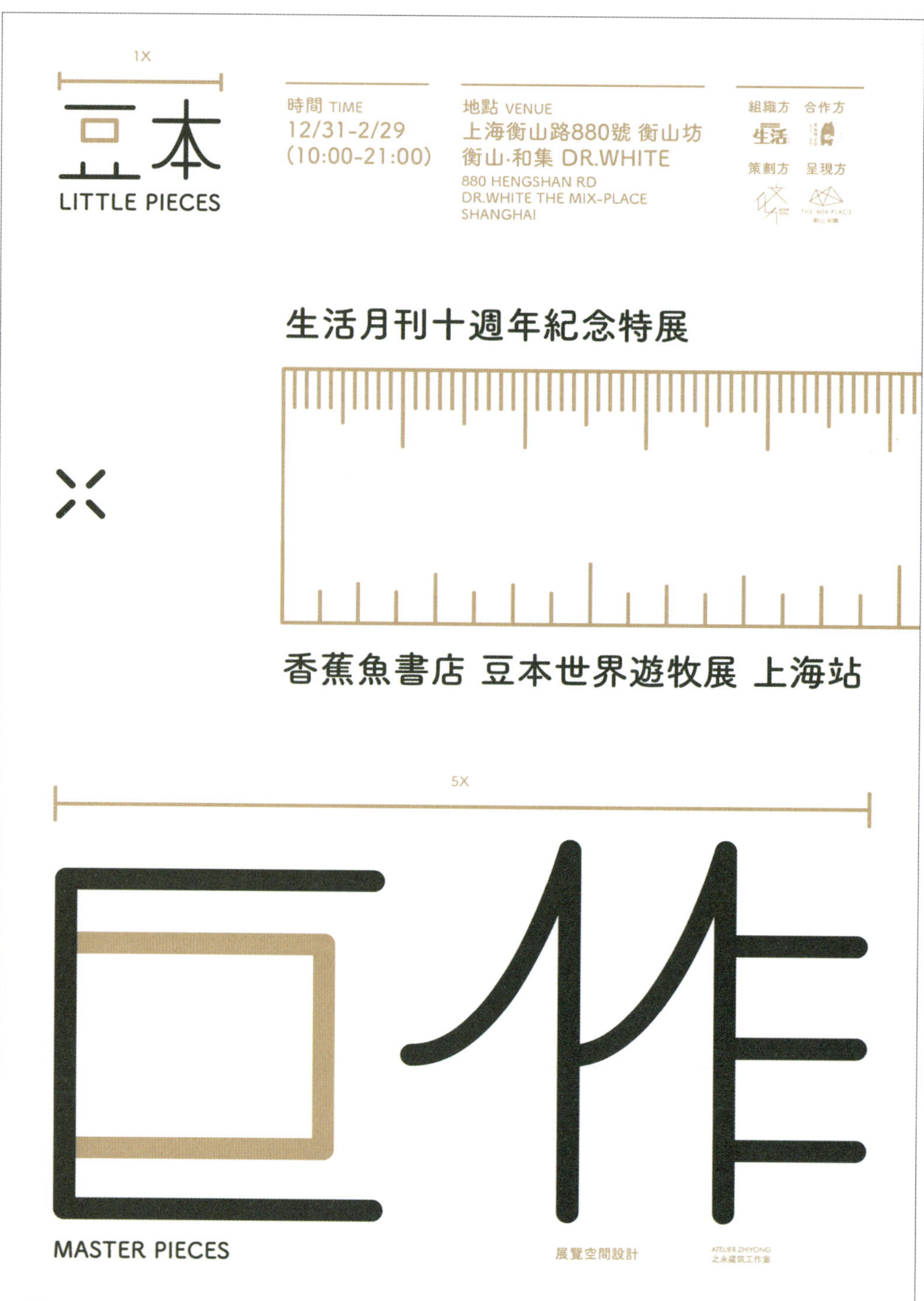

This specific visual identity created for the exhibition aims to raise public's awareness of print media through fun yet simple graphic solutions. The inspiration came from the paper size guide, the squares in which became the main feature of the identity to resemble the form of publications. Two sets of special rulers were also developed to encourage fun interaction anywhere and anytime.

Little Pieces X Master Pieces Collection

studio:
Ray KJ Chen

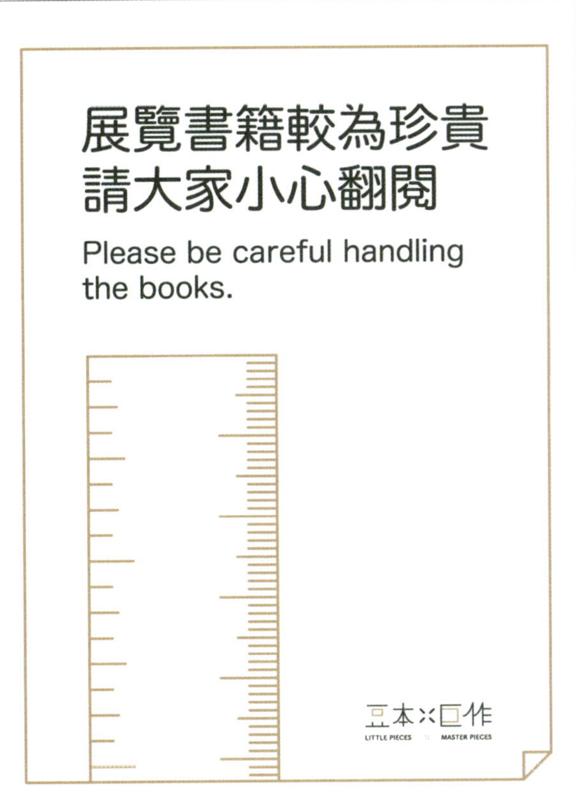

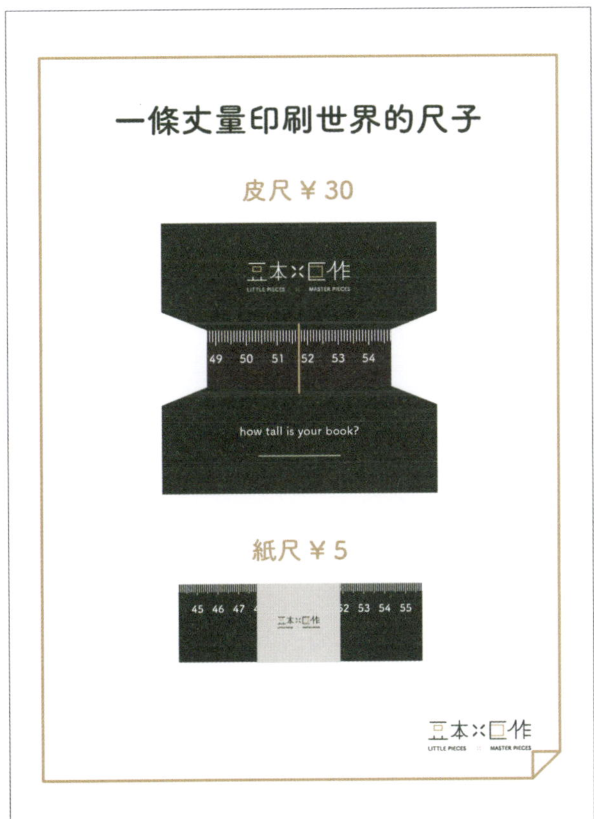

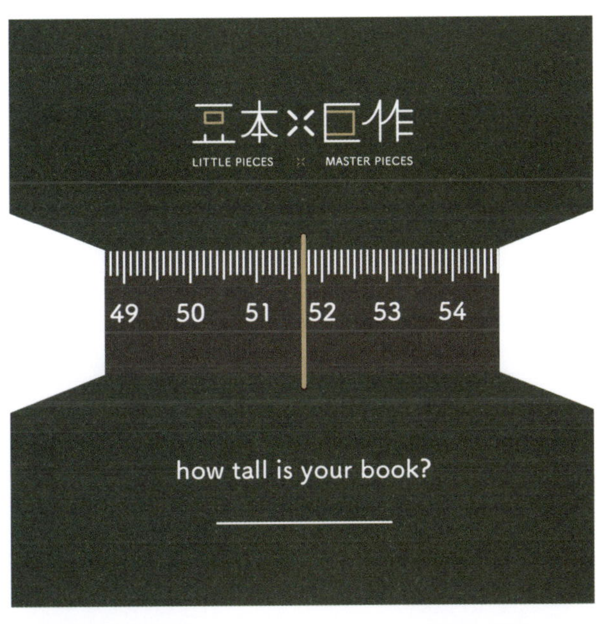

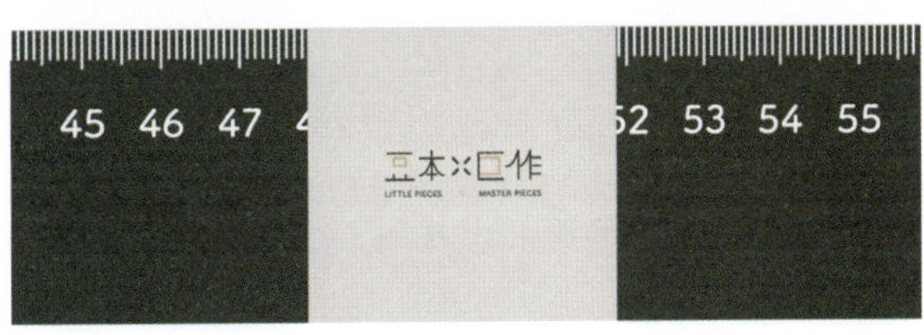

index

ACKNOWLEDGEMENTS

We would like to thank all the designers and contributors who have been involved in the production of this book. Their contributions have been indispensable in its compilation. We would also like to express our gratitude to all the producers for their invaluable opinions and assistance throughout this project. And to the many others whose names are not credited but have made specific input in this book, we thank you for your continuous support.

FUTURE COOPERATIONS

If you wish to participate in SendPoints' future projects and publications, please send your website or portfolio to
editor01@sendpoints.cn